Revelation

Preaching Verse by Verse

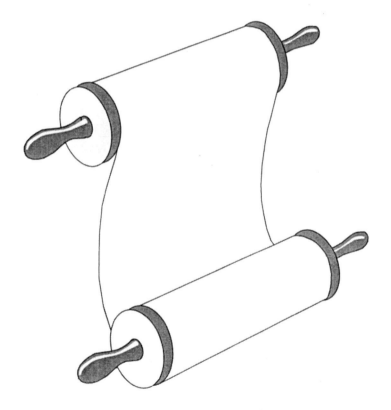

Pastor D. A. Waite, Th.D., Ph.D.

Published by

THE BIBLE FOR TODAY PRESS
900 Park Avenue
Collingswood, New Jersey 08108
U.S.A.

Church Phone: 856-854-4747
BFT Phone: 856-854-4452
Orders: 1-800-John 10:9
e-mail: BFT@BibleForToday.org
Website: www.BibleForToday.org
fax: 856-854-2484

We Use and Defend
the King James Bible

July, 2012
BFT3495

Copyright, 2012
All Rights Reserved

ISBN #978-1-56848-080-0

𝕬𝖈𝖐𝖓𝖔𝖜𝖑𝖊𝖉𝖌𝖒𝖊𝖓𝖙𝖘

**I wish to thank and to acknowledge the assistance
of the following people:**

- **The Congregation** of the 𝕭𝖎𝖇𝖑𝖊 𝕱𝖔𝖗 𝕿𝖔𝖉𝖆𝖞 𝕭𝖆𝖕𝖙𝖎𝖘𝖙 𝕮𝖍𝖚𝖗𝖈𝖍–for whom these messages were prepared, to whom they were delivered, and by whom they were published. They listened attentively and encouraged their Pastor.

- **Yvonne Sanborn Waite**–my wife, who encouraged the publication of these sermons, read the manuscript, developed the various boxes, suggested sentences to underline, and gave other helpful suggestions and comments; The boxes help the reader to see some of the more important topics that are covered in the various chapters.

- **Julie Monaghan**–a faithful church supporter and Internet attender who volunteered to spend the many hours required to type these sermons from the original cassette tapes, to put the words and Bible verses into paragraphs, and to put them into the computer. Julie volunteered to take this book of 22 chapters, knowing full well the time it would take. This was a huge time-consuming task that was necessary for the publishing of this book. She also did proofreading.

- **Anne Marie Noyle**–a faithful church supporter and Internet attender who proofread the book four times and gave many useful suggestions for improvement. Though she lives in Canada, she was able to give her suggestions over the phone. This also took many hours of reading and correcting.

- **Dr. Kirk DiVietro**–a computer expert in Word Perfect format who helped generate the **INDEX** for the book.

Foreword

- **The Beginning.** This book is the **ninth** in a series of books based on my expository preaching from various books of the Bible. It is an attempt to bring to the minds of the readers two things: (1) the **meaning** of the words in the verses and (2) the practical **application** of those words to the lives of both saved and unsaved people.

- **Preached Sermons.** These are messages that I have been preached to our **Bible For Today Baptist Church** in Collingswood, New Jersey. They were broadcast over the radio, over the Internet as they were being preached by streaming, and then placed afterwards on **http://www.BibleForToday.org/audio_sermons.htm.** This site allows people all over the world to listen. As the messages were originally preached, I took half a chapter during our Sunday morning services, spending about forty-five minutes on each message.

- **Other Verses.** In connection with both the **meaning** and **application** of the verses in this book, there are many verses from other places in the Bible that have been quoted for further elaboration of the teachings in this book. All the many verses of Scripture that are used to illustrate further truth are written out in full for easy reference.

- **A Transcription.** This entire book was typed into computer format by Julie Monaghan from the tape recordings of the messages as they were preached. These recordings are available in both audio and video formats (the **Audio cassettes are BFT#3169/1-22;** the **VHS Videos are BFT #3169VC1-11.** Though there has been some editing, the words in this book are basically the same as the ones I spoke as I preached these sermons.

- **The Audience.** The intended audience for this book is the same as the audience that listened to the messages in the first place. These studies are not meant to be overly scholarly, though there is some reference to various Greek Words used. My aim and burden is to try to help believers to understand the Words of God. It is my hope that my children, grandchildren, great grandchildren, and many others might profit from this study of the Book of Revelation.

Yours For God's Words,

D. A. Waite

Pastor D. A. Waite, Th.D., Ph.D.
Bible For Today Baptist Church

Table of Contents

Revelation
Chapter One

Introductory Remarks

A number of years ago, I preached verse by verse through the book of Revelation. I took half a chapter each Sunday morning. At that rate, since there are 22 chapters in the book, it took me a total of 44 weeks to preach and teach through it.

Though I have taken up other New Testament books in later years, I decided not to preach through Revelation again due to its length and for other reasons. I was willing to let the audio and video tapes that had been made of these messages to suffice for my treatment of this book.

A few months ago, as this is being written, Mrs. Julie Monaghan, one of our church's faithful Internet attenders to **The Bible For Today Baptist Church**, wrote me an e-mail and said she would be glad to take some of the audio cassettes of my preaching messages and prepare another book from them. She asked what book I would want her to work on. She asked me which book I would like to publish. I told her that Mrs. Waite would like to have Revelation published, but I said it was very long, and it would be difficult to do. I suggested, perhaps, a shorter book for her to work on.

However, Julie agreed with Mrs. Waite that she would be glad to put Revelation into a book, regardless of its length. She has done this huge task as a ministry for the Lord Jesus Christ. She has done an excellent job in paragraphing and formatting this book. There is very little need for change in wording other than looking over the words and ideas to make changes as might be needed.

I have dealt with Revelation on a verse by verse basis as I have done in my other books. I have sought to bring in many other verses that have a bearing on the themes that are being discussed in the Revelation book. I hope it will be a blessing to you who read and study this book. Sometimes I repeat various themes because these themes are repeated in Revelation as I took them up during forty-four different weeks.

Revelation 1:1

"The Revelation of Jesus Christ, which God gave unto him, to shew unto his servants things which must shortly come to pass; and he sent and signified *it* by his angel unto his servant John:"

The book of Revelation was written by John. He was used of the Lord to write five New Testament books: the *Gospel of John, 1 John, 2 John, 3 John, and Revelation.* Many Bibles say *"the Revelation of John."* It is really *"the Revelation of Jesus Christ."* The word Revelation (APOKALUPSIS) means, *"a laying bare concerning things before unknown; completely revealed."* John received from the Lord a photographic reproduction of the past, the present, and the future.

Four Personages Here

Notice that God the Father gave to God the Son the Revelation to show unto His servants the things which *must* (that is a definite necessity) shortly come to pass; and He sent and signified it by His angel. The angel here is the messenger that signified it unto His servant John. So we have four personages: the Lord Jesus Christ, God the Father, the angel/messenger (Angelos), and John himself.

The word *signified* (SEMAINO) is an interesting word. It means *"to give a sign, to signify, to indicate, to make known."* Some of the things in Revelation are signs or symbols. We take it wherever possible according to the Golden Rule of Bible Interpretation: *"Where the PLAIN SENSE of Scripture makes COMMON SENSE, SEEK NO OTHER SENSE"* unless, in the light of context, it is clearly a symbol.

The word *"revelation"* only occurs ten times in the New Testament.

- **Ephesians 3:3**
  "How that by **revelation** he made known unto me the mystery; (as I wrote afore in few words)"

Paul says, *"he made known unto me the **mystery**;"* It is an unfolding of something.

Concerning the angel, sometimes angels are human beings, sometimes they are superhuman beings.

- **Revelation 2:1**
  "Unto the angel of the church of Ephesus write; These things saith he that holdeth the seven stars in his right hand, who walketh in the midst of the seven golden candlesticks;"

This is probably the pastor of that local church. He is the messenger and he is called *"the angel."*

- **Revelation 22:8-9**
  "And I John saw these things, and heard *them*. And when I had heard and seen, I fell down to worship before the feet of the angel which shewed me these things. Then saith he unto me, See *thou do it* not: for I am thy fellowservant, and of thy brethren the prophets, and of them which keep the sayings of this book: worship God."

John fell down to worship before the feet of the angel. In that case it might have been a man—a messenger from the Lord. We are not to worship men or angels, but only the Lord.

These are things *"which shortly must come to pass."* That word *"must"* means it is certainly going to come to pass. Definitely, there is no question about it. God's *"must"* is often different from our *"must."*

- **2 Peter 3:8**
  "But, beloved, be not ignorant of this one thing, that one day *is* with the Lord as a thousand years, and a thousand years as one day."

Past, Present, And Future

The book of Revelation was written roughly in 96 A.D. and it will come to pass. I believe it is a prefiguration of what John saw in the past, what is presently in the church age in chapters 2 and 3, and then from chapter 4 through chapter 19, the things which are to come in the future. It is basically Daniel's 70th week, the 7-year great tribulation period, the judgment that God is going to rain upon the world because of their sins. (See Daniel 9:24-27.)

Revelation 1:2

"Who bare record of the word of God, and of the testimony of Jesus Christ, and of all things that he saw."

Here John says he *"bare record."* He is a witness. He heard things. He saw things. He sees the future, and He sees it exactly. He sees exactly what is going to come to pass.

Why did he use many symbols? John was in the Roman Empire. He was a prisoner on the isle of Patmos. He was banished there. Perhaps he did not want the people to know too much about the details, so he used all these different figures. But to us who understand these things, this was a revelation of, not only the church age which will end at the rapture, but also of things in the seven-year tribulation, of the millennial reign of the Lord Jesus Christ, and of eternity.

"Word" Vs. "Words" Of God

Notice, "*the word of God*" that he bare record of and "*the testimony of Jesus Christ.*" Both of these things are important. The "Word" of God has always meant to me the "Words" of God, but today we have some fundamentalist professors, writers, and pastors who say the "*Word*" of God does not mean the "*Words*" of God. They say it just means "*the message, the thoughts, the ideas, the teachings, and the concepts*" of God, but not the very Hebrew, Aramaic, and Greek "Words" of God.

A book came off the press in 2002 from Dr. Samuel Schnaiter, who is a professor at Bob Jones University. He is the present head of their ancient language department. He has written a book entitled *Bible Preservation and the Providence of God*. He believes that the exact original Hebrew, Aramaic, and Greek "*Words*" of God have not been preserved, but only the "*message.*"

- **Mark 7:13**
  "Making **the word of God** of none effect through your tradition, which ye have delivered: and many such like things do ye."

The Lord Jesus Christ accused the Pharisees of making the **Words of God** of none effect.

- **Luke 5:1**
  "And it came to pass, that, as the people pressed upon him to hear **the word of God,** he stood by the lake of Gennesaret,"

That is what we try to do in our church, to hear and preach the **Words of God.**

- **Luke 8:21**
  The Lord Jesus Christ said, "My mother and my brethren are these which hear **the word of God,** and do it."

Those are the real relationships. Those related to the Lord Jesus Christ are both hearing and doing His **Words.**

- **Acts 4:17**
  "But that it spread no further among the people, let us straitly threaten them, that they speak henceforth to no man in this name."

The council threatened the disciples not to speak anymore in the Lord Jesus Christ's Name.

- **Acts 4:19-20**
  "But Peter and John answered and said unto them, Whether it be right in the sight of God to hearken unto you more than unto God, judge ye. For we cannot but speak the things which we have seen and heard."

Those are the **Words of God** and the apostles did speak and preach the **Words** of God.

- **Acts 4:31**
  "And when they had prayed, the place was shaken where they were assembled together; and they were all filled with the Holy Ghost, and they spake **the word of God** with boldness."

We have to maintain boldness.

- **Acts 13:5**
  "And when they were at Salamis, they preached **the word of God** in the synagogues of the Jews: and they had also John to *their* minister."

Paul and Barnabas preached the **Words of God** in the synagogues of the Jews.

- **Acts 13:7**
  "Which was with the deputy of the country, Sergius Paulus, a prudent man; who called for Barnabas and Saul, and desired to hear **the word of God**."

Sergius Paulus desired to hear the **Words of God**. Many people do not desire to hear the **Words of God**. They say, "Why do we want to hear that?" It is boring to them. If the **Words of God** are boring to you, I wonder if you have new life in the Lord Jesus Christ. It is the message between you and the Heavenly Father, between you and the Saviour.

- **Acts 17:13**
  "But when the Jews of Thessalonica had knowledge that **the word of God** was preached of Paul at Berea, they came thither also, and stirred up the people."

When the **Words of God** are preached, they "stir up" some people, and get others to listen carefully.

We went into a drugstore and a lady saw us walk out. She walked behind us, saw the car, and saw the sign, "*Bible for Today Baptist Church*."

Then she called us on the telephone. She said, "*I would like to know how to be born-again. My preacher is a Methodist preacher in Haddonfield and I went to him and asked how to be born-again.*" He said they did not do that and that she would have to go to a Baptist church. I encouraged her to come out Sundays at 1:30 p.m. for our Bible study. I tried the best I could to lead her to the Lord Jesus Christ and be genuinely born-again.

Some do not like the **Words of God**, but sometimes the **Words of God** stir up people for good.

- **Acts 18:11**
  "And he continued *there* a year and six months, teaching **the word of God** among them."
- **Romans 10:17**
  "So then faith *cometh* by hearing, and hearing by **the word of God**."

You must have the **Words of God** to have faith to believe.

- **2 Corinthians 2:17**
  "For we are not as many, which corrupt **the word of God**: but as of sincerity, but as of God, in the sight of God speak we in Christ."

The Gnostic Critical Text-based new versions are corruptions of the **Words of God**.

- **2 Corinthians 4:2**
  "But have renounced the hidden things of dishonesty, not walking in craftiness, nor handling **the word of God** deceitfully; but by manifestation of the truth commending ourselves to every man's conscience in the sight of God."

Sometimes people use a proof text to deceitfully handle the Scriptures. That is not right either.

- **Ephesians 6:17**
  "And take the helmet of salvation, and the sword of the Spirit, which is **the word of God**:"

The word for "*word*" here is **RHEMA**, "*the spoken Words of God.*" We should memorize the **Words of God** and use them.

- **1 Thessalonians 2:13**
  "For this cause also thank we God without ceasing, because, when ye received **the word of God** which ye heard of us, ye received *it* not *as* the word of men, but as it is in truth, **the word of God**, which effectually worketh also in you that believe."

Paul thanked the Lord because that when they received the **Words of God**, they received them not as the words of men, but as the **Words of God**. The **Words of God** worked in the lives of the Thessalonian Christians.

- **Hebrews 4:12**
  "For **the word of God** *is* quick, and powerful, and sharper than any twoedged sword, piercing even to the dividing asunder of soul and spirit, and of the joints and marrow, and *is* a discerner of the thoughts and intents of the heart."
- **1 Peter 1:23**
  "Being born-again, not of corruptible seed, but of incorruptible, by **the word of God**, which liveth and abideth for ever."

Preserved Hebrew, Aramaic, & Greek

We must have these **Words**. That is why I believe God has preserved His **Hebrew, Aramaic, and Greek Words** which underlie the King James Bible. I also believe that we have these Divine Words truly, reliably, and accurately translated in our King James Bible. Those are the Words that will tell people how to come to the Lord Jesus Christ and be genuinely born-again. The Words of God can save souls. It saved our souls if we genuinely trusted in the Saviour.

- **1 John 2:14**
  "I have written unto you, fathers, because ye have known him *that is* from the beginning. I have written unto you, young men, because ye are strong, and **the word of God** abideth in you, and ye have overcome the wicked one."

He talks about the young men that are strong because the **Words of God** abide in them. That is what makes them strong.

- **Revelation 1:9**
  "I John, who also am your brother, and companion in tribulation, and in the kingdom and patience of Jesus Christ, was in the isle that is called Patmos, for **the word of God**, and for the **testimony** of Jesus Christ."

We have to have a "**testimony**" before the world. That means something we have seen and heard.

- **2 Timothy 1:8**
  "Be not thou therefore ashamed of the **testimony** of our Lord, nor of me his prisoner: but be thou partaker of the afflictions of the gospel according to the power of God;"

- **Hebrews 11:5**
  "By faith Enoch was translated that he should not see death; and was not found, because God had translated him: for before his translation he had this **testimony**, that he pleased God."

Importance Of Our Testimony

What is your testimony? What is mine? When people see us, what do they see? What do they hear?

Revelation 1:3

"Blessed *is* he that readeth, and they that hear the words of this prophecy, and keep those things which are written therein: for the time *is* at hand."

Again, "*the time is at hand*" means that it is ready. There is no prophecy to be fulfilled before these things take place. But there is a blessing to those who continue to "***read***" and continue to "***hear** the words of the prophecy and continue to keep those things that are written therein.*"

There are two words for "*time.*" CHRONOS is *chronological time,* such as Monday, Tuesday, Wednesday, and 1:00, 2:00, 3:00. But the word "*time*" in this verse is KAIROS, which is "*a particular season, an opportune time, a special time or fixed season that is at hand.*"

Keep What You Hear

Notice that it says to "*keep*" the things that you hear. There are different kinds of hearing. One is auditory–you hear words. But this hearing means to understand what you hear.

- **John 8:43**
  "Why do ye not understand my speech? *even* because ye cannot **hear** my word."

The Lord Jesus Christ said that the Pharisees could not **hear** His **Words**. They could listen and they could hear, but they did not genuinely believe. It must be both a hearing and an understanding.

- **John 8:47**
  "He that is of God heareth God's **words**: ye therefore hear *them* not, because ye are not of God."

So **hearing** is not simply listening. It is understanding. That is what John says we should do with this book of Revelation. Many people say they do not understand it. There are some things that I do not understand either, but I am going to preach it anyway and I will tell you what I do not understand. There are many things in the Bible, in the Old Testament and the New Testament that we may not understand, but God commands us to read them, keep them, and **hear** them. That is what we want to do with this precious Book. It is the **Word** of God, representing the **Words** of God, so we must be sure to **hear** them.

The time is at hand and we have to read. We have to **hear** in the proper way, and we have to keep that which is written.

Revelation 1:4

"John to the seven churches which are in Asia: Grace *be* unto you, and peace, from him which is, and which was, and which is to come; and from the seven Spirits which are before his throne;"

The seven churches in Asia are listed later on in the book. All of these churches were in Asia Minor: Ephesus, Smyrna, Pergamos, Thyatira, Sardis, Philadelphia, and Laodicea. This description of the One Who is, Who was, and Who is to come, I believe, is referring to God the Father. Later on, we are going to see the description in verse 8 of God the Son, the Lord Jesus Christ. The same dimensions are given for the Father as well as for the Son. The Son is the One before the throne of God. He is, He was, and He is to come. He is eternally in the present, eternally in the past, and eternally in the future.

Notice the seven Spirits which are before his throne. Here, I believe, is the Holy Spirit in His sevenfold attributes.

- **Isaiah 11:2**
  "And the spirit of the LORD shall rest upon him, the spirit of wisdom and understanding, the spirit of counsel and might, the spirit of knowledge and of the fear of the LORD;"

We see here the sevenfold attributes of the Holy Spirit of God. So God the Father, God the Son, and God the Holy Spirit are all equal Persons in the Divine Trinity.

- **Psalm 90:2**
  "Before the mountains were brought forth, or ever thou hadst formed the earth and the world, even **from everlasting to everlasting, thou *art* God**."

Here is the eternality of God, "*which is, which was, and which is to come*."

Grace is getting something that you and I do not deserve. "*Peace*" and other unmerited gifts are given to us through the Lord Jesus Christ. If we have God's "*peace*," we can understand it by the following definition: We can *"Fear nothing from God and be content with our earthly lot, of whatsoever sort it is."* These are the greetings that John gave to the seven churches.

Pre-Tribulation Church Rapture

The "true *church*," composed of all genuinely born-again Christians from the Day of Pentecost until the rapture, is never mentioned after chapter 3. It has been removed from earth to Heaven before the seven-year tribulation.

In the first three chapters of Revelation, the churches are mentioned, but you will not find the church after these chapters until chapter 19. The church has gone to Heaven. There are those who say they do not believe in the pre-tribulation rapture of the true church. Some believe that the rapture is going to take place either in the middle of the tribulation, or in the pre-wrath time, or at the end of the tribulation. All of these views are false views of the church's rapture. The seven-year tribulation is not for the church. It is called Daniel's 70th week of seven years each, making a total of 490 years. 69 weeks (483 years) have all come to pass exactly as Daniel prophesied. This 70th week is for the people of Israel, not for the church.

- Daniel 9:24
  "**Seventy weeks** are determined <u>upon thy people</u> and upon thy holy city, to finish the transgression, and to make an end of sins, and to make reconciliation for iniquity, and to bring in everlasting righteousness, and to seal up the vision and prophecy, and to anoint the most Holy."

"Thy people" refers to Daniel's people, that is, Israel. It has nothing whatsoever to do with the church. The true church will have been raptured to Heaven before this time ever begins.

Revelation 1:5

"And from Jesus Christ, *who is* the faithful witness, *and* the first begotten of the dead, and the prince of the kings of the earth. Unto him that loved us, and washed us from our sins in his own blood,"

The Lord Jesus Christ's Titles

Here is the Lord Jesus Christ. We have mention of God the Father, God the Holy Spirit (verse 4), and now in this verse, the Lord Jesus Christ, God the Son. Notice, the Lord Jesus Christ is called *"the faithful witness."* He is also called *"the first begotten of the dead."* This word, *first begotten*, is PROTOTOKOS. It is a title of honor, a title of privilege, a title of preeminence. He is the only One of His kind. He is the *"Prince,"* the King of the *kings of the earth* and the Leader of them.

- **Hebrews 2:17**
"Wherefore in all things it behoved him to be made like unto *his* brethren, that he might be a **merciful and faithful high priest** in things *pertaining* to God, to make reconciliation for the sins of the people."

Right now the Lord Jesus Christ is at the Father's right hand. He is our *"faithful high priest,"* interceding for those who are genuinely saved.

- **Hebrews 3:1-2**
"Wherefore, holy brethren, partakers of the heavenly calling, consider the Apostle and **High Priest** of our profession, Christ Jesus; Who was **faithful** to him that appointed him, as also Moses *was faithful* in all his house."

The Lord Jesus Christ never did anything against His Father's will. He was **faithful.** He is a **faithful** witness.

- **Revelation 3:14**
"And unto the angel of the church of the Laodiceans write; These things saith the Amen, the **faithful and true** witness, the beginning of the creation of God;"

Again, the Lord Jesus Christ is *"faithful"* and *"true."*

- **Revelation 19:11**
"And I saw heaven opened, and behold a white horse; and he that sat upon him *was* called **Faithful and True,** and in righteousness he doth judge and make war."

This is the Lord Jesus Christ Himself. He is *"faithful"* in all that He does.

That word, *"faithful,"* (PISTOS) means *"persons who show themselves faithful in the transaction of business, the execution of commands, or the discharge of official duties."*

Are we *"faithful"* in all these areas? This is Who the Lord Jesus Christ is—He is *"faithful."*

He is the **Prince** of the kings of the earth. That word, *"Prince,"* is ARCHON. It means *"the Leader, the One Who is over all."*

- **Acts 3:15**
  "And killed the **Prince** of life, whom God hath raised from the dead; whereof we are witnesses."

He is a *"Prince."* He is the *"King,"* but He is also the *"Prince,"* and the Leader.

- **Acts 5:31**
  "Him hath God exalted with his right hand *to be* a **Prince** and a Saviour, for to give repentance to Israel, and forgiveness of sins."

He is a *"Prince,"* and a powerful **Ruler** and Saviour.

- **Revelation 17:14**
  "These shall make war with the Lamb, and the Lamb shall overcome them: for he is **Lord of lords**, and **King of kings**: and they that are with him *are* called, and chosen, and faithful."

He is called the *"Lord of lords, and King of kings."* He is over them. He is the *"Prince over the kings of the earth."*

- **Revelation 19:16**
  "And he hath on *his* vesture and on his thigh a name written, **KING OF KINGS, AND LORD OF LORDS.**"

Here the terms are reversed – *"King of kings, and Lord of lords."* He is over all. Then notice, it's from the One who is the faithful witness, *"who loved us."* I am glad He **loved** us even when we were sinners, lost and Hell-bound.

- **John 3:16**
  "For God so **loved** the world, that he gave his only begotten Son, that whosoever believeth in him should not perish, but have everlasting life."

- **John 13:34**
  "A new commandment I give unto you, That ye **love** one another; as **I have loved you**, that ye also **love** one another."

He **loved** us. We are sinners, but He **loved** us.

- **John 15:9**
  "As the Father hath **loved** me, so have I **loved** you: continue ye in my **love**."
- **John 15:12**
  "This is my commandment, That ye **love** one another, as I have **loved** you."
- **Romans 8:37**
  "Nay, in all these things we are more than conquerors through him that **loved** us."
- **Galatians 2:20**
  "I am crucified with Christ: nevertheless I live; yet not I, but Christ liveth in me: and the life which I now live in the flesh I live by the faith of the Son of God, who **loved** me, and gave himself for me."
- **Ephesians 5:2**
  "And walk in **love**, as Christ also hath **loved** us, and hath given himself for us an offering and a sacrifice to God for a sweetsmelling savour."
- **Ephesians 5:25**
  "Husbands, **love** your wives, even as Christ also **loved** the church, and gave himself for it;"

Loving Our Wife As Christ Loves Us

That is a big order for us who are husbands. We are not successful in it, but God commands us to love our wives. No matter what they do, what they say, where they are, we husbands are to love them and continue to love them.

The sad thing about the **love** of the Lord Jesus Christ and the **love** of God is that the hyper-Calvinists (5-point Calvinists), like Harold Camping, president of Family Radio, do not believe God **loves** all the sinners of the world, but only the "*elect.*" That's a terrible, horrible, devilish doctrine. When the Bible says "*God so loved the world*," the hyper-Calvinists falsely interpret this to mean that God does not **love** the entire "*world*," but God just **loves** the world of the "*elect.*" So they falsely reinterpret and twist the Scripture. They are "*wresting*" the "*Scriptures*" unto "*their own destruction*" (2 Peter 3:16).

Christ Died For All People

We have to believe and preach that God loves all the sinners of the world, including us. Saved, lost, elect, non-elect –everybody. He loves us. That love is extended, and His provision for salvation is extended for all. He has given us Himself. He died for the sins of the whole world.

If you read the tract that Harold Camping has spread through Family Radio, you read that God's **love** is limited only to the *"elect."* They've spread that tract, representing their "Gospel," all over the world, in all the languages of the world. They asked for missionaries to go and pass out these false and untrue tracts. This is sad, indeed.

Notice also, in this verse, The Lord Jesus Christ *"washed us from our sins in His own blood."* We can partake of being *"washed from our sins"* by genuine faith in the Lord Jesus Christ Who shed His **blood** for all of us sinners on the cross of Calvary.

- **1 Corinthians 6:9-11**
  "Know ye not that the unrighteous shall not inherit the kingdom of God? Be not deceived: neither fornicators, nor idolaters, nor adulterers, nor effeminate, nor abusers of themselves with mankind, Nor thieves, nor covetous, nor drunkards, nor revilers, nor extortioners, shall inherit the kingdom of God. And such were some of you: but **ye are washed**, but ye are sanctified, but ye are justified in the Name of the Lord Jesus Christ, and by the Spirit of our God."

Can God **wash** all these people? Yes. If we genuinely come to the Lord Jesus Christ, He can **wash** us. Praise the Lord for that **washing**.

In pages 44-48 of my book *John MacArthur's Heresy on the Blood of Christ* (BFT #1400 @ $14.00 + $8.00 S&H), I list fourteen effects of the literal **blood** of the Lord Jesus Christ that are denied by John MacArthur. He says **blood** doesn't mean **blood**; it's just a metonym–a figure of speech–for death. No. Death is one thing, THANATOS; **blood** (HAIMA) is another. They're different words.

Through the **blood** of the Lord Jesus Christ the Scripture says we have:

1. **Redemption** (Leviticus 17:11; Matthew 26:28; Acts 20:28; Romans 5:9; Ephesians 1:7; Colossians 1:14; 1 Peter 1:18-19; Revelation 5:9)
2. **Propitiation** (Romans 3:25)
3. **Justification** (Romans 5:9)
4. **Fellowship** (Ephesians 2:13)

5. **Peace** (Ephesians 1:20)
6. **Forgiveness** (Ephesians 1:7; Colossians 1:14)
7. **Sanctification** (Hebrews 13:12)
8. **Reconciliation** (Colossians 1:20)
9. **Cleansing** (Hebrews 9:14; Hebrews 9:23; 1 John 1:7; Revelation 1:5; Revelation 7:14)
10. **Remembrance** (1 Corinthians 11:25)
11. **Boldness** (Hebrews 10:19)
12. **Maturity** (Hebrews 11:20)
13. **Punishment** (if we neglect the blood) (Hebrews 10:29; 1 Corinthians 11:29)
14. **Victory** (Revelation 12:11)

All fourteen of these Biblical effects of the literal "*blood*" of the Lord Jesus Christ cannot be understood like John MacArthur understands them as meaning only "*death*." This is one of the most serious heresies (among many others) that are held by John MacArthur.

As of this printing, we have over 3,009 messages on SermonAudio.com, but I have to be careful when I talk about John MacArthur. Apparently they have a participant who believes in MacArthur's false views on the **blood** of the Lord Jesus Christ. If I just bring it up in sermons, it's all right, but they've taken off about five of my messages on the **blood** of the Lord Jesus Christ. They also took off David Cloud's messages against Calvinism, because there are many Calvinists who participate in SermonAudio.com.

Plain Sense–Common Sense

When the Bible says we are washed by the blood of the Lord Jesus Christ, we are washed by "*the blood of Christ*" (Ephesians 2:13). If language means anything, in the Bible, "*Where the PLAIN SENSE makes COMMON SENSE, SEEK NO OTHER SENSE.*"

Yes, He died for the sins of the world. Yes, He shed His blood on the cross of Calvary. Sometimes the Bible talks about the death of the Lord Jesus Christ; sometimes it talks about the blood of the Lord Jesus Christ. All of these fourteen things about the blood of the Lord Jesus Christ are important and should never be minimized as John MacArthur and his followers do.

Revelation 1:6

"And hath made us kings and priests unto God and his Father; to him be glory and dominion for ever and ever. Amen."

- Revelation 5:10
  "And hast made us unto our God **kings and priests:** and we shall reign on the earth."

The Saved Are Believer-Priests

I don't believe in the Roman Catholic priesthood, but genuinely saved people have *"access"* (Ephesians 2:28) to God the Father through God the Son, the Lord Jesus Christ, just as the "high priest" of the Old Testament. One day genuinely saved people will be like *"kings."* This is because they will *"reign with Christ a thousand years"* during the Millennium (Revelation 20:4 & 6). They shall also *"reign for ever and ever"* (Revelation 22:5).

- Revelation 20:6
  "Blessed and holy *is* he that hath part in the first resurrection: on such the second death hath no power, but they shall be **priests** of God and of Christ, and shall **reign** with him a thousand years."
- Revelation 22:5
  "And there shall be no night there; and they need no candle, neither light of the sun; for the Lord God giveth them light: and **they shall reign for ever and ever.**"
- Luke 19:17-19
  "And he said unto him, Well, thou good servant: because thou hast been faithful in a very little, have thou **authority** over ten cities. And the second came, saying, Lord, thy pound hath gained five pounds. And he said likewise to him, Be thou also over five cities."

The Saved Will Reign With Christ

The thinking of many is that with our new resurrected bodies, during the millennial reign of the Lord Jesus Christ, the genuine believers will be helping the Lord Jesus Christ, reigning with Him for 1,000 years. What city is going to be yours? Philadelphia? Cherry Hill? Collingswood? Cleveland? New York City? Or where?

We who are genuinely born-again and truly saved will have new bodies. We'll not be like we are here with simple minds and often foolish actions. Our glorified bodies will be like unto the Lord Jesus Christ's body (Philippians 3:21; 1 John 3:2) and so we will be reigning with Him.

"*To Him be the glory and dominion*"—not to us—"*for ever and ever.*" When you praise yourself instead of the Lord and Saviour, something's amiss. That's what boasting and bragging does. We cannot boast, because we are saved by God's **grace**. We didn't save ourselves.

- **Ephesians 2:8-9**
  "For by **grace** are ye saved through faith; and that not of yourselves: it is the gift of God: **Not of works**, lest any man should boast."

Revelation 1:7

"**Behold, he cometh with clouds; and every eye shall see him, and they *also* which pierced him: and all kindreds of the earth shall wail because of him. Even so, Amen.**"

This is the second phase of the Lord Jesus Christ's second coming. At that time, "*every eye shall see Him.*" This is not the rapture when He snatches away all the true Christians, the genuinely saved and born-again ones. This second phase of His second coming in Glory will take place after the tribulation is over.

- **Zechariah 12:10**
  "And I will pour upon the house of David, and upon the inhabitants of Jerusalem, the spirit of grace and of supplications: and **they shall look upon me whom they have pierced**, and they shall **mourn for him**, as one mourneth for *his* only *son*, and shall be in **bitterness** for him, as one that is in bitterness for *his* firstborn."

All Shall "Wail" At Christ One Day

Israel will see the Lord Jesus Christ and mourn for Him as well. Why are they going to wail? They're going to "*wail because of Him,*" in the second phase of His second coming. At that time, His feet will touch the Mount of Olives (Zechariah 14:4). Then the mount will split, half to the north and half to the south. He will be the victor of war after the Battle of

Armageddon. When all the kings and all the nations gather in Israel against the Lord Jesus Christ and His people–the Jews who are there in Palestine–He will put down that rebellion in this Battle of Armageddon. At this time, "*all the kindreds of the earth shall wail because of Him.*" We'll see that in Chapters 16 and 19 as well. When He does come in the second phase of His second coming, His feet will touch that Mount of Olives from which He ascended.

Revelation 1:8

"I am Alpha and Omega, the beginning and the ending, saith the Lord, which is, and which was, and which is to come, the Almighty."

Here is the Lord Jesus Christ Himself. Remember in the earlier verse it was God the Father, "*Alpha and Omega,*" the first letter of the Greek alphabet, the last letter of the Greek alphabet, and everything in between. The "*beginning and the ending.*"

Christ Is Present, Past, & Future

There's nothing that is absent from the Lord Jesus Christ. He's everything that we need–present, past, and future. He supplies it. "*Which is, and which was, and which is to come.*" There's no time (as we understand it on earth) with the Lord Jesus Christ. Nor is there any time with God the Father, as it said in the earlier verse (verse 4).

He's called the "*Almighty*" (PANTOKRATOR). PANTO means "*all*" and KRATOR means "*powerful, reigning and ruling.*" It's He who holds sway over all things. Though He would like to, the Lord Jesus Christ does not hold sway over all people on this earth today, sad to say. Does He hold sway over you and me if we're genuinely born-again and truly saved? Is He the "*Almighty*" over us? That's what He demands. He demands that He be our Lord, that is, He to Whom we submit and obey (Romans 12:1-2). He's the "*Almighty*" Who has no beginning and no ending.

- **Micah 5:2**
  "But thou, Bethlehem Ephratah, *though* thou be little among the thousands of Judah, *yet* out of thee shall he come forth unto me *that is* to be ruler in Israel; whose **goings forth** *have been* from of old, **from everlasting.**"

This is talking about the Lord Jesus Christ.

The NIV's Heresy In Micah 5:2

The NIV mistranslates this horribly. It doesn't say, *"whose goings forth have been from of old,"* it just says *"from ancient days."* Not *"from everlasting,"* and not *"whose goings forth."* It says, *"whose origins,"* speaking of the Lord Jesus Christ having an *"origin."* He has no *"origin."* He always was—*"which is, and which was, and which is to come."* Micah 5:2 is a picture of Him Who is *"from everlasting."*

- John 8:56-59
  "Your father Abraham rejoiced to see my day: and he saw *it*, and was glad. Then said the Jews unto him, Thou art not yet fifty years old, and hast thou seen Abraham? Jesus said unto them, Verily, verily, I say unto you, **Before Abraham was, I am.** Then took they up stones to cast at him: but Jesus hid himself, and went out of the temple, **going through the midst of them, and so passed by.**"

Jehovah in the Old Testament revealed Himself to Moses as *"I am."* They took up stones to cast at the Lord Jesus Christ because they knew that He was saying He was the *"I am"* from all eternity past to all eternity future. They knew He was saying that He was Deity and to them it was blasphemy.

The Denial Of Christ's Omnipotence

The new versions leave out a phrase in this passage. They stop at the words: *"went out of the temple."* Not the Textus Receptus and the King James Bible. They both say, *"going through the midst of them, and so passed by."* The Gnostic heretics that doctored the *"B"* and *Aleph* (Vatican and Sinai) manuscripts did not believe in the omnipotence of the Lord Jesus Christ. They didn't see how that could be, because they thought He was just a man. How could He go "through the midst of them" when they hated Him and were ready to stone Him to death? The power of God is in our Bible. He's an omnipotent Saviour and He went right *"through the midst of them."*

- Hebrews 13:8
  "Jesus Christ the same yesterday, and to day, and for ever."

Christ, The Same Almighty Saviour

He's the same "Almighty." He's the same Saviour. He's the One Who can keep us and satisfy us from all eternity past, to the present, and on into the eternal future. He is the One Who is mentioned here in Revelation 1:8 as the everlasting Son of God, and God the Son.

Revelation 1:9

"I John, who also am your brother, and companion in tribulation, and in the kingdom and patience of Jesus Christ, was in the isle that is called Patmos, for the word of God, and for the testimony of Jesus Christ."

John was a humble man. He was an apostle, chosen by the Lord Jesus Christ. They had trouble even then in the New Testament times. John was banished to the isle of *"Patmos."* That island is in the Aegean Sea off the coast of Asia Minor or Turkey. He was banished to that little barren island with nothing much on it. His persecutors did not kill him, they just banished him. God revealed this book of Revelation to that banished prophet and apostle so that we would know what's going to happen in the future. God's right on His time schedule. Tribulation in general, either great or small, is a part of the genuine Christian walk. It is to be distinguished, however, from the seven-year tribulation period.

- **Matthew 13:20**
  "But he that received the seed into stony places, the same is he that heareth the word, and anon with joy receiveth it;"

The seed that fell on stony places just endured for a time. When **tribulation** and persecution came, these people were offended. I don't believe any of those first three soils or grounds were productive. It was only the good soil that brought forth fruit.

- **Matthew 24:21**
  "For then shall be great **tribulation**, such as was not since the beginning of the world to this time, no, nor ever shall be."

The Seven-Year Tribulation

The tribulation is seven years. I believe the great tribulation is the last half of that seven-year period.

- **John 16:33**
  "These things I have spoken unto you, that in me ye might have peace. In the world ye shall have **tribulation**: but be of good cheer; I have overcome the world."

Do you have any **tribulation**? If not, I wonder if you're His. If you're His, you will have **tribulation** in this world, but peace in Him.

- **Acts 14:22**
"Confirming the souls of the disciples, *and* exhorting them to continue in the faith, and that we must through much **tribulation** enter into the kingdom of God."

Godly Christians Receive Trouble

Tribulation involves trouble or trials. Trouble goes with genuine Christianity. Just like a glove and a hand, they go together. Love and marriage should go together. Sometimes they don't.

- **Romans 5:3**
"And not only *so*, but we glory in **tribulations** also: knowing that **tribulation** worketh patience;"

Trouble is not something we should try to escape. If it comes, it comes and we should realize that it works patience in us. Every time we have trouble, whatever it may be, we should be patient.

I lost my notes this morning and I couldn't figure out where they were. I was adjusting the microphone and I had laid them down at the piano. I never lay anything down at the piano. I looked all over the house. I had not lost my notes in five years, since the first service of this church. That little **tribulation** worked a little patience. When things don't go our way, we have to be patient. We have to learn patience in **tribulation**.

- **Romans 8:35**
  "Who shall separate us from the love of Christ? *shall* **tribulation**, or distress, or persecution, or famine, or nakedness, or peril, or sword?"

- **Romans 12:12**
  "Rejoicing in hope; patient in **tribulation**; continuing instant in prayer;"

Be patient in that trouble.

- **2 Corinthians 1:4**
  "Who comforteth us in all our **tribulation**, that we may be able to comfort them which are in any trouble, by the comfort wherewith we ourselves are comforted of God."

God comforts in all our **tribulation**. There's a comfort in trouble.

- **2 Corinthians 7:4**
  "Great *is* my boldness of speech toward you, great *is* my glorying of you: I am filled with comfort, I am exceeding joyful in all our **tribulation**."

Joy and trouble at the same time? That's right. Joy when you're having your teeth drilled? Yes, joy because you know it's going to be over soon – or at least sometime. Joy in **tribulation** is the joy the Spirit of God can give us.

- **1 Thessalonians 3:4**
  "For verily, when we were with you, we told you before that we should suffer **tribulation**; even as it came to pass, and ye know."

The Thessalonian Christians received **tribulation**. Paul warned them about it. The Lord Jesus Christ warns us about it.

Why was John on that little isle of Patmos in the Aegean Sea?
For two reasons:
1. *"For the Word of God"*; and
2. *"For the testimony of Jesus Christ."*

The *"Word of God"* always to us has meant *"the Words of God."* That's what it means. The **Words** of God. Not just simply messages, thoughts, concepts, ideas, or teachings, but the **Words** of God.

That's why John was there. The *"Words of God"* are important. If you believe the *"Words of God"* and stand for the "Words of God" in Scripture, you're going to have problems with some of the ones who are not standing for the *"Words of God."*

We've said many times, and I believe it, that the Roman Catholic Church is <u>not</u> standing for the *"Words of God."* They have their Latin Bible and they use their Latin translations which have many defects when compared to proper and precious Traditional Greek *"Words of God."*

Denial Of God-Breathed Words

The apostate, modernist liberals have no idea that the Words of God are even *"inspired"* and *"God-breathed"* even in the originals, much less in the Traditional Hebrew, Aramaic, and Greek <u>Words</u> that underlie our King James Bible. They have all kinds of modern Bibles that they use.

The new evangelicals don't have any stand on the *"Words of God"* being preserved in the Hebrew, Aramaic, and Greek Words underlying our King James Bible. They use all kinds of texts and versions.

For example, Billy Graham sells all kinds of versions and says, "This is the best," and then he says, "This one's the best." I don't know what his "best" means. Different people advertise different versions.

Then there are the fundamentalists. Some of us stand on the King James Bible in the right way. But some stand in a false way on the King James Bible. Peter Ruckman, Gail Riplinger, and their followers say that the King James Bible is *"inspired of God"* and *"God-breathed"* rather than being the only true, reliable, and accurate English translation of the *"inspired"* and *"God-breathed"* Hebrew, Aramaic, and Greek Words that underlie it. Their teaching on this doctrine is a serious heresy. These false teachers teach that the King James Bible is just like the originals and therefore that it supersedes the Hebrew, Aramaic, and the Greek Words from which it was taken. They even say that the King James Bible "corrects" the Hebrew, Aramaic, and Greek Words and that we should never use these languages. No. How can something that is the result and the product correct its source? That's heresy. Peter Ruckman, Gail Riplinger, and their followers say that the King James Bible is a direct revelation from God, not simply an excellent translation and that the Hebrew, Aramaic, and Greek Words should be trashed as unneeded.

There are some fundamentalist pastors and teachers who don't go as far as either Ruckman or Riplinger, but say the King James Bible is *"inspired"* or *"God-breathed"* in some way. This also is confusing and a serious error. Because of the King James Bible's true, faithful, and accurate translation into English of the proper Hebrew, Aramaic, and Greek Words, I have called the King James Bible, in the sub-title of my book, *Defending the King James Bible*, "God's Words Kept Intact In English." But it should never be called *"inspired."* That term must be confined to the Hebrew, Aramaic, and Greek Words that God gave us.

Denial Of Bible Preservation

There are fundamentalists who do not believe that the Hebrew, Aramaic, and Greek Words of God have been preserved, nor do they believe that there was even any promise in the Bible to the effect that these Words would be preserved. This is also a heresy. As I have said before, some of our fundamentalist friends are friends in many areas, but not in this area of the Bible. Bob Jones University (BJU) is the leader in this heresy, teaching that God has never even promised to preserve His

Hebrew, Aramaic, and Greek Words, much less that these Words have been preserved. Other fundamentalist schools have followed BJU in this heresy such as Detroit Baptist Seminary, Calvary Baptist Seminary, Central Baptist Seminary, Maranatha Baptist Bible College, and many other fundamentalist schools.

I was there at Maranatha Baptist Bible College three times, at least, when Dr. Myron Cedarholm was the president of that school. He had me speak about the Dean Burgon Society. He had me speak on the Textus Receptus and the King James Bible. When he turned it over to his nephew, all was changed. His nephew brought back the Gnostic Critical Westcott and Hort Greek text into the school.

We have some that are not in favor of the "*Words of God*" being preserved, even among fundamentalists, but I am glad that there are still some of us who have a proper understanding of the "*Word of God*" and the "*Words of God.*" I believe the Bible has been promised to be preserved–the Hebrew, Aramaic, and Greek **Words**. We have verses that show that. Here are some of them.

- **Matthew 5:18**
  "For verily I say unto you, Till heaven and earth pass, **one jot or one tittle** shall **in no wise pass** from the law, till all be fulfilled."
- **Matthew 24:35**
  "Heaven and earth shall pass away, but **my words shall not pass away.**"
- **Mark 13:31**
  "Heaven and earth shall pass away: but **my words shall not pass away.**"
- **Luke 21:33**
  "Heaven and earth shall pass away: but **my words shall not pass away.**"

Only Accurate English Translation

We hold to that. I believe that the King James Bible is the only true, reliable, and accurate English translation from those preserved Hebrew, Aramaic, and Greek Words.

Colonel Pedro Almeida, in Brazil, is working on an accurate Portuguese translation. The Trinitarian Bible Society has a Portuguese translation but the question is, "Is it proper and done right in every area?" The Trinitarian Bible Society in Brazil took out any reference on their website to the King James Bible, replacing it with *"the English Bible."* That could mean any version. They also no longer make any reference to the attacking of false versions in the Portuguese. Brother Almeida gave a good lecture to the Dean Burgon Society on the Portuguese Bible several years ago. That Portuguese Bible needs corrections because the Trinitarian Bible Society didn't do the whole thing properly. They also did not do the Spanish version completely right. At least the Trinitarian Bible Society has the right Hebrew, Aramaic, and Greek text, for now. We hope they always stay with that standard. Dr. Humberto Gomez has given us an accurate Spanish translation in his Reina-Valera-Gomez.

The Battle For The Words Of God

We have a battle *"for the Words of God"* and *"the testimony of Jesus Christ."* That's why John was banished to the isle of Patmos. He was a known Christian. He was not only a known Christian, but also a known disciple and apostle of the Lord Jesus Christ. He was known because he wrote a Gospel that told about the Lord Jesus Christ, His work, and His miracles.

- **John 20:30-31**
  "And many other signs truly did Jesus in the presence of his disciples, which are not written in this book: But these are written, that ye might believe that Jesus is the Christ, the Son of God; and that believing ye might have life through his name."

His enemies knew John was a strong follower of the Lord Jesus Christ. They knew he had written his Gospel as well as 1 John, 2 John, and 3 John–the epistles to genuine believers. Because he had a strong testimony for the Lord Jesus Christ, he was banished to that little island. We don't know how old he was when he died, but I'm sure he died *"with his boots on"* as they say, witnessing for the Lord Jesus Christ until death took him Home. John died after these things in this book were revealed to him by God the Father, by the Lord Jesus Christ, by His angel, and by God the Holy Spirit. John wrote all that was shortly to come to pass. He was faithful and had a *"testimony of Jesus Christ."* That's why he was banished.

We Could Also Be Banished

You and I may be banished one of these days because we do have a *"testimony of Jesus Christ"*—because we stand for the very Words of the living God. We must be faithful in all that what we do for our Saviour.

Revelation 1:10

"I was in the Spirit on the Lord's day, and heard behind me a great voice, as of a trumpet,"

The Lord's Day Defined

Some have said that the *"Lord's day"* means *"the day of the Lord."* No, I don't believe it's *"the day of the Lord."* I think it's the *"Lord's day"* like we worship on the first day of the week, Sunday—the *"Lord's day."* The reason I say that is, the word that's used here is KURIAKOS. It's not KURIOS. Every other time in the New Testament when it mentions *"the day of the Lord"* the Greek Words are HEMERA *(the day)* KURIOS *(of the Lord).* Here the Greek Word is KURIAKOS. It's a different word. I think it's the Lordly day and John was in the Spirit on the *"Lord's day."* I believe it was the first day of the week. I think that's when the disciples worshipped the Lord Jesus Christ just as we do today.

John heard behind him *"a great voice, as of a trumpet"*— possibly the voice of the Lord Jesus Christ. This *"great voice"* is going to tell him now what to say and what to write.

- **Deuteronomy 5:22**
  "These **words** the LORD spake unto all your assembly in the mount out of the midst of the fire, of the cloud, and of the thick darkness, with **a great voice**: and he added no more. And he wrote them in two tables of stone, and delivered them unto me."

- **Revelation 11:12**
  "And they heard **a great voice** from heaven saying unto them, Come up hither. And they ascended up to heaven in a cloud; and their enemies beheld them."

The Two Faithful Witnesses

These are the two witnesses. Some believe, as I do, that they are Moses and Elijah. Others believe they are Moses and Enoch, or Enoch and Elijah. These two witnesses were transported to Heaven, hearing "*a great voice.*"

- Revelation 21:3
  "And I heard **a great voice** out of heaven saying, Behold, the tabernacle of God *is* with men, and he will dwell with them, and they shall be his people, and God himself shall be with them, *and be* their God."

The Voice As A Trumpet

John says in the present verse that he heard behind him "*a great voice, as of a trumpet.*" Notice that word "*as.*" Whenever you see in Revelation "as," it means "*as or like, similar to.*" It's a figure of speech. The voice was "*like a trumpet.*" Not that he had a "*trumpet,*" but it was "*as a trumpet.*" So all the way through, whenever we see "*as*" or "like" we have to remember this is a picture – similar to, not exactly as. It's a symbol.

- 1 Corinthians 15:52
  "In a moment, in the twinkling of an eye, at the last **trump**: for the **trumpet** shall sound, and the dead shall be raised incorruptible, and we shall be changed."

The Rapture Trumpet

At the rapture of the true church, the snatching away of all the genuinely born-again Christians, there's going to be a "*trump.*" A "*trumpet*" shall sound. That's a real "*trumpet.*"

- 1 Thessalonians 4:16
  "For the Lord himself shall descend from heaven **with a shout**, with the voice of the archangel, and with the **trump** of God: and the dead in Christ shall rise first:"

The Lord Jesus Christ's Voice

There's the "*great voice,*" "*with a shout.*" That's why I think it's probably the voice of the Lord Jesus Christ that John heard. The voice of the archangel is another voice. After all, in

Revelation 1:1, this book is called *"the revelation of Jesus Christ."*

John is telling us what is, what was, and what shall be in the future. He's especially telling us that this is a Saviour that is, and was, and shall be–present, past, and future. The *"Alpha and Omega."* The *"beginning and the ending."* He who **loved** us and **washed** us from our sins in His own **blood**. That's the wonderful Gospel message that we should take to our fellow people, neighbors, and friends around the world–that He **loved** us and **washed** us from our sins.

Revelation 1:11

"Saying, I am Alpha and Omega, the first and the last: and, What thou seest, write in a book, and send *it* unto the seven churches which are in Asia; unto Ephesus, and unto Smyrna, and unto Pergamos, and unto Thyatira, and unto Sardis, and unto Philadelphia, and unto Laodicea."

The Alpha and Omega

This verse is from the *"Alpha and Omega,"* the Lord Jesus Christ Himself. He is the Author of this book, called *"the first and the last."* John is to write in a book what he sees. We have that book in the book of Revelation. He was to send it to the seven churches in Asia. That is Asia Minor in present-day Turkey.

These seven churches are also representative, I believe, of churches today. I believe we can apply the things directed to these churches to churches in our day as well. I also believe that these are prophetic churches. These are churches that also give us a picture of the course of church history from the apostolic time to the end of the church age before the Lord Jesus Christ comes in the rapture. I believe these are prophetic churches, as well as churches that actually existed in those days.

- **Revelation 1:8**
  "I am **Alpha and Omega**, the **beginning and the ending**, saith the Lord, which is, and which was, and which is to come, the Almighty."

The Lord Jesus Christ is called the *"Alpha and Omega,"* the first, and the last, and everything in between.

- Revelation 21:6
  "And he said unto me, It is done. I am *Alpha and Omega*, the **beginning and the end.** I will give unto him that is athirst of the fountain of the water of life freely."

The Beginning And The Ending

"Alpha and Omega" are Greek letters. The Lord is All that there is. He was in the *"beginning,"* at the first in the creation. He will be at the ending, when all is wiped away and changed. Again, this is the Lord Jesus Christ Himself.

- Revelation 1:17
  "And when I saw him, I fell at his feet as dead. And he laid his right hand upon me, saying unto me, Fear not; I am the **first and the last:**"

The Lord Jesus Christ–The Creator

He was before creation. He created all things. When this world is changed and there is a new Heaven and a new earth, He will be there as well.

- Revelation 22:13
  "I am Alpha and Omega, the beginning and the end, the **first and the last.**"
- Revelation 2:8
  "And unto the angel of the church in Smyrna write; These things saith the **first and the last,** which was dead, and is alive."

This is a title of our Saviour.

- John 1:1-3
  "In the beginning was the Word, and the Word was with God, and the Word was God. The same was **in the beginning with God.** All things were made by him; and without him was not any thing made that was made."

He's the living Word, and He was from the very **beginning.** All these titles belong to the Saviour.

The churches mentioned here were in Asia Minor (now called Turkey). Ephesus is mentioned seventeen times in Scripture; Smyrna, only two times; Pergamos, two times; Thyatira, four times; Sardis, three times; Philadelphia, two times; and Laodicea, four times. These churches were real churches.

John was to send this on to the churches of Asia Minor and to warn them. I believe the churches of today—our church and all other churches —need to be warned just like these in Revelation were. There were good things about them and there were bad things about them. We'll see that as we move along.

Revelation 1:12

"And I turned to see the voice that spake with me. And being turned, I saw seven golden candlesticks;"

It may seem a little strange to us that John turned to <u>see</u> the "*voice*," but he was referring to the Person speaking. This was the Lord Jesus Christ Himself that spake to him.

The Seven Golden Candlesticks

In Revelation 1:20, we learn that the seven "*candlesticks*" are the seven churches. They're called "*candlesticks.*" These should light up things. A "candlestick" with its lights should shine and bring light.

- **Matthew 5:14**
  "Ye are the **light** of the world. A city that is set on an hill cannot be hid."
- **John 8:12**
  "Then spake Jesus again unto them, saying, I am the **light** of the world: he that followeth me shall not walk in darkness, but shall have the light of life."
- **Exodus 25:31**
  "And thou shalt make a **candlestick** of pure gold: of beaten work shall the **candlestick** be made: his shaft and his branches, his bowls, his knops, and his flowers, shall be of the same."
- **Leviticus 24:2-4**
  "Command the children of Israel, that they bring unto thee pure oil olive beaten for the **light,** to cause the lamps to burn continually. Without the vail of the testimony, in the tabernacle of the congregation, shall Aaron order it from the evening unto the morning before the LORD continually: *it shall be* a statute for ever in your generations. He shall order the lamps upon the pure **candlestick** before the LORD continually."

This lamp was to be continually burning. It was placed right outside the vail before the holy of holies. This shows to us that our lamps–the lamp of this church, the lamp of any church–should be burning continuously. Not closing its doors, but continuously burning. The Lord Jesus Christ is the **light** of the world, and He tells us we are to let our **light** shine before men.

- **Matthew 5:16**
  "Let your **light** so shine before men, that they may see your good works, and glorify your Father which is in heaven."

This is what we have to do–not to glorify ourselves, but to glorify our Father which is in Heaven.

Revelation 1:13

"And in the midst of the seven candlesticks *one* like unto the Son of man, clothed with a garment down to the foot, and girt about the paps with a golden girdle."

Remember, in verse 20, the "**candlesticks**" are the seven churches of Ephesus, Smyrna, Pergamos, Thyatira, Sardis, Philadelphia, and Laodicea. There's the Lord Jesus Christ right in the midst of them. If He were in the midst of the churches today in this country, He would be sad –not only for the Roman Catholic system and churches that are far, far away, not only for the modernist liberal churches, not only for the new evangelical churches, but I'm sad to say, also for some of the fundamental churches (they that call themselves fundamental). He would be sad as well because of their departure from the true Words of God.

The "*garment*" from head to foot is a "*garment*" like that of a high priest. The Lord Jesus Christ is our High Priest gone into Heaven. It's the Heavenly vision.

- **Exodus 28:2-3**
  "And thou shalt make holy **garments** for Aaron thy brother for glory and for beauty. And thou shalt speak unto all *that are* wise hearted, whom I have filled with the spirit of wisdom, that they may make Aaron's **garments** to consecrate him, that he may minister unto me in the priest's office."

Christ Our Great High Priest

The Lord Jesus Christ was the Saviour and the Lamb of God at Calvary. Now He's making intercession for the genuine Christians at the right hand of the Father as our great High Priest.

- **Exodus 28:6**
  "And they shall make the **ephod** *of* gold, *of* blue, and *of* purple, *of* scarlet, and fine twined linen, with cunning work."
- **Exodus 35:19**
  "The cloths of service, to do service in the holy *place,* the holy **garments** for Aaron the priest, and the **garments** of his sons, to minister in the priest's office."

The High Priest's Garments

The garments of the Lord Jesus Christ are the garments of a High Priest. Not the high priesthood of Aaron, but the high priesthood of Melchisedec. He's our great High Priest who ever liveth to make intercession for us (Romans 8:34; Hebrews 7:25). This is what John saw as he turned, in the midst of the candlesticks. This is a picture of our Saviour. He's there, wanting to help genuinely saved people and to intercede for us.

- **1 John 2:1**
  "My little children, these things write I unto you, that ye sin not. And if any man sin, we have an **advocate** with the Father, Jesus Christ the righteous:"

Revelation 1:14

"His head and his hairs were white like wool, as white as snow; and his eyes were as a flame of fire;"

We're seeing a description of the Lord Jesus Christ at the right hand of the Father in Glory. First, *"His head and his hairs were white like wool, as white as snow."* This indicates His purity, and His sinlessness. It also indicates age and maturity, experience, and understanding. It commands respect.

- **Leviticus 19:32**
  "Thou shalt rise up before the **hoary head**, and honour the face of the **old man**, and fear thy God: I *am* the LORD."

The Asians, I think, take this too far. They worship the **old people.** When they die, they pray to the **old people.** I don't agree with that, but there should be respect for **old age**. These young "whippersnappers," as I call them, that yell and scream at **people, older** than they, and have no respect at all for them, is a terrible thing. It's an atrocity.

- **Proverbs 16:31**
  "The **hoary head** *is* a **crown of glory,** *if* it be found in the way of righteousness."

There's no fool like an old fool, if he's not in the way of righteousness. The **white hair** in itself doesn't mean anything, but if he's found in the way of righteousness, what a wonderful *"crown of glory."* Some people refer to *"white hair"* as "snow on the top" of the **head.** Some have a little bit less "snow" than others. The Lord Jesus Christ's **head** shows purity, age, experience, maturity, and understanding.

- **Isaiah 1:18**
  "Come now, and let us reason together, saith the LORD: though your sins be as scarlet, they shall be as **white as snow**; though they be red like crimson, they shall be **as wool.**"

"**Snow**" speaks of purity. Through Calvary, through genuine faith in the Lord Jesus Christ, our sins can be **washed** away and made *"white."*

- **Daniel 7:9**
  "I beheld till the thrones were cast down, and the Ancient of days did sit, whose **garment** *was* **white as snow,** and the hair of his **head** like the pure **wool:** his throne *was like* the fiery flame, *and* his wheels *as* burning fire."

This is a picture of the Lord Jesus Christ in Daniel's prophecy, whose **garment** was as *"white as snow"* and his **head** like pure *"wool."* This picture in Daniel is the same as that in Revelation that John saw.

- **Daniel 12:10**
  "Many shall be purified, and made **white,** and tried; but the wicked shall do wickedly: and none of the wicked shall understand; but the wise shall understand."

"White" is a symbol and picture of purification and purity.

- **Psalm 51:7**
  "Purge me with hyssop, and I shall be clean: wash me, and I shall be **whiter than snow.**"

This *"whiter than snow"* is the purging from sin. Our sins are forgiven by the Lord Jesus Christ, by genuine faith in Him, by redemption, by being genuinely born-again. We are given the righteousness of God and purity.

- **Lamentations 4:7**
  "Her Nazarites were purer than **snow,** they were **whiter** than milk, they were more ruddy in body than rubies, their polishing *was* of sapphire:"

The Nazarites were those who had vowed a vow of separation. These are pictures in Scripture of purity.

- **Mark 9:3**
  "And his **raiment** became shining, exceeding **white as snow**; so as no fuller on earth can **white** them."

Sometimes Snow Must Be Defined

Some of the translations that are wrong, in different versions all over the world, don't say in Isaiah 1:18, that your sins shall be as *"white as snow,"* because they say, "Well, the translators didn't know anything about "snow," so let's put another word in there." So they use some other word instead of snow. My conviction is, teach them what *"snow"* is. If they don't know what *"snow"* is, show them a picture of it. Show them on the television or on the Internet.

God uses the illustration of *"white as snow."* As the "snow" falls down it's *"white,"* it's pure. When it gets dirty on the ground after people walk on it, it's different.

- **Revelation 7:14**
  "And I said unto him, Sir, thou knowest. And he said to me, These are they which came out of great **tribulation**, and have **washed** their robes, and made them **white** in the **blood** of the Lamb."

These are the Biblical saints that have been either crucified or otherwise murdered during the future seven-year tribulation period. Again, the blood of the Lord Jesus Christ will cleanse them and make them *"white."*

The Lord's Eyes As Fire

Notice also the Lord Jesus Christ's *"eyes."* This is a picture of the risen Saviour, our Great High Priest in Glory. *"His eyes were as a flame of fire."* Remember that every time we see the word *"as,"* or *"like,"* it's a simile. It's a picture. It doesn't mean there was *"fire"* going out of *"His eyes,"* but it was *"as a flame of fire."*

"Fire" is piercing. *"Fire"* is also clearly seen. It would also speak of His being angry at sin. When He looks at us and the sin in our lives, there's *"fire"* in His *"eyes."* You've seen *"fire"* in the *"eyes"* of people when they're angry at you, or wanting to fight you or hit you.

- **Daniel 7:9**
  "I beheld till the thrones were cast down, and the Ancient of days did sit, whose **garment** *was* **white as snow**, and the **hair** of his **head** like the pure **wool**: his throne *was like* the fiery **flame**, *and* his wheels *as* burning **fire**."

This is the same vision that Daniel saw of the Lord Jesus Christ. The picture of *"fire"* is mentioned of the Lord in many places in the Bible.

- **Acts 7:30**
  "And when forty years were expired, there appeared to him in the wilderness of mount Sina an angel of the Lord in a **flame of fire** in a bush."

This is a picture of God's purity, God's holiness, and God's justice.

- **Hebrews 12:29**
  "For our God *is* a consuming **fire**."

That's a picture of God. Some people say that God is all love and goodness. No, He's also a *"fire"* that consumes.

We heard about a lady who set **fire** to her house and killed her mother at the same time because she had stolen hundreds of thousands of dollars from her employer. She wrote a note beforehand and then burned herself up. **Fire** is a terrible thing.

There is a book called *A Fearful Master* written several decades ago that talks about the dangers of government. The title came from a saying to the effect that *"Government, like fire, is a useful servant but a fearful master."*

Fire Can Consume

Fire can consume and our God is a consuming fire. He is absolutely pure. Without our new bodies we would never be able to stand before Him. That's why nobody who isn't genuinely saved and clothed with the righteous robes of the Lord Jesus Christ will ever enter Heaven. The Lord Jesus Christ is a consuming fire. We would burn up. That's why the people at Mount Sinai feared. The Lord thundered and was like the appearance of fire. They were afraid and told Moses to deal with the Lord. They didn't want to because they were impure and sinful.

- **Revelation 2:18**
  "And unto the angel of the church in Thyatira write; These things saith the Son of God, who hath his **eyes** like unto a **flame of fire**, and his feet *are* like fine brass;"

- **Revelation 19:12**
  "His **eyes** *were* as a **flame of fire**, and on his **head** *were* many crowns; and he had a name written, that no man knew, but he himself."
- **Hebrews 4:12-13**
  "For the word of God *is* quick, and powerful, and sharper than any twoedged sword, piercing even to the dividing asunder of soul and spirit, and of the joints and marrow, and *is* a discerner of the thoughts and intents of the heart. Neither is there any creature that is not manifest in his sight: but all things *are* naked and opened unto the **eyes** of him with whom we have to do."

The Lord sees all we do, hears all we say, knows all we think and our Lord is writing all the time, as the Negro spiritual says. The Lord Jesus Christ is at the Father's right hand with "*eyes . . . as flame of fire*" and everything is open and naked before His **eyes**. We can't hide from Him.

- **Psalm 139:2**
  "Thou knowest my downsitting and mine uprising, thou understandest my thought afar off."

The Lord Sees All

He's a Saviour with "*eyes . . . as a flame of fire.*" He sees all of us, knows all of us, and we can't fool Him. There's no hiding our sins from His sight.

Revelation 1:15

"And his feet like unto fine brass, as if they burned in a furnace; and his voice as the sound of many waters."

Here's further description. We see, first of all, the Lord Jesus Christ's "*head*" and "*hair*" in verse 14. We also see His "*eyes.*" Now we see His "*feet*" in verse 15, "*feet like unto fine brass.*" "*Brass*" in the Bible often speaks of judgment. His feet were permanently fixed. Nobody could move Him.

- **Exodus 39:39**
  "The **brasen** altar, and his grate of **brass**, his staves, and all his vessels, the laver and his foot,"

On that "*brasen altar*" they put the animals that were sacrificed as burnt offerings. That was a picture of judgment against sin.

- **Numbers 21:9**
  "And Moses made a serpent of **brass**, and put it upon a pole, and it came to pass, that if a serpent had bitten any man, when he beheld the serpent of **brass**, he lived."

This was another picture of "**brass**" as a picture of judgment. After the people were bitten by fiery serpents and were facing death, God told Moses to make a serpent of "**brass**." He didn't say "of tin." He didn't say "of iron." He didn't say "of wood." He said "*of brass*."

- **John 3:14-15**
  "And as Moses lifted up the **serpent** in the wilderness, even so must the Son of man be lifted up: That whosoever believeth in him should not perish, but have eternal life."

Sheltered & Not Perishing

That's the picture the Lord Jesus Christ spoke about to Nicodemus. The Lord Jesus Christ, on the cross of Calvary, was bearing all the sins of the world. All the fire of God's judgment was placed upon Him. If we're in Him, by genuine faith in the Lord Jesus Christ, we're sheltered from that judgment. Outside of Him, people die physically and one day they suffer the "*second death*" which puts them eternally in Hell, suffering the pain of the Lake of Fire. Just like the people in Moses' day, they died physically unless they looked at the "*serpent*." It was "life for a look."

I want to say also, that this "*serpent*" was available to everyone in the camp of Israel. There wasn't a single Israelite who was forbidden to look at the "*serpent*" lifted high on a pole. No matter where they were in the camps all around the tabernacle, it was high enough so that it could be seen. And so is the Lord Jesus Christ. Everyone can look at Him, truly trust Him, and be genuinely saved from the **judgment** of Hell, not only some "elect" group that the hyper-Calvinists have made up.

- **Deuteronomy 33:24-25**
  "And of Asher he said, *Let* Asher *be* blessed with children; let him be acceptable to his brethren, and let him dip his foot in oil. Thy shoes *shall be* iron and **brass**; and as thy days, *so shall* thy strength *be*."

Shoes of **brass** are strong and stable. I like the last part of this verse, "*as thy days, so shall thy strength be*." We've used that many times. Dr. M. R. DeHaan, founder and teacher of the Radio Bible Class, used to say that. I was in his class every single Friday night in Detroit, Michigan.

People would ask him, "*Dr. DeHaan when are you going to retire? When are you going to quit and stop?*" Then he quoted this verse. He died with his boots on. He just kept talking and speaking and preaching until he died. This is a good verse for those who are younger, and for those of us who are older as well.

- **Daniel 10:5-6**
  "Then I lifted up mine eyes, and looked, and behold a certain man clothed in linen, whose loins *were* girded with fine gold of Uphaz: His body also *was* like the beryl, and his face as the appearance of lightning, and his **eyes** as lamps of **fire**, and his arms and his feet like in colour to polished **brass**, and the voice of his words like the **voice** of a multitude."

Again, it's a picture of judgment. Daniel saw that vision clearly.

- **Revelation 2:18**
  "And unto the angel of the church in Thyatira write; These things saith the Son of God, who hath his **eyes** like unto a **flame of fire**, and his **feet** *are* like fine **brass**;"

The Lord Jesus Christ's **feet** are strong. He is able to judge.

Notice His "*voice as the sound of many waters.*" Think of Niagara Falls—a thunderous "*voice,*" as the "*sound of many waters.*" Strong, powerful and can be heard easily.

- **Psalm 29:3-5**
  "The **voice** of the LORD *is* upon the **waters**: the God of glory thundereth: the LORD *is* upon many waters. The *voice* of the LORD *is* powerful; the **voice** of the LORD *is* full of majesty. The **voice** of the LORD breaketh the cedars; yea, the LORD breaketh the cedars of Lebanon."

- **Psalm 93:4**
  "The LORD on high *is* mightier than the noise of many **waters**, *yea, than* the mighty waves of the sea."

Everyone can hear Him. He's sounding out throughout the world.

- **Ezekiel 43:2**
  "And, behold, the glory of the God of Israel came from the way of the east: and his **voice** *was* like a noise of **many waters**: and the earth shined with his glory."

- **Revelation 14:2**
  "And I heard a **voice** from heaven, as the **voice of many waters**, and as the **voice** of a great thunder: and I heard the **voice** of harpers harping with their harps:"

His "**voice**" thunders out, as it did when He was here upon earth.

- Matthew 11:28-29

The Promise Of Rest

"Come unto me, all *ye* that labour and are heavy laden, and I will give you rest. Take my yoke upon you, and learn of me; for I am meek and lowly in heart: and ye shall find rest unto your souls" (Matthew 11:28-29)

This is a voice that is powerful. A *"voice of many waters."* A "voice" that has sounded throughout the centuries. Over 2000 years it has sounded. That "**voice**" can still be heard in the Scriptures, the **Words** of God.

Revelation 1:16

"And he had in his right hand seven stars: and out of his mouth went a sharp twoedged sword: and his countenance *was* as the sun shineth in his strength."

We've seen His **hair**, His **eyes**, His **feet**. We've heard His **voice**. Now we see His **right hand**. That's the **hand** of strength. That's the **hand** of might. Who is in that **hand**? What is in that **hand**? The seven stars. We'll see in verse 20 that those seven stars are the angels of the seven churches. "Angel" means messenger (ANGELOS). In this case, it's probably the human messengers, the pastors, those who are preaching the **Words** of God in these seven different churches. That's whom the Lord Jesus Christ has in His **right hand**.

The Right Hand Of Protection

Preachers should not get out of the right hand of the Lord Jesus Christ. Those who are modernists, liberals, and unbelievers are out of His hand. They're not in His hand. He holds the hands of the preachers. A pastor must be in the right hand of the Son of God in order to stay straight, powerful, and right. It's a wonderful thing that in His right hand are the seven stars.

The *"sharp twoedged sword"* is used in many places in Scriptures.

- Psalm 149:6
  "Let the high *praises* of God *be* in their mouth, and a **twoedged sword** in their hand;"
  The **sword** is for judgment, and it is also for dividing asunder.

- **Hebrews 4:12**
  "For the **word** of God *is* quick, and powerful, and sharper than any **twoedged sword**, piercing even to the dividing asunder of soul and spirit, and of the joints and marrow, and *is* a discerner of the thoughts and intents of the heart."
- **Proverbs 5:3-4**
  "For the lips of a strange woman drop *as* an honeycomb, and her mouth *is* smoother than oil: But her end is bitter as wormwood, sharp as a **twoedged sword**."

Later on we will see, in the book of Revelation, that the same **sword** will be used to judge at the battle of Armageddon. He will smite with that sword.

- **Revelation 2:16**
  "Repent; or else I will come unto thee quickly, and will fight against them with the **sword** of my mouth."
- **Revelation 19:15**
  "And out of his mouth goeth a **sharp sword**, that with it he should smite the nations: and he shall rule them with a rod of iron: and he treadeth the winepress of the fierceness and wrath of Almighty God."
- **Revelation 19:21**
  "And the remnant were slain with the **sword** of him that sat upon the horse, which *sword* proceeded out of his mouth: and all the fowls were filled with their flesh."

At the battle of Armageddon, there will be a **sharp sword** out of the mouth of the Lord Jesus Christ. With it, He will slay the enemies that are gathered at Jerusalem so they will not hurt or harm His people.

Notice, not only the **sharp sword**, but also His "*countenance*" was as the **sun**. That is His face, His appearance.

- **John 8:12**
  "Then spake Jesus again unto them, saying, I am the **light** of the world: he that followeth me shall not walk in darkness, but shall have the **light** of life."

His **countenance** is **light**. It's bright with purity and truth.

- **Psalm 4:6**
  "*There be* many that say, Who will shew us *any* good? LORD, lift thou up the **light** of thy countenance upon us."

There's **light**. There's beauty and shining.

- **Psalm 44:3**
"For they got not the land in possession by their own **sword**, neither did their own arm save them: but thy **right hand**, and thine arm, and the **light** of thy **countenance**, because thou hadst a favour unto them."
- **Psalm 89:15**
"Blessed *is* the people that know the joyful sound: they shall walk, O LORD, in the **light** of thy **countenance**."

The **countenance** of the Lord Jesus Christ is bright. It's shining. It's **light**.

- **Matthew 17:2**
"And was transfigured before them: and his **face** did shine as the sun, and his raiment was white as the **light**."

The Transfigured Saviour

On the *Mount of Transfiguration*, the Lord Jesus Christ "was transfigured before them and His face did shine as the sun." That's what Moses received as he was in the mountain forty days and forty nights. He had to put a vail on his face because of the terrible shining.

I know some of you ladies have other means to get your shiny face off. Some of the men should use the same on their foreheads.

The Lord Jesus Christ's garment was white and His **face** did shine. He had a radiance about Him. He was transfigured before them.

- **Luke 9:29**
"And as he prayed, the fashion of his **countenance** was altered, and his raiment *was* white *and* glistering."

This is at a different time. This is during His prayer.

His **countenance** is as the sun shining in full strength. That's why no one can see the glory of the Lord Jesus Christ.

- **John 1:18**
"No man hath seen God at any time; the only begotten Son, which is in the bosom of the Father, he hath declared *him*."

The Father's Powerful Countenance

The Lord Jesus Christ has made known the Father and glorified Him. His countenance is too powerful. In these physical bodies, we couldn't see the Lord in all of His glory. We would die. That's why God hid Moses in the cleft of the rock and he saw only the after parts of the Lord as He passed by. He

hid him. Otherwise, he would have been slain. The glory of the
Lord Jesus Christ is shining as the sun.

Revelation 1:17

**"And when I saw him, I fell at his feet as dead. And he
laid his right hand upon me, saying unto me, Fear not; I am
the first and the last:"**

- **Revelation 2:8**
  "And unto the angel of the church in Smyrna write; These things
  saith **the first and the last,** which was dead, and is alive;"
- **Revelation 22:13**
  "I am Alpha and Omega, the beginning and the end, **the first
  and the last.**"

Stop Fearing!

John wondered who this was. The Lord Jesus Christ
identified Himself as *"the first and the last."* This is the Lord
of glory. John had rested on the Lord Jesus Christ's bosom at
the last supper. He had seen Him on the earth, but here, this
powerful resurrected Saviour, he did not know, and he was
afraid. In fact, that phrase, *"Fear not,"* is a present continuous
action, but it's a prohibition in the present, which means stop
an action already in process. *"Stop fearing."* John was afraid
when he saw the Lord Jesus Christ.

- **Matthew 10:28**
  "And **fear not** them which kill the body, but are not able to kill
  the soul: but rather **fear** him which is able to destroy both soul
  and body in Hell."
- **Luke 2:10**
  "And the angel said unto them, **Fear not**: for, behold, I bring
  you good tidings of great joy, which shall be to all people."
- **Acts 27:22-24**
  "And now I exhort you to be of good cheer: for there shall be no
  loss of *any man's* life among you, but of the ship. For there
  stood by me this night the angel of God, whose I am, and whom
  I serve, Saying, **Fear not**, Paul; thou must be brought before
  Caesar: and, lo, God hath given thee all them that sail with
  thee."

Believing God In The Storm

During the storm, when Paul saw the angel of God who said, *"Fear not,"* he believed God and all of the people were spared from that terrible shipwreck in Acts 27.

So the Lord Jesus Christ comforted John as He told him to stop fearing, do not fear, it is I, the first and the last.

Revelation 1:18

"*I am* he that liveth, and was dead; and, behold, I am alive for evermore, Amen; and have the keys of Hell and of death."

A key is something that is in charge. The keeper of the keys has the power to open and shut. It's a metaphor for power. The Lord Jesus Christ is the One Who **lives and was dead**.

- **Matthew 28:6**
  "He is not here: for **he is risen**, as he said. Come, see the place where the Lord lay."

- **Mark 16:6**
  "And he saith unto them, Be not affrighted: Ye seek Jesus of Nazareth, which was crucified: **he is risen**; he is not here: behold the place where they laid him."

- **Luke 24:6**
  "He is not here, but **is risen**: remember how he spake unto you when he was yet in Galilee,"

Denying That Jesus Christ Died

Some of the liberals say the Lord Jesus Christ didn't die. He just swooned and the cold recesses of the tomb revived Him. No, He did die. He says, *"I am he that liveth, and was dead."*

- **Romans 5:6**
  "For when we were yet without strength, in due time Christ **died** for the ungodly."

- **Romans 5:8**
  "But God commendeth his love toward us, in that, while we were yet sinners, Christ **died** for us."

He **died** for all sinners. Not just some sinners. Not just the elect sinners, but every sinner that ever walked on the face of the earth.

- **1 Corinthians 15:3**
  "For I delivered unto you first of all that which I also received, how that Christ **died** for our sins according to the scriptures;"

He **died** for our sins. The "*our*" includes everyone in the world, not just simply some.

- **2 Corinthians 5:15**
  "And *that* he **died** for all, that they which live should not henceforth live unto themselves, but unto him which **died** for them, and rose again."

He "**died** for all," but also He says, "*behold, I am alive for evermore.*"

- **Hebrews 7:25**
  "Wherefore he is able also to save them to the uttermost that come unto God by him, seeing he **ever liveth** to make intercession for them."

- **Hebrews 7:28**
  "For the law maketh men high priests which have infirmity; but the word of the oath, which was since the law, *maketh* the Son, who is consecrated for evermore."

He **lives forever**. There's no cessation of His life. He's the great high priest that **lives** forever.

- **Hebrews 13:8**
  "Jesus Christ the same yesterday, and to day, and for ever."

The Saviour Is Alive Forever

He's forever. The Lord Jesus Christ Who lives forever was dead, and behold He's alive forevermore. Amen.

Also, He has the "*keys of Hell and of death.* This word for **Hell** is a word in the Greek text that's called HADES, accurately translated as **Hell**. HADES is a place where the spirits and souls in the Old Testament abode before Jesus **rose** from the dead, before His crucifixion. It's called SHEOL in the Hebrew Old Testament. I believe these two words, HADES and SHEOL refer to the same place.

The Two Sections Of Sheol/Hades

There was a Paradise section in Sheol or Hades where the faithful went, and there was a section for the damned. There was a gulf between these two places. That's spoken of in Luke 16. After His bodily resurrection, the Lord Jesus Christ took the blessed dead out of Sheol/Hades, and took them to

Heaven. The Lord Jesus Christ has the keys of Hell. Those that are lost are still in that place of torment. Those who die without the Lord Jesus Christ today, their spirits and souls go immediately into that place. Also, their bodies, when they die, go to death. The Lord Jesus Christ has the keys. He has the keys both of Hell and of death.

- Luke 16:19-26
  "There was a certain rich man, which was clothed in purple and fine linen, and fared sumptuously every day: And there was a certain beggar named Lazarus, which was laid at his gate, full of sores, And desiring to be fed with the crumbs which fell from the rich man's table: moreover the dogs came and licked his sores. And it came to pass, that the beggar died, and was carried by the angels into Abraham's bosom: the rich man also died, and was buried; And in **Hell** he lift up his eyes, being in torments, and seeth Abraham afar off, and Lazarus in his bosom. And he cried and said, Father Abraham, have mercy on me, and send Lazarus, that he may dip the tip of his finger in water, and cool my tongue; for I am tormented in this flame.

    But Abraham said, Son, remember that thou in thy lifetime receivedst thy good things, and likewise Lazarus evil things: but now he is comforted, and thou art tormented. And beside all this, between us and you there is a great gulf fixed: so that they which would pass from hence to you cannot; neither can they pass to us, that *would come* from thence."

The beggar, Lazarus, died and was placed in Abraham's bosom. The rich man died and was buried, and in **Hell** he lifted up his eyes being in torments. That's a good translation of that word HADES. It's proper to translate it "*Hell*," rather than merely to transliterate it HADES as many of the new translations have done.

Hell's Torment In Two Phases

There are several phases of Hell. There's Gehenna, the lake of fire, which is the final phase, where the spirit, soul and body of the unsaved will reside for eternity. In the meantime, there's a Hell (Sheol/Hades) where their spirits and souls are dwelling. As soon as they die, they're in torments just like the rich man who died in Luke 16. Once dead, you can't go from the Hell section to the Paradise section. Once you're dead, you're dead and you can't change that.

We must warn our friends, our relatives, and other people of the torments of **Hell**. The Lord Jesus Christ alone has the keys of **Hell and of death**. He can take us out of that place.

- **Genesis 2:17**
  "But of the tree of the knowledge of good and evil, thou shalt not eat of it: for in the day that thou eatest thereof thou shalt surely die."

Death came, but the Lord Jesus Christ has the **keys** of death as well. If we're in the Lord Jesus Christ, we're genuinely saved. We don't have to die spiritually. We are eternally reconciled to God the Father through the Lord Jesus Christ.

- **Romans 5:12**
  "Wherefore, as by one man sin entered into the world, and **death** by sin; and so **death** passed upon all men, for that all have sinned:"

The Lord Jesus Has Death's Keys

That's why death is a reality. But the Lord Jesus Christ has the keys, not only of Hell, but also of death. No other person in this world can cause us to escape the second death or Hell. The Lord Jesus Christ alone can spare us.

- **Romans 6:23**
  "For the wages of sin *is* **death**; but the gift of God *is* eternal life through Jesus Christ our Lord."

The wages of sin is **death**, but the Lord Jesus Christ has the keys of death. It is eternal life that He can give to us through genuine faith in Him.

- **1 Corinthians 15:21**
  "For since by man *came* **death**, by man *came* also the resurrection of the dead."
- **1 Corinthians 15:55**
  "O **death**, where *is* thy sting? O grave, where *is* thy victory?"

The Saved No Longer Fear Death

The Lord Jesus Christ took off the wrappings of death just like He took off the wrappings of Lazarus who was bound hand and foot in grave clothes. The Lord Jesus Christ has the keys of death, so genuinely saved people no longer have to fear death. He took charge of it. He is able to give the genuine believers the victory.

- **2 Timothy 1:10**
  "But is now made manifest by the appearing of our Saviour Jesus Christ, who hath **abolished death**, and hath brought life and immortality to light through the gospel:"

This talks about what the Lord Jesus Christ did for us. He *"abolished death."* That couldn't mean physical **death** because we still die, unless the Lord Jesus Christ should return in the rapture. What does He mean?

Christ Abolished Death

He abolished that final death, the death of spirit, soul, and body in the lake of fire. He's abolished that and brought life and immortality to those who through the gospel have genuinely trusted the Lord Jesus Christ and are truly saved.

The Lord Jesus Christ has the **keys of death**. We don't have to wonder any longer. If people are genuinely saved and born-again, where are their spirits and souls? Are they in Hell? No, He has the key. If they're genuinely saved, they're with the Lord Jesus Christ in Heaven. What about their bodies? They're in the grave.

Transformed Bodies At The Rapture

What will happen to those bodies? Those bodies will be changed and transformed at the rapture of all those who are genuinely saved. The bodies of those who are genuinely born-again will be transformed like unto His glorious body (Philippians 3:21).

- **Hebrews 2:14**
  "Forasmuch then as the children are partakers of flesh and blood, he also himself likewise **took** **part** of the same; that through **death** he might destroy him that had the power of **death**, that is, the devil;"

Dr. M. R. DeHaan always took that to mean, not the **blood**, but just the flesh. He had **blood**, but it was eternal, everlasting, incorruptible blood.

- **Hebrews 10:5**
  "Wherefore when he cometh into the world, he saith, Sacrifice and offering thou wouldest not, but a **body** hast thou **prepared** me:"

The **body** of the Lord Jesus Christ that was **prepared** by the Father for the Son included every detail, including His sinews, His flesh, His **blood**, His feet, His hands, His arms, and every other **part** of His body. It was a special **body** through the miracle of the virgin birth of the Lord

Jesus Christ. Dr. M. R. DeHaan always took it to mean He took "**part**" of the same in Hebrews 2:14. He took on flesh, but it was sinless flesh, of course. But His **blood** was from God the Father. It was special, holy, and incorruptible **blood**. It was not mere "human **blood**."

That's the heresy of John MacArthur on his view of the **blood** of the Lord Jesus Christ. He says the Lord Jesus Christ had no different **blood** than yours and mine. He heretically teaches that the **blood** of the Lord Jesus Christ was just human **blood**. If that's the case, how could the **blood** of the Lord Jesus Christ cleanse us from sin? How could it genuinely save us? How could it redeem us? No. He had special Divine **blood** in that body that was "prepared" by God the Father through the virgin birth of the Lord Jesus Christ. We who are genuinely saved are redeemed by that special **blood** of the Lord Jesus Christ.

The Devil's Power Of Death

It says the Lord Jesus Christ took part of the same that through death He might destroy him that had the power of death, that is the Devil. Before He came and died for the sins of the world, before He took our sins in His own body, the Devil had the power of death. He was master of it. Everyone that's lost has the Devil as his master and god. The Devil is the one that's holding that person in his sway. Those people that reject our Saviour, and never genuinely trust Him as Saviour and Redeemer, will go to the place prepared for the Devil and his angels.

The Lord Jesus Christ through His **death** on the cross of Calvary has gotten a great victory over that old Devil. We no longer have to fear the Devil. We no longer have to fear Hell. If we're genuinely saved, we no longer have to fear **death**. The Lord Jesus Christ has the keys of **death** and of Hell. He has unlocked them and He will unlock all the fears of that place, as well. Wonderful Saviour!

Revelation 1:19

"Write the things which thou hast seen, and the things which are, and the things which shall be hereafter;"

Here is the outline of the book of Revelation. There are three points. It's good to have three points in an outline, although I don't always have three points.

1. *The things which thou hast seen.* This is Chapter 1. Write about the Lord Jesus Christ. Write about His glory. Write about

His descriptions. Write about Who He is–our Great High Priest. These are the **things which thou hast seen.**

2. *The things which are.* These things occur in Chapters 2 and 3. These Chapters describe the seven churches of Asia Minor or Turkey. As I said before, <u>I believe the book of Revelation should be interpreted in a futuristic fashion.</u> It's a picture not only of those seven churches, but they're also prophetic pictures. I believe they are a picture of the whole church age. Each one of those seven churches is a picture of the history of our churches for the last over 2,000 years. We are now in the last stage, the stage of the Laodicean apostate church.

3. *The things which shall be hereafter.* Those are things talked about in Chapters 4 through 22.

* **Revelation 4:1**

"After this I looked, and, behold, a door was opened in heaven: and the first voice which I heard *was* as it were of a trumpet talking with me; which said, **Come up hither**, and I will shew thee things which must be hereafter."

<u>The churches are mentioned in Chapters 2 and 3, but are never mentioned in Chapter 4 to the end of the book of Revelation, until the Lord Jesus Christ comes back and the genuinely saved ones come back with Him. The true church is gone.</u> Isn't it strange that some people have the true church going through either part of the tribulation, or up until the middle of the tribulation, or up until the pre wrath occurrence, even through the entire tribulation until its end? Daniel's 70th week is about seventy sevens of years, or 490 years.

Daniel's 70ᵗʰ Week Of Years

If the first sixty-nine of those weeks of years are about Israel, why wouldn't the 70ᵗʰ week of seven years be also for Israel? That's why there's no place whatever for the true church in the tribulation period.

Revelation 1:20

"The mystery of the seven stars which thou sawest in my right hand, and the seven golden candlesticks. The seven stars are the angels of the seven churches: and the seven candlesticks which thou sawest are the seven churches."

Here we have the mystery of the **seven stars** in His **right hand.** Here are the messengers or the "*angels.*" I believe these are human messengers. They're probably the pastors of those churches. They're in the Lord Jesus Christ's **right hand.**

The Candlesticks Are The Churches

The seven golden candlesticks are the seven churches of Asia Minor. This is the "*mystery.*" It was hard to understand, perhaps, for John, but the Lord Jesus Christ gives him the answer of who they are. Some of the things in Revelation are not as clearly described, but certainly these are described very clearly.

- **Psalm 98:1**
  "O sing unto the LORD a new song; for he hath done marvellous things: his **right hand,** and his holy arm, hath gotten him the victory."
- **Psalm 108:6**
  "That thy beloved may be delivered: save *with* thy **right hand,** and answer me."

Benjamin (BEN YAMIN in Hebrew) means "*the son of my right hand.*" That is what Jacob named his youngest son. His mother, Rachel, named him Benoni (BEN ONI in Hebrew). It means "*the son of my sorrow,*" because she died in childbirth. But Jacob called Benjamin the son of his **right hand.**

- **Psalm 138:7**
  "Though I walk in the midst of trouble, thou wilt revive me: thou shalt stretch forth thine hand against the wrath of mine enemies, and thy **right hand** shall save me."

In the powerful **right hand** of the Lord Jesus Christ–the pastors, the angels, the ones who are the messengers of the churches, should be there. They should not be outside of the Lord Jesus Christ's **hand.**

- **John 10:27-30**
  "My sheep hear my voice, and I know them, and they follow me:
  And I give unto them eternal life; and they shall never perish,
  neither shall any *man* pluck them out of **my hand.** My Father,
  which gave *them* me, is greater than all; and no *man* is able to
  pluck *them* out of **my Father's hand.** I and *my* Father are
  one."

In The Hand Of The Lord Jesus Christ

Pastors and leaders of the churches should and *must* be in
the hand of the Lord Jesus Christ. Otherwise, they're no
"*angels.*" They're no messengers. Woe unto the messengers
that are outside of the hand of the Lord Jesus Christ and who
either add to, or take away from the Words of God.

Revelation
Chapter Two

Revelation 2:1

"Unto the angel of the church of Ephesus write; These things saith he that holdeth the seven stars in his right hand, who walketh in the midst of the seven golden candlesticks;"

As I've said before, I believe the angel (ANGELOS), or the messenger, is referring to the pastor of this local church. He's the one that is the preacher and I think this is the one addressed here as *"the angel of the church of Ephesus."* He's the one to encourage his people.

The One who is the source of this message is the One *"that holdeth the seven stars in his right hand."* That's the Lord Jesus Christ. In Chapter 1, it talks about Him who holds these **"seven stars."** The **seven stars** are the pastors of the seven churches in Asia Minor or Turkey. He holds these seven stars in His right hand and He walks *"in the midst of the seven golden candlesticks."* Again, in Chapter 1 it mentions that the churches are these **golden candlesticks.**

Notice, He holds these stars. That word, KRATEO, is a very important word. It means *"to hold firmly; to hold strongly; to have power; to be powerful; to lay hand on"* these churches. The Lord Jesus Christ should be holding our church as well, strongly, so that we do not stray in any way, shape, or form.

Many feel, as I do, that these seven churches are pictures of the future of the church age. They are not simply churches that were then in the age of the early church. These seven churches are pictured as prophetic churches. Many have held this, others do not believe this. There are many different interpretations of the book of Revelation, but I believe this is the way it should be interpreted.

　　1. **Ephesus** is the church which pictures conditions up to the end of the Apostolic Age, which left its first love.

2. **Smyrna** is the picture of the great persecution of the churches which took place around 54–312 A.D.
3. **Pergamos** pictures the church that was teaching the doctrines of Balaam and the Nicolaitans, using the imperial power of the Roman Catholic system, and being settled in the world. This was around 312-606 A.D.
4. **Thyatira** speaks of the triumph of the teachings of Jezebel with just a remnant of genuine believers left. This was around 606–1520 A.D.
5. **Sardis** represents the period of the Reformation with some revival of truth, yet limited revival. This was around 1520–1739 A.D.
6. **Philadelphia** represents the true church and the professing church being together though with different emphases. This was around 1739 A.D.–the present.
7. **Laodicea** speaks of the final state of apostasy in the church. It is being seen in the days in which we live right now.

I believe these are prophetic pictures. I've always felt that. This view is contained in our old *Scofield Reference Bible* as well as in Bibles and books of other organizations. I taught this book of Revelation at the Bible Baptist Institute in Philadelphia and used the book by Dr. J. J. Van Gorder, *The ABC's of Revelation*. Others think that these seven churches have only reference to the churches themselves without any projected prophetic picture in the future.

"Ephesus" is mentioned seventeen times in the New Testament.

- **Acts 18:19**
  "And he came to **Ephesus**, and left them there: but he himself entered into the synagogue, and reasoned with the Jews."

- **Acts 19:1**
  "And it came to pass, that, while Apollos was at Corinth, Paul having passed through the upper coasts came to **Ephesus**: and finding certain disciples,"

- **Acts 19:10**
  "And this continued by the space of **two years**; so that all they which dwelt in Asia heard the word of the Lord Jesus, both Jews and Greeks."

Paul continued in **Ephesus** for at least three years. [See the verse Acts 20:31.]

- **Acts 20:17**
  "And from Miletus he sent to **Ephesus**, and called the elders of the church."

- **Acts 20:28-31**
  "Take heed therefore unto yourselves, and to all the flock, over the which the Holy Ghost hath made you overseers, to feed the church of God, which he hath purchased with his own blood. For I know this, that after my departing shall grievous wolves enter in among you, not sparing the flock. Also of your own selves shall men arise, speaking perverse things, to draw away disciples after them. Therefore watch, and remember, that by the space of **three years** I ceased not to warn every one night and day with tears."

Paul called for the elders (who are also called pastors and bishops) in **Ephesus** and told them to *"take heed."* The church of **Ephesus** did not always take heed.

Ephesus is the first church mentioned here in Chapter 2 of the book of Revelation. Paul was there many times. He set up that church, helped them, and warned them.

The Lord Jesus Christ walked among the church of **Ephesus**, as He does with all the other churches.

Revelation 2:2

"I know thy works, and thy labour, and thy patience, and how thou canst not bear them which are evil: and thou hast tried them which say they are apostles, and are not, and hast found them liars:"

Here the Lord Jesus Christ says, *"I know thy works."* He knows our **works**, what our church does and what we don't do. *"Labour"* is KOPOS. It's *"intense labour,"* not just book work or something from a desk.

- **John 6:27**
  "**Labour** not for the meat which perisheth, but for that meat which endureth unto everlasting life, which the Son of man shall give unto you: for him hath God the Father sealed."

- **1 Corinthians 15:58**
  "Therefore, my beloved brethren, be ye stedfast, unmoveable, always abounding in the work of the Lord, forasmuch as ye know that your **labour** is not in vain in the Lord."

- **1 Thessalonians 1:3**
  "Remembering without ceasing your work of faith, and **labour** of love, and patience of hope in our Lord Jesus Christ, in the sight of God and our Father;"

He also knows their *"patience"* (HUPOMONE). That word in the New Testament is *"characteristic of a man who is not swerved from his deliberate purpose and his loyalty to faith and piety by even the greatest trials, and troubles, and sufferings."* The church of **Ephesus** had **patience**. They had labour. They had works.

- **Romans 15:4**
  "For whatsoever things were written aforetime were written for our learning, that we through **patience** and comfort of the scriptures might have hope."
- **Hebrews 12:1**
  "Wherefore seeing we also are compassed about with so great a cloud of witnesses, let us lay aside every weight, and the sin which doth so easily beset *us,* and let us run with **patience** the race that is set before us,"

It's a great thing not to be fooling around with **evil** and this church was all right in that regard. They did not go along with **evil** people of any kind. What do we do with **evil** people? Do we take them in? No. We're to hate the **evil** and not *"to bear"* with them. Many people say we shouldn't **hate** anything. The Bible speaks contrary to that. We are to **hate** some things.

- **Psalm 34:14**
  "Depart from **evil**, and do good; seek peace, and pursue it."
- **Psalm 119:104**
  "Through thy precepts I get understanding: therefore I **hate** every false way.
- **Matthew 6:13**
  "And lead us not into temptation, but deliver us from **evil**: For thine is the kingdom, and the power, and the glory, for ever. Amen."

We should be delivered from that which is wrong, that which is **evil**, and that which is false. We're to **hate** every false way.

Notice, He says also, *"Thou hast tried them which say they are apostles and are not."* This refers to those in the early church who claimed to be **apostles**, but they weren't. They were **liars**.

- **2 Corinthians 11:13**
  "For such *are* **false apostles**, deceitful workers, transforming themselves into the **apostles** of Christ."

Even in Paul's time, in the day and age of the **apostles**, there were some that said they were **apostles** and they weren't. The Mormon church says right now they have **apostles**. That's an absolute **lie**. There are no more **apostles**. They're gone.

- **John 8:44**
  "Ye are of *your* father the Devil, and the lusts of your father ye will do. He was a murderer from the beginning, and abode not in the truth, because there is no truth in him. When he speaketh a **lie**, he speaketh of his own: for he is a **liar**, and the father of it."

Revelation 2:3

"And hast borne, and hast patience, and for my name's sake hast laboured, and hast not fainted."

The church at **Ephesus** had some good things. **Borne** means **borne** up with the burdens of the day. They had carried them.

- **Matthew 20:12**
  "Saying, These last have wrought *but* one hour, and thou hast made them equal unto us, which have **borne** the burden and heat of the day."

That word for "*labour*" is KOPIAO. It's "*to grow weary, tired, exhausted with toil and labour with effort.*" This is the **labour** which the church at **Ephesus** had. That's what our efforts should be, **laborious**, serving the Lord whether it's in witnessing, passing out tracts, or whatever it may be. It's doing what the Lord would have us to do, whether it's reading our Scriptures in the Bible or telling others about the Lord Jesus Christ.

They had not grown weary or **fainted** in any of these things.

- **Proverbs 24:10**
  "*If* thou **faint** in the day of adversity, thy strength *is* small. "

The time we need not to **faint** is when adversity and trouble come. That's when we should be strong and not **faint**.

- **Galatians 6:9**
  "And let us not be weary in well doing: for in due season we shall reap, if we **faint** not."

Their **labour** was not for themselves, it was for the sake of the Lord Jesus Christ. There should be no other motivation for serving the Lord but for the Lord Jesus Christ's Name sake, as the hymn writer James M. Black said in the last stanza of *When the Roll is Called Up Yonder.*

*"Let us **labour** for the Master from the dawn till setting sun,*
Let us talk of all His wondrous love and care;
Then when all of life is over, and our work on earth is done,
And the roll is called up yonder, I'll be there."

Revelation 2:4

"Nevertheless I have somewhat against thee, because thou hast left thy first love."

What does the Lord Jesus Christ have **against** our church? Does he have somewhat **against** us? Perhaps He does. He says the church at **Ephesus** had "*left its first love.*" The **first love** is the Lord Jesus Christ and the burning desire to please Him. Have you left your **first love**? Have I left mine? The **love** of the Lord Jesus Christ when we're first genuinely saved is very warm, precious, and holy. That word "*left*" (APHIEMI) means "*to send away, to disregard, to depart from, to go away leaving something behind, to abandon.*" The Lord Jesus Christ was angry at the church at **Ephesus**. He says, "*I have somewhat against thee.*" He was displeased with the church leaving its **first love**.

- **Luke 7:46-48**
  "My head with oil thou didst not anoint: but this woman hath anointed my feet with ointment. Wherefore I say unto thee, Her sins, which are many, are forgiven; for she **loved** much: but to whom little is forgiven, *the same* **loveth** little. And he said unto her, Thy sins are forgiven."

When you are first married, there is a **first love** that you have for your mate. That **love** should be warm for our mates, but especially for the Lord Jesus Christ Himself.

First love is first in the sense of rank. It means the **first love** that any of us should have should be for the Lord Jesus Christ, our Saviour. We should **love** one another as genuine believers. We should **love** our spouse. We should **love** our children. But the first in rank should be the Lord Jesus Christ. The church at **Ephesus** had left its **first love**. That's a sad thing against it, indeed.

Revelation 2:5

"Remember therefore from whence thou art fallen, and repent, and do the first works; or else I will come unto thee quickly, and will remove thy candlestick out of his place, except thou repent."

That word for "*repentance*" is METANOEO. META is "*to change.*" NOEO refers to "*the mind.*" It's a change of mind for the better, "*heartily to amend with abhorrence of one's past sins.*" The Lord Jesus Christ says to this church to **remember** from whence the people had **fallen**. If our church has any failings and **fallings**, He would say the same.

Repent and do the first works. Go back to square one. The first love is always maintained. Otherwise, the Lord Jesus Christ will **come quickly** and remove the **candlestick.** He'll destroy your church. He'll break it up. Certainly, the church at **Ephesus** is no more. It's a sad thing. I don't know how many years it lasted, but the Lord Jesus Christ gave them fair warning.

- **Luke 17:32**
  "**Remember** Lot's wife."

We have some things we need to **remember** in Scripture. They were to **remember** from whence they had **fallen.** We are to **repent.**

- **Luke 13:2-3**
  "And Jesus answering said unto them, Suppose ye that these Galilaeans were sinners above all the Galilaeans, because they suffered such things? I tell you, Nay: but, except ye **repent,** ye shall all likewise perish."

- **Acts 20:21**
  "Testifying both to the Jews, and also to the Greeks, **repentance** toward God, and **faith** toward our Lord Jesus Christ."

What Repentance Means

Repentance and genuine faith in the Lord Jesus Christ are both essentials. In "*repentance*," [METANOIA] the sinner must "*change his mind*" regarding two things: (1) He is a sinner before God and must be sent to Hell because of this. (2) The Lord Jesus Christ has paid the full price for the penalty of those sins and can deliver him from Hell and receive him into Heaven. After that "*change of mind*" on these two important details, he must genuinely believe on, accept, trust, and receive the Lord Jesus Christ as his Saviour from sin. This is how I balance true repentance and genuine faith.

Revelation 2:6

"But this thou hast, that thou hatest the deeds of the Nicolaitans, which I also hate."

Here again, is the **hate** factor. As we said before, many people say we don't **hate** anything. Some people don't even **hate** sin. The Lord Jesus Christ tells us differently. We are to hate **evil.**

- **Psalm 97:10**
  "Ye that love the LORD, **hate evil**: he preserveth the souls of his saints; he delivereth them out of the hand of the wicked."

We are to **hate evil** and wickedness, starting with ourselves. If we do not **hate** the **evil** in our own beings (that's where we start), we don't have the capacity to **hate evil** elsewhere. We start with our own wicked, sinful flesh. We must **hate** the evil of our flesh.

- **Psalm 119:104**
  "Through thy precepts I get understanding: therefore I **hate** every false way."

We should **hate** every false way.

- **Psalm 119:163**
  "I **hate** and abhor lying: *but* thy law do I love."

- **Proverbs 8:13**
  "The fear of the LORD *is* to **hate** evil: pride, and arrogancy, and the evil way, and the froward mouth, do I **hate**."

- **Amos 5:15**
  "**Hate the evil**, and love the good, and establish judgment in the gate: it may be that the LORD God of hosts will be gracious unto the remnant of Joseph."

The Lord Jesus Christ said He also **hates** the "*deeds of the Nicolaitans*" and He continues to **hate** them. The word, "*Nicolaitans*," comes from two Greek words. NIKAO is *to conquer* and LAOS is *the people.*

Nicolaitanism Explained

The conquering of the people is the situation in the Roman Catholic Church, where the Pope is the supreme power in the church. In the past, the people were not permitted to read or interpret the Bible. Now they say they can read it, but not interpret it. Years ago, they couldn't even have it or read it. The Roman Catholic leaders "*conquered the people*" so that the ordinary people couldn't come to the Lord Jesus Christ individually. They had to go through the Roman Catholic Church, and they still have to go through it. These are some of the deeds of the Nicolaitans.

Revelation 2:7

"He that hath an ear, let him hear what the Spirit saith unto the churches; To him that overcometh will I give to eat of the tree of life, which is in the midst of the paradise of God."

"He that hath an ear" is repeated seven times in Chapters 2 and 3. Notice *"what the Spirit saith."* That word *saith* is a continuous action, present tense. The Holy Spirit of God continues to say the things of the Words of God. We have to hear what He says. We must read, study, and know the Words of God.

The Understanding Of Overcoming

The word *"overcome"* is used several times in the letters to the churches. Some may feel that this is a special reward, but because of the way it's phrased—both here and also in verse 11—I believe this *"overcoming"* is the overcoming of Satan, that is, overcoming the Devil, and his power over them. I think, in this case, it's salvation. They will *"eat of the tree of life"* because they're truly saved and they've overcome the evil one, the wicked one, and are now genuinely saved. I believe that's the meaning of this.

- **Genesis 3:22-24**
  "And the LORD God said, Behold, the man is become as one of us, to know good and **evil**: and now, lest he put forth his hand, and take also of the **tree of life**, and eat, and live for ever: Therefore the LORD God sent him forth from the garden of Eden, to till the ground from whence he was taken. So he drove out the man; and he placed at the east of the garden of Eden Cherubims, and a flaming sword which turned every way, to keep the way of **the tree of life**."

They could not go back and eat and live forever in their fallen state. The Lord was very careful about that.

Some believe this is a **reward** or a crown of some kind.

- **James 1:12**
  "Blessed *is* the man that endureth temptation: for when he is tried, he shall receive the **crown** of life, which the Lord hath promised to them that love him."

- **Revelation 2:10**
  "Fear none of those things which thou shalt suffer: behold, the devil shall cast *some* of you into prison, that ye may be tried; and ye shall have tribulation ten days: be thou faithful unto death, and I will give thee a **crown** of life."

Those of us who have **overcome** the world, the flesh, and the Devil and have been genuinely saved and truly born-again will eat of that **tree of life** as well. We will have eternal life. We have it right now. <u>That **tree** in the midst of the paradise of God in Heaven is for the blessings of Christians who are genuinely saved</u>. That's how we would interpret that *overcoming* in this verse.

Revelation 2:8

"And unto the angel of the church in Smyrna write; These things saith the first and the last, which was dead, and is alive;"

Notice that in each church, the Lord Jesus Christ identifies Himself by one of the identifying marks found in Chapter 1. In one instance, He's the One who has the **keys**, in another, the One who walks in the midst of the seven golden **candlesticks**. Here the identification is the One Who is the **first and the last**. He's the beginning. He's the end. He's the Alpha and the Omega.

Notice, the Lord Jesus Christ **was dead**–died for our sins, and He's **alive**–a living Saviour. Later on in this church of **Smyrna**, we'll see that they will have persecution ten days.

Many feel that this is the tenfold persecution of the churches in that time period of 54-312 A.D. The time period had a total of ten persecutions.

Ten Personages Of History

1. Nero – 54 A.D.
2. Domitian – 81 A.D.
3. Trajan – 98 A.D.
4. Antonius – 117 A.D.
5. Severus – 195 A.D.
6. Maximinius – 235 A.D.

7.	Decius – 249 A.D.
8.	Valerian – 254 A.D.
9.	Aurelian – 270 A.D.
10.	Diocletian – 284 A.D.

Under Diocletian's persecution the Romans burned genuine Christians and their Bibles. They burned all the Scriptures that they had. It was a terrible persecution. Some feel that this church at **Smyrna** was a picture of these persecutions during this time frame from 54-284 A.D. **Smyrna** means *myrrh,* which was used for the embalming of the dead.

The Lord Jesus Christ is identified here as *"the first and the last"* as well as in Revelation 1:17 and Revelation 22:13. He says to the **Smyrna** church that He *"was dead and is alive."* If we do not genuinely believe the Lord Jesus Christ is **alive**–physically **alive**–at the Father's right hand in His resurrected body, woe unto us! He's **alive**.

- **Acts 7:55**
"But he, being full of the Holy Ghost, looked up stedfastly into heaven, and saw the glory of God, and Jesus standing on the right hand of God,"

He's **alive**–raised and glorified in His resurrected body.

- **Romans 8:34**
"Who is he that condemneth? *It is* Christ that **died**, yea rather, that is **risen** again, who is even at the right hand of God, who also maketh intercession for us."

That is a present work. The Lord Jesus Christ is **living** at the right hand of God the Father.

- **Colossians 3:1**
"If ye then be **risen** with Christ, seek those things which are above, where Christ sitteth on the right hand of God."

The Lord Jesus Christ is sitting there in Heaven. He's **alive**. Unbelievers don't believe this. They have no faith in a risen **living** Saviour. They don't believe He's coming back again at the rapture, to put down sinners at the battle of Armageddon, and to set up His millennial kingdom.

I had a lady call me who said she had a 60-page book. She wanted to know if I would read it if she sent it to me. She was against the Millennium. I said, *"Well ma'am, I guess I could flip through it. If you want to send it, it's up to you."* She didn't believe there was going to be a Millennium. How can you believe in a Millennium if the Lord Jesus Christ is not **living**? She thought that it was all figurative, and so on.

He is **living** and one day He will come back and set up His glorious kingdom.

- **Hebrews 7:25**
  "Wherefore he is able also to save them to the uttermost that come unto God by him, seeing he ever **liveth** to make intercession for them."
- **Hebrews 12:2**
  "Looking unto Jesus the author and finisher of *our* faith; who for the joy that was set before him endured the cross, despising the shame, and is set down at the right hand of the throne of God."

How can we look unto a dead man? He has sat down at the right hand of God the Father. He's there in Heaven. He's not dead, He's **alive**.

Revelation 2:9

"I know thy works, and tribulation, and poverty, (but thou art rich) and I know the blasphemy of them which say they are Jews, and are not, but are the synagogue of Satan."

The Lord Jesus Christ knows their **works** and all that they do at this church of **Smyrna**. They had **tribulation** – a lot of trouble.

- **John 16:33**
  "These things I have spoken unto you, that in me ye might have peace. In the world ye shall have **tribulation**: but be of good cheer; I have overcome the world. "
- **2 Corinthians 1:4**
  "Who comforteth us in all our **tribulation**, that we may be able to comfort them which are in any trouble, by the comfort wherewith we ourselves are comforted of God."

Notice also their **poverty**. This church was impoverished. They didn't have much. They didn't have lavish homes and all the things that we have in our society today. How could they be in **poverty**, but *rich*? Well, that's very easy.

- **2 Corinthians 6:10**
  "As sorrowful, yet alway rejoicing; as **poor**, yet making many **rich**; as having nothing, and *yet* possessing all things."

Paul was **poor**–dirt poor. The Lord Jesus Christ was **poor**. He had nowhere to lay His head. Yet Paul says the Lord was *"making many rich."* Our church, though we may be **poor** in smallness, can make many **rich**. Our missionaries can help us. We can send out the gospel. We do send out the gospel with radio, Internet, verses, tapes, DVD recordings, videos and *Defined King James Bible*. We have to realize that though genuine Christians may be in **poverty** physically, they can be **rich** spiritually and can be making many **rich**.

- **2 Corinthians 8:9**
  "For ye know the grace of our Lord Jesus Christ, that, though he was **rich**, yet for your sakes he became **poor**, that ye through his **poverty** might be **rich**."

Physical **poverty** and spiritual **poverty** are two different things. Physical **riches** and spiritual **riches** are two different things as well.

- **James 2:5**
  "Hearken, my beloved brethren, hath not God chosen the **poor** of this world **rich** in faith, and heirs of the kingdom which he hath promised to them that love him?"

We're **rich** if we have the Lord Jesus Christ as our Saviour. We're **rich** and the Lord Jesus Christ has given us these riches even in **poverty**. **Poverty** is relative. The **poor** of this United States of America, whatever the **poverty** level is now, used to be big money in 1940. We used to be able to buy a house for $7,000. We went through a store the other day. My son Dick said, *"Here, Dad, here's a book that tells all about the prices in 1927 when you were born."* It tells how much eggs were; how much for a quart of milk; how much a house was; how much a car was. I tell you, this was something.

The Relativity of Poverty

Poverty is relative. Go to Africa, as Mrs. Waite and I have, if you want to see poverty. Go to Iran. Go to Iraq. Go to China. Go to all these other places. Can the poverty-stricken nations be rich in faith? Yes, they can. They can be rich in the things of the Lord Jesus Christ. That's what God wants every one of us to be, regardless of our pocketbooks.

Many people say they are **Jews**. The British-Israelite faction of the church believes that the Anglo-Saxon white people are the **Jews** and the present **Jews** are just impostors. They teach that the ten lost tribes never came back to Israel from Assyria, but that the white Anglo-Saxon Celtic people are the **Jews**. For example, they say that the word, *British*, comes from *"Brit"* (Hebrew, short for *"covenant"*) and *"Ish"* (Hebrew for *"man"*). Therefore, they say that the *"covenant of the man"* means that the British people are the real **Jews**. No, the white people are not the **Jews** as the Nazis, British Israelites, and others say. The **Jews** are God's people, many of whom are in Palestine. They are in unbelief, but the white Anglo-Saxons are not the **Jews**.

This was probably the case there at the church of **Smyrna**. They said they were **Jews** and they were not. They were of the "*synagogue of Satan.*" I believe the **Jews** are God's earthly people and they're still alive. They're still here. I do not believe that they're some of the white races. In fact, we see in the book of Revelation there will be 144,000 evangelists who are **Jews**. They're real **Jews**, 12,000 from each of the twelve tribes of Israel.

Revelation 2:10

"Fear none of those things which thou shalt suffer: behold, the devil shall cast some of you into prison, that ye may be tried; and ye shall have tribulation ten days: be thou faithful unto death, and I will give thee a crown of life."

The Lord Jesus Christ said to this church in **Smyrna**, representing the persecution period of the churches in 54-312 A.D., to "*fear none of those things which they would suffer.*" We may be **suffering** as things continue to wax worse and worse in our country and in the world, but this certainly was the case there. They were in **prison** for their faith. We may be put in **prison** for our faith, too. We have to be reminded of this. They were **tried** in the sense of *tested*.

The **tribulation** of **ten days** were the waves of persecution of the Roman emperors as the history of the church developed. They endured torture and very painful deaths. Crucifixion is always painful, just as it was in the days of the Lord Jesus Christ. There were death chambers and people going into closets with spikes impaling them and all kinds of things.

Martyrs Faithful Unto Death

There were some Christians in the early church that *Fox's Book of Martyrs* writes about who suffered terrible, painful deaths. Some relinquished and said they were going to renounce the Lord Jesus Christ in order to have their lives spared. But the Lord says, "*be thou faithful unto death,*" if that's what it takes. Do not renounce. Do not ever say I don't belong to my Saviour. If you do belong to Him, own up to Him faithful, even unto death.

- 2 Timothy 1:7
  "For God hath not given us the spirit of **fear**; but of power, and of love, and of a sound mind."

The Holy Spirit has not given us a spirit of **fear**. We're not to **fear** these things.

- **Job 23:10**
  "But he knoweth the way that I take: *when* he hath **tried** me, I shall come forth as gold."

Job was **tried**. He was **tested**, was he not? His children were killed. His oxen and all his other animals were gone. His health was gone. His wife told him to "*curse God and die*" (Job 2:9b).

- **Psalm 66:10**
  "For thou, O God, hast proved us: thou hast **tried** us, as silver is **tried**."

- **Hebrews 11:17**
  "By faith Abraham, when he was **tried**, offered up Isaac: and he that had received the promises offered up his only begotten *son*,"

- **James 1:12**
  "Blessed *is* the man that endureth temptation: for when he is **tried**, he shall receive the **crown of life**, which the Lord hath promised to them that love him."

- **1 Peter 1:7**
  "That the trial of your faith, being much more precious than of gold that perisheth, though it be **tried** with fire, might be found unto praise and honour and glory at the appearing of Jesus Christ:"

- **1 Corinthians 4:2**
  "Moreover it is required in stewards, that a man be found **faithful**."

All the genuinely saved are stewards of God and the things that God has given to us.

- **1 Timothy 1:12**
  "And I thank Christ Jesus our Lord, who hath enabled me, for that he counted me **faithful**, putting me into the ministry;"

God called Paul. He had been a wicked murderer of genuine Christians, but He counted him **faithful** and put him into the ministry.

- **2 Timothy 2:2**
  "And the things that thou hast heard of me among many witnesses, the same commit thou to **faithful** men, who shall be able to teach others also."

There are five **crowns** in Scripture. Remember the memory hint, **"R GIRL."**

The Five Bible Crowns

1. "R" – the <u>crown</u> of righteousness (2 Timothy 4:8)
2. "G" – the <u>crown</u> of glory (1 Peter 5:4)
3. "I" – the incorruptible <u>crown</u> (1 Corinthians 9:25)
4. "R" – the <u>crown</u> of rejoicing (1 Thessalonians 2:19)
5. "L" – the <u>crown</u> of life (James 1:12 and Revelation 2:10)

These are rewards. Those who receive these **crowns**, will cast them at the feet of the Lord Jesus Christ (Revelation 4:10).

Revelation 2:11

"He that hath an ear, let him hear what the Spirit saith unto the churches; He that overcometh shall not be hurt of the second death."

The Lord Jesus Christ gave the Words of the Bible to the **Holy Spirit** and the **Holy Spirit** gave those Words to the human writers. We are to **hear** what the **Holy Spirit** has said.

- **1 Corinthians 2:13**
  "Which things also we speak, not in the **words** which man's wisdom teacheth, but which the **Holy Ghost** teacheth; comparing spiritual things with spiritual."

The **Spirit** of God teaches that the Bible has His **Words**. The command of the Lord Jesus Christ to the church at **Smyrna** and to the church at **Ephesus** and to our church is to hear what the **Spirit** of God says to the churches.

"He that overcometh." I think this means to **overcome** the Devil. I think this means if they're saved they shall not be hurt of the **second death**. The **second death** will not hurt the ones that are genuinely saved.

- **Revelation 20:6**
  "Blessed and holy *is* he that hath part in the first resurrection: on such the **second death** hath no power, but they shall be priests of God and of Christ, and shall reign with him a thousand years."

The **second death** is the Lake of Fire in Hell. **Death** is a separation.

Three Kinds Of Death

There are three kinds of death.

(1) Spiritual death is a separation of the spirit and soul of unsaved people from fellowship with God.

(2) Physical death, is a separation of the spirit and soul from the body when people die, whether genuinely saved or lost.

(3) Eternal death is a separation of the spirit, soul, and body of all the unsaved people from the presence of God.

- **Revelation 20:14**
  "And death and Hell were cast into the **lake of fire**. This is the **second death**."

The ones who are **overcoming**, who are genuinely saved, will escape that **lake of fire**.

- **Revelation 21:8**
  "But the fearful, and unbelieving, and the abominable, and murderers, and whoremongers, and sorcerers, and idolaters, and all liars, shall have their part in the **lake** which burneth with **fire** and brimstone: which is the **second death**."

Literal Fire In Hell

You might ask if I believe there's literal fire in Hell? Absolutely. It is a lake of fire and brimstone. Was there fire that came down and wiped out Sodom and Gomorrah? Oh yes–fire and brimstone, turned them to ashes. Lot's wife looked back and was turned into a pillar of salt. We're to remember that.

We're glad the Lord Jesus Christ will deliver those who are truly born-again from the pains of that **second death**, the **lake of fire**, and **Hell** itself. Praise the Lord for that!

Now, you don't get genuinely saved just as a "fire escape from **Hell**." That's not the purpose of God in saving us. It's true we will escape the **lake of fire**, but He has more than that for us who are genuinely saved and truly born-again. We must labor for the Master. We must serve Him acceptably and be among His **faithful**.

Revelation 2:12

"And to the angel of the church in Pergamos write; These things saith he which hath the sharp sword with two edges;"

The angel again is the messenger. Many times the word *angel* is used for human messengers. I believe that this again refers to the pastor, the one who is the preacher of that church, the pastor/bishop/elder. All three words are for the same person, different offices but the same person.

In Chapter One, the Lord Jesus Christ was identified as having a *"sharp sword with two edges."* This is a revelation of the Lord Jesus Christ to us human beings through the Apostle John to us.

The word **Pergamos** is an interesting word. I believe it represents the status of the churches from 312 to 606 A.D. **Pergamos** is from two Greek Words. PER is *thoroughly* and GAMOS is *married.* *"Thoroughly married"* implies the marriage of the church and the world. Rome with big cathedrals, big churches, big pompous statues, and idols. I believe that's the period of time this church represents.

This church was under imperial favor. In that day and age the churches very often obeyed the imperial government. If the government said, "Don't do this," they didn't do it. They just sat idly by.

Roman Catholic Heresies

I believe we have right now in the Roman Catholic system the quintessence—the very most elaborate form—of this type of imperial church. It is the church of Rome. Their leaders have power. They have money. They have instruments and vestments. They have all kinds of idols and idolatry. They have their cathedrals. But they do not have the pure gospel of the Lord Jesus Christ. I believe this is what this church of Pergamos represents.

Revelation 2:13

"I know thy works, and where thou dwellest, even where Satan's seat is: and thou holdest fast my name, and hast not denied my faith, even in those days wherein Antipas was my faithful martyr, who was slain among you, where Satan dwelleth."

Here again, the Lord Jesus Christ **knows** their **works**. You can't hide from Him. He knows our **works** of our church–whether absent or present. Either we have them or we don't. He knows.

He also knows where they **dwell** and it's *"where Satan's seat is."* Satan is the powerful *"god of this world"* (2 Corinthians 4:4). This church was right in the midst of that. If it's a picture of the imperial situation from those dates mentioned, this is certainly where **Satan's seat** is. There were more than 50-million **martyrs** of Rome–many millions were slaughtered because they were not Roman Catholics. It's still going on to this day.

Holding Fast Bible Doctrines

We must hold fast the Name of the Lord Jesus Christ and the faith taught in the Bible, no matter what comes. We must hold the doctrines of our Bible–no matter what comes. Part of the doctrine taught in the Bible involves two things: (1) the verbal, plenary inspiration (VPI) and (2) the verbal, plenary preservation (VPP) of the Hebrew, Aramaic, and Greek Words that underlie our King James Bible. Faithful translations, like our English King James Bible, God has made possible from those verbal, plenary preserved Hebrew, Aramaic, and Greek Words. We must *"hold fast"* to all the doctrines of the faith as they are taught in the Bible.

Here are some of these important Biblical doctrines we must *"hold fast"*:

- **Christology–the doctrine of Christ.** Everything about Him. His Deity, His virgin birth, His bodily resurrection, His miracles, His second coming, the rapture, the millennial reign.
- **Pneumatology–the doctrine of the Holy Spirit.** What we believe. Not the tongues type of thing. Not the wildfire. Not the charismatics.
- **Soteriology–the doctrine of salvation.** By grace through faith plus nothing.

- Eschatology—the doctrine of last things. Prophetic events.
- Ecclesiology—the doctrine of the church.
- Satanology—the doctrine of Satan.
- Hamartiology—the doctrine of sin.
- Angelology—the doctrine of angels.
- Theology Proper—the doctrine of the Trinity.

In all of these doctrines, and many others, we in our church **hold fast** the doctrines of the Bible's faith. We do not move. No matter who moves on the religious scene, we stay the same. That's what the Lord Jesus Christ urged the church of Pergamos to do.

- **1 Thessalonians 5:21**
  "Prove all things; **hold fast** that which is good."
- **2 Timothy 1:13**
  "**Hold fast** the form of sound words, which thou hast heard of me, in faith and love which is in Christ Jesus."
- **Hebrews 10:23**
  "Let us **hold fast** the profession of *our* faith without wavering; (for he *is* faithful that promised;)"
- **James 1:6**
  "But let him ask in faith, nothing wavering. For he that wavereth is like a wave of the sea driven with the wind and tossed."

Satan is a powerful person. He's not all powerful, but he's powerful. Don't think that he isn't.

- **Mark 8:33**
  "But when he had turned about and looked on his disciples, he rebuked Peter, saying, Get thee behind me, **Satan:** for thou savourest not the things that be of God, but the things that be of men."

Satan can't indwell genuine believers, but he can use them like he used Peter to try to thwart the things of the Lord Jesus Christ. We must savour the things that be of God.

- **Luke 22:31-32**
  "And the Lord said, Simon, Simon, behold, **Satan** hath desired to have you, that he may sift you as wheat: But I have prayed for thee, that thy faith fail not: and when thou art converted, strengthen thy brethren."

Satan wants to control the genuine believers.

- **Acts 26:16-18**
  "But rise, and stand upon thy feet: for I have appeared unto thee for this purpose, to make thee a minister and a witness both of these things which thou hast seen, and of those things in the which I will appear unto thee; Delivering thee from the people, and *from* the Gentiles, unto whom now I send thee, To open their eyes, *and* to turn *them* from darkness to light, and *from* the power of **Satan** unto God, that they may receive forgiveness of sins, and inheritance among them which are sanctified by faith that is in me."

That's part of the gospel, to turn them from **Satan** and all the **Satanic** works.

- **2 Corinthians 2:11**
  "Lest **Satan** should get an advantage of us: for we are not ignorant of his devices."

Paul says he knows how **Satan** handles people. We have to be on our guard.

- **2 Corinthians 11:14**
  "And no marvel; for **Satan** himself is transformed into an angel of light."

We have to be careful.

Satan As A Roaring Lion

We can tell a roaring lion, but we cannot always tell when Satan comes as an angel of light. That will get us. Beware. Satan can transform himself.

- **2 Thessalonians 2:9**
  "*Even him,* whose coming is after the working of **Satan** with all power and signs and lying wonders,"

This is the man of sin. What's he going to do in that tribulation seven-year period – Daniel's 70th week? *With all power and signs and lying wonders.* They're false miracles.

Antipas was the Lord Jesus Christ's **faithful martyr**. He was **faithful** unto death. Steven was the first **martyr**.

- **Acts 22:20**
  "And when the blood of thy **martyr** Stephen was shed, I also was standing by, and consenting unto his death, and kept the raiment of them that slew him."

Paul was probably the Pharisee in charge of the stoning of Stephen.

- **Revelation 17:6**
  "And I saw the woman drunken with the blood of the saints, and with the blood of the **martyrs** of Jesus: and when I saw her, I wondered with great admiration."

There will be many more **martyrs**. The **martyr** Antipas was there in that church in **Pergamos**.

Revelation 2:14

"But I have a few things against thee, because thou hast there them that hold the doctrine of Balaam, who taught Balac to cast a stumblingblock before the children of Israel, to eat things sacrificed unto idols, and to commit fornication."

Here were **Balac** and **Balaam**. **Balac** said to **Balaam** words to this effect: "Now **Balaam**, there's a people that's going against us, and the Lord is with them. They've conquered all their foes. And lest they come and conquer us, I want you to curse them. You just go ahead and curse them on this mountain and on that mountain." **Balaam** went. The Lord didn't want him to go, but finally, by His permissive will, He allowed him to go. You'll probably remember, the ass he was riding on tried to stop him.

- **Numbers 31:8**
  "And they slew the kings of Midian, beside the rest of them that were slain; *namely,* Evi, and Rekem, and Zur, and Hur, and Reba, five kings of Midian: **Balaam** also the son of Beor they slew with the sword."

- **Numbers 31:16**
  "Behold, these caused the children of Israel, through the counsel of **Balaam**, to commit trespass against the LORD in the matter of Peor, and there was a plague among the congregation of the LORD."

Because **Balaam** was not separated from these wicked people that he was in with, the Israelites slew him with the sword. He was right in among the unbelievers and when the unbelievers were slain by the Israelites, **Balaam** was also killed.

- **Nehemiah 13:2**
  "Because they met not the children of Israel with bread and with water, but hired **Balaam** against them, that he should curse them: howbeit our God turned the curse into a blessing."

- **2 Peter 2:15**
  "Which have forsaken the right way, and are gone astray, following the way of **Balaam** *the son* of Bosor, who loved the wages of unrighteousness;"

What was **Balaam's** purpose? He was out for the wages – the money.

- **Jude 11**
  "Woe unto them! for they have gone in the way of Cain, and ran greedily after the error of **Balaam** for reward, and perished in the gainsaying of Core."

The Doctrine Of Balaam

This doctrine of Balaam was in the church at Pergamos. Baal worship included prostitution and homosexuality. Money was paid to engage in the sins of homosexuality, adultery, and fornication. That money was given to their gods. This is the evil. This is the falseness of Baal and Baal worship. That's what Balaam taught the children of Israel to do.

Revelation 2:15

"So hast thou also them that hold the doctrine of the Nicolaitans, which thing I hate."

That's another thing the Lord Jesus Christ has against them. The doctrine of the **Nicolaitans** was the power of the priests, rabbis, pastors, or others over the people.

Revelation 2:16

"Repent; or else I will come unto thee quickly, and will fight against them with the sword of my mouth."

The Lord Jesus Christ told the church at **Pergamos** to repent. The word *"repent"* (METANOEO) means *"to change one's mind for the better; heartily to amend with an abhorrence of the past."* That's what **repentance** is. When we repent of our sin we know that it was wrong and wicked. If we don't **repent**, if we don't change our minds regarding sin, the Lord Jesus Christ says He will come quickly and fight against us.

As I said before, I believe that these churches not only represent the seven churches that were then in Asia Minor but also are prophetic of the church Age.

The Pergamos Picture

Pergamos was the church under imperial power, settled in the world, from 312–606 A.D. The Pergamos church was a picture of the church that was thoroughly married to the world. Certainly Rome and the era of Roman imperialism was a type of that.

When the Lord Jesus Christ starts **fighting** against us, we're in trouble. It's bad enough for the Devil to **fight** against us. They had to **repent** and we have to **repent** if we have sin.

The **sword** of his **mouth** is judgment from the Lord Jesus Christ.

- **Jeremiah 18:8**
  "If that nation, against whom I have pronounced, turn from their evil, I will **repent** of the evil that I thought to do unto them."

- **Ezekiel 18:30**
  "Therefore I will judge you, O house of Israel, every one according to his ways, saith the Lord GOD. **Repent**, and turn *yourselves* from all your transgressions; so iniquity shall not be your ruin."

- **Luke 17:3**
  "Take heed to yourselves: If thy brother trespass against thee, rebuke him; and if he repent, forgive him."

Forgiveness After Repentance

Here's forgiveness after repentance. If seven times a day he says, "I repent, I change my mind," forgive him. That's what God wants us to do. This church at Pergamos had to repent and change their ways.

Revelation 2:17

"He that hath an ear, let him hear what the Spirit saith unto the churches; To him that overcometh will I give to eat of the hidden manna, and will give him a white stone, and in the stone a new name written, which no man knoweth saving he that receiveth *it*."

I think this *overcoming* is used in each one of these churches for true Christian believers—the genuinely saved people.

- **1 John 2:13-14**
  "I write unto you, fathers, because ye have known him that is from the beginning. I write unto you, young men, because ye have **overcome** the wicked one. I write unto you, little children, because ye have known the Father. I have written unto you, fathers, because ye have known him *that is* from the beginning. I have written unto you, young men, because ye are strong, and the word of God abideth in you, and ye have overcome the wicked one."

The **Holy Spirit's Words** are in the Scriptures. We are to hear what He says and continue to stay in His Words.

- **1 Corinthians 2:12-13**
  "Now we have received, not the spirit of the world, but the spirit which is of God; that we might know the things that are freely given to us of God. Which things also we speak, not in the **words** which man's wisdom teacheth, but which the **Holy Ghost** teacheth; comparing spiritual things with spiritual."

The White Stone's Meaning

These are the spiritual Words of the Lord Jesus Christ. To the one that's overcoming, He said He will give a white stone. White is a very glistening stone. This is the Greek word LEUKOS which is a *brilliant whiteness*. The stone is a small worn-out stone or pebble. In the ancient courts of justice the accused were condemned by black pebbles and the acquitted went free by white pebbles. It was a vote, on account of the use of pebbles in voting. You've heard of being *"black balled."* That's the black vote where you're condemned.

New Names For The Saved

This white stone will be for those of us who are genuinely saved and truly born-again, standing before the throne with our sins forgiven. Our sins are forgiven by genuine faith in the Lord Jesus Christ. On that stone there will be a new name written which no man knows. You've heard that gospel song, *A New Name Written Down in Glory*. All of us who are saved will have new names. We don't know what that name is going to be, but the Lord Jesus Christ is going to give us a new name.

Revelation 2:18

"And unto the angel of the church in Thyatira write; These things saith the Son of God, who hath his eyes like unto a flame of fire, and his feet *are* like fine brass;"

The Lord Jesus Christ is speaking to this church of **Thyatira**. I believe that it's a picture of the Dark Ages 606 – 1520 A.D. There was the triumph of Balaamism and Nicolaitanism. There was also a believing remnant. They were in trouble.

The Lord Jesus Christ's Eyes

Notice the Lord's eyes are *like unto a flame of fire*. The piercing eyes of the Lord Jesus Christ show that He can see everything in clarity and in judgment. He has penetrating eyes. *His feet are like fine brass*. This pictures feet of judgment that are ready to go.

The Lord Jesus Christ is looking at our church as well, with His flaming **eyes** and His **feet** as fine brass, to **see** what we measure up to and what we don't measure up to. Is He pleased with us? Is He displeased? It's very important indeed that we see this.

Revelation 2:19

"I know thy works, and charity, and service, and faith, and thy patience, and thy works; and the last *to be* more than the first."

Here the Lord Jesus Christ looks at the church at **Thyatira**, this church in the Dark Ages when Rome was very powerful and light was very scarce. He commends them. He knows their **works**.

What are we doing for the Lord Jesus Christ? Does He know our **works**? If we're genuinely saved, He expects us to have good **works**. Not that **works** will save us. **Works** can't get us genuinely saved, but once we're truly saved we must have **works** unto His glory.

The second thing the Lord Jesus Christ sees in that church at **Thyatira** is **charity**. Does He **see** that in our church? **Charity** is love.

- **1 Corinthians 16:14**
  "Let all your things be done with **charity**."

That's **our** love for the brethren and **love** for the things of the Lord.

- **Colossians 3:12-14**
  "Put on therefore, as the elect of God, holy and beloved, bowels of mercies, kindness, humbleness of mind, meekness, longsuffering; Forbearing one another, and forgiving one another, if any man have a quarrel against any: even as Christ forgave you, so also *do* ye. And above all these things *put on* charity, which is the bond of perfectness."

There Are Quarrels In Churches

This is for churches like ours. There are quarrels in churches–all kinds of quarrels. If you don't think there are quarrels you've never been in many churches. We are to put on charity like a garment. The love or charity that churches have is the bond that ties things together for perfectness.

- **2 Thessalonians 1:3**
  "We are bound to thank God always for you, brethren, as it is meet, because that your faith groweth exceedingly, and the **charity** of every one of you all toward each other aboundeth;"

This means there's room for growth in **charity** as genuine believers in the church. That church in **Thyatira** had love abounding. That should be our goal as well in our church.

The third thing the Lord Jesus Christ sees in the church at **Thyatira** was their **service**. What are we doing for the Lord?

- **Romans 12:1-2**
  "I beseech you therefore, brethren, by the mercies of God, that ye present your **bodies** a living sacrifice, holy, acceptable unto God, *which is* your reasonable **service**. And be not conformed to this world: but be ye transformed by the renewing of your mind, that ye may prove what *is* that good, and acceptable, and perfect, will of God."

It is reasonable to present our **bodies** unto the Lord. The Lord Jesus Christ bought us with His precious blood and genuinely saved us. He has made us truly born-again and given us new life. He demands we **serve** Him with our **bodies** – all of our **bodies**.

- **Psalm 144:9**
  "I will sing a new song unto thee, O God: upon a psaltery *and* an instrument of **ten strings** will I sing praises unto thee."

We should praise the Lord with our **bodies.**

Ten strings of our **body:**

- ✦ **Two eyes**
- ✦ **Two ears**
- ✦ **One mouth**
- ✦ **Two hands**
- ✦ **Two feet**
- ✦ **One heart**

In 1965, I was in Reno, Nevada, under treatment for Hodgkins disease (cancer of the lymph glands.) Laetrile was used. While I was in Reno, I preached a message in one of the Baptist churches there. The pastor asked me to preach for him. I preached on presenting your **body.** I didn't know whether my **body** was going to live or die. This was a very strong sermon that I preached for weeks and months whenever churches asked me to come and minister to them. I didn't know how much time I had left.

The Lord raised me up, but I didn't know if I had one more month or one more year. I still don't know. Our oldest son, Don, got a house with a second floor so that Mrs. Waite could move in there when I went Home to be with the Lord. The whole situation was serious business.

Don't be conformed to the world. Our **service** must be perfect before the Lord.

- **Ephesians 6:5-7**
  "Servants, be obedient to them that are *your* masters according to the flesh, with fear and trembling, in singleness of your heart, as unto Christ; Not with eyeservice, as menpleasers; but as the **servants** of Christ, doing the will of God from the heart; With good will doing **service,** as to the Lord, and not to men:"

Our **service** should be to the Lord and this was the **service** of the people in the church of **Thyatira.** Also notice their **faith.** It's important to have genuine **faith.**

- **Romans 1:8**
  "First, I thank my God through Jesus Christ for you all, that your **faith** is spoken of throughout the whole world."

Faith Spoken Throughout The World

Is our faith in our church spoken of throughout the whole world? Do they know us? Do they know what we stand for? This is what Thyatira had. What is genuine faith?

- **Hebrews 11:1**
  "Now **faith** is the substance of things hoped for, the evidence of things not seen."
- **1 Corinthians 16:13**
  "Watch ye, stand fast in the **faith**, quit you like men, be strong."

Stand fast in the true **faith** of the Scriptures and the doctrines of the Bible. Don't let anybody push you around on that. Be diligent, be strong, be unbending.

- **Colossians 1:3-4**
  "We give thanks to God and the Father of our Lord Jesus Christ, praying always for you, Since we heard of your **faith** in Christ Jesus, and of the love *which ye have* to all the saints,"

We ought to thank God for people that have **faith**. It's an important thing to have.

- **Colossians 2:5**
  "For though I be absent in the flesh, yet am I with you in the spirit, joying and beholding your order, and the stedfastness of your **faith** in Christ."

The Colossian church had **faith** and so this church at **Thyatira** did as well. Notice the sixth thing – **patience**. The Lord Jesus Christ saw their **patience**. In the midst of the Dark Ages they were **patient**.

- **2 Corinthians 6:4**
  "But in all *things* approving ourselves as the ministers of God, in much **patience**, in afflictions, in necessities, in distresses,"

Paul with all the afflictions, troubles, and trials was still **patient**.

- **Colossians 1:11**
  "Strengthened with all might, according to his glorious power, unto all **patience** and longsuffering with joyfulness;"

Longsuffering is putting up with people. We have to be longsuffering as well. People let us down. People say one thing and do another. **Patience** is putting up with things, difficulties, trials, and adversities, like the **patience** of Job. He lost his animals, family, health, and friends but he didn't lose his faith.

- **2 Thessalonians 1:4**
"So that we ourselves glory in you in the churches of God for your **patience** and faith in all your persecutions and tribulations that ye endure:"

May we have patience in the midst of trials and troubles.

- **Hebrews 10:36**
"For ye have need of **patience**, that, after ye have done the will of God, ye might receive the promise."

God does not answer immediately. When He gives something in His Words or He says something in His Words, He will keep it. We must have **patience** to believe that He will keep it and just wait **patiently** for Him to fulfill that which He has promised.

Revelation 2:20

"Notwithstanding I have a few things against thee, because thou sufferest that woman Jezebel, which calleth herself a prophetess, to teach and to seduce my servants to commit fornication, and to eat things sacrificed unto idols."

There were good things about **Thyatira**, but the Lord had some things **against** them. The Lord Jesus Christ tells it like it is. He tells it like it is with our church. I'm sure He has things **against** us.

Jezebel was King Ahab's wife. Ahab was a wicked king.

- **1 Kings 16:31**
"And it came to pass, as if it had been a light thing for him to walk in the sins of Jeroboam the son of Nebat, that he took to wife **Jezebel** the daughter of Ethbaal king of the Zidonians, and went and served Baal, and worshipped him."

- **1 Kings 18:13**
"Was it not told my lord what I did when **Jezebel** slew the prophets of the LORD, how I hid an hundred men of the LORD'S prophets by fifty in a cave, and fed them with bread and water?"

Jezebel Was A Murdering Idolater

Jezebel was a murderer. She was not only a worshipper of Baal with all the false idols and sexual immorality that went along with that worship, she slew the prophets of the LORD.

- **1 Kings 21:5-8**
  "But **Jezebel** his wife came to him, and said unto him, Why is thy spirit so sad, that thou eatest no bread? And he said unto her, Because I spake unto Naboth the Jezreelite, and said unto him, Give me thy vineyard for money; or else, if it please thee, I will give thee *another* vineyard for it: and he answered, I will not give thee my vineyard. And Jezebel his wife said unto him, Dost thou now govern the kingdom of Israel? arise, *and* eat bread, and let thine heart be merry: I will give thee the vineyard of Naboth the Jezreelite. So she wrote letters in Ahab's name, and sealed *them* with his seal, and sent the letters unto the elders and to the nobles that *were* in his city, dwelling with Naboth."

Ahab was downhearted because Naboth had a vineyard that he wanted. He had all kinds of vineyards but he had the itch for more. He wanted that vineyard. **Jezebel** usurped the authority of the king. That's what **Jezebel** does – she usurps authority that's not rightfully hers. She found false witnesses against Naboth and they stoned him to death. That's **Jezebel** – a sly killer.

- **1 Kings 21:15**
  "And it came to pass, when **Jezebel** heard that Naboth was stoned, and was dead, that **Jezebel** said to Ahab, Arise, take possession of the vineyard of Naboth the Jezreelite, which he refused to give thee for money: for Naboth is not alive, but dead."

Jezebel was the one that gave the plan and plot to get that vineyard. Who would want to kill for a vineyard?

- **1 Kings 21:25**
  "But there was none like unto Ahab, which did sell himself to work wickedness in the sight of the LORD, whom **Jezebel** his wife stirred up."

Jezebel Was A Terrible Wife

Wickedness is always in the sight of the LORD. Jezebel was a "stirrer-upper" of wickedness and evil. She was a terrible, terrible wife. I wouldn't want a wife like that, would you? I wouldn't want a wife to stir up evil.

- **2 Kings 9:22**
  "And it came to pass, when Joram saw Jehu, that he said, *Is it peace, Jehu?* And he answered, What peace, so long as the whoredoms of thy mother **Jezebel** and her witchcrafts *are so many?*"

- **2 Kings 9:30-33**
  "And when Jehu was come to **Jezreel, Jezebel** heard *of it;* and she painted her face, and tired her head, and looked out at a window. And as Jehu entered in at the gate, she said, *Had* Zimri peace, who slew his master? And he lifted up his face to the window, and said, Who *is* on my side? who? And there looked out to him two *or* three eunuchs. And he said, Throw her down. So they threw her down: and *some* of her blood was sprinkled on the wall, and on the horses: and he trode her under foot."

Jezebel, that **evil woman**, met her end. It was a horrible sight.

Women Preachers Unbiblical

What about women preachers? Are women preachers biblical? Jezebel was a woman who usurped authority that was not hers. Women preachers usurp authority that is not theirs. Are there very many women preachers in the world? Recent statistics showed women preachers to represent 7.9% of the preachers in the United States. There are probably more now this year.

Prior to about 1966, **Women preachers** in the United States numbered approximately 16,648, broken down as follows:

- ◆ **United Methodists**—4,743
- ◆ **Assemblies of God**—4,000
- ◆ **Presbyterian U.S.A.**—2,419
- ◆ **United Church of Christ**—1,803
- ◆ **Southern Baptists**—1,225
- ◆ **Evangelical Lutheran**—1,358
- ◆ **Episcopal**—1,000
- ◆ **Church of Scotland**—100

Since 1986, the number of **women preachers** increased to 20,730 in this country. That's an increase over 1977 when there were only 10,000. In nine years the number increased from 10,000 to 20,000 **women preachers**. What does the **Bible for Today Baptist Church** have to say about **women preachers**? We're against them. Why are we against them? Because God is against them as the King James Bible clearly teaches.

- **Acts 20:17**
  "And from Miletus he sent to Ephesus, and called the elders of the church."

Elders Are Always Masculine

That's a masculine word (PRESBUTEROS). Elders are always masculine.

- **Acts 20:28**
  "Take heed therefore unto yourselves, and to all the flock, over the which the Holy Ghost hath made you **overseers**, to feed the church of God, which he hath purchased with his own blood."

The word **overseers** (EPISKOPOS) is a **masculine** word. They're males.

- **1 Corinthians 14:34**
  "Let your **women** keep silence in the churches: for it is not permitted unto them to speak; but *they are commanded* to be under obedience, as also saith the law."

Women are certainly not to **preach**. This is clear. People say this was just historical, just what they did in those days and now we can reinterpret that and it's no problem. They say it doesn't really mean that for this day. Yes, it does. The principles are there.

- **1 Corinthians 14:35**
  "And if they will learn any thing, let them ask their husbands at home: for it is a shame for **women** to **speak** in the church."

Women are certainly not to **preach** in the church. If they can't speak, they certainly can't **preach** in the pulpits.

- **1 Timothy 2:11-12**
  "Let the **woman** learn in **silence** with all subjection.
  But I suffer not a **woman** to **teach**, nor to **usurp**
  authority over the man, but to be in **silence**."

Timothy was pastor of the church at Ephesus. The apostle Paul was training this pastor in the things of the Lord to be a good pastor. **Women preachers** are against the Scriptural stand.

- **1 Timothy 3:1**
  "This is a true saying, If a **man** desire the office of a bishop, he desireth a good work."

Bishops Are Always Masculine

Bishop is a masculine word (EPISKOPOS). There are no female bishops. It's a masculine Greek Word. If you get some of these Bibles that are gender neutral they'll change the word *he* into *one* or something else.

- 1 Timothy 3:2
  "A **bishop** then must be blameless, the **husband** of one wife, vigilant, sober, of good behaviour, given to hospitality, apt to teach;"

What could be clearer than that? **Husband is male. Wife is female.** The **pastor** must be a **husband.** I believe that the Scriptures imply that a **pastor** must be married.

- Titus 1:5
  "For this cause left I thee in Crete, that thou shouldest set in order the things that are wanting, and ordain **elders** in every city, as I had appointed thee:"

Again, *elders* are all **masculine. There's no feminine gender in this.** The Greek text is clear.

- Titus 1:6
  "If any be blameless, the **husband** of one wife, having faithful children not accused of riot or unruly."

The Bible repeats this twice, emphasizing it. There is no **woman preacher** who can be "*the husband of one wife.*" That leaves out **lesbians.** It has nothing to do with that.

- 1 Peter 5:1-4
  "The **elders** which are among you I exhort, who am also an elder, and a witness of the sufferings of Christ, and also a partaker of the glory that shall be revealed: Feed the flock of God which is among you, taking the oversight thereof, not by constraint, but willingly; not for filthy lucre, but of a ready mind; Neither as being lords over God's heritage, but being ensamples to the flock. And when the chief Shepherd shall appear, ye shall receive a crown of glory that fadeth not away."

Again, *elders* is a **masculine** word. **Pastor, bishop,** and **elder** are three words for the same office. This is what I believe the Scriptures teach us. An **elder** is a mature genuine Christian in the things of the Lord Jesus Christ. A **bishop** is an **overseer** that oversees the ministry of the Lord Jesus Christ. A **pastor** is a **shepherd** who guides the sheep. Peter says he was also an **elder.** He tells them to *Feed the flock of God.* That's the word for **shepherd.** *Taking the oversight thereof* is being a bishop. These **pastors/bishops/elders** were to be *ensamples to the flock.*

The *chief Shepherd* is again a **masculine** word – the Lord Jesus Christ. Regardless of what the **lesbian** Virginia Mollenkott says, that He's a man/woman. That's what she calls the Lord Jesus Christ. She calls Him–that is, a half-man and half-woman. That is what she calls the Lord *androgynous* Jesus Christ in order to push **lesbianism** and **homosexuality**. No, He's **masculine**.

"**Jezebel**" is a symbolic name for a **woman** who pretended to be a **prophetess** and who was addicted to antinomianism–against any law–claimed her Christian liberty of eating things **sacrificed to idols.** That's what she made these people at **Thyatira** do. She **seduced** the others in that church. That word for **seduced** (PLANAO), like a planet moving all over the place, means *to cause to go astray, to lead astray from the right way.* That's what this **Jezebel** did to lead them from the truth into error, to deceive them.

When things were **sacrificed to idols**, the flesh that was left over from the heathen **sacrifices** was either eaten at the feast or sold by the poor in the market. You're not to eat anything offered to **idols**, but this **woman** said it was all right.

Revelation 2:21

"And I gavo hor spaco to repent of her fornication; and she repented not."

The Lord Jesus Christ gave this **woman, Jezebel**, whether it was a real name or a person in that church, **space to repent**, but she didn't **repent** of her **fornication**, either physical or spiritual. Baalimism was physical **fornication** or adultery, including homosexuality. Spiritual **fornication** is being disloyal to the Lord Jesus Christ.

When the Lord puts a finger on you and on me in our sin, we'd better **repent**. We'd better change our minds and our ways. We'd better do it, otherwise we're in trouble with the Lord. He will fight **against** us and that's a bad thing.

Revelation 2:22

"Behold, I will cast her into a bed, and them that commit adultery with her into great tribulation, except they repent of their deeds."

This woman wants to commit all this wickedness and sin. The word for *them that commit adultery with her* has a Hebrew idiom, in addition to the physical **adultery**. This Hebrew idiom says it's used of *"those who at a woman's solicitation are drawn away to idolatry and the eating of things sacrificed to idols."* You've heard the expression, "Well, he's made his bed, he'll lie in it." The Lord Jesus Christ is going to judge that **woman Jezebel**. He's going to judge any **woman** here in our church that would be out of line as well.

Jezebels are all around us and certainly in this terrible plague of **women preachers** and pastors. **Gail Riplinger**, along with many other **women**, is like a **woman preacher** in our own day. She is usurping authority over men who are pastors and church leaders in violation of 1 Timothy 2:12. It's a terrible thing indeed. There are over 20,000 **women preachers** in the United States alone. Someone who says there's nothing wrong with **women preachers** will say that Paul was against **women** and that he hated them. Therefore he wrote against them and it was only cultural. <u>No, it's not cultural. It's Scriptural.</u> The qualifications for a pastor/bishop/elder are very clear in Scripture. <u>Many orientals believe in **women preachers**</u>. They think there's nothing wrong with it. Just think how many **women preachers** there are all over the world. These are modern day **Jezebels**.

Revelation 2:23

"And I will kill her children with death; and all the churches shall know that I am he which searcheth the reins and hearts: and I will give unto every one of you according to your works."

The Lord Jesus Christ said He would **kill her children with death**. Do you want the Lord to **search** your heart? <u>This is not open theism, which is the new theology that says that God doesn't know everything and can't know everything</u>. No, He is **omniscient**. He searches the hearts.

- **Psalm 139:1-4**
  "To the chief Musician, A Psalm of David. O LORD, thou hast **searched** me, and known *me*. Thou **knowest** my downsitting and mine uprising, thou **understandest** my thought afar off. Thou compassest my path and my lying down, and art **acquainted** *with* all my ways. For *there is* not a word in my tongue, *but*, lo, O LORD, thou **knowest** it altogether."

- **Jeremiah 17:9-10**
  "The heart *is* deceitful above all *things*, and desperately wicked: who can **know** it? I the LORD **search** the heart, *I* try the reins, even to give every man according to his ways, and according to the fruit of his doings."

That word *reins* is the word for kidneys (KILYAH). It is used of *the inmost thoughts; the feelings or purposes of the soul.* The Lord is able to **search** those things and He does **search** them. He also **searches** the heart (LEB), which is *the soul; the mind; the desires; the appetites; the affection; the understanding; the seat of intelligence.*

God Searches Secrets

Let me ask you, are we open for search or does the Lord need a search warrant? No, He needs no search warrant. He searches right now, yesterday, tomorrow, all the time. He searches our church. He searches our hearts.

Revelation 2:24

"But unto you I say, and unto the rest in Thyatira, as many as have not this doctrine, and which have not known the depths of Satan, as they speak; I will put upon you none other burden."

There were others in **Thyatira** who had not *known the depths of Satan* like this **woman Jezebel** was teaching and **seducing** with all the false doctrines.

- **Proverbs 9:13**
  "A foolish woman is clamorous: she is simple, and knoweth nothing."
- **Proverbs 9:18**
  "But he knoweth not that the dead *are* there; *and that* her guests *are* in the **depths of Hell**."

This is the *depths of Satan.* The Lord has **deep things.**

- **1 Corinthians 2:10**
  "But God hath revealed *them* unto us by his Spirit: for the Spirit searcheth all things, yea, the **deep things** of God."

We can know the **deep things** of God – the truths of Scripture – by the Holy Spirit alone.

Some in **Thyatira** had not gone after this **woman Jezebel.** Satan is **deep.** He has wickedness and it's rampant.

- **Isaiah 14:12-15**
  "How art thou fallen from heaven, O **Lucifer,** son of the morning! *how* art thou cut down to the ground, which didst weaken the nations! For thou hast said in thine heart, I will ascend into heaven, I will exalt my throne above the stars of God: I will sit also upon the mount of the congregation, in the

sides of the north: I will ascend above the heights of the clouds; I will be like the most High. Yet thou shalt be brought down to Hell, to the sides of the pit."

Here we see a picture of **Satan**. **Lucifer** is a good translation of the Hebrew Word (HEYLEL) meaning, *light bearer; light giver; shining one*. This is a good translation, not like the NIV and the others.

There are five "I wills" of **Satan**:

Satan's Five "I Wills"

1.   I will ascend into Heaven
2.   I will exalt my throne above the stars of God
3.   I will sit also upon the mount of the congregation
4.   I will ascend above the heights of the clouds
5.   I will be like the most High

The fifth one is the most dangerous. That's a terrible, terrible tragedy. **Satan** wants to be just like God. **Satan** will be judged. There's no question about that.

- **Acts 10:38**
  "How God anointed Jesus of Nazareth with the Holy Ghost and with power: who went about doing good, and healing all that were oppressed of the **devil**; for God was with him."

- **Ephesians 4:27**
  "Neither give place to the **devil**."

Don't give the **Devil** any elbow room. Just push him away and get away from him.

- **Ephesians 6:11**
  "Put on the whole armour of God, that ye may be able to stand against the wiles of the **devil**."

Wiles means cleverness. The **Devil** is cagey. He's clever.

- **2 Timothy 2:26**
  "And *that* they may recover themselves out of the snare of the **devil**, who are taken captive by him at his will."

The Devil Has Snares

The Devil has snares. A snare is a trap that you don't see until you get into it. We have to be very careful where we walk. Look down, look around, look everywhere. Examine the whole thing.

- **James 4:7**
  "Submit yourselves therefore to God. Resist the **devil**, and he will flee from you."

Don't accept the **Devil** or make a covenant with him. Don't even have a dialogue with him. <u>Resist him</u>. God promises that the **Devil** will flee from you.

- **1 Peter 5:8-9**
  "Be sober, be vigilant; because your adversary the **devil**, as a roaring lion, walketh about, seeking whom he may devour:
  Whom resist stedfast in the faith, knowing that the same afflictions are accomplished in your brethren that are in the world."

- **2 Corinthians 2:11**
  "Lest **Satan** should get an advantage of us: for we are not ignorant of his devices."

Satan has many strategies. Paul was well-versed in every strategy of the **Devil**. He was not ignorant.

- **2 Corinthians 11:13-15**
  "For such *are* false apostles, deceitful workers, transforming themselves into the apostles of Christ. And no marvel; for **Satan** himself is transformed into an angel of light. Therefore *it is* no great thing if his ministers also be transformed as the ministers of righteousness; whose end shall be according to their works."

These are pastors and missionaries called Christians, but they're not genuinely saved. There are ministers and preachers in churches all over the world that are lost. The **Devil** comes not only as *a roaring lion*, but also as *an angel of light*. The ministers and pastors in the modernistic churches are **Satan's** men. They seem righteous on the outside, but they're wolves in sheep's clothing. So we have the World Council of Churches, the Roman Catholic Church, the Muslims, and all the false religions. **Satan** is interested in deceiving and he has deceived these leaders.

Here are seven things about **Satan:**

Seven Characteristics Of Satan

1. He's the prince of evil spirits, the adversary of God.
2. He incites apostasy and sin.
3. Worshippers of idols are under his control

> 4. By his devils, he's able to take possession of men and inflict them with diseases.
> 5. By God's assistance, he's overcome.
> 6. At Christ's return, he will be bound with chains for 1,000 years.
> 7. A Satan-like man can be called Satan.

Do you know any **Satan-like** men? Be careful. Maybe it's someone around you, someone near where you live or where you shop. We have to be careful.

Revelation 2:25

"But that which ye have *already* hold fast till I come."
There were those in **Thyatira** that hadn't gone after **Jezebel** and the false **idols** and teachings.

- **1 Thessalonians 5:21**
  "Prove all things; **hold fast** that which is good."

The word here is KATECHO, which means *to take hold; hold fast.* Don't let go. Be faithful. Continue to hold and retain sound words.

- **Hebrews 4:14**
  "Seeing then that we have a great high priest, that is passed into the heavens, Jesus the Son of God, let us **hold fast** *our* profession."

- **Hebrews 10:23**
  "Let us **hold fast** the profession of *our* faith without wavering; (for he *is* faithful that promised;)"

The Lord Jesus Christ wants us to **hold fast**. These people in **Thyatira** had not gone over to the false teachings of **Jezebel**. The Lord Jesus Christ says He will be **coming**.

- **1 Corinthians 15:51-52**
  "Behold, I shew you a mystery; We shall not all sleep, but we shall all be changed, In a moment, in the twinkling of an eye, at the last trump: for the trumpet shall sound, and the dead shall be raised incorruptible, and we shall be changed."

This is the **rapture** of the Church, the first phase of the Lord Jesus Christ's second coming.

- **1 Thessalonians 4:16-17**
  "For the Lord himself shall **descend from heaven** with a shout, with the voice of the archangel, and with the trump of God: and the dead in Christ shall rise first: Then we which are alive *and* remain shall be caught up together with them in the

clouds, to meet the Lord in the air: and so shall we ever be with the Lord."

This is also a picture of the **rapture**.

- **1 Thessalonians 5:23**
"And the very God of peace sanctify you wholly; and *I pray God* your whole spirit and soul and body be preserved blameless unto the **coming** of our Lord Jesus Christ."

We must have *blamelessness* until He **comes**. When is He going to **come back** for the genuine believers? When will He take us Home to Glory? We don't know. It could be at any moment. We don't know the exact time or the hour.

Revelation 2:26

"And he that overcometh, and keepeth my works unto the end, to him will I give power over the nations:"

Again, this is the genuine believers who keep, hold, and attend carefully to observe His Words unto the end. We will have *"power over the nations"* as the Lord Jesus Christ has promised.

- **Luke 19:17**
"And he said unto him, Well, thou good servant: because thou hast been faithful in a very little, have thou **authority** over ten cities."

In the millennial reign of the Lord Jesus Christ, genuinely born-again Christians in their glorified bodies will reign with Him.

- **2 Timothy 2:12**
"If we suffer, we shall also **reign** with *him:* if we deny *him,* he also will deny us:"

- **Revelation 5:10**
"And hast made us unto our God kings and priests: and we shall **reign** on the earth."

The Saved Will Reign On The Earth

We who are genuinely saved will reign on the earth. Not in these old bodies with minds that are very weak, but with minds like unto the Lord Jesus Christ and new bodies.

- **Revelation 20:6**
"Blessed and holy *is* he that hath part in the first resurrection: on such the second death hath no power, but they shall be priests of God and of Christ, and shall **reign** with him a thousand years."
- **Revelation 22:5**
"And there shall be no night there; and they need no candle, neither light of the sun; for the Lord God giveth them light: and they shall **reign** for ever and ever."

Revelation 2:27

"And he shall rule them with a rod of iron; as the vessels of a potter shall they be broken to shivers: even as I received of my Father."

The Lord Jesus Christ is spoken of in the Old Testament as **ruling** over the nations. This is a picture of that.

- **Psalm 2:9-10**
"Thou shalt **break them** with a rod of iron; thou shalt **dash them in pieces** like a potter's vessel. Be wise now therefore, O ye kings: be instructed, ye judges of the earth."

When the Lord Jesus Christ comes back at the end of the seven-year period of the tribulation, the Battle of Armageddon will be taking place. He will see the **nations** from the north, south, east, and west assembled in Jerusalem to **fight** against Israel and fight against His own people. He will *"destroy them with the brightness of His coming"* (2 Thessalonians 2:8) and **break them** as vessels of a potter. The birds of the air will come and feast themselves on the blood and the flesh of those that will be slain at that **Battle** of Armageddon, on the hill of Megiddo.

- **Revelation 11:15**
"And the seventh angel sounded; and there were great voices in heaven, saying, The kingdoms of this world are become *the kingdoms* of our Lord, and of his Christ; and he shall **reign** for ever and ever."

The Lord Jesus Christ The Ruler

The Lord Jesus Christ is going to be the Ruler. The first time He came as a Saviour. Whosoever cometh unto Him can have everlasting life and be genuinely saved. The Gospel is still open. Once the rapture takes place and the genuinely saved Christians are gone, He's coming back a second time – the

> second phase of His second coming – as the Ruler and the Judge and will *"rule"* the nations *"with a rod of iron."*

- **Revelation 19:16**
  "And he hath on *his* vesture and on his thigh a name written, KING OF KINGS, AND LORD OF LORDS."

That's when He comes back in power and glory. That's **rulership** – King of all the kings, **Lord** of all the lords.

- **Revelation 20:6**
  "Blessed and holy *is* he that hath part in the first resurrection: on such the second death hath no power, but they shall be priests of God and of Christ, and shall **reign** with him a thousand years."

He will **reign.**

Revelation 2:28

"And I will give him the morning star."

The Lord Jesus Christ is called the *"Morning Star."* That's one of His titles. That's why the New International Version and some of the other versions are wrong in their translation of Isaiah 14:12. The Lord Jesus Christ is the *"Morning Star."*

- **Isaiah 14:12**
  "How art thou fallen from heaven, O Lucifer, son of the morning! *how* art thou cut down to the ground, which didst weaken the nations!"

The New International Version falsely translates this, *"How you have fallen from heaven, morning star, son of the dawn!"* There's no Hebrew Word there for morning (SHACHAR) and there's no star (KOKAB). It's Lucifer – *light bearer; shining one.* They've given the title "morning star" to Lucifer, the Devil. This is blasphemy. In fact, some people worship Lucifer. Some of the false religions and the New Age movement worship Lucifer.

- **Revelation 22:16**
  "I Jesus have sent mine angel to testify unto you these things in the churches. I am the root and the offspring of David, *and* the bright and **morning star.**"

The NIV's translation states that the false antichrist wants to take unto himself and usurp to himself the title of *"morning star."* The Lord Jesus Christ is the only *"Morning Star"* that we have.

Revelation 2:29

"He that hath an ear, let him hear what the Spirit saith unto the churches."

The Lord talks to the church at **Thyatira**. He can talk to the church here–𝕭𝖎𝖇𝖑𝖊 𝖋𝖔𝖗 𝕿𝖔𝖉𝖆𝖞 𝕭𝖆𝖕𝖙𝖎𝖘𝖙 𝕮𝖍𝖚𝖗𝖈𝖍. Do we have an **ear to hear**? The Bible is clear. We have it in our excellent King James Bible. The **Holy Spirit** is the One who has given us the Words that the Lord Jesus Christ has given Him (John 16:13-15).

- **1 Corinthians 2:12-13**

  "Now we have received, not the spirit of the world, but the spirit which is of God; that we might know the things that are freely given to us of God. Which things also we speak, not in the words which man's wisdom teacheth, but which the **Holy Ghost** teacheth; comparing spiritual things with spiritual."

I believe that the Words of God were given by God. There is an idea of biblical inspiration that is against verbal inspiration in the sense that they don't want to think that God caused the human writers to put down every Word that God told them. They say the writers chose out of their own vocabulary what to write. No. The vocabulary may have been the writer's, but the Words from the vocabulary were given by God Himself. That's what Paul means. We have it in the Bible and we have to have an **ear to hear.**

The Preservation Of God's Words

That word *"saith"* is in the present tense – continuous action. It's what the Spirit *continues* to say. As long as our Bibles are here, as long as we have the Words of God, if you have an ear, you're urged to hear what the Spirit of God says unto you. Woe be unto us if we have in our church and in our hearts that which is displeasing to the Lord. This is important to see.

May we be blessed by the reading of His Words. May we be blessed by holding fast to things of Scripture and having an ear for His Words that He may bless and use us–our families, our homes, and our church.

Revelation
Chapter Three

Revelation 3:1

"And unto the angel of the church in Sardis write; These things saith he that hath the seven Spirits of God, and the seven stars; I know thy works, that thou hast a name that thou livest, and art dead."

The **angel**–the messenger–I believe is the pastor of this church at **Sardis**. All these seven churches were in Asia Minor. As I said before, this is in the area of Turkey. It represents the period of the Reformation with only a remnant of genuine believers again (1520-1739 A.D.)

The *seven spirits of God* are the sevenfold fullness of the Spirit of God. We saw in Chapter One that the *seven stars* are the pastors of these churches. The Lord Jesus Christ holds those **seven stars**, those pastors.

How can they be **living** and **dead** at the same time?

- **Ephesians 2:1-2**
  "And you *hath he quickened,* who were **dead** in trespasses and sins; Wherein in time past ye walked according to the course of this world, according to the prince of the power of the air, the spirit that now worketh in the children of disobedience:"

There's a way of being **dead** in trespasses and sins yet **living** in physical life.

- **1 Timothy 5:6**
  "But she that liveth in pleasure is **dead** while she **liveth.**"

This talks about the young widows who have strayed away from their pledge to serve the Lord in the local church. There's no communication with the Lord. She's out of fellowship with the Lord.

Contrast Between Death And Living

There's the contrast between death and living. Death is a separation. That's basically what death is. At physical death, it's a separation of our spirits and souls from our bodies. That's physical death. Spiritual death, on the part of all those that are lost, is separation of their spirits and souls from God. They can't communicate with God when they're dead in sin and not genuinely saved. Eternal death will be the separation of the spirits, souls, and bodies–all three–in Hell, the lake of fire for those that reject the Lord Jesus Christ.

This church has *a name that thou livest*. Every church in Collingswood, Cherry Hill, Philadelphia, Pensacola, or wherever churches may be, have a name that they **live**. Whether it's a Methodist, Baptist, or any other denomination. Many times (although not all) the Methodist churches no longer hold to that name. They no longer believe the doctrines of John Wesley or Charles Wesley that were Biblically sound. Not all Baptist churches believe in the Baptist distinctives of years gone by. Many of them are apostates and liberals. This is true of other denominations as well. This is the same as the church at **Sardis**, having *a name that thou livest, and art dead*, spiritually separated from the blessings of the Lord Jesus Christ.

Revelation 3:2

"Be watchful, and strengthen the things which remain, that are ready to die: for I have not found thy works perfect before God."

As the Lord Jesus Christ talks to these churches, He's talking to our church, the 𝕭𝖎𝖇𝖑𝖊 𝖋𝖔𝖗 𝕿𝖔𝖉𝖆𝖞 𝕭𝖆𝖕𝖙𝖎𝖘𝖙 𝕮𝖍𝖚𝖗𝖈𝖍, and all churches of this present age as well. Be **watchful**. That's a continuous action. Continue to **watch**. That word for *"watch"* is *to give strict attention; be cautious; be alive; to take heed lest through remission and indolence some destructive calamity suddenly overtakes you*. In our church, we must **watch**. That's why we have our literature rack with all kinds of things to **watch** about. There are various issues of the churches and things we ought to continue to **watch**.

"Strengthen" is also in the present tense. This church may be off-base, but they are to **strengthen**, establish, hold on to, and make firm the things that are good and that do remain in their church. We ought to keep sound doctrinal things as well.

- **Matthew 24:42**
  "**Watch** therefore: for ye know not what hour your Lord doth come."
- **Matthew 26:41**
  "**Watch** and pray, that ye enter not into temptation: the spirit indeed *is* willing, but the flesh *is* weak."
- **Acts 20:29-31**
  "For I know this, that after my departing shall grievous wolves enter in among you, not sparing the flock. Also of your own selves shall men arise, speaking perverse things, to draw away disciples after them. Therefore **watch**, and remember, that by the space of three years I ceased not to warn every one night and day with tears."

Watch Out For Wolf-Sheep

We have to watch for wolves in sheep's clothing in our churches, as well as those that are without, trying to damage the cause of the Lord Jesus Christ.

- **1 Corinthians 16:13**
  "**Watch** ye, stand fast in the faith, quit you like men, be strong."

We have to be careful of unbelief coming into our hearts, our lives, our church, and the churches in our nation.
- **1 Thessalonians 5:6**
  "Therefore let us not sleep, as *do* others; but let us **watch** and be sober."
- **2 Timothy 4:5**
  "But **watch** thou in all things, endure afflictions, do the work of an evangelist, make full proof of thy ministry."

Watch For All Compromises!

Watch. Open your eyes and see. Modernism, apostasy, heresy, and compromise do not come overnight. Modernism, apostasy, heresy, and compromise come gradually. That's what New Evangelicalism was called by Harold Ockenga in 1948, as he said we have a "*new evangelicalism.*" They don't want to be separatists from apostasy any more. They're going to try to win those apostates over and go in with them. That's not God's way.

- **2 Corinthians 6:17-18**
  "Wherefore come out from among them, and be ye separate, saith the Lord, and touch not the unclean *thing;* and I will receive you, And will be a Father unto you, and ye shall be my sons and daughters, saith the Lord Almighty."

Watch Out For Apostasy!

We need to watch in all things lest apostasy and compromise come in. We must also watch in our own hearts, lest our hearts become cold and we compromise truth.

- **Psalm 31:24**
  "Be of good courage, and he shall **strengthen** your heart, all ye that hope in the LORD."

The Lord, if we're genuinely saved, will **strengthen** our hearts.

- **Luke 22:31-32**
  "And the Lord said, Simon, Simon, behold, Satan hath desired *to have* you, that he may sift *you* as wheat: but I have prayed for thee, that thy faith fail not: and when thou art converted, **strengthen** thy brethren."

The Lord Jesus Christ talked to Simon Peter who was going to forsake Him.

- **Ephesians 6:10-11**
  "Finally, my brethren, be **strong** in the Lord, and in the power of his might. Put on the whole armour of God, that ye may be able to stand against the wiles of the devil."

That's the only **strength** that we have spiritually–in the Lord Jesus Christ. A lady called me who was seeing all kinds of Satanic things and visions. She was scared to death. She was hearing voices. I said if this person is saved, she has to be **strong** in the Lord. She has to resist the Devil and he will flee from her. This is a terrible situation. The strength must come from the Lord Jesus Christ and we are to put on all the armour of God. I hope that gave a comfort to this woman, and I trust that it did. We have to be **strong** in the Lord Jesus Christ, not in our own strength. The Devil is powerful but he's not all-powerful.

- **1 John 4:4**
  "Ye are of God, little children, and have overcome them: because **greater** is he that is in you, than he that is in the world."

- **1 Peter 5:10**
  "But the God of all grace, who hath called us unto his eternal glory by Christ Jesus, after that ye have suffered a while, make you perfect, stablish, **strengthen**, settle *you.*"

We have to be **strong** in the Lord Jesus Christ. That's what this church at Sardis didn't have and needed.

- **2 Timothy 2:1**
  "Thou therefore, my son, be **strong** in the grace that is in Christ Jesus."

If we're going to be spiritually **strong** at all, it has to be in the grace of the Lord Jesus Christ. We have to be in the Scriptures, the Words of God, following, practicing, and confessing all known sin if we're genuinely saved, that we may be **strong** and established in the things of the Lord Jesus Christ.

This church was ready to **die**. All these churches had names, but the names are fast becoming **dead** even though they say they're **alive**. **Death** sometimes comes slowly. People don't **die** all of a sudden many times. It's a slow process and we must see that.

My wife reads the obituaries to see if there's anybody that's **died** recently that she knows. Many times it says in the obituaries *"after a long illness."* After a long illness they **die**. Churches are that same way. You take the **strongest** church that you can think of in the past. They were **strong**, vibrant, and evangelistic. Slowly things creep in and they begin to **die** gradually. They get the new worship-type of thing and the charismatic-type of thing, change the versions of the Bible, and move on to all kinds of music changes. Contemporary ideas come in and it's a gradual **death**. I believe that's what the Lord Jesus Christ was saying about this church at Sardis. May our church never **die**, whether gradually or instantaneously. May everyone of you keep your eyes upon the Lord Jesus Christ and be **strengthened** in the grace which is in Christ Jesus our Lord.

- **Ephesians 6:13-17**
  "Wherefore take unto you the whole armour of God, that ye may be able to withstand in the evil day, and having done all, to stand. Stand therefore, having your loins girt about with truth, and having on the breastplate of righteousness; And your feet shod with the preparation of the gospel of peace; Above all, taking the shield of faith, wherewith ye shall be able to quench all the fiery darts of the wicked. And take the helmet of salvation, and the sword of the Spirit, which is the Word of God:"

Revelation 3:3

"Remember therefore how thou hast received and heard, and hold fast, and repent. If therefore thou shalt not watch, I will come on thee as a thief, and thou shalt not know what hour I will come upon thee."

The Lord Jesus Christ tells this church at **Sardis** to continue to remember. All of our churches must remember. This church **heard** and **received** the truth of God. He tells them to **remember** what they have **received**. We've **received** things.

Reference To The "Received" Text

This talks, I believe, about the Received Greek Text. It's called the Received Text, or the Textus Receptus. That's one thing we've received. We have to hear it. We have to fight for it and hold fast the things we've received. We've received the doctrines of the faith–the Deity of the Lord Jesus Christ, being born-again by grace through genuine faith in His death and the shedding of His blood on the cross of Calvary. All of these doctrines we've received, as well as His virgin birth, His coming again, and His miracles. What we've received and heard, we have to hold fast just like this church at Sardis.

Hold fast is the Word TEREO. It means *to carefully take care of and attend to; to guard.* We are to **guard** the things which we have **received** and **keep** them in the state in which we're in. That's why I, as a Bible-believing pastor, want to **guard** and **keep** the things that I have **received**.

Dr. Mark Minnick, one of the writers in the book, *From the Mind of God to the Mind of Man* and the sequel to it, *God's Word In Our Hands* (written by many who are connected to Bob Jones University), sent me an e-mail and asked me what type of text I hold to. I told him it was the exact Masoretic Hebrew, Aramaic, and Greek Words that underlie our King James Bible. Then he wrote another e-mail to me and said some of his friends believe this way and he wanted to know what version of the **Received** Text I mean. I said, "There are many **Received** Texts, but basically *Beza's Fifth Edition of 1598* is what our King James Bible translators used." He said, "Weren't they just a law unto themselves using anything they wanted?" I told him, "No." According to Dr. Scrivener, in only 190 places does the *Beza's Fifth Edition of 1598* depart from our King James Bible. That's a very small percentage out of more than 140,000 Words in the New Testament Traditional Greek Text.

Hold On To Truth Received

We have to hold that which we've received and heard. This church at Sardis was to repent and change their ways. If not, if they don't watch, the Lord Jesus Christ says He is going to come unto them as a thief, and take away their church from them. That's exactly what happened historically.

- **Acts 17:11**
  "These were more noble than those in Thessalonica, in that they **received** the word with all readiness of mind, and searched the scriptures daily, whether those things were so."

We have to hold fast what we **receive**. Don't forget it. Don't throw it away.

- **1 Corinthians 15:1**
  "Moreover, brethren, I declare unto you the gospel which I preached unto you, which also ye have **received**, and wherein ye stand;"

- **Colossians 2:6**
  "As ye have therefore **received** Christ Jesus the Lord, *so* walk ye in him:"

Stay by the stuff. Don't change.

- **1 Thessalonians 2:13**
  "For this cause also thank we God without ceasing, because, when ye **received** the word of God which ye heard of us, ye **received** *it* not *as* the word of men, but as it is in truth, the word of God, which effectually worketh also in you that believe."

- **2 Thessalonians 3:6**
  "Now we command you, brethren, in the name of our Lord Jesus Christ, that ye withdraw yourselves from every brother that walketh disorderly, and not after the tradition which he **received** of us."

We have **received** things and we have to guard them.

Revelation 3:4

"Thou hast a few names even in Sardis which have not defiled their garments; and they shall walk with me in white: for they are worthy."

Keep Pure From Defilement

There were a few that didn't defile themselves. That word defile is an interesting term. MOLUNO means *to pollute; to stain; to contaminate.* It's used in the New Testament of those who have not kept themselves pure from the defilements of sin. They've soiled themselves by fornication and adultery. The Lord Jesus Christ mentioned at least thirteen things that defile in the Gospel of Mark.

- **Mark 7:20-23**
  "And he said, That which cometh out of the man, that **defileth** the man. For from within, out of the heart of men, proceed evil thoughts, adulteries, fornications, murders, Thefts, covetousness, wickedness, deceit, lasciviousness, an evil eye, blasphemy, pride, foolishness: All these evil things come from within, and **defile** the man."

- **James 3:6**
  "And the tongue *is* a fire, a world of iniquity: so is the tongue among our members, that it **defileth** the whole body, and setteth on fire the course of nature; and it is set on fire of Hell."

I'm glad that there were a few in **Sardis** that were not **defiled**. I hope there are many more than just a few in our church here that have not *"defiled their garments."*

- **Colossians 1:10**
  "That ye might walk **worthy** of the Lord unto all pleasing, being fruitful in every good work, and increasing in the knowledge of God;"

The Lord alone is **worthy**. We'll see that in Chapter 4 of this book of Revelation. The Lord Jesus Christ is **worthy** and He wants us to walk in a **worthy** manner of Him who has truly saved us. That's a tall order, but that's what God would have us to do.

Revelation 3:5

"He that overcometh, the same shall be clothed in white raiment; and I will not blot out his name out of the book of life, but I will confess his name before my Father, and before his angels."

I believe every time the phrase "**He that overcometh**" is used, it's talking about the believers, the genuinely saved people. NIKAO is *the conqueror; the ones that continue to overcome.* These shall be "*clothed in white raiment.*" In Glory, that's what our raiment will be. "*The book of life*" is used five other times in Scripture and it always referred to those that are genuinely saved, those who are born-again by genuine faith in the Lord Jesus Christ.

- **Philippians 4:3**
  "And I intreat thee also, true yokefellow, help those women which laboured with me in the gospel, with Clement also, and *with* other my fellowlabourers, whose names *are* in **the book of life.**"

The names of those that are genuinely saved are in **the book of life.** God has a **book.** You say, "Does He keep **books**?" Yes. He keeps good **books.** Some people in business have two sets of **books**—one for the investigators to look at and another, that are the real **books.** One of the ministries I have known about had a Certified Public Accountant (CPA) who kept the **books.** He's with the Lord Jesus Christ now. He said there were two sets of **books.** The Lord Jesus Christ has one set of **books** and He keeps them straight.

- **Revelation 13:8**
  "And all that dwell upon the earth shall worship him, whose names are not written in **the book of life** of the Lamb slain from the foundation of the world."

Those whose names are not written in **the book of life** shall worship the beast during the tribulation.

- **Revelation 17:8**
  "The beast that thou sawest was, and is not; and shall ascend out of the bottomless pit, and go into perdition: and they that dwell on the earth shall wonder, whose names were not written in **the book of life** from the foundation of the world, when they behold the beast that was, and is not, and yet is."

- **Revelation 20:12**
  "And I saw the dead, small and great, stand before God; and the books were opened: and another book was opened, which is *the book* of life: and the dead were judged out of those things which were written in the books, according to their works."

- **Revelation 20:15**
  "And whosoever was not found written in **the book of life** was cast into the lake of fire."

The Book Of Life

Is your name there? Are you sure you're genuinely saved and born-again? Are you trusting the Lord Jesus Christ as your Saviour and Redeemer? If so, your name is in the book of life. If not, you will be cast into Hell, into the lake of real, literal, burning fire for all eternity to come.

- **Revelation 22:19**
  "And if any man shall take away from the words of the book of this prophecy, God shall take away his **part** out of **the book of life**, and out of the holy city, and *from* the things which are written in this book."

I don't believe God will take out the "*name*" out of **the book of life** so that he loses his salvation. That which is taken out of **the book of life** is his "*part*." I interpret that "*part*" to be his reward. I believe all these versions that have taken away the Words of **the book of life**, or added to the Words of **the book of life** are going to have their "*part*" removed from the book of life. Not their names, their "*part*"–their rewards. I believe that's what it's speaking of in Revelation 22:19.

- **Matthew 10:32**
  "Whosoever therefore shall **confess me** before men, him will I **confess** also before my Father which is in heaven."

That's what the Lord Jesus Christ says to the church at **Sardis**. We should never be ashamed of our Lord Jesus Christ. We should **confess** Him and should not draw back. If somebody asks you, "Are you a Christian? Are you saved? Are you born-again? Are you a Bible-believing Christian?" If you are, I hope your answer will always be, "YES." Unequivocally, yes. Not "I hope so," or "Maybe," or "Ask me some other question," or whatever. Don't be ashamed. **Confess** Him before men.

Revelation 3:6

"He that hath an ear, let him hear what the Spirit saith unto the churches."

This is a refrain that ends the messages to every one of these seven churches. It's in the present tense continuous action. "Let him continue to **hear**."

- **1 Corinthians 2:12-13**
  "Now we have received, not the spirit of the world, but the **spirit** which is of God; that we might know the things that are freely given to us of God. Which things also we speak, not in the words which man's wisdom teacheth, but which the **Holy Ghost** teacheth; comparing spiritual things with spiritual."

The Words that the **Spirit of God says** to these churches are said to our church as well. The **Holy Spirit** of God has given to us the Lord Jesus Christ's Words (John 16:13-15)–Old Testament **Words** in Hebrew and a little Aramaic, and New Testament **Words** in Greek.

Accurate Translations Needed

We must have accurate translations of those Words in all the languages of the world. We do have an accurate translation of God's Hebrew, Aramaic, and Greek Words in our King James Bible. I believe it is the only accurate translation in the English language today. God expects us to hear what the Holy Spirit of God says to our church and to us. Not only must we read His Words, but also we must heed the Words of God. This is important.

Revelation 3:7

"And to the angel of the church in Philadelphia write; These things saith he that is holy, he that is true, he that hath the key of David, he that openeth, and no man shutteth; and shutteth, and no man openeth;"

This is the pastor of the church at **Philadelphia**. As we said before, Philadelphia represents the true church and the professing church from 1739 to the present. This is a church where missionary endeavors began to multiply and grow. It's also a church which represents the era when Bible institutes were founded and grew to take the place of modernistic seminaries. Now, sad to say, those Bible institutes are turning into either colleges or universities and are drifting from the truth badly. It's a different situation. They no longer want to be called Bible institutes. They have to be *colleges*. They don't all want to be called colleges. That's not big enough for them. They want to be called *universities*. Now we have universities. What used to be Cedarville Baptist College is now Cedarville University. It's the same way with Grand Rapids Baptist Theological Seminary. Now its Cornerstone University.

The Lord has given a powerful **open door** to our church and we pray that He would keep it that way. So far He has **opened** our church and He has not yet shut the **door** of the 𝔅𝔦𝔟𝔩𝔢 𝔣𝔬𝔯 𝔗𝔬𝔡𝔞𝔶 𝔅𝔞𝔭𝔱𝔦𝔰𝔱 ℭ𝔥𝔲𝔯𝔠𝔥.

The Lord Opens & Shuts Doors

It is the Lord Jesus Christ Who has opened the door, and He can shut it anytime He sees fit. We must realize that. When the Lord Jesus Christ shuts the door, no matter if they keep having services, if the Lord Jesus Christ is outside that church, they might as well shut the doors. That's what the liberals and modernistic churches have done. They keep on going with their programs and so on, but the Lord Jesus Christ is not there. He has shut the doors.

The Lord Jesus Christ has the "*keys*" to open and shut the **doors**. He is the One Who has this **power**.

- **Matthew 28:18**
  "And Jesus came and spake unto them, saying, All **power** is given unto me in heaven and in earth."
- **2 Corinthians 12:9**
  "And he said unto me, My grace is sufficient for thee: for my strength is made perfect in weakness. Most gladly therefore will I rather glory in my infirmities, that the **power** of Christ may rest upon me."
- **Colossians 1:11**
  "Strengthened with all might, according to his glorious **power**, unto all patience and longsuffering with joyfulness;"

The Lord Jesus Christ has **power**. He can **open doors** and He can **close doors**.

- **Colossians 2:10**
  "And ye are complete in him, which is the head of all principality and **power**:"

He's the head of all kinds of **power**.

- **2 Thessalonians 1:9**
  "Who shall be punished with everlasting destruction from the presence of the Lord, and from the glory of his **power;**"
- **Hebrews 1:3**
  "Who being the brightness of *his* glory, and the express image of his person, and upholding all things by the word of his **power**, when he had by himself purged our sins, sat down on the right hand of the Majesty on high;"

He's in control of the entire universe. He created Mars. He created the earth. He created the billions of stars. He created man. He has the **power** over creation.

- **2 Peter 1:16**
  "For we have not followed cunningly devised fables, when we made known unto you the **power** and coming of our Lord Jesus Christ, but were eyewitnesses of his majesty."

Revelation 3:8

"I know thy works: behold, I have set before thee an open door, and no man can shut it: for thou hast a little strength, and hast kept my word, and hast not denied my name."

Jesus Christ the Lord and our Saviour, says He knows their works. The church of **Philadelphia** represents the church of the Reformation. Our Baptist churches never went through the Reformation. The Baptist-kind of churches have always been in existence from the time of Paul in the New Testament right on to the present. We never came out of Rome. We never came out of the Lutheran church or the Episcopal church. Baptist churches have never been a part of the Reformation.

The Reformation Stopped Short

The Reformation didn't go far enough, as far as I'm concerned. Luther still maintained many of the rags of Rome, as my wife's grandfather used to refer to them. Lots of things are still there and haven't changed.

Our church has been **opened** by the Lord Jesus Christ. I believe strongly in that. It's an **open door**, even as Philadelphia had an open door and no man is able to shut it.

- **Acts 14:27**
  "And when they were come, and had gathered the church together, they rehearsed all that God had done with them, and how he had **opened** the **door** of faith unto the Gentiles."
- **1 Corinthians 16:9**
  "For a great **door** and effectual is **opened** unto me, and *there are* many adversaries."

Open Door Adversaries

There are always adversaries when God's open door is there.

- **2 Corinthians 2:12**
  "Furthermore, when I came to Troas to *preach* Christ's gospel, and a **door** was **opened** unto me of the Lord,"
- **Acts 16:9**
  "And a vision appeared to Paul in the night; There stood a man of Macedonia, and prayed him, saying, Come over into Macedonia, and help us."

God's Open Door To Europe

That's the door to Europe. Asia had the Gospel, but now Europe was opened up. That was the door that Paul speaks of. The Lord Jesus Christ opened the door. We can't open doors. The Lord can.

- **Colossians 4:3**
  "Withal praying also for us, that God would **open** unto us a **door** of utterance, to speak the mystery of Christ, for which I am also in bonds:"

Here Paul was praying in jail. He was in prison in the book of Colossians.

God wants us to **keep His Words**. Our church should **keep His Words**. We should not depart from the **Words** of God in any way.

- **John 14:15**
  "If ye love me, **keep** my commandments."
- **John 14:23**
  "Jesus answered and said unto him, If a man love me, he will **keep** my words: and my Father will love him, and we will come unto him, and make our abode with him."

- **John 15:10**
  "If ye **keep** my commandments, ye shall abide in my love; even as I have **kept** my Father's commandments, and abide in his love."
- **1 John 5:3**
  "For this is the love of God, that we **keep** his commandments: and his commandments are not grievous."
- **1 Timothy 6:20**
  "O Timothy, **keep** that which is committed to thy trust, avoiding profane *and* vain babblings, and oppositions of science falsely so called:"

The title of David Cloud's paper, *O Timothy*, is from this verse. We're to keep that which is committed to our trust. <u>The Traditional Received Greek and Traditional Hebrew/Aramaic Words are the Words that are committed to our trust.</u> We're to **keep** all the doctrines of Scripture.

This church of **Philadelphia** did not **deny** the **Name** of the Lord Jesus Christ, nor should our church or any church today.

- **Matthew 10:33**
  "But whosoever shall deny me before men, him will I also **deny** before my Father which is in heaven."

May we never **deny** the Lord Jesus Christ!

- **Matthew 26:34**
  "Jesus said unto him, Verily I say unto thee, That this night, before the cock crow, thou shalt **deny** me thrice."

The church at Philadelphia had a little strength. They had not **denied** the Lord's **Name**.

What about our **open door**? In October, 1998, the Lord **opened** this **door** of the church in our house. Until now, the Lord has kept this **door open**. Praise the Lord for that! Currently, we have nine missionaries that we support each month. This is part of our **open door**. God has **opened** up that **door** to help and assist in these missionary endeavors. The Lord Jesus Christ has opened our radio ministry. We're also on the Internet. As of this writing, we're getting computer downloads each month from over 60 foreign countries and from all 50 states in the USA. The Lord Jesus Christ has **opened** a **door**. He's **opened** a **door** for services here, and for our video families around this country, and around the world. The Lord Jesus Christ has also **opened** a **door** for books. Our church has been able to publish many books through the offerings that are given to this ministry. <u>I don't take a salary, but the salary I would normally take goes into the books and our support of our missionaries support. The books have reached out along with the calendar tracts and pens for our ministry.</u> Pray that the **door** will stay **open** for the **Bible for Today Baptist Church**. We have an **open door**. We ought to thank the Lord Jesus Christ for it.

If the Lord Jesus Christ sets an **open door** before you or before me, we'd better walk through that **door**. Don't cease. You have all kinds of **open doors** in your ministry and in your life, wherever you are. When the Lord Jesus Christ is in it, walk through it and don't stop. I believe the Lord Jesus Christ has **opened** this **door**. He leads us in all of our endeavors.

Revelation 3:9

"Behold, I will make them of the synagogue of Satan, which say they are Jews, and are not, but do lie; behold, I will make them to come and worship before thy feet, and to know that I have loved thee."

We've seen a program in the morning called *The Key of David*. This refers to Herbert W. Armstrong. Armstrong is a cross between British Israelism and Jehovah's Witnesses. It's a terrible heresy. He says that the present-day **Jews** are not **Jews**, but the **Jews** are citizens of Britain, the United States, and Germany. He says that Anglo-Saxon Celtic people are the **Jews**. This practice was present in the church at **Philadelphia**. People were saying they were **Jews** and were not.

Harold Camping with his Family Radio program taught that the promises of **Israel** have been transferred to the church. This is absolutely and totally false. **Israel's** promises are going to be maintained and fulfilled by national **Israel**. The true church is separate and distinct.

The Jews Rights In Palestine

I believe that the Jews that are in Palestine now are the Jews that God has given the right to that land. They are in unbelief, but one day God is going to raise them up as a people. They're going to come in genuine faith and truly believe.

- **Romans 11:26**
  "And so all **Israel** shall be saved: as it is written, There shall come out of Sion the Deliverer, and shall turn away ungodliness from **Jacob**:"

Revelation 3:10

"Because thou hast kept the word of my patience, I also will keep thee from the hour of temptation, which shall come upon all the world, to try them that dwell upon the earth."

I believe this is referring to the tribulation period or Daniel's 70th Week. Daniel's 70th Week is for Daniel's people (Daniel 9:24). That's why it's so important that we distinguish between **Israel**, God's people of the Old Testament, and the true church, God's born-again people of the New Testament. You can't mix them. The tribulation period will be for the judgment against the **Jews** at that time.

Pre-Tribulation Church Rapture

The genuine believers in the church at Philadelphia, like any true believers, are kept from that hour. I believe in a Pre-tribulation rapture of the true Church, taking away the truly born-again Christians before this terrible tribulation takes place.

- **1 Thessalonians 5:1-6**
  "But of the times and the seasons, brethren, ye have no need that I write unto you. For yourselves know perfectly that the day of the Lord so cometh as a thief in the night. For when they shall say, Peace and safety; then sudden destruction cometh upon them, as travail upon a woman with child; and they shall not escape. But ye, brethren, are not in darkness, that that day should overtake you as a thief. Ye are all the children of light, and the children of the day: we are not of the night, nor of darkness. Therefore let us not sleep, as *do* others; but let us watch and be sober."

We will not be overtaken. We will be **kept** from the hour of this tribulation period. That's a promise.

Revelation 3:11

"Behold, I come quickly: hold that fast which thou hast, that no man take thy crown."

This is talking about the **return** of the Lord Jesus Christ . We're to **hold fast**. That's the word KRATEO, which means *to grab hold of; to lay hands on and be master of.* We should hold on to the things and doctrines that we have. We should not discard our sound standards of music, the Words of God, our sound **standards** of preaching, and our sound doctrinal **standards**.

Christ's Imminent Return

I believe in the imminent rapture of our Lord Jesus Christ. No prophecy needs to be fulfilled before He comes in the air for all of His truly born-again Christians and transforms their bodies into immortal bodies. The bodies of the genuinely saved ones who are in corruption now (in the grave) will be transformed into incorruption. One day the Lord Jesus Christ will come quickly.

- **1 Thessalonians 5:21**
  "Prove all things; **hold fast** that which is good."
- **2 Timothy 1:13**
  "**Hold fast** the form of sound words, which thou hast heard of me, in faith and love which is in Christ Jesus."

That's why we **hold fast** to the Received Words in the Hebrew, Aramaic, and Greek that underlie our King James Bible in English.

God speaks in this verse about a "*crown.*" There are five **crowns** in Scripture. I have summed up these five **crowns** by the following memory hint: "R GIRL."

Five Crowns For Believers

1. "R"—the crown of righteousness—loving His appearing. (2 Timothy 4:8)
2. "G"—the crown of glory—a faithful shepherd of the flock. (1 Peter 5:4)
3, "I"—the incorruptible crown—running the race successfully. (1 Corinthians 9:25)
4. "R"—the crown of rejoicing—for winning souls. (1 Thessalonians 2:19)
5. "L"—the crown of life—being faithful unto death. (James 1:12 and Revelation 2:10)

- **Revelation 4:10**
  "The four and twenty elders fall down before him that sat on the throne, and worship him that liveth for ever and ever, and cast their **crowns** before the throne, saying,"

I believe this is a picture of the true church in **Glory**.

- **Revelation 4:11**
  "Thou art worthy, O Lord, to receive **glory** and honour and power: for thou hast created all things, and for thy pleasure they are and were created."

God has set before us an **open door** as in this poem by Martha Snell Nicholson:

The Red Sea

When the children of Israel crossed the Red Sea
It comforts my heart to know,
That there must have been many timorous ones
Who faltered and feared to go;
Feared the ribbon of road which stretched
Ahead like a narrow track,
With the waves piled high on the other side,
And nothing to hold them back
Nothing to hold them back but a Hand
They could neither see nor feel;
Their God seemed distant and far away,
and only the peril real.
Yet the fearful ones were as safe as the brave,
For the mercy of God is wide.
Craven and fearless, He lead them all
Dry shod to the other side.
And I think of the needless pain and terror
We bring to our own Red Sea.
Strengthen Thy timorous ones dear Lord,
And help us to trust in Thee.

May we ask our God to keep our church **door open** to serve Him, to trust in Him and ask His help for all these things. He is able. He **opened** this **door** of our church just like He did for the church at **Philadelphia**. He set before them an **open door** that no man can shut. May we keep that **door open** and may we continue to pray for Him to guide us.

Revelation 3:12

"Him that overcometh will I make a pillar in the temple of my God, and he shall go no more out: and I will write upon him the name of my God, and the name of the city of my God, *which is* new Jerusalem, which cometh down out of heaven from my God: and *I will write upon him* my new name."

Here is the Lord Jesus Christ speaking to the **overcomers** at the church of **Philadelphia**.

- 1 Timothy 3:15
  "But if I tarry long, that thou mayest know how thou oughtest to behave thyself in the house of God, which is the church of the living God, the **pillar** and ground of the truth."

The Church As A Pillar

The pillar that holds things up is the church. Genuine believers are going to be made pillars in the temple of God. In Heaven we will no longer go out into the highways and byways of this world. This temple of God and the new Jerusalem that comes down out of Heaven is mentioned many times in Scripture.

- Revelation 21:2
  "And I John saw the holy **city, new Jerusalem,** coming down from God **out of heaven,** prepared as a bride adorned for her husband."

The New Jerusalem

This new Jerusalem is going to be suspended during the millennial Reign of the Lord Jesus Christ directly over the earthly Jerusalem. We'll see that, as we come into the later part of the book of Revelation.

- Revelation 21:10
  "And he carried me away in the spirit to a great and high mountain, and shewed me that great **city,** the holy **Jerusalem,** descending **out of heaven** from God,"

That's a miracle. Nobody can believe that, unless they believe the Bible. How can a huge **city**–1,500 miles long, 1,500 miles high and 1,500 miles

deep– foursquare–come down **out of Heaven?** That takes faith that
God has given to us in the Scripture.

- **Revelation 21:14-23**
  "And the wall of the **city** had twelve foundations, and in them
  the names of the twelve apostles of the Lamb. And he that
  talked with me had a golden reed to measure the **city**, and the
  gates thereof, and the wall thereof. And the **city** lieth
  foursquare, and the length is as large as the breadth: and he
  measured the city with the reed, twelve thousand furlongs. The
  length and the breadth and the height of it are equal. And he
  measured the wall thereof, an hundred *and* forty *and* four
  cubits, *according to* the measure of a man, that is, of the angel.
  And the building of the wall of it was *of* jasper: and the city *was*
  pure gold, like unto clear glass. And the foundations of the wall
  of the **city** *were* garnished with all manner of precious stones.
  The first foundation *was* jasper; the second, sapphire; the third,
  a chalcedony; the fourth, an emerald; The fifth, sardonyx; the
  sixth, sardius; the seventh, chrysolite; the eighth, beryl; the
  ninth, a topaz; the tenth, a chrysoprasus; the eleventh, a jacinth;
  the twelfth, an amethyst. And the twelve gates *were* twelve
  pearls; every several gate was of one pearl: and the street of the
  city *was* pure gold, as it were transparent glass. And I saw no
  temple therein: for the Lord God Almighty and the Lamb are the
  temple of it. And the city had no need of the sun, neither of the
  moon, to shine in it: for the glory of God did lighten it, and the
  Lamb *is* the light thereof."

This describes that **city.** Gold is precious and this whole **Heavenly
city,** miraculously coming down, is made of pure gold. There will be no
need of the temple, or of the sun, or the moon.

- **Revelation 2:17**
  "He that hath an ear, let him hear what the Spirit saith unto the
  churches; To him that overcometh will I give to eat of the
  hidden manna, and will give him a white stone, and in the stone
  a **new name** written, which no man knoweth saving he that
  receiveth *it.*"

The *new name* will be given in Glory when the Lord Jesus Christ
reigns on this earth.

Revelation 3:13

"He that hath an ear, let him hear what the Spirit saith unto the churches."

This is the refrain after the messages to every one of these seven churches. The Lord Jesus Christ speaks to us as well. Do you have an **ear**? Do I have an **ear**? Do we have an **ear** to **hear**? What are we supposed to **hear**? Not what the preacher says with his words, but *what the Spirit saith unto the churches.* As the preacher preaches the Words of God, that's what we're to **hear**. The **Spirit** of God is the One who is speaking and every church must **hear** what the **Spirit** of God saith. That's continuous action—what He continues to say to the churches.

- **1 Corinthians 2:12-13**
  "Now we have received, not the **spirit** of the world, but the **spirit** which is of God; that we might know the things that are freely given to us of God. Which things also we speak, not in the **words** which man's wisdom teacheth, but which the Holy Ghost teacheth; comparing spiritual things with spiritual."

The desire of the Lord Jesus Christ is for every one of these churches (and ours is not an exception), is to **hear** what the **Spirit** of God says to the **churches**. He speaks it in His **Words**. He speaks it in the Hebrew, Aramaic, and Greek **Words** that underlie the King James Bible.

The King James Bible Is Best

The King James Bible is the clearest, the best and the only accurate representation of those Words. God wants us to be in the Scriptures, reading day by day from Genesis to Revelation. Some people say they don't want to read the Old Testament, that it's too difficult. It may be hard, but if you just keep plowing along, you'll find something that you'll understand and something that will bless your heart and soul. If you don't believe it, try it. Read through those Scriptures from Genesis to Revelation. Hear what the Spirit of God says unto the churches.

That's the trouble with the modernist and apostate churches. They're not listening to what the Spirit of God says. They're not listening to the Scriptures. They're following man and not the Words of God. This is a danger in every church in every age. They must listen to only what the Scriptures say — what the Spirit of God says unto the churches.

Revelation 3:14

"And unto the angel of the church of the Laodiceans write; These things saith the Amen, the faithful and true witness, the beginning of the creation of God;"

In the prophetic picture, the **Laodiceans'** church is the church of **apostasy**, which we are living in today. The **apostate** churches are growing rapidly. Whether it's the **apostasy** in the National Council of Churches in this country, or the World Council of Churches all over the world, the Roman Catholic church with all of its **apostasy**, the emerging church **apostasy**, or the charismatic **apostasy**, we're living in a mixed-up situation.

The Lord Jesus Christ is called the *Amen*. **Amen** means *I believe it*. It's true.

- **2 Corinthians 1:20**
  "For all the promises of God in him *are* yea, and in him **Amen**, unto the glory of God by us."

- **Revelation 1:18**
  "*I am* he that liveth, and was dead; and, behold, I am alive for evermore, **Amen**; and have the keys of Hell and of death."

The Laodicean Church Is Here

The Lord Jesus Christ is addressing the Laodicean church. LAOS is *people* and DOKEO is *to say or to think*. It's *what the people think*. My friends, who cares what the people think? What does God think? That's the important issue. The Laodicean church was a lackadaisical church.

- **Revelation 1:5**
  "And from Jesus Christ, *who is* the **faithful witness**, *and* the first begotten of the dead, and the prince of the kings of the earth. Unto him that loved us, and washed us from our sins in his own blood,"

The Lord Jesus Christ is the **true and faithful witness**. He will not lie. Somebody might come on the **witness** stand to get somebody else off and they lie. They change the story. Not the Lord Jesus Christ.

- **Matthew 27:11**
  "And Jesus stood before the governor: and the governor asked him, saying, Art thou the King of the Jews? And Jesus said unto him, **Thou sayest**."

- **1 Timothy 6:13**
  "I give thee charge in the sight of God, who quickeneth all things, and *before* Christ Jesus, who before Pontius Pilate witnessed a **good confession;"**

Notice also He's *the beginning of the creation of God.* He was there at the **creation.** He had no beginning. He was the **Creator** Himself–the **Creator** of the ends of the earth.

- **John 1:3**
  "All things were **made** by him; and without him was not any thing made that was **made."**

He is not only *the Amen,* not only *the faithful and true witness,* but also the *beginning of the creation of God.*

- **Ephesians 3:9**
  "And to make all *men* see what *is* the fellowship of the mystery, which from the beginning of the world hath been hid in God, who **created** all things by Jesus Christ:"

Denial Of Christ As The Creator

Those three words–*"by Jesus Christ"*–are eliminated in the Westcott and Hort false Greek text. The Gnostic Critical Text takes out *"by Jesus Christ"* because the Gnostics who formed that text of "B" and Aleph (Vatican and Sinai) did not believe the Lord Jesus Christ was the Creator.

I read the Bob Jones University book that is the sequel to *From the Mind of God to the Mind of Man.* It's called *The Word of God in Our Hands.* These people are saying, over and over again, that those of us who stand for the Received Greek Text, and the Traditional Hebrew Masoretic Text, and the King James Bible, are making too much of the issues. They say there's really nothing wrong whatever with all these different versions. They claim the doctrines are pure and there's not a doctrine that's changed.

Why 356 Doctrinal Perversions

My friend, *"creation"* is a doctrine. When they take out the Lord Jesus Christ, creating all things "by Jesus Christ," I'm up in arms. I will continue to be up in arms. No, my friend, that's only one doctrine of the 356 doctrines that these perversions have in their Bibles. Why? Because they've followed a perverted text of the Gnostics of Egypt who denied the Deity of the Lord Jesus Christ. They denied the bodily resurrection of the Lord Jesus Christ. They denied His virgin birth and His miracles. Those heretics in Egypt doctored manuscripts "B" and Aleph (Vatican and Sinai). Westcott and Hort in 1881 came out with their version of the Greek text to change it. This is one of the changes they made. They take out Jesus Christ as the Creator in Ephesians 3:9. It certainly does make a difference which version of the Bible we use.

- **Colossians 1:16**
"For by him were all things **created**, that are in heaven, and that are in earth, visible and invisible, whether *they be* thrones, or dominions, or principalities, or powers: all things were **created** by him, and for him:"

The Lord Jesus Christ was the **Creator** – *the beginning of the creation of God.*

Revelation 3:15

"I know thy works, that thou art neither cold nor hot: I would thou wert cold or hot."

This **Laodicean** church was neither **hot nor cold**. The Lord Jesus Christ wishes they were one or the other.

- **Judges 6:39**
"And Gideon said unto God, Let not thine anger be **hot** against me, and I will speak but this once: let me prove, I pray thee, but this once with the fleece; let it now be dry only upon the fleece, and upon all the ground let there be dew."

- **Psalm 39:2-4**
"I was dumb with silence, I held my peace, *even* from good; and my sorrow was stirred. My heart was **hot** within me, while I was musing the fire burned: *then* spake I with my tongue, LORD, make me to know mine end, and the measure of my days, what it *is; that* I may know how frail I *am.*"

- **Matthew 24:12**
"And because iniquity shall abound, the love of many shall wax **cold**."

Coldness In Our Churches

"Cold" in what sense? There was no warm genuine Christian faith nor a desire for holiness. We have this coldness in churches in our country and all over the world today. May our church never be cold.

Revelation 3:16

"So then because thou art lukewarm, and neither cold nor hot, I will spue thee out of my mouth."

The Lord Jesus Christ wants nothing to do with this **lukewarm** church. What does **lukewarm** mean? According to the dictionary, it's *barely or moderately warm (said of liquids); not very warm or enthusiastic.* This church was not enthusiastic. It was tepid, lacking warmth, and without enthusiasm. A person who is *Laodicean* is *"indifferent or lukewarm in religion as the early professing Christians of Laodicea."*

- **Leviticus 20:22**
  "Ye shall therefore keep all my statutes, and all my judgments, and do them: that the land, whither I bring you to dwell therein, **spue you not out.**"

That's the word for **vomit.** This is a terrible thing. Is the Lord Jesus Christ too strong on this church? No. The Lord Jesus Christ is never too strong on any church. What He says, He means. This is the church of the **apostasy** of our day.

Revelation 3:17

"Because thou sayest, I am rich, and increased with goods, and have need of nothing; and knowest not that thou art wretched, and miserable, and poor, and blind, and naked:"

Roman Catholic Empty Formalism

The Roman Catholic church has a form of godliness but denies the power thereof. Think of the richness of the Roman Catholic system with millions upon millions of dollars. They can pay millions of dollars to buy off the people that the priests have done homosexual or pedofile acts upon. They buy off the families. This is a terrible thing. They don't know that they're wretched and miserable. The same is true of some non-Roman Catholic groups as well.

- **Romans 7:24**
  "O wretched man that I am! who shall deliver me from the body of this **death?**"

- **1 Corinthians 15:19**
  "If in this life only we have hope in Christ, we are of all men most **miserable**."

They don't know that they're **miserable**. They don't know that they're poor.

- **Matthew 15:14**
  "Let them alone: they be **blind** leaders of the blind. And if the blind lead the **blind**, both shall fall into the ditch."

Across the street from us, a Lutheran church had a bishop ordain the pastor of the church. I don't know what that church preaches, but many Lutheran churches in this country preach heresy, denying the doctrines of the genuine faith. Twenty or thirty years ago when our sons went over there one Christmas to see what they were singing, there was nothing but apostasy there. Whether it's changed or not, who knows?

- **Matthew 23:16**
  "Woe unto you, *ye* **blind** guides, which say, Whosoever shall swear by the temple, it is nothing; but whosoever shall swear by the gold of the temple, he is a debtor!"

The **Laodicean** people don't know that they're **blind**. The Lord Jesus Christ sets them straight. They're **blind**–spiritually **blind**.

- **Matthew 23:17**
  "*Ye* fools and **blind**: for whether is greater, the gold, or the temple that sanctifieth the gold?"

That's strong language. No one likes to be called a fool.

- **Matthew 23:24**
  "*Ye* **blind** guides, which strain at a gnat, and swallow a camel."

- **Matthew 23:26**
  "*Thou* **blind** Pharisee, cleanse first that *which is* within the cup and platter, that the outside of them may be clean also."

- **John 9:39-41**
  "And Jesus said, For judgment I am come into this world, that they which see not might see; and that they which see might be made **blind**. And *some* of the Pharisees which were with him heard these words, and said unto him, Are we **blind** also? Jesus said unto them, If ye were **blind**, ye should have no sin: but now ye say, We see; therefore your sin remaineth."

If they were to be humble and say, "We're **blind** and lost sinners and we need Thy salvation," He would have healed their spiritual blindness. That's the trouble with the **Laodicean** church. They don't know that they're **blind**. It's a terrible state if you don't know you're **blind**. Also, they're **naked**–without the proper clothing.

- **Genesis 3:7**
  "And the eyes of them both were opened, and they knew that they *were* **naked**; and they sewed fig leaves together, and made themselves aprons."

Adam & Eve's Nakedness

They had the glory of God over them. When they sinned, the glory of God was gone. There they were, stark naked. The Lord changed their aprons into coats of skins. This is a picture of Calvary, the shedding of innocent blood as a substitute to clothe those that were and are in need of clothing.

- **Genesis 3:21**
  "Unto Adam also and to his wife did the LORD God make coats of skins, and **clothed** them."

The Laodicean Disgrace & Misery

These people at Laodicea were a terrible disgrace to the Lord Jesus Christ. We have professing Christians of Laodicea in our own day, not only here, but all over the world. They have all these things. They don't see it, but the Lord Jesus Christ sees the heart. He sees their wretchedness, misery, poverty, blindness, and spiritual nakedness. That's why He wants to spue them out of His mouth. That's why He wants to take their candlestick out of its place.

Revelation 3:18

"I counsel thee to buy of me gold tried in the fire, that thou mayest be rich; and white raiment, that thou mayest be clothed, and *that* the shame of thy nakedness do not appear; and anoint thine eyes with eyesalve, that thou mayest see."

The Lord Jesus Christ says, "*I counsel thee*" to this **Laodicean** church. He counsels all the churches of the world that are **apostate** even today to **buy gold** of Him.

- **1 Corinthians 3:11-13**
  "For other foundation can no man lay than that is laid, which is Jesus Christ. Now if any man build upon this foundation **gold**, silver, precious stones, wood, hay, stubble; Every man's work shall be made manifest: for the day shall declare it, because it

shall be revealed by **fire**; and the **fire** shall try every man's work of what sort it is."

- **2 Timothy 2:20**
"But in a great house there are not only vessels of **gold** and of silver, but also of wood and of earth; and some to honour, and some to dishonour."

- **1 Peter 1:7**
"That the trial of your faith, being much more precious than of gold that perisheth, though it be tried with **fire**, might be found unto praise and honour and glory at the appearing of Jesus Christ:"

The Lord Jesus Christ has **gold** and riches by salvation. By genuine faith in Him, He can give us worthy spiritual **gold**.

He tells them also to buy of Him *white raiment*–proper **clothing**.

- **Psalm 45:13-14**
"The king's daughter *is* all glorious within: her **clothing** *is* of wrought **gold**. She shall be brought unto the king in **raiment** of needlework: the virgins her companions that follow her shall be brought unto thee"

My mother-in-law, Gertrude Sanborn, always referred to her three girls as *"King's daughters."* We have to have the **raiment**, the **cloke** of the Lord Jesus Christ, or we aren't going into Heaven.

- **Isaiah 61:10**
"I will greatly rejoice in the LORD, my soul shall be joyful in my God; for he hath clothed me with the **garments** of salvation, he hath covered me with the **robe** of righteousness, as a bridegroom decketh *himself* with ornaments, and as a bride adorneth *herself* with her jewels."

We need to be **clothed** with His **garments** of salvation. We need right **clothing**. By genuine faith in the Lord Jesus Christ, His redemption can give us that **clothing**.

- **Revelation 3:5**
"He that overcometh, the same shall be **clothed** in **white raiment**; and I will not blot out his name out of the book of life, but I will confess his name before my Father, and before his angels."

The Lord Jesus Christ can **clothe** those of us who are genuinely saved in **white raiment**.

- **Ezekiel 16:13**
"Thus wast thou **decked** with **gold** and silver; and thy **raiment** *was of* fine linen, and silk, and broidered work; thou didst eat fine flour, and honey, and oil: and thou wast exceeding beautiful, and thou didst prosper into a kingdom."

God-Provided Raiment

When God called Israel, He gave them all the raiment that they needed. They forsook the raiment and the Lord. They disappointed the Lord and He had to judge them.

- **Zechariah 3:4**
"And he answered and spake unto those that stood before him, saying, Take away the filthy **garments** from him. And unto him he said, Behold, I have caused thine iniquity to pass from thee, and I will **clothe** thee with change of **raiment**."

Clothed In Christ's Righteousness

We must be clothed in the righteousness of the Lord Jesus Christ if we're going to be in Heaven. The church at Laodicea needed some raiment to cover their nakedness.

Also, their eyes were **blind**. They needed salve.

- **Psalm 32:8**
"I will instruct thee and teach thee in the way which thou shalt go: I will guide thee with mine **eye**."

Eyes Open For Guidance

If He's guiding us with His eye, we have to have our eyes open to see that guidance.

- **Psalm 32:9**
"Be ye not as the horse, or as the mule, *which* have no understanding: whose mouth must be held in with bit and bridle, lest they come near unto thee."

We must have **eyesalve for our eyes** so we can **see** His **eyes** guiding us and leading us.

- **Psalm 101:3**
"I will set no wicked thing before mine **eyes**: I hate the work of them that turn aside; *it* shall not cleave to me."

Our **eyes** are important. Our **eyes** need to be seeing for the Lord Jesus Christ, not for wickedness.

- **Psalm 119:18**
  "Open thou mine **eyes**, that I may behold wondrous things out of thy law."

Eyesalve And Raiment Needed

The Words of God can give us the things we need. We need eyesalve that we may be able to follow the Lord Jesus Christ and to be what He wants us to be.

The church at Laodicea needed to be rich with gold. They needed to have raiment to clothe their nakedness. They needed to have eyesalve that they might be able to see. They were horribly blind.

Revelation 3:19

"As many as I love, I rebuke and chasten: be zealous therefore, and repent."

This is a present tense continuous action–as many as He continues to **love**. It's not that He still doesn't love these terrible apostates in the Laodicean church, nor does He stop **loving** the apostates in our churches all over the world today. He continues to love.

Rebuke And Chastening Needed

As many as He really loves, He rebukes and chastens. You say, "I don't like rebuke." Well, if the Lord Jesus Christ really loves you, you'd better get used to it. That Word for rebuke is ELEGCHO, which is *to reprimand severely; to chide; to admonish; to reprove; to call to account; to show one is at fault and demand an explanation.*

- **Deuteronomy 28:20**
  "The LORD shall send upon thee cursing, vexation, and **rebuke**, in all that thou settest thine hand unto for to do, until thou be destroyed, and until thou perish quickly; because of the wickedness of thy doings, whereby thou hast forsaken me."
- **Psalm 6:1**
  "To the **chief Musician on Neginoth upon Sheminith, A Psalm of David.** O LORD, **rebuke** me not in thine anger, neither **chasten** me in thy hot displeasure."

David knew that a **rebuke** was coming, but he didn't want it to be in anger.

- **Psalm 39:11**
  "When thou with **rebukes** dost correct man for iniquity, thou makest his beauty to consume away like a moth: surely every man *is* vanity. Selah."
- **Proverbs 9:8**
  "Reprove not a scorner, lest he hate thee: **rebuke** a wise man, and he will love thee."

When we get **rebuked** and we don't love the person, what does that say about our wisdom?

- **Proverbs 28:23**
  "He that **rebuketh** a man afterwards shall find more favour than he that flattereth with the tongue."

We like flattery, do we not? If there's something that needs to be **rebuked**, we must **rebuke**.

- **Mark 8:33**
  "But when he had turned about and looked on his disciples, he **rebuked** Peter, saying, Get thee behind me, Satan: for thou savourest not the things that be of God, but the things that be of men."

Peter was out of line. The Lord Jesus Christ had told them He was going to be crucified and would rise from the dead on the third day. Why didn't Peter shut his mouth? He didn't know what was happening. He was not omniscient. The Lord Jesus Christ **rebuked** him. Satan was using Peter. It wasn't that he indwelled Peter, but he was using him to speak the falsities through his mouth.

- **Luke 17:3**
  "Take heed to yourselves: If thy brother trespass against thee, **rebuke** him; and if he **repent**, forgive him."

Forgiveness Follows Repentance

There's no leeway in either of those commands. When a person repents, you forgive him. You wipe the slate clean and go on to the next point. Then if he repents again, forgive him again.

- **1 Timothy 5:1**
  "**Rebuke** not an elder, but intreat *him* as a father; *and* the younger men as brethren;"

We have to be careful to intreat elders as fathers.

- 1 Timothy 5:20
  "Them that sin **rebuke** before all, that others also may fear."
This talks about sinning pastors/bishops/elders. That's what God intends, that we make it a public **rebuke**.

Rebuke Of A Drinking Pastor

We mentioned the fall into drink of a fundamentalist pastor in Virginia Beach. He realized that is a sin. He has since made the whole thing public. He rebuked himself. Really, that's the proper way to do it.

- 2 Timothy 4:2
  "Preach the word; be instant in season, out of season; reprove, **rebuke**, exhort with all longsuffering and doctrine."
The Lord Jesus Christ not only **rebukes**, but He **chastens** those He loves. The word is PAIDEUO. It means *to bring up a child; to chastise and castigate with words; to correct.* In fact, it also means *to chastise with blows.* Sometimes the words *to scourge* are used of a father punishing his son, or of a judge ordering one to be scourged. The word *"chasten"* is only used 24 times in Scripture.

- Deuteronomy 8:5
  "Thou shalt also consider in thine heart, that, as a man **chasteneth** his son, so the LORD thy God **chasteneth** thee."
He **chastens** us for our good.

- Job 5:17
  "Behold, happy *is* the man whom God correcteth: therefore despise not thou the **chastening** of the Almighty:"

- Psalm 94:12
  "Blessed *is* the man whom thou **chastenest**, O LORD, and teachest him out of thy law;"
We should be glad when the Lord corrects us that we may straighten ourselves out, please Him, and serve Him.

- Proverbs 13:24
  "He that spareth his rod hateth his son: but he that loveth him **chasteneth** him betimes."
That word *betimes* means early.

- Proverbs 19:18
  "**Chasten** thy son while there is hope, and let not thy soul spare for his crying."
Sometimes children cry even before you **chasten** them. I have four sons and one daughter to prove that.

- **1 Corinthians 11:32**
  "But when we are judged, we are **chastened** of the Lord, that we should not be condemned with the world."
- **Hebrews 12:5-7**
  "And ye have forgotten the exhortation which speaketh unto you as unto children, My son, despise not thou the **chastening** of the Lord, nor faint when thou art **rebuked** of him: For whom the Lord loveth he **chasteneth**, and scourgeth every son whom he receiveth. If ye endure **chastening**, God dealeth with you as with sons; for what son is he whom the father **chasteneth** not?"

Children Need Chastening

That's the problem right there. We have altogether too many sons whose fathers do not chasten them. If you don't believe it, just try to teach them in the school district of Philadelphia for nineteen years. You'll see the children and the result of no father's chastening. Many of the children are spoiled brats–not all of them, but a good portion of them.

- **Hebrews 12:11**
  "Now no **chastening** for the present seemeth to be joyous, but grievous: nevertheless afterward it yieldeth the peaceable fruit of righteousness unto them which are exercised thereby."
- **Titus 2:14**
  "Who gave himself for us, that he might redeem us from all iniquity, and purify unto himself a peculiar people, **zealous** of good works."

This church should be **zealous** with interest in doing the will of the Lord Jesus Christ. I hope our church is **zealous**. Then He says, *"repent."* This is METANOEO, *a change of mind; a change of action.* Change your ways.

- **Luke 5:32**
  "I came not to call the righteous, but sinners to **repentance**."
- **Acts 3:19**
  "**Repent** ye therefore, and be converted, that your sins may be blotted out, when the times of refreshing shall come from the presence of the Lord;"
- **Acts 20:21**
  "Testifying both to the Jews, and also to the Greeks, **repentance** toward God, and faith toward our Lord Jesus Christ."

A change of our ideas against our sin is important. In Dallas Theological Seminary we were told and were taught by Dr. Chafer's 8-volume theology, *Systematic Theology,* that genuine faith is the essential without any additional thing. So he was very clear to point out it's not faith plus baptism; it's not faith plus joining a church; it's not faith plus anything else. It's genuine faith in the Lord Jesus Christ. He also said it's not faith plus **repentance**. I always say this, however: "Justifying faith, obedient faith, purified faith must be preceded by a **repentant** attitude."

Changing Your Mind About Sin

How can you want to genuinely trust the Lord Jesus Christ who died for your sins if you don't know that you're a sinner and change your mind about your sins and about the Saviour? My belief is that genuine faith and repentance are concomitant. They go together. They're concurrent. A justifying, saving faith in the Lord Jesus Christ must have a change of mind about sin and about the Saviour. The sin we used to love, now we must hate. If we don't hate it, how can we have genuine faith in the Lord Jesus Christ, the Sin-bearer that took our sins? That's how I've resolved faith and repentance. They go together.

- **Acts 26:20**
  "But shewed first unto them of Damascus, and at Jerusalem, and throughout all the coasts of Judaea, and *then* to the Gentiles, that they should **repent** and turn to God, and do works meet for **repentance**."

This is not that I believe in lordship salvation. You have to define it correctly. John MacArthur is one who believes in the heresy of lordship salvation. If you define it as MacArthur and others define it, lordship salvation means that you cannot be genuinely saved until you first make the Lord Jesus Christ the Lord of your life in everything you say, everything you do, and everything you think. Now my question is, "How can a sinner, lost and bound for Hell, make the Lord Jesus Christ the Lord of his life before he is genuinely saved?" Lordship first, then salvation next, means if you don't make the Lord Jesus Christ the Lord of your life, then you're not genuinely saved. That's a horrible heresy. However, salvation lordship—switch the order of those words—that's the proper order.

Salvation Before Lordship

That's what the Bible teaches. Salvation must come first, then, and only then, can you make Him Lord of your life. He'll make you able to do that. The Holy Spirit of God can convict you and make it possible for you to do that. That's what Paul did. He was genuinely saved first. Then he said, "Lord what wilt thou have me to do?"

Revelation 3:20

"Behold, I stand at the door, and knock: if any man hear my voice, and open the door, I will come in to him, and will sup with him, and he with me."

Here is the Lord Jesus Christ standing outside a closed **door**, knocking. That's continuous action. It's not that you can't hear him **knocking**. The church at **Laodicea** has shut Him out, but He's still willing to come in. The world, which is like the Laodicean church, has also rejected the Lord Jesus Christ and **shut Him out**.

Shutting Out The Lord

The genuine Christian that rejects full-time service and obedience to the Lord Jesus Christ has shut Him out. He still wants to come in. We must open our doors to our Saviour's will, not only for genuine salvation but also for service. It's very important.

Notice in this verse, it's a *"whosoever will."* He says, *"if any man hear my voice, and* **open the door,** *I will come in to him and will sup with him, and he with me."* That's not simply for the elect.

The Lord Jesus Christ is standing at the **closed door**. Let's take a look at a few **doors** in Scripture.

- **Genesis 6:16**
    "A window shalt thou make to the ark, and in a cubit shalt thou finish it above; and the **door** of the ark shalt thou set in the side thereof; *with* lower, second, and third *stories* shalt thou make it"

There's the **door** of the ark to save the entire world. Eight souls were the only ones to come in at that **door**. I'm sure it was a *"whosoever will."* I'm sure Noah preached the gospel that the Lord Jesus Christ was the Saviour, and that through His Seed all the nations of the earth are going to be genuinely saved. That is just like the gospel that was preached to

Abraham. The people of Noah's day didn't want to have anything to do
with it, so they were slain in the flood.

- **Genesis 7:16**
  "And they that went in, went in male and female of all flesh, as
  God had commanded him: and the LORD **shut him in**."

Here's the **closed door**. It's too late. The **door** of the ark was **open**. All
the animals went in two by two, seven sets of clean ones and two sets of
unclean ones. Noah and his family went in–Shem, Ham, Japheth, their
wives, and Noah's wife. There were eight people and all the animals.
Then the Lord **shut the door**. It should be **shut**. It was too late. Maybe
somebody was pounding on that **door**, but it was closed.

- **Genesis 8:15-16**
  "And God spake unto Noah, saying, Go forth of the ark, thou,
  and thy wife, and thy sons, and thy sons' wives with thee."

The **door** now was **open**. The flood was over after a year and Noah went
out.

- **Genesis 19:5-6**
  "And they called unto Lot, and said unto him, Where *are* the
  men which came in to thee this night? bring them out unto us,
  that we may know them. And Lot went out at the **door** unto
  them, and **shut the door** after him,"

That's a **door** that should have been **shut**.

- **John 10:9**
  "I am the **door**: by me if any man enter in, he shall be saved,
  and shall go in and out, and find pasture."

The Lord Jesus Christ is the **door**. The **door** of the **Laodicean** church
was **closed** and He stood at the outside, **knocking**. The **door** must be
opened before it's too late.

In the Song of Solomon we have a beautiful picture of this.

- **Song of Solomon 5:2**
  "I sleep, but my heart waketh: *it is* the voice of my beloved that
  knocketh, *saying,* Open to me, my sister, my love, my dove,
  my undefiled: for my head is filled with dew, *and* my locks with
  the drops of the night."

- **Song of Solomon 5:5-6**
  "I rose up to **open** to my beloved; and my hands dropped *with*
  myrrh, and my fingers *with* sweet smelling myrrh, upon the
  handles of the lock. I **opened** to my beloved; but my beloved
  had withdrawn himself, *and* was gone: my soul failed when he
  spake: I sought him, but I could not find him; I called him, but
  he gave me no answer"

There's a time when the **knocking** will cease. We must open the **door** when the Lord Jesus Christ calls for salvation, or for service. There's a saying in Shakespeare's *Julius Caesar:*

> *There is a tide in the affairs of men*
> *Which, taken at the flood, leads on to fortune;*
> *Omitted, all the voyage of their life*
> *Is bound in shallows and in miseries.*

We have a time to hear. When the Lord Jesus Christ **knocks**, we must answer for genuine salvation, or for service. We must **hear**.

- **John 5:25-26**
  "Verily, verily, I say unto you, The hour is coming, and now is, when the dead shall **hear** the voice of the Son of God: and they that **hear** shall live. For as the Father hath life in himself; so hath he given to the Son to have life in himself;"

Your Door Must Be Opened

That's eternal life from spiritual deadness. Many people can hear the voice of the Lord Jesus Christ, but the door remains closed. It's not enough to hear. The door must be opened for genuine salvation or for service. His promise is that He will come in. He will take charge of us and we will have fellowship with Him.

- **John 10:9**
  "I am the **door**: by me if any man enter in, he shall be saved, and shall go in and out, and find pasture."

There is your fellowship. The sheep need food and the pasture is there.

- **John 15:5**
  "I am the vine, ye *are* the branches: He that **abideth** in me, and I in him, the same bringeth forth much fruit: for without me ye can do nothing."

- **1 John 1:7**
  "But if we walk in the light, as he is in the light, we have **fellowship** one with another, and the blood of Jesus Christ his Son cleanseth us from all sin."

The Lord Jesus Christ is standing without in this **Laodicean** church of apostasy and unbelief. It represents closing Him off for service as well as closing Him off for genuine salvation.

Revelation 3:21

"To him that overcometh will I grant to sit with me in my throne, even as I also overcame, and am set down with my Father in his throne."

We're going to share the **throne** of the Lord Jesus Christ.

* **Revelation 5:10**
  "And hast made us unto our God kings and priests: and we shall **reign** on the earth."

* **Revelation 20:4**
  "And I saw **thrones**, and they sat upon them, and judgment was given unto them: and *I saw* the souls of them that were beheaded for the witness of Jesus, and for the word of God, and which had not worshipped the beast, neither his image, neither had received *his* mark upon their foreheads, or in their hands; and they lived and reigned with Christ a thousand years."

The Saved Will Reign With Christ

If we're genuinely saved, we will sit down with the Lord Jesus Christ in His millennial reign–the thousand-year reign of the Lord Jesus Christ–and reign with Him as He has overcome and is set down in His Father's throne.

Revelation 3:22

"He that hath an ear, let him hear what the Spirit saith unto the churches."

Again, this is continuous action–continuously to **hear** what the **Spirit saith**.

* **1 Corinthians 2:13**
  "Which things also we speak, not in the **words** which man's wisdom teacheth, but which the **Holy Ghost** teacheth; comparing spiritual things with spiritual."

What we must hear is what the **Words** of God are teaching us. That's important as we read and study the **Words** of God. This is the final church, the church at **Laodicea**. He's still speaking through His **Words** –not through visions as the charismatics say, but through His **Words**. There's a hymn called *O Jesus Thou Art Standing,* written by William W. How.

Jesus And The Fast-Closed Door

O Jesus, Thou art standing, outside the fast closed door,
In lowly patience waiting to pass the threshold o'er:
Shame on us, Christian brothers, His name and sign who bear,
O shame, thrice shame upon us, to keep Him standing
there!
O Jesus, Thou art pleading in accents meek and low,
I died for you, My children, and will you treat Me so?
O Lord, with shame and sorrow we open now the door;
Dear Savior, enter, enter, and leave us nevermore.

Our Lord's **closed door** must be opened by the ones who hear that knock. We must **open** the **door** for salvation by genuine faith in the Lord Jesus Christ. Those of us who are genuinely saved, He's calling us for service. *What wilt Thou have me to do?* May our God bless our service for Him and our church. May we not be like the **Laodicean** church.

Revelation
Chapter Four

Revelation 4:1

"After this I looked, and, behold, a door *was* opened in heaven: and the first voice which I heard was as it were of a trumpet talking with me; which said, Come up hither, and I will shew thee things which must be hereafter."

I believe this is a reference to the **rapture** of all of the true church–the snatching away of the bride of Christ, the genuinely saved ones, the believers, the born-again ones from the day of Pentecost to the rapture. It's a controversial subject, no question about it, <u>but it must be pre-millennial and must be pre-tribulational</u>, I believe very clearly. It cannot be post-millennial or pre-wrath. These are false prophetic positions.

The **rapture** of the true church is the very first event in this portion of the book of Revelation. I believe this must be before the seven-year period of the tribulation.

- **Titus 2:13**
  "Looking for that **blessed hope**, and the glorious appearing of the great God and our Saviour Jesus Christ;"

How can we be looking for "*that blessed hope,*" if we're going to be looking for the tribulation period? Harold Camping is wrong on that subject. He thinks we're in the tribulation today. He says we've been in the tribulation for some time. That's his amillennial approach.

- **1 Thessalonians 4:16-17**
  "For the Lord himself shall descend from heaven with a shout, with the voice of the archangel, and with the trump of God: and the dead in Christ shall rise first: Then we which are alive *and* remain shall be **caught up** together with them in the clouds, to meet the Lord in the air: and so shall we ever be with the Lord."

There is a real tribulation. I believe the **rapture** is pre-tribulational. That's what we were taught at Dallas Theological Seminary and that's what is taught in the Scriptures. The believers, or genuinely saved ones, will be **caught up** in the clouds to meet the Lord Jesus Christ in the air.

Some people believe in a mid-tribulation **rapture**. They say the genuine Christians are going to go halfway through this terrible, terrible judgment on the earth. That's not Scriptural.

Then somebody else comes along with a pre-wrath **rapture**. This is not a mid-tribulation **rapture**, but a little bit later, before the real wrath comes. Then, they say the true church is going to be taken off into Heaven.

Finally, there are those that teach a post-tribulation **rapture**. They think the true church—all the genuine born-again believers—are going to go all the way through the tribulation and at the end, they'll be **taken up** to Heaven.

No, the **rapture** of the true church is pre-tribulational. Notice John says, *"I looked, and, behold, a door was opened in heaven; and the first voice which I heard was as it were of a trumpet talking with me."* I believe this was the Lord Jesus Christ talking and saying, *"Come up hither, and I will shew thee things which must be hereafter."* John, representing the Church—the genuine believers—is **caught up**. This is why I believe Revelation 4:1 is the pre-tribulation **rapture**.

Why is there a pre-tribulation **rapture**? First of all, Daniel's 70th **week** is for Israel, not for the church. There are 490 years in all to be fulfilled—**70 weeks** of **seven years** each. There have been seven such weeks already, plus 434. That's 483 years fulfilled. There is one more week of **seven years** to go.

- **Daniel 9:24**
  "**Seventy weeks** are determined upon **thy people** and upon thy holy city, to finish the transgression, and to make an end of sins, and to make reconciliation for iniquity, and to bring in everlasting righteousness, and to seal up the vision and prophecy, and to anoint the most Holy."

This has nothing to do with the true church. It is restricted to *"thy people"* which refers to the Jews only, not the genuinely saved in the church.

- **Daniel 9:25**
  "Know therefore and understand, *that* from the going forth of the commandment to restore and to build Jerusalem unto the Messiah the Prince *shall be* seven weeks, and threescore and two weeks: the street shall be built again, and the wall, even in troublous times."

Daniel's Prediction Of Christ's Birth

The commandment to rebuild Jerusalem was in the time of Ezra and Nehemiah when they were in Babylonian captivity. *Seven weeks* of years is 49 years. *Threescore and two weeks* are 434 more years, which would be 483 years altogether. The book of Daniel predicted the actual coming into the world of the Lord Jesus Christ, right to the year that He would be born, and that He would suffer, bleed, and die at the cross of Calvary.

- **Daniel 9:26**
  "And after threescore and two weeks shall Messiah be **cut off**, but not for himself: and the people of the **prince that shall come** shall destroy the city and the sanctuary; and the end thereof *shall be* with a flood, and unto the end of the war desolations are determined."

Christ's Crucifixion Predicted

This is the Lord Jesus Christ at the crucifixion of Calvary. The *"people of the prince that shall come"* is the Roman Empire. The Roman emperor *"cut off"* the Lord Jesus Christ. He died at the cross of Calvary at Roman hands. The Jewish method of execution was stoning, but the Romans used crucifixion.

- **Daniel 9:27**
  "And he shall confirm the covenant with many for **one week**: and in the **midst of the week** he shall cause the sacrifice and the oblation to cease, and for the overspreading of abominations he shall make *it* desolate, even until the consummation, and that determined shall be poured upon the desolate"

The Antichrist Breaks His Covenant

This is referring to the antichrist. *"One week"* is seven years. The seven-year period of tribulation will have an antichrist reigning. He's going to confirm a covenant with Israel. The genuinely saved in the true church will have already been raised into Heaven. *"In the midst of the week"* is right in the middle of that seven-year period at three and a half years. This antichrist is going to break the covenant with

Israel in the middle of the tribulation. Israel will think this antichrist is a great ruler. He's going to be taking the place of the Lord Jesus Christ. "Anti" has two meanings: it means *against* the Lord Jesus Christ; and it also means *instead of or in place of* the Lord Jesus Christ.

Daniel's 70ᵗʰ Week has nothing to do with the genuinely saved in the true church. I am a Dispensationalist. Our church is a dispensational church and I believe in the Dispensations. The Dispensation of Law is one thing, the Dispensation of Grace is another. The Dispensation of the millennial Kingdom is another.

The Church–Gone Chapter 4 & After

The true church doesn't even appear on the earth after Chapters 2 and 3 of the book of Revelation. We see the churches– the seven churches of Asia–in Chapters 2 and 3. After that time, from Revelation 4:1 on through to the end, the true church is not on the earth. We do see twenty-four elders that represent the true church in Heaven.

What is the procedure of the pre-tribulation **rapture?** That is found, first of all in the *trumpet* as it says in Revelation 4:1. John, being representative of the true church or genuinely saved ones, hears the voice as of a trumpet.

- **Revelation 1:10**
  "I was in the Spirit on the Lord's day, and heard behind me a great voice, as of a **trumpet**,"
Notice, *as of a trumpet* means *similar* to a **trumpet**. It's not a trumpet, but a figure of speech–*as, like, similar*.
- Revelation 1:11
  "Saying, I am Alpha and Omega, the first and the last: and, What thou seest, write in a book, and send *it* unto the **seven churches** which are in Asia; unto **Ephesus**, and unto **Smyrna**, and unto **Pergamos**, and unto **Thyatira**, and unto **Sardis**, and unto **Philadelphia**, and unto **Laodicea**."

Christ Said "Come Up Hither"

Here's what the *voice, as of a trumpet* said. It's the Lord Jesus Christ speaking *as a trumpet*. I believe the trumpet voice is the Lord Jesus Christ Himself. The Lord Jesus Christ is saying to John, as representative of the true church, "*Come up hither.*"This is not the trumpet judgments. In the book of Revelation you'll find seven seals, seven trumpet judgments, and seven vials.

- **Revelation 8:2**
  "And I saw the seven angels which stood before God; and to them were given **seven trumpets.**"
- **Revelation 8:6**
  "And the seven angels which had the **seven trumpets** prepared themselves to sound."
- **Revelation 8:13**
  "And I beheld, and heard an angel flying through the midst of heaven, saying with a loud voice, Woe, woe, woe, to the inhabiters of the earth by reason of the other voices of the **trumpet** of the three angels, which are yet to sound!"

These are the **trumpets** of judgment. The *voice, as of a trumpet* that John heard in Revelation 4:1 is the **trumpet** of the assembly of the true believers, those that are genuinely saved, up to Glory.

Harold Camping, and others who believe in either a mid-tribulation, pre-Wrath, or post-tribulation **rapture**, see all these **trumpets** in Revelation as the **rapture** of the true church. No, these are not the **trumpets** of the **rapture**.

- **1 Corinthians 15:49-52**
  "And as we have borne the image of the earthly, we shall also bear the image of the heavenly. Now this I say, brethren, that flesh and blood cannot inherit the kingdom of God; neither doth corruption inherit incorruption. Behold, I shew you a mystery; We shall not all **sleep,** but we shall all be **changed,** In a moment, in the twinkling of an eye, at the last **trump**: for the **trumpet** shall sound, and the dead shall be raised incorruptible, and we shall be **changed.**"

There's no way that our flesh and blood bodies can go up into Heaven. There has to be a **transformation.** The meaning of *sleep* here is death. It's not soul **sleep,** as the Jehovah's Witnesses and others falsely believe.

- **John 11:11-14**
  "These things said he: and after that he saith unto them, Our friend Lazarus **sleepeth**; but I go, that I may awake him out of **sleep.** Then said his disciples, Lord, if he **sleep,** he shall do well. Howbeit Jesus spake of his **death**: but they thought that he had spoken of taking of rest in **sleep.** Then said Jesus unto them plainly, Lazarus is **dead.**"

The Living Saved Will Be Changed

Some believers will not *sleep* in death. You and I might be among them. When the Lord Jesus Christ comes in the rapture to take us Home to Heaven, we will not have died yet, but we will all be changed. This flesh and blood body can never go to Heaven. It can't even go up into the atmosphere a few thousand feet. We will have to be changed.

How is this change going to take place? It's going to be "*In a moment, in the twinkling of an eye.*" How can these old bodies of ours be changed into glorified ones just like unto the Lord Jesus Christ's body in a moment? No problem with God! There are many problems with us. We couldn't do it, but God is omnipotent and He's able to do it.

- **1 Corinthians 15:53**
  "For this corruptible must put on **incorruption**, and this mortal *must* put on **immortality**."

When anyone is buried, the body corrupts. At the **rapture** of the true church, before the tribulation period takes place, those corruptible bodies will be instantaneously changed to **incorruption**, nevermore to corrupt.

- **John 11:25-26**
  "Jesus said unto her, I am the resurrection, and the life: he that believeth in me, though he were **dead**, yet shall he live: And whosoever liveth and believeth in me shall never **die**. Believest thou this?"

We who are genuinely born-again will never **die** spiritually, even though we may **die** physically.

- **1 Thessalonians 4:15-18**
  "For this we say unto you by the word of the Lord, that we which are alive *and* remain unto the coming of the Lord shall not prevent [or precede] them which are asleep. For the Lord himself shall descend from heaven with a shout, with the voice of the archangel, and with the trump of God: and the dead in Christ shall rise first: Then we which are alive *and* remain shall be caught up together with them in the clouds, to meet the Lord in the air: and so shall we ever be with the Lord. Wherefore comfort one another with these words."

The Order Of The Rapture

The Words of God here give us the order of the rapture. If we're genuinely saved and we're living when the Lord Jesus Christ comes, we will not go up first. The bodies of genuinely saved people that are dead, and are in corruption, will put on incorruption. Then they will rise first. After that, the genuinely saved who are living, will be raised up. When He summons us, we who are genuinely saved will not be able to say, "Not interested." Those that are lost, who are living at that time, are going to stay right here on this earth. They will go through the tribulation period. It will be a terrible thing.

The believers or genuinely saved ones will go up to Heaven before any part of this judgment comes to pass on the earth. It's going to be a terrible judgment. We haven't seen anything yet. There will be persecutions, troubles, and problems that we'll see as we move along through the book of Revelation.

Revelation 4:2

"And immediately I was in the spirit: and, behold, a throne was set in heaven, and *one* sat on the throne."

John wasn't taken up to **Heaven** in the flesh. He was *in the Spirit*. It was a spiritual experience to go to **Heaven** to be with the Lord. He makes it very clear.

God the Father is sitting on the **throne** of **Heaven**. A **throne** is a *place of rule; a place of reigning and authority.*

- **Matthew 5:34**
  "But I say unto you, Swear not at all; neither by **heaven**; for it is God's **throne**:"

Does this mean when we say, "*For Heaven's sake*" that it's swearing? Yes, that's swearing. Don't swear by **Heaven**. Don't swear by anything.

Heaven Is God's Throne

Heaven is God's throne. That's the place where God rules and reigns—where He controls things. Is He out of control now because the world is so bad and so wicked? No, He's permitting the wickedness of men to continue until such a time as He says He's had enough. That's when He will draw the curtain on this old earth. That's when the rapture will take place. The genuine Christians will be gone and the judgments will pour out from Heaven, twenty-one-fold. There will be seven seals, seven trumpets, and seven vials—twenty-one judgments upon this earth.

When God said it was going to rain from **Heaven** and told Noah to prepare an ark, Noah obeyed and prepared an ark. Noah preached for 120 years to that generation. They probably thought he was a fool, I'm sure. Nobody came into the ark except Noah, Mrs. Noah, Shem, Ham, Japheth, and their wives—eight people. There came a time when God had enough of the wickedness, the homosexuality, the filthiness, and all the other sins of that wicked world. There's going to come a time when God will have no more patience with this earth. He's longsuffering, not willing that any should perish. He wants all to come to repentance, but He does not force people to accept His Son as their Saviour.

- **Matthew 23:22**
  "And he that shall **swear** by heaven, sweareth by the **throne** of God, and by him that sitteth thereon."

Swearing is rampant in our country, as you know. It's a terrible thing. God's Name is taken in vain.

I don't listen to Oprah very much on the TV, but I just happened to walk through the room, and there she was. She said, "Holy Jesus." I've never heard that expression in years and years. They usually **swear** by God's Name all the time, but here's the Name of Jesus being used to swear. Don't swear by Heaven because it's the **throne** of God. If you swear by **Heaven** it's as if you're swearing by God Himself.

"Minced Oaths" Should Be Avoided

There are such things as "minced oaths." You don't say, "God," but you might use "Gosh" or "Golly." You don't say, "Jesus," but you say, "Gee." These are minced oaths. They mean the same thing. We have to be careful of our language.

- **Acts 7:49**
  "Heaven *is* my **throne**, and earth *is* my footstool: what house will ye build me? saith the Lord: or what *is* the place of my rest?"

The Lord's **throne** is in **Heaven**. The earth is His footstool. One day the Lord Jesus Christ is going to come back and put His feet upon this earth. He's going to judge this earth.

- **Hebrews 8:1**
  "Now of the things which we have spoken *this is* the sum: We have such an high priest, who is set on the right hand of the throne of the Majesty in the **heavens;**"

The Lord Jesus Christ is at the right hand of God the Father in **Heaven.**

- **Hebrews 12:2**
  "Looking unto Jesus the author and finisher of *our* faith; who for the joy that was set before him endured the cross, despising the shame, and is set down at the right hand of the **throne** of God."

- **Revelation 1:4**
  "John to the seven churches which are in Asia: Grace *be* unto you, and peace, from him which is, and which was, and which is to come; and from the seven Spirits which are before his **throne;**"

John was taken to the Father's **throne.** He was immediately in the place where all power originated. He saw this **throne** and the One that sat upon it.

The Lord Jesus Christ will also have a **throne** upon this earth, the **throne** of his father David, when he reigns and rules for a thousand years.

Revelation 4:3

"And he that sat was to look upon like a jasper and a sardine stone: and there was a rainbow round about the throne, in sight like unto an emerald."

A Simile Is Used Here Again

Here again is a simile. John couldn't describe God the Father, but he was able in the Spirit to see something of the Father. We know that no man *"hath seen God at any time"* (John 1:18; 1 John 4:12), so the best he could do was to describe in word pictures what it was like to behold God the Father sitting on that throne. He couldn't put it into words. He was speechless as to describe in detail, but he says He was *"like a jasper."* A jasper is a green quartz. Then he says, *"a sardine stone."* A sardine stone is a deep orange-red variety of chalcedony used in jewelry. Here is a mixture of colors. Of course, a rainbow has all the colors.

- **Genesis 9:13**
  "I do set my **bow** in the cloud, and it shall be for a token of a covenant between me and the earth."

The Lord put a **rainbow** in the sky to remind those who dwell on earth that He will never again judge the earth by a universal flood. By fire, yes, but not a flood.

The Rainbow Is Like An Emerald

The rainbow here is similar to *"an emerald,"* which is a bright green, transparent, precious stone. We have all these different colors to picture the Lord. John saw these colors. I don't think any of us would be shocked at these colors. They're beautiful colors. We sometimes see rainbows at the end of a storm coming down from the Heavens to the earth. This is a pleasant sight.

The Lord Jesus Christ continues to sit on that **throne**. Some people have asked if God is really on the **throne** of control and power. Ones like Harold Camping, who say that we're in the Millennium right now, say that the Lord Jesus Christ is effectively reigning right now. If the Lord Jesus Christ is effectively reigning today, I would simply say, "He's doing a very poor job." Look at the wars. Look at the terrorists. Look at the killings and slaughter. No. He's not effectively reigning. The amillennial people and the post-millennial people and the spiritualizing people are wrong in this, but God is still on that **throne**. He knows when to draw in the likes of men and He will put a stop to their reigning and their ruling. He will one day Himself be the Ruler, but not yet. He's still on that **throne** and He has ultimate power. Just wait a while and be patient. He will show what that power is.

Revelation 4:4

"And round about the throne were four and twenty seats: and upon the seats I saw four and twenty elders sitting, clothed in white raiment; and they had on their heads crowns of gold."

Here are the **four and twenty elders**. Many believe, and I believe also, that this is a representation of the true believers–the genuinely saved ones–that are in Heaven. Why do I say that? Well, I say it first of all because these four and twenty elders were *"clothed in white raiment."* This **white raiment** is the clothing of the true saints–the genuine believers. I believe this is a representation of the true church in

Heaven. That's where they belong. The believers are raptured in Revelation 4:1.

- **Revelation 3:5**
  "He that overcometh, the same shall be **clothed in white raiment**; and I will not blot out his name out of the book of life, but I will confess his name before my Father, and before his angels."

- **Revelation 3:18**
  "I counsel thee to buy of me **gold** tried in the fire, that thou mayest be rich; and **white raiment**, that thou mayest be **clothed**, and *that* the shame of thy nakedness do not appear; and anoint thine eyes with eyesalve, that thou mayest see."

Laodiceans Need To Get Saved

The Lord Jesus Christ advised the Laodicean church to get genuinely saved–truly born-again, trusting in the Lord Jesus Christ–so that they would have *white raiment*. The fact that the elders were in *white raiment*, I believe, represents the genuinely saved ones that are in Heaven.

- **Revelation 4:10-11**
  "The **four and twenty elders** fall down before him that sat on the **throne**, and worship him that liveth for ever and ever, and cast their **crowns** before the throne, saying, Thou art worthy, O Lord, to receive glory and honour and power: for thou hast created all things, and for thy pleasure they are and were created."

I believe this is what the genuinely saved ones are going to do when they get to Heaven. They'll worship before the Lord and, if they have a **crown**, they'll cast those **crowns** before the Lord Jesus Christ's feet.

The Five Biblical Crowns

There are five crowns in Scripture. Remember the memory hint, "R GIRL."

1. "R"–the crown of righteousness (2 Timothy 4:8)
2. "G"–the crown of glory (1 Peter 5:4)
3. "I"–the incorruptible crown (1 Corinthians 9:25)
4. "R" – the crown of rejoicing (1 Thessalonians 2:19)
5. "L"–the crown of life (James 1:12 & Revelation 2:10)

- **Revelation 5:5**
  "And one of the **elders** saith unto me, Weep not: behold, the Lion of the tribe of Juda, the Root of David, hath prevailed to open the book, and to loose the seven seals thereof."

The elders are there in Heaven and telling John not to weep.

- **Revelation 5:6**
  "And I beheld, and, lo, in the midst of the throne and of the four beasts, and in the midst of the **elders**, stood a Lamb as it had been slain, having seven horns and seven eyes, which are the seven Spirits of God sent forth into all the earth."

The **elders** are there with these *"four beasts"* or four living creatures. We're going to take up those **elders** more in detail, later on. I believe those four beasts, or the four living creatures, represent special angelic beings–the lead angels like the seraphim and the cherubim. I believe these four beasts, the living creatures, as in the book of Ezekiel, represent those features.

- **Revelation 5:8**
  "And when he had taken the book, the **four beasts** and **four** *and* **twenty elders** fell down before the Lamb, having every one of them harps, and golden vials full of odours, which are the prayers of saints."

Here are the elders with *"the prayers of the saints."* I believe they are saints. They represent the genuine believers in this picture.

- **Revelation 5:11**
  "And I beheld, and I heard the voice of many angels round about the **throne** and the beasts and the elders: and the number of them was ten thousand times ten thousand, and thousands of thousands"

Here are millions of angels and millions of the "elders" (representing those who are genuinely saved).

- **Revelation 5:14**
  "And the four beasts said, Amen. And the **four** *and* **twenty elders** fell down and worshipped him that liveth for ever and ever."

The word *beasts* in 1611 talked about a living creature. It's not a beast like we think about, a horrible monster, but it represents something like a normal animal that is a called a living creature. These **twenty-four elders** are worshipful people.

- **Revelation 7:11**
  "And all the angels stood round about the **throne**, and *about* the elders and the four beasts, and fell before the throne on their faces, and worshipped God,"

Worship is what the saints of God will be doing in Heaven. If you're genuinely saved, if you're genuinely born-again, you'll be worshipping God the Father and the Lord Jesus Christ. That will be the place of worship in Heaven. There will be no inhibitions. We'll have new bodies. I believe these **twenty-four elders** represent the believers doing just that.

- **Revelation 7:13**
  "And one of the elders answered, saying unto me, What are these which are arrayed in **white robes**? and whence came they?"

These are the ones that are martyred during the tribulation period. They are tribulation saints—Christians that are genuinely saved. Again, these **elders** represent the church.

- **Revelation 14:3**
  "And they sung as it were a new song before the **throne**, and before the four beasts, and the **elders**: and no man could learn that song but the hundred *and* forty *and* four thousand, which were redeemed from the earth"

144,000 Jewish Evangelists

These hundred and forty-four thousand Jews are gospel preachers and evangelists during the tribulation period. They will be singing with the elders in Heaven.

- **Revelation 19:4**
  "And the **four and twenty elders** and the four beasts fell down and worshipped God that sat on the **throne**, saying, Amen; Alleluia."

---

24 Elders Represent The Church

These twenty-four elders, I believe, represent the believers, the genuinely saved ones in Heaven, not on the earth. As I said before, there's not a single reference to the true church any more after Revelation 4:1. This, of course, is important to see as it shows that the true church will not be here on this earth.

In this modern day in which we live, some pastors and churches are emphasizing worship more. They're having worship services and worship leaders. They're up there with instruments, drums, trumpets, and many other things. I don't believe that's appropriate. They talk about worship, worship, worship. They have many contemporary songs, soft rock, and sometimes rock music. I don't think most of them know the first thing about worship.

The Worship Of The 24 Elders

These twenty-four elders in Glory, I believe, represent the genuine believers. They know about worship. We'll know about worship when we get to Heaven and it will be the right worship. We'll worship the right Person. We'll worship in the right manner. We'll worship with the right songs of Zion, and the Lord Jesus Christ will accept such worship. God cannot accept worship from unbelievers. He can't do it. He doesn't like the worship from unbelievers. He does not hear the voices of sinners and lost people except for one plea for forgiveness and acceptance of His Son as their Saviour.

- **Matthew 11:28**
  "Come unto me, all *ye* that labour and are heavy laden, and I will give you rest."

The Lord Jesus Christ will hear that plea and they can be saved by genuine faith in Him, but the Lord does not hear the voices of unbelievers. All over the country and all over the world we have people that are claiming to worship God whose hearts are still black with sin. They never have repented of their sins, never have genuinely trusted the Lord Jesus Christ as Saviour, have never been redeemed, and they claim to worship. In the Roman Catholic Church, for instance, they enter the church, they bow, and call it worship. My friends, worship is more than the attitude of bowing the knees. Worship is something of the heart. When we who are genuinely saved get to Glory, with these **twenty-four elders** being the picture of it, we will know how to worship the Lord. The word worship means *worth*-ship. It comes from the word *worth*.

- **Revelation 5:12**
  "Saying with a loud voice, Worthy is the Lamb that was slain to receive power, and riches, and wisdom, and strength, and honour, and glory, and blessing."

We will see His worthiness. Those modernists, liberals, unbelievers, apostates, and their churches that don't believe in the Deity of our

Saviour can't worship Him. It's a terrible thing. It reminds me of the Lord's Words about worship in Israel's time.

- **Isaiah 1:13**
  "Bring no more vain oblations; incense is an abomination unto me; the new moons and sabbaths, the calling of assemblies, I cannot away with; *it is* iniquity, even the solemn meeting."

There was hypocrisy connected with that form of wrong worship. In Heaven, in Glory, we'll worship right.

Revelation 4:5

"And out of the throne proceeded lightnings and thunderings and voices: and *there were* seven lamps of fire burning before the throne, which are the seven Spirits of God."

Here is the picture of the **throne** of God, with *lightnings and thunderings and voices.* This is a picture of God's absolute holiness. Notice the *seven lamps of fire.* We met up with the **seven Spirits of God** earlier in the book of Revelation. This is the seven-fold manifestation of **God the Holy Spirit.**

- **Revelation 1:4**
  "John to the seven churches which are in Asia: Grace *be* unto you, and peace, from him which is, and which was, and which is to come; and from the **seven Spirits** which are before his **throne;**"
- **Revelation 3:1**
  "And unto the angel of the church in Sardis write; These things saith he that hath the **seven Spirits of God**, and the seven stars; I know thy works, that thou hast a name that thou livest, and art dead."
- **Revelation 5:6**
  "And I beheld, and, lo, in the midst of the throne and of the four beasts, and in the midst of the elders, stood a Lamb as it had been slain, having seven horns and seven eyes, which are the **seven Spirits of God** sent forth into all the earth."
- **Isaiah 11:2**
  "And the spirit of the LORD shall rest upon him, the spirit of wisdom and understanding, the spirit of counsel and might, the spirit of knowledge and of the fear of the LORD;"

This is the **seven-fold** picture of the plenitude and fullness of the **Holy Spirit of God.** You have the Deity of the Lord Jesus Christ there. You have the Deity of God the **Holy Spirit**. You have the Deity of God the Father. The Trinity is there in Glory.

Voices Out Of God's Throne

Notice, in Revelation 4:5, the *lightnings and thunderings and voices* out of God's throne. When John described (Revelation 4:3) the Lord as like a jasper, a sardine stone, a rainbow and an emerald, that was beautiful. God has beautiful, wonderful traits. God is love, but He's also holy. This is the holiness aspect of the Lord. This is the same God on the throne, but here out of the throne proceed *lightnings and thunderings and voices.*

- **Ezekiel 1:13-14**
  "As for the likeness of the living creatures, their appearance *was* like burning coals of fire, *and* like the appearance of lamps: it went up and down among the living creatures; and the fire was bright, and out of the fire went forth **lightning**. And the living creatures ran and returned as the appearance of a flash of **lightning**."

As I said before, these four living creatures are called *"four beasts"* in Revelation. They are like the cherubim and the seraphim, a special type of angelic beings. The lightning represents the holiness and purity of the Lord.

- **Exodus 19:12-13**
  "And thou shalt set bounds unto the people round about, saying, Take heed to yourselves, *that ye* go *not* up into the mount, or touch the border of it: whosoever toucheth the mount shall be surely put to death: There shall not an hand touch it, but he shall surely be stoned, or shot through; whether *it be* beast or man, it shall not live: when the trumpet soundeth long, they shall come up to the mount."

- **Exodus 20:18-19**
  "And all the people saw the **thunderings, and the lightnings**, and the noise of the trumpet, and the mountain smoking: and when the people saw *it,* they removed, and stood afar off. And they said unto Moses, Speak thou with us, and we will hear: but let not God speak with us, lest we die."

The Purity Of God Pictured

This was a picture of the God of righteousness, the God of holiness, the God of purity. That's why we must flee to the Lord Jesus Christ and hide ourselves from the wrath of God and the wrath of the Lamb. He is the only One that can protect us from God's holiness and power.

The people removed and stood afar off. I'd stand afar off, too. Wouldn't you, if you saw and heard the **lightnings and thunderings**, the noise of a trumpet, and the mountain smoking? He's powerful. He's terrifying unless the Lord Jesus Christ His Son comes and genuinely saves us. Now we have no more terror of God the Father. If we're in the Lord Jesus Christ, if we're genuinely saved, there's no more fear, dread, or terror of God the Father. Without the Lord Jesus Christ, there's a very terrible fear. This is a very important point. Only as we're covered in the Lord Jesus Christ can we talk with God the Father. Otherwise, we die.

- **Exodus 19:8**
  "And all the people answered together, and said, All that the LORD hath spoken we will do. And Moses returned the words of the people unto the LORD."

"Do" Versus "Done"

In the book of Exodus, the people forsook the Lord and His rule over them. This was a "do" type of religion. When you come to the Lord Jesus Christ, it's a "done" religion. He said, *"It is finished"* (John 19:30). All of the sins that we have committed—past, present and future—all the sins of the world have been placed upon the Lord Jesus Christ, the spotless, sinless Lamb. Now He has done the work. All the other religions of the world stress "do." They do this, do this, do this, then they hope to be saved at the end of their lives. No, "doing" won't do it. The Lord Jesus Christ has done it. It's finished. It's completed.

- **John 19:30**
  "When Jesus therefore had received the vinegar, he said, It is finished: and he bowed his head, and gave up the ghost."

I'm glad that we have in the Scriptures His Words. I think, as I've said before, that the Lord Jesus Christ is the Author of all the Hebrew, Aramaic, and Greek Words of Scripture.

- **John 16:12-13**
  "I have yet many things to say unto you, but ye cannot bear them now. Howbeit when he, the **Spirit** of truth, is come, he will guide you into all truth: for he shall not speak of himself; but whatsoever he shall hear, *that* shall he speak: and he will shew you things to come."

The Lord Jesus Christ is the Author of the Old Testament Words, I believe, just like the New Testament Words. He has given to us His Bible and I believe we have His Words in the Hebrew, Aramaic, and Greek Words that underlie our King James Bible. Now we can say, "Let God speak to us through His Words." Not through visions, not through dreams, but through His Words.

The Catching Away Of Believers

God's purity and absolute holiness is evidenced by the lightnings and thunderings in Revelation 4:5. One day the Lord Jesus Christ will return. These things must definitely come to pass. Everything in the book of Revelation historically will come to pass in the future. Before all that takes place, the Lord Jesus Christ is going to snatch away the believers.

My mother-in-law, Gertrude Sanborn, wrote a poem called

Expectation

My heart doth wait;
My Lord will soon be coming.
My heart doth wait
To see His lovely face.
My heart doth wait
To hear His voice so beautiful.
For His return
So longs my yearning heart.
My heart doth wait;
This song, keeps ringing on.
He's coming soon,
And this thought spurs me on.
For Him I wait,
But He alone doth know the time.
My heart doth wait and sings its song.
He's coming soon;
He's coming soon.

My heart doth wait;
My heart doth wait.

Are You Born-Again?

We don't know the time or the hour of the Lord Jesus Christ's return. It could happen before we close this study. The Lord Jesus Christ will snatch up the true believers, the genuinely saved ones, and leave all the unsaved people right here on this earth. It could happen today. We must be ready. Are you ready? Are you genuinely saved? Are you truly born-again? Are you sure?

We must be sure, because The Lord Jesus Christ is coming before any part of that tribulation comes. I believe this is scripturally true and we fight against many in the churches that are teaching false mid-tribulation, pre-wrath, or post-tribulation raptures. I believe that's wrong. We must be ready.

Revelation 4:6

"And before the throne *there was* a sea of glass like unto crystal: and in the midst of the throne, and round about the throne, *were* four beasts full of eyes before and behind."

John is seeing this vision of Heaven. He was taken up in Revelation 4:1 when the voice, which I believe is the voice of the Lord Jesus Christ, said *"Come up hither."* John was on the isle of Patmos, which is off the coast of Greece. He was banished to that little island because he was a genuine Christian, because he was an apostle of the Lord Jesus Christ, and because he was preaching the Words of God. The Lord Jesus Christ revealed to him the present state of the churches in Chapters 2 and 3. Then in Chapter 4, the true church–the genuine believers or the Body of the Lord Jesus Christ–is snatched away. I believe that is the rapture of the true church. Now we're seeing a picture of the future in Heaven. John was taken up there in the Spirit.

This also talks of the living creatures. That word *"beast"* is not the same as we use it today as far as a horrible, monstrous type of thing.

- **Isaiah 6:1-3**
  "In the year that king Uzziah died I saw also the Lord sitting upon a throne, high and lifted up, and his train filled the temple. Above it stood the seraphims: each one had six wings; with twain he covered his face, and with twain he covered his

feet, and with twain he did fly. And one cried unto another, and said, Holy, holy, holy, *is* the LORD of hosts: the whole earth is full of his glory"

The picture here is of the **throne** of God in Heaven. SARAPH means *to burn; the burning ones*. Apparently, these are the same creatures as those in the book of Revelation. "*Holy, holy, holy*" is their theme. I believe that the **four beasts** are angelic beings. The Lord has millions of angels, Heavenly messengers, but I believe that seraphim and cherubim are special, maybe the leading angels. They're very close to the Lord. They're holy angels. They aren't unholy angels. These angelic beings are worshipping the Lord.

The throne of God is a very important place. The throne is where the judgments and decisions of the Lord Jesus Christ are made.

- **Matthew 5:34**
  "But I say unto you, Swear not at all; neither by Heaven; for it is God's **throne:**"

That's where He lives. That's where His edicts are pronounced

- **Matthew 23:22**
  "And he that shall swear by heaven, sweareth by the throne of God, and by him that sitteth thereon."

It's bad to take the Name of the Lord in vain, or to swear by Heaven. I know people say, "for Heaven's sake." They're swearing by Heaven.

- **Hebrews 4:16**
  "Let us therefore come boldly unto the **throne** of grace, that we may obtain mercy, and find grace to help in time of need."

That **throne** is in Heaven. That's where those of us who are genuinely saved take our prayers and burdens–to the **throne** of grace.

- **Hebrews 8:1**
  "Now of the things which we have spoken *this is* the sum: We have such an high priest, who is set on the right hand of the **throne** of the Majesty in the heavens;"

The Lord Jesus Christ died for our sins on the cross and rose again. Now He's interceding for those that are genuinely saved. The Lord Jesus Christ is at the place of honor. The right hand is always a place of honor. He is at the right hand of the **throne** of God the Father.

- **Hebrews 12:2**
  "Looking unto Jesus the author and finisher of *our* faith; who for the joy that was set before him endured the cross, despising the shame, and is set down at the right hand of the **throne** of God."

Christ On David's Throne One Day

The Lord Jesus Christ will one day assume His throne upon this earth, the throne of His father David. He will reign and rule over this earth during the millennial reign of the Lord Jesus Christ as we'll see in Revelation 19 and following.

- **Job 37:18**
  "Hast thou with him spread out the sky, *which is* strong, *and* as a molten looking **glass**?"

- **1 Corinthians 13:12**
  "For now we see through a **glass**, darkly; but then face to face: now I know in part; but then shall I know even as also I am known."

- **Exodus 38:8**
  "And he made the laver *of* brass, and the foot of it *of* brass, of the **lookingglasses** of *the women* assembling, which assembled *at* the door of the tabernacle of the congregation."

This was the place where the priests washed their hands and feet before they ministered to the Lord in the holy place and the most holy place. The laver was made of the polished **looking glasses** of the women.

- **2 Corinthians 3:18**
  "But we all, with open face beholding as in a **glass** the glory of the Lord, are changed into the same image from glory to glory, *even* as by the Spirit of the Lord."

The Mirror Of God's Words

As we who are genuinely saved look into the Scriptures, the Words of God, we can see this mirror of the Lord Jesus Christ and we can be transformed into His image by the Spirit of God—and only by the Spirit of God.

- **James 1:23-24**
  "For if any be a hearer of the word, and not a doer, he is like unto a man beholding his natural face in a **glass**: For he beholdeth himself, and goeth his way, and straightway forgetteth what manner of man he was."

- **Psalm 68:17**
  "The chariots of God *are* twenty thousand, *even* thousands of angels: the Lord *is* among them, *as in* Sinai, in the holy *place*."

- **Psalm 148:2**
  "Praise ye him, all his angels: praise ye him, all his hosts."

- **Revelation 5:11**
  "And I beheld, and I heard the voice of many angels round about the **throne** and the beasts and the elders: and the number of them was ten thousand times ten thousand, and thousands of thousands"

The living creatures around God's **throne** are full of eyes. Perhaps they're guardian angels that take care of the genuine Christian believers that are truly saved.

Revelation 4:7

"And the first beast *was* like a lion, and the second beast like a calf, and the third beast had a face as a man, and the fourth beast *was* like a flying eagle."

Again, I believe these are special angelic beings. We don't know what these things represent. Many have said they represent the four gospels. Maybe that's the case.

- **Ezekiel 1:10**
  "As for the likeness of their faces, they four had the **face** of a man, and the face of a **lion**, on the right side: and they four had the face of an ox on the left side; they four also had the **face** of an **eagle**."

This apparently speaks about the same individuals as in Revelation 4:7. I believe they're angelic beings. They're either cherubim or seraphim. The cherubim were in the tabernacle.

- **Exodus 25:20**
  "And the cherubims shall stretch forth *their* wings on high, covering the mercy seat with their wings, and their **faces** *shall look* one to another; toward the mercy seat shall the **faces** of the cherubims be."

- **Exodus 26:31**
  "And thou shalt make a vail *of* blue, and purple, and scarlet, and fine twined linen of cunning work: with cherubims shall it be made:"

If indeed these angelic beings represent the four gospels, Matthew certainly would speak about the **lion**. The **Lion** of the tribe of Judah talks about the Lord Jesus Christ, speaking of His kingliness. Mark would be the **calf**, showing the Lord Jesus Christ as a Servant. Mark is the shortest gospel. Always it says, *"anon"* or *"immediately."* Luke speaks of the Lord Jesus Christ as the Son of Man and His perfect Manhood and perfect ability as a virgin-born Man. The flying **eagle** is possibly the gospel of John, showing the Lord Jesus Christ as the Son of God with Heavenly pictures and so on.

Four Pictures Of Christ

These are four different pictures that some have said the angelic beings represent. Maybe they're speaking of the Lord Jesus Christ in all of His fullness. If they are angelic beings, if they are speaking of the four gospels, which speak of the Lord Jesus Christ in His earthly ministry, maybe they're to represent what He has given to us on this earth when he was on the earth. All are pointing to the Lord Jesus Christ as the Saviour of the world.

I don't know for certain what these **four beasts** are, but they seem like they are angelic beings. They certainly are with the Lord. They're not unholy angels, which were banished from Heaven. They're there in the very presence of God, so they have to be holy. You can't get close to the Lord and be unholy. I don't believe they represent the true Christians or genuinely saved people. I believe those are represented by the **twenty-four elders.**

Revelation 4:8

"And the four beasts had each of them six wings about *him*; and *they were* full of eyes within: and they rest not day and night, saying, Holy, holy, holy, Lord God Almighty, which was, and is, and is to come."

The **four beasts** with the **lion**, the **calf**, the **man**, and the flying **eagle** with **six wings** are similar to those in the book of Isaiah Chapter 6.

- **Isaiah 6:1-3**
   "In the year that king Uzziah died I saw also the Lord sitting upon a throne, high and lifted up, and his train filled the temple. Above it stood the seraphims: each one had **six wings**; with twain he covered his face, and with twain he covered his feet, and with twain he did fly. And one cried unto another, and said, Holy, holy, holy, *is* the LORD of hosts: the whole earth *is* full of his glory."

The Call Of Isaiah

This was the call of Isaiah. God called Isaiah to be His prophet and His minister to the children of Israel, wayward as they were. He had a vision of Heaven and of the Lord sitting on His throne. These seraphim with six wings apparently are the same four beasts in the book of Revelation. They are angelic beings, as we said before, and Isaiah seems to point that out as well.

Notice, *they were full of eyes.* They're able to see things that are going on down on earth. Are angels watching us? Yes, I believe that they are.

Notice also, *they rest not day and night.* We usually have a **rest**, whether it's eight hours or seven. Some of us get more **rest** than others. Some of us are restless and don't get too much **rest**, <u>but these living creatures or angelic beings, as I believe, do not have any **rest** day or night. They're on 24-hour call as it were, just like doctors and preachers usually are.</u> These angelic beings are not only on 24-hour call, they don't sleep. They're sleepless. Therefore, what are they doing? They're saying, *"Holy, holy, holy, Lord God Almighty."* This is exactly the same that seraphim uttered in Isaiah 6. The Trinity is pictured here–the Father, Son, and Holy Spirit, the holiness of God.

I believe it's important to see in the book of Revelation the context and the continuity that the Lord must be recognized as holy before we can see the judgments that are going to come upon this wicked earth. Once the genuine believers are taken away, there are twenty-one serious judgments. There are seven seal judgments, seven trumpet judgments and seven vial judgments. There are twenty-one judgments in seven years. They're going to be horrific. These angelic beings, the seraphim, are setting the stage to realize <u>the Lord is **holy** and He cannot stand unholiness.</u> He's gracious now. We've read that even in the Old Testament. He's full of mercy, but when He's had enough, He's had enough. He's going to judge this wicked world for the wickedness and sins. The holiness of God is important to see.

Holy angels are in Heaven. They worship and praise the Lord.

- **Hebrews 1:6**
  "And again, when he bringeth in the firstbegotten into the world, he saith, And let all the angels of God worship him."

- **Hebrews 12:22**
  "But ye are come unto mount Sion, and unto the city of the living God, the heavenly Jerusalem, and to an innumerable company of angels,"

If the angels can praise the Lord and say, "*Holy, holy, holy,*" should we not, as genuine believers on this earth also do the same? God has told us to do that. We should give constant praise and thanks.

- **Psalm 7:17**
  "I will praise the LORD according to his righteousness: and will sing praise to the name of the LORD most high."

- **Psalm 33:2**
  "Praise the LORD with harp: sing unto him with the psaltery *and* an instrument of ten strings."

They had harps. They just started making the ten-string harp again. A harp is a stringed instrument, just like a piano has strings and it's played. There's a book written by William Pettingill, called *I Will Praise Him on an Instrument of Ten Strings*. He makes the ten strings apply to the bodies of genuinely saved people. We have:

- Two eyes—what we see.
- Two ears—what we hear.
- Two hands—what we do.
- Two feet—where we walk.
- One mouth—what we speak unto Him.
- One heart—that is given over unto Him.

We can praise Him with our ten-stringed instrument. We should praise the Lord of Heaven and earth.

- **Psalm 34:1**
  "*A Psalm* of David, when he changed his behaviour before Abimelech; who drove him away, and he departed." I will bless the LORD at all times: his praise *shall* continually *be* in my mouth."

Praising God Continually Is Hard

That's difficult to do, but remember, He is praiseworthy. Our God is worthy and He should be in our lips, and in our hearts, and in our thoughts praising Him continually. If David could do it in the Old Testament before the Lord Jesus Christ came to suffer and die for sinners, should we not also do that? We may not speak it outwardly but silently, praise to the Lord.

·   **Psalm 40:3**
    "And he hath put a new song in my mouth, *even* praise unto our
    God: many shall see *it,* and fear, and shall trust in the LORD."
When we praise and glorify the Lord Jesus Christ, they will see it.
Yesterday, we went over to *The Breadboard* restaurant. While there, my
wife and I made different phone calls to different people. We talked to
one another about different things. A lady came up from her seat and
said, "You're a pastor. How nice it is to meet you." We told her where our
services were. She said she goes to a different Bible-believing church
somewhere but might come to a Bible study. As we praise the Lord,
people will see. Some of them will be happy and some of them will be
sad.

•   **Psalm 51:15**
    "O Lord, open thou my lips; and my mouth shall shew forth thy
    praise."

Praise God With Our Mouth

We have to praise Him with our mouth. Of course, our
hearts must be genuinely saved and moving along with the
Lord, otherwise we can't praise Him. Our lips sometimes do
not praise the Lord. Our lips are sometimes bad or wrong. We
have to confess it to the Lord when we sin with our lips. It's
easy to shoot off our mouth. That's tempting to all of us with
the flesh. We have the old nature. If we're genuinely saved, we
have a new nature and God should control our mouth and our
lips to show forth His praise.

•   **Psalm 56:10**
    "In God will I praise *his* word: in the LORD will I praise *his*
    word."
We should be glad that we have God's Words. His Hebrew, Aramaic, and
Greek Words underlying the King James Bible are preserved for us. Our
English King James Bible is translated accurately from those Words.

We Must Have His Words To Praise

How can we praise His Words if we don't have His
Words? Books that have been written by some of our
fundamentalist brethren have said that we don't have the
Words of God. They say we just have the message and don't

> have His Words. How can we praise His Words if we just have His message? A message is just a general thing. The Words of God are here and they have been preserved. I believe this strongly.

Dr. Thomas Strouse wrote an excellent review of the book *The Word of God in Our Hands* put out by Bob Jones University people and others. Dr. Strouse shows very clearly that God has promised to preserve His Hebrew, Aramaic, and Greek Words. We have those preserved Words and we can praise Him as David could.

- **Psalm 63:5**
  "My soul shall be satisfied as *with* marrow and fatness; and my mouth shall praise *thee* with joyful lips:"

Praise is with joyful lips. It's not just, "Well, I have to do this and drag myself to do it." No. Joyful lips are important.

- **Psalm 86:12**
  "I will praise thee, O Lord my God, with all my heart: and I will glorify thy name for evermore."

Heart And Lips Working Together

That's an interesting point. It's not just the lips but the heart must be involved. The lips can say anything. Lips can fool people. They can talk glibly and say, "Oh, how I love the Lord," but their heart may be far from Him.

- **Matthew 23:25-27**
  "Woe unto you, scribes and Pharisees, hypocrites! for ye make clean the outside of the cup and of the platter, but within they are full of extortion and excess. *Thou* blind Pharisee, cleanse first that *which is* within the cup and platter, that the outside of them may be clean also. Woe unto you, scribes and Pharisees, hypocrites! for ye are like unto whited sepulchres, which indeed appear beautiful outward, but are within full of dead *men's* bones, and of all uncleanness."
- **Psalm 100:4**
  "Enter into his gates with thanksgiving, *and* into his courts with praise: be thankful unto him, *and* bless his name."
- **Revelation 4:10**
  The four and twenty elders fall down before him that sat on the throne, and worship him that liveth for ever and ever, and cast their crowns before the throne, saying,

The angelic beings worship and say, "Holy, holy, holy" and the elders fall down before Him and worship Him. We have to do the same thing.

- **Matthew 21:15-16**
  "And when the chief priests and scribes saw the wonderful things that he did, and the children crying in the temple, and saying, Hosanna to the Son of David; they were sore displeased, And said unto him, Hearest thou what these say? And Jesus saith unto them, Yea; have ye never read, Out of the mouth of babes and sucklings thou hast perfected praise?"

Can little ones praise the Lord? Absolutely. I remember in Sunday School we used to sing *Can a little one like me thank the Father fittingly?* I was in a modernistic Methodist church. They used to sing that. It's certainly true. Once I was genuinely saved I could understand it. Little ones can praise the Lord.

- **Hebrews 13:15**
  "By him therefore let us offer the sacrifice of praise to God continually, that is, the fruit of *our* lips giving thanks to his name."

He speaks of praise as a sacrifice. For what have we been thankful today? For what have we been thankful yesterday, last week, last month? What will we be thankful for tomorrow? This sacrifice of praise and thanks is to be continual.

- **Psalm 69:30**
  "I will praise the name of God with a song, and will magnify him with thanksgiving."

We sing in our church. Some sing better than others. There is no question about that. But we still sing. That's an important part of our service.

- **Psalm 92:1**
  "A Psalm *or* Song for the sabbath day." *It is a* good *thing* to give thanks unto the LORD, and to sing praises unto thy name, O most High:"

- **Psalm 95:2**
  "Let us come before his presence with thanksgiving, and make a joyful noise unto him with psalms."

Some people have noise instead of melodious beautiful singing, but we're to come before His presence with thanksgiving. Thank the Lord. We should be thankful unto His Name at all times.

- **1 Corinthians 15:57**
  "But thanks *be* to God, which giveth us the victory through our Lord Jesus Christ."

1 Corinthians 15 is the Resurrection chapter. One day our bodies will be changed and glorified.

- **2 Corinthians 2:14**
  "Now thanks *be* unto God, which always causeth us to triumph in Christ, and maketh manifest the savour of his knowledge by us in every place."

The triumph must be in the Lord Jesus Christ. He always causes us to be victorious.

- **2 Corinthians 9:15**
  "Thanks *be* unto God for his unspeakable gift."

A gift that's unspeakable can't be put into words. It's great, wonderful, and glorious indeed. Give thanks.

- **Ephesians 5:20**
  "Giving thanks always for all things unto God and the Father in the name of our Lord Jesus Christ;"

Always is mentioned in many places. It means *daily, continually.*

- **Romans 8:28**
  "And we know that all things work together for good to them that love God, to them who are the called according to *his* purpose."

Some things are better than others, but God says we're to give thanks for all things unto Him, the good as well as the bad. We should be able to learn from the things that come our way that are bad.

- **Philippians 4:6**
  "Be careful for nothing; but in every thing by prayer and supplication with thanksgiving let your requests be made known unto God."

This is the constant petition that we should have before the Lord.

- **Colossians 2:7**
  "Rooted and built up in him, and stablished in the faith, as ye have been taught, abounding therein with thanksgiving."

Help The Angels Praise The Lord

We should not leave it to the angels to praise Him and say, "Holy, holy, holy." We should at this time do it ourselves, while we're still here.

- **Colossians 3:17**
  "And whatsoever ye do in word or deed, *do* all in the name of the Lord Jesus Christ, giving thanks to God and the Father by him."

In everything we do we should say, "Thank you, Lord."

- **1 Thessalonians 5:18**
  "In every thing give thanks: for this is the will of God in Christ Jesus concerning you."
- **Hebrews 13:15**
  "By him therefore let us offer the sacrifice of praise to God continually, that is, the fruit of *our* lips giving thanks to his name."

The **four beasts** say, "Holy, holy, holy" day and night. They praise the Lord Jesus Christ which was, which is, and which is to come. They're talking about the eternal past and the eternal future of the Lord God of Heaven and earth and thanking Him.

Revelation 4:9

"And when those beasts give glory and honour and thanks to him that sat on the throne, who liveth for ever and ever,"

These angelic beings—the seraphim or the cherubim—**give glory and honour and thanks** to the Lord Jesus Christ. There's no ending to the Lord Jesus Christ. *My God and I shall go on forever,* as the hymn writer has said.

Revelation 4:10

"The four and twenty elders fall down before him that sat on the throne, and worship him that liveth for ever and ever, and cast their crowns before the throne, saying,"

While the **beasts** are there, resting neither day nor night, saying, "**Holy, holy, holy,** Lord God Almighty, which was, and is, and is to come," at the same time the **four and twenty elders** fall down before Him. As I've said before, I believe the four and twenty elders represent the glorified church, the true believers, the genuinely saved ones that are in Heaven. No longer are they on the earth. They are not going to go through any part of the tribulation period. I believe in the pre-tribulation rapture of the believers.

Saved Fall Down Before The Throne

Now they fall down before God the Father as He sits on the throne. That's what we're going to be doing in Glory, worshipping Him that liveth forever and ever. There's no end to His life. He was in eternity past, He is now, and He will be

forever. Time is just a dispensation of grace. When the
dispensations are finished, from the creation of the world
right on through to the end, then eternity will remain again.
Time is just a fleeting moment of eternity.

- **Revelation 5:5**
  "And one of the elders saith unto me, Weep not: behold, the
  Lion of the tribe of Juda, the Root of David, hath prevailed to
  open the book, and to loose the seven seals thereof."

One of the elders, representative of the genuine believers, will say that
there's finally Someone that will come to open the seven-sealed book.
That's the book of the judgments upon this earth.

- **Revelation 5:6**
  "And I beheld, and, lo, in the midst of the throne and of the four
  beasts, and in the midst of the elders, stood a Lamb as it had
  been slain, having seven horns and seven eyes, which are the
  seven Spirits of God sent forth into all the earth."
- **Revelation 5:11**
  "And I beheld, and I heard the voice of many angels round
  about the throne and the beasts and the elders: and the number
  of them was ten thousand times ten thousand, and thousands
  of thousands;"

A Special Class Of Angels

The reason that I say that the *beasts* are a special class of
angels, maybe the lead angels, is because here around the
throne are the *angels, the beasts, and the elders*. They're
separate, so they must be leading angels.

- **Revelation 5:14**
  "And the **four beasts** said, Amen. And the **four and** twenty
  elders fell down and worshipped him that liveth for ever and
  ever."

Heavenly Beings Worship God

We have over and over again in Revelation the angelic
beings–the beasts or living creatures–and the twenty-four
elders, representing the true church, praising and
worshipping the Lord together around the throne.

- **Revelation 7:13**
  "And one of the elders answered, saying unto me, What are these which are arrayed in white robes? and whence came they?"

These elders, again, represent the true church, the genuine believers that are up in Heaven.

- **Revelation 14:3**
  "And they sung as it were a new song before the **throne**, and before the **four beasts**, and the elders: and no man could learn that song but the hundred *and* forty *and* four thousand, which were redeemed from the earth."

- **Revelation 19:4**
  "And the **four and twenty elders** and the **four beasts** fell down and worshipped God that sat on the **throne**, saying, Amen; Alleluia."

Various Crowns in The Bible

These four angels worship the Lord. The elders will cast their crowns before the throne. We've talked about the five crowns that genuine believers can have. That's why I believe that the elders are true Christians that are in Heaven.

There are five crowns in Scripture. Remember the memory hint, "R GIRL."

1. "R"–the crown of righteousness (2 Timothy 4:8)
2. "G"–the crown of glory (1 Peter 5:4)
3. "I"–the incorruptible crown (1 Corinthians 9:25)
4. "R"–the crown of rejoicing (1 Thess. 2:19)
5. "L"–the crown of life (James 1:12, Revelation 2:10)

- **Psalm 29:2**
  "Give unto the LORD the glory due unto his name; worship the LORD in the beauty of holiness."

- **Psalm 95:6**
  "O come, let us worship and bow down: let us kneel before the LORD our maker."

- **John 4:24**
  "God *is* a Spirit: and they that worship him must worship *him* in spirit and in truth."

There's a hymn that I've heard many times before, a gospel song that differentiates between the angels worshipping the Lord and the true believers, the genuinely saved ones, the redeemed ones, in Heaven. Here is a hymn by Johnson Oatman, Jr. written in 1894.

Holy, Holy, Is What the Angels Sing

There is singing up in Heaven such as we have never known,
Where the angels sing the praises of the Lamb upon the throne,
Their sweet harps are ever tuneful, and their voices always clear,
O, that we might be more like them while we serve the Master here!
(Refrain)
Holy, holy, is what the angels sing
And I expect to help them make the courts of Heaven ring;
But when I sing redemption's story, they will fold their wings,
For angels never felt the joys that our salvation brings.
But I hear another anthem, blending voices clear and strong,
"Unto Him Who hath redeemed us and hath bought us," is the song;
We have come through tribulation to this land so fair and bright,
In the fountain freely flowing, He hath made our garments white.
Then the angels stand and listen, for they cannot join that song,
Like the sound of many waters, by that happy, blood-washed
throng,
For they sing about great trials, battles fought and vict'ries won,
And they praise their great Redeemer, who hath said to them, "Well
done."
So, although I'm not an angel, yet I know that over there
I will join a blesséd chorus that the angels cannot share;
I will sing about my Savior, who upon dark Calvary
Freely pardoned my transgressions, died to set a sinner free.

The Lord Jesus Christ did not die for the sins of angels. He died for the sins of men, women, boys, and girls.

The four living creatures can say, "**Holy, holy, holy to the Lord God Almighty.**" They know He's holy, but they cannot join in the songs of the Lamb, the songs of the redeemed in Heaven, because they've never been redeemed themselves and never have known the joy that our salvation brings.

Revelation 4:11

"**Thou art worthy, O Lord, to receive glory and honour and power: for thou hast created all things, and for thy pleasure they are and were created.**"

Our God is **worthy**. Is He **worthy** to you? Is He **worthy** to me? This is the Father, I believe. It's the Heavenly Father, the One that is on the throne. If people come to the Lord Jesus Christ, God's Son, they will understand and agree that God is **worthy**. He's **worthy** to be praised,

worthy to be believed, and worthy to be worshipped. These genuine believers, the **four and twenty elders** representing the true believers that are in Glory, are praising the Lord God the Father of the genuine believers. We can praise Him here on the earth, but in our glorified bodies we'll sing even more His praises and His worth.

- **Genesis 32:10**
  "I am not worthy of the least of all the mercies, and of all the truth, which thou hast shewed unto thy servant; for with my staff I passed over this Jordan; and now I am become two bands."

Jacob could say he was not worthy. None of us are worthy. Jacob was a sinner, like all the rest of us are sinners, and he admits it.

- **Psalm 18:3**
  "I will call upon the LORD, *who is worthy* to be praised: so shall I be saved from mine enemies."

We can praise one another, but the Lord is the only One **worthy** to be praised.

- **Matthew 8:8**
  "The centurion answered and said, Lord, I am not **worthy** that thou shouldest come under my roof: but speak the word only, and my servant shall be healed."

The centurion, though he commanded a hundred men in the Roman army, knew he was not **worthy**. The problem with many people in this world that are lost is that they think that they are **worthy** and that they themselves can take themselves to Heaven apart from genuine faith in the Lord Jesus Christ. The problem with some genuine believers that are truly saved Christians is the thought that, in our own selves, we are **worthy**. That's wrong. In the Lord Jesus Christ, we are **worthy**. He made us **worthy**, but in ourselves we're not **worthy**.

- **John 1:27**
  "He it is, who coming after me is preferred before me, whose shoe's latchet I am not **worthy** to unloose."

John The Baptist's Attitude

John the Baptist had a right relationship to the Lord Jesus Christ. John was first on the earth to minister and preach the kingdom of Heaven and say, "Repent, the kingdom of heaven is at hand," but as soon as he saw the Lord Jesus Christ, he shrunk back and said, "I'm not worthy even to take off the shoestrings off His feet." That's the proper analysis.

- **John 3:30**
  "He must increase, but I *must* decrease."
So many of the followers of John the Baptist went to the Lord Jesus
Christ and followed Him.
- **James 2:7**
  "Do not they blaspheme that **worthy** name by the which ye are
  called?"
This talks about the lost rich people in James' time that had no faith in
the Lord Jesus Christ and that hurt and harmed those that were poor.
- **Revelation 3:4**
  "Thou hast a few names even in Sardis which have not defiled
  their garments; and they shall walk with me in white: for they
  are worthy."
The white garments of salvation show that the redeemed believers have
been made **worthy** of the Lord Jesus Christ.
- **Revelation 5:12**
  "Saying with a loud voice, Worthy is the Lamb that was slain to
  receive power, and riches, and wisdom, and strength, and
  honour, and glory, and blessing."
The Lamb is **worthy**. The true believers that are genuinely saved are
worthy in salvation, not in their flesh.
   The Lord Jesus Christ was there at the **creation**.
- **Genesis 1:1**
  "In the beginning God **created** the heaven and the earth."
- **John 1:1-3**
  "In the beginning was the Word, and the Word was with God,
  and the Word was God. The same was in the beginning with
  God. All things were **made** by him; and without him was not
  any thing **made** that was **made**."
- **John 1:10-12**
  "He was in the world, and the world was **made** by him, and the
  world knew him not. He came unto his own, and his own
  received him not. But as many as received him, to them gave he
  power to become the sons of God, *even* to them that believe on
  his name:
- **Ephesians 3:9**
  "And to make all *men* see what *is* the fellowship of the mystery,
  which from the beginning of the world hath been hid in God,
  who **created** all things **by Jesus Christ**:"
God the Father **created**, but it's also *by Jesus Christ*. As we've said
before, those three words are not in the false Greek texts. The NIV, the

NASV, the ESV, the RSV, the NRSV, and the other new versions drop out *"by Jesus Christ."* The Father and the Son **created** all things.

- **Colossians 1:16**
  "For by him were all things **created**, that are in heaven, and that are in earth, visible and invisible, whether *they be* thrones, or dominions, or principalities, or powers: all things were **created** by him, and for him:"

Both Father & Son Were Creators

God the Father, as well as God the Son, created all things. Because He is Creator of all things for His pleasure, and for the pleasure of His Son, He is worthy to receive glory, honor and power. There's no superfluous amount of honor, glory, and power that we can attribute to our God and to our Saviour the Lord Jesus Christ. There's no way we can glorify Him sufficiently or more than He ought to receive. He is glorious. He is worthy of our praise, our honor, and of all the power and authority that we give unto Him. There's no way that we should stop praising Him.

As the **four beasts** in Heaven, representing the angelic beings, praise Him as "Holy, holy, holy," and as the **twenty-four elders**, representing the believers in Glory, are worshipping Him, and **casting their crowns** before Him, praising Him, and thanking Him, we should do the same today. Our God has given us great things and He is **worthy** to be praised, not to be blasphemed, but to be glorified in all that we do and say. That should be done continually, not simply once in a while, but all the time – our lips, our hearts, and our mouths giving praise unto our God.

𝕽𝖊𝖛𝖊𝖑𝖆𝖙𝖎𝖔𝖓
𝕮𝖍𝖆𝖕𝖙𝖊𝖗 𝕱𝖎𝖛𝖊

Revelation 5:1

"And I saw in the right hand of him that sat on the throne a book written within and on the backside, sealed with seven seals."

This is God the Father. He is there in Glory. The true believers, the genuinely saved ones, the redeemed ones, the truly born-again ones, have been raptured and taken Home to Heaven. Judgments are going to come upon the earth. There will be a total of twenty-one judgments after the genuine believers are snatched away and gone.

Twenty-One Judgments

There will be seven seals, seven trumpets, and seven vials. These twenty-one judgments will happen within a seven-year period. That is eighty-four months. Dividing eighty-four months by twenty-one judgments you get (on average) one judgment every four months. In other words, every 120 days, after the believers are gone, there will be judgments upon this earth.

God the Father, the Lord God of Heaven and earth, is sitting on the throne in Heaven. He has a **book** of the earth's judgment. God the Father is a God of righteousness, a God of justice and a God of judgment. He will not let things go unjudged. Therefore, He has this **book**.

- **2 Peter 3:9**
  "The Lord is not slack concerning his promise, as some men count slackness; but is longsuffering to us-ward, not willing that any should perish, but that all should come to repentance."

God is longsuffering. He wants everyone to be genuinely saved. A gentleman called us and wanted to know if I believed in salvation only for the "elect." I told him the Lord Jesus Christ says, "*Come unto me, all ye that labour and are heavy laden, and I will give you rest*" (Matthew 11:28). He also said, "*And whosoever will, let him take the water of life freely*" (Revelation 22:17b).

The Lord Jesus Christ is not now judging this world. The Father is not judging the world. He is longsuffering. He wants as many sinners to come to the Lord Jesus Christ as possible before the rapture, before He calls the genuine believers, the truly saved ones, Home.

THESE ARE THE SEVEN SEALS:

1. **The white horse of conquering power.**
2. **The red horse of war.** We have had enough wars all over the world, but this is going to be a special, very serious war.
3. **The black horse of famine.** There will be no food, nothing to eat, and a scourge of famine throughout the world.
4. **The pale horse of pestilence and death.** All sorts of different diseases will come upon them that may never have been seen before.
5. **The souls under the altar.** Many that are saved will be slain on this earth during these seven years. They will be martyrs for the Lord Jesus Christ. As soon as they say, "*I believe in the Lord Jesus Christ,*" they will be slaughtered by the antichrist. If they are genuinely saved, but are quiet, and do not want to confess Him, then the Lord Jesus Christ Himself will judge them.
6. **Physical changes in the earth and the sky.** The sky will not be the same. Neither the earth nor the sun will be the same. There will be terrible changes.
7. **Silence in Heaven.** There is always a reason for silence. They say "*silence is golden.*" Sometimes that is true, sometimes it is not. In this case, it is not "*golden.*"

What is a **seal**? A **seal** (SPHRAGIS) is "*something that is an inscription; an impression made by a seal; that which signifies anything that is to be confirmed, approved or authenticated by a seal; a token or proof.*" That is this seal. It is authenticated, it is proven, and it is sure. These judgments will take place.

- **1 Kings 21:8**
  "So she wrote letters in Ahab's name, and sealed *them* with his **seal**, and sent the letters unto the elders and to the nobles that *were* in his city, dwelling with Naboth."

This was Jezebel. She was a liar and a conniver. She wanted to get the vineyard of Naboth for her husband, Ahab. Ahab was angry and weeping in his bed. Jezebel, the wicked woman, came and asked him what was the matter with him. Ahab had plenty of vineyards, but he wanted Naboth's vineyard. She said she would fix that. She wrote

letters and **sealed** them with the king's name and caused Naboth to be stoned. Ahab then took the vineyard.
- **Matthew 27:66**
  "So they went, and made the sepulchre sure, **sealing** the stone, and setting a watch."

The Lord's Sealed Tomb

The tomb of the Lord Jesus Christ was sealed to authenticate that it was not to be tampered with. The Lord had other plans. As you know, that stone was rolled away by the angel. I am sure the Lord Jesus Christ Himself did not need the stone to be rolled away. He came out of that tomb and went right straight through the stone. His resurrection body had no need to roll back tomb stones or open doors as our earthly bodies do. Our bodies, like any earthly object, are made up of atoms. Atoms are made of neutrons, protons, electrons, and a lot of space. Our problem is we cannot go through the spaces. The Lord Jesus Christ's body could. The people needed to have the stone rolled away, so the angel did roll it away.

- **John 20:26**
  "And after eight days again his disciples were within, and Thomas with them: *then* came Jesus, the doors being shut, and stood in the midst, and said, Peace *be* unto you."
- **Matthew 28:5-6**
  "And the angel answered and said unto the women, Fear not ye: for I know that ye seek Jesus, which was crucified. He is not here: for he is risen, as he said. Come, see the place where the Lord lay."
- **Ezekiel 2:9-10**
  "And when I looked, behold, an hand *was* sent unto me; and, lo, a roll of a **book** *was* therein; And he spread it before me; and it *was* written within and without: and *there was* written therein lamentations, and mourning, and woe."

The judgment of the book of Ezekiel is similar to the judgments of the book of Revelation. This is not a pleasant book to open. It is a figure of a **book** because a **book** can be opened like a scroll can be rolled down. All seven of these seal judgments, when they are opened, are God's means of judging the earth and the world. They are terrific judgments. The Lord Jesus Christ is a righteous Judge, there is no question about that.

- **Genesis 18:25**

  "That be far from thee to do after this manner, to slay the righteous with the wicked: and that the righteous should be as the wicked, that be far from thee: Shall not the Judge of all the earth do right?"

Abraham was pleading about Sodom and Gomorrah that the Lord would not destroy the righteous with the wicked.

<u>We have Sodomites all over the place today.</u> They are apparently almost ruling the country. You do not dare speak out against them anymore. Many preachers have closed their mouths about sodomites and lesbians. Not this preacher. I might be put in jail and fined in due time in the future because I will never stop preaching about these lifestyles as being sinful and against God's Words. I do not know how much our government here in the city of Collingswood is influenced by the homosexuals. All I know is we have them here. Our mayor has said that Collingswood is a "gay friendly" community and he is welcoming them into our town. They come from all over. Those who come from Pennsylvania say that Collingswood is more friendly than Pennsylvania. It is a sad thing.

Looking For Righteous People

God told Abraham that, if He could find fifty righteous people, He would not destroy Sodom and Gomorrah. Abraham said, Suppose you cannot find fifty? Maybe just forty-five? How about forty? How about thirty? How about twenty? What if even ten are righteous? The Lord said He would spare the cities for ten righteous people. If He could find ten, they would not be destroyed (Genesis 18:22-32). As you know, He could not find them.

<u>He found Lot</u>, Mrs. Lot, and two daughters. Mrs. Lot did not even come out alive. She looked back (Genesis 19:26). She had so many relatives, so many possessions, so many things of memory back there in that wicked city of Sodom with the Sodomites and all the filth that was there, that she looked back. God had said, "*Look not behind thee*" (Genesis 19:17). She looked back. She hesitated, and she became a pillar of salt (verse 26). The pitch and "*brimstone and fire*" must have landed upon her (verse 24). Only three escaped from that terrible thing.

God Always Does Right

The Lord is righteous. Abraham's statement was a question: *"Shall not the Judge of all the earth do right?"* (See Genesis 18:25.) That is true. God will do right. Whether you or I understand it, when God judges the wicked, He is right. He is always right. People will say the Lord cannot be right because He has prepared Hell, a lake of fire. *"That is not right,"* they say. No, it is right. God is righteous in His judgment. He has given us a Saviour, the Lord Jesus Christ. He has urged both men and women, as well as boys and girls, to come unto Him and be genuinely saved, to truly trust in Him, to receive Him as Saviour and Redeemer. If they do so, they are redeemed and they do not go to that place of torment.

Hell was not prepared for men, women, boys, and girls. It was *"prepared for the devil and his angels"* (Matthew 25:41). These are fallen creatures. There are no other places to go. There are only two places in the Bible to go after our death—either Heaven or Hell. There is no third place, such as limbo or purgatory. There is no such a place taught in Scripture.

There are only two destinies. It is either going to Heaven with the Lord Jesus Christ, God the Father, God the Holy Spirit, and all the redeemed; or it is going to the place *"prepared for the devil and his angels"* in the lake of fire. What would Heaven be like if wickedness was there? It would be horrible. It would not be Heaven. He has to punish those who reject His Son, and this is what He does.

This **seven-sealed book** was in the **right hand of Him that sat upon the throne**. The **right hand** is a place of honor and authority. The right hand of God the Father held this **book**.

Revelation 5:2

"And I saw a strong angel proclaiming with a loud voice, Who is worthy to open the book, and to loose the seals thereof?"

The Only Worthy Person

"Who is worthy"? This is the book of judgment. Who is worthy to be the judge and to pour out these judgments, the seven seals, upon this wicked world during that seven-year

> period of tribulation? He had to be worthy. Just anybody could not do it, any more than just anybody can do many other things. He had to be worthy to loose these seven seals of judgment.

- John 5:22
  "For the Father judgeth no man, but hath committed all judgment unto the Son:"

The Lord Jesus Christ will be there for true believers, the genuinely saved ones, at the Judgment Seat of the Lord Jesus Christ. He will be there with the lost ones, those that have rejected the Lord Jesus Christ, at the Great White Throne Judgment. He is the *"Judge of all the earth"* (Genesis 18:25).

- Genesis 32:10
  " I am **not worthy** of the least of all the mercies, and of all the truth, which thou hast shewed unto thy servant; for with my staff I passed over this Jordan; and now I am become two bands."

Certainly, those who are **not worthy** could not open the seals, and judge other people, if they themselves were sinners and wicked. Jacob knew he was **not worthy**.

- Luke 3:16
  "John answered, saying unto *them* all, I indeed baptize you with water; but one mightier than I cometh, the latchet of whose shoes I am **not worthy** to unloose: he shall baptize you with the Holy Ghost and with fire:"

John the Baptist knew he was **not worthy** compared to the Lord Jesus Christ. The Lord Jesus Christ was **worthy**, but John the Baptist was not.

- Luke 7:6
  "Then Jesus went with them. And when he was now not far from the house, the centurion sent friends to him, saying unto him, Lord, trouble not thyself: for I am **not worthy** that thou shouldest enter under my roof:"

The centurion who had a hundred men under him, a commander in the Roman army, had someone in his family that was sick. He said to the Lord Jesus Christ not to come to his house to heal him. Every one of us must say, "I am **not worthy** of the Lord Jesus Christ." We are **not worthy**, but He can make us **worthy** by genuinely trusting the Lord Jesus Christ in giving eternal life and righteousness—not our own, but His righteousness.

- James 2:6-7
  "But ye have despised the poor. Do not rich men oppress you, and draw you before the judgment seats? Do not they **blaspheme** that **worthy** Name by the which ye are called?"

Blaspheming God's Name

The Name of the Lord is worthy. It is a terrible disgrace that men blaspheme His Name. We see that, on every hand, people are blaspheming the Name of God the Father and blaspheming the Name of God the Son.

I do not know whether or not people swear by the Holy Spirit. I do not know that I have ever heard that, but maybe they do not realize that the Holy Spirit is God also. They do swear all the time by the Lord Jesus Christ, and by God the Father. They take Their Names *"in vain"* (Exodus 20:7).

They **blaspheme** that **worthy** Name. He is **worthy**. His Name is **worthy**. He is a **worthy** God and has a **worthy** Name.

- Revelation 3:4
  "Thou hast a few names even in Sardis which have not defiled their garments; and they shall walk with me in white: for they are **worthy**."

One of the seven churches in Asia Minor had a few which had not defiled their garments. God alone can make people **worthy**. The Lord alone is **worthy**. These who had come out of a lost and dying world and had been genuinely saved, truly born-again, and regenerated, had been made **worthy** by God the Father. They had been made righteous by God the Father through faith in His Son. He has given us who are genuinely saved, a righteousness not our own, but His own imputed righteousness.

A *"strong angel"* with "a loud voice," proclaimed that message. *"Who is worthy to open the book?"* It has to be a **worthy** One, otherwise He cannot open this book of judgment. This word for proclaiming is KERUSSO. It means *"like a herald; to proclaim with the manner of a herald, always with a suggestion of formality, gravity and authority, which must be listened to and obeyed."* That is the force of this word, KERUSSO, that is used here.

The Book In The Father's Hand

There was, in the Father's right hand, a book of judgment with seven seals. These are seven judgments that will come upon this earth during the seven-year period of tribulation.

> The genuinely born-again Christians will be in Heaven, taken and raptured away. Who is worthy to open those seals and start the judgments?

Revelation 5:3

"And no man in heaven, nor in earth, neither under the earth, was able to open the book, neither to look thereon."

Nobody could "*open the book*" or "*look thereon.*" The opening of that "*book*" will begin the opening of the seven seals, to start the seven-sealed judgments on this wicked world. <u>The One who opens the "*book*" had to be Himself spotless, pure, and sinless. A sinner could not judge someone else.</u> It must be someone Who could take care of things in a righteous manner.

- Job 9:33
  "Neither is there any daysman betwixt us, *that* might lay his hand upon us both."

That word, *daysman,* means an *umpire.* The Lord Jesus Christ is that umpire that can lay His hand upon God and man. He came not to judge but to genuinely save. He is perfect.

- John 8:3-11
  "And the scribes and Pharisees brought unto him a woman taken in adultery; and when they had set her in the midst, They say unto him, Master, this woman was taken in adultery, in the very act. Now Moses in the law commanded us, that such should be stoned: but what sayest thou? This they said, tempting him, that they might have to accuse him. But Jesus stooped down, and with *his* finger wrote on the ground, *as though he heard them not.* So when they continued asking him, he lifted up himself, and said unto them, He that is without sin among you, let him first cast a stone at her. And again he stooped down, and wrote on the ground. And they which heard *it,* being convicted by *their own* conscience, went out one by one, beginning at the eldest, *even* unto the last: and Jesus was left alone, and the woman standing in the midst. When Jesus had lifted up himself, and saw none but the woman, he said unto her, Woman, where are those thine accusers? hath no man condemned thee? She said, No man, Lord. And Jesus said unto her, Neither do I condemn thee: go, and sin no more."

The Gnostic Critical Greek Text

The Gnostic Critical Westcott and Hort false Greek text removes, doubts, and questions this incident about the woman taken in adultery. Among the over 8,000 other changes that this Gnostic Critical Greek Text makes in the Words underlying our King James Bible, it omits these twelve verses: John 7:53 to John 8:11. The NIV questions it. The New American Standard questions it. The Revised and New Revised Standard versions question it. The English Revised Version questions it. Almost every modern version of the Bible, both in English and in all of the other languages in the world question it. Our King James Bible includes it because it has unquestioned authenticity.

Dr. Kim from the National Institute of Health in the Washington, D.C. area in Maryland visited our church. He got a number of books. He came with Dr. Jung many years ago when Dr. Jung was here. Dr. Kim asked me a question before he left. He said, "*Pastor Waite, why was not David stoned for adultery?*" That is a good question. Well, God evidently pardoned him, just as the Lord Jesus Christ pardoned this adulterous woman. Under the law of Moses, the command was that such should be stoned. David was a murderer. He was also an adulterer. He should have been stoned. That was a good question. I do not know whether he was satisfied with my answer. I just simply said that the Lord's mercies and grace were there in the Old Testament, operating in David, just as He is operating with us today.

Christ Died For Every Person

The Lord Jesus Christ is the only One Who is without sin. He is sinless and spotless. That is why He could take all the sins of all the world in His body on the cross (1 Peter 2:24). That is one thing I discussed with a gentleman who called me on the phone. I said the question is, "For whom did the Lord Jesus Christ die?" John Calvin, even in his book on Romans, said the Lord Jesus Christ died for the sins of the world. The hyper-Calvinists who were raised up after John Calvin changed his view to say He only died for the "*elect*" and that He did not die for the sins of every person in the world.

I interpret the word "*world*" in John 3:16 as the world of all people who ever lived. "*God so loved the world.*" That means all of us sinners —black, white, and all other colors, big and small, men and women, boys and girls, rich and poor, and sick and well–the whole world. This is not just simply the "*world of the elect.*" This is a very serious misinterpretation of the Bible! That is where we part company with the hyper-Calvinists who say He only died for, and only loved just part of the world.

- 1 Timothy 2:5
  "For there is one God, and one mediator between God and men, the man Christ Jesus;"

The only One to open the book and to open the seals that is **worthy** is the only One Who is without sin and perfect. He is the One Who can be a Judge. Remember what God told Abraham, "*Shall not the Judge of all the earth do right?*" (See Genesis 18:25). Yes. The Lord Jesus Christ is the only One Who is **worthy**.

People have many kinds of contests. They wonder, "*Who is worthy to do this?*" and "*Who is worthy to do that?*" There are some things that not everyone can do. Not everyone can pole vault over a bar which is fifteen feet high in the air. Not everyone can high jump over a bar six or seven feet in the air. To judge the world and to open the seals in this book of judgment, the Lord Jesus Christ was the only One qualified.

Revelation 5:4

"And I wept much, because no man was found worthy to open and to read the book, neither to look thereon."

John says he **wept**, not just a "little," but he "wept much." Why was John **weeping**? He knew full well that there was sin that had to be judged in this world. He knew also that the Lord Jesus Christ and God the Father is a just God. Who is going to open this? Who is going to get this started? Who is going to begin this judgment upon the earth and upon the wickedness of men and women?

God Is Longsuffering To Sinners

God has let these sins go unjudged for over 2,000 years. He *was longsuffering* in the days of the flood. He was *longsuffering* in the days of Sodom and Gomorrah. He is *longsuffering* today. He has let murder go on. He has let rapes go on. He has let homosexuality go on. He has let stealing and all kinds of sins and wickedness go on. He has never judged this world as it ought to be judged.

I found in Scripture <u>twenty-seven different people that **wept**</u>. Is it wrong to **weep**? There are reasons for weeping. Here are some of the people in the Bible that **wept**:

1. Hagar
2. Esau
3. Jacob
4. Isaac
5. Joseph
6. The baby Moses
7. The children of Israel in the wilderness
8. Samson's wife
9. Ruth and Orpah
10. Hannah
11. David and Jonathan
12. Saul
13. David
14. David's sons
15. David's servants
16. Elisha
17. Joash the king
18. Hezekiah
19. The priests and the Levites
20. Nehemiah
21. Job's three friends
22. Peter
23. People at funerals in the New Testament
24. The Lord Jesus Christ
25. Mary Magdalene
26. The Ephesian pastors
27. The Apostle John

Revelation 5:5

"And one of the elders saith unto me, Weep not: behold, the Lion of the tribe of Juda, the Root of David, hath prevailed to open the book, and to loose the seven seals thereof."

I believe, as I said earlier, <u>the twenty-four elders represent the born-again, saved, believers—the church in Glory</u>. One of the members of the body of the Lord Jesus Christ, the genuinely saved ones, said to John, *"Weep not."* As I have said many times before, there are two different Greek structures in a command like this. One is the present tense prohibition. Another is the aorist tense prohibition. If it is the aorist tense, it means, *"Don't even begin to weep."* If it is the present tense, it means to stop an action already in progress.

Here is the Lord Jesus Christ. He is called the *"Lion of the tribe of Juda."* **Lions** devour. **Lions** are not friends to men.

A Lamb First, A Lion Next

The Lord Jesus Christ did not come as a *"Lion"* the first time. He came as a *"Lamb"* (John 1:29b) to die for sinners. Because He came as a *"Lamb"* Who was *"slain from the foundation of the world"* (Revelation 13:8) for sinners, He is qualified to be the *"Lion"* to judge the sinners in this judgment of the seals. He is called *"the Lion of the tribe of Juda, the Root of David."* To fulfill the prophesies of the Messiah of Israel, the Lord Jesus Christ had to come through the line of David.

- **Genesis 49:9**
  "Judah *is* a **lion's** whelp: from the prey, my son, thou art gone up: he stooped down, he couched as a **lion**, and as an old **lion**; who shall rouse him up?"

Judah was called a **lion**. The Lord Jesus Christ is called the **Lion** of the tribe of Juda.

- Hosea 5:14
  "For I *will be* unto Ephraim as a **lion**, and as a young **lion** to the house of Judah: I, *even* I, will tear and go away; I will take away, and none shall rescue *him*."

This is talking about another lion. Ephraim was the northern ten tribes.

The Lion Will Judge

As a lion who tears and devours, this is the picture of the Lord Jesus Christ, the One Who is going to judge. He did not come the first time *"to judge the world."* He came *"to save the world"* (John 12:47). This verse describes the world which is about to be judged. During this judgment of the seven years of tribulation on this earth, the genuine believers are in Heaven. The Lord Jesus Christ is the One Who is going to be acting as the Lion.

- 1 Peter 5:8
  "Be sober, be vigilant; because your adversary the devil, as a roaring **lion**, walketh about, seeking whom he may devour:"

The Devil, as a roaring **lion,** is out to punish and to hurt those that are genuinely saved. We should *"resist"* him, *"stedfast in the faith"* (James 4:7; 1 Peter 5:9).

The Lord Jesus Christ is called the **Lion** of the tribe of Juda, the Root of David. He had to be from David's line. He came forward and opened the book and began to loose the seven seals of judgment.

Revelation 5:6

"And I beheld, and, lo, in the midst of the throne and of the four beasts, and in the midst of the elders, stood a Lamb as it had been slain, having seven horns and seven eyes, which are the seven Spirits of God sent forth into all the earth."

Here John saw God the Father seated on the **throne** and in the midst of the **four beasts.** I believe these four living creatures are special angels, cherubim or seraphim. The **elders** are a picture of the genuine believers that are saved in Heaven.

The Lord Jesus Opens The Seals

It is given to us what is meant by the seven horns and seven eyes. The Holy Spirit of God will apparently be active in this judgment upon the earth. The Lord Jesus Christ will open the seals to begin the seven-sealed judgment, but the Holy Spirit will go forth and help as these judgments are enacted.

- **Isaiah 11:2**
  "And the **spirit** of the LORD shall rest upon him, the **spirit** of wisdom and understanding, the **spirit** of counsel and might, the **spirit** of knowledge and of the fear of the LORD;"

This is the sevenfold fullness of the **Holy Spirit.** He is going to be with the Lord Jesus Christ during this **judgment** when it comes.

- **Genesis 22:7-8**
  "And Isaac spake unto Abraham his father, and said, My father: and he said, Here am I, my son. And he said, Behold the fire and the wood: but where is the **lamb** for a burnt offering? And Abraham said, My son, God will provide himself a **lamb** for a burnt offering: so they went both of them together."

Abraham was sure that God would provide Himself a **lamb.** The Lord Jesus Christ Himself was the **Lamb.**

- **Hebrews 11:17-19**
  "By faith Abraham, when he was tried, offered up Isaac: and he that had received the promises **offered up** his only begotten son, Of whom it was said, That in Isaac shall thy seed be called: Accounting that God was **able to raise him up**, even from the dead; from whence also **he received him in a figure**."

God Raised Isaac In A Figure

In obedience to God's command, Abraham was willing to sacrifice his son. Abraham figuratively slew his son and God raised him up from the dead, "in a figure." The faith of Abraham was great. This is a picture of Calvary, when God spared not His own Son, but delivered Him up for us all.

- **Exodus 12:3**
  "Speak ye unto all the congregation of Israel, saying, In the tenth *day* of this month they shall take to them every man a **lamb**, according to the house of *their* fathers, a **lamb** for an house: "

After the tenth plague, on the tenth day of the first month, the Israelites were to take a **lamb** and wait for four days. On the fourteenth day, they were to offer it up, making sure it was clean. Then they were to kill it in the evening. When the Lord saw the blood of that **lamb** on the top and side posts of the doors, He passed over that house. The blood of the **lamb** was to protect.

- **John 1:29**
  "The next day John seeth Jesus coming unto him, and saith, Behold the **Lamb** of God, which taketh away the sin of the world."

The Lord Jesus Christ is called the **Lamb** of God.

- **John 1:36**
  "And looking upon Jesus as he walked, he saith, Behold the **Lamb** of God!"

The Lamb Of God Named

This is the second time John the Baptist called the Lord Jesus Christ the Lamb of God. He is the Lamb that God sent into this world as the sacrificial offering for the sinners of all the world.

· **1 Peter 1:18-19**
"Forasmuch *as* ye know that ye were not redeemed with corruptible things, as silver and gold, from your vain conversation *received* by tradition from your fathers; But with the precious blood of Christ, as of a **lamb** without blemish and without spot:"

Redeemed By The Lamb's Blood

We are redeemed by the blood of the Lamb. The death of the Lord Jesus Christ was necessary, but the shedding of His blood was also necessary. Redemption was by His blood.

That is where John MacArthur is wrong in his assessment, saying that blood does not mean blood. He says we were not redeemed by the precious blood of the Lord Jesus Christ, meaning real blood. According to him, blood just means His death. God says it was blood and that is what God means. HAIMA is blood. THANATOS is death. You cannot twist the two and make one mean the other.

The Passover Lamb–Death & Blood

It is just like the Passover lamb. The lamb was to be slain on the fourteen day of the first month. The blood was to be put into a basin. Hyssop, an ordinary weed, was to be dipped in that basin and the blood was to be put on the top and the side posts of the door. The Lord Jesus Christ was the Lamb slain. The Father said, "When I see the blood, I will pass over you. I will protect you." One did not die in that home. They did not put the lamb on the door post, they applied the blood. The death and the blood are separate all through the offerings. They slew the offering, and they applied the blood.

- **Revelation 5:12**
"Saying with a loud voice, Worthy is the **Lamb** that was slain to receive power, and riches, and wisdom, and strength, and honour, and glory, and blessing."

- **Revelation 7:14**
"And I said unto him, Sir, thou knowest. And he said to me, These are they which came out of great tribulation, and have washed their robes, and made them white in the blood of the **Lamb**."

Christ's Blood Makes White

The Lamb that was slain is the Lord Jesus Christ. How can blood make somebody white? Spiritually speaking, white means clean from sin. That means forgiveness of sin. That means cleanliness. That means washed clean by the blood of the Lamb.

- **Revelation 12:11**
  "And they overcame him by the blood of the **Lamb**, and by the word of their testimony; and they loved not their lives unto the death."
- **Revelation 13:8**
  "And all that dwell upon the earth shall worship him, whose names are not written in the book of life of the **Lamb** slain from the foundation of the world."

Yes, the **Lamb** was slain from the foundation of the world. God sent Him into this world when the fulness of the time was come to redeem them that were under the law and also the Gentiles.

This was the picture of the One Who was to come forth and to open the **seals**. John beheld in the midst of the throne and the **four beasts** (the angelic beings—cherubim or lead angels) and the **elders** (those that represent the church), there stood a **Lamb** as it had been slain. This is a picture and a title. We sing the hymn *Just As I Am*. One of the stanzas says, "O **Lamb** of God, I come." He is called the **Lamb** of God.

A gentleman called me recently. We agreed on many things. We agreed on Billy Graham. He was also opposed to Evangelicals and Catholics together. He and his wife were former Catholics. He had gotten into a tangle with Charles Colson who is for Roman Catholic ecumenism and so forth. I told him that Charles Colson wrote me up in his book called *The Body*. My name is right in there.

We agreed on that, but we could not agree on for whom did the Lord Jesus Christ die. Was it just for the elect or did He die for the sinners of the whole world? We also could not agree on who could genuinely trust the Lord Jesus Christ as Saviour. Granted, the Holy Spirit of God, through the Words of God, must lead, guide, direct, and minister to the needs.

Paul's Answer To His Jailor

When the Philippian jailor asked Paul, "What must I do to be saved?" Did Paul have to scratch his head and say, "If

you are elect, you can be saved"? No, he said, "Believe on the
Lord Jesus Christ, and thou shalt be saved, and thy house."
"Whosoever will" may genuinely trust Him. He is the Lamb.
There was a provision for the sins of the world.

Revelation 5:7

"And he came and took the book out of the right hand of him that sat upon the throne."

He came. That is the Lord Jesus Christ. The One who is **worthy**
went to the **throne** of God the Father, put out His nail-pierced hand of
His resurrected body, and took that seven-sealed **book** out of the hand
of God the Father. This shows that it is, as they say, "curtain time." The
show must go on. It is terrible. This is not a pleasant "curtain time"
performance, but the seven-seal judgment of the world will begin. God
is pouring out His wrath upon the sins of this world.

He promised Noah that never again would He judge the world by
water. He put the rainbow in the sky as a token of that promise. Never
again by water. But by fire? Yes, indeed. We see these coming
judgments. They will be horrific judgments.

A Rescuer From Judgments

I am glad that there is a Rescuer that can take us out of
these judgments—all twenty-one of them. There are seven
seals, seven trumpets, and seven vials. The Lord Jesus Christ
is that Lamb Who was slain for your sins, my sins, and for the
sins of the whole world. By genuinely trusting Him, a person
can be free from these judgments that will be upon this earth.
The genuine born-again Christians will be gone to Heaven.

The Pre-Tribulation Rapture

That is why, as I have said before, I cannot accept
anything but a pre-tribulation rapture of the true church
before any part of that tribulation. It is not mid-tribulation,
going through half of it. It is not pre-wrath, going through up
to the wrath. It is not post-tribulation, going through the
whole tribulation. We are not going to be here.

We have a **Lamb** that was slain for our sins. We who are genuinely
saved will be gone. We are free. He is the **Lamb** of God that takes away

the sins of the world. He was slain from the foundation of the world to give salvation and eternal life to those that genuinely receive Him.

In this time of judgment, He is the **Lion** of the tribe of Judah, ready to devour and to righteously judge those who dwell upon the earth who have never been genuinely saved and have rejected the Saviour, the Lord Jesus Christ, the **Lamb** of God that takes away the sin of the world.

- **John 1:29b**
  "Behold the **Lamb** of God, which taketh away the sin of the world."

Meaning Of "The Sin Of The World"

Again, I take that "world" to mean all the people in the world. That means now it is not a question of sin. The sins of all people have been "taken away." Now the issue is, "What will you do with the Son of God who took those sins away?" You must genuinely receive this Saviour to claim this gift as your own.

Will you accept Him or reject Him? He bore your sins in His own body on the tree. Now you must accept and take that salvation by faith. We are not Universalists at all. We do not believe everybody is genuinely saved because the Lord Jesus Christ took the sins of the world upon Him. The sin question has now become the Son question. What will you do with the Son of God? Will you genuinely trust Him or reject Him?

Revelation 5:8

"And when he had taken the book, the four beasts and four *and* twenty elders fell down before the Lamb, having every one of them harps, and golden vials full of odours, which are the prayers of saints."

John the apostle is there in a vision and is taken up to Glory. The true church, the genuine believers, have been raptured before the tribulation takes place upon this earth. John has been taken up and he sees many things. As we said before, this is the preparation of the first of twenty-one judgments. There are seven seal judgments, seven trumpet judgments, and seven vial judgments.

The Only Worthy One In Heaven

The Lord Jesus Christ had taken the book. He is the only One in Heaven worthy to open up that book and to judge this world, because He is perfect. Only ones that are perfect can judge others and He is the perfect Lamb of God.

The four beasts or living creatures, I think, are pictures of the lead angels, probably the seraphim or the cherubim. The four and twenty elders are probably pictures and representatives of the true believers, the genuinely saved people, that are taken up to Heaven. Someone asked me if these would possibly be some of the leaders, such as pastors, that these particular elders represent. They may possibly be certain pastors or maybe the apostles, but they are representatives of the church, the ones that are genuinely saved.

They Worshipped Before The Lamb

Notice what they did. They fell down before the Lamb. They worshipped the Lord Jesus Christ in Heaven. When true believers that are genuinely saved are raptured and taken to Heaven, that is what they will be doing all through eternity. They will be worshipping the Lord Jesus Christ and the Father. Notice also, they had every one of them harps and golden vials full of odours. These harps in their hands are stringed instruments.

- **Psalm 33:2**
  "Praise the LORD with **harp**: sing unto him with the psaltery and an instrument of ten strings."
These are instruments of praise.
- **Psalm 71:22**
  "I will also praise thee with the psaltery, *even* thy truth, O my God: unto thee will I sing with the **harp**, O thou Holy One of Israel."
- **Psalm 137:2-4**
  "We hanged our **harps** upon the willows in the midst thereof. For there they that carried us away captive required of us a song; and they that wasted us required of us mirth, saying, Sing us one of the songs of Zion.
  How shall we sing the LORD'S song in a strange land? "

Singing The Lord's Songs

When Israel was in captivity in Babylon, they did not want to have their harps with them. They were no longer singers. That is what we have to do. We are in a strange land, this world. We have to sing the Lord's songs.

The elders not only had **harps** but they also had **golden vials full of odours**, which is like **incense**. The **incense** and the **odors** are linked with prayers throughout the Scriptures.

- **Exodus 30:1**
  "And thou shalt make an altar to burn **incense** upon: *of* shittim wood shalt thou make it."

- **Exodus 30:7**
  "And Aaron shall burn thereon sweet **incense** every morning: when he dresseth the lamps, he shall burn **incense** upon it."

The **incense** was to be burning every morning. The fragrance and the wonderful **odor** going up to the Lord.

- **Psalm 141:2**
  "Let my prayer be set forth before thee *as* **incense**; *and* the lifting up of my hands *as* the evening sacrifice."

Praying Is Like Incense

If you are on praying ground, if you are genuinely saved and truly born-again, and you pray unto the Lord, that is sweet incense just like the altar of incense going up before the Lord.

- **Luke 1:10**
  "And the whole multitude of the people were **praying** without at the time of **incense**."

The Time Of Incense

That was when the priest Zacharias, John the Baptist's father, was in the temple. They were praying at the time of incense. That is when the prayers were made. Prayers and incense go together.

- **Revelation 8:3**
  "And another angel came and stood at the altar, having a golden censer; and there was given unto him much **incense**, that he should offer *it* with the prayers of all saints upon the golden altar which was before the throne."
- **Revelation 8:4**
  "And the smoke of the **incense**, *which came* with the **prayers** of the saints, ascended up before God out of the angel's hand."

Here again, **prayer** and **incense** are a wonderful fragrance given before the Lord.

Revelation 5:9

"And they sung a new song, saying, Thou art worthy to take the book, and to open the seals thereof: for thou wast slain, and hast redeemed us to God by thy blood out of every kindred, and tongue, and people, and nation;"

In 1611, *sung* was the past tense of *sing*. Now we say *sang*. It is not a mistake in grammar. The living creatures and the twenty-four elders, representing the genuine believers, the truly saved ones, sang a **song** in Glory saying, "**Thou art worthy.**" They were speaking of the **Lamb**, the Lord Jesus Christ. He is **worthy**.

Slain And Redeemed By His Blood

He can open the seals and judgments can be poured out upon this earth during that seven-year period of tribulation after the genuine believers are snatched away because of two things:

1. He was slain.
2. He has redeemed them by His blood.

These twenty-four elders represent the true church, the genuine believers. Some people say we are going to amalgamate with everybody else. We are going to get one nation, one tongue, one people, and so on. No. Nations and people are going to be separate all the way through until eternity as we see here in Revelation 5.

Notice there are two phases:

1. Slain
2. Redeemed by thy blood

That is one of the things on which John MacArthur is in error. We have said that many times. *Slain* was the first thing and after He was **slain**, *the* _blood_ was applied. There are two phases, just like the Passover lamb. The **lamb** was **slain** and the **blood** was applied on the top and side posts of the door.

- **James 2:7**
  "Do not they blaspheme that **worthy** name by the which ye are called?"
- **Revelation 4:11**
  "Thou art **worthy**, O Lord, to receive glory and honour and power: for thou hast created all things, and for thy pleasure they are and were created."

The Lord Jesus Christ is **worthy**. There is no question about that.

- **Revelation 5:2**
  "And I saw a strong angel proclaiming with a loud voice, Who is worthy to open the **book**, and to loose the **seals** thereof?"

It is the Lord Jesus Christ Himself who is **worthy** to open the **seals**.

- **Revelation 5:5**
  "And one of the elders saith unto me, Weep not: behold, the **Lion** of the tribe of Juda, the Root of David, hath prevailed to open the book, and to loose the seven **seals** thereof."

He is **worthy** to open this **book** and to loose the **seals**. The **Lamb** that was slain speaks of His death at the cross of Calvary.

- **Acts 2:23**
  "Him, being delivered by the determinate counsel and foreknowledge of God, ye have taken, and by wicked hands have crucified and **slain**:"

By God the Father's "determinate counsel and foreknowledge," the Lord Jesus Christ was **slain**.

- **Revelation 5:6**
  "And I beheld, and, lo, in the midst of the throne and of the four beasts, and in the midst of the elders, stood a **Lamb** as it had been **slain**, having seven horns and seven eyes, which are the seven Spirits of God sent forth into all the earth."
- **Revelation 5:12**
  "Saying with a loud voice, **Worthy** is the **Lamb** that was **slain** to receive power, and riches, and wisdom, and strength, and honour, and glory, and blessing."

The Lord Jesus Christ has **redeemed** truly born-again people to God the Father by His **blood**.

- **1 Peter 1:18-19**
  "Forasmuch as ye know that ye were not **redeemed** with corruptible things, *as* silver and gold, from your vain conversation *received* by tradition from your fathers; But with the precious **blood** of Christ, as of a **lamb** without blemish and without spot:"

We are not **redeemed** with corruptible things, that is, with things that wax old and waste away. The way this is phrased would imply that His **blood** is not a "*corruptible thing*," and therefore "incorruptible."

A man from Manchester, England e-mailed me and said, "Dr. Waite, what a joy and thrill it is to find your decent and unadulterated teaching. I listened to your sermon on the fourteen effects of the **blood** of Christ and was very concerned to hear about John MacArthur's confused view."

Then he sent me John MacArthur's article where he said he believed in the precious **blood**, as if that clears it up. In that article, which I sent back to this man, I put in bold letters some of things John MacArthur says in the article. For instance, he says the word **blood** is the chief term the New Testament uses to refer to the atonement.

MacArthur does not believe that **blood** means **blood**. He believes that **blood** is a metonym or figure of speech for death. According to MacArthur, there is nothing supernatural in the **blood** of the Lord Jesus Christ that sanctifies. He believes it was just human, natural, normal **blood** with nothing supernatural or divine about it.

MacArthur also says there is no bowl of **blood** in Heaven. He says we are sanctified by the Lord Jesus Christ's sacrificial *death*. Then he says it is not the actual liquid that cleanses us from our sins, but the work of redemption. He is always saying that *blood means death*.

Here in this verse of Revelation 5:9, I believe, is the clearest picture of the two terms, "**death**" and "**blood**." First of all, it says that the Lord Jesus Christ was **slain**. Second, it says that the Lord Jesus Christ has **redeemed** us to God the Father by His **blood**. The **death** of Christ was important, but **redemption** was by the shedding of His **blood**.

---

14 Things Fulfilled By His Blood

There are at least fourteen different things that are mentioned in Scripture that are accomplished by the blood of the Lord Jesus Christ. When God's Words say that it is the blood of the Lord Jesus Christ that cleanses us from sin, it is the blood of the Lord Jesus Christ that cleanses us from sin. There is no question about it. Death is THANATOS. Blood is HAIMA. The two words are different, separate, and distinct from one another. They cannot and must not be combined or confused as John MacArthur and his many followers have done and are doing even today!

John MacArthur says that death means **blood** and **blood** means death. Therefore he would imply that "Thou wast **slain** and hast **redeemed** us to God by thy *death*." That is a serious heresy. John MacArthur is moaning on his website about the terrible people who are misrepresenting him. People that do not read his article carefully think he means **blood** like we mean **blood**. He does not. He says it right in the article, but he is a clever deceiver as he seeks to explain his heretical view on the **blood** of the Lord Jesus Christ. This is a sad and harmful position.

The Lord Jesus Christ, praise the Lord, was **slain** and has **redeemed** those who are genuinely saved by His **blood**, out of every kindred and nation all over the world.

Revelation 5:10

"And hast made us unto our God kings and priests: and we shall reign on the earth."

The 24 Elders Are The Saved Ones

Here again, this is another reason that I believe the twenty-four elders represent the genuine believers, the saved ones, the true church. The redemption by blood was not speaking of angels, but of the twenty-four elders that were there.

- **1 Peter 2:5**
  "Ye also, as lively stones, are built up a spiritual house, an holy **priesthood**, to offer up spiritual sacrifices, acceptable to God by Jesus Christ."

We are told that we who are genuinely saved are **priests**—believer priests—who can go directly into the presence of God. We do not need any intermediary, rabbi, priest, pastor, or anyone else.

- **1 Peter 2:9**
  "But ye *are* a chosen generation, a royal **priesthood**, an holy nation, a peculiar people; that ye should shew forth the praises of him who hath called you out of darkness into his marvellous light:"

Genuinely saved people are a royal **priesthood**. It says, in the verse below, that He has made us **kings and priests**.

- **Revelation 1:6**
  "And hath made us **kings and priests** unto God and his Father; to him *be* glory and dominion for ever and ever. Amen."

Christians Will Reign With Christ

You may not feel like a king or a queen down here on this earth, but as far as the Lord Jesus Christ is concerned, genuine believers have been made kings and priests.

We shall reign on the earth. That is why, again, I say the twenty-four elders are representatives of the genuinely saved people. It is the genuine believers who are up in Glory.

- **Luke 19:12**
  "He said therefore, A certain nobleman went into a far country to receive for himself a kingdom, and to return."

The Lord Jesus Christ talks about the nobleman who gave ten pounds to his ten servants. These servants were wisely to invest this money and gain interest on it.

- **Luke 19:17**
  "And he said unto him, Well, thou good servant: because thou hast been faithful in a very little, have thou authority over ten cities."

This is a picture. The man that received the kingdom is the Lord Jesus Christ and the ten cities will be **ruled** by those that are faithful. If we are genuinely saved people, we will **reign** with Him in Glory and we will have authority.

- **Luke 19:19**
  "And he said likewise to him, Be thou also over five cities."

Here is another man who had gained five pounds. This is the illustration of the millennial **reign** of the Lord Jesus Christ and genuine believers that will be **reigning** with Him.

- **Revelation 20:4**
  "And I saw thrones, and they sat upon them, and judgment was given unto them: and *I saw* the souls of them that were beheaded for the witness of Jesus, and for the word of God, and which had not worshipped the beast, neither his image, neither had received *his* mark upon their foreheads, or in their hands; and they lived and **reigned** with Christ a thousand years."

What will be the duties of genuine believers in Heaven? During the millennial reign of the Lord Jesus Christ, the thousand-year **reign**, we will reign with Him a thousand years. The genuinely saved ones will be in their new, resurrected, and glorified bodies.

- **Revelation 20:6**
  "Blessed and holy *is* he that hath part in the first resurrection: on such the second death hath no power, but they shall be **priests** of God and of Christ, and shall **reign** with him a thousand years."

We will not be the main **kings** over this earth, but we will **reign** with Him. You may say, "Can He trust Christians to **reign** with Him on this earth? We are not now presidents, emperors, **kings**, or queens." With new bodies, we will **reign** with Him a thousand years and it will be possible. There is no question about it. This is what God has prepared for those that are genuinely saved.

The New Jerusalem Our Home

Where will we go at the end of each day? As we will see later, the new Jerusalem will be our home. It will be suspended over this earth. It will be foursquare—1500 miles north, south, east, and west. The genuinely saved people will go home there and come back the next day and reign over this earth. For a thousand years we will rule with the Lord Jesus Christ.

Revelation 5:11

"And I beheld, and I heard the voice of many angels round about the throne and the beasts and the elders: and the number of them was ten thousand times ten thousand, and thousands of thousands;"

There were many angels. How many **angels** are there? Can they take care of things?

- **Hebrews 1:14**
  "Are they not all **ministering spirits**, sent forth to minister for them who shall be heirs of salvation?"

We may call them "guardian **angels**." They are **angels** who will help us. If you multiply ten thousand times ten thousand you get a **hundred million**. Then this verse says, "and **thousands of thousands**." In other words, there are myriads of **angels**.

Not All Angels Are Holy

Not all angels are holy. Some are unholy and fallen angels. These are holy angels in Heaven. They praise the Lord. They are not human beings. They have never been redeemed or genuinely saved. They do not know the joy of salvation. They were created by God, probably on the first day of Creation.

- **Genesis 1:1**
  "In the beginning God created the heaven and the earth."

God created the Heaven and the earth and all the Heavenly things. The **angels** were there. The **angels** saw the Lord as He created the rest of the earth and the things of the second, third, fourth, fifth, and sixth days of Creation.

Praising Around God's Throne

All of these holy angels were beside the throne and around the throne. The beasts were also there, which I believe are probably the lead angels. The twenty-four elders were there, representing the genuine believers and the true church. These were all praising the Lord with loud voices. Notice what they are saying:

Revelation 5:12

"Saying with a loud voice, Worthy is the Lamb that was slain to receive power, and riches, and wisdom, and strength, and honour, and glory, and blessing."

This brings us to the sevenfold **worthiness** of the Lord Jesus Christ. Let us look at this sevenfold **worthiness**.

1. Christ Is Worthy To Receive Power.

The first thing the Lord Jesus Christ is **worthy** to receive is **power**.

- **Matthew 28:18**
  "And Jesus came and spake unto them, saying, All **power** is given unto me in heaven and in earth."
- **Mark 13:26**
  "And then shall they see the Son of man coming in the clouds with great **power** and glory."
- **1 Corinthians 1:24**
  "But unto them which are called, both Jews and Greeks, Christ the **power** of God, and the wisdom of God."

- **1 Timothy 6:14-15**
  "That thou keep *this* commandment without spot, unrebukeable, until the appearing of our Lord Jesus Christ: Which in his times he shall shew, *who is* the blessed and only **Potentate**, the King of kings, and Lord of lords"

That is *power*. The Lord Jesus Christ is a **powerful** ruler. He will be King of kings and Lord of lords. All the hosts of Heaven, the thousands and millions of angels, the genuine believers, and the cherubim will say, "**Worthy is the Lamb that was slain to receive power.**"

---

2. Christ Is Worthy To Receive Riches.

Notice the second thing the Lord Jesus Christ is **worthy** to receive is *riches*.

- **Romans 11:33**
  "O the depth of the **riches** both of the wisdom and knowledge of God! how unsearchable *are* his judgments, and his ways past finding out!"

The Lord Jesus Christ has great **riches**. Do you feel impoverished? He has glorious **riches** in Heaven.

- **2 Corinthians 8:9**
  "For ye know the grace of our Lord Jesus Christ, that, though he was **rich**, yet for your sakes he became poor, that ye through his poverty might be **rich**."

If the Lord Jesus Christ had not left His **riches** in Heaven, come down to this earth, taken upon Himself a perfect sinless body, suffered, bled, and died for our sins, shedding His blood for the redemption of the world, we would never be able to be spiritually **rich**. He became poor. He became One of us, yet without sin. The Lord Jesus Christ (God the Son), in eternity past, was always Spirit. God the Father is Spirit. God the Holy Spirit is Spirit. God the Son was always Spirit and He became flesh. God became flesh and dwelled among us so born-again people could be made **rich** with His **riches**, even though He was "poor" at Calvary.

- **Ephesians 1:7**
  "In whom we have redemption through his blood, the forgiveness of sins, according to the **riches** of his grace;"

Forgiveness is part of His **riches**. He is worthy to receive **riches**. We do not get these **riches** by our works, but by His grace through genuine faith. It is by His grace alone.

- **Ephesians 1:18**
  "The eyes of your understanding being enlightened; that ye may know what is the hope of his calling, and what the **riches** of the glory of his inheritance in the saints,"

Christ has **worthy riches** of glory in the saints. There is no one in all the universe that is more **rich** than the Lord Jesus Christ. The Father has given Him all things—every single thing in Heaven and in earth. If we are genuinely saved and truly born-again by genuine faith in the Lord Jesus Christ, we have a share in those **riches** in Glory.

- **Ephesians 3:8**
  "Unto me, who am less than the least of all saints, is this grace given, that I should preach among the Gentiles the unsearchable **riches** of Christ;"

Paul Was A Humble Man

Paul was not a proud, arrogant man. He was a humble man. He was glad for the grace of God that stopped his journey on the way to Damascus to imprison and kill Christians. Paul was made a preacher instead of a persecutor. Then notice that he was to preach "the unsearchable riches of Christ." The Lord Jesus Christ has unsearchable riches—riches that cannot even be searched out. We do not even know where they come from. He owns the cattle upon a thousand hills (Psalm 50:10).

- **Philippians 4:19**
  "But my God shall supply all your need according to his **riches** in glory by Christ Jesus."

Paul worked as a tentmaker to care for his own needs. Whenever he needed something, he made some tents and got enough money for food, clothing, and lodging. Occasionally, churches gave him an offering of some funds. The Philippian church was one of those churches that gave. They gave out of their need and out of their poverty. They gave to Paul to help him continue his ministry and his apostleship.

God Supplies The Christian's Needs

The Lord God of Heaven and earth will supply our need with the riches that He has. He supplies the needs of our church and of our missionaries that we support. Praise the Lord for the riches in Glory by Christ Jesus.

The Lord Jesus Christ has gone to Heaven, but He is still giving **riches** to those that are genuinely trusting Him. He will not necessarily make us wealthy beyond all means, but He will provide for us. He will take care of us and meet our needs.

3. Christ Is Worthy To Receive Wisdom.

The third thing that the Lord Jesus Christ is worthy to receive is *wisdom*.

- **Romans 11:33**
  "O the depth of the riches both of the **wisdom** and knowledge of God! how unsearchable are his judgments, and his ways past finding out!"

God the Son is included here. There is no person more **wise** than the Lord Jesus Christ.

- **1 Corinthians 1:24**
  "But unto them which are called, both Jews and Greeks, Christ the power of God, and the **wisdom** of God."

The Lord Jesus Christ is made **wisdom** unto us who are truly born-again and genuinely saved.

- **James 1:5**
  "If any of you lack **wisdom**, let him ask of God, that giveth to all *men* liberally, and upbraideth not; and it shall be given him."

The **wisdom** of the Lord Jesus Christ is given unto the genuinely saved people.

- **1 Corinthians 1:30**
  "But of him are ye in Christ Jesus, who of God is made unto us **wisdom**, and righteousness, and sanctification, and redemption:"

- **1 Corinthians 1:21**
  "For after that in the **wisdom** of God the world by wisdom knew not God, it pleased God by the foolishness of preaching to save them that believe."

The world did not receive the **wisdom** of the Lord Jesus Christ.

4. Christ Is Worthy To Receive Strength.

The fourth thing that the Lord Jesus Christ is worthy to receive is *strength*.

- **Ephesians 6:10**
  "Finally, my brethren, be **strong** in the Lord, and in the power of his might."

The Lord Jesus Christ is the Christian's source of **strength**. We do not have to be weak in the things of faith.

- **2 Timothy 2:1**
  "Thou therefore, my son, be **strong** in the grace that is in Christ Jesus."

We need spiritual **strength** to stand against the world, the flesh and the Devil. If they laugh at you, ask the Lord for **strength** to be a good witness and to have a good testimony.

5. Christ Is Worthy To Receive Honour.

The fifth thing that the Lord Jesus Christ is worthy to receive is *honour.*

- **Matthew 13:57**
  "And they were offended in him. But Jesus said unto them, A prophet is not without **honour**, save in his own country, and in his own house."

The Lord Jesus Christ was in His own area and the people did not know Him. When He left His area, people worshipped Him and went with Him and accepted Him. He is a prophet that is worthy of **honour**.

- **1 Timothy 6:14-16**
  "That thou keep this commandment without spot, unrebukeable, until the appearing of our Lord Jesus Christ: Which in his times he shall shew, who is the blessed and only Potentate, the King of kings, and Lord of lords; Who only hath immortality, dwelling in the light which no man can approach unto; whom no man hath seen, nor can see: to whom be **honour** and power everlasting. Amen."

Do you **honor** the Lamb if you are genuinely saved? Do you **honor** the Lord Jesus Christ? He is worthy of our **honor**.

- **Hebrews 2:9**
  "But we see Jesus, who was made a little lower than the angels for the suffering of death, crowned with glory and **honour**; that he by the grace of God should taste death for every man."

The Lord Jesus Christ tasted death for every man, woman, and child. We do not go along with the hyper-Calvinists who say He only tasted death for the "elect." He tasted death for *every* man. It is up to everyone genuinely to accept and receive that everlasting life and salvation.

When the Lord Jesus Christ was here upon earth, He was crowned with thorns. God the Father has crowned Him with glory and **honor**. He is worthy of **honor**.

---

6. Christ Is Worthy To Receive Glory.

The sixth thing that our Lord Jesus Christ, the Lamb, is worthy to receive is *glory*. The Lord Jesus Christ is the King of **Glory**.

- **Matthew 19:28**
  "And Jesus said unto them, Verily I say unto you, That ye which have followed me, in the regeneration when the Son of man shall sit in the throne of his **glory**, ye also shall sit upon twelve thrones, judging the twelve tribes of Israel."

This is the Lord Jesus Christ when He comes back. He is going to come in **glory**.

- **Matthew 24:30**
  "And then shall appear the sign of the Son of man in heaven: and then shall all the tribes of the earth mourn, and they shall see the Son of man coming in the clouds of heaven with power and great **glory**."

The genuinely saved will not be here to see Him coming in **glory**. The true believers, or saved ones, will be snatched up before the seven-year tribulation comes. At the end of that time, the Lord Jesus Christ will come back in power and **glory**. The unsaved world will see Him coming in power and great **glory**.

- **Mark 13:26**
  "And then shall they see the Son of man coming in the clouds with great power and **glory**."
- **Luke 9:26**
  "For whosoever shall be ashamed of me and of my words, of him shall the Son of man be ashamed, when he shall come in his own **glory**, and *in his* Father's, and of the holy angels."

The Battle For The Words Of God

Let us pause right here. Ashamed of His Words? That is the battle of the Bible today. Men are battling over what are the Words of the Lord Jesus Christ. I believe He is the Author of all the Words of the Old Testament Hebrew text and all the Words of the New Testament Greek text. Those are His Words, translated accurately we think, in the King James Bible.

Some people say they do not know where the Words of God are. There is a whole book that has come out from Bob Jones University and their professors, teachers, and writers. Writers in this book from ten different fundamental schools are represented. Dr. Strouse has written an excellent article in review of that particular book. It is called

Preservation: The Word of God in Our Hands. The men that have written this book, from ten different fundamental Bible-believing schools, say that the Word of God is not the same as the Words of God. Some of them say it is simply the message, thoughts, ideas, or concepts of God, but not His very Words. Then they say the Word of God is preserved in all the Hebrew manuscripts and in all the Greek manuscripts all over the world. Think about that. Yet they say in the title, *"God's Word In Our Hands."* How can it be in our hands if it is only in

manuscripts all over the world? It is inconsistent. They do not believe that God has promised to preserve His Hebrew, Aramaic, and Greek Words.

The Lord Jesus Christ is coming one day in glory. May He never be ashamed of you or of me because we are ashamed of His Words. If you do not know His Words, how can you obey His Words?

- **Matthew 4:4**
  "But he answered and said, It is written, Man shall not live by bread alone, but by every word that proceedeth out of the mouth of God."

It is important that we have the Words of God. <u>I believe, by faith, that God has not only promised to preserve His Hebrew and Greek Words of the Old and New Testaments, but that He has also preserved them in the Hebrew, Aramaic, and Greek Words that underlie our King James Bible.</u> To me, that is my faith. These fundamentalist teachers and preachers can rant and rave. They can say they do not know where the Words are. Just because they are insecure, is no reason for me to be insecure. If they do not know anything, I am not going to join the crowd and say that I do not know anything either. I must be positive. How can I preach the Words of God if I have doubt as to what those Words are? The Lord Jesus Christ said that whosoever is ashamed of Him and of His Words, the Son of man will be ashamed of him also.

- **John 1:14**
  "And the Word was made flesh, and dwelt among us, (and we beheld his **glory**, the **glory** as of the only begotten of the Father,) full of grace and truth."

The Lord Jesus Christ's **glory** was manifested on the Mount of Transfiguration.

- **John 17:24**
  "Father, I will that they also, whom thou hast given me, be with me where I am; that they may behold my **glory**, which thou hast given me: for thou lovedst me before the foundation of the world."

This was the High Priestly prayer of the Lord Jesus Christ. His **glory** was hidden while He was here on this earth. His body hid that **glory**, but within Him was **glory**. That is where, on the Mount of Transfiguration, the apostles, Peter, James and John, saw His **glory** as His garments became white and glistering. He is worthy of **glory**.

---
7. Christ Is Worthy To Receive Blessing.

The seventh and final thing that the Lord Jesus Christ is worthy to receive is *blessing*.

- **Matthew 23:39**
  "For I say unto you, Ye shall not see me henceforth, till ye shall say, **Blessed** *is* he that cometh in the name of the Lord."

Looking On Him Whom They Pierced

One day the Jews will look upon Him whom they have pierced and they will say, "Blessed." The 144,000 evangelist Jews during the tribulation period will one day say, "Blessed is He that cometh in the name of the Lord."

- **Mark 11:9**
  "And they that went before, and they that followed, cried, saying, Hosanna; **Blessed** is he that cometh in the name of the Lord:"

This was during the seven days before the crucifixion. The Lord Jesus Christ is worthy of **blessing**. They called Him **blessed** and He is **blessed**.

- **Luke 19:38**
  "Saying, **Blessed** *be* the King that cometh in the name of the Lord: peace in heaven, and glory in the highest."

- **Acts 3:26**
  "Unto you first God, having raised up his Son Jesus, sent him to **bless** you, in turning away every one of you from his iniquities."

He is worthy of **blessing**. He was sent to **bless** you. Are you familiar with the **blessings** of God? That is the purpose of His Son's coming.

- **Romans 9:5**
  "Whose *are* the fathers, and of whom as concerning the flesh Christ *came*, who is over all, God **blessed** for ever. Amen."

He is God the Son. He is also **blessed** forever. He is worthy of **blessing**. God **blessed** Him and put His stamp of approval upon His Son, the Lord Jesus Christ.

- **1 Timothy 6:14-15**
  "That thou keep *this* commandment without spot, unrebukeable, until the appearing of our Lord Jesus Christ: Which in his times he shall shew, *who is* the **blessed** and only Potentate, the King of kings, and Lord of lords; "

The Lord Jesus Christ is **blessed**. He is worthy of **blessing**.

- **Revelation 5:13**
  "And every creature which is in heaven, and on the earth, and under the earth, and such as are in the sea, and all that are in them, heard I saying, **Blessing**, and honour, and glory, and power, *be* unto him that sitteth upon the throne, and unto the Lamb for ever and ever."

They will bless the Lamb. Is He a **blessing** to you? Has He made your life a **blessing**? The Lord Jesus Christ is in the business of **blessing** those of us that trust Him as Saviour and Redeemer. The Lord Jesus Christ is **worthy** of all these seven things.

Revelation 5:13

"And every creature which is in heaven, and on the earth, and under the earth, and such as are in the sea, and all that are in them, heard I saying, Blessing, and honour, and glory, and power, be unto him that sitteth upon the throne, and unto the Lamb for ever and ever."

Here all the **creatures** gather together in Heaven. That includes the Heavenly angels, the four beasts or cherubim, and the twenty-four elders representing the genuine believers. Those that are still on the earth will also at this time praise the Lord. Those under the earth are perhaps those that may be in Hell itself. These fourfold blessings are with God the Father and with the Lamb seated next to Him on the throne.

The **fourfold blessings** of God the Father are here. They are **blessing, honour, glory, and power** unto the One that sits on the throne. It is the **Heavenly Father** that is sitting on the throne. They are also unto the **Lamb**, the Lord Jesus Christ, God the Son. To the Father and the Lamb is this fourfold worthiness that is **blessing, honour, glory, and power**. They leave off the other three of the sevenfold blessing, glory, and worthiness of the Lamb mentioned in verse 12. They leave off riches, wisdom, and strength. As it was already mentioned, the Lord Jesus Christ is **worthy** of all seven of these.

These **creatures** of Heaven and earth, and under the earth, and in the sea will be bowing and worshipping the Lord Jesus Christ, the Lamb. There are many verses on that.

- Isaiah 45:23
  "I have sworn by myself, the word is gone out of my mouth *in* righteousness, and shall not return, That unto me every knee shall **bow**, every tongue shall swear."

One Day All Will Bow To Jesus

When it says, "*under the earth,*" maybe those in Hell one day will have to bow before the Lord Jesus Christ, as well as those that are on the earth. One day both saved and lost will bow. If you bow before Him and accept Him as your Saviour and Redeemer while you are living, and you are genuinely saved, that is the way to go. Those that are lost, whether on this earth during the tribulation period, or at the Great White Throne Judgment where the lost will be judged and sent into the lake of fire for all eternity, will have to bow and declare before the Lord Jesus Christ, honor and glory.

- Romans 14:11
  "For it is written, *As* I live, saith the Lord, every knee shall **bow** to me, and every tongue shall confess to God."

This is quoting from Isaiah 45. They do not want to do it now, but they are going to do it some time. It is better to do it now and accept Him as Saviour and Redeemer rather than to **bow** then, realizing that it is too late.

- Philippians 2:10
  "That at the name of Jesus every knee should **bow**, of *things* in heaven, and *things* in earth, and *things* under the earth; "

He came as the Son of man, in the form of a servant, made in the likeness of man and suffered the death of the cross. Wherefore God has highly exalted Him. This is the context here in Philippians 2:10. One day the whole world, saved and lost, will have to **bow**. The true believers who are genuinely saved in this life should **bow** before the Lord Jesus Christ and worship Him and adore Him and say to the glory of God that He is our Saviour and Redeemer. Even the lost, one day will have to **bow** before Him as Sovereign. Then after they **bow**, He will send them to the lake of fire because they rejected His love and His grace.

Revelation 5:14

"And the four beasts said, Amen. And the four *and* twenty elders fell down and worshipped him that liveth for ever and ever."

Again, the **four beasts**, these living creatures, are probably the cherubim or seraphim. After all the worthiness is declared, the **four and twenty elders worship**.

- **Genesis 22:5**
    "And Abraham said unto his young men, Abide ye here with the ass; and I and the lad will go yonder and **worship**, and come again to you."

They were going to have a ram slain in the place of Isaac.

- **Psalm 45:11**
    "So shall the king greatly desire thy beauty: for he *is* thy Lord; and **worship** thou him."

The only One to **worship** is the Lord, not man or angels, but the Lord.

- **Matthew 2:11**
    "And when they were come into the house, they saw the young child with Mary his mother, and fell down, and **worshipped** him: and when they had opened their treasures, they presented unto him gifts; gold, and frankincense, and myrrh."

The wise men came from the east when the Lord Jesus Christ was about two years old. When they saw the young child with Mary his mother, did they fall down and **worship** her? No. They did not **worship Mary. That is the sin of the Roman Catholic Church—mariolatry. It is a horrible thing.** That is one of the things mentioned in Don Jasmin's paper, *The Fundamentalist Digest,* about a film that has come out about Jesus. There is mariolatry there and the mariolatrous priests are praising that thing as a great depiction because of the Mary-**worship**.

No, these wise men fell down and worshipped Him, the Lord Jesus Christ. He alone is worthy of **worship**.

- **Luke 24:52**
    "And they **worshipped** him, and returned to Jerusalem with great joy:"

After the Lord Jesus Christ was resurrected, the disciples **worshipped** Him. The Lord Jesus Christ is **worthy** of our **worship**. He has a sevenfold **worthiness**.

- **Revelation 5:12**
  "Saying with a loud voice, **Worthy** is the Lamb that was slain to receive **power**, and **riches**, and **wisdom**, and **strength**, and **honour**, and **glory**, and **blessing**."

Trust The Saviour's Worthiness

Can you say all these things? Can you realize that in the Lord Jesus Christ, if He is your Saviour, He has all these things? He is worthy because He has all these things. He can give us great grace, great peace, great honor, great blessing and great riches in Glory. We trust that this may be your situation, that you are trusting this Saviour and His worthiness today.

Revelation
Chapter Six

Revelation 6:1

"And I saw when the Lamb opened one of the seals, and I heard, as it were the noise of thunder, one of the four beasts saying, Come and see."

We begin now the **seven seal** judgments. Then there will be **seven trumpet** judgments and **seven vial** judgments. There will be twenty-one judgments in a matter of eighty-four months or seven years of the tribulation period. That is an average of one every four months. I am glad that the genuine believers—the truly saved ones—are going to be out of here and not a part of these terrible plagues.

As John was looking at the **Lamb**, the Lord Jesus Christ, opening the first seal, he heard a **noise of thunder**. Notice that one of the **four beasts**, which we think are maybe the lead angels, cherubim, or seraphim, told John the apostle to come and see. Those words, "**Come and see**" are repeated in every one of the first four **seal** judgments, in verses one, three, five, and seven.

Come And See

Why did the angel, one of these living creatures, tell John the apostle to come and see? It was because John had to see with his own eyes this which was going to take place so that he could put upon his heart and mind for us to see what the future is going to be in this world. Every one of these things will be fulfilled.

Notice, he says he heard the noise of thunder. God uses thunder in the Old Testament and New Testament in many places.

- **Exodus 9:23**
  "And Moses stretched forth his rod toward heaven: and the LORD sent **thunder** and hail, and the fire ran along upon the ground; and the LORD rained hail upon the land of Egypt."

This is one of the plagues when the Israelites were in Egypt and in bondage. **Thunder** is certainly a shocking thing. I know all the little ones, the little children, as they are growing up, when they hear that thunder, the general question is, "Mom and Dad, what is that?" They are frightened. It is a terrible thing.

  - **1 Samuel 12:18**
    "So Samuel called unto the LORD; and the LORD sent **thunder** and rain that day: and all the people greatly feared the LORD and Samuel."

The Lord sent **thunder** and rain. They needed some rain. It was parched. When the **thunder** comes, many times the rain comes. Of course, there is also, with the **thunder**, the **lightning**. That is also a fearful thing. Of course, **lightning** when it strikes does a lot of damage.

This voice that John heard was as **thunder**. It was the Lord trying to get people's attention. It got John's attention, I am sure, as any **thunder** would get our attention, especially when you hear the crack!

Speed Of Sound And Light

I have always known that the speed of light and the speed of sound are different. The speed of sound is eleven hundred feet per second which is slow compared to the speed of light which is 186,000 miles per second. Because of this, you can always see the flash of the lightning before you hear the sound of the thunder which is a part of it. I always say this, "If you can count five seconds roughly, between the lightning and the thunder, you know the lightning is at least one mile away." I always told that to my children when they were growing up. If the thunder comes immediately right after the lightning, then you know that the dangerous lightning is very close to your location.

  - **Psalm 77:18**
    "The voice of thy **thunder** *was* in the Heaven: the lightnings lightened the world: the earth trembled and shook."

The Lord's power is in Heaven.

- Isaiah 29:6
  "Thou shalt be visited of the LORD of hosts with **thunder**, and with earthquake, and great noise, with storm and tempest, and the flame of devouring fire."

God's Thunder And Lightning

People that are atheists are naturalistic and do not believe God is in charge of the thunder and lightning, but He is. This noise that was like thunder awakened John the apostle, I am sure, as he saw this.

Revelation 6:2

"And I saw, and behold a white horse: and he that sat on him had a bow; and a crown was given unto him: and he went forth conquering, and to conquer."

The first **seal** that is opened, the first judgment, is this **white horse**. There are different colored horses—the **white horse** here, the red horse in verse 4, the black horse in verse 5 and the pale horse in verse 8.

The Bow Of War

The bow here is like a bow and arrow. It is an element of war. It is a weapon. There is also a crown. Crowns were given to kings and various others. He went forth conquering and to conquer. He was continuously conquering and a weapon for the battle was being raised here of a conquering power.

- **Genesis 48:22**
  "Moreover I have given to thee one portion above thy brethren, which I took out of the hand of the Amorite with my sword and with my **bow**."

We do not use **bows** too often for hunting, but there are some hunters that do hunt with **bow** and arrow. They have special **bows** that can aim exactly and that is what they use. They do not use guns of any kind. Of course, **bows** are also used for target practice and so on. This was a war **bow**.

- **1 Samuel 18:4**

    "And Jonathan stripped himself of the robe that *was* upon him, and gave it to David, and his garments, even to his sword, and to his **bow**, and to his girdle."

When David was fleeing from Jonathan's father, Saul, Jonathan gave him his armaments and equipment. David had his **bow**. It was for battle.

- **2 Kings 13:15**

    "And Elisha said unto him, Take **bow** and arrows. And he took unto him **bow** and arrows."

This is a weapon of war that was used to conquer. He was to smite with that **bow** so many times. He smote only three times and he should have smitten six or seven times to conquer this enemy on that many occasions.

- **1 Chronicles 12:2**

    "*They were* armed with **bows**, and could use both the right hand and the left in *hurling* stones and *shooting* arrows out of a **bow**, *even* of Saul's brethren of Benjamin."

The Benjamites were both right-handed and left-handed. They were ambidextrous, having two right hands, as it were.

- **2 Chronicles 17:17**

    "And of Benjamin; Eliada a mighty man of valour, and with him armed men with **bow** and shield two hundred thousand."

Their armaments included **bows**.

- **Psalm 7:11-12**

    "God judgeth the righteous, and God is angry *with the wicked* every day. If he turn not, he will whet his sword; he hath bent his **bow**, and made it ready."

The Lord Jesus Christ is ready with His **bow** bent, ready to shoot at the wicked and one day will take them to Hell. It is a terrible situation.

The Crown For A King

The man on the white horse also has a crown. I believe that when he finishes conquering all the different nations and rulers, he is going to crown one of them in order to be the victor in that battle. A crown is used for a king.

- **2 Samuel 1:10**

    "So I stood upon him, and slew him, because I was sure that he could not live after that he was fallen: and I took the **crown** that *was* upon his head, and the bracelet that *was* on his arm, and have brought them hither unto my lord."

Here the Amalekite lied when he was speaking about Saul out in the battlefield with his **crown**. Some of the kings went out to battle without their **crown** so they could be incognito. Otherwise, the enemy will shoot that king because he is the first leader. Of course, David punished this Amalekite because Saul was the Lord's anointed. The Amalekite should not have slain him, but Saul had begged him.

- **2 Samuel 12:30**
  "And he took their king's **crown** from off his head, the weight whereof *was* a talent of gold with the precious stones: and it was *set* on David's head. And he brought forth the spoil of the city in great abundance."

The **crown** meant that this was the ruler. I think this man on the white horse, when he went forth conquering and to conquer, had this **crown** in hand to **crown** the one who was the victor.

- **2 Kings 11:12**
  "And he brought forth the king's son, and put the **crown** upon him, and *gave him* the testimony; and they made him king, and anointed him; and they clapped their hands, and said, God save the king."

Little Joash was only seven years old. Athaliah the queen was trying to take over the kingdom and was thwarted. The **crown** is to be given to the ones that are rulers after the conquering.

Revelation 6:3

"**And when he had opened the second seal, I heard the second beast say, Come and see.**"

Here now is the **second seal**. It is the **red horse**, the horse of war. The Lord Jesus Christ is opening the **seals**. The **seals** are the judgments on this world that are meted out by the Lord Jesus Christ. The Lord Jesus Christ is the righteous Judge. God the Father has given to the Son all judgment and He will take care of it. Because He was the **Lamb** slain before the foundation of the world, He is worthy to be the Judge. He can open the **seals**. The second beast or living creature again wanted John to see and observe what was going to take place in this **second seal**. We have to observe it as well.

The Pre-Tribulation Rapture

Although the book of Revelation is gloom and doom in many places, it is real and it will take place. We must understand. That is why it is so important to me that I teach the proper picture of the rapture of genuine believers—the truly saved ones. When the Lord Jesus Christ takes us out of this world, it must be before any part of the tribulation period takes place. Otherwise, the genuine Christians would be a part of this judgment on the earth.

The Great Tribulation

This is Daniel's 70th week, as we have said before. This is the last week of the seventy weeks of seven years, or 490 years. It is not at all for the genuine believers of the church age. Genuine born-again Christians are going to escape this if they are truly saved. If you are not genuinely saved, you will be a part of this tribulation, if you are still living at that time, after the rapture takes place.

Revelation 6:4

"And there went out another horse *that was* red: and *power* was given to him that sat thereon to take peace from the earth, and that they should kill one another: and there was given unto him a great sword."

Just think, "to kill one another." We have **killing** all the time. Four women in Philadelphia were murdered at the time of this writing. In Israel there are bombs and suicide bombers. There is **killing** in Iran and Iraq.

Taking Peace From The Earth

There is going to be given to him that sat on the red horse power to take peace from the earth. We have relative peace in our country, although not in the streets of Philadelphia, New York, or Camden, where murders take place almost every day. There is not peace in those areas. There is not peace in Baghdad, where they tried to kill four Baptist pastors who tried to set up a church.

This **second seal** judgment is the **judgment of war**.

- **Psalm 46:9-10a**
  "He maketh **wars** to cease unto the end of the earth; he breaketh the bow, and cutteth the spear in sunder; he burneth the chariot in the fire. Be still, and know that I *am* God;"

One day the Lord Jesus Christ will make **wars** to cease. That will take place during the millennial reign of the Lord Jesus Christ.

- **Luke 21:9**
  "But when ye shall hear of **wars** and commotions, be not terrified: for these things must first come to pass; but the end *is* not by and by."

War is a part of the **judgments** during this tribulation.

There have been many **wars** in the history of our world. Here are just a few of them:

1. **Revolutionary War—1775**
2. **Quasi War—1798**
3. **Barbary Wars—1801**
4. **War of 1812**
5. **Slave Trade Patrols—1820**
6. **Anti-Piracy Patrols—1822**
7. **Indian Wars—1835**
8. **Mexican War—1846**
9. **Civil War—1861**
10. **Spanish American War—1898**
11. **Philippine Insurrection—1899**
12. **China Relief Boxer Rebellion—1900**
13. **Latin American Campaigns—1906**
14. **World War I—1917**
15. **Yangtze Service—1926**
16. **China Service—1937**
17. **World War II—1941**
18. **Korean Conflict—1950**
19. **Vietnam Service—1962**
20. **Desert Shield—1991**
21. **Kosovo Conflict—1999**
22. **Global War on Terrorism—2001**
23. **And many, many more wars**

One Day Peace Will Come

Now there is the war in Afghanistan, Iraq, and many other places that continue to multiply. It goes on and on, but one day, there is going to be a war of all wars, and peace will be taken from the earth. It is a terrible thing when peace is gone, taken away from the earth completely. When the Prince of Peace is gone and when the genuine believers in the Lord Jesus Christ are raptured and pulled out of this world, peace will be taken from the earth. This is the second seal judgment of war.

- **Psalm 119:165**
  "Great **peace** have they which love thy law: and nothing shall offend them."

There is no **peace**. People have rejected the law of the Lord. They have rejected the Lord Jesus Christ, the Prince of **Peace**. **Peace** will be taken from off this earth.

Peace Defined

The word peace is an interesting word. In the genuine Christian faith, it has been defined as follows: *peace is the tranquil state of the soul assured of its salvation through the Lord Jesus Christ and, so fearing nothing from God and content with its earthly lot, of whatsoever sort it is.* That is God's peace, but peace will be taken from the earth.

- **John 14:27**
  "Peace I leave with you, my **peace** I give unto you: not as the world giveth, give I unto you. Let not your heart be troubled, neither let it be afraid."

Get Saved Before The Tribulation

The peace that the Lord Jesus Christ has offered will no longer be open for reception. During the tribulation period, there will be some who will be genuinely saved, but those that have had an opportunity to accept the peace of the Lord Jesus Christ and have rejected Him, according to 2 Thessalonians 2:12, many feel that they will not have any further opportunity to be genuinely saved. Among those that have never heard, certainly there are going to be some that will be genuinely saved during that tribulation period, but they must go through the Prince of Peace. Peace will be taken from the earth.

- **2 Thessalonians 2:12**
  "That they all might be damned who believed not the truth, but had pleasure in unrighteousness."

- **Romans 5:1**
  "Therefore being justified by faith, we have **peace** with God through our Lord Jesus Christ:"

We who are truly born-again have **peace**. The only way to make **peace** with God the Father who is at war with us as sinners, is through the Lord Jesus Christ. We are justified, declared righteous in God's eyes by the Lord Jesus Christ and what He did for us at the cross of Calvary. **Peace** taken from the earth means that the **peace** of the Lord Jesus Christ is gone from the world. It is a terrible thing. There will be war, not **peace**.

Secret Cold Wars

One definition of peace is *the absence of war.* Many times there is no peace but there is no war either. There is what is called a "cold war." We suffered through that just before World War II and a little after. There are secret wars. Cold war involves espionage and taking secrets from different countries and then infiltration. That is, of course, a terrible thing. Rome fell from within, not from without. Nobody conquered Rome, but it was from within. That is the way the United States of America, if and when it falls, will fall not from without but from within.

- **Colossians 1:20**
  "And, having made **peace** through the blood of his cross, by him to reconcile all things unto himself; by him, *I say,* whether *they be* things in earth, or things in Heaven."

This is speaking of the Lord Jesus Christ and the **peace** by the blood of His cross. There is the way that God can make **peace** with sinners such as we are, through the cross of the Lord Jesus Christ. He suffered for us, bled, and died in our place.

No Peace During The Tribulation

During the tribulation, peace will be taken from the earth. There will be war and they are going to kill one another. There is a great sword with which to do this. A great sword is a weapon of war, whatever that might be. Whether it is the literal sword or a weapon different than the sword, either way it is understandable.

Revelation 6:5

"And when he had opened the third seal, I heard the third beast say, Come and see. And I beheld, and lo a black horse; and he that sat on him had a pair of balances in his hand."

Here is the **third seal**. It is the **black horse of famine**. We will take up the subject of **famine** in detail a little bit later as we come to the fourth seal in verse 8. Why do I say this is **famine** in verses 5 and 6? It is **famine** because he has some **balances** in his hand and we will see in the next verse what happens to those **balances**.

Balances are to weigh out things. When we go to the store for meat or cheese, or whatever it is, we might say, "Give me half a pound of this" or, "Give me a quarter of a pound of this." The store clerk then puts it on the scale and weighs it. The **balances** show that there will be very, very high prices for very little food.

- **Leviticus 19:36**
  "Just **balances**, just weights, a just ephah, and a just hin, shall ye have: I *am* the LORD your God, which brought you out of the land of Egypt."

Israel, according to the law, and even we today, should have just **balances**. We should have **balances** that actually add up. An ounce is an ounce, not a little half an ounce. That is why we have the standard of **weights** and measures in Washington, D.C. I do not know whether it is kept up as it should be, but I would take it that it would be. God wants us to be just.

- **Proverbs 11:1**
  "A false balance *is* abomination to the LORD: but a just **weight** *is* his delight."

We have to have just **balances** and not false.

- **Proverbs 16:11**
  "A just **weight** and **balance** *are* the LORD'S: all the **weights** of the bag *are* his work."

Even Little Things Are Important

Even the little thing of how much things weigh is a work of God. He is interested in justice in weights and measures.

- **Proverbs 20:23**
  "Divers **weights** *are* an abomination unto the LORD; and a false **balance** *is* not good."
- **Daniel 5:27**
  "TEKEL; Thou art weighed in the **balances, and art found wanting.**"

This was at the feast of Belshazzar when they were all drunk and the handwriting was on the wall. They were all amazed and their knees were knocking together. One of the things on the wall was "TEKEL." The weights of things, whether they are good or bad, show up.

- **Matthew 24:7**
  "For nation shall rise against nation, and kingdom against kingdom: and there shall be **famines**, and pestilences, and earthquakes, in divers places."

Famines Were Predicted By The Lord

The famines are predicted by the Lord Jesus Christ. The Lord Jesus Christ wrote the Bible—the Old Testament Hebrew and Aramaic Words as well as the New Testament Greek Words. He is the Author—the Originator of the Words of Scripture. The Holy Spirit gave those Words to the writers and the writers wrote them down. The Lord Jesus Christ knew about famines. They were predicted by Him in Matthew 24 and other places.

- **Romans 8:35**
  "Who shall separate us from the love of Christ? *shall* tribulation, or distress, or persecution, or **famine**, or nakedness, or peril, or sword?"

Nothing Separates Us From Christ

Nothing can separate us from the love of Christ. Famine is one of these things that has come upon this earth and will come upon them, as well.

Revelation 6:6

"And I heard a voice in the midst of the four beasts say, A measure of wheat for a penny, and three measures of barley for a penny; and *see* thou hurt not the oil and the wine."

The Famine Seal

Here in this third seal, the famine seal, you get the famine because of what is said in verse 6. A measure (CHOINIX) is a dry measure. It contains a little bit less than a quart. A penny (DENARION) means containing ten. It is a Roman coin used in the New Testament. It has a certain number of grains of silver in it. It was the principal silver coin of the Roman Empire and from the parable of the labourers in the vineyard, it would seem that a denarius was then the ordinary pay for a day's wages. It was a whole day's wages for one penny.

- **Matthew 20:2**
  "And when he had agreed with the labourers for a **penny** a day, he sent them into his vineyard."

You will remember at the first hour the man said, "Will you work for me for a **penny**?" The labourer said, "Yes, I will." At the sixth hour, somebody said, "Will you work for me for a **penny**?" Then at the eleventh hour, "Will you work for me for a **penny**?" When everybody got a penny, the people that started the first hour complained, "Wait a minute! We worked the whole day for a **penny**." Then the man said, "I contracted with you for a **penny**. I have every right to do that. You agreed to me." A penny was a whole day's wages.

Can you imagine a whole day's wages, whatever you make per day whether it is $50, $60, $100, or $200, that you would only get less than a quart of food for that whole day's pay? If you have a family, how are you going to feed them with that much **wheat**? **Barley** perhaps is a little cheaper–a whole day's wages for less than three quarts of barley. **Barley** and **wheat** are good, but there is poverty because they do not have the money and they do not have the ability to get the money. There is going to be **famine** because things are going to be scarce. Of course, that is what makes **famine**– when the food is not there and the money is not there. How many people would give a whole day's wages for less than a quart of **wheat** or for less than three quarts of **barley**?

Don't Hurt The Oil And Wine

The last part of this verse, "*see* thou hurt not the oil and wine," is, perhaps, a reference to those that are well-to-do, those that are rich, those that have plenty of money and those that do not need to worry about a penny. They have plenty of pennies. If it takes one day's wages for a quart of wheat and three measures of barley for another penny, they have ten or fifteen pennies. They are not going to be hurt. The oil and the wine—the rich people—will not be hurt, but the poor people definitely will be hurting at this time. I will talk a little bit more about famine when we come to verse 8, but I wanted to at least open it up here.

Revelation 6:7

"And when he had opened the fourth seal, I heard the voice of the fourth beast say, Come and see."

Pestilence and death are the fourth seal judgment upon this earth during the seven-year tribulation period. Again, there are the same words to John the apostle, "Come and see." When the Lamb opened this fourth seal, the fourth beast said, "John, I want you to come. I want you to see what will happen to this earth."

I'm Glad The Saved Will Be Raptured

John was able to come and to observe and he has written this down so that people would know what is going to befall them in the latter days and times. It is important to know that these things will not come to pass partially. They will be coming to pass in full. That is why, as I have said, I am glad that I will not be there during that time of those seven years of the tribulation and undergo the seven seal judgments, the seven trumpet judgments, and the seven vial judgments.

Revelation 6:8

"And I looked, and behold a pale horse: and his name that sat on him was Death, and Hell followed with him. And power was given unto them over the fourth part of the earth, to kill with sword, and with hunger, and with death, and with the beasts of the earth."

Here is the terrible **fourth seal**, the **pale horse** of **pestilence** and **death**. Notice that "**Hell followed with him.**" **Hell** is **Hades**. The spirits and souls of those that are lost go into **Hell**, to **Hades**, even during this time. One in four will meet **death**.

What does that amount to? What is the world's population. At the time of this writing, it is 6.9 billion people–almost 7 billion people.

Billions Of People To Die

What would one fourth of that be? It would be about 1.7 billion people that would be dead. What if the Lord Jesus Christ does not return immediately and we have more population? For instance, if we would go to 2050 (which I do not see how we could go that long before the Lord Jesus Christ comes) they are predicting not 6.9 billion people, but 9 billion people. What would a fourth of that be? That would be 2.2 billion people who would be *immediately* dead. There is no question about it. It will be instantaneous death by these different means that are listed here. Over 90% of population growth takes place in developing countries, we are told, many of which have serious social, economic, and environmental problems. They are going to be killed by this fourth plague. Notice how they are going to be killed. There is the sword. We know what that would be. Then hunger and famine, which is a terrible way to die. They say that bellies swell up, and all kinds of things take place. Famine and hunger occurred in the Old Testament.

- **Jeremiah 14:12**

   "When they fast, I will not hear their cry; and when they offer burnt offering and an oblation, I will not accept them: but I will consume them by the sword, and by the **famine**, and by the pestilence."

Here was apostate Israel that had turned from the law of God, turned from the Lord of Heaven and earth and the Saviour that one day would come. I believe that during the tribulation period the basic people that will be judged will be the people of Israel. They have rejected the Saviour. Daniel's 70th week is upon "thy people" as it says in Daniel 9. God will consume them, not only by the **sword** but also by the **famine** and the pestilence.

- **Jeremiah 21:9**
  "He that abideth in this city <u>shall die by the **sword**</u>, and by the famine, and by the pestilence: but he that goeth out, and falleth to the Chaldeans that besiege you, he shall live, and his life shall be unto him for a prey."

Cannibalism Prevailed In Jerusalem

This is when the Babylonians were encircling Jerusalem. God predicted death by the famine and the pestilence. In fact, one of the things that took place during the Babylonian surrounding of Jerusalem, during the siege before they took over, was that the women would kill their own babies and eat them. It was a terrible thing. There was cannibalism at the time when Babylon was surrounding Jerusalem, before they took them over to Babylon as captives. This was predicted and it was true.

- **Jeremiah 24:10**
  "And <u>I will send the **sword**, the **famine**</u>, and the pestilence, among them, till they be consumed from off the land that I gave unto them and to their fathers."

<u>God's judgments of the **famine** and the **sword** are in His hands.</u> You may say, "Is not that a terrible God that would bring the **sword** and the **famine** to people?" Well, that is part of His judgment. The Devil does this all the time for no reason.

The Lord's Punishments Vary

<u>The Lord sometimes punishes by famine and by sword.</u> <u>These are punishments from the Lord Jesus Christ. We must never try to judge or question His integrity, His honesty, and His equality of judgment.</u> He is not unequal in His judgments, but He knows what He is doing. Otherwise, how could He send the lost world to Hell? How could He send them to the lake of fire? He is just in His judgments and He is gracious. He has given opportunity to every one of these in this tribulation period, to every one of them before this comes upon them. He has extended the gospel to them by radio, by Internet, by preachers, by churches, and by many other means.

They could come unto the Lord Jesus Christ, and they could be genuinely saved. They do not have to endure this tribulation period. That is why we have to get the Words of God out to the world, so that people do not end up in this lost state.

Then He says, "**I will kill one fourth of the earth.**" <u>One of every four persons will die with the **sword**, with **hunger**, with **all kinds of death**.</u> There might atomic radiation. There could be all kinds of things.

Then there are the **beasts of the earth.** You might say, "Do **beasts** eat people?" Ferocious **beasts slay** people.

- **1 Samuel 17:46**

    "This day will the LORD deliver thee into mine hand; and I will smite thee, and take thine head from thee; and I will give the carcases of the host of the Philistines this day unto the fowls of the air, and to the wild **beasts** of the earth; that all the earth may know that there is a God in Israel."

This was when David confronted Goliath. The **beasts** certainly do devour people.

I remember on that same television program about lions, there was a big buffalo that was being killed. Once that buffalo went down, that was the end. Then there were other animals that came. Big elephants came to this water hole. Here were the **tigers** eating the buffalo, but those elephants frightened them away because they wanted the water. Then after the elephants left that particular kill, the tigers came back. Then twenty-five or thirty vultures just pounced on the carcass. It was a terrible thing.

The **beasts** of the earth will **slay.** As we know, later on in the book of Revelation we are going to see that the **fowls** of the air and the beasts of the earth will come at the Battle of Armageddon and they will eat the flesh of all those that will be **slain** by the Lord Jesus Christ when He returns.

- **Jeremiah 19:7**

    "And I will make void the counsel of Judah and Jerusalem in this place; and I will cause them to fall by the **sword** before their enemies, and by the hands of them that seek their lives: and their carcases will I give to be meat for the **fowls** of the Heaven, and for the **beasts** of the earth."

People today talk about getting rid of the **beasts** of the earth, for instance **foxes.** The animal protection league does not want them to be killed, but the **foxes** have been eating chickens and different things. They talk about killing some of the **bears** because there are too many of them around eating different things. These carnivorous **beasts** still eat, and they will continue to eat, but in that day God will cause the evil beasts to consume the people. **One fourth** of the people on earth will be killed. Part of them will be killed by **beasts**.

- **Ezekiel 5:17**
  "So will I send upon you **famine** and evil **beasts**, and they shall bereave thee; and pestilence and blood shall pass through thee; and I will bring the **sword** upon thee. I the LORD have spoken *it*."

A Few To Babylon At A Time

You know, that is one of the reasons that God did not take away all of the people of Israel from the land at first. You will remember that the Lord took away the two tribes of Judah, the southern two tribes, into Babylon. He did not take them all at once, lest the beasts would come in and take over the land. He waited because when people are there, apparently the beasts do not come in as much.

I said I would talk a little bit about **famine**. One of the things that will kill a **fourth part** of the earth (one in four meet **death**) is **famine** or **hunger**. There are three instances that I would like to mention to you.

1. Irish famine, 1845—1850. More than a million people in Ireland died, starved to death, while massive quantities of food were being exported from their country. They gave it to others. They were almost forced to give the food and they died. One million plus is many people dying. There was disease—typhus, scurvy, and dysentery—because of the **famine** and **hunger** at that time in Ireland. It was called the potato **famine**. Potatoes contain nutrients, carbohydrates, and vitamin C, which are necessary for a healthy diet.

2. Ukrainian famine, 1932—1933. There were six to seven million dead in that **famine**. It was a **famine** that engulfed the Ukraine, the northern Caucusus, and the lower Volga River. It was a result of Joseph Stalin's policy of forced collectivization. Stalin was determined to crush all vestiges of Ukrainian nationalism. They were going to rise up and be free, which is what they deserved to be. Stalin said, "No. We want to make you under our system." According to a Soviet author, "Before they died, people often lost their senses and ceased to be human beings." One of Stalin's lieutenants in the Ukraine stated in 1933 that the famine was a great success. It showed the peasants "who is the master here. It costs millions of lives but the collective farm system is here to stay."

3. Sudan famine, July 1998. Sudan is one of the largest African countries. In that **famine,** 2.6 million people were at risk of starvation out of a population of 25 million. In Africa, there was civil war. There were all kinds of things that were taking place.

Different ones have used **famine** throughout the world in different places and areas, but the Lord Jesus Christ is going to use this as one of the means of taking the lives of one out of four, meeting death, there in this **fourth seal** of **famine** and pestilence.

Death And Hell

Notice, he that sat upon that horse "was Death, and Hell followed with him." When those that are without the Lord Jesus Christ die, Hell follows after. There is no let-up there. After death, comes Hell. Right now, when a person has never genuinely trusted the Lord Jesus Christ as Saviour and Redeemer, spirit and soul go immediately to Hades or Hell and he is in conscious torment. Unsaved people do not go to Purgatory. Roman Catholicism says there is an intermediate limbo, an in between things. Purgatory is not there. It is direct. Following Death, Hell was there and power was given unto them over the fourth part of the earth.

We do not want anybody to be killed. That is not our desire, but this is in the Lord Jesus Christ's hands. He has determined that He will have a judgment upon this earth. In fact, there will be twenty-one different judgments. There are the seven seal judgments, seven trumpet judgments, and seven vial judgments upon the earth. I would hope that people who are in this world who are lost, would read the words of Revelation. This is the reason for the Revelation, that people would read and he that hath ears to hear, let him hear what the Spirit saith to the churches. If people could read what is to befall this earth when the Lord Jesus Christ takes His people Home, they may come to the Lord Jesus Christ and be genuinely saved. That is what they should do, that they would not be one of these that are taken in **death.**

Many people on television say, "Well, this man was near **death** but he came back from **death** and he has this story to tell." He will say, "I heard beautiful music. I saw wonderful light and I came back. Everything is fine and peachy." This is Satan's mirage and lies in order to make people think that there is no fear in **death** and that no **Hell** follows

death for those that are lost and have never genuinely trusted the Lord Jesus Christ as Saviour. There is fear in **death**. Believe me, you had better fear **death** if you are lost, if you have never been truly saved by genuine faith in the Lord Jesus Christ and you are not really born-again, but to the genuine believers, there is no fear in **death**.

- **Hebrews 2:15**
  "And deliver them who through fear of **death** were all their lifetime subject to bondage."

Christ Broke The Fear Of Death

The Lord Jesus Christ has broken that fear of death. You may have fear of dying, the process, even if you are genuinely saved. The pain is there. God is able through His grace to overcome that pain. He is able to take care of that. Some of you may not have the suffering of pain. I hope that is the case. Some people go immediately, whether by heart attack or whatever. Some go after a long illness. Whatever it is, if you are genuinely saved and born-again, you ask God to give you dying grace. There is living grace and there is dying grace. There is grace to take care of whatever the need.

My wife's father **died** instantly. He was out doing the lawn work, as he always did, in Florida. He was out there in his lawn and just keeled over. The neighbor said he saw him there. He had just got off his tractor and he had a smile on his face. Dad Sanborn knew the Lord Jesus Christ as Saviour. He was ready to go. He was willing to go and join Mom Sanborn, his wife, who had **died** eight weeks earlier. That was quick. It was apparently a heart attack. He had a heart problem. There was no long suffering. His wife, my wife's mother, had a longer illness. She was in the hospital and different things.

We have to be praising the Lord that He can be our "no fear in **death**." People that are lost must be told that when **death** comes, **Hell** comes next. We have a gospel and we have the peace of the Lord Jesus Christ that we can give to people.

- **Romans 5:1**
  "Therefore being justified by faith, we have peace with God through our Lord Jesus Christ:"

We who are genuinely saved will never come into these terrible judgments upon this earth.

Revelation 6:9

"And when he had opened the fifth seal, I saw under the altar the souls of them that were slain for the word of God, and for the testimony which they held:"

There are seven **seal** judgments. We have talked about the first four seals.

1. The white horse, or conquering power. Some have called him "the great faker," which is true. He is a counterfeit judge.

2. The red horse, the peace taker. Peace is taken from the earth.

3. The black horse, famine. The unemployed baker, someone has said.

4. The pale horse, pestilence, and death. The overworked undertaker.

These are the four horsemen. We are now going to talk about the **fifth** and sixth seals. The **fifth seal** is souls under the altar. The sixth seal is physical changes in the earth and sky. The seventh **seal** will not be until chapter 8. Chapter 7 is parenthesis between the sixth and the seventh **seals**.

Opening The Fifth Seal

Here, the Lord Jesus Christ, the Lamb, is opening this fifth seal. Notice why the souls under the altar were slain, *"for the word of God."* They stood for the Words of God and that is why they were slain. The verse says, "under the altar." That indicates that there is an altar in Heaven.

- **Revelation 11:1**
  "And there was given me a reed like unto a rod: and the angel stood, saying, Rise, and measure the temple of God, and the **altar**, and them that worship therein."
- **Revelation 11:19**
  "And the temple of God was opened in Heaven, and there was seen in his temple the **ark** of his testament: and there were lightnings, and voices, and thunderings, and an earthquake, and great hail."
- **Exodus 25:40**
  "And look that thou make them after their **pattern**, which was shewed thee in the mount."

This was God's instruction to Moses when he built the tabernacle. The **pattern** on earth was like the original, genuine **pattern** in Heaven. I believe the holy of holies is there. I believe the mercy seat is there. Everything in the tabernacle here is up there in Heaven, including the altar. The souls under the **altar** were the martyrs that were **slain**. They were in Heaven.

- **Genesis 4:8**
  "And Cain talked with Abel his brother: and it came to pass, when they were in the field, that Cain rose up against Abel his brother, and **slew** him."

The first martyr was Abel. He was the first **slain** in Scripture.

- **Acts 22:20**
  "And when the blood of thy martyr Stephen was shed, I also was standing by, and consenting unto his **death**, and kept the raiment of them that **slew** him."

Stephen was a martyr in the New Testament, **slain** for his testimony.

- **Revelation 2:13**
  "I know thy works, and where thou dwellest, *even* where Satan's seat *is*: and thou holdest fast my name, and hast not denied my faith, even in those days wherein Antipas *was* my faithful martyr, who was **slain** among you, where Satan dwelleth."

The **fifth seal** judgment in Revelation seems to be that the people would be **slain**. One of the possible reasons they were **slain** is that the earth perhaps was very angry against the Lord Jesus Christ because they had been judged in the first four seal judgments. Just think, twenty-five percent of the earth **slain** by **famine**, by earthquake, and by fire. Who knows, maybe an atomic radiation bomb. They were angry, and possibly because of that, they turned on the genuine Christians and slew them during the seven-year time of tribulation.

- **Revelation 13:15**
  "And he had power to give life unto the image of the beast, that the image of the beast should both speak, and cause that as many as would not worship the image of the beast should be **killed**."

Death In The Tribulation

Those who will not worship this antichrist, this beast, in the seven-year tribulation period, will be killed.

I say again, the genuine believers, the saved ones, are not going to be here during that time. If you are truly born-again and saved by genuine faith in the Lord Jesus Christ, you will be gone. You will be taken up in the rapture before any part of that tribulation. If you are here during that seven years, if you have rejected Christ as your Saviour, and are still living, you will have to go through the tribulation. The false prophet will cause as many as do not worship the image of the beast (who is probably the antichrist himself, the actual political ruler), should be **killed**. There are going to be more martyrs under the altar because of this.

- **Revelation 16:6**
  "For they have shed the **blood** of saints and prophets, and thou hast given them **blood** to drink; for they are worthy."

Death–The Seed Of The Church

The blood of the genuine saints and the martyrs is sometimes called the seed of the church. In the early Christian days there were many martyrs that were slain because of their good testimonies.

- **Revelation 18:24**
  "And in her was found the **blood** of prophets, and of saints, and of all that were **slain** upon the earth."

Slaughter By False Religionists

This talks about Babylon's false religionists and the "Great Whore," which is probably the Roman Catholic Church, apostate Protestant churches, and all the different world religions. There is going to be a slaughter. Not a particularly indiscriminate slaughter, but of the genuine believers, the ones who are truly saved during that tribulation and come to the Lord Jesus Christ.

- **Revelation 20:4**
  "And I saw thrones, and they sat upon them, and judgment was given unto them: and *I saw* the souls of them that were **beheaded** for the witness of Jesus, and for the word of God, and which had not worshipped the beast, neither his image, neither had received *his* mark upon their foreheads, or in their hands; and they lived and reigned with Christ a thousand years."

Notice the reason they are **slain**. It is because they witnessed for the Lord Jesus Christ and the Words of God. They are going to be **slain** because of their stand for the Words of God and for the testimony that they hold.

- **Revelation 1:9**
  "I John, who also am your brother, and companion in tribulation, and in the kingdom and patience of Jesus Christ, was in the isle that is called Patmos, for the word of God, and for the **testimony** of Jesus Christ."

Why was John banished? It was because of **the Words of God**, and standing **for the Words of God**, and the **testimony** of the Lord Jesus Christ.

- **1 Peter 4:16**
  "Yet if *any man suffer* as a Christian, let him not be ashamed; but let him glorify God on this behalf."

There is going to be suffering. Make sure that the suffering and **testimony** is because of our love for the Lord Jesus Christ and for His **Words**. We stand for the King James Bible in English and the Hebrew, Aramaic, and Greek Words that underlie it. I believe these are the **Words of God**, which have been preserved for us. There is great criticism, even among fundamental fellow believers, because we stand for these things.

Revelation 6:10

"**And they cried with a loud voice, saying, How long, O Lord, holy and true, dost thou not judge and avenge our blood on them that dwell on the earth?**"

The Cry Of The Slain Martyrs

Here are the people who are martyrs. Those that were slain cry out continuously. This is in the imperfect tense—continuous past action. They were continually crying out with a loud voice. They wanted judgment to fall on those that slew them. That is a normal reaction. The Lord Jesus Christ is a Judge, but He is also a God of mercy. He is waiting. How long? Not yet. It is not yet time. God is merciful. He is waiting before this slaughter takes place.

- **Exodus 34:6-7**
  "And the LORD passed by before him, and proclaimed, The LORD, The LORD God, merciful and gracious, longsuffering, and abundant in goodness and **truth**, Keeping mercy for thousands, forgiving iniquity and transgression and sin, and that will by no means clear *the guilty*; visiting the iniquity of the fathers upon the children, and upon the children's children, unto the third and to the fourth *generation*."

God is going to judge, but He is patient and **merciful** before He does. We wonder why He waited so long to judge Sodom and Gomorrah, but He waited. Finally, He judged. It was the same way with the flood.

- **Psalm 103:8**

  "The LORD *is* **merciful** and **gracious**, slow to anger, and plenteous in mercy."

These souls cried out, "**How long before thou dost avenge us?**" He is waiting.

- **Jonah 4:2**

  "And he prayed unto the LORD, and said, I pray thee, O LORD, *was* not this my saying, when I was yet in my country? Therefore I fled before unto Tarshish: for I knew that thou *art* a **gracious** God, and **merciful**, slow to anger, and of great kindness, and repentest thee of the evil."

Jonah was escaping the judgment that he was told to proclaim against Nineveh. Jonah did not want to go to Nineveh to proclaim the judgment. He was disobedient, but he said, "Lord, you are **gracious**." He is **gracious**.

- **2 Peter 3:9**

  "The Lord is not slack concerning his promise, as some men count slackness; but is **longsuffering** to us-ward, not willing that any should perish, but that all should come to repentance."

Before the Lord Jesus Christ comes in the rapture, and the tribulation begins, He wants all the sinners to come to repentance and be saved by faith. This is His **longsuffering**. This is why He waited and did not judge immediately those that had slain these genuine Christians under the altar.

- **Deuteronomy 32:43**

  "Rejoice, O ye nations, *with* his people: for he will **avenge the blood** of his servants, and will render **vengeance** to his adversaries, and will be **merciful** unto his land, *and* to his people."

He will **avenge**, but not now. He is not yet ready. God will **avenge** those that do wrong. There is going to be judgment. These souls cried out, "Why not do it immediately?"

- **2 Kings 9:7**

  "And thou shalt smite the house of Ahab thy master, that I may **avenge the blood** of my servants the prophets, and the **blood** of all the servants of the LORD, at the hand of Jezebel."

Jezebel slew many servants, the prophets of God. God said He was going to send Jehu to **avenge** them. The souls under the altar say, "When will

you judge and **avenge** our **blood** upon them that dwell on the earth?"
God is the Judge.

- **Genesis 18:25**
  "That be far from thee to do after this manner, to slay the
  righteous with the wicked: and that the **righteous** should be as
  the wicked, that be far from thee: Shall not the Judge of all the
  earth do right?"

Abraham pled for Sodom and Gomorrah, "If you find fifty **righteous**,
forty, thirty, right down to ten **righteous**, wilt Thou not spare?" The
Lord said He would spare the city if He found ten righteous. God the
Father is Judge. The Lord Jesus Christ is the Judge also. He is going to
be judging the believers.

- **2 Corinthians 5:10**
  "For we must all appear before the judgment seat of Christ; that
  every one may receive the things *done* in *his* body, according to
  that he hath done, whether *it be* good or bad."

He is going to judge the lost as well.

- **Revelation 20:11**
  "And I saw a great white throne, and him that sat on it, from
  whose face the earth and the Heaven fled away; and there was
  found no place for them."

The Lord Jesus Christ will be the Judge of all the unsaved and they
will be thrown into the lake of fire.

Those souls that were slain ask the Lord, "Why was not **vengeance**
made immediately?"

Revelation 6:11

**"And white robes were given unto every one of them;
and it was said unto them, that they should rest yet for a
little season, until their fellowservants also and their
brethren, that should be killed as they *were*, should be
fulfilled."**

The Lord Jesus Christ just simply said to these martyrs, "Wait a
while." There are others that are coming. More are going to be killed in
this tribulation time. Then, judgment will be poured out.

White robes were given unto them, to every one of these that are
genuinely saved. The **white robes** are mentioned repeatedly in the book
of Revelation.

- **Revelation 3:4**
"Thou hast a few names even in Sardis which have not defiled their garments; and they shall walk with me in **white**: for they are worthy."
- **Revelation 3:5**
"He that overcometh, the same shall be clothed in **white** raiment; and I will not blot out his name out of the book of life, but I will confess his name before my Father, and before his angels."
- **Revelation 3:18**
"I counsel thee to buy of me gold tried in the fire, that thou mayest be rich; and **white** raiment, that thou mayest be clothed, and *that* the shame of thy nakedness do not appear; and anoint thine eyes with eyesalve, that thou mayest see."

The Laodicean church needed **white** raiment.

- **Revelation 4:4**
"And round about the throne *were* four and twenty seats: and upon the seats I saw four and twenty elders sitting, clothed in **white raiment**; and they had on their heads crowns of gold."

I believe the twenty-four elders are representatives of the true church, the genuine believers—the saved ones. They are clothed in **white** and sitting around the throne.

- **Revelation 7:9**
"After this I beheld, and, lo, a great multitude, which no man could number, of all nations, and kindreds, and people, and tongues, stood before the throne, and before the Lamb, clothed with **white robes**, and palms in their hands;"

The picture of **white** is the picture of purity. Because they are genuinely saved and redeemed, they have **white robes**.

- **Revelation 7:13**
"And one of the elders answered, saying unto me, What are these which are arrayed in **white robes**? and whence came they?"

White Robes In Glory

God clothes the people that are in Glory in white robes. What is that a picture of? It is a picture of holiness, purity, and righteousness. Those that are genuinely saved and are in Heaven have absolute purity and righteousness.

- **Genesis 15:6**
  "And he believed in the LORD; and he counted it to him for **righteousness**."

This talks about Abraham, the father of the faith. Abraham believed in the Lord and He counted it to him for **righteousness**. Genuine faith is equal to **righteousness**. In the Old Testament, Abraham found it. That is why it says in the New Testament that he is the father of the faithful. Those that have genuine faith, as Abraham, can also have **righteousness**.

- **Romans 3:22**
  "Even the **righteousness** of God *which is* by faith of Jesus Christ unto all and upon all them that believe: for there is no difference:"

Notice, the **righteousness** is offered *unto* all, but it is *upon* only those that genuinely believe.

- **Romans 4:5**
  "But to him that worketh not, but believeth on him that justifieth the ungodly, his faith is counted for **righteousness**."

This is a tremendously important gospel verse. We are not saved by works. That is where the **white robes** come. The whiteness is the **purity** of God's **righteousness**. How did this all happen, that by genuine faith in the Lord Jesus Christ we could be **righteous**?

- **2 Corinthians 5:21**
  "For he hath made him *to be* sin for us, who knew no sin; that we might be made the **righteousness** of God in him."

God the Father has made the Lord Jesus Christ to be sin for us. A perfect, sinless Saviour, the Lord Jesus Christ died so that sinners could be genuinely saved, have everlasting life, and be made **righteous**.

Resting A While In Glory

Notice also, in Revelation 6:11 it says that every one of them should rest for a little while until their fellowservants and their brethren should be killed. There are going to be more martyrs that will be coming, but these are going to be resting for a while. It is wonderful that in Glory there is going to be rest. We are going to serve the Lord, but there is also going to be rest.

- **Genesis 8:9**
  "But the dove found no **rest** for the sole of her foot, and she returned unto him into the ark, for the waters *were* on the face of the whole earth: then he put forth his hand, and took her, and pulled her in unto him into the ark."

This is one of the first times that the word **rest** is found in Scripture.

- **Psalm 37:7**
  "**Rest** in the LORD, and wait patiently for him: fret not thyself because of him who prospereth in his way, because of the man who bringeth wicked devices to pass."

The souls under the altar had **rest**.

- **Isaiah 57:20-21**
  "But the wicked *are* like the troubled sea, when it cannot **rest**, whose waters cast up mire and dirt. *There is* no peace, saith my God, to the wicked."

The wicked do not have any **rest**. The waves of the sea just keep pounding and pounding.

- **Matthew 11:28-29**
  "Come unto me, all *ye* that labour and are heavy laden, and I will give you **rest**. Take my yoke upon you, and learn of me; for I am meek and lowly in heart: and ye shall find **rest** unto your souls."

The Lord Jesus Christ says this to all. The Jews rejected Him, so He turned to all of us. The gospel is for all, not just simply for some group of "the elect," but for anyone who labors. They can come unto Him and He will give them the **rest** of salvation. Put genuine trust in the Lord Jesus Christ and be truly saved. Then there is the **rest** of service, *Take my yoke upon you.* Serve the Lord and ye shall find **rest** unto your souls.

- **Revelation 4:8**
  "And the four beasts had each of them six wings about *him*; and *they were* full of eyes within: and they **rest** not day and night, saying, Holy, holy, holy, Lord God Almighty, which was, and is, and is to come."

The Four Beasts Praise The Lord

Talking about rest, the four beasts or living creatures, (which I believe are cherubim or seraphim), *"rest not day and night."* Why do they not rest? The Lord does not rest. The genuine believers are going to rest. The living creatures do not rest day and night. What are they doing? They are saying,

"Holy, holy, holy, Lord God Almighty, which was, and is, and is to come." They do not rest because they praise the Lord. This word for rest (ANAPAUSIS) means, *"to cause or to permit one to cease from any movement or labor in order to recover and collect his strength."*

<u>It is wonderful that in Glory there is going to be rest.</u> We have a little bit of rest every day. Some of us get eight hours, some seven, some six, some less, some more. In Glory in Heaven, there is going to be rest from our labors.

Revelation 6:12

"And I beheld when he had opened the sixth seal, and, lo, there was a great earthquake; and the sun became black as sackcloth of hair, and the moon became as blood;"

Here is the **sixth seal**. There are physical changes on the earth and in the sky. John beheld the Lord Jesus Christ opening this **sixth seal** of judgment. First of all, there was a **great earthquake**. That word *earthquake* is only mentioned sixteen times in the King James Bible.

- **1 Kings 19:11**
  "And he said, Go forth, and stand upon the mount before the LORD. And, behold, the LORD passed by, and a great and strong wind rent the mountains, and brake in pieces the rocks before the LORD; *but* the LORD *was* not in the wind: and after the wind an **earthquake**; *but* the LORD was *not* in the **earthquake**:"

The Lord was talking to Elijah. This is one of the first references to the **earthquake**, to show who was the Lord. He **shook** the earth. The Lord is able to **shake** the earth. He will **shake** the earth in this sixth seal judgment.

- **Matthew 24:7**
  "For nation shall rise against nation, and kingdom against kingdom: and there shall be famines, and pestilences, and **earthquakes**, in divers places."

Earthquakes In Divers Places

It is not that there were never earthquakes. There are all kinds of earthquakes in this world. In fact, I have seen a chart with all the different earthquakes showing the date, time, and place, and so on. The Lord Jesus Christ says that there are going to be earthquakes *in divers places*, apparently at the same time. There will be earthquakes all over the world. This is going to take place during this sixth seal. There will be physical changes in the earth and sky during this judgment of God. "High Frequency Active Auroral Research Program (HAARP)" has caused many man-made earthquakes in recent years, but these earthquakes in Revelation 6 will be caused by the Lord Jesus Christ Himself.

- **Matthew 27:54**
  "Now when the centurion, and they that were with him, watching Jesus, saw the **earthquake**, and those things that were done, they feared greatly, saying, Truly this was the Son of God."

After the resurrection of the Lord Jesus Christ, many of the saints in the earth arose and went out into Jerusalem. There was an **earthquake** there on that occasion.

- **Matthew 28:2**
  "And, behold, there was a **great earthquake**: for the angel of the Lord descended from Heaven, and came and rolled back the stone from the door, and sat upon it."

  This is after the bodily resurrection of the Lord Jesus Christ. There was a **great earthquake** then on that occasion.

- **Luke 21:11**
  "And **great earthquakes** shall be in divers places, and famines, and pestilences; and fearful sights and great signs shall there be from Heaven."

The Lord Jesus Christ, while He was here on the earth, predicted **great earthquakes**.

- **Acts 16:26**
  "And suddenly there was a **great earthquake**, so that the foundations of the prison were shaken: and immediately all the doors were opened, and every one's bands were loosed."

Paul and Silas were in prison because Paul cast out a spirit of divination from a girl. God uses **earthquakes** and He used them even in Acts 16 to release Paul and Silas from their prison.

- **Revelation 8:5**
  "And the angel took the censer, and filled it with fire of the altar, and cast *it* into the earth: and there were voices, and thunderings, and lightnings, and an **earthquake**."

- **Revelation 11:13**

  "And the same hour was there a **great earthquake**, and the tenth part of the city fell, and in the **earthquake** were slain of men seven thousand: and the remnant were affrighted, and gave glory to the God of Heaven."

You will remember in the Old Testament when Korah, Dathan, and Abiram had a big revolution against Moses. The Lord opened up the earth and it swallowed them up, they and their families, because they had perverted the things of the Lord. Here, in this **earthquake**, seven thousand were dead.

- **Revelation 11:19**

  "And the temple of God was opened in Heaven, and there was seen in his temple the ark of his testament: and there were lightnings, and voices, and thunderings, and an **earthquake**, and great hail."

- **Revelation 16:18**

  "And there were voices, and thunders, and lightnings; and there was a **great earthquake**, such as was not since men were upon the earth, so mighty an **earthquake**, *and* so great."

Earthquakes & Sun & Moon Changes

This will not be a small earthquake. That word for earthquake is SEISMOS. From this we get the word *seismograph*, which gives the measure of an earthquake. The great earthquake, the judgment, will take place on this earth.

There will also be changes in the sun and in the moon. The sun will become *black as sackcloth of hair*. Sackcloth is the word SAKKOS, which is *dark coarse cloth, made especially from the hair of animals.*

- **Isaiah 13:10**

  "For the stars of Heaven and the constellations thereof shall not give their light: the **sun** shall be darkened in his going forth, and the **moon** shall not cause her light to shine."

This is in the day of the Lord, which is this tribulation period. The **sun** and the **moon** are involved in this **sixth seal judgment**.

- **Joel 2:10**

  "The earth shall quake before them; the heavens shall **tremble**: the **sun** and the **moon** shall be dark, and the stars shall withdraw their shining:"

This is again in the day of the Lord, which is Daniel's Seventieth Week. There are going to be cataclysmic changes in the heavens at the time of the **sixth seal** judgment of God.

- **Joel 2:31**
  "The **sun** shall be turned into darkness, and the **moon** into blood, before the great and the terrible day of the LORD come."

The **moon** is going to be like unto **blood**. It is not necessarily going to be **blood** itself, but it is going to be a figure, as red as **blood**. It says here in Revelation 6:12, *"the moon became as blood."*

John MacArthur says that **blood** does not mean literal **blood**, but it is only figurative. This is one place where it is figurative. *"As blood"* is a figure of speech, but almost all other times, with very few exceptions, it is literal **blood** that has been given in the Scriptures.

- **Matthew 24:29**
  "Immediately after the tribulation of those days shall the **sun** be darkened, and the **moon** shall not give her light, and the stars shall fall from Heaven, and the powers of the Heavens shall be shaken:"

This is all predicted by the Lord Jesus Christ Himself.

- **Luke 21:25-26**
  "And there shall be signs in the **sun**, and in the **moon**, and in the stars; and upon the earth distress of nations, with perplexity; the sea and the waves roaring; Men's hearts failing them for fear, and for looking after those things which are coming on the earth: for the powers of Heaven shall be shaken."

All of these things will be true and it will be a terrible day indeed.

- **Acts 2:20**
  "The **sun** shall be turned into darkness, and the **moon** into blood, before that great and notable day of the Lord come:"

Terrible Judgments To Come

This day of the Lord is a picture that has come in the book of Revelation with the terrible judgments that will take place upon this earth. There will be shaking of the Heavens. The sun will be different. The moon will be different. What do you think the people on this earth are going to think about it? They are going to be wondering, I am sure.

Revelation 6:13

"And the stars of heaven fell unto the earth, even as a fig tree casteth her untimely figs, when she is shaken of a mighty wind."

Not only were the **sun** and **moon** different, but also the **stars**. There are millions upon billions of **stars** in the universe. One article on the Internet stated: *"The Hubble telescope has found there may be 125 galaxies in the universe."* Another article in NASA's "IMAGINE THE UNIVERSE" in 2002 stated, regarding galaxies: *"A recent German super-computer simulation estimates that the number may be as high as 500 billion."* One of the Internet articles stated that there were possibly **100 billion stars** in our own Milky Way Galaxy. Another Internet article placed the number of stars in our Milky Way Galaxy at **200 billion stars**.

In an article dated August 24, 2009, the following estimates were given. If there are only **350 billion galaxies** and if our Milky Way Galaxy, with **200 billion stars** is *"an average size galaxy,"* that means that there are an estimated **70 billion-trillion stars** in the entire universe. The Lord made all of these **stars**. What a powerful, omnipotent God the Bible tells us about!

This verse predicts that many of the **"stars of Heaven"** will fall to earth. Serious results will take place when this happens. When a meteorite comes down, people estimate where it might hit, and how many will be killed.

An unripe **fig** that grows during the winter and that does not come to maturity, falls off in the spring. That is called an **untimely fig**. That is what will happen to the **stars** in the changes in the heavens.

- **Genesis 1:16**
  "And God made two great lights; the greater light to rule the day, and the lesser light to rule the night: *he made* the **stars** also."

Our Little Daughter's Memory Verse

A little section of that verse was one of our daughter's memory verses. *"He made the stars also"* is short, so Dianne could remember it when she was just a little girl.

- **Isaiah 13:10**
  "For the **stars** of heaven and the constellations thereof shall not give their light: the **sun** shall be darkened in his going forth, and the **moon** shall not cause her light to shine."

This is in the day of the Lord.

- **Ezekiel 32:7-8**

  "And when I shall put thee out, I will cover the heaven, and make the **stars** thereof dark; I will cover the sun with a cloud, and the moon shall not give her light. All the bright lights of heaven will I make dark over thee, and set darkness upon thy land, saith the Lord GOD."

- **Daniel 8:10**

  "And it waxed great, *even* to the host of heaven; and it cast down *some* of the host and of the **stars** to the ground, and stamped upon them."

  Stars will fall. One of the expressions of Bob Jones, Sr., the founder of Bob Jones University, was "Do right until the **stars** fall." That is what we all ought to do. The **stars** one day will fall.

- **Joel 3:15**

  "The **sun** and the **moon** shall be darkened, and the **stars** shall withdraw their shining."

  Again, this is a prediction in the Old Testament about the **stars**. The **sun** is the closest **star** to our earth. They say it is 93 million miles away. It is a red-hot **sun**. If that **sun** were any closer, we would probably burn up. If it were any farther away, we would be cold. It is just exactly where God wanted that **sun**. The **sun** and the **stars** will withdraw their shining.

- **Matthew 24:29**

  "Immediately after the tribulation of those days shall the **sun** be darkened, and the **moon** shall not give her light, and the **stars** shall fall from heaven, and the powers of the heavens shall be shaken:"

- **Mark 13:24-25**

  "But in those days, after that tribulation, the **sun** shall be darkened, and the **moon** shall not give her light, And the **stars** of heaven shall fall, and the powers that are in heaven shall be shaken."

Why Don't The Stars Fall?

Why don't the stars fall now? Because the Lord has put them in a fixed place. The planets move around. The stars in heaven are there because God put them there to stay. He has rules and regulations just like in everything else. The law of gravity is there. The stars keep their place. The sun keeps its position. The planets rotate in a certain movement.

Everything is as it should be, right from the creation of the world, about six thousand years ago. The world does not believe it was six thousand years as the Bible teaches. They say it has been millions and millions of years. That cannot be. It is impossible. The **sun**, the **moon**, and the **stars** were placed where God wanted them to be. One day, at this **sixth seal** judgment, the earth, the heaven, the **sun**, the **stars**, and the moon will make some changes. He is going to abrogate and do away with that law of the **sun** and the **stars** and they will fall. Not all of them—you could not have billions and even trillions of them falling, or the whole earth would be burned up—but there will be **stars** coming down.

The Meaning Of Earthquake

The word earthquake (SEISMOS) comes from the word SEIO, which means *to tremble*. This is going to happen one day. At the right time, the Lord Jesus Christ will do it.

Revelation 6:14

"**And the heaven departed as a scroll when it is rolled together; and every mountain and island were moved out of their places.**"

Here is the **heaven** departing, **rolled** up just like a **scroll**. The **heavens** departing is also predicted in the Old Testament at this day of the Lord. God forecast what would happen in this tribulation period, the day of the Lord, as it is called.

- **Isaiah 13:13**
  "Therefore I will shake the **heavens**, and the earth shall **remove** out of her place, in the wrath of the LORD of hosts, and in the day of his fierce anger."

- **Isaiah 34:4**
  "And all the host of **heaven** shall be **dissolved**, and the **heavens** shall be **rolled together as a scroll**: and all their host shall fall down, as the leaf falleth off from the vine, and as a falling *fig* from the fig tree."

- **Isaiah 51:6**
  "Lift up your eyes to the **heavens**, and look upon the earth beneath: for the **heavens** shall vanish away like smoke, and the earth shall wax old like a garment, and they that dwell therein shall die in like manner: but my salvation shall be for ever, and my righteousness shall not be abolished."

- **Haggai 2:21**
  "Speak to Zerubbabel, governor of Judah, saying, I will shake the **heavens** and the earth;"
  God is going to shake them. We do not want any baby shaking syndrome. You know what that is. If you shake them too hard, they die. We heard about a fellow who was shaking a little baby and he killed him. It was murder and it is terrible. God is going to shake the **heavens** during this tribulation period.
- **Matthew 24:29**
  "Immediately after the tribulation of those days shall the **sun** be darkened, and the **moon** shall not give her light, and the **stars** shall fall from heaven, and the powers of the heavens shall be shaken:"
- **2 Peter 3:7**
  "But the **heavens** and the earth, which are now, by the same word are kept in store, reserved unto fire against the day of judgment and perdition of ungodly men."
The **heavens** that we have now are reserved for judgment. God is one day going to judge them.
- **2 Peter 3:12**
  "Looking for and hasting unto the coming of the day of God, wherein the **heavens** being on fire shall be dissolved, and the elements shall melt with fervent heat?"
One day, God is going to burn up the old **heavens** and the old earth. Will you be where your soul should be, safely trusting in the Lord Jesus Christ? I trust that is the case.
- **2 Peter 3:13**
  "Nevertheless we, according to his promise, look for new **heavens** and a new earth, wherein dwelleth righteousness."
God is going to renovate this earth and make it new. He is going to renovate the heavens and make new **heavens** as well.
- **Isaiah 51:6**
  "Lift up your eyes to the **heavens**, and look upon the earth beneath: for the **heavens** shall vanish away like smoke, and the earth shall wax old like a garment, and they that dwell therein shall die in like manner: but my salvation shall be for ever, and my righteousness shall not be abolished."
- **Isaiah 65:17**
  "For, behold, I create new **heavens** and a new earth: and the former shall not be remembered, nor come into mind."

Heavenly Changes Promised

In both the Old Testament and the New Testament, the Bible talks about the heavens changing. Then it talks here in Revelation 6:14 about the mountains and the islands being moved out of their places. An island is the little bit of land that is jutting up out of the water, as we know. If the islands are moved, they apparently go down under the water. There are going to be cataclysmic changes.

At the flood, the water was over all the earth. It was a universal flood. Here, at this judgment, there is going to be a shifting of mountains and islands.

- **Isaiah 40:4**
  "Every **valley** shall be exalted, and every **mountain** and hill shall be made low: and the crooked shall be made straight, and the rough places plain:"

This is one of the things that John the Baptist predicted. He quoted from Isaiah 40:4. If the **valleys** shall be exalted, that means God is going to change the whole topography of this earth. The valleys are going to be jutting up like **mountains**. The **mountains** will go flat. Every hill shall be made low. The **crooked** will be made **straight**. The Lord Jesus Christ is going to do this in His time and in His way.

- **Revelation 16:20**
  "And every island fled away, and the **mountains** were not found."

Now what does that mean? That means there are no more islands. We have islands right here in New Jersey. If this took place at this time, what happens to these islands? They would just flee away. That means they would sink to the bottom and would be no longer there. The water would cover them. That is what is going to happen one day. What about all the houses on these islands? They will perish. What about the people? They will perish. God is going to shake the earth and the **heavens** and reconstitute what is down here on this earth.

Physical Changes To The Earth

The mountains were not found. One day, the Lord Jesus Christ is going to take away the mountains and the islands and change this old earth. That is a sad situation. The judgment will be physical changes on the whole earth and in the sky.

Revelation 6:15

"And the kings of the earth, and the great men, and the rich men, and the chief captains, and the mighty men, and every bondman, and every free man, hid themselves in the dens and in the rocks of the mountains;"

Notice, there are seven different categories of people:

1. The kings

2. The great men

3. The rich men

4. The chief captains

5. The mighty men

6. The bondman

7. The free man

Hiding In The Rocks And Mountains

What do they do? They hide themselves. These were hiding in the rocks and in the mountains. Kings are high people. The great men would be the princes (MEGISTANES). They are the ones who are *associates or couriers of the king.* The chief men (CHILIARCHOS) are *commanders over a thousand soldiers.* All of these people are trying to hide from the Lord Jesus Christ.

- **Genesis 3:18**
  "And they heard the voice of the LORD God walking in the garden in the cool of the day: and Adam and his wife **hid** themselves from the presence of the LORD God amongst the trees of the garden."

Adam and Eve tried to **hide** themselves. They were not successful.

- **Exodus 33:18-22**
  "And he said, I beseech thee, shew me thy glory. And he said, I will make all my goodness pass before thee, and I will proclaim the name of the LORD before thee; and will be gracious to whom I will be gracious, and will shew mercy on whom I will shew mercy. And he said, Thou canst not see my face: for there shall no man see me, and live. And the LORD said, Behold, *there is* a place by me, and thou shalt stand upon a rock: And it shall come to pass, while my glory passeth by, that I will put thee in a clift

of the rock, and will **cover** thee with my hand while I pass by: And I will take away mine hand, and thou shalt see my back parts: but my face shall not be seen"

The Lord hid Moses in the rock. He was **hiding** in a rock from the Lord's glory, not because he did not love the Lord, but to protect him from the glory. He would have been killed if he had seen the full glory of God.

God's Hiding Place

The Lord has provided us a place of hiding in the Lord Jesus Christ. We can hide in Him. We cannot hide from Him. These kings and all the other people could not hide from the Lord. How can you hide from the Lord? There is no way to hide from the Lord.

- **Psalm 119:114**
"Thou *art* my **hiding** place and my shield: I hope in thy word."
The Lord is the only place we can **hide** from His wrath.
- **Psalm 32:7**
"Thou *art* my **hiding** place; thou shalt preserve me from trouble; thou shalt compass me about with songs of deliverance. Selah."

These **seven groups** of people could not find any **hiding** place in the Lord Jesus Christ because they had rejected Him. They were **hiding** *from* the Lord Jesus Christ.

- **Psalm 139:7-10**
"Whither shall I go from thy spirit? or whither shall I **flee** from thy presence? If I ascend up into heaven, thou *art* there: if I make my bed in Hell, behold, thou *art there. If* I take the wings of the morning, *and* dwell in the uttermost parts of the sea; Even there shall thy hand lead me, and thy right hand shall hold me."
    Up into heaven—that is North.
    In Hell—that is South.
    Wings of the morning—that is East, where the sun comes up.
    Uttermost parts of the sea—that is West, the Mediterranean Sea.

There is no way to **hide** from the Lord.

- **Hebrews 4:13**
"Neither is there any creature that is not manifest in his sight: but all things *are* **naked** and **opened** unto the eyes of him with whom we have to do."

Revelation 6:16

"And said to the mountains and rocks, Fall on us, and hide us from the face of him that sitteth on the throne, and from the wrath of the Lamb:"

This is what these seven classifications of people were saying. They cannot flee from the **wrath of the Lamb**.

- **Luke 3:7**

  "Then said he to the multitude that came forth to be baptized of him, O generation of vipers, who hath warned you to flee from the **wrath** to come?"

We have to flee from God's **wrath**. People that are lost must flee.

- **John 3:36**

  "He that believeth on the Son hath everlasting life: and he that believeth not the Son shall not see life; but the **wrath** of God abideth on him."

God's **wrath** abides on you if you are not genuinely saved. This is a terrible thing.

- **Romans 1:18**

  "For the **wrath** of God is revealed from heaven against all ungodliness and unrighteousness of men, who hold the truth in unrighteousness;"

- **Romans 5:9**

  "Much more then, being now justified by his blood, we shall be saved from **wrath** through him."

If we are justified by genuine faith in the Lord Jesus Christ, accepting Him and trusting Him as our Saviour and Redeemer, we will be saved from this **wrath** of tribulation and the **wrath** of Hell.

- **Ephesians 5:6**

  "Let no man deceive you with vain words: for because of these things cometh the **wrath** of God upon the children of disobedience."

- **Colossians 3:6**

  "For which things' sake the **wrath** of God cometh on the children of disobedience:"

- **1 Thessalonians 1:10**

  "And to wait for his Son from heaven, whom he raised from the dead, *even* Jesus, which delivered us from the **wrath** to come."

The Lord Jesus Christ is the only One that can deliver us from the **wrath** to come. He is the Lamb and He can deliver us.

- **1 Thessalonians 5:9**

  "For God hath not appointed us to **wrath**, but to obtain salvation by our Lord Jesus Christ,"

People on this earth do not have to endure the **wrath** of the Lamb. They can trust Him and be genuinely saved. What about the love of the Lamb? There is not only the wrath of the Lamb, but there is also the love of the Lamb.

- **John 1:29**

  "The next day John seeth Jesus coming unto him, and saith, Behold the **Lamb** of God, which taketh away the sin of the world."

That is His love.

- **1 Peter 1:18-19**

  "Forasmuch *as* ye know that ye were not redeemed with corruptible things, as silver and gold, from your vain conversation *received* by tradition from your fathers; But with the precious blood of Christ, as of a **lamb** without blemish and without spot:"

The Lamb's Love Or His Wrath?

This is the love of the Lamb. He offers salvation to those who will genuinely trust Him, and receive Him, and be truly saved. That is His love. You do not have to face His wrath. If you are lost and unsaved, you will face His wrath one day. The Lord Jesus Christ pleads with you and I plead with you, that anyone who reads this who is not in the Lord Jesus Christ, would genuinely trust Him and be truly saved.

Revelation 6:17

"For the great day of his wrath is come; and who shall be able to stand?"

This is the end of the line. This **sixth seal**, the great day of His **wrath**, is come. It is a wrathful day. How are we going to stand?

- **Romans 5:2**

  "By whom also we have access by faith into this grace wherein we **stand**, and rejoice in hope of the glory of God."

If we are genuinely saved, we can **stand** in the Lord Jesus Christ. It is not in our own merits, but in His merits.

- **1 Corinthians 15:1**
  "Moreover, brethren, I declare unto you the gospel which I preached unto you, which also ye have received, and wherein ye **stand**;"

We have to **stand** in this gospel, the good news that the Lord Jesus Christ died for us who are sinners.

- **Galatians 5:1**
  "**Stand** fast therefore in the liberty wherewith Christ hath made us free, and be not entangled again with the yoke of bondage."

- **Ephesians 6:11**
  "Put on the whole armour of God, that ye may be able to **stand** against the wiles of the devil."

The Devil is filled with wiles and we are able to **stand** with God's weapons and His armour, not with our own. Only those who are in the Lord Jesus Christ can **stand**.

Any Saved During The Tribulation?

Are there any genuine believers in the seven-year tribulation period? Yes, there will be true believers. I will talk about the great multitude of saints that are genuinely saved because of the preaching of the 144,000 Jews. There will be 12,000 from each of the twelve tribes. We will see that great multitude of true believers in Heaven that were able to stand against the wiles of the Devil. Many of them will be slaughtered, as we saw in Revelation 6:9, but many will be spared and will be evangelists for the Lord Jesus Christ.

We have seen that those who are mighty and those who are rich could not use their might and their wealth to spare them from the **wrath** of the **Lamb**. They had to seek for **rocks**, **caves**, and crevices to **hide**. There is no **hiding** place from the **Lamb** and from God's **wrath**. You cannot **hide** from His **wrath**, but there is **hiding** in the Lord Jesus Christ. He is a great **hiding** place that makes us safe and enables us to **stand** for Him.

𝕽𝖊𝖇𝖊𝖑𝖆𝖙𝖎𝖔𝖓 𝕮𝖍𝖆𝖕𝖙𝖊𝖗 𝕾𝖊𝖇𝖊𝖓

Revelation 7:1

"And after these things I saw four angels standing on the four corners of the earth, holding the four winds of the earth, that the wind should not blow on the earth, nor on the sea, nor on any tree."

Chapter 7 is a parenthesis. Chapter 6 had to do with the **seven seal** judgments. The **first seal** was the white horse, the conquering power. The **second seal** was the red horse of war. The **third seal** was the black horse of famine. The **fourth seal** was the pale horse of pestilence and death. The **fifth seal** was the martyred souls under the altar. The **sixth seal** was physical changes in the earth and the sky. The **seventh seal** will not be taken up until Chapter 8.

Daniel's Seventieth Week

The Lord Jesus Christ does not do anything here to judge in Chapter 7. This is <u>Daniel's Seventieth Week</u> and it is for the Jews or the Israelites. In fact, each one of the tribes are going to be included.

We will see that two tribes are left out of the twelve. Joseph and Levi are substituted for Dan and Ephraim. One explanation for that is Jeroboam's two golden calves. One was placed in the area of Bethel, which is where Ephraim dwelled. The other was placed in the area of Dan. These were leaders in idolatry. Some feel that these two tribes, Dan and Ephraim, were left out from the 144,000 that we will talk about later because of this idolatry.

After the physical changes during the sixth seal, John saw **four angels** standing on the four corners of the earth. The earth, as we know it, does not have **four corners**, but there are four areas. We have north, south, east, and west. That is where these **angels** were standing, holding the **four winds** of the earth. The word for **wind** here is ANEMOS. It means *a very strong wind; a violent agitation; a stream of air*. It also means *a strong, tempestuous wind*. This is a negative thing. These **four angels** were in charge of the **winds** that they should not blow until everything was taken care of that we will see in the next verse.

You know that when the **winds** blow on the sea there is a storm. When **wind** blows on trees, they crack and fall over. We had a big **wind** storm fifteen or twenty years ago. A big tree fell right on the sun room because of the **wind**. There was a strong **wind** in Baltimore, Maryland that tipped over a boat with twenty-five people on board. One person died and two or three were missing. The boat was about thirty-six feet long. Winds are dangerous, indeed.

- **Matthew 7:26-27**
  "And every one that heareth these sayings of mine, and doeth them not, shall be likened unto a foolish man, which built his house upon the sand: And the rain descended, and the floods came, and the **winds** blew, and beat upon that house; and it fell: and great was the fall of it."

If you build a house on sand it is not going to last too long. Some people do not have the knowledge of the terrain and they have built houses on sand and other things that are not proper. The Lord Jesus Christ said it is a foolish man that does that.

If you do not build your spiritual house on the Lord Jesus Christ and His Words, do what He says, be genuinely saved, and build upon Him who is the Rock, you are going to be in serious trouble.

The Power Of Winds

Let me just explain to you what winds can do. I looked up hurricanes on the Internet. A hurricane is *a tropical cyclone with winds of at least seventy-four miles an hour*. A hurricane blows counter-clockwise in the northern hemisphere and clockwise in the southern hemisphere. They are formed from simple complexes of thunderstorms. These thunderstorms can grow into hurricane strength with cooperation from the ocean and the atmosphere. First, the ocean itself has to be warmer than 81° Fahrenheit. You know that will be in the summer. A hurricane cannot come in the winter. It is interesting, but winds can destroy. They can take down homes and tear things apart.

Here in Chapter 7, the winds were withheld in God's grace and mercy.

- **Matthew 8:26-27**
  "And he saith unto them, Why are ye fearful, O ye of little faith? Then he arose, and rebuked the **winds** and the sea; and there was a great calm. But the men marvelled, saying, What manner of man is this, that even the **winds** and the sea obey him!"

The disciples were in a storm on the Sea of Galilee. What manner of man is this? The Lord Jesus Christ is the Creator of the **winds** and the seas. He is God the Son as well as the Son of man. He has power over the **winds**. He can speak and bring peace. As He can bring peace from the **winds** of the storm, He can also bring peace to our souls that are stormy and blowing around in sadness and distress. He can do that and He has done it if we are genuinely saved.

- **Matthew 11:28**
  "Come unto me, all *ye* that labour and are heavy laden, and I will give you rest."

There will be no **winds**, no storm, no blowing, no tempest, but rest and peace.

- **Isaiah 57:20-21**
  "But the wicked *are* like the troubled sea, when it cannot rest, whose waters cast up mire and dirt. *There is* no peace, saith my God, to the wicked."

The storms, the **winds**, and the tempest will upset the wicked and there is no peace at all in them.

- **Acts 27:14**
  "But not long after there arose against it a tempestuous **wind**, called Euroclydon."

Paul was on a journey. He was being sent to Rome because he was a prisoner. On the voyage to Rome, there was a big storm that came up. It took them off course and the soldiers almost killed the prisoners. The Lord spared Paul and all the other prisoners. This Euroclydon was a strong **wind** that took the ship off course and drove it to a small island. They were about to kill the prisoners because if the prisoners had fled, the Roman guards and centurions that were guarding them would be slain.

- **Acts 27:20**
  "And when neither sun nor stars in many days appeared, and no small **tempest** lay on *us*, all hope that we should be saved was then taken away."

Winds and the **tempest** almost slew Paul and the prisoners that were with him on his way to Rome. He had already had three missionary journeys. This was the fourth journey. It was a missionary journey because when he got to Rome he was able to speak and to teach the things of the Lord Jesus Christ there in his own hired house and wherever he was in prison. The Lord used this **tempest** to give faith and support for Paul as a missionary and a man of God. God spoke to him at that time and warned him that there would be no loss of life, and there was not any loss of life in that **storm**.

- **Acts 27:23-25**
  "For there stood by me this night the angel of God, whose I am, and whom I serve, Saying, Fear not, Paul; thou must be brought before Caesar: and, lo, God hath given thee all them that sail with thee. Wherefore, sirs, be of good cheer: for I believe God, that it shall be even as it was told me."

Paul told them that there would be no loss of life to any person, because the Lord would spare them. A tempestuous **wind** was the means of Paul saying, "I believe God," and that it would be just as the Lord told him it would be.

- **James 3:4**
  "Behold also the ships, which though *they be* so great, and are driven of fierce **winds**, yet *are* they turned about with a very small helm, whithersoever the governor listeth."

A ship is supposed to have a rudder. If the rudder works, it can be driven and controlled and you can take it where it is supposed to be. Without the rudder, even though it is a small helm or rudder, it would be driven by fierce **winds** and turned around.

We have had sailing experience with different sailboats that we have had through the years. My dad had a small one called a *National* sailboat. It had a rudder, a tiller, and everything else to go with it. We got into bad **storms**. Then he got another one, a *Great Lakes 21*. That is a twenty-one footer. It had a keel on it. When the **wind** is strong and blowing, those center-board boats, those *National* boats, will go right over if you do not watch yourself. The nice thing about the *Great Lakes 21*, is that it had a keel on it and it would never go over. As soon as that lead keel came out of the water it went back down and the boat was stabilized. It just would not tip over, so that was an encouraging thing.

Safety In Paul's Ship

Paul's ship was safe as long as the Lord Jesus Christ, the Master of the seas, was in charge. That ship rammed up onto the shore. Some took boats and some took boards, but they got ashore on Melita, or Malta, and were all safe and spared. It could have been a terrible, great catastrophe, indeed.

Revelation 7:2

"And I saw another angel ascending from the east, having the seal of the living God: and he cried with a loud voice to the four angels, to whom it was given to hurt the earth and the sea,"

Headship Among The Angels

Apparently, in the angelic areas, just like in other areas, there is a headship. One angel is over another. This angel was a stronger angel than the other four angels. He had charge over them. He told these four angels not to hurt the earth or the sea. These angels had the power to hurt the earth and the sea. There was no question about their power to hurt. The angel forbade these other four angels to do this.

He **ascended from the east.** Notice what he had. He had the **seal of the living God** in his hand. Later on, we will see how they will use that **seal.** The word for **seal** is SPHRAGIS. It means, *that by which anything is confirmed or proved or authenticated; a seal, a token, or a proof.* This was the **seal of the living God.** The Lord God of Heaven and earth is the One that can **seal** those that are genuinely saved, those that are true believers. This **seal** was going on those genuine believers, those that were to come to the Lord Jesus Christ and to be His. He waited until that **seal** was upon them and they were not supposed to **hurt the earth and the sea** until that happened. That is exactly what took place. The **four angels** did not strike, **hurt,** or do anything that would harm the **earth and the sea.** No judgment was made upon them.

Revelation 7:3

"Saying, Hurt not the earth, neither the sea, nor the trees, till we have sealed the servants of our God in their foreheads."

This was the purpose: until they had **sealed the servants of our God**. It says in the New Testament that every genuine believer who is truly born-again, saved, and genuinely trusting the Lord Jesus Christ as Saviour and Redeemer, has been **sealed** by the Holy Spirit. The **seal** is something that God has given to us in order to make us His. This makes us genuine. There are many people who claim to be Christians who have never been **sealed** by the Holy Spirit of God. They have never been truly born-again. They have never had new life and have never been regenerated. They do not have the **seal** of the Holy Spirit. God has given to those who are genuine believers to be **sealed** by the Spirit of God.

The Meaning Of Sealing

Sealing gives an authentication, which means we are His, born of the Spirit of God. We are Christians or *Christ ones*. They were first called Christians at Antioch. It also means that we will never be lost. A seal is for certainty and for assurance. You do not get sealed one day and then lose the seal the next. When God seals the genuine believers who are truly saved, born-again, and regenerated, the Holy Spirit indwells them.

He does not remove the Holy Spirit like He did in the Old Testament. David prayed, "Take not thine Holy Spirit from me." In the New Testament, the age of grace is different. The Holy Spirit of God never will depart. We are His and we are His forever. He has **sealed** us. We may not always follow His will, genuine believers and true Christians many times do not, but we are **sealed** and He wants us to go back to Him from whatever it may be. This is an important thing, the **seal** of the living God.

The **four angels** had the power to **hurt** and to harm the **earth**. They could make typhoons, hurricanes, cyclones, and everything else with these winds. The angel over them says, "**Hurt not the earth. Do not hurt the sea. Do not hurt the trees, until we have sealed the servants of our God in their foreheads.**" God was, in His grace, waiting for this thing to happen upon the earth.

Daniel's Seventieth Week Of Years

As we have said before, the tribulation period is Daniel's Seventieth Week. It is seven years in length. Seventy years were determined upon Israel. They were years of sevens. There were 490 years altogether. This is the last week of years.

Notice, when it says, *"Hurt not,"* it is a prohibition. There are two kinds of prohibitions. One is a present prohibition, meaning *to stop hurting* the earth. The aorist tense means *do not even begin to do something.* This one is in the aorist tense. It means, *do not even begin to* hurt the **earth**, or the **sea**, or the **trees**. Do not start. Do not begin. It does not mean, "Stop doing it." They had not begun. One **angel** had the power over the other four, to have them stop until they had **sealed** the servants of God in their foreheads.

Jewish Evangelists Commissioned

We will see a little bit later, that these ones that are sealed will be Jews. They will be of the twelve tribes of Israel. You might ask, "How can Jews be servants of our God?" They were servants of God in the Old Testament. They disappointed the Lord. The ten tribes of the north were taken into Assyrian captivity about 700 B.C. The two tribes in the south, Benjamin and Judah, were taken into the Babylonian captivity about 600 B.C., but they were servants of the most high God.

Now, in Daniel's Seventieth Week, Israel is back in line. Israel is back in the picture and these servants are going to be **sealed** by the Lord. When they are sealed, they are going to be genuinely saved. Salvation and sealing are one and the same. God would not **seal** a person and not genuinely save them. He does not **seal** the Devil's children. He only **seals** the genuine believers, the truly saved ones. They are called *"the servants of our God."* They will be **sealed** in their foreheads.

During this tribulation period, as we will see later on, there will be a **seal** of the antichrist. This will be a **seal** in the right hand or in the **forehead**. It will be the *mark of the beast.* That is not the **seal** here. This is the **seal** that is genuine. It is the **seal** from our **living God** upon His servants.

As we have said, in Chapter 7 there is a parenthesis. God has stopped His judgments. The Lord is able to stop things that He begins. The first **six seal** judgments upon the earth occur in Chapter 6. He could continue, but He said, "Now, just wait." He is merciful. He is longsuffering. Remember, if we take a look at the total picture of the twenty-one different judgments (seven seals, seven trumpets, and seven vials), we see a total of one every four months, on average, during the seven-year period of the tribulation. Here, the Lord Jesus Christ is saying, "I am going to wait a while. I am going to be **sparing**."

- **Numbers 14:18**
"The LORD *is* **longsuffering**, and of great mercy, forgiving iniquity and transgression, and by no means clearing *the guilty*, visiting the iniquity of the fathers upon the children unto the third and fourth *generation*."

Perhaps more can be genuinely saved during this time. He is just **waiting**. It is not that God is not just. It is not that God is not going to visit the sin of the fathers upon the children. In other words, when the father sins and teaches it to the child, the child sins. God is going to judge for that sin, but He is also **longsuffering** and of great mercy. His **longsuffering** is seen in this Chapter 7 parenthesis. No more of these judgments will be during this time, not even the **seventh seal**. It will wait until Chapter 8.

- **Psalm 86:15**
"But thou, O Lord, art a God full of compassion, and **gracious**, **longsuffering**, and plenteous in mercy and truth."

Our Just And Righteous God

The graciousness and longsuffering of God are some of his characteristics. He is a just God. He is a righteous God. He judges sin, but He is also gracious, longsuffering, and full of mercy and compassion. That is why He stops in the parenthesis of Chapter 7. That is why He stops the judgments on this earth. The genuine believers that are truly saved will be gone. Everyone that is genuinely saved and born-again will be in Heaven during these judgments upon the earth of unbelievers, but God's compassion is what makes Him to stop.

- **Psalm 103:8**
"The LORD *is* merciful and **gracious**, slow to anger, and plenteous in mercy."

Again, we see the Lord is merciful, **gracious**, and slow to anger. He does have anger. There is the **wrath** of the **Lamb** that they will flee from, but He is slow to anger and plenteous in **mercy**. He has plenty of mercy to go around.

- Luke 18:10-13
  "Two men went up into the temple to pray; the one a Pharisee, and the other a publican. The Pharisee stood and prayed thus with himself, God, I thank thee, that I am not as other men are, extortioners, unjust, adulterers, or even as this publican. I fast twice in the week, I give tithes of all that I possess. And the publican, standing afar off, would not lift up so much as his eyes unto Heaven, but smote upon his breast, saying, God be **merciful** to me a sinner."

Mercy is *not getting something you deserve.* That is God's **mercy.** When He withholds Hell, damnation, and judgment, that is His **mercy.** He is full of and plenteous in **mercy.**

- Hebrews 2:17
  "Wherefore in all things it behoved him to be made like unto *his* brethren, that he might be a **merciful** and faithful high priest in things *pertaining* to God, to make reconciliation for the sins of the people."

This talks about the Lord Jesus Christ, our High Priest appearing now in Heaven. The Lord Jesus Christ was made Man, perfect Man as well as perfect God, in order that He might understand. He was made *like unto* his brethren. He was not made exactly the same as His brethren. He was not made as we are that He would have sin, but He is like us. He is perfect Man as well as perfect God, that He might be a merciful and faithful High Priest. He is in Heaven above, at the Father's right hand. He can be merciful unto us because He knew what it was like as He walked this earth. He saw the people and their condition and the terrible wickedness, the sin, the sickness, and the poverty. He saw all of these things. Now in Heaven above, at the right hand of God the Father, He looks down at those of us who are genuinely saved and He is merciful to us. I am glad that He is, because when we fail Him, He does not snap in judgment. He is **merciful** and He is a faithful High Priest Who can intercede for us.

Christ, The Believer's Advocate

First of all, the Lord Jesus Christ does not want us to sin, but if we do sin, He is an advocate–an attorney, or lawyer–that genuinely saved people have at the right hand of the Father.

- **1 Peter 3:20**
  "Which sometime were disobedient, when once the **longsuffering** of God waited in the days of Noah, while the ark was a preparing, wherein few, that is, eight souls were saved by water."

This talks about the early years of this earth up until Genesis, Chapters 5 and 6. Here is an illustration of the **longsuffering** of God. He waited to judge. He waited for the flood until the ark was ready. He could have judged at any moment. I would have wiped out Noah, Mrs. Noah, Shem, Ham, Japheth, and their three wives, but He waited. I believe that He made that ark big enough. It had three decks. It was very long–three times the length of a football field. It was big enough, not only for every animal species, two of every one and seven pairs of every clean beast, but I believe there was room for anyone who wanted to come into that ark, as far as the human beings were concerned. I believe it was an open invitation. I believe that was what Noah preached for 120 years. He was a preacher of righteousness for 120 years. "Whosoever will, let him come. It is going to rain." But they said, "Me, go into a boat? I have never seen any rain." (The mist came up to water the earth and there was no such thing as rain.) "Why should I come into your boat? You are crazy, Noah!"

Noah's Provision Was Made

I believe, although there is no Scripture to show it, there was room enough. He made provision, but nobody came. Finally, when it was time to go into the ark, the Lord shut the door. Noah came in because he believed the Lord. Mrs. Noah came in. Shem came in. Ham came in. Japheth and the three wives came in. Eight people were saved. God is longsuffering and waited while the ark was being prepared.

Can you imagine, without the tools we have today, how long it would take to prepare a big ship, three times the length of a football field, and wide and tall with three decks, and so on? There were only three workers plus Noah. I am sure no one else helped him. God waited and was **longsuffering**.

- **2 Peter 3:9**
  "The Lord is not slack concerning his promise, as some men count slackness; but is **longsuffering** to us-ward, not willing that any should perish, but that all should come to repentance."

His **longsuffering** right now is awaiting His judgment. When the rapture takes place and the genuine believers are taken up off this earth and into Heaven and Glory, there is going to be judgment on this earth.

Before that happens, God wants as many as possible to be genuinely saved. He wants everyone to come to repentance and not to perish. He is not going to force them, but He wants them to come and He is **longsuffering.** That is what He is here in Chapter 7, **longsuffering.**

Revelation 7:4

"And I heard the number of them which were sealed: **and there were sealed an hundred and forty and four thousand of all the tribes of the children of Israel."**

The Seven Biblical Dispensations

As I said before, God is not through with the children of Israel. He is not through with them. We must be dispensationalists. These are the three major dispensations:

The Dispensation of Law. That is when Moses was there.

The Dispensation of Grace. That is what we are living in now.

The Dispensation of the Kingdom. That is of the future Millennial reign and glory of the Lord Jesus Christ.

There were also four other dispensations:

The Dispensation of Innocence

The Dispensation of Conscience

The Dispensation of Human Government

The Dispensation of Promise

I believe in these dispensatons. God is not through with His people, Israel.

That is not what the British Israelites teach. British Israelism says that the white race is the ten lost tribes. They say the ten tribes were lost; therefore, the white race is now **Israel.** No, that is not right. There is still an **Israel.** They are still confirmed. One of the things they say about British Israelism concerning the words, *"Brit"* and *"Ish"* is the following: *Ish* in Hebrew is *man. Brit* (short for Berith) is a *covenant.* Therefore, they say *"the man of the covenant"* is British, the white Anglo-Saxon people. It's a form of Nazi white supremacy. They are against the Negroes and the Jews. They think God is through with them.

It is not as Harold Camping taught all over the world on all of his thousands of stations with millions of listeners. He said that God is through with **Israel** and now **Israel** is the same as the church. He said that the promises of Israel in the Old Testament are equal to the promises of the church in the New Testament.

Israel Is Not The Church

No, a thousand times, no. <u>The promises to Israel will be fulfilled literally to Israel.</u> That means Israel is going to be revived and Israel is going to be a nation again. Right now, there is a nation, but they are going to be a nation accepting the Lord Jesus Christ and genuinely trusting Him one day. The promises to Israel are not fulfilled in the church.

There is a rule of interpretation. Some have called it the Golden Rule of Interpretation: "Where the PLAIN SENSE makes COMMON SENSE, SEEK NO OTHER SENSE," except in the light of context that it is clearly otherwise a figure of speech.

It says here in Verse 4 that John heard the number of them that were **sealed**, *"of all the tribes of the children of Israel."* There were nine and a half tribes on the west side of the Jordan River. Gad, Reuben, and the half tribe of Manasseh were on the other side of the Jordan River. There are **twelve tribes** that inhabited the land and when they go back to the land (and some are back in the land now), when they understand what their tribes are, they will be somewhere in **Israel**. Right now, they are dispersed. The ones that are **sealed** have not come back yet, but they are all over the world. God knows who they are. God knows where they are. They are **Jews**. They are **Israelites**. Some are U.S. citizens. Some are British citizens. Some are Russian citizens. They are all over the world, but one day God is going to **seal** these servants of His from every tribe. There will be 144,000 altogether.

By the way, the 144,000 are not the Jehovah's Witnesses. They declare, "We are the 144,000." One thing we are going to see, a little bit later in the book of Revelation, is that every one of them is a virgin. Ask the people who are Jehovah's Witnesses if all of them are virgins. Have they ever been married? Are they single? These 144,000 evangelists are not Jehovah's Witnesses, by any means. They are 12,000 from each of the twelve tribes of **Israel**.

Revelation 7:5

"Of the tribe of Juda *were* sealed twelve thousand. Of the tribe of Reuben *were* sealed twelve thousand. Of the tribe of Gad *were* sealed twelve thousand."

Here the children of Israel are numbered and listed by their tribes. Each of these successive verses 5, 6, 7, and 8 have three in each. There are twelve altogether. We need to refresh our memories about the sons of Israel. There were twelve of them and the birth order is as follows:

1. **Reuben was the firstborn (Genesis 29).** He was born of Leah. Reuben disappointed his father. He lay with his father's concubine. It was a terrible atrocity so he did not get the blessing of the firstborn. Firstborns always get double portions. That double portion was split, I believe. Probably Joseph was the one to receive it. Ephraim and Manasseh were the two sons of Joseph and they were the ones that had the blessing. Jacob loved Rachel first. Leah was not favored, but she had the first son.

2. **Simeon** was the second son born to Leah.

3. **Levi** was the third son, also born to Leah. She was the "hated" wife. Her father, Laban, switched his daughters on the wedding night so that Jacob was given Leah instead of Rachel. Jacob had to serve Laban seven more years to get Rachel.

4. **Judah** was also Leah's son. The first four sons and tribes were from Leah, the one who was less respected.

- **Deuteronomy 21:15-17**
  "If a man have two wives, one beloved, and another hated, and they have born him children, *both* the beloved and the hated; and *if* the firstborn son be hers that was hated: Then it shall be, when he maketh his sons to inherit *that* which he hath, *that* he may not make the son of the beloved firstborn before the son of the hated, *which is indeed* the firstborn: But he shall acknowledge the son of the hated *for* the firstborn, by giving him a double portion of all that he hath: for he *is* the beginning of his strength; the right of the firstborn *is* his."

In the Old Testament, they were permitted to have two wives. (That does not mean we are permitted to have two wives in the New Testament.) The one that was hated was not to be "short changed." If she was the first wife, she should be the one that has the honor. Just because you love the other one, you do not short change the one that is hated.

5. **Dan** was the son of Rachel's handmaid, Bilhah.
6. **Naphtali** was also the son of Bilhah.
7. **Gad** was the son of Leah's handmaid, Zilpah.
8. **Asher** was also the son of Zilpah.
9. **Issachar** was another son of Leah.
10. **Zebulon was another son of Leah.** (Dinah was the only daughter listed in Scripture, who was also born to Leah.)
11. **Joseph** was born to Rachel. She was finally able to have a son.
12. **Benjamin** was also born to Rachel. She died giving birth to him.

These are the order of the twelve tribes. The tribes of Joseph and Levi are substituted for Dan and Ephraim in the list of the 144,000. As I said before, some have felt that the reason probably is because Jeroboam's golden calves were in Ephraim's territory and in Dan's territory.

The Tribes Around The Tabernacle

During the wilderness wanderings, every one of the tribes had a place around the tabernacle. The front side of the tabernacle was always facing east. The back side would be to the west. The right side would be on the north, and the left side would be south. The tabernacle moved forty-three times in the forty years of the wilderness wanderings. When God's guiding cloud arose, every one of the Levites had a job to do. They had to pick up the tabernacle, grab it up, and move it to the next place. As the cloud moved, they moved. Around that tabernacle area, were the Levites and the other tribes:

Judah, Issachar, and Zebulon were on the east side, behind Moses, and Aaron and his sons.

Reuben, Simeon, and Gad were on the south side, behind the Kohathites.

Ephraim, Manasseh, and Benjamin were on the west side, behind the Gershonites.

Dan, Asher, and Naphtali were on the north side, behind the Merarites.

As they moved, God insisted that it be done in that formation. Every time they moved, they had to move in order. Many times we wonder, "Is God an orderly God?" He certainly is. He expects us to be following His orders and His Words as well. That is what they did as they moved and went from place to place.

Revelation 7:6

"Of the tribe of Aser *were* sealed twelve thousand. Of the tribe of Nepthalim *were* sealed twelve thousand. Of the tribe of Manasses *were* sealed twelve thousand."

Here are 12,000 of each of these tribes (12,000 times three, or 36,000), just like Judah, Reuben, and the tribe of Gad were sealed in the previous verse.

Revelation 7:7

"Of the tribe of Simeon *were* sealed twelve thousand. Of the tribe of Levi *were* sealed twelve thousand. Of the tribe of Issachar *were* sealed twelve thousand."

Here we see that Levi is a part of this. Levi is sealed also. Normally, Levi was more or less left out. The Levites were dispersed among all the tribes of Israel, as you may know. During the time of the judges, there were forty-eight Levitical cities. I remember that, because we used to have forty-eight states. All of these Levites were scattered throughout Israel. There were Levitical cities on the east side of the Jordan River and on the west side. Normally, Levi was not mentioned too much. Here, the tribe of Levi is going to be among the 144,000 that will be sealed by the Spirit of God and will be raised up as evangelists in this tribulation time.

Revelation 7:8

"Of the tribe of Zabulon *were* sealed twelve thousand. Of the tribe of Joseph *were* sealed twelve thousand. Of the tribe of Benjamin *were* sealed twelve thousand."

As I said before, Joseph normally does not enter into the picture either. It is usually Ephraim and Manasseh, the sons of Joseph. When he was in Egypt, he had these two sons. But now, the tribe of Joseph is alive and well during this time of the seven-year period of the tribulation. Half of his tribe will be sealed. Ephraim and Manasseh are his sons, but only Manasseh will be sealed under that 12,000 as well.

Revelation 7:9

"After this I beheld, and, lo, a great multitude, which no man could number, of all nations, and kindreds, and people, and tongues, stood before the throne, and before the Lamb, clothed with white robes, and palms in their hands;"

This is the great **multitude** standing before the **Lamb** and before the throne. They are saved people. Where do they come from? It is not from the New Testament age of grace. There are **multitudes** that are genuinely saved and born-again, during the age of grace, but here in this seven-year tribulation period there will also be a great **multitude** that will be genuinely saved. I believe that the reason they are truly saved is because of these 144,000 Jews that are world-wide evangelists. These evangelists will have led these people to the Lord Jesus Christ. They will have turned and looked upon their Messiah, Whom they crucified. They will now say, "Blessed is He that cometh in the name of the Lord." This is the reason for the great **multitude.** In effect, the Jewish evangelists in less than seven years are able to accomplish what the Gentiles could not accomplish in over 2,000 years during the age of grace. This is because it will be God's will and God's timing to perform this.

Notice, in Verse 9 that it was *"out of every nation."* There is not going to be one government all over the world as the internationalists want to have. At this time, there are going to be nations, <u>plural</u>, not one big world government that some strive for today. The people are not going to be one race. There is not going to be one language. Many today are now trying to figure out one language and push that language on the whole world. There is not going to be one language, because this verse speaks about people of all different nations and "tongues."

The Multitude Before God's Throne

These that are genuinely saved, the multitude, stood before the throne. They are in Heaven. There is no question about it, they are in Heaven. They are truly saved because of the work, I believe, of these evangelists who were faithful to the Lord Jesus Christ and the gospel that was preached during that seven-year period of the tribulation.

Notice, they are clothed with white robes. They are pure. They are righteous. They have the white robes just like other true believers in other places in the book of Revelation. They will stand before the Lamb and before the throne. God the Father is on the throne. The Lamb is at His right hand. This multitude is standing before them both, clothed in white.

What a wonderful place to be! Are you going to be there in Heaven? Will you be clothed in a robe of white righteousness–not your own–the righteousness of the Lord Jesus Christ? That is very important.

- **Matthew 7:14**
  "Because strait *is* the gate, and narrow *is* the way, which leadeth unto life, and few there be that find it."

The Lord Jesus Christ said that in this age in which we live there are going to be few that find the right way. There is not going to be a **multitude**.

- **2 Timothy 3:13**
  "But evil men and seducers shall wax worse and worse, deceiving, and being deceived."

There is not going to be a great revival at the end of the age of grace. Many people say there is going to be a revival. This verse seems to say, "No." There will not be a revival.

There will be a revival here in Revelation 7:9. There certainly will be **multitudes**, *a great* **multitude** *which no man could number.* They could not even count them because there will be so many genuinely saved, standing before the Lord, and before the Lamb. This will be the result of the gospel preaching of the 144,000 Jewish evangelists.

What about salvation after the Rapture? People say, "When the Lord Jesus Christ takes away the genuine believers, can anybody be genuinely saved if they have heard the gospel and have rejected it?" Many feel that these people cannot be truly saved. However, I believe that those that never heard the gospel before and never rejected the Lord Jesus Christ before, can be genuinely saved during the tribulation. But those who have heard the gospel, and rejected it before the rapture, cannot be genuinely saved. Why do I say this?

- **2 Thessalonians 2:6-12**
  "And now ye know what withholdeth that he might be revealed in his time. For the mystery of iniquity doth already work: only he who now letteth *will let*, until he be taken out of the way. And then shall that Wicked be revealed, whom the Lord shall consume with the spirit of his mouth, and shall destroy with the brightness of his coming: *Even him*, whose coming is after the working of Satan with all power and signs and lying wonders, And with all deceivableness of unrighteousness in them that

perish; because they received not the love of the truth, that they might be saved. And for this cause God shall send them strong delusion, that they should believe a lie: That they all might be damned who believed not the truth, but had pleasure in unrighteousness."

The Removal Of The Holy Spirit

The Holy Spirit will be removed when the rapture of the true church takes place. The hindering against sin will no longer be present strongly in the world. In some of these miracle workers, Benny Hinn and some of the others, Satan has his lying wonders as well. Many believe that their eyes will be so blinded when the genuine believers are gone, raptured from this place, they will believe the lie of the antichrist who comes and deceives. The chance for them to be genuinely saved is before the Lord Jesus Christ comes back in the rapture, not afterwards. As I said before, many of the people all over the world who have never heard the gospel can and will be genuinely saved. These 144,000 evangelists will permit this to happen.

- **Exodus 23:2**
  "Thou shalt not follow a **multitude** to *do* evil; neither shalt thou speak in a cause to decline after many to wrest *judgment*:"

Just because the **multitude** says, "Come on, do it," do not follow them.

- **Matthew 21:8-9**
  "And a very great **multitude** spread their garments in the way; others cut down branches from the trees, and strawed *them* in the way. And the **multitudes** that went before, and that followed, cried, saying, Hosanna to the Son of David: Blessed *is* he that cometh in the name of the Lord; Hosanna in the highest."

That was on Palm Sunday. **Multitudes** were there, but look in Matthew 26:47.

- **Matthew 26:47**
  "And while he yet spake, lo, Judas, one of the twelve, came, and with him a great **multitude** with swords and staves, from the chief priests and elders of the people."

The Lord Jesus Christ was in the garden of Gethsemane. There was a big **crowd**. What did they have with them? They had swords and staves. They were out to crucify the Lamb of God that taketh away the sin of the world.

- **Matthew 27:20**
  "But the chief priests and elders persuaded the **multitude** that they should ask Barabbas, and destroy Jesus."
- **Zechariah 12:10**
  "And I will pour upon the house of David, and upon the inhabitants of Jerusalem, the spirit of grace and of supplications: and they shall look upon me whom they have pierced, and they shall mourn for him, as one mourneth for *his* only *son*, and shall be in bitterness for him, as one that is in bitterness for *his* firstborn."

The Jewish Evangelists

God will put his hand upon every one of the twelve tribes of these evangelists. They will go forth throughout the whole world. As I said before, the Jewish evangelists, sealed with the power of God, will do more in seven years than the Gentiles have been able to do in over 2,000 years, as far as winning souls to the Lord Jesus Christ. That does not mean we should stop trying. Praise God, one day He will cause these Jews to be redeemed, to be genuinely saved, to come back to their Messiah and to look upon Him whom they have pierced, as it says in the book of Zechariah.

God will use these Jewish Christians in the evangelizing of the world through God's written Words, through video, through audio, through radio, through Internet, through word of mouth, and through any other means that God may approve.

Revelation 7:10

"And cried with a loud voice, saying, Salvation to our God which sitteth upon the throne, and unto the Lamb."
This was the redeemed multitude that were genuinely saved from that tribulation period, out of the terrible slaughters and judgments. They are the ones that **cried with a loud voice**. The word *saying* is a present continuous action. They continuously say, *"Salvation to our God which sitteth upon the throne and unto the Lamb."* It is interesting that **salvation** is of the Lord. That certainly is true. It is not by our works or our deeds, but by genuine faith we can enter into that **salvation**, by trusting the Lord Jesus Christ as Saviour and Redeemer.

The Train's Entrance Platform

An illustration was given by Chaplain Maddox when I was in the Navy chaplain corps. He said that God's salvation is like a powerful train. The train represents the power of God. That is like salvation. To step onto the train, we step onto the platform and then step onto the train. That platform by which we step onto the train is faith. It is genuine faith in the Lord Jesus Christ that gets us onto God's powerful train of His salvation.

- **Exodus 14:13**
  "And Moses said unto the people, Fear ye not, stand still, and see the **salvation** of the LORD, which he will shew to you to day: for the Egyptians whom ye have seen to day, ye shall see them again no more for ever."

The Lord is the only One Who can genuinely **save** us and nobody else.

- **Exodus 15:2**
  "The LORD is my strength and song, and he is become my **salvation**: he is my God, and I will prepare him an habitation; my father's God, and I will exalt him."

- **2 Chronicles 20:17**
  "Ye shall not *need* to fight in this *battle*: set yourselves, stand ye *still*, and see the **salvation** of the LORD with you, O Judah and Jerusalem: fear not, nor be dismayed; to morrow go out against them: for the LORD *will be* with you."

Salvation is of the Lord. The saved multitude in Heaven are continuously saying, *"Salvation to our God!"*

- **Psalm 3:8**
  "**Salvation** *belongeth* unto the LORD: thy blessing is upon thy people. Selah."

- **Psalm 51:12**
  "Restore unto me the joy of thy **salvation**; and uphold me *with thy* free spirit."

This was after David had sinned in the adultery with Bathsheba and then murdered Uriah the Hittite. It is always God's **salvation**. We have many people today that are running around trying to **save** themselves, whether by good works, or by baptism, or by joining a church, or by some other means—but this is not the way.

- **Jonah 2:9**
  "But I will sacrifice unto thee with the voice of thanksgiving; I will pay *that* that I have vowed. **Salvation** *is* of the LORD."

Jonah, from the whale's belly said, *"Salvation is of the LORD."* When he finally found out that salvation is of the Lord, then that great fish vomited him up. He was spared, but **salvation is of the Lord.**

- **Acts 4:12**
  "Neither is there **salvation** in any other: for there is none other name under Heaven given among men, whereby we must be **saved.**"

- **Romans 1:16**
  "For I am not ashamed of the gospel of Christ: for it is the power of God unto **salvation** to every one that believeth; to the Jew first, and also to the Greek."

The gospel of the Lord Jesus Christ concerning His death, His burial, and resurrection, is **salvation** by faith. **Salvation is of the Lord.**

- **Titus 2:11**
  "For the grace of God that bringeth **salvation** hath appeared to all men,"

The grace of God brought **salvation.** If the Lord Jesus Christ had never come to this earth to bring **salvation,** dying on the cross for our sins, we would never have had it.

- **Titus 2:12-13**
  "Teaching us that, denying ungodliness and worldly lusts, we should live soberly, righteously, and godly, in this present world; Looking for that blessed hope, and the glorious appearing of the great God and our Saviour Jesus Christ;"

We have the **salvation** of God. That is what these redeemed people were saying around the throne.

Revelation 7:11

"And all the angels stood round about the throne, and *about* the elders and the four beasts, and fell before the throne on their faces, and worshipped God,"

Here you have the **angelic** host, and the **elders,** representing the true church or the believers, the genuinely saved in Heaven, and the **four beasts.**

The Meaning Of Worship

Worship is important. That word for worship, by the way, is PROSKUNEO. It means literally, *to kiss the hand in token of reverence.* The picture is like a dog licking his master's hand. That is the worship. Among the Asians, especially to the

> Persians, it means *to fall upon the knees and touch the ground with the forehead.* This is profound reverence. In the New Testament, it is *kneeling or prostration to do homage.* This is what that word *worship* means.

- **Exodus 34:14**
  "For thou shalt **worship** no other god: for the LORD, whose name is Jealous, is a jealous God:"

We are not to **worship** any other god.

- **Psalm 96:9**
  "O **worship** the LORD in the beauty of holiness: fear before him, all the earth."

This is the attitude of **worship**. We might not be able to fall down with our forehead on the ground, but our attitude should be submission to the Lord Jesus Christ and bowing in **worship**. That is what **worship** means.

- **Matthew 4:9-10**
  "And saith unto him, All these things will I give thee, if thou wilt fall down and **worship** me. Then saith Jesus unto him, Get thee hence, Satan: for it is written, Thou shalt **worship** the Lord thy God, and him only shalt thou serve."

Satan wanted the Lord Jesus Christ to **worship** him. If you remember, He was in the wilderness in the temptation forty days and forty nights without food. The Lord Jesus Christ owns all the kingdoms and all the power, anyway. Satan claimed that he owned them and he would give them to the Lord Jesus Christ if He would **worship** him.

- **John 4:24**
  "God *is* a Spirit: and they that **worship** him must **worship** *him* in spirit and in truth."

This woman at the well had told the Lord Jesus Christ that her people **worshipped** at the mountain in Samaria and the Jews at Jerusalem. The Lord Jesus Christ told her that the time would come when they would not **worship** at any mountain. We must not possess any physical things, idols, images, or likenesses. We **worship** *in spirit and in truth.*

- **Acts 17:23**
  "For as I passed by, and beheld your devotions, I found an altar with this inscription, TO THE UNKNOWN GOD. Whom therefore ye ignorantly **worship**, him declare I unto you."

Paul was in Athens. They had altars to all kinds of gods. He said, "You have all these idols and you **worship** someone you do not even understand." He preached the Lord Jesus Christ to them.

- **Hebrews 1:6**
"And again, when he bringeth in the firstbegotten into the world, he saith, And let all the angels of God **worship** him."
This talks about the Lord Jesus Christ. He is the only One that merits our **worship**. All the elders and the four beasts fell down before the throne and **worshipped** the Lord Jesus Christ.

Revelation 7:12

"Saying, Amen: Blessing, and glory, and wisdom, and thanksgiving, and honour, and power, and might, *be* unto our God for ever and ever. Amen."

These are the seven different attributes of **worship** of the Lord, the God of Heaven and earth, and God the Father. In Chapter 5 of the book of Revelation, these are ascribed to the worthiness of the Lamb. He is **worthy**, the Lord Jesus Christ, the Lamb of God. These who were falling down and **worshipping** were saying, *"Amen."* They began with **Amen** and they end with **Amen**.

Seven Attributes Of Worship

1. **Blessing**
When we **bless**, we should **bless** the Lord. That means we are thinking that He is worthy of our **blessing**. We should always ask the Lord to **bless** our food before we eat breakfast, lunch, or supper. The **blessing** is of the Lord. This is important.

2. **Glory**
He is the only One Who has **glory**. We have no **glory** of our own. He is the Shekinah glory, so much so that when the Lord Jesus Christ came on this earth He had to veil His **glory**. That is the reason for the incarnation, God becoming flesh and dwelling among us. The **glory** was unveiled on the Mount of Transfiguration. He was **glorified** and His garments glistened and were **glorious**.

3. **Wisdom**
The **wisdom** of God is found in the Scriptures. There is no one like Him in **wisdom** or knowledge. He is **omniscient**, all wise.

4. **Thanksgiving**
We should never forget to **thank** the Lord, not simply at **Thanksgiving** time and season, but always.

5. Honour

We should **honor** the Lord with our firstfruits, with our service, with our bodies.

6. Power

We should attribute **power** and might to Him.

7. Might

- **Matthew 28:18-19**
  "And Jesus came and spake unto them, saying, All **power** is given unto me in Heaven and in earth. Go ye therefore, and teach all nations, baptizing them in the name of the Father, and of the Son, and of the Holy Ghost:"

- **Acts 2:21**
  "And it shall come to pass, *that* whosoever shall call on the name of the Lord shall be saved."

This is the **power** and the **might** that are His. We should put on the armour of God. All of these attributes are given unto the Father and to the Son by these who are genuinely saved and redeemed.

Revelation 7:13

"And one of the elders answered, saying unto me, What are these which are arrayed in white robes? and whence came they?"

Here again are the people in **white robes**. **White** is the color that represents redeemed people. These are redeemed people in Glory, in Heaven, and they are arrayed in **white**. It speaks of purity.

- **Revelation 6:11**
  "And **white robes** were given unto every one of them; and it was said unto them, that they should rest yet for a little season, until their fellowservants also and their brethren, that should be killed as they *were*, should be fulfilled."

- **Revelation 3:4**
  "Thou hast a few names even in Sardis which have not defiled their garments; and they shall walk with me in **white**: for they are worthy."

- **Revelation 3:5**
  "He that overcometh, the same shall be clothed in **white** raiment; and I will not blot out his name out of the book of life, but I will confess his name before my Father, and before his angels."

- **Revelation 3:18**
  "I counsel thee to buy of me gold tried in the fire, that thou mayest be rich; and **white raiment**, that thou mayest be clothed, and *that* the shame of thy nakedness do not appear; and anoint thine eyes with eyesalve, that thou mayest see."

The church of Laodicea, which was a hypocritical and apostate church, was told by the Lord Jesus Christ to clothe themselves in **white raiment**, not their own good works.

- **Revelation 4:4**
  "And round about the throne *were* four and twenty seats: and upon the seats I saw four and twenty elders sitting, clothed in **white raiment**; and they had on their heads crowns of gold."

The twenty-four elders are a picture of the true church, the genuine believers.

- **Revelation 7:9**
  "After this I beheld, and, lo, a great multitude, which no man could number, of all nations, and kindreds, and people, and tongues, stood before the throne, and before the Lamb, clothed with **white robes**, and palms in their hands;"

This is a picture of purity and righteousness. We speak of brides coming in **white**. Sometimes they are not pure. They are impure, but they still wear the **white**. I do not understand that. **White** is a picture of righteousness.

- **Genesis 15:6**
  "And he believed in the LORD; and he counted it to him for righteousness."

Abraham believed in the LORD and He counted it to him for righteousness. This is the purity, the **white robes**. When we get to Heaven we will have the **white robes** upon us.

- **Romans 3:22**
  "Even the **righteousness** of God *which is* by faith of Jesus Christ unto all and upon all them that believe: for there is no difference:"

Unto all means the gospel is to everyone who wants to trust the Lord Jesus Christ as Saviour, but *upon all* is only for those who genuinely believe. The invitation is given to all, but only those who genuinely believe are truly saved.

- **Romans 4:5**
  "But to him that worketh not, but believeth on him that justifieth the ungodly, his faith is counted for righteousness."

That is the **white** robes, the righteous robes, the pure robes.

- 2 Corinthians 5:21
  "For he hath made him *to be* sin for us, who knew no sin; that
  we might be made the righteousness of God in him."

God the Father made God the Son "*to be sin for us,*" in our place. If we
are trusting Him and redeemed and genuinely born-again, we have His
righteousness and we will deserve the **white robes** in Glory.

Revelation 7:14

**"And I said unto him, Sir, thou knowest. And he said to
me, These are they which came out of great tribulation,
and have washed their robes, and made them white in the
blood of the Lamb."**

John, the one who is writing this, said to the angel, "**Thou
knowest**" who these are. They came out of great tribulation. They were
slaughtered by the antichrist, the beast, and the false prophet. Here are
the **white robes** again. They made them **white in the blood of the
Lamb.**

- Isaiah 1:18
  "Come now, and let us reason together, saith the LORD: though
  your sins be as scarlet, they shall be as **white** as snow; though
  they be red like crimson, they shall be as wool."

Red, the **blood of the Lamb**, equals **white**. John MacArthur has a
heresy on the **blood** of the Lord Jesus Christ. He says that the **blood** in
Scripture does not mean blood. It is just a metonym, or a figure of
speech, for death. No. **Blood** means **blood.** His death was one thing,
but the application of His **blood** was another. There are at least fourteen
Biblical effects of the literal **blood** of the Lord Jesus Christ. It is not the
death of the Lord Jesus Christ, although He shed His **blood** at His
death. That is true, but God says **blood** does fourteen things. First there
is redemption, or atonement, substitution, remission, salvation,
purchase through the literal **blood** of the Lord Jesus Christ.

- Leviticus 17:11
  "For the life of the flesh *is* in the **blood**: and I have given it to
  you upon the altar to make an atonement for your souls: for it *is*
  the **blood** *that* maketh an atonement for the soul."

Blood, Not Death, Makes Atonement

It is the blood that makes atonement. The death of the
substitute in the sacrifices of the Old Testament was not it, but
the blood properly applied. If God says it is the blood, I believe

it is the blood. We must not twist the Scriptures as John
MacArthur and his many followers do.

- **Matthew 26:28**
  "For this is my **blood** of the new testament, which is shed for
  many for the remission of sins."

He is talking about the literal **blood** of the Lord Jesus Christ shed.

- **Mark 14:24**
  "And he said unto them, This is my **blood** of the new testament,
  which is shed for many."

- **Luke 22:20**
  "Likewise also the cup after supper, saying, This cup *is* the new
  testament in my **blood**, which is shed for you."

- **Acts 20:28**
  "Take heed therefore unto yourselves, and to all the flock, over
  the which the Holy Ghost hath made you overseers, to feed the
  church of God, which he hath purchased with his own **blood**."

Here is a purchase with His **blood**. God says that the Lord Jesus Christ's
blood is important. By the way, John MacArthur is in error when he
teaches that the **blood** of the Lord Jesus Christ is just human **blood**,
just like your **blood** and my **blood**. No. It is not just human **blood**. It
is incorruptible **blood**. It is the **blood** that God provided for Him when
He gave Him His body in the virgin birth of the Lord Jesus Christ.

- **Hebrews 10:5**
  "Wherefore when he cometh into the world, he saith, Sacrifice
  and offering thou wouldest not, but a **body** hast thou prepared
  me:"

In the incarnation, when God became man, God the Father prepared a
special **body** for the Lord Jesus Christ through the virgin birth. That
included His muscles, His head, His feet, His **blood**, His nerves–all the
parts of His body. The **blood** of the Lord Jesus Christ is not simply
human **blood**. Human **blood** could never atone for anything. We use
human **blood** for **blood** transfusions. It is all right for that, but it will
never genuinely save the soul. It is the Lord Jesus Christ who died for us.

- **Romans 5:9**
  "Much more then, being now justified by his **blood**, we shall be
  saved from wrath through him."

*Justified by His **blood**.* God talks about the literal **blood** of the Lord
Jesus Christ.

- **Ephesians 1:7**
  "In whom we have redemption through his **blood**, the
  forgiveness of sins, according to the riches of his grace;"

- **Colossians 1:14**
  "In whom we have redemption through his **blood**, *even* the forgiveness of sins:"

The Bible Speaks Often About Blood

God speaks throughout His Scripture about the blood of the Lord Jesus Christ being for redemption, for atonement, for forgiveness, for purchase. The death of the Lord Jesus Christ is one thing, that is true, but the shedding of His blood is for the purchase and for the redemption.

- **1 Peter 1:18-19**
  "Forasmuch as ye know that ye were not redeemed with corruptible things, *as* silver and gold, from your vain conversation *received* by tradition from your fathers; But with the precious **blood** of Christ, as of a lamb without blemish and without spot:"

We are bought with the precious **blood** of the Lord Jesus Christ. We are not redeemed with corruptible things. That is where, by analogy, we see that the **blood** of the Lord Jesus Christ is incorruptible. If it says we are not redeemed with corruptible things, such as silver, gold, or precious stones, but with the precious **blood** of the Lord Jesus Christ, it is incorruptible. That is the contrast–not with corruptible things, but with the precious **blood**.

I believe that incorruptible blood is on the mercy seat of God in Heaven and it speaks as we trust the Lord Jesus Christ as Saviour. Satan tempts the genuine Christians on this earth and points the finger in accusation, "That person there sinned!" God the Father simply points to the **blood** of the Lord Jesus Christ on the mercy seat and says, "No, that sinner has sinned, but I have forgiven his sin by the **blood** of my Son, the Lord Jesus Christ."

Christ's Blood Is Without Blemish

The precious blood of the Lord Jesus Christ is without blemish and without spot. If it is the *precious blood of Christ, as of a lamb without blemish and without spot,* how could it be mere human blood? Our blood is with blemish. Our blood has sickness, disease, and other things are carried with it. I believe, in fact, after Adam was created by God and he sinned, that sin nature was passed on through Adam's blood line to all of us today. The sin nature and wickedness of sin comes

through the blood line. We have a sinful nature through Adam
and because of Adam's sin, all die.

- **Revelation 5:9**
  "And they sung a new song, saying, Thou art worthy to take the
  book, and to open the seals thereof: for thou wast slain, and hast
  redeemed us to God by thy **blood** out of every kindred, and
  tongue, and people, and nation;"

The Lord Jesus Christ, the **Lamb**, is worthy. That verse shows
clearly how John MacArthur's heresy is completely wrong. In this same
verse, it talks about *thou wast slain*, talking about the Lord Jesus Christ.
That is His death. Then it says, *and redeemed us to God by thy **blood***.
Here is the death and the **blood** in the same verse. **Blood** is not a
metonym for death. **Blood** is **blood** in the Scriptures. John MacArthur
points to only a very few places in the Scripture where "**blood**" is used
as a figure of speech. Sometimes it is, but all the way through,
predominantly, when the **blood** is shed in the sacrifices of the Old
Testament, all the **blood** of lambs, and goats, and so on, it is literal
blood. It is not a figure of speech at all.

   1. The first effect of the blood of Christ is redemption.
   2. The second effect of the blood of Christ is propitiation.
Propitiation means God is satisfied. He is satisfied with the death and the
work of His Son.

- **Romans 3:25**
  "Whom God hath set forth *to be* a propitiation through faith in
  his **blood**, to declare his righteousness for the remission of sins
  that are past, through the forbearance of God;"

   3. The third effect of the blood of Christ is justification.

- **Romans 5:9**
  "Much more then, being now **justified** by his **blood**, we shall
  be saved from wrath through him."

God declares us righteous by the **blood** of Christ. That was the sacrifice.
That was the thing that atones for sin.

   4. The fourth effect of the blood of Christ is fellowship.

- **Ephesians 2:13**
  "But now in Christ Jesus ye who sometimes were far off are
  made nigh by the **blood** of Christ."

We are made nigh. That means close. That means **fellowship**. We can
have **fellowship** with the Lord by the **blood** of the Lord Jesus Christ.

5. <u>The fifth effect of the blood of Christ is peace</u>.
- **Colossians 1:20**
  "And, having made **peace** through the **blood** of his cross, by him to reconcile all things unto himself; by him, *I say*, whether *they be* things in earth, or things in Heaven."

6. <u>The sixth effect of the blood of Christ is forgiveness</u>.
- **Ephesians 1:7**
"In whom we have redemption through his **blood**, the **forgiveness** of sins, according to the riches of his grace;"
- **Colossians 1:14**
"In whom we have redemption through his **blood**, *even* the **forgiveness** of sins:"

7. <u>The seventh effect of the   blood of Christ is sanctification</u>. It means setting us apart.
- **Hebrews 13:12**
  "Wherefore Jesus also, that he might **sanctify** the people with his own **blood**, suffered without the gate."

8. <u>The eighth effect of the literal blood of Christ is reconciliation</u>.
- **Colossians 1:20**
  "And, having made peace through the **blood** of his cross, by him to **reconcile** all things unto himself; by him, *I say*, whether *they be* things in earth, or things in Heaven."

9. <u>The ninth effect of the blood of Christ is cleansing, purging, washing, or purifying</u>. There are five different Scriptures that show us that.
- **Hebrews 9:14**
  "How much more shall the **blood** of Christ, who through the eternal Spirit offered himself without spot to God, **purge** your conscience from dead works to serve the living God?"
- **Hebrews 9:23**
  "*It was* therefore necessary that the patterns of things in the Heavens should be **purified** with these; but the Heavenly things themselves with better sacrifices than these."
- **1 John 1:7**
  "But if we walk in the light, as he is in the light, we have fellowship one with another, and the **blood** of Jesus Christ his Son **cleanseth** us from all sin."

- **Revelation 1:5**
  "And from Jesus Christ, *who is* the faithful witness, *and* the first begotten of the dead, and the prince of the kings of the earth. Unto him that loved us, and **washed** us from our sins in his own **blood**,"
- **Revelation 7:14**
  "And I said unto him, Sir, thou knowest. And he said to me, These are they which came out of great tribulation, and have **washed** their robes, and made them **white** in the **blood** of the Lamb."

10. The tenth effect of the blood of Christ is remembrance.

- **1 Corinthians 11:25**
  "After the same manner also *he took* the cup, when he had supped, saying, This cup is the new testament in my **blood**: this do ye, as oft as ye drink it, in **remembrance** of me."

11. The eleventh effect of the blood of Christ is boldness and access to God's throne.

- **Hebrews 10:19**
  "Having therefore, brethren, **boldness** to enter into the holiest by the **blood** of Jesus,"

12. The twelfth effect of the blood of Christ is maturity in doing God's will.

- **Hebrews 13:20-21**
  "Now the God of peace, that brought again from the dead our Lord Jesus Christ, that great shepherd of the sheep, through the **blood** of the everlasting covenant, Make you **perfect** in every good work to do his will, working in you that which is wellpleasing in his sight, through Jesus Christ; to whom *be* glory for ever and ever. Amen."

13. The thirteenth effect of the blood of Christ is punishment—sometimes sickness, or weakness, through the mistreatment of the blood of Christ.

- **Hebrews 10:29**
  "Of how much sorer **punishment**, suppose ye, shall he be thought worthy, who hath trodden under foot the Son of God, and hath counted the **blood** of the covenant, wherewith he was sanctified, an **unholy** thing, and hath done despite unto the Spirit of grace?"

God is going to judge for this. This is exactly what John MacArthur has said about the **blood** of Christ, that it is **common** (KOINOS) and **unholy**. That is the Greek word used in this verse for "unholy."

MacArthur counts the **blood** of the Lord Jesus Christ as just a **common** thing, as if the **blood** of the Lord Jesus Christ is just **common blood** and human **blood** like yours and mine. This is serious heresy! I think this verse focuses on this very heresy of John MacArthur, saying the **blood** of the Lord Jesus Christ is just like our **blood, common** and just **human blood.** He is in serious trouble, as far as I am concerned, and is going to have some sore **punishment** when he stands before the Lord Jesus Christ in judgment. If he is a genuinely saved man, he is going to stand before the judgment seat of the Lord Jesus Christ.

- **1 Corinthians 11:27**
  "Wherefore whosoever shall eat this bread, and drink *this* cup of the Lord, **unworthily,** shall be **guilty** of the body and **blood** of the Lord."

We have to be careful that we are not drinking **unworthily.** Unsaved people should never partake of the Lord's Supper.

- **1 Corinthians 11:29-30**
  "For he that eateth and drinketh **unworthily,** eateth and drinketh **damnation** to himself, not discerning the Lord's body. For this cause many *are* weak and sickly among you, and many sleep."

God killed some of the early Christians who were carousing around at the Lord's Supper, drunk and disorderly, and not walking with the Lord Jesus Christ. There are some judgments involved with that, as well.

14. The fourteenth effect that we have through the blood of Christ is victory over Satan.

- **Revelation 12:11**
  "And they **overcame** him by the **blood** of the Lamb, and by the word of their testimony; and they loved not their lives unto the death."

The one that they are **overcoming** is the Devil, or Satan, or the serpent.

The Blood Of Christ Is Important

These fourteen things in Scripture talk about the blood of the Lord Jesus Christ. We have to take all of them by genuine faith. Not one of them says, "the death" in any of these fourteen different times. It is the blood of the Lord Jesus Christ. God considers the blood of the Lamb to be important. These who were genuinely saved, washed their robes and made them white in the blood of the Lamb, because they had genuinely trusted Him. They were truly saved. They were born-again believers. They were genuine

Christians. As such, they could have white robes, washed in the blood of the Lamb.

- **Isaiah 1:18**
  "Come now, and let us reason together, saith the LORD: though your sins be as **scarlet**, they shall be as white as snow; though they be red like crimson, they shall be as **wool**."

Here is the washing by the **blood** of the cross and by the **blood** of the Lamb. There is a poem that my mother-in-law, Gertrude Sanborn, has written from Colossians 1:20 entitled,

The Blood of His Cross.

*The **Blood** of His cross—*
O how precious and holy!
It covers the sin
Of the lost, guilty one.

It avails for the souls
Of our innocent children
And those who are sick
And weak and undone.

*The **Blood** of His cross—*
That blest cleansing flow—
We are by its crimson
Made whiter than snow.

It availeth forever;
Its power will abide.
That life-stream from Calvary
That flowed from His side.

It is important that these who are genuinely saved are washed and cleansed by the blood of the Lord Jesus Christ. <u>Are you washed and cleansed by the **blood** of the Lord Jesus Christ</u>? Have you genuinely trusted, accepted, and received Him as Saviour and Redeemer? That is important.

Slaying Of Christians By Antichrist

These who *came out of great tribulation* came out of the seven years of judgments upon this earth. They were genuinely saved. The antichrist, the one who was an evil monster upon this earth at that time, slew these genuine

Christians and they were taken to Heaven. They were praising the Lord Jesus Christ. They washed their robes and made them white in the blood of the Lamb.

Revelation 7:15

"Therefore are they before the throne of God, and serve him day and night in his temple: and he that sitteth on the throne shall dwell among them."

These who are genuinely saved and have their robes washed **white** in the **blood** of the **Lamb** are before the throne of God. Nobody can get before the throne of God who is not genuinely saved. The lost will not be in Heaven. If you have never genuinely trusted the Lord Jesus Christ as your Saviour and Redeemer, you are not going to be there. Nobody is going to be there who is not genuinely born-again. It is going to be a special place, a holy place, an exclusive place for only those who have been redeemed.

What They Do In Heaven

Notice what they do there in Heaven. Notice these who were saved out of great tribulation and washed their robes in the blood of the Lamb. They serve Him. That is a present tense, continuously serving Him. Not just for a second, but every day. Not just every day, but every day and every night. Of course, it says in the Scripture later that there will be no night there, but they will be continuously serving the Lord. Where? In His temple in Heaven.

- **Acts 20:18-19**
  "And when they were come to him, he said unto them, Ye know, from the first day that I came into Asia, after what manner I have been with you at all seasons, **Serving** the Lord with all humility of mind, and with many tears, and temptations, which befell me by the lying in wait of the Jews:"

Paul was a **servant.** We are going to be **serving** the Lord Jesus Christ up in Heaven. Do you serve Him here? God wants us to **serve** the Lord Jesus Christ here as well. In Heaven, we are going to **serve** the Lord Jesus Christ night and day.

- **Acts 27:23**
  "For there stood by me this night the angel of God, whose I am, and whom I **serve,**"

When Paul was shipwrecked, the people were afraid. The storm was ready to dash that ship against the rocks. The Lord Jesus Christ was the One whom Paul **served**.

- **Romans 1:9**
  "For God is my witness, whom I **serve** with my spirit in the gospel of his Son, that without ceasing I make mention of you always in my prayers;"

We are here to **serve**. We are not here to just soak up the things of the Lord, but to **serve** the Lord Jesus Christ in all the ways that we can.

- **Romans 12:1**
  "I beseech you therefore, brethren, by the mercies of God, that ye present your bodies a living sacrifice, holy, acceptable unto God, *which is* your reasonable **service**."

God Wants Our Bodies For Himself

God wants our bodies. You may ask, "He wants my body?" That is right. You might say, "Well, I have to work." All right, but while you work, He wants you to use your body to witness–your hands, your eyes, your mouth, and your feet to walk in His ways. He wants you and beseeches you to give Him your "reasonable service."

- **Romans 12:11**
  "Not slothful in business; fervent in spirit; **serving** the Lord;"

We can **serve** the Lord Jesus Christ no matter what we are doing or where we are. We can be **serving** the Lord Jesus Christ in some way whether at work, at play, at school, or anywhere else.

- **Ephesians 6:7**
  "With good will doing **service**, as to the Lord, and not to men:"

Is our **service** only to men or is it to the Lord Jesus Christ? It is important to **serve** the Lord.

- **Colossians 3:24**
  "Knowing that of the Lord ye shall receive the reward of the inheritance: for ye **serve** the Lord Christ."

Service for the Lord Jesus Christ is what we need be about.

- **1 Thessalonians 1:9**
  "For they themselves shew of us what manner of entering in we had unto you, and how ye turned to God from idols to **serve** the living and true God;"

Here were pagans in Thessalonica that worshipped idols. The gospel is powerful enough to get people away from idols. Then what? **Serve** the living and true God.

- **Hebrews 9:14**
  "How much more shall the blood of Christ, who through the eternal Spirit offered himself without spot to God, purge your conscience from dead works to **serve** the living God?"

God wants us to **serve** Him here. These that came out of the tribulation **served** the Lord Jesus Christ day and night before the throne.

Dwelling With God For Eternity

Then it says, *"he that sitteth on the throne shall dwell among them."* He dwells with us now, but we will dwell with Him. God is dwelling with the genuine believers, the ones who are genuinely saved, in His omnipresence. One day, if we are genuinely saved, we are going to be dwelling with Him.

- **Psalm 23:6**
  "Surely goodness and mercy shall follow me all the days of my life: and I will **dwell** in the house of the LORD for ever."
- **Matthew 1:23**
  "Behold, a virgin shall be with child, and shall bring forth a son, and they shall call his name **Emmanuel**, which being interpreted is, God **with us**."

This talks about the fulfillment of Isaiah 7:14, the virgin birth of the Lord Jesus Christ, *Emmanuel*. "IM" is *with*, "U" is *us*, "EL" is *God*. God is **with us.** The Lord Jesus Christ was *"God-with-us"* here on this earth. He is perfect God, **dwelling** in a body, come from Heaven to save sinners such as we.

- **Matthew 28:20**
  "Teaching them to observe all things whatsoever I have commanded you: and, lo, I am **with you** alway, *even* unto the end of the world. Amen."

The presence of the Lord Jesus Christ promises to be **with us** who are genuinely saved to the end of the world.

- **Revelation 21:3**
  "And I heard a great voice out of Heaven saying, Behold, the tabernacle of God *is* with men, and he will **dwell** with them, and they shall be his people, and God himself shall be **with them**, *and be* their God."

Heaven will be made up of people **dwelling** with the Lord and the Lord **dwelling** with people. People may say, "I don't want to be in the presence of the Lord." The people at Mount Sinai, at the giving of the law, said to Moses, "We are not going to go over that mount. It is shaking and quivering. There are earthquakes, lightning, and thunder. We are afraid. You go up and represent us." Those people did not want to be in the presence of the Lord. I would not want to be in the **presence** of thunder and lightning either. In our unsaved bodies no one in this world can be in the **presence** of God and live. We would die. When we have our new bodies, just like the resurrected, glorified body of the Lord Jesus Christ, we not only will be able to be with the Lord but we will be rejoicing in His **presence**. We will be glad to be with the Lord. We will dwell with Him and He will dwell with us.

The Millennial Reign Of Christ

In the millennial reign of the Lord Jesus Christ there will be a change of attitude and a change of many other things. There will be a change in topography, a change in mountains, rivers, and plains. There will also be a change in the nature of the beasts. God can change that nature and He will do so. The lion will lie down with the lamb in peace.

He is going to change nature. That is what makes us able to be with and dwell with the Lord. We who are genuinely born-again will be able to be with Him because our natures will be changed and our whole bodies. We will have our robes washed white in the blood of the Lamb.

Revelation 7:16

"They shall hunger no more, neither thirst any more; neither shall the sun light on them, nor any heat."

In Heaven, He will take care of **hunger** and **thirst**. Right now, we **thirst**. We drink water and we are refreshed. We **hunger** and we eat food, but in Heaven our bodies will not be like these bodies. They will not need water and food. We will not **hunger**. We will not **thirst**. The sun shall not **light** on us, nor any **heat**. We will not have any sunburn or problems in that area.

- **John 4:14**
  "But whosoever drinketh of the water that I shall give him shall never **thirst**; but the water that I shall give him shall be in him a well of water springing up into everlasting life."

The woman at the well met the Lord Jesus Christ. He asked her for some water. He offered her water if she wanted it. She wondered how He could get water. The well was deep and He had nothing to draw with. The Lord Jesus Christ could, and did, give the water of life to that woman. She came to draw water. She forgot what she came for because now she had living water. She was a prostitute and had five husbands. The one she was living with was not her husband. She dropped her pot of water and went back to the city and said, "Come, see a man, which told me all things that ever I did: is not this the Christ?" He gave her living water. She did not **thirst** anymore, spiritually.

- **John 6:35**
  "And Jesus said unto them, I am the bread of life: he that cometh to me shall never **hunger**; and he that believeth on me shall never **thirst**."

We will not **thirst** or **hunger** spiritually. He satisfies the **hungry** heart. If you have genuinely trusted the Lord Jesus Christ, you understand what that means and what it is.

- **John 7:37-38**
  "In the last day, that great *day* of the feast, Jesus stood and cried, saying, If any man **thirst**, let him come unto me, and drink. He that believeth on me, as the scripture hath said, out of his belly shall flow rivers of living water."

- **Revelation 6:8**
  "And I looked, and behold a pale horse: and his name that sat on him was Death, and Hell followed with him. And power was given unto them over the fourth part of the earth, to kill with sword, and with **hunger**, and with death, and with the beasts of the earth."

The Judgment Of Great Hunger

In this seal judgment there is going to be great hunger on earth. But the Lord Jesus Christ in Heaven will satisfy those of us who are genuinely saved. He will provide for us the food and drink–the water. He will take care of us in Heaven for all eternity.

Revelation 7:17

"For the Lamb which is in the midst of the throne shall feed them, and shall lead them unto living fountains of waters: and God shall wipe away all tears from their eyes."

This is a great thing. The **Lamb**, the Lord Jesus Christ, Whose **blood** washed our robes and made them **white**, is **in the midst of the throne**. He shall **feed them and lead them**. These two things are necessary.

- **Psalm 23:1-2**
  "A Psalm of David. The LORD is my shepherd; I shall not want. He maketh me to lie down in **green pastures**: he **leadeth** me beside the still waters."

He maketh me to lie down in **green pastures**. There is the **feeding**. God has promised to **feed** us. *He* **leadeth** *me beside the still waters.* There is the **leading**. The Shepherd feeds in the green pastures. The Shepherd leads. Here it says the Lamb shall **feed** them and **lead** them unto living fountains of waters.

Wiping Away Tears

Then it talks about God wiping away tears from their eyes. You cannot wipe away what you do not have. Apparently, as people have come out from the great tribulation on this earth, there are tears and they are wiped away by the Lord. There are a number of tears in Scripture.

- **2 Kings 20:5**
  "Turn again, and tell Hezekiah the captain of my people, Thus saith the LORD, the God of David thy father, I have heard thy prayer, I have seen thy **tears**: behold, I will heal thee: on the third day thou shalt go up unto the house of the LORD."

Hezekiah was doomed to death. He was told he had so many years and he was going to die. Hezekiah prayed and wept and God said, *"I have heard thy prayer, I have seen thy* **tears**.*"* God did heal Hezekiah and gave him fifteen extra years to live.

- **Psalm 6:6**
  "I am weary with my groaning; all the night make I my bed to swim; I water my couch with my **tears**."

God is going to **wipe away** all of these **tears** from our eyes in Glory.

- **Psalm 116:8**
  "For thou hast delivered my soul from death, mine eyes from **tears**, *and* my feet from falling."

These are **tears** of sadness. There are also **tears** of joy, of course.

- **Isaiah 25:8**
  "He will swallow up death in victory; and the Lord GOD will **wipe away tears** from off all faces; and the rebuke of his people shall he take away from off all the earth: for the LORD hath spoken *it*."

- Jeremiah 14:17
"Therefore thou shalt say this word unto them; Let mine eyes run down with **tears** night and day, and let them not cease: for the virgin daughter of my people is broken with a great breach, with a very grievous blow."

Jeremiah was a **tearful** prophet. He was a strong preaching prophet, but also a **weeping** prophet.

- Acts 20:19
"Serving the Lord with all humility of mind, and with many **tears**, and temptations, which befell me by the lying in wait of the Jews:"

Why Did Paul Have Tears?

Why would Paul have many tears? Because the people whom he served brought tears to his eyes. He was burdened with tears.

- Acts 20:31
"Therefore watch, and remember, that by the space of three years I ceased not to warn every one night and day with **tears**."

Paul was talking to the elders, bishops, and pastors at the church at Ephesus. He was warning them, but with **tears**. There is an emotional feeling because evil was coming upon these people. Evil comes upon us. We must be warned, but with **tears**.

- 2 Timothy 1:4
"Greatly desiring to see thee, being mindful of thy **tears**, that I may be filled with joy;"

Paul was in prison. He was martyred after his last letter to Timothy. He wanted to see Timothy. He had many tears. He was a pastor. Pastors have burdens and **tears**. Whatever the **tears** were, Paul wanted to see Timothy and to be filled with joy. Timothy did visit Paul in prison and he was made happy and rejoiced because of his fellow preacher.

- Revelation 21:4
"And God shall **wipe away all tears** from their eyes; and there shall be no more death, neither sorrow, nor crying, neither shall there be any more pain: for the former things are passed away."

No Tears In Heaven

This is Glory. This is Heaven. God, indeed, shall wipe away tears from their eyes. These are the saints in Glory, the multitude who were genuinely saved because of the 144,000

Jewish evangelists that were faithful during that seven-year tribulation period, preaching the Words of God. They washed their robes and made them white in the blood of the Lamb. Praise God for that cleansing blood that can genuinely save us, help us, and cleanse us.

Revelation
Chapter Eight

Revelation 8:1

"And when he had opened the seventh seal, there was silence in Heaven about the space of half an hour."

Have you ever thought about **silence**? It is interesting. Why would there be **silence in Heaven** for **half an hour**? I want to look at some verses on **silence** and see if we can figure out some of the meanings of it.

- **Judges 3:19**
  "But he himself turned again from the quarries that *were* by Gilgal, and said, I have a secret errand unto thee, O king: who said, Keep **silence**. And all that stood by him went out from him."

Ehud was one of the judges. He was out to slay the evil king of Moab.

- **Psalm 31:18**
  "Let the lying lips be put to **silence**; which speak grievous things proudly and contemptuously against the righteous."

There are no lying lips in Heaven.

- **Psalm 50:3**
  "Our God shall come, and shall not keep **silence**: a fire shall devour before him, and it shall be very tempestuous round about him."

When the Lord Jesus Christ judges, there is no **silence**. There is tempestuous wind, rain, thunders, and lightnings, but no **silence** when the Lord Jesus Christ is judging.

- **Psalm 83:1**
  "A Song *or* Psalm of Asaph. Keep not thou **silence**, O God: hold not thy peace, and be not still, O God."

When you are listening for the things of the Lord, or you are listening for His voice, listening for what to do next; if you are listening for guidance, the psalmist says, "Do not be **silent**. Tell me what I should do." The Lord can speak and help us.

- **Ecclesiastes 3:7**
  "A time to rend, and a time to sew; a time to keep **silence**, and a time to speak;"

Silence Not Always Golden

The old saying is, "Silence is golden," but sometimes it is yellow. In fact, I think it was Abraham Lincoln who said, "To sin by silence, when they should speak up, makes cowards of men." There is a time to keep silence, but there is a time to speak.

In the **seventh seal** judgment in Heaven there was **silence about a half an hour**. I do not know whether any of us can take pure **silence** for **half an hour** in this life.

If you go into the recesses of the big caves, it is not only dark but I guess it is **silent**. It is hard to keep **silence**. We can hear our heart, we can hear our breathing.

- **Isaiah 62:6**
  "I have set watchmen upon thy walls, O Jerusalem, *which* shall never hold their peace day nor night: ye that make mention of the LORD, keep not **silence**,"

God gave to the prophet Isaiah a charge. Watchmen are to watch for the enemy coming. We have watchmen that need to be watching at the walls for the enemies coming as far as doctrine in the Bible and the different false doctrines. He was a watchman for the enemy soldiers coming in. We needed a watchman on 9-11. There was no watchman. In all the interviews on 9-11 they were trying to blame one another. The Clinton regime did not do enough. The Bush regime did not do enough. The FBI did not do enough. Well, who did do enough? There was no watchman. They knew and they had heard about and read about how that planes could be used to bomb and kill people. Did they tell anyone about it? Did they try anything to protect? No.

Isaiah Was A Watchman

Isaiah was a watchman upon the walls of Jerusalem. The duty of a watchman is to be crying out. People say, "What are you shouting about? Why are you so angry about modernism, unbelief, apostasy, compromise, and things that are wrong in the world? Why do you preach the truth of Scripture?" It is because God has put those of us who are preachers and genuine Christians as watchmen. All of us should be watchmen, watching on the walls.

We should not hold our peace day nor night when we see evidences of evil coming upon us, evidence of different doctrine, things that are tearing apart our Bibles, all these different Bible versions and perversions, and things coming upon us. It is even in the fundamentalist ranks. It is not only in the Roman Catholic or the apostate ranks of the different world religions. It is not only in the liberal, modernist, apostate, and the middle-of-the-road new evangelicals, but fundamental Bible-believing Christians have to be on guard for apostasy and compromise, as watchmen on the walls. We are not to hold our peace. "To sin by silence, when we should speak up, makes cowards of men," as Abraham Lincoln said.

Dr. McIntire, who is with the Lord now, sounded out the alarm here in Collingswood and all over the world with his radio programs. He is gone now. Collingswood would be better if he were still here. I am sure that he would not be homosexual-friendly as they are today. I am sure that many things would be different. I was with him as an associate for several years assisting his radio broadcast and teaching at Shelton College, Cape May, New Jersey. That is why I am in Collingswood, New Jersey.

Watchmen on the walls should not hold their peace day nor night. We cannot keep **silence** if we know the Lord. Speak up!

- **Lamentations 2:10**
  "The elders of the daughter of Zion sit upon the ground, *and* keep **silence**: they have cast up dust upon their heads; they have girded themselves with sackcloth: the virgins of Jerusalem hang down their heads to the ground."

They were imprisoned. They were in captivity. Jeremiah wrote Lamentations. They were **silent** because they were in misery. Sometimes misery and pain do make us **silent**. Sometimes it makes us scream in pain and agony, but here they were silent.

- **Amos 5:13**
  "Therefore the prudent shall keep **silence** in that time; for it *is* an evil time."

Sometimes you speak up when you should be **quiet.** This gets you in trouble. For instance, I remember when we were in the courtroom here in Haddon Township. One man tried to approach the judge and ask him some questions. That policeman spoke right up, "Get back! Sit down!" He did not keep **silent.** I suppose, under the situation and the way

things are, he might have attacked the judge. He might have had a knife
or a gun. They just wanted to keep him back from that area. I noticed
that even when anyone had a paper, or a letter–or anything else–the
officer was to go, and take that paper from the person, and hand it to the
judge. It is very cautious. The prudent shall keep **silence** in the evil day.

- **Habakkuk 2:20**
  "But the LORD *is* in his holy temple: let all the earth keep
  silence before him."

We hear that verse many times. Many churches have that on the top of
their walls for a time of **silence** before the service begins.

- **Matthew 22:34**
  "But when the Pharisees had heard that he had put the
  Sadducees to **silence**, they were gathered together."

There is a way to put people to **silence** as well. The Lord Jesus Christ
was so wise, so honest, and so able, by what He said, to shut them up.
The Pharisees were out to get Him. The Sadducees were out to get Him.
He put them to **silence**. They could not talk. He had answered their
question. To answer anything back would make them look foolish. He
put them to **silence**.

- **Acts 15:12**
  "Then all the multitude kept **silence,** and gave audience to
  Barnabas and Paul, declaring what miracles and wonders God
  had wrought among the Gentiles by them."

It was wonderful when Paul and Barnabas came back to Jerusalem from
their missionary journey and gave a report. The multitudes were **quiet**.

I taught in the Philadelphia school district for nineteen years;
eighteen years in the junior high and one year in the senior high. Believe
you me, when the teacher is teaching in Philadelphia public schools,
there is not **silence**. I think there is probably not **silence** in
Collingswood public schools. I do not think there is **silence** in Haddon
Township, or in Haddon Heights, or in the public schools of any other
towns. I understand from two of my sons, it is not much better in
Christian schools where they both taught. It is probably getting worse.

I am glad for the people of the Lord that I can talk in the church. I
can hear myself talking and thinking. When Paul told about his journey,
the people were **silent**.

- **Acts 21:40**
  "And when he had given him licence, Paul stood on the stairs,
  and beckoned with the hand unto the people. And when there
  was made a great **silence**, he spake unto *them* in the Hebrew
  tongue, saying,"

Paul was on trial. They were amazed that he knew Hebrew as he talked to the Jews that were out to kill him.

- **1 Corinthians 14:28**
  "But if there be no interpreter, let him keep **silence** in the church; and let him speak to himself, and to God."

Tongues Not Scriptural Now

Foreign languages were spoken until the Bible was completed. That was a way of getting the gospel out. In the day of Pentecost, twelve apostles were speaking at least twelve different foreign languages. That was a way of preaching the gospel. They did not understand these languages. They did not learn the languages. The Lord gave these to them as a special gift. These gifts of speaking in other languages, so people could be genuinely saved, was in the true church, I believe, until the Bible was completed. After the Bible was completed, that gift ceased, although the Charismatics and Pentecostals differ with us on that. I believe it ceased. Now we have the Bible. We do not need the special foreign languages.

When the languages were in effect, even in 1 Corinthians 14, they were still special gifts. Even when the gifts were in the true church, they were to be used properly and to have an interpreter.

- **1 Corinthians 14:34**
  "Let your women keep **silence** in the churches: for it is not permitted unto them to speak; but *they are commanded* to be under obedience, as also saith the law."

Here is a verse on women preachers. Women preachers abound in these days in which we live. In fact, I heard this morning on the news that there was a preaching conference of women for two days in this area. It is amazing.

- **1 Timothy 2:11-12**
  "Let the woman learn in **silence** with all subjection. But I suffer not a woman to teach, nor to usurp authority over the man, but to be in **silence**."

There is a hymn called *Be Still, My Soul.* The words were written by Katharina von Schlegel in 1697. We need the **silence** of stillness.

> *Be still, my soul! the Lord is on thy side;*
> *Bear patiently the cross of grief or pain;*
> *Leave to thy God to order and provide;*
> *In ev'ry change, He faithful will remain.*

Be still, my soul! thy best, thy heav'nly Friend
Thru thorny ways leads to a joyful end.

I think the **silence** for half an hour was preparing Heaven for the judgments of the seven trumpets. We have seen that the first part of Revelation had to do with the seven churches, speaking prophetically. Then we had the seven seals. Now we come into the seven trumpets, and following that, the seven vials later on. These are judgments and I believe the silence was preparing for that purpose.

Revelation 8:2

"And I saw the seven angels which stood before God; and to them were given seven trumpets."

Angels Standing Before God

Here are angels standing before God. These are holy angels. Not all the angels can stand before God. Lucifer was an angel, a created being, Satan. He could not stand. He left the Lord, so he was shut out. Holy angels are standing before God.

- **Matthew 25:31**
  "When the Son of man shall come in his glory, and all the holy **angels** with him, then shall he sit upon the throne of his glory:"
The holy **angels** have access to Heaven.
- **Mark 8:38**
  "Whosoever therefore shall be ashamed of me and of my words in this adulterous and sinful generation; of him also shall the Son of man be ashamed, when he cometh in the glory of his Father with the holy **angels**."
There are holy **angels**, as well as unholy **angels**.
- **Revelation 14:10**
  "The same shall drink of the wine of the wrath of God, which is poured out without mixture into the cup of his indignation; and he shall be tormented with fire and brimstone in the presence of the holy **angels**, and in the presence of the Lamb:"
The holy **angels** will be there in the presence of the Lord as people are being tormented. They are there before God. Other things happen before God.
- **Romans 3:19**
  "Now we know that what things soever the law saith, it saith to them who are under the law: that every mouth may be stopped, and all the world may become guilty before God."

At the Great White Throne judgment, when the unbelievers are judged because they rejected the Lord Jesus Christ, and never genuinely received Him as Saviour, their mouths will be stopped. They will have nothing to say.

- **Romans 4:2**
  "For if Abraham were justified by works, he hath *whereof* to glory; but not before God."

Before God is holiness. That is why only the holy **angels** are before Him.

- **1 Thessalonians 3:13**
  "To the end he may stablish your hearts unblameable in holiness before God, even our Father, at the coming of our Lord Jesus Christ with all his saints."

The Presence Of God

   Everyone who is genuinely saved, as a truly born-again Christian, has the very presence of God. We are in His presence. There is no way to escape His presence. You cannot hide from Him. You cannot turn the lights off so He cannot see you. He can see everyone. He sees our hearts. He is omniscient. He knows every heart. We have to be blameless in holiness before Him. These angels stood before God.

- **2 Timothy 4:1-2**
  "I charge *thee* therefore before God, and the Lord Jesus Christ, who shall judge the quick and the dead at his appearing and his kingdom; Preach the word; be instant in season, out of season; reprove, rebuke, exhort with all longsuffering and doctrine."

We read this every Sunday. That is why we try to preach faithfully the Words of God.

Revelation 8:3

   "And another angel came and stood at the altar, having a golden censer; and there was given unto him much incense, that he should offer *it* with the prayers of all saints upon the golden altar which was before the throne."

   Here is another **angel** that came and stood at the altar. He had a **golden censer**. A **censer** is something that has **incense** in it. This word is used only ten times in the entire Bible. The word for **censer** is LIBANOTOS. It is *the gum exuding from a frankincense tree*. The **censer** itself had a very pleasant aroma to it. It is a special container.

- **Leviticus 10:1**
  "And Nadab and Abihu, the sons of Aaron, took either of them his **censer**, and put fire therein, and put **incense** thereon, and offered strange fire before the LORD, which he commanded them not."

Nadab and Abihu were evil sons of Aaron. The Lord slew them.

- **Leviticus 16:12**
  "And he shall take a **censer** full of burning coals of fire from off the altar before the LORD, and his hands full of sweet **incense** beaten small, and bring *it* within the vail:"

This was on the day of atonement, when the high priest went in before the Lord only once a year. The smoking **censer** was to be brought inside the holy of holies. There are two vails. One is the outer vail and one is the inner vail. That inner vail could only be come into once a year by the high priest, sacrificing first for his own sins with the bullock, then the goat for the sins of the people. He then took the blood and put it upon the mercy seat in the holy of holies. He had to come in first with that **censer**. What about the **incense**?

- **Exodus 30:1**
  "And thou shalt make an altar to burn **incense** upon: *of* shittim wood shalt thou make it."

This was a special altar so that the perfume or aroma could be brought before the Lord.

- **Exodus 40:26-27**
  "And he put the **golden altar** in the tent of the congregation before the vail: And he burnt sweet **incense** thereon; as the LORD commanded Moses."

- **Leviticus 16:12-13**
  "And he shall take a **censer** full of burning coals of fire from off the altar before the LORD, and his hands full of sweet **incense** beaten small, and bring *it* within the vail: And he shall put the incense upon the fire before the LORD, that the cloud of the **incense** may cover the mercy seat that *is* upon the testimony, that he die not:"

The Day Of Atonement

On the day of atonement, when the high priest went in once a year, he took the burning coals in the censer and brought it within the vail. Inside the holy of holies you had the mercy seat on top of the ark of the covenant. Inside the ark of the covenant there were the ten commandments, Aaron's rod that budded, and the golden pot of manna. On top of that ark was a mercy seat. It was a place to put the blood of the offerings. Before the high priest could go in to that mercy seat, into the very presence of God, he had to take the incense that he die not. This incense before the mercy seat covered that. In the holy of holies, that is where the presence of the Lord was throughout the entire Israelite journeys. Throughout the forty years in the wilderness, that was where God dwelled. It was a very special place.

That was why Nadab and Abihu offering strange **incense** were slain. That was why the high priest had to be very careful. That is why they say, according to tradition, that when the high priest went in there once a year on the day of atonement (*Yom Kippur* in the Hebrew), he had to have a rope tied to his leg in case he would sin and God would slay him. Who could go in there? Nobody could. They would all die, so they had to pull him out. Whether true or not, it sounds reasonable to me. The incense protected the high priest.

Incense and **prayer** go together. These are things that go up to the Lord, just like the smoke of the **incense**.

- **Psalm 5:3**
  "My voice shalt thou hear in the morning, O LORD; in the morning will I direct *my prayer* unto thee, and will look up."

The Lord wants to hear our voices like **incense** coming up to Him.

- **Acts 2:42**
  "And they continued stedfastly in the apostles' doctrine and fellowship, and in breaking of bread, and in **prayers**."

Prayers In The Apostolic Churches

Prayers were part of what was done in the apostolic local churches. That is why we pray in our church as well.

- **Romans 1:9**
  "For God is my witness, whom I serve with my spirit in the gospel of his Son, that without ceasing I make mention of you always in my **prayers**;"

Paul was talking to the true church, the genuine Christians, at Rome.

- **Ephesians 1:16**
  "Cease not to give thanks for you, making mention of you in my **prayers**;"

Here again is the **incense** of **prayers** going before the Lord.

- **Philippians 4:6**
  "Be careful for nothing; but in every thing by **prayer** and supplication with thanksgiving let your requests be made known unto God."
- **Colossians 4:2**
  "Continue in **prayer**, and watch in the same with thanksgiving;"
- **1 Thessalonians 5:17**
  "**Pray** without ceasing."
- **James 5:16**
  "Confess *your* faults one to another, and **pray** one for another, that ye may be healed. The effectual fervent **prayer** of a righteous man availeth much."
- **1 Peter 3:12**
  "For the eyes of the Lord *are* over the righteous, and his ears *are open* unto their **prayers**: but the face of the Lord *is* against them that do evil."

If we are genuinely saved, He can hear our **prayers**. He wants us to **pray**.

- **Revelation 5:8**
  "And when he had taken the book, the four beasts and four *and* twenty elders fell down before the Lamb, having every one of them harps, and golden vials full of odours, which are the **prayers** of saints."

How Much Prayer-Incense Goes Up?

How much incense is going up because of your prayers and my prayers? The incense going up to Heaven, just like the smoke goes up, are the prayers before the Lord.

Revelation 8:4

"And the smoke of the incense, *which came* with the prayers of the saints, ascended up before God out of the angel's hand."

Here is the picture again of **prayers of the saints** that **ascended up** before the throne of God. It is like **incense**. That is a picture or a figure of speech. The altar of **incense** that God told Moses to make in the tabernacle was a picture of **prayer**. They were to keep that **incense** going day in and day out, all the time, in memorial before the Lord. That is what we must do before the Lord, as far as **prayers** are concerned.

My mother-in-law, Gertrude Sanborn, wrote a poem about **prayer**.

Stop Awhile

When the Holy Spirit speaks to me
*Saying stop awhile and **pray**,*
Many times I say "TOO BUSY,"
And I go along my way.

That day is full of trials,
And the labor seems so long;
The cares of it oppress me,
And I find I have no song.

BUT–When the Holy Spirit speaks to me
And I stop my course and pray
And heed His voice so tender,
I kneel down to God and say:

"Thank You, Lord, for calling me!
I am so bent to sin,
*And I know I'd soon forget to **pray***
But for Him who dwells within."

*And so I **pray**, and praise, and learn*
Sweet lessons at His Feet;
I find it's there I get the strength
The daily tasks to meet!

The Lord Wants Us To Pray

Prayers are as the incense going up to the Lord. The Lord wants us to pray. That is why the disciples went to the Lord Jesus Christ and said, "Lord, teach us to pray." That is why the Lord Jesus Christ spent all night in prayer to God the Father before choosing His disciples.

Do you wonder why He chose Judas Iscariot? It was a part of the plan of God. It was needful that one be there to teach us that there are traitors in our midst. Judas was that traitor. As the Lord Jesus Christ said, "*it had been good for that man if he had not been born.*" (Matthew 26:24).

Revelation 8:5

"And the angel took the censer, and filled it with fire of the altar, and cast *it* into the earth: and there were voices, and thunderings, and lightnings, and an earthquake."

Here is the presence of God. The scene is in Heaven. It is just before the first trumpet sounds in verse 7. This is where God is. The **fire of the altar** was cast on the earth with **voices, thunderings, lightnings, and an earthquake.**

Why We Should Fear God

This is a picture of why we should fear God. There is fear. Those that are lost should not shake their fists and say, "There is no such thing as God." They should not say, "I do not want your Saviour, the Lord Jesus Christ." They should accept Him. There is no fear, but this is a fearful thing to fall into the hands of the living God. There should be a fear of God's presence unless we are in the Lord Jesus Christ.

If we are in the Lord Jesus Christ, there should be no fear because we have an insulated suit, as it were. We have an suit to shield us. While up in space, the people must have special suits so they can exist. The only way we can exist in the presence of God is to have new glorified bodies. We will have new bodies if we are genuinely saved and born-again. God will give us new bodies.

- Exodus 9:23
  "And Moses stretched forth his rod toward Heaven: and the LORD sent **thunder** and hail, and the fire ran along upon the ground; and the LORD rained hail upon the land of Egypt."

God's Special Thunder

This was special thunder sent from God. He makes the thunder in a general way, but sometimes there is special thunder for judgments. This plague of thunder was one of them.

- Exodus 20:18
  "And all the people saw the **thunderings**, and the lightnings, and the noise of the **trumpet**, and the mountain smoking: and when the people saw *it*, they removed, and stood afar off."

This was at Mount Sinai when the Lord gave the law of Moses. They were afraid. Did they approach? No, they removed, and stood afar off. Their fear of the Lord was intense.

- **2 Samuel 22:14**
  "The LORD **thundered** from Heaven, and the most High uttered his voice."

In order to take care of people in battle, there was special **thunder** from Heaven.

- **Isaiah 29:6**
  "Thou shalt be visited of the LORD of hosts with **thunder**, and with **earthquake**, and great noise, with storm and tempest, and the flame of devouring fire."

This is part of the presence of the Lord.

- **Revelation 4:5**
  "And out of the throne proceeded **lightnings** and **thunderings** and voices: and *there were* seven lamps of **fire** burning before the throne, which are the seven Spirits of God."

- **Revelation 11:19**
  "And the temple of God was opened in Heaven, and there was seen in his temple the ark of his testament: and there were **lightnings**, and voices, and **thunderings**, and an **earthquake**, and great hail."

- **Revelation 16:18**
  "And there were **voices**, and **thunders**, and **lightnings**; and there was a great **earthquake**, such as was not since men were upon the earth, so mighty an **earthquake**, *and* so great."

The Lord's Presence

The Lord's presence is very awful, a very *awe-filled* presence. We ought not to just jump into His presence and think that He's just a little Person like we are. No, my friends, the One who stretched forth the Heavens, the stars, and the galaxies, and made us in His own image, is not Someone who is just an insignificant Person like we are. We should never talk about Him frivolously by calling Him "the Man upstairs" and other demeaning terms. No. He is a God of power, might, awe, and majesty.

Notice, not only were there voices and **thunderings** there at the altar in Heaven, but also **lightnings**. Sometimes the Lord uses special **lightnings**. We have **lightning** all the time. Of course, that is special because the earth needs **lightning**. Do you know why He has lightning? I understand that it is the only way that nitrogen can be taken out of the earth and made usable for the plants. When the rain comes and the **lightnings** come, the nitrogen in the air can be then transformed to be useful for plants. That is what they tell us, anyway.

- **Exodus 20:18**
  "And all the people saw the **thunderings**, and the **lightnings**, and the noise of the trumpet, and the mountain smoking: and when the people saw *it*, they removed, and stood afar off."
- **2 Samuel 22:15**
  "And he sent out arrows, and scattered them; **lightning**, and discomfited them."

This was the special **lightning** for discomfiting and making the Israelites to win battles.

- **Revelation 4:5**
  "And out of the throne proceeded **lightnings** and **thunderings** and voices: and *there were* seven lamps of fire burning before the throne, which are the seven Spirits of God."

The Lord's Presence

This is part of what the Lord's presence is. You cannot describe what God is. You cannot draw a picture of Him. That is why He says we are to have no other gods before him nor any images or likenesses. We do not know what He is. There are all these different figures. He is lightning. He is thundering. He is voices and earthquakes. He is powerful. That is our terminology, so that we on earth can understand His might and His power.

- **Revelation 11:19**
  "And the temple of God was opened in Heaven, and there was seen in his temple the ark of his testament: and there were **lightnings**, and voices, and **thunderings**, and an **earthquake**, and great hail."
- **Revelation 16:18**
  "And there were voices, and **thunders**, and **lightnings**; and there was a great **earthquake**, such as was not since men were upon the earth, so mighty an **earthquake**, *and* so great."

There are not only the **thunderings** and **lightnings**, but also an **earthquake**. It was a special **earthquake**.

- **Luke 21:11**
  "And great **earthquakes** shall be in divers places, and famines, and pestilences; and fearful sights and great signs shall there be from Heaven."

This is in the last days, when the time of judgment will come upon the earth.

- **Isaiah 29:6**
  "Thou shalt be visited of the LORD of hosts with **thunder**, and with **earthquake**, and great noise, with storm and tempest, and the flame of devouring **fire**."

This is preparatory to the trumpet judgments as they come. The scene is in Heaven and the **censer** is there with fire on the altar. The **thunderings**, the **lightnings**, and the **earthquake** is a picture of the power and the might of Almighty God.

Revelation 8:6

"And the seven angels which had the seven trumpets prepared themselves to sound."

Here begins the **seven trumpet** judgments. This is a **preparation** time. Before you do something great, or even if it is not great, I hope you get **prepared**. The Boy Scout motto is *"Be prepared."* We must prepare. When women invite you to dinner there must be **preparation**. When a preacher invites you to come to church, he is going to be **prepared** or there is something wrong with him. There has to be **preparation** in anything we do. If it is a very important thing, we must have **preparation**.

Sounding The Seven Trumpets

These angels were going to sound the seven trumpet judgments upon the earth. We will see these are terrible, awful judgments with people dying, fish dying, and other things. There must be preparation. Does that mean the angels have to prepare, too? Yes.

It has been many years since our four sons and one daughter were little and we had to discipline them. I hope that as parents, before that happens, you **prepare**. Be sure you give them what it takes, but not more than what it should take. Discipline should be applied **only** when it is necessary, and **always** when it is necessary.

- **John 14:2-3**
  "In my Father's house are many mansions: if *it were* not so, I would have told you. I go to **prepare** a place for you. And if I go and **prepare** a place for you, I will come again, and receive you unto myself; that where I am, *there* ye may be also."

He is **preparing** a place of beauty, harmony, and peace in Heaven. It is a wonderful **preparation** for us who are genuine Christians.

- **1 Corinthians 2:9**
  "But as it is written, Eye hath not seen, nor ear heard, neither have entered into the heart of man, the things which God hath **prepared** for them that love him."

God has a **preparation**. He is **preparing** a place in Heaven for those that love Him, those who are genuinely saved, those that have trusted the Lord Jesus Christ, and are truly born-again.

- **1 Corinthians 14:8**
  "For if the trumpet give an uncertain sound, who shall **prepare** himself to the battle?"

Preparation for battle has to be the right sound. We have to use the Scriptures that are proper Scriptures, the right sound. We have to preach the right gospel, not a false gospel, so that people can **prepare** themselves for the battle of this life and a battle for the truth.

- **Hebrews 10:5**
  "Wherefore when he cometh into the world, he saith, Sacrifice and offering thou wouldest not, but a body hast thou **prepared** me:"

The Lord Jesus Christ is speaking to the Father. The **prepared** body of the Lord Jesus Christ, every part—the sinews, the muscles, the nerves, the blood, the hair—every part was specially **prepared**. That is why the blood of the Lord Jesus Christ is so important.

- **Hebrews 11:7**
  "By faith Noah, being warned of God of things not seen as yet, moved with fear, **prepared** an ark to the saving of his house; by the which he condemned the world, and became heir of the righteousness which is by faith."

There were 120 years of preparation. You may say, "That is an awfully long time. Most of us are not around for 120 years." Noah was over 600 years of age. He had plenty of time. He was a preacher of righteousness **preparing** the ark.

Revelation 8:7

"The first angel sounded, and there followed hail and fire mingled with blood, and they were cast upon the earth: and the third part of trees was burnt up, and all green grass was burnt up."

Seven trumpet judgments begin right here. The first angel sounded. This is the **first trumpet**. The **second trumpet**, a burning mountain, is in verses 8 and 9. The **third trumpet**, a falling star called Wormwood, is in verses 10 and 11. The **fourth trumpet**, the sun smitten, is in verses 12 and 13. The **fifth trumpet**, the plague of locusts, is in chapter 9, verses 1 to 12. The **sixth trumpet**, the plague of horsemen, is in chapter 9, verses 13 to 21. The **seventh trumpet**, the judgment of angry nations, is in chapter 11, verses 15 to 19.

Twenty-One Judgments From God

These twenty-one judgments (seven seals, seven trumpets, and seven vials) occur at the average rate of one every four months. The believers, the genuinely saved ones, will not be here. If you are truly born-again and genuinely saved, you are not going to be here during these terrible judgments on the earth. We do not go along with those who believe that the genuinely saved people will go through part of the tribulation, or half of the tribulation, or a pre-wrath tribulation, or all of the tribulation. No. The genuinely born-again Christians will be raptured before any part of the tribulation.

Notice, in verse 7 what happened when the **hail and fire mingled with blood** were cast upon the earth. The **third part of the trees was burnt up.** You might say, "Well, so what? I have some **trees**. I can spare a few." We had a big **tree** fall on our house. We were glad to have it taken away. Fortunately, it did not damage our house.

Trees are important in Scripture.

- **Genesis 3:2**
  "And the woman said unto the serpent, We may eat of the fruit of the **trees** of the garden:"

Fruit **trees** are for eating. For those of us who love fruit, without **trees** we would have no fruit.

- **Exodus 10:15**
  "For they covered the face of the whole earth, so that the land was darkened; and they did eat every herb of the land, and all the fruit of the **trees** which the **hail** had left: and there remained not any green thing in the **trees**, or in the herbs of the field, through all the land of Egypt."
- **Leviticus 19:23**
  "And when ye shall come into the land, and shall have planted all manner of **trees** for food, then ye shall count the fruit thereof as uncircumcised: three years shall it be as uncircumcised unto you: it shall not be eaten of."
- **Leviticus 26:4**
  "Then I will give you rain in due season, and the land shall yield her increase, and the **trees** of the field shall yield their fruit."

That is part of what God has given–the fruit **trees**. What if a third of the **trees** perish?

- **Leviticus 26:20**
  "And your strength shall be spent in vain: for your land shall not yield her increase, neither shall the **trees** of the land yield their fruits."

If the people sin, then the **trees** of the land will not yield their fruits. This is a judgment of the Lord. The fruit **trees** will be barren.

Often, people may have apple **trees,** cherry **trees,** and different types of fruit **trees.** I remember in our yard we had apple **trees** with very little apples. We had sweet cherries and sour cherries in Ohio. We used to pick those. They were good fruit **trees.**

- **Deuteronomy 6:11**
  "And houses full of all good *things*, which thou filledst not, and wells digged, which thou diggedst not, vineyards and olive **trees,** which thou plantedst not; when thou shalt have eaten and be full;"

Olive **trees** produce olive oil, which is useful in cooking and different things.

- **Deuteronomy 8:8**
  "A land of wheat, and barley, and vines, and fig **trees,** and pomegranates; a land of oil olive, and honey;"

- **Deuteronomy 20:19**
  "When thou shalt besiege a city a long time, in making war against it to take it, thou shalt not destroy the **trees** thereof by forcing an axe against them: for thou mayest eat of them, and thou shalt not cut them down (for the tree of the field *is* man's *life*) to employ *them* in the siege:"

They could make a siege and make ramparts against the walls with **trees** that were not fruit **trees**. They were not to cut down the fruit **trees** because they were going to eat the fruit of these **trees**.

- **Deuteronomy 34:3**
  "And the south, and the plain of the valley of Jericho, the city of palm trees, unto Zoar."

There is a usefulness in the palm **trees**: palm fruit and palm oil. You may say, "Palm **trees**? What are they for?" There are coconuts and different fruits. A third of these **trees** will be gone.

- **2 Samuel 5:23**
  "And when David enquired of the LORD, he said, Thou shalt not go up; *but* fetch a compass behind them, and come upon them over against the mulberry **trees**."

- **Nehemiah 9:25**
  "And they took strong cities, and a fat land, and possessed houses full of all goods, wells digged, vineyards, and oliveyards, and fruit **trees** in abundance: so they did eat, and were filled, and became fat, and delighted themselves in thy great goodness."

Fruit **trees** were used of the Lord to feed the people. They are very important.

- **Ecclesiastes 2:5**
  "I made me gardens and orchards, and I planted **trees** in them of all *kind of* fruits:"

Solomon even remarks about **trees**. Think of all the fruits. There are cherries, apples, peaches, and figs—all kinds of fruits. Solomon was one that was wise.

Notice also in verse 7, this first trumpet judgment, that not only a **third of the trees was burnt up**, but all the **green grass** was burnt up. You might say, "Well, that would be good. I would not have to mow it. So what?" Well, let us think about that.

- **Deuteronomy 11:15**
  "And I will send **grass** in thy fields for thy cattle, that thou mayest eat and be full."

Cattle is a general term for four-legged animals. It includes the cows and the sheep. Just think, if all the **grass** were gone, what are they going to eat? They will die. For those who are meat-eaters, there will be no meat. After a while there will be trouble.

- **1 Kings 18:5**
  "And Ahab said unto Obadiah, Go into the land, unto all fountains of water, and unto all brooks: peradventure we may find **grass** to save the horses and mules alive, that we lose not all the beasts."

There was a famine and no rain. God had shut up the rain and Elijah was doing battle with Ahab. They went out to look at the land. Everything was dried up. **Grass** is important for animals. Those of you who know about horses, and other animals, know that they need **grass** for food.

- **Job 6:5**
  "Doth the wild ass bray when he hath **grass**? or loweth the ox over his fodder?"

The wild asses need **grass** to feed, as well.

- **Job 40:15**
  "Behold now behemoth, which I made with thee; he eateth **grass** as an ox."

Though we don't know for sure, a behemoth was probably a dinosaur.

- **Psalm 104:14**
  "He causeth the **grass** to grow for the cattle, and herb for the service of man: that he may bring forth food out of the earth;"

All the cattle would die without **grass**.

- **Jeremiah 14:5-6**
  "Yea, the hind also calved in the field, and forsook *it*, because there was no **grass**. And the wild asses did stand in the high places, they snuffed up the wind like dragons; their eyes did fail, because *there was* no **grass**."

They had to move on to another pasture. That was what people used to do in the Old West. The cattle grazers were all angry at the sheep grazers because the sheep cut the **grass** closer than the cows. The sheep herders and the cattle men were all at odds. They were fighting. They moved the pastures.

We have many deer. I understand there are too many that are eating up all kinds of things. They go into your vegetable gardens. Of course, there are people that are against the slaughter of deer, but you have to keep the population down.

This judgment will affect the people living on the earth at that time. It may take a while, but soon the cattle will die off. They will have no meat and the food will be cut off. There will be no fruit from a third of the **trees**. We do not know where that is going to hit, whether in the United States of America, or in Russia, or China, or wherever.

A Judgment Against Food

This first trumpet judgment will be a catastrophic judgment against food and things that are necessary to eat.

Praise the Lord, we have a wonderful Saviour that can take us out of this judgment on the earth! We have enough **food** here. We have enough water here. We have enough **grass**, and so on. I am glad that the Lord who saved us, if we are genuinely saved and born-again, will take us to Heaven where there is no need for **grass, trees**, or food. The Lord Jesus Christ, the Lamb of God, is our water of life and bread of life. We will be safe with Him in Glory when this takes place.

Revelation 8:8

"And the second angel sounded, and as it were a great mountain burning with fire was cast into the sea: and the third part of the sea became blood;"

This is the **great mountain** that was **burning.** *As it were* means it would be a figure. A tremendous amount of some substance came down. It was a burning substance. There are a number of burning **mountains** in Scripture.

- **Deuteronomy 4:11**
  "And ye came near and stood under the **mountain**; and the **mountain burned** with fire unto the midst of Heaven, with darkness, clouds, and thick darkness."

This was Mount Sinai. The presence of God is a **burning** fire. It is part of His nature of purity and judgment.

- **Deuteronomy 5:23**
  "And it came to pass, when ye heard the voice out of the midst of the darkness, (for the **mountain did burn** with fire,) that ye came near unto me, *even* all the heads of your tribes, and your elders;"

That same **mountain**, Mount Sinai, is referred to here. When the law of Moses was given, Mount Sinai was a **burning mountain**.

Here in Revelation 8:8, is a **great mountain burning** with **fire** cast into the sea.

- **2 Kings 6:17**
  "And Elisha prayed, and said, LORD, I pray thee, open his eyes, that he may see. And the LORD opened the eyes of the young man; and he saw: and, behold, the **mountain** *was* full of horses and chariots of **fire** round about Elisha."

Here is a **mountain** full of chariots of **fire**.

Notice also when that **burning mountain** went into the sea, part of it became **blood**. Again, this is in many places in Scripture, where water becomes **blood**.

- **Exodus 4:9**
  "And it shall come to pass, if they will not believe also these two signs, neither hearken unto thy voice, that thou shalt take of the water of the river, and pour *it* upon the dry *land*: and the **water** which thou takest out of the river shall become **blood** upon the dry *land*."

This was one of the judgments on the Egyptians.

- **Exodus 7:17**
  "Thus saith the LORD, In this thou shalt know that I *am* the LORD: behold, I will smite with the rod that *is* in mine hand upon the **waters** which *are* in the river, and they shall be turned to **blood**."

It was a miracle. You cannot turn **water** into **blood**. The Lord Jesus Christ turned **water** into wine. This was good grape juice. Here are **waters** turned into **blood**.

- **Exodus 7:19**
  "And the LORD spake unto Moses, Say unto Aaron, Take thy rod, and stretch out thine hand upon the **waters** of Egypt, upon their streams, upon their rivers, and upon their ponds, and upon all their pools of water, that they may become **blood**; and *that* there may be **blood** throughout all the land of Egypt, both in *vessels of* wood, and in *vessels of* stone."

Judgment was solid on that score.

- **Exodus 7:21**
  "And the fish that *was* in the river died; and the river stank, and the Egyptians could not drink of the **water** of the river; and there was **blood** throughout all the land of Egypt."

Here we see the results of this judgment. The fish that was in the river died. When you turn **water** into **blood** you cannot sustain life, as far as fish are concerned.

- **Revelation 11:6**
  "These have power to shut Heaven, that it rain not in the days of their prophecy: and have power over **waters** to turn them to **blood**, and to smite the earth with all plagues, as often as they will."

Many of us feel that one of the two witnesses will be Elijah, and the other one will be Moses because of the miracles. There were ten plagues in Egypt.

- **Revelation 16:3-4**
  "And the second angel poured out his vial upon the **sea**; and it became as the **blood** of a dead *man*: and every living soul died in the sea. And the third angel poured out his vial upon the rivers and fountains of **waters**; and they became **blood**."

The **blood** upon the sea is a miracle that will be repeated not only in chapter 8, but also in chapter 16.

Revelation 8:9

"And the third part of the creatures which were in the sea, and had life, died; and the third part of the ships were destroyed."

Judgment Upon The Sea

Here is the judgment upon the sea. One third of the creatures were destroyed. You may say, "What kind of creatures are we talking about?" There are all kinds of creatures in the sea. We could name many of them, but there are tuna fish, lobster, whales, sharks, bass, turtles, stingrays, octopus, snails, perch, barracuda, and all kinds of other fish. A third of them die. Some people go out and fish. When a third of the fish die there will be hunger here on the earth. I am glad I am not going to be here to see it.

Notice also in this judgment, the **third part of the ships were destroyed**. I do not understand the chemistry of the **waters** being turned into **blood**, but there was **the third part of the ships** as well as the creatures. Whether **blood** would not sustain them or if they just sink because there is a different viscosity, I do not know, but the third part of the **ships** were destroyed.

Destruction Of Various Ships

What kind of ships are there? There are fishing ships; people will fish. They are not going to have much fish because a third of them will be gone. There are also sailboats, pleasure boats, passenger ships, and all kinds of warships. A third of them will be destroyed. There are destroyers, battleships, cruisers, transport ships, submarines, aircraft carriers, and all kinds of ships. A third of them will be gone because of the second trumpet judgment of the mountain burning with fire cast into the sea.

These are things that are going to be upon this earth. Certainly, people will say, "How can this happen? It has never been done before." The Lord Jesus Christ is able to do things that have never been done before. The Lord Jesus Christ was born of a virgin. That was never done before. He came into this world. All these things are miracles of God.

Revelation 8:10

"And the third angel sounded, and there fell a great star from Heaven, burning as it were a lamp, and it fell upon the third part of the rivers, and upon the fountains of waters;"

Here is the **angel** that had the **great star** falling from Heaven, **burning as a lamp**. **Stars** normally do not fall. There are meteors, and so on, but this is a special **star** that has been sent by the Lord Jesus Christ.

- **Genesis 1:16**
  "And God made two great lights; the greater light to rule the day, and the lesser light to rule the night: *he made* the **stars** also."
Here we see the origin of the **stars**.

Falling Stars

What is a falling star? I looked it up on the Internet, and among other things, they are solid bodies that enter the earth's atmosphere as they travel through space. These stars are commonly called meteors. Meteors can enter the atmosphere with a velocity that ranges from ten to seventy kilometers per second. That is very fast. They plunge into the atmosphere and consequently, the friction that is created by the atmosphere

> causes the meteor to begin burning out. This produces a great light. That is what it says in Revelation 8:10, *"burning as a lamp."*

A **meteor** is a falling **star**. **Meteor** showers occur when hundreds of **meteors** fall simultaneously. Therefore, the atmosphere acts as a buffer that protects the earth's surface. Many **meteors** burn up as they travel through the atmosphere, but in space there is no such barrier. These **meteors** do not burn up in space, just on the earth as they come toward it.

Meteors that come to the earth are called meteorites. There are different types of these. There are iron, stony iron, chondrites—all different materials. In 1908, a meteor struck Siberia and left a big crater. It flattened out the **trees**, and so on. This in Revelation 8:10 is going to be a **star** falling from Heaven. It is going to impact this earth and cause a lot of damage.

Another article from the Internet describing falling or shooting **stars** indicates that during certain times of the year there are greater numbers of **meteors** in the sky than other times. The **showers** are given names, based on the constellations present in the sky from whence they appear. Here is a partial list:

1. Quadrantids, January 1 – 6
2. Lyrids, Apr 19 - Apr 24
3. Alpha Capricornids, Jul 3 - Aug 15
4. Perseids, Jul 17 - Aug 24
5. Epsilon Geminids, Oct 14 - Oct 27

All of these different types of **meteor** showers are given names by people on this earth.

The Falling Star From Heaven

This star in Revelation 8:10 is going to be a falling star from Heaven and God is going to do it. It is the third trumpet judgment. The angel gave the trumpet sound and the star came, *burning as it were a lamp and fell upon the third part of the rivers and upon the fountains of waters.*

You may say, "How can a **star** that is **burning** fall upon a third part of the waters if it falls just in one place?" This is not going to be like regular **meteors**. It is going to be a **meteor**, or falling **star**, that is broken up, apparently in all different places and ways. It will fall on a third of the rivers and also on the fountains of waters, the source of the streams. There will be problems, I am sure, with drinking and with things needed to sustain life because of this third trumpet judgment of the burning **star.**

Revelation 8:11

"And the name of the star is called Wormwood: and the third part of the waters became wormwood; and many men died of the waters, because they were made bitter."

Wormwood is the name of this falling, burning **star.** It is named that because of the **bitter water** that it produces. Many times people may say, "I want soda pop, tea, milk, or some other beverage," but they will not be able to drink of the **water** of sustaining life. When they drink that **water** there is death.

It is just like sailors when they are shipwrecked or out at sea and they run out of **water.** Sometimes they can get it from the rain. They can drink that rain, but if they try to drink the salt **water** they will die. Our bodies cannot use salt **water.**

These **waters** will be made **bitter** because of this burning, fiery **Wormwood star** that falls from Heaven. We are told that there are about 60,000 impurities in **water.** That is what one man says who advertised and talked about *"Penta Water."* In the elimination of these impurities from our regular water that we drink in our towns, only about 45 or 50 are taken out (probably less than that) of the 60,000 impurities. It does not get them all by any means.

- **Exodus 15:23**
  "And when they came to Marah, they could not drink of the **waters** of Marah, for they *were* **bitter**: therefore the name of it was called Marah."

The Meaning Of Marah

That word Marah means *bitter.* Because they could not drink the waters, they had to go somewhere else. Sometimes enemies of a company or a nation purposefully make the waters undrinkable. They might pour salt in them or something else so that the people cannot drink. This was true in the Old Testament when they stopped up the wells and made them so they were not usable. Water is important. It has to be pure water.

- **Numbers 5:18**
  "And the priest shall set the woman before the LORD, and uncover the woman's head, and put the offering of memorial in her hands, which *is* the jealousy offering: and the priest shall have in his hand the **bitter water** that causeth the curse:"

Here was the **bitter water** that had to do with seeing whether or not a woman had committed adultery with some other man. If she had been adulterous, she would suffer very great pain and suffering. We do not know what this **bitter water** was, but it was a special one that God made to test whether or not a woman was unfaithful to her husband in the Old Testament.

- **Ruth 1:20-21**
  "And she said unto them, Call me not Naomi, call me **Mara**: for the Almighty hath dealt very **bitterly** with me. I went out full, and the LORD hath brought me home again empty: why *then* call ye me Naomi, seeing the LORD hath testified against me, and the Almighty hath afflicted me?"

Naomi had lost her husband and her sons in the country of Moab. She was very, very sad. Her name was Naomi, which means *pleasant*. The word **Mara** means *bitter* in Hebrew. The Lord was able to make that up to her, and He did. Boaz became Ruth's husband and she became a mother in the lineage of King David. Naomi thought that she was no longer "pleasant" because she had lost her husband and her two sons, Mahlon and Chilion. Orpah stayed in Moab. Ruth was faithful. She came with Naomi from Moab and was blessed in that action.

- **Ruth 1:16-17**
  And Ruth said, Intreat me not to leave thee, *or* to return from following after thee: for whither thou goest, I will go; and where thou lodgest, I will lodge: thy people *shall be* my people, and thy God my God: Where thou diest, will I die, and there will I be buried: the LORD do so to me, and more also, *if ought* but death part thee and me."

- **Proverbs 27:7**
  "The full soul loatheth an honeycomb; but to the hungry soul every **bitter** thing is sweet."

Why would they loathe a sweet honeycomb? If you are too full, you cannot eat anything more. We ought to be thankful for even the **bitter** things when we are hungry. We say that sometimes when people complain about the food. I know someone who recently said, "I cannot stand the food. It is terrible." I said, "Well, maybe you ought to just be thankful to the Lord for giving you food." To the hungry soul every bitter thing is sweet. That is why people that are starving eat roots, leaves, and various other things. They are hungry.

- **Isaiah 5:20**
  "Woe unto them that call evil good, and good evil; that put darkness for light, and light for darkness; that put **bitter** for sweet, and sweet for **bitter!**"

Bitter Should Be Called Bitter

We cannot change bitter for sweet, and sweet for bitter. If something is bitter, we are going to call it bitter. If something is darkness, we ought to call it darkness. If something is light, we ought to call it light. If it is evil, we call it evil. God does not want us to shade things just for publicity or to be necessarily "politically correct." We ought to be honest.

- **James 3:11**
  "Doth a fountain send forth at the same place sweet *water* and **bitter**?"

This talks about the fountain of our tongue. Are we able to say sweet things and then also **bitter** things? Our tongue and our lives should be for the Lord and not mixed. If we are genuinely saved, we ought to have sweet **water** on our lips and on our tongue and not **bitter water**.

This **Wormwood** will be **bitter**, as far as the **waters** that are on this earth. They will be **poisoned**. Many **men died** because they were made **bitter**. We do not know the **bitterness** or the type of poison, but it will cause people to die. Whether it is arsenic or some other poison we are not told, but the Lord Jesus Christ is going to make this **Wormwood** come to the **waters** so that **many men die**. It does not say how many. Can you imagine? Unexpectingly, you drink **water** and death occurs. When you go to your tap and you draw out the **water**, you just drink it by faith. What if it were poison? You would not know the difference.

Revelation 8:12

"And the fourth angel sounded, and the third part of the sun was smitten, and the third part of the moon, and the third part of the stars; so as the third part of them was darkened, and the day shone not for a third part of it, and the night likewise."

Here is the fourth trumpet judgment, having to do with the **sun**. God made that **sun**. He put the **stars** there. He put the **moon** there.

Now, the Lord is going to go contrary to His creative nature.

In Genesis 1:13-18 we see the Creation by God of the **sun** and the **moon** and the **stars**. It is interesting, He does not call it **sun** in Genesis. He does not call it **moon**. They are not named. (It is called *the sun* later on.)

- **Genesis 1:14**
  "And God said, Let there be **lights** in the firmament of the Heaven to divide the day from the night; and let them be for signs, and for seasons, and for days, and years:"

Signs And Seasons Lights

These are lights for signs, seasons, and days. We talk about a month which come from the word, *moon*. As soon as the moon gets full and it goes to the next one, that is one "moon", or month. In the Old Testament the dating usually was 30 days for a month, rather than 31, or whatever. We have a lunar year, which is 360 days instead of 365 and a fourth. The lights are for signs, and for seasons, and for days, and years.

- **Genesis 1:15-18**
  "And God made two great **lights**; the greater **light** to rule the day, and the lesser **light** to rule the night: he made the **stars** also. And God set them in the firmament of the Heaven to give light upon the earth, And to rule over the day and over the night, and to divide the light from the darkness: and God saw that it was good."

The greater light to rule the day would be the **sun** and the lesser light to rule the night would be the **moon**. This judgment will cause **a third** of the light to go. Normally, a light is there and we can depend upon it. The **sun** is there.

God Is A Divider

God is a divider. He divided the light from the darkness. When light comes into a room there is no more darkness. Darkness is the absence of light. Just turn all the lights off to make it dark. The Lord is a divider and He is a separatist of evil and good, darkness and light.

If this happens, as far as the **sun** not shining for **a third** of the time, just think what will happen. Many people may freeze. We depend upon the **sun's** light for heat. The crops and grass may die, also. They are dependent upon the **sunlight** along with the trees, as well. These are some of the problems due to the **sun**.

What about problems due to the **moon**? The tides would be uneven. I am not sure about the science of it, but the tides have to do with the **moon**. Sometimes the tides are ebb tides, sometimes high tides. They go up and down. When **a third** of the time the **moon** is gone, tides may be uneven and flooding might occur.

I looked up some of the things about the **sun**, because this is the thing that God is going to touch in this fourth trumpet judgment. A **third** part of the **sun** was smitten. What about our **sun**?

It is one of more than 100 billion **stars** in our galaxy—just in our galaxy. There are thousands and thousands of galaxies. Who put those **stars** up there? Certainly, the Lord is the only One that could create them. Man with his investigation, going to the **moon**, Saturn, and so on, cannot create. All he can do is go visit.

The Sun Is A Huge Object

The sun is the largest object in the solar system. It is the biggest of anything up there among these billions of stars. In fact, it contains more than 99.8% of the mass of our entire solar system. Jupiter contains most of the rest. The sun is huge. People sometimes say the sun is an ordinary star. Certainly, there are many smaller stars, but the sun is the top 10% by mass.

It is made up of about 70% hydrogen, 28% helium, different metals and so on. As far as the rotation of the **sun**, at the equator, the **sun** rotates once every 25.4 days. At the poles, it rotates as much as 36 days. You may ask, "Why does it rotate differently at the center than it does at the poles?" That is because it is not a symmetrical body. It is not a solid body like the earth, so it has differences in rotation.

The surface of the **sun** is called the photosphere. It has a temperature of about 5800 K, which is *kelvin*. Sunspots are cool regions. They are only 3,800 K. The **sun** is certainly hot.

The **sun** and the **moon** orbit the earth according to Ticho Brahe, rather than having (as most believe) the earth orbits the sun. Tycho Brahe was a Danish astronomer who believed that it is not the **sun** that is the center of our solar system, but the earth is the center. He believed that the planets go around the earth. I agree with the Brahe position. We are told that all astronomy can be explained by either of these two positions, either (1) the heliocentric position (sun the center) or the geocentric position (earth the center).

Be that as it may, the **sun** and the **moon** appeared. The **moon** orbits the earth. Sometimes the **moon** comes in front of the **sun** and there is an eclipse. When the **moon** comes between the earth and the **sun** it is called a solar eclipse. Sometimes the eclipse is partial and sometimes it is full.

The **sun's** magnetic field is very powerful and very strong. When a third of the **sun** is touched, the magnetic field will probably be affected as well. It is very strong by terrestrial standards.

The Sun's Solar Wind

In addition to heat and light, the sun emits a low density stream of charged particles known as solar wind. The sun's output is not entirely constant. Sometimes it is hotter than others. In the 17th century there was the Maunder Minimum that coincided with an abnormally cold period in northern Europe, sometimes known as the "Little Ice Age." There are all different kinds of intensities of the sun.

The **sun's** satellites, those things that go around it, used to number nine, but now many think Pluto has disappeared so there are only eight planets at present. When a **third** of the **sun** is smitten in this judgment, I wonder if that will affect the planets. The eight present planets are Mercury, Venus, Earth, Mars, Jupiter, Saturn, Uranus, and Neptune. Uranus was discovered in 1781. Neptune was discovered in 1846. If the sun is struck on this judgment, it may affect the planets. I am not sure, but it is certainly possible that would be the case.

Notice also in Revelation 8:12, the **third part** of the **moon** was smitten. Again, I looked it up to see a little bit about the **moon**. By viewing it even by the naked eye, we can discern two major types of terrain. There are bright islands and darker plains. As you remember, in July, of 1969, the first man went up to the moon. Neil Armstrong was the first man to set foot on the **moon** in the Apollo 11 mission, followed by Buzz Aldrin. The lunar sky is always black. I wonder what will happen when **a third** of the **moon** is struck. Of course, the **moon** is the light of the **sun**. That is what gives the **moon** its light.

Also, the **moon's** gravity is different than it is here. It is one-sixth of the earth's gravity. In other words, if a man weighs 180 pounds here on earth, he will weigh only 30 pounds up on the **moon**. That gives that picture of weightlessness.

The Moon And The Earth

The rotation of the moon and its revolution around the earth takes 27 days, 7 hours and 43 minutes to go around. When they were up there on the Apollo mission, they planted four nuclear-powered seismic stations. They wanted to collect the seismic data on the moon, so they put those up there. They found out that the crust of the moon is 37 miles thick. That is a big crust. What happens when a third of the moon is struck?

There are some **meteoric** impacts on the **moon**. That is where you would see the seismic effects. Since the **moon** has no atmosphere, they hit very hard. There is nothing to stop them.

The average length of a lunar month is 29.5 days. The surface of the **moon** during the day is 107º centigrade. It has a hot surface. You can see why you would need those **moon** suits to go up there. The surface temperature at night is -153º centigrade. It is completely cold, as you can see.

Striking The Third Part Of The Sun

The Lord Jesus Christ in His judgment, here in this fourth trumpet judgment, is going to strike the third part of the sun, the third part of the moon and the stars also, so that a third part of them is darkened. If you go to the North Pole or the South Pole, they have longer days and longer nights, as you know.

Here in our area, people living in Collingswood, all the sinners will not be taken up with the Lord Jesus Christ in the rapture. Those that are lost—all the lost people whatever they may be, whatever their status – they will have **a third** of the day darkened. There are 24 hours in a day. **A third** of it is 8 hours. So there are 16 hours of light and 8 hours of darkness when you would expect that it would be light. In other words, instead of getting dark at 6:00, let us say, it gets dark 8 hours earlier. Just think of that. Suppose it gets dark at 8:00, as it does when the days get longer. Eight hours earlier would be at 12:00 noon. There would be darkness at noon. The **sun** and the **moon** will have an effect. Believe you me, when that happens those sinners that are upon this earth are going to take notice, I am sure. Would you not take notice when the sun does not stay lighted the third part of the day that normally it is there? They will say, "What is happening?" I hope they turn to the Lord Jesus Christ. I hope they understand what is happening.

Revelation 8:13

"And I beheld, and heard an angel flying through the midst of Heaven, saying with a loud voice, Woe, woe, woe, to the inhabiters of the earth by reason of the other voices of the trumpet of the three angels, which are yet to sound!"

Here is an **angel flying** through the midst of Heaven. He is a **warning messenger**. That is the express purpose of the **angel**. That word *flying* is a present tense. He is continuously **flying** through the **midst of Heaven**. He is speaking to the earth. I do not know how they are going to hear, whether it is a loudspeaker system or just a miracle of the Lord Jesus Christ, but they are going to listen to the pronouncing **woe** warning of judgments. This is judgment number four. There are five, six, and seven **trumpet** judgments yet. Here is the warning.

The Lord in His Word always issues a warning before He pronounces judgment. He is a gracious God. We saw on television the thirtieth anniversary of a tremendous hurricane season. In 1974, hundreds died and there was very little warning. They warned, they said on the radio afterwards, when it was almost too late. One little boy, who was nine years old at the time, is now a meteorologist. He was talking about people getting warnings of hurricanes. God gives warnings in the **woes** of Revelation.

- **Revelation 9:12**
  "One **woe** is past; *and,* behold, there come two **woes** more hereafter."

There are **three woes**.

- **Revelation 11:14**
  "The second woe is past; *and,* behold, the **third woe** cometh quickly."

- **Revelation 12:12**
  "Therefore rejoice, *ye* Heavens, and ye that dwell in them. **Woe** to the inhabiters of the earth and of the sea! for the Devil is come down unto you, having great wrath, because he knoweth that he hath but a short time."

The Final Woe

Here is the final woe. It says here that the angel was coming *by reason of the other voices* and he says, *"Woe to the inhabiters of the earth."* There are going to be three more trumpet judgments.

God **warns**. How did He **warn** in His Bible of other things coming? If you take, for instance, Noah and the flood. That was the first **warning** that God gave.

- **Genesis 6:3**
  "And the LORD said, My spirit shall not always strive with man, for that he also *is* flesh: yet his days shall be an hundred and twenty years."

In other words, God **warned** the people 120 years before the flood that the flood was coming. There was a **warning**.

- **Hebrews 11:7**
  "By faith Noah, being **warned** of God of things not seen as yet, moved with fear, prepared an ark to the saving of his house; by the which he condemned the world, and became heir of the righteousness which is by faith."

He was warned of God about that flood and he prepared the ark. The ark was large enough to contain all of the animals, two of each species, and seven pairs of the clean animals. They did not have to be giants. They could be babies or small ones. There were three large decks, wide enough to take care of every one.

- **1 Peter 3:20**
  "Which sometime were disobedient, when once the longsuffering of God waited in the days of Noah, while the ark was a **preparing**, wherein few, that is, eight souls were saved by water."

God waits before judgment comes. He was waiting until the ark was **prepared** before the judgment of the flood.

- **2 Peter 2:5**
  "And spared not the old world, but saved Noah the eighth *person*, a preacher of righteousness, bringing in the flood upon the world of the ungodly;"

Noah was a preacher. I am sure, during those 120 years, he would preach unto the people that the flood was coming. They did not believe him. His sons–Shem, Ham, and Japheth–did believe him. Their wives believed him. Mrs. Noah believed him. They were spared. The animals went in, then as soon as that door was shut, the flood came.

The Rich Man And Lazarus Warning

There is another warning in the Bible concerning judgment to come. That is in Luke 16 concerning the rich man and Lazarus. I believe this is an actual story. It was not a parable or fictional story. These were real people.

- Luke 16:19-21

  "There was a certain rich man, which was clothed in purple and fine linen, and fared sumptuously every day: And there was a certain beggar named Lazarus, which was laid at his gate, full of sores, And desiring to be fed with the crumbs which fell from the rich man's table: moreover the dogs came and licked his sores."

Here are the two men–the rich man, and Lazarus. Lazarus apparently was a genuine believer. He was trusting in the Lord. He was in bad shape.

- Luke 16:22-23

  "And it came to pass, that the beggar died, and was carried by the angels into Abraham's bosom: the rich man also died, and was buried; And in Hell he lift up his eyes, being in torments, and seeth Abraham afar off, and Lazarus in his bosom."

Lazarus was genuinely saved. He was trusting in the Lord Jesus Christ as Saviour and Redeemer Who one day would come. The rich man was lost. He rejected the Saviour, the Messiah. He was in torments. There were two different compartments of the world of the people that had died. There was the Paradise section and then there was the tormented, the damned section. Abraham was in the Paradise part and Lazarus was there, too.

- Luke 16:24

  "And he cried and said, Father Abraham, have mercy on me, and send Lazarus, that he may dip the tip of his finger in water, and cool my tongue; for I am tormented in this flame."

The Flame Was A Real Flame

There was real flame. There was real torment. That is one of the reasons why I believe there is an intermediate body. It is not the final body, but the intermediate body that can feel pain. For the genuine believers, there is an intermediate body that can go to Heaven before we get our final resurrected body. It is a body that can be known and seen, one that can talk and fellowship with the Lord Jesus Christ.

- **Luke 16:25**
  "But Abraham said, Son, remember that thou in thy lifetime receivedst thy good things, and likewise Lazarus evil things: but now he is comforted, and thou art tormented."

Lazarus trusted the Lord Jesus Christ, but the rich man did not.

- **Luke 16:26**
  "And beside all this, between us and you there is a great gulf fixed: so that they which would pass from hence to you cannot; neither can they pass to us, that would come from thence."

You cannot leave the tormented section of Hell and move on to Paradise. There is a great gulf fixed.

- **Luke 16:27-28**
  "Then he said, I pray thee therefore, father, that thou wouldest send him to my father's house: For I have five brethren; that he may testify unto them, lest they also come into this place of torment."

He was concerned, but too late, for his five brothers. He did not want them to come to the place of torment.

- **Luke 16:29-31**
  "Abraham saith unto him, They have Moses and the prophets; let them hear them. And he said, Nay, father Abraham: but if one went unto them from the dead, they will repent. And he said unto him, If they hear not Moses and the prophets, neither will they be persuaded, though one rose from the dead."

The Lord Jesus Christ rose bodily from the dead. Are people flocking genuinely to trust Him as Saviour and Redeemer? There was a newscast where one of the men was an atheist. He began to write against the Lord Jesus Christ and against God. In searching and studying, he became converted to the Lord Jesus Christ. The thing that hit him was that the Lord Jesus Christ rose from the dead. It was miraculous. That resurrection changed His disciples and His apostles. It overturned their lives. If people would not hear Moses and the prophets they will not hear even if one rose from the dead. That is powerful. The Lord Jesus Christ did rise.

The Flying Angel's Warning

The Lord Jesus Christ has given this trumpet judgment. Before judgments five, six, and seven, the flying angel is crying out to the inhabiters of the earth, those that are still living on this earth. I trust and I hope that the unsaved at that time will take heed to the warning that woes are coming, these three trumpet judgments yet to come, and they will turn to the Lord Jesus Christ and forsake the antichrist who will then be ruling and reigning on this earth. This is God's wonderful grace and longsuffering in that He warns us before the woes come. He has warned us who are here and all over the world.

- **Romans 6:23**
  "For the wages of sin *is* **death**; but the gift of God *is* eternal life through Jesus Christ our Lord."
- **Hebrews 9:27**
  "And as it is appointed unto men once to **die**, but after this the judgment:"

Hell And Heaven Are Both Real

Hell is real, but Heaven is also real. We trust that every one of those reading this has accepted, in a real, genuine fashion, the Lord Jesus Christ as their Saviour. Otherwise, there is judgment down the line.

Rebelation
Chapter Nine

Revelation 9:1

"And the fifth angel sounded, and I saw a star fall from Heaven unto the earth: and to him was given the key of the bottomless pit."

This **star falling from Heaven**, I believe, according to Revelation 9:2 that says *"and he opened,"* will apparently be a personified **star**–a person. This is what I believe.

- **Revelation 9:11**
  "And they had a king over them, *which is* the **angel** of the bottomless pit, whose name in the Hebrew tongue *is* Abaddon, but in the Greek tongue hath *his* name Apollyon "

Apparently, the falling **star** was the **angel**.

The Key To The Bottomless Pit

Notice, he has the key to the bottomless pit. Keys in Scripture are used at different times for different things. Keys, of course, open up things. They have access to things. This Satanic angel had the key to the bottomless pit.

- **Isaiah 22:22**
  "And the **key** of the house of David will I lay upon his shoulder; so he shall open, and none shall shut; and he shall shut, and none shall open."

This is speaking of the Lord Jesus Christ. He has the **key** of the house of David. When a person has genuine faith in the Lord Jesus Christ, Heaven can open for that person. The Lord Jesus Christ has power to **open** up Heaven and to shut it so that no man can **open** it. Once death occurs, our opportunity is over from ever receiving the Lord Jesus Christ as Saviour. It is too late. Now, while we are living, the **door** to Heaven is open if we have genuine faith in the Lord Jesus Christ as our Saviour.

- **Matthew 11:28**
  "Come unto me, all *ye* that labour and are heavy laden, and I will give you rest."
- **Luke 11:52**
  "Woe unto you, lawyers! for ye have taken away the **key** of knowledge: ye entered not in yourselves, and them that were entering in ye hindered."

The lawyers were those that had to do with the law of Moses. They added many things. They were not interested in Heaven. It was a terrible thing, hindering people that wanted to come to the Lord Jesus Christ. People wanted to come to the Lord Jesus Christ by genuine faith in Him, but these lawyers hindered them and took away the **key** of knowledge.

- **Revelation 1:18**
  "*I am* he that liveth, and was dead; and, behold, I am alive for evermore, Amen; and have the **keys** of Hell and of death."

This is the Lord Jesus Christ Himself. He is alive for evermore.

The Keys Of Heaven

The Lord Jesus Christ holds in His hands the keys of Heaven, the keys of Hell, and the keys of death. People must genuinely trust Him in order to evade and escape Hell when they die and enter into Heaven. This certainly is a key of our Saviour.

- **Revelation 3:7**
  "And to the angel of the church in Philadelphia write; These things saith he that is holy, he that is true, he that hath the **key** of David, he that openeth, and no man shutteth; and shutteth, and no man openeth;"

This is a reference back to Isaiah 22:22. It speaks of the Lord Jesus Christ again. The Lord Jesus Christ is the One Who can open up Heaven. Popes cannot do it. Saints cannot do it. Pastors cannot do it. Rabbis cannot do it. No individual can open up Heaven. The Lord Jesus Christ is the only One that has the key that can open up that wonderful, glorious Place. It is for those who are redeemed, those who say, "Christ has redeemed us once for all." He has that key that opens up the door and He also has the **key** that "shutteth, and no man openeth." We have to be sure that we are in the Lord Jesus Christ, right here on this earth before we die, otherwise there is no hope of anything in the future.

The Bottomless Pit

As far as that bottomless pit, the abyss, ABUSSOS is the Greek word for it. It is *a very deep gulf, or chasm; the lowest part of the earth, used as the common receptacle of the dead, and especially as the abode of devils.* This abyss is where the devils are and when this bottomless pit is opened with this key that the angel has, all these devils come out. It is a terrible thing.

Then there is the word, PHREAR, the pit of the abyss. In the nether world, it is thought to increase in size the further it extends from the surface of the earth, and so resembles a cistern, the orifice of which is narrow. Here is the pit, just like a cistern, small at the top and then it just opens right up. That is the place, I believe, where Hell is and it will be created a special place for the judgment of the ones that are dead and have not genuinely trusted the Lord Jesus Christ. They are there even today in the bottomless pit.

Revelation 9:2

"And he opened the bottomless pit; and there arose a smoke out of the pit, as the smoke of a great furnace; and the sun and the air were darkened by reason of the smoke of the pit."

This **pit** was opened and **smoke** appeared, first of all.

- **Genesis 19:28**
  "And he looked toward Sodom and Gomorrah, and toward all the land of the plain, and beheld, and, lo, the **smoke** of the country went up as the **smoke** of a **furnace**."

Sodom And Gomorrah's Judgment

This was God's judgment on Sodom and Gomorrah for their wickedness of sodomy and all their other filthiness and sin. God's judgment was as a smoke of a furnace. The judgment here of this trumpet is going to be *smoke of a great furnace.*

- **Exodus 19:18**
  "And mount Sinai was altogether on a smoke, because the LORD descended upon it in fire: and the **smoke** thereof ascended as the **smoke of a furnace**, and the whole mount quaked greatly."

This was Mt. Sinai when the law was given. The **smoke** was the holiness of God.

- **2 Samuel 22:8-9**
  "Then the earth shook and trembled; the foundations of Heaven moved and shook, because he was wroth. There went up a **smoke** out of his nostrils, and fire out of his mouth devoured: coals were kindled by it."

God was wroth. God was angry. There was the **smoke** of God, the judgment of God. Hell itself, the lake of fire, is a very great penalty and judgment.

- **Isaiah 4:5**
  "And the LORD will create upon every dwelling place of mount Zion, and upon her assemblies, a cloud and **smoke** by day, and the shining of a flaming fire by night: for upon all the glory *shall be* a defence."

He will have a *smoke by day* just like on the tabernacle in the wilderness. Forty years, He led them by day with a pillar of cloud and **smoke,** and at night by a pillar of fire. The Lord's presence sometimes is referred to as **smoke**.

- **Isaiah 6:4-5**
  "And the posts of the door moved at the voice of him that cried, and the house was filled with **smoke**. Then said I, Woe *is* me! for I am undone; because I *am* a man of unclean lips, and I dwell in the midst of a people of unclean lips: for mine eyes have seen the King, the LORD of hosts."

Here is Isaiah's call to the ministry of a prophet. This again is the holiness of the Lord. Sometimes smoke is for holiness.

God's Use Of Smoke For Judgment

The Lord sometimes uses smoke for judgment, as in Sodom and Gomorrah. Other times there is smoke that comes out of His nostrils. Other times, smoke is used to show His presence and His holiness. In this case, it is the release out of

> the smoke, as we will see in verse 3, of the locusts. It was smoke that darkened the whole air. I am glad I am not going to be here to see all this darkening of the air.

Revelation 9:3

"And there came out of the smoke locusts upon the earth: and unto them was given power, as the scorpions of the earth have power."

Here the **locusts** have come out, millions of them **smoking** up the whole earth. **Locusts** only occur sixteen times in Scripture.

- **Exodus 10:12**
  "And the LORD said unto Moses, Stretch out thine hand over the land of Egypt for the **locusts**, that they may come up upon the land of Egypt, and eat every herb of the land, *even* all that the hail hath left."

This is one of the ten plagues on Egypt. The **locusts** eat up the crops. That is their goal. These **locusts** in Revelation 9:3 do not do that, but normal locusts eat up every green thing.

- **2 Chronicles 6:28-30**
  "If there be dearth in the land, if there be pestilence, if there be blasting, or mildew, **locusts**, or caterpillers; if their enemies besiege them in the cities of their land; whatsoever sore or whatsoever sickness *there be*: *Then* what prayer *or* what supplication soever shall be made of any man, or of all thy people Israel, when every one shall know his own sore and his own grief, and shall spread forth his hands in this house: Then hear thou from Heaven thy dwelling place, and forgive, and render unto every man according unto all his ways, whose heart thou knowest; (for thou only knowest the hearts of the children of men:)"

Here is a plague of **locusts** upon the people and Solomon prays, "Please Lord, forgive us," because of the **locusts**.

There was a plague of **locusts** recently in Australia. This is a terrible thing.

- **2 Chronicles 7:13-14**
  "If I shut up Heaven that there be no rain, or if I command the **locusts** to devour the land, or if I send pestilence among my people; If my people, which are called by my name, shall humble themselves, and pray, and seek my face, and turn from their wicked ways; then will I hear from Heaven, and will forgive their sin, and will heal their land."

Here is a command by the Lord that **locusts** devour the land. The **locusts** could be prayed away in that case.

- **Psalm 105:34-35**
  "He spake, and the **locusts** came, and caterpillers, and that without number, And did eat up all the herbs in their land, and devoured the fruit of their ground."

This is speaking of the Egyptian bondage and judgment. This judgment on Egypt was a direct result from God. God is in control of these plagues.

- **Mark 1:6**
  "And John was clothed with camel's hair, and with a girdle of a skin about his loins; and he did eat **locusts** and wild honey;"

This is something that I would not favor. Some people do eat **locusts**. They fry them and put salt on them and eat them. They are "clean," as far as the law of Moses in the Old Testament was concerned.

Notice, these **locusts** in Revelation 9:3 had power *as the scorpions of the earth have power*. **Scorpions** are only mentioned nine times in Scripture altogether.

- **Deuteronomy 8:15**
  "Who led thee through that great and terrible wilderness, *wherein were* fiery serpents, and **scorpions**, and drought, where *there was* no water; who brought thee forth water out of the rock of flint;"

In that wilderness for forty years, there were **scorpions**.

- **1 Kings 12:11**
  "And now whereas my father did lade you with a heavy yoke, I will add to your yoke: my father hath chastised you with whips, but I will chastise you with **scorpions**."

Rehoboam was the wicked son of Solomon. God rent ten tribes of the kingdom to Jeroboam and gave only two to Rehoboam.

- **Ezekiel 2:6**
  "And thou, son of man, be not afraid of them, neither be afraid of their words, though briers and thorns *be* with thee, and thou dost dwell among **scorpions**: be not afraid of their words, nor be dismayed at their looks, though they *be* a rebellious house."

Preaching To Disobedient People

Every time a prophet preached to a people that were disobedient there was a possibility of fear. Whenever a pastor preaches to people, sometimes there is a fear. Ezekiel was

warned to be not afraid. Sometimes they say, "Looks can kill."
Sometimes they can, sometimes they cannot. Ezekiel was not
to be afraid of their looks.

- Luke 10:19
  "Behold, I give unto you power to tread on serpents and
  scorpions, and over all the power of the enemy: and nothing
  shall by any means hurt you."

The Lord Jesus Christ sent out the seventy disciples after the twelve were
sent out. This was apostolic power. We do not believe that the
Charismatics are right in saying that these powers are present with us
today. This was during the apostolic time. Now that the Scriptures are
completed (in 90 to 100 A.D.), all these signs of the apostles are gone.
They had power to tread on serpents and **scorpions**.

What is a **locust**? I looked up a few things. First of all, it is any large
grasshopper, specifically a migratory **grasshopper**, often traveling
in great swarms and destroying nearly all vegetation in the area that it
visits. They often cause extensive and serious damage to crops in many
parts of Africa and Asia. These **locusts** in Revelation 9:3 will not
damage the crops. **Locusts** are well known for invading cropping areas
in swarms of millions.

Just think—swarms of millions of **locusts**! Can you imagine
locusts in the millions? They leave behind devastated fields and
plantations. There are different ways of controlling **locusts** and
grasshoppers now.

Locusts As Scorpions

The locusts in this verse will be as scorpions of the earth.
I looked up a few things on scorpions. I think we ought to
know what a scorpion is. They are called common arachnids
and considered relatives of spiders, mites, ticks, and
harvesters. There are approximately 1,300 species of
scorpions worldwide. They are characterized by an elongated
body and a segmented tail that is tipped with a venomous
stinger.

What about their range? They are commonly thought of as
desert animals. In fact, they occur in many other habitats,
including grasslands, savannahs, deciduous forests, pine
forests, and so on. Scorpions have been found even under
snow-covered rocks in elevations of over 12,000 feet. Even in
the snow, there are some scorpions in the Andes Mountains of

South America and the Himalayas of Asia. About ninety species of scorpions occur in the United States. All but four of these naturally occur west of the Mississippi River.

What about their description? As arachnids, **scorpions** have mouth parts called chelicercae, a pair of pedipalps, and four pairs of legs. (I am sure that will be of great interest to those of us interested in spiders and **scorpions**.) The pincer-like pedipalps are used primarily for the capture of prey and for defense. They are also covered with various types of sensory hairs. The body is divided into two main regions. The abdomen consists of twelve distinct segments. The last five form what most people refer to as the tail. We will see about these tails a little bit later. At the end of the abdomen is the telson, which bears a bulb-shaped structure containing the venom glands and a sharp, curved aculeus to deliver the venom. On the underside, the **scorpion** bears a pair of unique sense organs called pectines. The male bears more teeth than the female.

Characteristics Of Scorpions

They are nocturnal predatory animals and they feed on a variety of insects, spiders, centipedes, and other scorpions. They eat each other. The larger scorpions occasionally feed on vertebrates, such as small lizards, snakes, and mice. Scorpions fall prey to many types of creatures, such as the centipedes, tarantulas, insectivorous lizards, birds (especially owls) and mammals, including shrews, mice and bats. Scorpions have other enemies, as well. On the average, a female gives birth to about twenty-five to thirty-five young. They ride on her back until a week or two after the birth.

The venom of **scorpions** is for the capture of prey and for defense. The venom contains complex neurotoxins, affecting the victim's nervous system. Despite their bad reputation, only one species in the United States and about twenty others worldwide have venom potent enough to be considered dangerous to humans. The venom of the **scorpion** may produce severe pain, swelling at the site of the sting, numbness, frothing at the mouth, difficulties in breathing, including respiratory paralysis, muscle twitching, and convulsions. Death is rare, especially in more recent times, and anti-venom is available. The world's most dangerous scorpions live in northern Africa, the Middle East, India, and Mexico. Typically, mortality rises up to about four percent in hospital cases. Sometimes death by **scorpion** sting, if it occurs, is a result of heart or respiratory failure some hours after the incident. When it says that **locusts** are dangerous and have the power of the **scorpion**, that is what is involved with all this pain and poison.

Descriptions of Locusts

The word for locust is AKRIS. It occurs in various Oriental countries, stripping fields and trees. Numberless swarms of them almost every spring are carried by the winds from Arabia into Palestine. Having devastated the country, they migrate to regions farther north until they perish by falling into the sea. I guess they are a little stupid, to go into the sea and die. The Orientals are accustomed to feed upon locusts, either raw or roasted. Now, what are you going to have, raw or roasted ones? I do not want either one, pardon me. They are seasoned with salt and prepared in other ways. Israelites are permitted to eat them. That is what John the Baptist fed on–locusts and wild honey.

Revelation 9:4

"And it was commanded them that they should not hurt the grass of the earth, neither any green thing, neither any tree; but only those men which have not the seal of God in their foreheads."

Contrary to their nature, eating all the **green things**, this was not the purpose of these **locusts**. The **seal of God** is given to true believers that are genuinely saved.

- **2 Corinthians 1:21-22**
  "Now he which stablisheth us with you in Christ, and hath anointed us, *is* God; Who hath also **sealed** us, and given the earnest of the Spirit in our hearts."
- **Ephesians 1:13**
  "In whom ye also *trusted*, after that ye heard the word of truth, the gospel of your salvation: in whom also after that ye believed, ye were **sealed** with that holy Spirit of promise,"

Locusts Won't Hurt The Saved

If any genuine believers are truly saved through the preaching of the 144,000 in the tribulation period, these locusts will not hurt them or harm them. They have been sealed by the Lord Jesus Christ.

- **Ephesians 4:30**
"And grieve not the holy Spirit of God, whereby ye are **sealed** unto the day of redemption."

That is why I believe you cannot lose your salvation once you have been genuinely saved. You have been **sealed** by the Holy Spirit of God.

- **Revelation 7:2-4**
"And I saw another angel ascending from the east, having the seal of the living God: and he cried with a loud voice to the four angels, to whom it was given to hurt the earth and the sea, Saying, Hurt not the earth, neither the sea, nor the trees, till we have **sealed** the servants of our God in their foreheads. And I heard the number of them which were **sealed**: *and there were* sealed an hundred *and* forty *and* four thousand of all the tribes of the children of Israel."

No Hurt To The Sealed Ones

These locusts, according to this verse, were not to hurt or do anything to the ones who were sealed. The ones who have not the seal of God in their foreheads are the ones that are going to be affected. Those that are sealed will be exempt from any danger or harm from these locusts coming out of the abyss—the bottomless pit—led by the Devil and his Satanic forces.

Revelation 9:5

"And to them it was given that they should not kill them, but that they should be tormented five months: and their torment *was* as the torment of a scorpion, when he striketh a man."

Scorpions To Torment People

Again, the scorpions are about to come forth, but not to kill people. They were to torment people for five months. The Greek word for torment is BASANISMOS. It means *to torture; to vex with grievous pains of body and mind; to torment.* That is what God has destined for those that are not sealed, those that are lost, those that are worshipping the Devil and idols.

This word for **torment** is an interesting term.

- **Matthew 8:28-29**
  "And when he was come to the other side into the country of the Gergesenes, there met him two possessed with devils, coming out of the tombs, exceeding fierce, so that no man might pass by that way. And, behold, they cried out, saying, What have we to do with thee, Jesus, thou Son of God? art thou come hither to **torment** us before the time?"

They knew that their destiny was the lake of fire in **torment**, torture, and terrible pain.

- **Luke 16:22-28**
  "And it came to pass, that the beggar died, and was carried by the angels into Abraham's bosom: the rich man also died, and was buried; And in Hell he lift up his eyes, being in **torments**, and seeth Abraham afar off, and Lazarus in his bosom. And he cried and said, Father Abraham, have mercy on me, and send Lazarus, that he may dip the tip of his finger in water, and cool my tongue; for I am **tormented** in this flame. But Abraham said, Son, remember that thou in thy lifetime receivedst thy good things, and likewise Lazarus evil things: but now he is comforted, and thou art **tormented**. And beside all this, between us and you there is a great gulf fixed: so that they which would pass from hence to you cannot; neither can they pass to us, that *would come* from thence. Then he said, I pray thee therefore, father, that thou wouldest send him to my father's house: For I have five brethren; that he may testify unto them, lest they also come into this place of **torment**."

The rich man denied the Lord Jesus Christ. Lazarus apparently genuinely trusted Him and was in Paradise. Hell is not a picnic. <u>Hell is for those that have rejected the Lord Jesus Christ as their Saviour.</u> They are not genuinely saved and redeemed. There is **torment**. It will be eternal **torment**. This should motivate each one of us to tell our friends, neighbors, and relatives about the Saviour, the Lord Jesus Christ, that lives in Glory, willing to save those who come to Him by genuine faith. The flames are real. The flames are genuine. It is not a figure of speech.

Hell Fire Denied By Billy Graham

I know different ones have taken the fire out of Hell. Billy Graham is one. In 1950, he said that there is no fire in Hell. Various new evangelicals have taken fire out of Hell. The Lord Jesus Christ speaks of it as everlasting fire. He speaks of it as the lake of fire. This is reality. It is not just a parable. I do not care what the Pope says in the Council of Trent about Purgatory. They say you wait in Purgatory, and through penance and other means, come out and pass up to Heaven. No, you cannot.

The rich man was thinking about his relatives too late. Think about your relatives and your friends that are lost now. Do not wait until it is too late, until they die. Think about them now. This should be a motivation for all of us to remember that **torment** is there. Hell is real. The Lord Jesus Christ has given those who are genuinely saved–deliverance from Hell, and deliverance from the grave, suffering, and **torment**. He has given us the wonderful bliss of Heaven and Glory in His presence. We ought to praise the Lord for that.

Revelation 9:6

"And in those days shall men seek death, and shall not find it; and shall desire to die, and death shall flee from them."

We have people here that will **seek death**. This pain, this **torment** of these locusts, will be so great, like the **scorpion's** pain, that they will want to **die**, but they cannot. They will be forbidden to **die**. **Death** shall flee from them. Many of us remember the pictures on television of the 9-11 fires coming from the two towers. We saw the bodies of some people falling from those towers, hurling themselves down. Why? The pain and **torment** was so great they wanted to end it immediately. They knew they were going to **die,** but the pain caused them to **seek death.** They found it and they **died.** In this case, the **torment** is going to be so great, that they **seek death**, but **death** shall flee from them. Euthanasia means "pleasant **death**" for those who want to die because of pain.

- **Job 1:21**
  "And said, Naked came I out of my mother's womb, and naked shall I return thither: the LORD gave, and the LORD hath taken away; blessed be the name of the LORD."

This verse seems to be a reference against euthanasia or mercy **killing**. The Lord permitted Job's possessions and children to be taken away. When the Lord's time comes to take our life, that is His prerogative.

- **Luke 23:46**
  "And when Jesus had cried with a loud voice, he said, Father, into thy hands I commend my spirit: and having said thus, he gave up the ghost."

The Lord Jesus Christ gave up His life. He had the power to take His life. After His suffering was finished, He said, "It is finished." He gave up His life and it was completed.

Euthanasia Defined

Euthanasia and mercy killing, might be defined as the intentional killing by an act or omission of a dependant human for his or her alleged benefit. There is voluntary euthanasia where somebody has requested to be killed. There is non-voluntary where no request was made. There is involuntary euthanasia, where a person says, "Do not kill me," and they kill them. Assisted suicide is another thing, euthanasia by action, euthanasia by omission. It is not euthanasia, unless the death is intentionally caused by what is done or not done.

I found something about the history of euthanasia on the Internet.

In B.C. 400, Hippocrates said, "I will give no **deadly** medicine to anyone, if asked, or suggest any such counsel." He was against euthanasia.

From the fourteenth to the twentieth century, English law forbade euthanasia. For over 700 years, in the Anglo-American common law tradition, euthanasia was punished or otherwise disapproved of. This included both **suicide** and assisted **suicide**.

Assisting Suicide Outlawed

In 1828, the early American statutes explicitly outlawed assisted suicide.

In 1920, a book came out permitting the destruction of life if it is not deemed worthy of life. The author argued that patients who ask for **death** assistance should, under very carefully controlled conditions, be able to obtain it from a physician. The book helped support involuntary euthanasia by Nazi Germany. Involuntary, they did not want it, but they were **killed.**

Promoting Mercy Killing

In 1935, the Euthanasia Society of England was formed to promote euthanasia or mercy killing.

---

http://www.nightingalealliance.org/pdf/state_grid.pdf Is a LINK that shows the current status of each of our states regarding euthanasia.

As of 2011, the following states either authorize euthanasia under certain conditions (such as physician-assisted suicide), or else have no laws prohibiting euthanasia: Alabama, the District of Columbia, Idaho, Massachusetts, Montana, North Carolina, Ohio, Oregon, Utah, Vermont, Washington, West Virginia, and Wyoming. All the remaining states have laws which prohibit euthanasia.

In 1939, in Nazi Germany, Hitler ordered widespread mercy **killing** of the sick and disabled. Life not deemed worthy of life was how he defined this. He started with very young children with symptoms of mental retardation or physical deformity. They just **killed** them. That was what he believed. The Nazi euthanasia program quickly expanded to include older disabled children and adults.

In 1995, Australia's northern territory approved a euthanasia bill. It took effect in 1996, but fortunately the Australian Parliament overturned it in 1997.

In 1999, Dr. Jack Kevorkian was sentenced to ten to twenty-five years in prison for giving a lethal injection to Thomas Youk.

In 2000, the Netherlands legalized euthanasia.

In 2002, Belgium legalized euthanasia.

There is an international task force for euthanasia and assisted **suicide** list of frequently asked questions. There are about twelve pages of frequently asked questions on how to go ahead and **kill** yourself. It is a sad thing when men **seek death**, or euthanized **death**, and people are saying it is all right. Pretty soon, I am sure it will become legal, not only in Oregon, but also in other states in the United States of America. Note the above list of states that either permit physician assisted suicide or have no laws against euthanasia. This is sad.

Will we be turned into Nazi Germany, whereby there are not just those that want to be euthanized because of the pain they are undergoing, but also those who will be forced to be **killed**? It is an important thing.

Men Will Seek Death

In Revelation 9:6, these men, because of the torment of the locusts, this terrible plague upon them, will seek death and shall not find it. There will be no Dr. Kevorkians around at that time. You cannot do it. There will be no way to do it. None of the societies will be able to do it. They will desire to die and death shall flee from them.

The Lord Jesus Christ, though He was not necessarily eager to **die**, gave up His life and did **die**. It was the fulfillment of the Old Testament prophecy that the Messiah would give His life for the ransom of many. That is what He did willingly.

Revelation 9:7

"And the shapes of the locusts *were* **like unto horses prepared unto battle; and on their heads** *were* **as it were crowns like gold, and their faces** *were* **as the faces of men."**

The picture of these **locusts** was like **horses prepared for battle.** In other words, they had armor plate so they would not be hurt. Nobody could kill them. They had very important **heads** with **crowns like gold.** They had **faces like men.** Can you imagine the devils with **faces of men?** Promotional pictures on television that advertised *The Passion* showed you a picture of Satan. It was a woman with a horrible, grotesque face. These **locusts** will have **faces of men.** Can you imagine thousands and millions of them? They will have **faces of men** and will be wounding and tormenting the people that are lost and refuse to come to the Lord Jesus Christ as Saviour in genuine faith. This is a picture of these **locusts.**

Revelation 9:8

"And they had hair as the hair of women, and their teeth were as *the teeth* **of lions."**

They must have had long **hair**, not shaved off like some **women** do today. Their **teeth** were as the **teeth of lions.** I would not want to be in the mouth of a **lion.** Would you? I looked up **lions' teeth**, just to be on the safe side, to see what their **teeth** are like.

In fact, just the other day Mrs. Waite and I were looking at one of the Discovery Channel programs, I think it was. There was a father **lion** who was too old. Two young **lions** came to drive him out of the pride. While he was there, you could see his **teeth.** I told my wife, "See those front **teeth?** They are separated. They have a big gap in there." That fits in with what I looked up about their **teeth.**

The Lion's Killing Teeth

The lion's teeth are well-adapted for killing their prey and eating it. The great canine teeth, the two teeth in the front, are spaced such as they can slip between the cervical vertebrae, that is the neck vertebrae, of their favorite-sized prey animals and sever the spinal cord. That is why they have this gap. The shape of the back teeth, which are called carnassials instead of molars, makes them work like a pair of scissors.

Their **teeth** were as the **teeth of lions**. You can imagine the pain that will be inflicted. It does not say how, but if these critters that are shaped like **horses prepared for battle,** that are like the sting of **scorpions** and pain, have **teeth** like **lions**, with the **faces of men,** you can imagine the bites, or whatever it may be, will be a terrible thing. Men, women, and children will seek death and will not be able to find it. How much better were they to have genuinely accepted the Lord Jesus Christ, the Prince of Life, to save them and take them to Heaven. They would then have the **seal of God** in their foreheads, so that they would not be harmed. The only people that will be harmed, **tormented,** and tortured by these **locusts,** are those that do not have the **seal of God** in their foreheads, those who are lost, those who have rejected the Lord Jesus Christ as Saviour.

Revelation 9:9

"And they had breastplates, as it were breastplates of iron; and the sound of their wings was as the sound of chariots of many horses running to battle."

Description Of Locusts

Locusts are flying creatures. They had breastplates for protection. You can imagine sounds of the pounding by the way they flap their wings. Not only would there be fear in the hearts of those that were not sealed on their foreheads with the seal of God, but they would fear as the locusts attacked, and at the sound of the approach of these terrible creatures.

Breastplates in Scripture are for protection and for beauty.

- **Exodus 28:4**
  "And these *are* the garments which they shall make; a **breastplate,** and an ephod, and a robe, and a broidered coat, a mitre, and a girdle: and they shall make holy garments for Aaron thy brother, and his sons, that he may minister unto me in the priest's office."

The first instance of **breastplates** was on the garments of Aaron, the high priest. He had a special **breastplate** designed and wonderfully decked out.

- **Ephesians 6:14**
  "Stand therefore, having your loins girt about with truth, and having on the **breastplate** of righteousness;"

The Protecting Breastplate

The only way we can get a breastplate to protect us from the evil of the Devil is the righteousness of the Lord Jesus Christ and by genuinely trusting in Him to be saved. Only then can a person have His righteousness.

- 1 Thessalonians 5:8
  "But let us, who are of the day, be sober, putting on the **breastplate** of faith and love; and for an helmet, the hope of salvation."

Those of us who are genuinely saved have a **breastplate** of protection from the world, the flesh, and the Devil.

Revelation 9:10

"And they had tails like unto scorpions, and there were stings in their tails: and their power *was* to hurt men five months."

Just think, it is going to be a **five-month torment** by these locusts with **teeth like lions, faces like men**, shaped like **horses** prepared for battle. The **sound** will be **like chariots** of many horses **running** to battle. They will bring terrible **torments**. The Greek word for **sting**, by the way, is KENTRON. The **sting** is as that of bees, scorpions, and locusts. Such insects wound by their **sting** and even cause death. Paul attributes death personified as a **sting** like a deadly weapon.

- 1 Corinthians 15:55
  "O death, where *is* thy **sting**? O grave, where *is* thy victory?"

Allergies To Stinging Insect Venom

As far as stings are concerned, I thought we should look at a few of these things. There are approximately between one and two million people in the United States who are severely allergic to stinging insect venom. Imagine the torment for five months of this type of thing. Each year, ninety to a hundred deaths from sting reactions are recorded. Many more deaths may be occurring, mistakenly diagnosed as heart attacks, sunstrokes, and attributed to other causes. More people die each year from the effects of insect venom than from spider or snake bites. Extreme human sensitivity to stings, resulting in serious or fatal reactions is confirmed almost entirely to cases involving bees, wasps, hornets, bumblebees, and ants. In this case, death will be from these locusts.

Insect allergies can cause life-threatening disruptions of breathing and circulatory systems, called anaphylactic shock. For one person in a hundred, the sting of an insect can be fatal. Most people that are stung have a local reaction such as redness, pain, swelling, and some itching. The reaction progresses quickly to sites other than the sting bite, followed by difficult breathing and choking of the throat. The person experiences systemic allergic reaction, anaphylaxis, requiring emergency medical treatment. What if all these symptoms prevailed and these people sought **death** and could not find it? Just these symptoms are horrible, indeed. If you are **stung** on the hand and your face begins to swell, or hives break out all over your body, this is a serious condition requiring emergency room attention. **Stings** usually last just a few hours, sometimes with only local reactions, but severe allergic reactions can come within a few minutes after the **sting** occurs. The whole body might be involved. A person may feel dizzy, lightheaded, nauseated, weak, have stomach cramps, diarrhea, itching around the eyes, a warm feeling, coughing, hives breaking out, followed with vomiting, swelling, wheezing, difficult breathing, shortness of breath, hoarse speech, a drop in blood pressure, shock, and so on.

The Symptoms Of Being Stung

It is an important thing that these who are stung will have symptoms, I am sure, similar to the stings of animals and insects even of today. They will seek death from the torture-symptoms of these stings by these locusts. These are Satanic-type of beings that are developed, and will hurt those who are not sealed in their foreheads by the Spirit of God.

Revelation 9:11

"And they had a king over them, *which* is the angel of the bottomless pit, whose name in the Hebrew tongue *is* Abaddon, but in the Greek tongue hath *his* name Apollyon."

They had a **leader**. They had a **king**. These **locusts** were probably regimented. **Kings** usually regiment their subjects. They have an order.

They know what to do. They know who to attack and who not to attack. Just think, the only ones spared are the ones who have the **seal** of God in their foreheads. The 144,000 Jewish evangelists were **sealed**. Other believers that will be led to the Lord Jesus Christ will also have the **seal** of God. These will be prevented from being **stung** by these terrible **locusts** with pain for **five months**.

That king in **Hebrew** is **Abaddon** and in **Greek** is **Apollyon**, which means *destruction* and *the destroyer*. That **Abaddon** is the name of the **angel** prince of the infernal regions, a minister of death, and the author of havoc on the earth. That is what **Abaddon** means. Here the leader is this one who causes the **torment** and the **pain** of those who dwell on the earth who are not truly born-again Christians. If you are reading this, wherever you may be, and are not genuinely saved, not walking with the Lord Jesus Christ, genuinely converted, and born-again, I trust you will get truly saved immediately. Get ready! The Lord Jesus Christ could come at any moment. Tribulation would then begin with seven years of suffering and **torment**.

Five Months Of Pain

This particular trumpet judgment will come and bring five whole months of pain inflicted by these terrible inhuman locusts. The pain will be for those who have rejected the Lord Jesus Christ as their Saviour. May you be ready and prepared.

People will be **seeking death** and cannot find it. Sometimes people are so pained that they want to **die**. Job, I think, would have just as soon **died** with all of his **pain**, but the Lord said, "No. Not yet, Job." He got out of that idea and was blessed. He lived for probably double the more years of his life. He had more children and his wife was back with him.

- **1 Corinthians 15:55-56**
  "O death, where *is* thy **sting**? O grave, where *is* thy victory? The **sting** of death is sin; and the strength of sin is the law."

Safe In The Arms Of Jesus

Blessed be the name of the Lord Jesus Christ, Who has risen and has given us who are genuinely saved, victory and justification by faith in His wonderful Words. He has been able to spare us from these terrible sufferings–the torment of locusts, or Hell, or any of these devastations. We will be safe in the arms of the Lord Jesus Christ if we are genuinely trusting in Him as our Saviour and Redeemer.

Revelation 9:12

"One woe is past; *and,* **behold, there come two woes more hereafter."**

The Seven Trumpet Judgments

We are continuing to talk about the seven trumpet judgments. These judgments are announced in the book of Revelation during the tribulation period which is Daniel's 70th Week. Those who are genuinely saved and born-again, will be caught up to Heaven before this ever takes place. They will be separated from all of the tribulation and have nothing to do with it. They will be in Heaven.

The First Trumpet–hail, fire, and blood (Rev. 8:7)

The Second Trumpet–a burning mountain (Rev. 8:8-9)

The Third Trumpet–a falling star (Rev. 8:10-11)

The Fourth Trumpet–the smitten sun (Rev.8:12-15)

The Fifth Trumpet–the locust plague (Rev. 9:1-12)

The Sixth Trumpet–the horsemen plague (Rev. 8:14-19)

The Seventh Trumpet–finishing the mystery (Rev. 10:7)

The first woe was, perhaps, the locusts. The second woe will be the horsemen that are talked about in the last part of Revelation 9. There are many woes in Scripture. God pronounces woes on various things.

- **Proverbs 23:29-30**
  "Who hath **woe?** who hath sorrow? who hath contentions? who hath babbling? who hath wounds without cause? who hath redness of eyes? They that tarry long at the wine; they that go to seek mixed wine."

The drunkards have a **woe** against them.

- **Isaiah 3:11**
  "**Woe** unto the wicked! *it shall be* ill *with him*: for the reward of his hands shall be given him."

There are **woes** against wicked people.

- **Isaiah 5:11**
  "**Woe** unto them that rise up early in the morning, *that* they may follow strong drink; that continue until night, *till* wine inflame them!"

Again, there is **woe** against drink and drunkards.

- Isaiah 5:20-21
  "**Woe** unto them that call evil good, and good evil; that put darkness for light, and light for darkness; that put bitter for sweet, and sweet for bitter! **Woe** unto them *that are wise* in their own eyes, and prudent in their own sight!"

For those that are stuck on themselves, God says there is a **woe** against them.

- Isaiah 5:22
  "**Woe** unto *them that are* mighty to drink wine, and men of strength to mingle strong drink:"

Again, God is pronouncing **woe** against drinkers. Alcoholic beverages in any form are terrors to the body and the soul. God pronounces **woe** unto them.

- Isaiah 31:1
  "**Woe** to them that go down to Egypt for help; and stay on horses, and trust in chariots, because *they are* many; and in **horsemen**, because they are very strong; but they look not unto the Holy One of Israel, neither seek the LORD"

Egypt A Picture Of The World

Egypt is a picture of the world. We ought not to go down to the world. The Lord Jesus Christ is stronger than any people in the world. We ought not to put confidence in horses and chariots, or tanks, or missiles, or any other thing in our day. The Lord Jesus Christ is the One Whom we should seek, not the might of nations, horses, and battlements.

- Jeremiah 23:1
  "**Woe** be unto the pastors that destroy and scatter the sheep of my pasture! saith the LORD."

Here is a **woe** against the pastors, the shepherds of the flock of Israel. These were probably the kings. The shepherds were kings, no doubt, in that sense. The pastors were probably the prophets, maybe the priests, those that care for the people. Those pastors who speak lies and do not believe the truth scatter the sheep of the Lord.

- Ezekiel 34:2
  "Son of man, prophesy against the shepherds of Israel, prophesy, and say unto them, Thus saith the Lord GOD unto the shepherds; **Woe** *be* to the shepherds of Israel that do feed themselves! should not the shepherds feed the flocks?"

Pastors and shepherds do have some feed from the flock, but to feed just themselves with more money, more food, and so on, brings a **woe** against such shepherds.

- **Habakkuk 2:15**
  "**Woe** unto him that giveth his neighbour drink, that puttest thy bottle to *him*, and makest *him* drunken also, that thou mayest look on their nakedness!"

Woe To The Drunkards

Again, there is woe to the drunkards. You may not drink yourself, but if you give a neighbor to drink there is woe. <u>Does this mean we should not be a bartender?</u> I guess that would be the situation. If you give your neighbor to drink, God says there is woe unto you. There is a lot of drinking that leads to nakedness and sexual immorality as well.

- **Matthew 23:27**
  "**Woe** unto you, scribes and Pharisees, hypocrites! for ye are like unto whited sepulchres, which indeed appear beautiful outward, but are within full of dead *men's* bones, and of all uncleanness."

The Duties Of The Scribes

The scribes were the ones that wrote down the verses of the Scriptures, but they did not follow them. <u>Hypocrites are people that say one thing and do another</u>, or do one thing and say another. The Lord Jesus Christ pronounced a woe on the Pharisees because they were hypocrites.

- **Luke 6:26**
  "**Woe** unto you, <u>when all men</u> shall speak well of you! for so did their fathers to the false prophets."

Here is a **woe** on those who are politically correct. That is one of the things that we talk about all the time–being politically correct. Is it right to be politically correct? Does the Lord think it is? Do we want people to speak well of us? Of course, we do. <u>Notice the words, *all men*.</u> We hope that some men and women will speak well of us, but **woe** when all men do. You do not rattle a single cage. You do not ruffle a single feather of anybody. That is the basis of this new movement in church growth. That is the movement of Rick Warren, Joel Osteen, and others. Rick Warren says the church should get rid of the pillars of the churches, the old-timers. They just "hold things up." That is what they do. Get rid of them, says Rick Warren.

I talked to a man that I used to know when I was a member of a nearby Baptist church. I was a teacher in the Berean Sunday school class for many years. There were from 90 to 100 in the class. The man said the entire Berean class is gone, the ones whom I taught. He said the pastor told these people: "If you don't like what's going on, you don't have to be here." So they left. He said if it had not been for his wife, he would have left, but the wife was interested in the music and other things. So they stayed. It is a sad thing.

We Ought To Speak The Truth

We ought to speak the truth. We ought to speak in love, but still speak the truth. That does not make all people our friends.

- **1 Corinthians 9:16**
  "For though I preach the gospel, I have nothing to glory of: for necessity is laid upon me; yea, **woe** is unto me, if I preach not the gospel!"

Paul said he had a **woe** on him if he preached not the gospel. The Lord Jesus Christ called him, knocked him to the ground, blinded him, and told him to go preach to the Gentiles.

- **Revelation 8:13**
  "And I beheld, and heard an angel flying through the midst of Heaven, saying with a loud voice, **Woe, woe, woe**, to the inhabiters of the earth by reason of the other voices of the trumpet of the three angels, which are yet to sound!"

- **Revelation 11:14**
  "The second **woe** is past; *and,* behold, the third **woe** cometh quickly."

- **Revelation 12:12**
  "Therefore rejoice, *ye* Heavens, and ye that dwell in them. **Woe** to the inhabiters of the earth and of the sea! for the devil is come down unto you, having great wrath, because he knoweth that he hath but a short time."

The Final Woe Of Revelation

This is the final woe of Revelation. Woe to the inhabiters of the earth when the Devil is cast out of Heaven and down to this earth during this seven-year period of tribulation. Heaven will be rid of him, but the earth will not. He will be bound after the seven years are over for one thousand years. He will not be

completely helpless. They will have the world and the flesh, but not the Devil. During the entire millennial period, he will be bound. At the end he will be loosed for a season, but his time is short.

Revelation 9:13

"And the sixth angel sounded, and I heard a voice from the four horns of the golden altar which is before God,"

Here is the **golden altar**. I believe it is the **altar of incense**. The **altar of incense** is in Heaven.

- **Exodus 30:1-3**
  "And thou shalt make an **altar** to burn **incense** upon: *of* shittim wood shalt thou make it. A cubit *shall be* the length thereof, and a cubit the breadth thereof; foursquare shall it be: and two cubits *shall be* the height thereof: the horns thereof *shall be* of the same. And thou shalt overlay it with pure gold, the top thereof, and the sides thereof round about, and the horns thereof; and thou shalt make unto it a crown of gold round about."

Here is the **golden altar** of incense. That **incense**, or perfume, was to be burned morning and evening, all the time.

- **Exodus 37:25**
  "And he made the **incense altar** *of* shittim wood: the length of it *was* a cubit, and the breadth of it a cubit; *it was* foursquare; and two cubits *was* the height of it; the horns thereof were of the same."

Moses was first told by the Lord to make it, then he did. In Heaven, there is an **altar of incense**. There was an **altar of incense** on the earth in the tabernacle, just in front of the vail that separated between the holy place and the holy of holies. I believe, as it says in Scripture in Revelation, in Heaven there is a temple. There is an **altar**. Here is the **altar of incense**. This is the Heavenly **altar of incense**. We talked about the **altar of incense** and the prayers of the saints. The incense ascends and gives a beautiful fragrance on that **altar**.

I believe there is also a mercy seat in Heaven. On that mercy seat in Heaven is the blood of the Lord Jesus Christ. Just like the Old Testament priest once a year, on the day of atonement, was to take the blood of the bullock for his own sin and then the blood of the goat for the sins of the people and put that blood on the mercy seat. By the same token, I believe the Lord Jesus Christ, after His sacrifice at Calvary, also took of His blood and put it on the mercy seat in Heaven.

Revelation 9:14

"Saying to the sixth angel which had the trumpet, Loose the four angels which are bound in the great river Euphrates."

Here is the **sixth angel**. These four **angels** were bound, but they are going to be **loosed** to judge this earth. I am glad I am not going to be here. I know you are not going to be here if you are genuinely saved, as well. They are going to be loosed. They are **bound in that great river Euphrates**.

- **Revelation 7:1-2**
"And after these things I saw **four angels** standing on the four corners of the earth, holding the four winds of the earth, that the wind should not blow on the earth, nor on the sea, nor on any tree. And I saw another angel ascending from the east, having the seal of the living God: and he cried with a loud voice to the **four angels**, to whom it was given to hurt the earth and the sea,"

The Four Angels

These are probably the same four angels. These four angels are in that great river Euphrates. That river goes all the way from up in the mountains of Turkey and flows down through Assyria and Syria to Babylon and empties into the Persian Gulf. It is interesting that the river Euphrates is where these four angels were bound. That is the very same section of this earth that is at war today, Iran (Persia), Iraq (Assyria and Babylonia), all these different areas. It is amazing, but that is where these angels were bound. They are going to be loosed.

The **Euphrates River** has always been dependable for navigation, better than the Tigris. More than two-thirds of it is navigable, some 1,200 miles, in fact.

An article I got from the Internet talked about the **Euphrates** in mythology. They think the Bible is a myth. I do not. The Bible is truth. They said in Genesis the river **Euphrates** was one of the four rivers that flowed from the garden of Eden. This is according to Genesis 2:14. It is the fourth river. That is a fact.

The Dried Up River

Then they said that in John's Revelation, it was prophesied in the "poetic vision" that in the end-times it will dry up in preparation for the battle of Armageddon. I believe that whole river Euphrates will dry up so that the kings of the east can come across and do battle at Jerusalem. The Lord Jesus Christ will come back and slay them with the brightness of His coming. That is no mythology. That is fact and truth. It is interesting how the world paints it.

This river Euphrates is where these angels were bound up at this time. It is a large river in Assyria, Syria, Mesopotamia, Babylon, and flowing into the Gulf of Persia.

Revelation 9:15

"And the four angels were loosed, which were prepared for an hour, and a day, and a month, and a year, for to slay the third part of men."

Here is preparation for battle. Once before, it was said that the **angels** were **prepared**. We have to be **prepared** for things that are coming. Even though these **angels** were for slaughter, they have **preparation**. There is always a **preparation**. Notice, it took them a long time to **prepare**. I do not know how long it would take you to prepare to **slaughter one-third** of the earth's population, but these **four angels** were prepared. When they were thinking about invading that area over there in Iraq, some commentator said, "Maybe the president will say, Let's do it this weekend." Who knows?

Killing A Third Part Of Men

That word *"slay"* is in the continuous present tense. They are going to **slay** constantly. It takes a long time to **kill** a **third part of men.**

As far as **preparation** is concerned, the Lord has good **preparation**, too.

- **John 14:2-3**
  "In my Father's house are many mansions: if *it were* not *so*, I would have told you. I go to **prepare** a place for you. And if I go and **prepare** a place for you, I will come again, and receive you unto myself; that where I am, *there* ye may be also."

The Lord Jesus Christ is **preparing** a place for those that are genuinely saved.

- **1 Corinthians 2:9**
"But as it is written, Eye hath not seen, nor ear heard, neither have entered into the heart of man, the things which God hath **prepared** for them that love him."

God **prepared** good things. These angels are **prepared** for bad things on this wicked world.

- **1 Corinthians 14:8**
"For if the trumpet give an uncertain sound, who shall **prepare** himself to the battle?"

We have to be straight in our sounds for war.

- **Hebrews 10:5**
"Wherefore when he cometh into the world, he saith, Sacrifice and offering thou wouldest not, but a body hast thou **prepared** me:"

Christ's Prepared Body

This is the Lord Jesus Christ speaking to His Father. God the Father prepared a body for the Lord Jesus Christ through the miracle of the virgin birth–His sinews, His blood, His hands, His arms–that was an entirely prepared body. He was a true and perfect Human, but yet prepared. Just as Adam was created by God, so this body was specially prepared by the Lord Himself.

- **Hebrews 11:7**
"By faith Noah, being warned of God of things not seen as yet, moved with fear, **prepared** an ark to the saving of his house; by the which he condemned the world, and became heir of the righteousness which is by faith."

Noah had some **preparation** to do. He was a preacher of righteousness for 120 years, **preparing** that ark. That was a huge ark. All he had was himself, his three sons, their three wives, and his own wife. The rest of the world would not **prepare** that ark. It had never rained. He said it was going to rain. They thought he was crazy, but he **prepared**.

As far as **a third** of the earth is concerned, in 2004, the world's population was 6.3 billion. A **third** would be 2.1 billion **dead** if this would happen today. In 2014, it is estimated that the world population will be 7.1 billion. A third of that is 2.3 billion **dead**. If the earth lasts until 2024, there will be 7.7 billion. That would be 2.5 billion **dead.**

When we came to Collingswood, there were only 3.3 billion people in this world. As of July 1, 2011, the world's population is now 6.9 billion. If the Lord Jesus Christ should tarry His coming and the population continues to increase all the way down to the end of 2050, they project the population of the world will be 9 billion people. A **third** of them (3 billion people) would be destroyed by these **four angels**. They are going to continuously kill in this judgment upon the earth.

Revelation 9:16

"And the number of the army of the horsemen *were* two hundred thousand thousand: and I heard the number of them."

The Army Of Slaughter

Here is the army that is going to be slaughtering the third of this world's population. There are two million of them. A third of the whole population is going to be slain. The horsemen are riding on horses. It is not clear whether it is the horsemen that are doing the killing or the horses. It is entirely possible that it is the horses. I am just going to take these horses as horses. They could be any number of things. They could be all kinds of jet planes, they could be rockets, they could be anything, but the Lord Jesus Christ is calling them horses, so I am going to deal with them as horses.

Revelation 9:17

"And thus I saw the horses in the vision, and them that sat on them, having breastplates of fire, and of jacinth, and brimstone: and the heads of the horses *were* as the heads of lions; and out of their mouths issued fire and smoke and brimstone."

These **horses** had the **breastplates**, the armament, of **fire**. **Jacinth** is red, almost close to black. It is sort of reddish-black. **Brimstone** is sulfur. The Lord Jesus Christ is called the **Lion** of the tribe of Judah, but beware. The Devil is also a "roaring **lion**." Notice that word *issued*. Again, it is a present tense, continuously issued. It belches out of their mouths. Whether it is the horses' mouths or the riders' mouth (probably the horses), it belches **fire** continuously. **Fire** in Scripture is used of God's judgment in many places.

- **Genesis 19:24**
  "Then the LORD rained upon Sodom and upon Gomorrah brimstone and **fire** from the LORD out of Heaven;"

These were terrible wicked cities.

- **Matthew 25:41**
  "Then shall he say also unto them on the left hand, Depart from me, ye cursed, into everlasting **fire**, prepared for the devil and his angels:"

God did not make Hell for people. He prepared Hell for the Devil and for his angels. It is everlasting **fire** and we cannot say **fire** in Hell is going to be just for a minute, a day, a week, a month, a year, a decade, or a Millennium. It is going to be just as everlasting, as everlasting life will be for the genuinely saved people. Those that have rejected the Lord Jesus Christ as their Saviour, God says they will be in that everlasting fire. It is prepared for the Devil and his angels and those that follow the Devil will follow in that path.

- **Mark 9:45**
  "And if thy foot offend thee, cut it off: it is better for thee to enter halt into life, than having two feet to be cast into Hell, into the **fire** that never shall be quenched:"

The Lord Jesus Christ was a Hell-**fire** preacher. We have all kinds of new evangelicals and even some of the fundamentalists who are saying there is no real literal **fire** in Hell. They say that it is just a figure of speech. The Lord Jesus Christ talked about *the fire that shall never be quenched*. That is a serious thing, as far as I am concerned. Billy Graham never believed in **fire** way back in the 1950's. I wrote him up in sermons that he preached. He said that **fire** is not there. It is just a figure of speech. It is just to be banished from God's presence.

- **2 Thessalonians 1:7-8**
  "And to you who are troubled rest with us, when the Lord Jesus Christ shall be revealed from Heaven with his mighty angels, In flaming **fire** taking vengeance on them that know not God, and that obey not the gospel of our Lord Jesus Christ:"

The 2ⁿᵈ Phase Of Christ's Coming

This is when the Lord Jesus Christ comes in the second phase of His second coming in power. The first phase is the rapture, snatching away the genuine believers that are truly saved. After that comes the tribulation. When the tribulation is over, His glorious coming will be in flaming fire taking vengeance on His enemies. He came the first time as the Saviour. He is coming the second time to judge. If you will not accept Him as your Saviour, He will be your Judge. It is a terrible thing, but the choice is yours.

- **Hebrews 12:29**
  "For our God *is* a consuming **fire**."

This is different from the liberals and modernists when they say, "God is love." It is true that one of His attributes is love, but He is also a consuming **fire** as far as judgment is concerned.

- **Revelation 14:10**
  "The same shall drink of the wine of the wrath of God, which is poured out without mixture into the cup of his indignation; and he shall be tormented with **fire** and brimstone in the presence of the holy angels, and in the presence of the Lamb:"

Fire is a part of the Lord Jesus Christ's judgment. One of the three ways that these **four angels** will destroy one-third of the earth is with **fire**. As I said before, we saw on television the terrible catastrophe of 9-11 in New York City. There were bodies falling out of the top floors in **fire** and flames. The pain was so great they wanted to meet death immediately. When God is judging in Hell it is going to be with **fire**.

- **Revelation 20:10**
  "And the devil that deceived them was cast into the lake of **fire** and brimstone, where the beast and the false prophet *are*, and shall be **tormented** day and night for ever and ever."

Not Burned Up In 1,000 Years

Notice, they are still there. After 1,000 years the beast and the false prophet are still in the lake of fire. They did not burn up. They will have "unburnable" bodies. They will be bodies that will be not able to burn up, but they will feel the pains of Almighty God in Hell. That is their judgment.

- **Revelation 20:14**
  "And death and Hell were cast into the lake of **fire**. This is the second death."

Notice, the second thing with which they are going to judge the earth is **smoke**. That is how some of the firemen that go into buildings are killed, not by the **fire**, but by **smoke** inhalation.

- **Genesis 19:28**
  "And he looked toward Sodom and Gomorrah, and toward all the land of the plain, and beheld, and, lo, the **smoke** of the country went up as the **smoke** of a furnace."

There is death by **smoke** by the four angels of the **sixth trumpet** judgment.

- **Exodus 19:18**
  "And mount Sinai was altogether on a **smoke**, because the LORD descended upon it in **fire**: and the **smoke** thereof ascended as the **smoke** of a furnace, and the whole mount quaked greatly."

I am glad we who are genuinely saved have the Lord Jesus Christ to intercede for us so that we do not have to be in the **fire** and **smoke** of God's wrath. The law of Moses was put into effect when God had no Saviour. He had not come yet, so there was the **smoke, fire,** and judgment. The Mosaic law could never save anybody. Only by God's grace, through genuine faith in the Lord Jesus Christ, can we be redeemed.

The third cause of **one-third** of the people being dead is **brimstone**. That is a sulfurous and poisonous type of thing.

- **Psalm 11:6**
  "Upon the wicked he shall rain snares, **fire** and **brimstone**, and an horrible tempest: *this shall be* the portion of their cup."

Here is God's judgment using **brimstone**.

- **Luke 17:29**
  "But the same day that Lot went out of Sodom it rained **fire** and **brimstone** from Heaven, and destroyed *them* all."

When will God rain **fire** and **brimstone** upon the Sodomites of our day? I do not know. Maybe He will not, but in that seven-year period of tribulation there is going to be **smoke**, there is going to be **fire**, and there is going to be **brimstone**. That is going to be the cause of 2.1 billion that will meet their **death**. I am sure they will not be expecting it. These angels will go ahead, continuously issuing out this **fire**.

Revelation 9:18

"By these three was the third part of men killed, by the fire, and by the smoke, and by the brimstone, which issued out of their mouths."

Again, this word for *issued* is present tense continuous action. These are continuously issuing out of their **mouths**, these **horses** (or whatever they were, but the Lord Jesus Christ says they were in the figure of **horses**) in order to destroy. As I have said before, suppose the Lord Jesus Christ would come back today and this tribulation would begin. The world population is around 6.9 billion. That would mean 2.3 billion would die continuously, one at a time. That is a lot of people. It is one out of every three. This is a terrible judgment, the judgment of these **horsemen** and these **horses**.

Revelation 9:19

"For their power is in their mouth, and in their tails: for their tails *were* like unto serpents, and had heads, and with them they do hurt."

God's Protective Hands

Again, these words *they do hurt* are a continuous present tense. They continue to hurt. There is no let up in this pain that they will inflict before they die. The Lord is able to protect people. There are many places in Scripture where there is no hurt, but here there will be hurt. They will be hurting because of the judgment of God.

- **Isaiah 11:9**
  "They shall **not hurt** nor destroy in all my holy mountain: for the earth shall be full of the knowledge of the LORD, as the waters cover the sea."

This is during the millennial reign of the Lord Jesus Christ.

- **Isaiah 65:25**
  "The wolf and the lamb shall feed together, and the lion shall eat straw like the bullock: and dust *shall be* the serpent's meat. They shall **not hurt** nor destroy in all my holy mountain, saith the LORD."

Again, this is speaking of the millennial reign of the Lord Jesus Christ. Normally, a wolf would eat the lamb, but not during the Millennium. There is a time and a place when God will **not hurt**.

- **Daniel 3:25**
  "He answered and said, Lo, I see four men loose, walking in the midst of the fire, and they have **no hurt**; and the form of the fourth is like the Son of God."

Shadrach, Meshech, and Abednego would not bow down and worship this image, because it was against the commandments of God (*Thou shalt have no other gods before me*). They were thrown into the fiery furnace. The king saw four men walking in the **fire**: Shadrach, Meshech, Abednego, and the Son of God, the Lord Jesus Christ, Who was there to protect them. The other versions say, "like unto a son of the gods." They take away the Deity of the Lord Jesus Christ and take away the reference to the Lord Jesus Christ there in the **fire**. They had **no hurt** because the Lord Jesus Christ was there to protect them.

- **Daniel 6:22**
  "My God hath sent his angel, and hath shut the lions' mouths, that they have not hurt me: forasmuch as before him innocency was found in me; and also before thee, O king, have I done **no hurt**."
- **Luke 10:19**
  "Behold, I give unto you power to tread on serpents and scorpions, and over all the power of the enemy: and nothing shall by any means **hurt** you."

This is not for us today. This is apostolic miracles and power. The Bible is completed now.

Horse Tails Like Serpents

The tails of these horses in Revelation 9 are going to be like serpents, vipers, and all the different snakes that are poisonous–including the copperheads, and the rattlesnakes of all varieties. It is going to be a painful type of death. They will continuously hurt the people that are on the earth.

Revelation 9:20

"And the rest of the men which were not killed by these plagues yet repented not of the works of their hands, that they should not worship devils, and idols of gold, and silver, and brass, and stone, and of wood: which neither can see, nor hear, nor walk:"

Can you imagine those two-thirds that are **not killed**, the four billion that are not killed? You would think that they would get the point and **repent** of their sins and genuinely come to the Lord Jesus Christ and be truly saved, but no they do not. The rest of them that were not killed yet **repented not**. Of what did they **repent not**? The works of their hands.

The Devil And His Helpers

They continued to worship the devil and his helpers. All false religion, whatever it is and wherever it is, whether in the United States of America, China, Russia, or anywhere, are worshipping Satan and the devils. Notice these idols of gold, silver, brass, stone, and wood *neither can see, nor hear, nor walk*. Why would you worship something that could neither see, nor hear, not walk?

The Lord God of Heaven and earth can see all of the world. He can hear all the prayers of all the world. He can walk and go anywhere. He is omnipresent. He is everywhere present. The Lord Jesus Christ is the only Saviour. He is the One to worship, but these people will not repent.

- **Luke 5:32**
  "I came not to call the righteous, but sinners to **repentance**."
  The Lord Jesus Christ had something to say about **repentance**. He came not to call the righteous, that is, those that think they are righteous, but sinners to **repentance** [METANOIA], *a change of mind* about sin—hating sin, not loving it like before. This also implies a *"change of mind"* concerning the fact that the Lord Jesus Christ can genuinely save you from your sins.

- **Acts 3:19**
  "**Repent** ye therefore, and be converted, that your sins may be blotted out, when the times of refreshing shall come from the presence of the Lord;"
  These sinners would not **repent** so that their sins would be blotted out.

- **2 Peter 3:9**
  "The Lord is not slack concerning his promise, as some men count slackness; but is longsuffering to us-ward, not willing that any should perish, but that all should come to **repentance**."

They Still Did Not Repent

These people who were still alive, would you not think that they would be so happy that they were spared the painful death of the fire, the smoke, the brimstone, and terrible continuous serpent or rattlesnake bites that they would say, "We had better repent of our sins. We had better be ready"? That should be what anyone would say, but they did not. They did not repent.

- **Psalm 106:36-37**
  "And they served their **idols**: which were a snare unto them. Yea, they sacrificed their sons and their daughters unto **devils**,"
- **Psalm 135:15-18**
  "The **idols** of the heathen *are* **silver and gold**, the work of men's hands. They have mouths, but they speak not; eyes have they, but they see not; They have ears, but they hear not; neither *is* there *any* breath in their mouths. They that make them are like unto them: *so is* every one that trusteth in them."

There is nothing good about **idolatry** and there is nothing good about unrepentance. Men facing death **unrepentant** is serious indeed.

Revelation 9:21

"Neither repented they of their murders, nor of their sorceries, nor of their fornication, nor of their thefts."

Here are four other things. They did **not repent** of their idolatry. They did **not repent** of worshipping idols and devils. Now there are four other things of which they did **not repent**. They did not change their minds. They kept right on with their **murders**, their **sorceries**, their **fornication**, and their **thefts**. **Murder** is only used thirty-seven times in Scripture.

- **Numbers 35:30**
  "Whoso **killeth** any person, the **murderer** shall be put to death by the mouth of witnesses: but one witness shall not testify against any person *to cause him* to die."

This is capital punishment in the Old Testament. It is carried over in the New Testament.

- **Romans 13:1-4**
  "Let every soul be subject unto the higher powers. For there is no power but of God: the powers that be are ordained of God. Whosoever therefore resisteth the power, resisteth the ordinance of God: and they that resist shall receive to themselves damnation. For rulers are not a terror to good works, but to the evil. Wilt thou then not be afraid of the power? do that which is good, and thou shalt have praise of the same: For he is the minister of God to thee for good. But if thou do that which is evil, be afraid; for he beareth not the sword in vain: for he is the minister of God, a revenger to *execute* wrath upon him that doeth evil."

- **Numbers 35:31**
  "Moreover ye shall take no satisfaction for the life of a **murderer**, which *is* guilty of death: but he shall be surely put to death."

In other words, there is no penance, no offering, no money to take for him. No one could die in his place like the Lord Jesus Christ did for Barabbas the **murderer**.

- **Matthew 15:19**
  "For out of the heart proceed evil thoughts, **murders**, adulteries, fornications, thefts, false witness, blasphemies:"

This is where **murder** proceeds, out of the unconverted, unrepentant heart.

- **Matthew 19:18**
  "He saith unto him, Which? Jesus said, Thou shalt do no **murder**, Thou shalt not commit adultery, Thou shalt not steal, Thou shalt not bear false witness,"

The Lord Jesus Christ was speaking to the rich young man. One of the commandments was, "Thou shalt do no **murder**."

- **Romans 1:29**
  "Being filled with all unrighteousness, fornication, wickedness, covetousness, maliciousness; full of envy, **murder**, debate, deceit, malignity; whisperers,"

These are the sins of the unsaved heathen world. Among other things, they are filled with **murder**.

No Repentance About Drugs

The second thing they will not repent of is their sorceries. The word sorceries [PHARMAKEIA], as in pharmacy or drugs, means not only *the use of sorcery for worshipping the Devil,* but also *the administering of drugs.* They will not repent of drug addiction. It also means, *sorcery and magical arts of idolatry,* and so on.

- **Exodus 7:11**
  "Then Pharaoh also called the wise men and the **sorcerers**: now the magicians of Egypt, they also did in like manner with their enchantments."

When Moses performed all these miracles before Pharaoh to get his people to go out of Egypt into the wilderness, Pharaoh also called his **sorcerers**. Sorcery was even right in the book of Exodus, the second book of the Bible.

- **Isaiah 47:9**
  "But these two *things* shall come to thee in a moment in one day, the loss of children, and widowhood: they shall come upon thee in their perfection for the multitude of thy **sorceries**, *and* for the great abundance of thine enchantments."

Judgment Was Coming

Judgment was coming because of sorcery. Sorcery brought judgment to Israel. There will be judgment also to these people in the tribulation.

- **Acts 8:9**
  "But there was a certain man, called Simon, which beforetime in the same city used **sorcery**, and bewitched the people of Samaria, giving out that himself was some great one:"

The word *simony* is used today. He tried to buy the gift of the Holy Spirit.

- **Acts 13:8**
  "But Elymas the **sorcerer** (for so is his name by interpretation) withstood them, seeking to turn away the deputy from the faith."

Sorcerers do not want people to come to the Lord Jesus Christ as Saviour and Redeemer.

These were not repentant of **murders** and **sorceries**, whether drug addiction or worship of Satan, nor of their **fornication**. They kept right on, not abstaining from it. The Lord has many things to say about **fornication** which means sexual relations by those that are not married to one another.

- **Acts 15:20**
  "But that we write unto them, that they abstain from pollutions of idols, and *from* **fornication**, and *from* things strangled, and *from* blood."

There were only four things from which they were to abstain from the law of Moses. **Fornication** was one of them.

- **Romans 1:29**
  "Being filled with all unrighteousness, **fornication**, wickedness, covetousness, maliciousness; full of envy, murder, debate, deceit, malignity; whisperers,"

The whole unsaved Gentile world was being filled with all unrighteousness. **Fornication** was one of these things.

- **1 Corinthians 5:1**
  "It is reported commonly *that there is* **fornication** among you, and such **fornication** as is not so much as named among the Gentiles, that one should have his father's wife."

Even in the church of Corinth there was incest and God judged that.

- **1 Corinthians 6:13**
  "Meats for the belly, and the belly for meats: but God shall destroy both it and them. Now the body *is* not for **fornication**, but for the Lord; and the Lord for the body."

Fornication is not what we should do with our bodies.

- **1 Corinthians 6:18**
  "Flee **fornication**. Every sin that a man doeth is without the body; but he that committeth **fornication** sinneth against his own body."

God tells us to flee **fornication**, run away from it.

- **1 Corinthians 7:2**
  "Nevertheless, *to avoid* **fornication**, let every man have his own wife, and let every woman have her own husband."

God has an answer to **fornication**. He has a remedy for that.

- **Hebrews 13:4**
  "Marriage is honourable in all, and the bed undefiled: **but whoremongers** and adulterers God will judge."

- **2 Corinthians 12:21**
  "*And* lest, when I come again, my God will humble me among you, and *that* I shall bewail many which have sinned already, and have not repented of the uncleanness and **fornication** and lasciviousness which they have committed."

In the Corinthian church, following the suit of this incestuous man that had his own father's wife, this spread like wildfire. Once sin begins, it spreads.

- **Galatians 5:19**
  "Now the works of the flesh are manifest, which are *these*; Adultery, **fornication**, uncleanness, lasciviousness,"

Fornication–A Work Of The Flesh

One of the works of the flesh is fornication. A believer who is genuinely saved and born-again has the Spirit of God indwelling him or her. But, he or she also has the flesh, which has the possibility of the works of the flesh. One of these works is fornication.

- **Ephesians 5:3**
  "But **fornication**, and all uncleanness, or covetousness, let it not be once named among you, as becometh saints;"

He did not want to have the church at Ephesus repeat what was happening in Corinth. Cappadocia, Corinth, and Crete were the three most wicked cities in all the ancient world because of the sins, one of which was **fornication**.

- **Colossians 3:5**
  "Mortify therefore your members which are upon the earth; **fornication**, uncleanness, inordinate affection, evil concupiscence, and covetousness, which is idolatry:"

Paul tells the church at Colosse the same thing. He says, "Mortify your members which are upon the earth." Put them to death. Biblical Christians with the old flesh, must put these to death. One thing they were to mortify in this list was **fornication**.

- **1 Thessalonians 4:3**
  "For this is the will of God, *even* your sanctification, that ye should abstain from **fornication**:"

Abstaining From Fornication

The sanctified life includes abstaining from fornication, to absolutely quit it, just as Joseph fled from the presence of Potiphar's wife. He fled!

Not only did these people not repent of murders, sorceries, and fornication, but also they did not repent of their thefts. Thievery was rampant. They did not repent of that. They kept stealing.

- **Exodus 20:15**
  "Thou shalt not **steal**."
- **Matthew 15:19**
  "For out of the heart proceed evil thoughts, murders, adulteries, fornications, **thefts**, false witness, blasphemies:"
- **Matthew 19:18**
  "He saith unto him, Which? Jesus said, Thou shalt do no murder, Thou shalt not commit adultery, Thou shalt not **steal**, Thou shalt not bear false witness,"
- **Ephesians 4:28**
  "Let him that **stole steal** no more: but rather let him labour, working with *his* hands the thing which is good, that he may have to give to him that needeth."

They had thieves in the church at Ephesus. Paul says, "If you used to **steal**, do not **steal** any more." What are you going to do then? Do not steal from somebody, give to somebody that needs it.

As far as the **repentance** of **murders**, all across the nation they have been rising. **Murders** and rapes are going up. As of the late 1990's statistics, of all the cities that have the top **murder** rate percentage-wise in the whole United States of America, our nation's capital is **murder** capital number one. The highest percentage of **murders**, with 69.3 **murders** out of 100,000, is in Washington, D.C., the **murder** capital. What is the second one? Philadelphia, Pennsylvania, with 27.4 **murders** out of 100,000. What is the third one? Dallas, Texas, with 24.8 **murders** out of 100,000. What is the fourth one? Los Angeles, California, with 22.8 **murders** out of 100,000. The fifth one is Chicago, Illinois, with 20.5 **murders** out of 100,000. What is the sixth one? Phoenix, Arizona, with 19.1 **murders** out of 100,000.

They do not **repent** of these **murders**. They do not repent of their sorceries. Satanism is going high, wide, and handsome all over the world. In fact, they now even have chaplains that are Satanists in the chaplain corps of the Army, Navy, Air Force, and Marines. It is a terrible thing.

Drug traffic is mushrooming. What about the sin of **fornication**? In a recent study, the Centers for Disease Control found that among ninth graders, forty percent had committed **fornication**. The numbers rise to seventy-two percent by the time the children have reached the twelfth grade. Seventy-two percent are committing **fornication**. Whether actual sex or oral sex, it is still **fornication**. The consequences of this behavior are staggering. Every year, three million teens acquire a sexually-transmitted disease. Every year, more than one million teens become pregnant. That is one out of every nine women aged fifteen to nineteen. Studies indicate that while church children do not participate in sexual activity at quite the rate worldly children do, our children in the churches only lag about twenty points behind the national averages. Satan is preaching a sermon about sex that kids want to hear and they are willingly falling into his trap of lies and deception.

The Crime Of Theft

As far as theft, all kinds of theft, larceny makes up fifty-six percent of all the crime committed in America. They are not going to repent of these thefts. That includes pickpocketing, purse snatching, shoplifting, theft of motor vehicles, theft from buildings, theft from coin machines, theft of bicycles. Whatever it may be, it is fifty-six percent of all crime. These people, having seen one-third of all people and their friends die, the two-thirds do not repent of all their sins. There is a poem by Norman Trott, *No Time For God?*

No time for God?

What fools we are to clutter up
Our lives with common things
And leave without heart's gate
The Lord of life and life itself - our God!

No time for God?
As soon to say no time
To eat or sleep or love or die.
Take time for God
Or you shall dwarf your soul,
And when the angel death
Comes knocking at your door,
A poor misshapen thing you'll be
To step into eternity!

No time for God?
That day when sickness comes
Or troubles find you out
And you cry out for God;
Will he have time for you?

No time for God?
Some day you'll lay aside
This mortal self and make your way
To worlds unknown,
And when you meet Him face to face
Will he - should He
Have time for you?

People Unrepentant Facing Death

Here are people facing death unrepentant. I trust that every person reading this has repented of sin and genuinely come in solid faith in the Lord Jesus Christ to live a holy and godly life. This is my prayer.

Revelation
Chapter Ten

Revelation 10:1

"And I saw another mighty angel come down from Heaven, clothed with a cloud: and a rainbow *was* upon his head, and his face *was* as it were the sun, and his feet as pillars of fire:"

John sees another angel, a **mighty angel clothed with a cloud** and **a rainbow on his head**. This was a **mighty angel**. As we will see later, he puts one foot on the land, and one foot on the sea. The **rainbow** is something in Scripture that we should think about. We cannot go into what all the symbols of this **angel** and how he was clothed would mean, but God set a **rainbow** in His Heaven and in the **clouds** after the flood.

- **Genesis 9:13**
  "I do set my **bow** in the cloud, and it shall be for a token of a covenant between me and the earth."

This is the **rainbow** that this angel had around his head.

- **Genesis 9:14-15**
  "And it shall come to pass, when I bring a **cloud** over the earth, that the **bow** shall be seen in the **cloud**: And I will remember my covenant, which *is* between me and you and every living creature of all flesh; and the waters shall no more become a flood to destroy all flesh."

No more will there be a flood. God is going to bring **fire** on the earth to destroy this world, but not a flood.

- **Genesis 9:16-17**
  "And the **bow** shall be in the **cloud**; and I will look upon it, that I may remember the everlasting covenant between God and every living creature of all flesh that *is* upon the earth. And God said unto Noah, This *is* the token of the covenant, which I have established between me and all flesh that *is* upon the earth."

- **Revelation 4:1**
  "After this I looked, and, behold, a door *was* opened in Heaven: and the first voice which I heard *was* as it were of a trumpet talking with me; which said, Come up hither, and I will shew thee things which must be hereafter."

This is the rapture of the church when we are taken up out of this wicked world before this tribulation period begins. That *"Come up hither"* is the rapture, the snatching away of the genuine believers.

- **Revelation 4:2-3**
  "And immediately I was in the spirit: and, behold, a throne was set in Heaven, and *one* sat on the throne. And he that sat was to look upon like a jasper and a sardine stone: and *there was a* **rainbow** round about the throne, in sight like unto an emerald."

The Lord has a **rainbow** in Heaven around His throne. I looked up a few things about the **rainbow**.

What Is A Rainbow

What is a rainbow? One author describes a rainbow as "one of the most spectacular light shows observed on earth." Indeed, the traditional rainbow is sunlight spread out into its spectrum of colors and diverted to the eye of the observer by water droplets. The bow part describes the fact that the rainbow is a group of nearly circular arcs of color, all having a common center. Mrs. Waite and I saw a rainbow as we were flying home one time. It was a beautiful rainbow.

Where Is The Sun In A Rainbow?

Where is the sun when you see a rainbow? The sun is always behind you when you face a rainbow. The center of the circular arc of the rainbow is the direction opposite to that of the sun. The rain is in the direction of the rainbow.

What makes the **bow**? Back in 1637, Descartes said, "This bow appears not only in the sky but also in the air around us and near us whenever there are drops of water illuminated by the sun and we can see it in certain fountains, for example." The drops of the water make the **rainbow**.

What makes the color? It is made up of seven colors. That is the light. There are really more than that. There are red, orange, yellow, green, blue, indigo, and violet. Actually, the **rainbow** is the whole spectrum of colors from red to violet and even beyond the colors that our eyes can see.

This picture of the **rainbow** is the covenant that God will no longer destroy this world by a flood. There are floods that are local floods, but never a universal flood that floods the whole earth and destroys all living creatures on this earth. That was His promise, and yet that **rainbow** is around the throne of God. He remembers that covenant. It is an everlasting covenant. This angel was clothed with a **rainbow** upon his head.

Revelation 10:2

"And he had in his hand a little book open: and he set his right foot upon the sea, and *his* left *foot* on the earth,"

He must have had a long leg span to stand on the **sea** and the **earth**, unless he was right at the edge of the sea, which is possible. Notice, he had in his hand a **little book open**. Later on in this chapter we will see what happens with this **book**. It is just like what happened to Ezekiel.

- **Ezekiel 2:8-10**
  "But thou, son of man, hear what I say unto thee; Be not thou rebellious like that rebellious house: open thy mouth, and eat that I give thee. And when I looked, behold, an hand *was* sent unto me; and, lo, a roll of a **book** *was* therein; And he spread it before me; and it *was* written within and without: and *there was* written therein lamentations, and mourning, and woe."

God was going to give him a **book** to eat. This was a **book** of woe that Ezekiel was told to eat.

- **Ezekiel 3:1-3**
  "Moreover he said unto me, Son of man, eat that thou findest; eat this roll, and go speak unto the house of Israel. So I opened my mouth, and he caused me to eat that **roll**. And he said unto me, Son of man, cause thy belly to eat, and fill thy bowels with this roll that I give thee. Then did I eat *it*; and it was in my mouth as honey for sweetness."

The Sweet And Bitter Book

The book, the Scriptures, of the judgment that is going to come from this angel is going to be sweet, maybe to the one that is eating, and using, and understanding it like John, but it is going to be bitter to those that partake of this judgment.

It is a bittersweet type of a **book** that is mentioned here in the **book** of Revelation. We will see a little more detail later on. I do not know about you, but I do not know that I would be interested in eating a **book**. Some people probably eat paper. That is one of the things that some people eat, but this was a spiritual experience. This **little book** was open and we will see about what happens later on, as far as the eating of this **book** that John was told to do.

Revelation 10:3

"And cried with a loud voice, as *when* a lion roareth: and when he had cried, seven thunders uttered their voices."

This angel was a **mighty angel** with a **mighty voice**. Some of us have mighty voices. Some of us have smaller voices. This was a **mighty voice** just like a **lion**. You have perhaps seen **lions** at the zoo and heard some of the roars that they make.

We do not know what the **seven thunders** would say. We will see later that we are not going to know what the **seven thunders** say when they utter their **voices**. Normally, **seven thunders** cannot speak, but God has a way of speaking through these **thunders**, whatever they may be.

I want to look at the **lion roaring**. There are many verses about **lions** and their **roaring**. I thought that we could look at some of them at least.

- **Job 4:10-11**
  "The roaring of the **lion**, and the voice of the fierce **lion**, and the teeth of the young **lions**, are broken. The old **lion** perisheth for lack of prey, and the stout **lion's** whelps are scattered abroad."

Here is a picture of **lions** that roar. The Devil is a **lion**. He is a **roaring lion**. The Lord Jesus Christ is the **Lion** of the tribe of Judah. **Lions roar** when you see them in the zoo, perhaps, before they eat. When they are hungry, they roar. I am sure that Daniel's **lions** were **roaring lions**, but God shut their mouths and they did not harm Daniel.

- **Psalm 22:13**
  "They gaped upon me *with* their mouths, as a ravening and a **roaring lion**."

This is a picture of the Lord Jesus Christ on the cross of Calvary. It talks about the people looking at Him as He was being crucified. People were anxious that He be crucified. The chief priests, rulers, and the people cried out all at once "Let Him be crucified!" and "Crucify Him!" Psalms

21, 22, 23, and 24 speak of the past, the present, and the future of the Lord Jesus Christ.

- **Proverbs 19:12**
  "The king's wrath is as the **roaring** of a **lion**; but his favour is as dew upon the grass."

This pictures the **roaring** of a **lion** just like a king who is angry. That king that put Daniel into the **lion's** den did it because he had promised that whosoever prayed and asked anything of anyone either human or divine would be thrown into the den of **lions**. We think of Saddam Hussein and all the wrath that he poured upon people just like a **roaring lion**–killing, murdering, and torturing his people.

- **Proverbs 28:15**
  "As a **roaring lion**, and a ranging bear; so is a wicked ruler over the poor people."

Wicked Rulers Like Roaring Lions

Wicked rulers over poor people are just like **roaring lions** who are killing, robbing, stealing, taking their homes, and so on. This right of eminent domain is a right that has been granted as proper. It is very, very hard to understand sometimes. Here is a town of three or four people in charge, or even one person in charge, they have a meeting and they say by eminent domain, "We are going to take your house." The poor people cannot fight it. They cannot do anything about it. There is a man who is going to have his whole business taken over on Collings Avenue in Collingswood, New Jersey, and he cannot do anything about it. He said, "I have built up this business. It is my business. It is my life. They will pay me a little, but I cannot remake this whole thing. I am out of business." I believe sometimes wicked rulers have plans and they push people over like roaring lions.

- **Isaiah 5:29**
  "Their **roaring** shall be like a **lion**, they shall roar like young **lions**: yea, they shall roar, and lay hold of the prey, and shall carry it away safe, and none shall deliver it."

The **roaring lion,** when he is hungry, makes a very, very strong sound. This angel and the loud voice that he makes is as when a **lion roars**. He is **roaring loudly**. He is going to bring some thunderous words as well.

- **Amos 3:4**
  "Will a **lion roar** in the forest, when he hath no prey? will a young **lion** cry out of his den, if he have taken nothing?"

When Does A Lion Roar?

When does a lion roar? The roar, apparently, is after he gets the prey, after he kills the lamb, or the deer, or whatever he is after. That is victory for him. This angel roared like a lion.

- **Amos 3:8**
  "The **lion** hath **roared**, who will not fear? the Lord GOD hath spoken, who can but prophesy?"

I tell you, if some **lion** came up in our area and started **roaring**, who would not fear? Just the thunderous sound of his voice would make us to be afraid.

- **1 Peter 5:8**
  "Be sober, be vigilant; because your adversary the devil, as a **roaring lion**, walketh about, seeking whom he may devour:"

Here we see the Devil as a **lion**. Peter says to the believers to be sober. That means to think, use your brain. To be vigilant means to look around, all over. The Devil is our adversary. He is real. He is not just an influence. The Devil is a person. He is against the things of God. There are no holds barred, as far as the Devil is concerned, when he is out after the genuine believers.

Peter is talking to Biblical Christians. We have our flesh that is after us to sin. Every one of us is possessed with that, even if we are genuinely saved. We have the Holy Spirit of God inside, but we also have the old nature. The flesh is still with us until we die. We have the world around us that wants us to sin. They want us to do everything that is evil and wicked. Then we have the Devil. Sometimes the Devil comes *as a roaring lion,* but sometimes the Devil comes as an *angel of light,* as it says in the book of 2 Corinthians.

- **2 Corinthians 11:14**
  "And no marvel; for Satan himself is transformed into an **angel of light**."

The **angel of light** seems like a good person. He is a bad person, no matter if he comes in light or if he **roars** like a **lion**. By the **roar** of the **lion** you can tell, or you should be able to tell, that he means ill against you. He is our adversary and he devours many, many Biblical Christians. He is not limited to ordinary Christian men and women, or boys and girls, but to leaders especially. The Devil is after leaders. He is after deacons. He is after pastors. He is after missionaries. He is after those who are in the Lord's work in some way or another, as well as genuine believers generally. He is seeking whom he may devour.

Satan's Evil Ministries

Did he seek to devour the Lord Jesus Christ? Yes, he did. Was he successful? No, he was not. Did he seek to devour Adam and Eve in the garden? Yes, he did. Did he succeed? Yes, he succeeded. Because Eve ate of the fruit that was forbidden, and gave it to Adam. Then Adam ate of it. Adam had heard the Lord say, "Don't you dare eat that fruit! All the other fruit trees in the garden you can have. There is no question about it. You will not go hungry. You will not starve."

- **Genesis 2:16-17**
  "And the LORD God commanded the man, saying, Of every tree of the garden thou mayest freely eat: But of the tree of the knowledge of good and evil, thou shalt not eat of it: for in the day that thou eatest thereof thou shalt surely die."

Satan quoted the verse to Eve, but he put a period where God went on to say but of the tree in the center of the garden thou shalt not eat thereof.

- **Genesis 3:1**
  "Now the **serpent** was more subtil than any beast of the field which the LORD God had made. And he said unto the woman, Yea, hath God said, Ye shall not eat of every tree of the garden?"

Satan quoted partially and convinced Eve that it was all right to eat of all the trees, so she took the fruit and ate it. Adam ate it also. Their eyes were opened and sin was put upon the whole race. You and I die because Adam sinned. <u>Death passed upon all men because of one man</u>.

- **Romans 5:12**
  "Wherefore, as by one man sin entered into the world, and **death** by sin; and so **death** passed upon all men, for that all have sinned:"

In the Lord Jesus Christ's case, He was out there in the wilderness with nothing to eat for forty days. **Satan** came and tempted Him.

- **Matthew 4:3**
  "And when the **tempter** came to him, he said, If thou be the Son of God, command that these stones be made bread."

Satan, the **angel of light**, knew that the Lord Jesus Christ was capable of making stones into bread. You and I cannot do that. But, though He could have done it, He did not do it.

- **Matthew 4:4**
  "But he answered and said, It is written, Man shall not live by bread alone, but by every word that proceedeth out of the mouth of God."

Satan's Three Temptations Of Christ

Three different times the Devil tempted the Lord Jesus Christ and the Lord Jesus Christ refused. The adversary, the Devil, sought to devour the Lord Jesus Christ. He tried to get Him to worship him. He tried to get Him to cast Himself down from the temple. The Lord Jesus Christ was faithful.

The **Devil** said he would give Him all the worlds if He would worship him. **Satan** is the **prince of this world**. He is the **ruler** and leader of this world. God has given him the world in this life, but the Lord Jesus Christ is predominantly the Master of all things. **Satan** did not have Him under his control. He could not give the world to the Lord Jesus Christ. God has let Satan, as the prince of the power of the air, be the ruler of darkness in this life.

- **Revelation 5:5**
  "And one of the elders saith unto me, Weep not: behold, the **Lion** of the tribe of Juda, the Root of David, hath prevailed to open the book, and to loose the seven seals thereof."

Book Of The Earth's Redemption

This is the book of the earth's redemption. The Lord Jesus Christ is called the Lion of the tribe of Juda. We must distinguish between the Lord Jesus Christ and the antichrist. They are both lions. One is a roaring lion seeking whom he may devour. The other is the King of kings and Lord of lords. He is the Saviour of those that come unto Him by genuine faith and truly trust Him.

As far as these thunders that this angel had uttered, his voice was loud like when a **lion roars** and **seven thunders** uttered their voices. We do not know what this **thunder** is, but the Lord used **thunders** in Exodus. For instance:

- **Exodus 9:33-34**
  "And Moses went out of the city from Pharaoh, and spread abroad his hands unto the LORD: and the **thunders** and hail ceased, and the rain was not poured upon the earth. And when Pharaoh saw that the rain and the hail and the **thunders** were ceased, he sinned yet more, and hardened his heart, he and his servants."

This was one of the miracles that Moses was able to perform. Pharaoh had what is known as "foxhole religion," you might say. He prayed to please take these away. When there was no more thunder, hail, or rain, he was just as evil and wicked as he was before.

- **Exodus 19:16**
  "And it came to pass on the third day in the morning, that there were **thunders** and lightnings, and a thick cloud upon the mount, and the voice of the trumpet exceeding loud; so that all the people that *was* in the camp trembled."

The Thunder At Mount Sinai

This was the thunder of the Lord at Mount Sinai when He was delivering the law unto Moses. This thunder was very severe and loud. It was the power of the Lord. When the Lord thunders in this world and we see the lightning and the rain, this is the Lord's doing. He is the One that makes that thunder. He has special thunders in judgment as well.

Revelation 10:4

"And when the seven thunders had uttered their voices, I was about to write: and I heard a voice from Heaven saying unto me, Seal up those things which the seven thunders uttered, and write them not."

What The Thunders Said

Apparently, John was able to discern what the thunders said and he was going to write it. Sometimes things are for public use and sometimes they are not. Sometimes they are private. In this case, John was forbidden to write what the thunders had uttered.

- **2 Samuel 1:20**
  "Tell *it* not in Gath, publish *it* not in the streets of Askelon; lest the daughters of the Philistines rejoice, lest the daughters of the uncircumcised triumph."

When Christian Leaders Fall

They were not to utter that King Saul had been killed by the Philistines. Sometimes, when genuine Christian leaders fall, it is better maybe not to tell the world. They just laugh and say, "Oh, another one of those fundamentalists or Bible-believing Christians is dead, or has sinned, or has gone astray."

- 2 Samuel 18:27-29
  "And the watchman said, Me thinketh the running of the foremost is like the running of Ahimaaz the son of Zadok. And the king said, He *is* a good man, and cometh with good tidings. And Ahimaaz called, and said unto the king, All is well. And he fell down to the earth upon his face before the king, and said, Blessed be the LORD thy God, which hath delivered up the men that lifted up their hand against my lord the king. And the king said, Is the young man Absalom safe? And Ahimaaz answered, When Joab sent the king's servant, and *me* thy servant, I saw a great tumult, but I knew not what *it was*."

Here is some news that David the king was interested in. Absalom, his son, had rebelled against him. He fought against him and wanted to bring David's kingdom down. Joab was out there after Absalom. There was another runner that Joab sent out named Cushi, who had bad news. Ahimaaz had good news. King David was interested in one thing. He said, "Is the young man Absalom safe?" He was the one that had rebelled against his father. The mercy and grace of David is why, I believe, he is a man after God's own heart. He loved ones who hated him. He was interested in Absalom. Absalom was out to kill him. Ahimaaz had no news. Cushi came and said that he was slain. Joab put three darts into him and slew him.

Some Things Are Sealed

There are some things that are sealed and some things that cannot be uttered. This was one of the things that John was told not to write. He gave us the Revelation of the Lord Jesus Christ. Many things he has revealed, but not what the thunders said.

- **Daniel 9:24**
  "Seventy weeks are determined upon thy people and upon thy holy city, to finish the transgression, and to make an end of sins, and to make reconciliation for iniquity, and to bring in everlasting righteousness, and to **seal** up the vision and prophecy, and to anoint the most Holy."

These are weeks of years. Seventy sevens are 490 years. All these things have taken place but for seven more years. There are seven years that have not been fulfilled. The seventh year is this seven-year period of tribulation. Notice, it says, "Seventy weeks are determined upon **thy people.**" That is why I do not believe the true church has any part of the tribulation. We are gone before it ever starts.

The 70th Week Of Daniel

This is the 70th week of Daniel. It is the 70th week of Israel, so the true church, the genuine believers in this dispensation, are not part of that tribulation period. Many people are teaching against the pre-tribulation rapture. They say the genuinely saved people will be raptured in the middle of the tribulation, or they're going to go partly through, or they're going pre-Wrath, or they're going all the way through (a post-tribulation rapture). No, this is upon *thy people.*

There was a **seal** that was put upon Daniel's vision as well. Everything that is known is not always able to be uttered.

- **2 Corinthians 12:4**
  "How that he was caught up into paradise, and heard unspeakable words, which it is not lawful for a man to utter."

Paul was stoned in Lystra in Acts 14, about fourteen years before he wrote this in 2 Corinthians 12. He was hauled out of the city, supposing he was dead. I believe he was dead. I believe the Lord Jesus Christ took him to Heaven and then brought him back for more work and more ministry.

Unspeakable Words

Notice what he heard in Heaven. He heard the words, but the words are unspeakable. He was not to repeat them. In this case, just like in the case of the angel and the thunders, John was not to talk about these thunders and Paul was not to talk about the glories of Heaven. Maybe if he talked about it, everybody would want to go to Heaven and nobody would be down here on the earth to serve the Lord.

Revelation 10:5

"And the angel which I saw stand upon the sea and upon the earth lifted up his hand to Heaven,"

He was going to have an **oath.**

- **Genesis 14:22**
  "And Abram said to the king of Sodom, I have lift up mine hand unto the LORD, the most high God, the possessor of **Heaven** and **earth**,"
- **Ezekiel 20:15**
  "Yet also I lifted up my hand unto them in the wilderness, that I would not bring *them* into the land which I had given them, flowing with milk and honey, which *is* the glory of all lands;"

The Lord in the Old Testament permitted **oaths**. In the New Testament, He forbids **oaths**.

- **Matthew 5:34-37**
  "But I say unto you, Swear not at all; neither by Heaven; for it is God's throne: Nor by the earth; for it is his footstool: neither by Jerusalem; for it is the city of the great King. Neither shalt thou swear by thy head, because thou canst not make one hair white or black. But let your communication be, Yea, yea; Nay, nay: for whatsoever is more than these cometh of evil."

Many of us who are genuine Christians in this dispensation that do not believe we should **swear**, affirm when we appear before the court to give testimony. They let us do that. They know that we are not supposed to swear. You can say, "*I affirm that the testimony before me is going to be the truth, the whole truth, and nothing but the truth.*"

Revelation 10:6

"And sware by him that liveth for ever and ever, who created Heaven, and the things that therein are, and the earth, and the things that therein are, and the sea, and the things which are therein, that there should be time no longer:"

He lifted up his **hand** and **sware**. In the Old Testament, this was taking an **oath**. I want to just mention two things in this verse. First, he swears by Him that liveth for ever and ever.

We worship a God Who is an eternal God, from eternity past to eternity future. He is not a God that comes in for a season and goes out, like our presidents. They are in four years, and maybe four more, but no more than eight. Our Lord Jesus Christ is forever. We can count on Him. He does not stop being Lord for ever and ever.

- **Exodus 15:18**
  "The LORD shall reign for ever and ever."

Now He is not reigning specifically on this earth, but He is reigning as far as the overall picture. He is in charge. The Lord Jesus Christ one day will reign physically upon this earth for 1,000 years. That will be the millennial reign of the Lord Jesus Christ.

- **Psalm 10:16**
  "The LORD *is* King for ever and ever: the heathen are perished out of his land."

Denying Christ's Millennial Reign

Those that do not believe in the millennial reign of the Lord Jesus Christ say that He is reigning now. No, there is a sense in which He reigns over the genuine believers who have trusted Him as Saviour and Redeemer. We have made Him our King. He should rule our hearts. He should rule our lives. In that sense, He is reigning, but one day, He will reign over the earth during the millennial reign of the Lord Jesus Christ. He is King of kings and Lord of lords.

- **Psalm 45:6**
  "Thy throne, O God, *is* for ever and ever: the sceptre of thy kingdom *is* a right sceptre."

The throne will never stop. He will never abdicate that throne. Nobody will usurp the throne. Nobody will kick Him off the throne. He is in charge forever and ever on His throne.

- **Psalm 48:14**
  "For this God *is* our God for ever and ever: he will be our guide *even* unto death."

- **Psalm 23:4**
  "Yea, though I walk through the valley of the shadow of death, I will fear no evil: for thou *art* with me; thy rod and thy staff they comfort me."

The genuine believer has just a shadow of death. If we are genuinely saved, we have no real spiritual **death** or separation from the Lord, because we go Home to be with the Lord Jesus Christ, which is far better.

Should a genuine believer renounce the Lord Jesus Christ at his **death**? No! Should a true believer be mean and ugly at his **death**? No. I realize some genuine believers, before they die, lose their minds. Sometimes their minds are not in control of their bodies and their tongues, but should we glorify God at our death? Yes! Every single one of us will meet death unless the Lord Jesus Christ returns and takes us up to Heaven in the Rapture.

Be Prepared For Death

We must be prepared for death. David said in the Psalms that God will be our guide until the point of death, whenever that will be. Whether it is in Iraq where these young men are being killed, slaughtered, and maimed by the hundreds. Whether it is a slow death, or a quick death, or a hard death, we must be guided by our Lord Jesus Christ unto death.

- **Hebrews 1:8**
  "But unto the Son *he saith*, Thy throne, O God, *is* for ever and ever: a sceptre of righteousness *is* the sceptre of thy kingdom."
Here is the Deity of the Lord Jesus Christ. God the Father speaks to His Son. The Lord Jesus Christ is the One Who is on that throne as well as the Father. It is the Father's throne and one day it will be the Lord Jesus Christ's throne. He is God forever and ever.

- **Hebrews 13:8**
  "Jesus Christ the same yesterday, and to day, and for ever"
He is an eternal Saviour. We have an eternal God.

- **1 Peter 4:11**
  "If any man speak, *let him speak* as the oracles of God; if any man minister, *let him do it* as of the ability which God giveth: that God in all things may be glorified through Jesus Christ, to whom be praise and dominion for ever and ever. Amen."

The Lord Jesus Christ Is Eternal

The Lord Jesus Christ had no beginning. He was from all eternity past. He has no ending. He is in all eternity future. He is forever and ever.

- **Revelation 4:9**
  "And when those beasts give glory and honour and thanks to him that sat on the throne, who liveth for ever and ever,"
We have an eternal God. He does not sleep. He does not slumber.

- **Psalm 121:4**
  "Behold, he that keepeth Israel shall neither slumber nor sleep."
- **Revelation 4:10**
  "The four and twenty elders fall down before him that sat on the throne, and worship him that liveth for ever and ever, and cast their crowns before the throne, saying,"

These, again, are representative of the genuine believers, the true church worshipping the Lord God that lives forever and ever.

- **Revelation 5:14**
  "And the four beasts said, Amen. And the four *and* twenty elders fell down and worshipped him that liveth for ever and ever."

We Have An Eternal God

We have an eternal God. He does not stop. He does not sleep. He does not die. He is always with us wherever we are. Not only is He forever, but He is also Omnipotent (all powerful), Omniscient (all knowing), and He will take care of us.

The second thing in this verse, this **angel** sware by Him Who **created Heaven and earth and the sea and the things that are therein.** We have an eternal **Creator.** Our God is an eternal **Creator.** That word **creator** and **created** is used forty times in the Bible.

- **Genesis 1:1**
  "In the beginning God **created** the Heaven and the earth."

Notice, He **created** the Heaven and the earth. This angel sware by Him that **created** the Heaven and the earth.

- **Genesis 1:21**
  "And God **created** great whales, and every living creature that moveth, which the waters brought forth abundantly, after their kind, and every winged fowl after his kind: and God saw that *it was* good."

This is not evolution as some people are taught in schools. That is not the way it happened.

- **Genesis 1:27**
  "So God **created** man in his *own* image, in the image of God created he him; male and female **created** he them."

We are creatures of God Himself. The everlasting God **created** man in His own image. <u>We are spirit, soul, and body</u>. In that sense it is in His image, a trinity as the Father, Son, and Holy Spirit.

God Did Not Create Homosexuals

Notice, *male and female created he them.* This was no unisex situation. That situation is rising higher and higher, is it not? As I was being driven to the airport in Chicago, a brother said that the homosexuals in Chicago especially, thousands upon thousands, have big parades every year. They are just taking over the city. God made them male and female and that is the way it is.

- **Genesis 2:3-4**
  "And God blessed the seventh day, and sanctified it: because that in it he had rested from all his work which God **created** and made. These *are* the generations of the Heavens and of the earth when they were **created**, in the day that the LORD God made the earth and the Heavens,"

God is the **Creator**, over and over in Scripture. That is why I preach it. That is why I believe it. That is why I am against evolution, whether naturalistic evolution, or theistic evolution. There are two branches of this evolutionary battle. Naturalistic evolution says that life came from nothing, just from a spark, or a big bang, or something else.

Theistic Evolution Is False

Theistic evolution is just as unscriptural. It teaches that man was made from a two-legged ape-like creature and then God breathed into his nostrils the breath of life. That is, they teach that man (really a subman) evolved up to two legs looking like an ape. Then, at that time, God breathed into his nostrils the breath of life. He evolved up to a point then God sort of did the rest. No. That is just as wrong. He created them male and female.

- **Genesis 5:1-2**
  "This *is* the book of the generations of Adam. In the day that God **created** man, in the likeness of God made he him; Male and female **created** he them; and blessed them, and called their name Adam, in the day when they were **created.**"

Adam means *dust.* It also means *red.*

- **Genesis 6:7**
  "And the LORD said, I will destroy man whom I have **created** from the face of the earth; both man, and beast, and the creeping thing, and the fowls of the air; for it repenteth me that I have made them."

This was just before He destroyed this earth with the flood. He takes credit for **creating** man. God made them and He had a right to destroy them, but He spared Noah and Mrs. Noah, Shem and Mrs. Shem, Ham and Mrs. Ham, Japheth and Mrs. Japheth, along with two (male and female) of all the species of animals that were then in existence, and of the clean ones, seven pairs. He put them in that huge ark. It had three decks, able to house every single pair of man and animals that were made. For one whole year plus, it was upon the waters. God spared them, but He was going to destroy those who would not repent, and would not trust Him. He did this in the flood.

- **Isaiah 40:26**
  "Lift up your eyes on high, and behold who hath **created** these *things*, that bringeth out their host by number: he calleth them all by names by the greatness of his might, for that *he is* strong in power; not one faileth."

This is talking about all the stars of Heaven and all the planets of Heaven. Never one fails. Oh, they have these shooting stars, meteorites that fall, but that is all part of the plan to keep things clean up there, I guess. Not one fails because of His power. He is omnipotent.

- **Isaiah 42:5**
  "Thus saith God the LORD, he that **created** the Heavens, and stretched them out; he that spread forth the earth, and that which cometh out of it; he that giveth breath unto the people upon it, and spirit to them that walk therein:"

He is the One that **made** the earth. He is the One that **made** the Heavens. God is the **Creator**, our eternal God.

- **Isaiah 45:12**
  "I have made the earth, and **created** man upon it: I, *even* my hands, have stretched out the Heavens, and all their host have I commanded."

Remember, it says He spake and there was light. He just **commanded**, and these things took place. Imagine the power, imagine the omnipotence of a God that can make not only this earth, which is huge and monstrous, but also all the planets, and the millions and millions of stars that are up there. Just imagine the power. It was not by chance alone. It was not by a spark of something that blew up all of a sudden.

Almighty God, Who is our God if we are genuinely saved believers and we are truly trusting the Lord Jesus Christ as Saviour, made it all.

- **Isaiah 45:18**
  "For thus saith the LORD that **created** the Heavens; God himself that **formed** the earth and **made** it; he hath established it, he **created** it not in vain, he formed it to be inhabited: I *am* the LORD; and *there is* none else."

Geocentricity Vs. Heliocentricity

That is where I believe many who are geocentrists rather than heliocentrists believe that the earth is the center, not the sun. It is called geocentricity versus heliocentricity. One of the verses they use is right here. God has established the earth. It is fixed, not revolving or rotating. This is a big issue, but we will not get into it now.

God **formed** the earth to be inhabited. He did not say He **formed** the moon, or Mars, or Jupiter, or Saturn, or Venus, or any of the planets to be inhabited, but the earth. It is a special **creation** with special light and special heat so that we can live here. Before the flood, the earth was beautiful. The whole earth was inhabited. The whole earth was tropical. All of a sudden after the flood, everything changed. No longer was it all tropical. There was a North Pole and a South Pole that were frozen. We see evidences of tropical vegetation on the North and South Poles. How did it get there? That was before the flood. God judged this earth, but He made it to be inhabited. It is still inhabited. One day He is going to burn it up, and have a new earth and a new Heaven. Believers that are genuinely saved will go to be with the Lord Jesus Christ.

- **1 Corinthians 11:9**
  "Neither was the man **created** for the woman; but the woman for the man."

Sometimes women think that man was **created** for them, but God's order must be respected. It was not good that man should be alone. He looked around at the animals and there was no help that was fitted, or suited, or "*meet*" for Adam, so God **made** woman out of Adam's rib.

- **2 Corinthians 5:17**
  "Therefore if any man *be* in Christ, *he is* a new **creature**: old things are passed away; behold, all things are become new."

Here is another type of creation. Any man or woman that is genuinely saved and born-again is a new **creature** or a new **creation**. This is about being born-again, having new life. He says we are new **creatures**.

- **Ephesians 2:10**
  "For we are his workmanship, **created** in Christ Jesus unto good works, which God hath before ordained that we should walk in them."

Those of us who are genuinely saved believers, are **created** in the Lord Jesus Christ. This is another **creation**. Not the Heavens, not the earth, not the sea, not the animals, or men, or women, but these are genuinely saved people whether they are men, women, boys, or girls, redeemed by His workmanship and **created**.

- **Ephesians 3:9**
  "And to make all *men* see what *is* the fellowship of the mystery, which from the beginning of the world hath been hid in God, who **created** all things by Jesus Christ:"

Denial Of Christ As Creator

The Lord Jesus Christ is the Creator. Did you know that those three words are gone from the false texts that make the foundation of the new versions? The New International Version does not have *by Jesus Christ*. The New American Standard Version does not have *by Jesus Christ*, nor the Revised Standard Version, nor any of these modern versions. Why? Because they have a false Greek text. It is not our Textus Receptus, the Received Text that underlies our King James Bible. They have the false text, Westcott's and Hort's text, Nestle-Aland's text, the United Bible Society's text.

Call it what you will, it is the text of the Gnostics of Egypt. We talked about that in our King James Bible Seminar at Fairhaven Baptist College and Church in Indiana. The Gnostics of Egypt were centered in Alexandria. That was the headquarters. Clement of Alexandria was the first Gnostic. He taught Origen–another Gnostic. Then Eusebius, another Gnostic, read the writings of Origen, and was influenced by him. The library of Alexandria is filled with Gnosticism. Gnosticism is a theology and a philosophy. It is a theology that denies all the Person and work of the Lord Jesus Christ. It denies that the Lord Jesus Christ was and is God. It denies He was virgin born. It denies His Deity, His miracles, and denies the fact that He could create anything. It denies that He arose bodily from the dead, and is coming again.

Gnostic Text False Manuscripts

Because of this, these manuscripts, Vatican and Sinai, B and Aleph, tainted by Gnosticism in Alexandria, take out things, wherever they find them, to conform to their heresies. This is one of their heresies in Ephesians 3:9. They remove the phrase, *"by Jesus Christ."* Why? Because they do not believe He could create anything. He is just a man according to the Gnostics, so they took it out.

- **Colossians 1:16**
  "For by him were all things **created**, that are in Heaven, and that are in earth, visible and invisible, whether *they be* thrones, or dominions, or principalities, or powers: all things were **created** by him, and for him:"

This is speaking of the Lord Jesus Christ. Even the atoms that you cannot see–electrons, protons, and neutrons–were **created** by Him, and for His benefit.

- **Colossians 3:10**
  "And have put on the new *man*, which is renewed in knowledge after the image of him that **created** him"

These are genuinely saved people. Again, true believers are called **created** beings, new **creations**, something new.

- **Revelation 4:11**
  "Thou art worthy, O Lord, to receive glory and honour and power: for thou hast **created** all things, and for thy pleasure they are and were **created**."

Born-Again Ones Are New People

Praise God that, if we are genuinely saved, the eternal Creator is our God. He made us, not by chance, but by purpose. If we are genuinely trusting the Lord Jesus Christ as Saviour and Redeemer, if we have been born-again, He has created a new thing. We are new people, new creatures in the Lord Jesus Christ. We are His workmanship, created in Christ Jesus to glorify Him and to serve Him forever. If you do not know Him as Saviour and Redeemer, you should genuinely trust Him, and be created a new creature in the Lord Jesus Christ.

Revelation 10:7

"But in the days of the voice of the seventh angel, when he shall begin to sound, the mystery of God should be finished, as he hath declared to his servants the prophets."

This **seventh angel** has not **sounded**, but he is beginning to **sound**. That word **mystery** is MUSTERION. It is *a secret*, God's special secret. We do not know which **mystery** this is, but as it has been declared to his servants the prophets, He is going to stop the **mystery**.

- **Ephesians 3:2-5**
  "If ye have heard of the dispensation of the grace of God which is given me to you-ward: How that by revelation he made known unto me the **mystery**; (as I wrote afore in few words, Whereby, when ye read, ye may understand my knowledge in the **mystery** of Christ) Which in other ages was not made known unto the sons of men, as it is now revealed unto his holy apostles and prophets by the Spirit;"

That is what a **mystery** is: something that is not made known, something that is secret, something that is hidden. This verse says that the **mystery** "should be finished, as he hath declared to his servants the prophets." These servants were the ones that received this sacred secret. What is the **mystery**?

- **Ephesians 3:6**
  "That the Gentiles should be fellowheirs, and of the same body, and partakers of his promise in Christ by the gospel:"

The promise, the **mystery** here that Paul revealed, was revealed by the Lord Jesus Christ. It was that the Jews and the Gentiles, if they are genuinely saved, would be in one body. They would be no longer separated, divided, or alienated. That is one **mystery** that has been made clear.

- **Colossians 1:25-26**
  "Whereof I am made a minister, according to the dispensation of God which is given to me for you, to fulfil the word of God; *Even* the **mystery** which hath been hid from ages and from generations, but now is made manifest to his saints:"

God's Hidden Mystery

This mystery is again mentioned. This is a sacred secret, as we said before. Paul was made a minister because the Lord

Jesus Christ called him to minister unto the Gentiles and unto the world. The mystery was hid from generations. The Old Testament knew nothing of the Gentiles and the Jews becoming one in the Lord Jesus Christ. It was a secret. It was hidden from all the people. They had things in the Old Testament that spoke of the Lord Jesus Christ at His first coming. They spoke of the Lord Jesus Christ at His second coming, but this intermediate of more than 2,000 years of the Gentiles, the church age, was not in the Old Testament. Paul was given that special secret. It was revealed unto him and he made it known.

- **Colossians 1:27**
  "To whom God would make known what *is* the riches of the glory of this **mystery** among the Gentiles; which is Christ in you, the hope of glory:"

Paul is writing to the Gentiles at Colosse. Paul, a Jew, Biblically saved by grace through genuine faith in the Lord Jesus Christ, and who now is a genuine Christian, is writing to these Gentiles. He says that is the **mystery**. That is the thing that was kept secret. As we speak to people that are lost and unsaved, bound for Hell, when they come to the Lord Jesus Christ, and genuinely trust Him as Saviour and Redeemer, the Lord Jesus Christ resides in them. It is true that God the Holy Spirit is indwelling the genuine Christians. We speak of the Holy Spirit's indwelling foremost, but it is also true that the Lord Jesus Christ indwells the genuine believers.

- **John 14:23**
  "Jesus answered and said unto him, If a man love me, he will keep my words: and my Father will love him, and we will come unto him, and make our abode with him."

The Father, Son, and Holy Spirit indwell the genuine believers. That does not make us God, but it means that we have the power of God inside. It is a wonderful thing that the Lord Jesus Christ could inhabit wicked and sinful people such as we are. The old nature does not change, but God the Father, God the Holy Spirit, and God the Son (the Lord Jesus Christ) reside in us when we are genuinely saved and regenerated by true faith, repenting of our sins. We realize we are sinners and we genuinely trust the Lord Jesus Christ. Christ is in us, the hope of Glory.

What does that mean, the hope of Glory? That means if we have Him, one day we will have glory. As the hymn writer said, Only Glory By and By. We will have the glory of Heaven, the glory of God's grace and the glory of His presence. That is the **mystery**.

The Mystery Of The Gospel

There is another mystery. We are not sure what this mystery is, but it says in Revelation 10:7, "the mystery of God should be finished, as he hath declared to his servants the prophets." The second mystery is the mystery of the gospel.

- **Ephesians 6:19-20**
  "And for me, that utterance may be given unto me, that I may open my mouth boldly, to make known the **mystery** of the gospel, For which I am an ambassador in bonds: that therein I may speak boldly, as I ought to speak."

Paul says to these Gentiles, "Pray for me." The sacred secret of the gospel was not known in old ages. The gospel of the Lord Jesus Christ was that He should come into the world and not be a king and reign, which is the Old Testament picture of the coming of the Lord Jesus Christ, but that He should suffer and bear the sins of the world. That was also in the Scriptures in the Old Testament in Psalm 22, Isaiah 53, and other places, but this **mystery** of the gospel is that those who are genuinely trusting in Him could be truly saved.

Paul was an ambassador because the Lord Jesus Christ made him an ambassador. He made him a minister. He made him an apostle. When the gospel is preached, it is not always popular. Paul prayed and asked the people in Ephesus to pray that he might be bold in his proclamation of the gospel. People do not like to hear that they are sinners. People do not like to hear that they are lost. They do not like to hear that God's Words say that all the lost ones that refuse to genuinely receive the Lord Jesus Christ will end up in an eternal Hell in the lake of fire.

- **Colossians 4:3**
  "Withal praying also for us, that God would open unto us a door of utterance, to speak the **mystery** of the Christ, for which I am also in bonds:"

Paul also asked for prayer from the Colossian Christians. The book of Colossians was one of the prison epistles. Paul wrote it from jail. He was in prison when he wrote all four of the prison epistles: Ephesians, Philippians, Colossians, and Philemon. Paul says that because of this mystery of the Lord Jesus Christ, because of this gospel that he preached, he was in prison. He would not stop. He would not shut up. When the Romans said, "Do not preach the Lord Jesus Christ," he did not obey.

- **Acts 5:29**
  "Then Peter and the *other* apostles answered and said, We ought to obey God rather than men."

Paul Obeyed God Rather Than Men

Paul did obey God rather than men, so he continued to preach the mystery of the Lord Jesus Christ. All these mysteries, the mystery of the gospel, the mystery of the Jews and Gentiles in one body in the Lord Jesus Christ, "should be finished as he hath declared to his servants the prophets" (Revelation 10:7).

That word for declared is EUAGGELIZO. It means *to evangelize.* God put special note onto His **prophets.** His **prophets** are important, both the Old Testament **prophets** and the New Testament **prophets** as well.

We do not have **prophets** any more. We do not believe with the Mormons that they still have the apostles or **prophets.** We do not believe that. I believe that we have the Scriptures. God called His *servants the prophets.*

The Meaning Of DOULOS

There are many words for prophets, but this one here is the word DOULOS. It is the regular word for slavery, a bond slave, one who gives himself up to another's will. The prophets in the Old Testament gave themselves up to God's will, whose service is used by the Lord Jesus Christ. It means, *devoted to another to the disregard of one's own interests.* Paul was a prophet in the New Testament.

- **Jeremiah 25:4**
  "And the LORD hath sent unto you all his servants the **prophets**, rising early and sending *them*; but ye have not hearkened, nor inclined your ear to hear."

God sent many **prophets** in the Old Testament. But they did not want to do what they said.

- **Jeremiah 26:5**
  "To hearken to the words of my servants the **prophets**, whom I sent unto you, both rising up early, and sending *them*, but ye have not hearkened;"

I tell you, it is something when God sends His **servants,** the prophets, and we do not hearken. We do not listen. That was true in the Old Testament.

- **Jeremiah 35:15**
  "I have sent also unto you all my servants the **prophets**, rising up early and sending *them*, saying, Return ye now every man from his evil way, and amend your doings, and go not after other gods to serve them, and ye shall dwell in the land which I have given to you and to your fathers: but ye have not inclined your ear, nor hearkened unto me."

That is the message of the **prophet**. Change your ways, return from sin and come back to the Lord. The Israelites, the northern kingdom and the southern kingdom, did not hearken to the Lord.

- **Amos 3:7**
  "Surely the Lord GOD will do nothing, but he revealeth his secret unto his servants the **prophets**."

They had a special inside revelation-track from the Lord. He did not do anything without first revealing it to the prophets.

<u>Abraham was a **prophet.**</u> We do not normally think of him as a prophet. But God revealed to Abraham that He was going to kill all those in Sodom and Gomorrah, except those that came out, the righteous ones. Lot did not seem too righteous.

- **Genesis 18:20-21**
  "And the LORD said, Because the cry of Sodom and Gomorrah is great, and because their sin is very grievous; I will go down now, and see whether they have done altogether according to the cry of it, which is come unto me; and if not, I will know."

I do not know how long it will be, before God will call our country, and other countries in the world—Sodom and Gomorrah.

Abraham pled with the Lord, as you know. He knew that his nephew, Lot, was there. The Lord could not even find ten righteous people. Finally, the angels of the Lord had to grab Lot and his wife and two daughters and pull them out. It was a terrible scene.

Prophets Were Told The Future

God reveals unto His servants, the prophets, what is going to happen. That is why John, who was an apostle and also a prophet, was given all the future. That is what we have in the book of Revelation, what is going to happen. We see the future that God has planned because He revealed it to His servant, the prophet, John.

Revelation 10:8

"And the voice which I heard from Heaven spake unto me again, and said, Go *and* take the little book which is open in the hand of the angel which standeth upon the sea and upon the earth."

Here he is going to take this **little book**. Later on we are going to see what he does with it.

We Must Read & Heed God's Words

We have a book: the Bible, the Words of God. We have to take our book and we have to read it. We have to use it. It is open. We have it in our own language. We have it in our English language. I believe the closest, most accurate translation, is our King James Bible based on the proper Greek text and proper Hebrew text. We are to read and use it. What good does it do if we do not use it?

- **Deuteronomy 31:23-26**
  "And he gave Joshua the son of Nun a charge, and said, Be strong and of a good courage: for thou shalt bring the children of Israel into the land which I sware unto them: and I will be with thee. And it came to pass, when Moses had made an end of **writing** the words of this law in a **book**, until they were finished, That Moses commanded the Levites, which bare the ark of the covenant of the LORD, saying, Take this **book** of the law, and put it in the side of the ark of the covenant of the LORD your God, that it may be there for a witness against thee."

Moses wrote the law that God had commanded him in a **book**. It was something that could be read by others.

This angel said to John to go and take the **little book** that was open. This is what Moses told Joshua, to take the **book** of the law and put it inside the ark of the covenant. That law that was given was a witness against their sins and against their wickedness. Moses was a prophet. He knew that, after he died, the Israelites would go even more foul than ever.

- **Joshua 1:8-9**
  "This **book** of the law shall not depart out of thy mouth; but thou shalt meditate therein day and night, that thou mayest observe to do according to all that is written therein: for then thou shalt make thy way prosperous, and then thou shalt have

good success. Have not I commanded thee? Be strong and of a good courage; be not afraid, neither be thou dismayed: for the LORD thy God *is* with thee whithersoever thou goest."

Meditate On God's Words

We have to take that book, use it, meditate on it, and then we will have good success. We have to take our Bibles and read and study.

- **Joshua 23:6**
  "Be ye therefore very courageous to keep and to do all that is written in the **book** of the law of Moses, that ye turn not aside therefrom "*to* the right hand or *to* the left;"

Keep Everything That Is There

This word *all* means keep everything that is there. We are Biblical Christians in the New Testament. We do not keep the Old Testament law. We are not under the law. We are under grace, but we have a New Testament. We have a new Bible and a New Testament. We should keep all the words that are there. That is why it is important that all be preserved. The Old Testament Hebrew text and the New Testament Greek text should be preserved and all the words should be accurately translated so that we can keep them.

- **2 Kings 22:8-9**
  "And Hilkiah the high priest said unto Shaphan the scribe, I have found the **book** of the law in the house of the LORD. And Hilkiah gave the **book** to Shaphan, and he read it. And Shaphan the scribe came to the king, and brought the king word again, and said, Thy servants have gathered the money that was found in the house, and have delivered it into the hand of them that do the work, that have the oversight of the house of the LORD"

A scribe was the one that copied the Words of God. Shaphan brought the book to King Josiah.

- **2 Kings 22:11**
  "And it came to pass, when the king had heard the words of the **book** of the law, that he rent his clothes."

He ripped his clothes in mourning because he knew he was a sinner. He knew that all the people in his reign had committed sin.

We must take the **book** of God. We must take the Scriptures, read them, study them, and know them, so that we can repent of our sins when we have gone astray. We know what God expects of us as Josiah did at that time.

- **2 Kings 22:13**
  "Go ye, enquire of the LORD for me, and for the people, and for all Judah, concerning the words of this **book** that is found: for great *is* the wrath of the LORD that is kindled against us, because our fathers have not hearkened unto the words of this **book,** to do according unto all that which is written concerning us."

God is wrathful also, I am sure, at those of us who do not follow His Words in the New Testament. If we do not take it, if we do not study it, if we do not read it, and do not follow it, this is a serious matter.

- **2 Chronicles 34:21**
  "Go, enquire of the LORD for me, and for them that are left in Israel and in Judah, concerning the words of the **book** that is found: for great *is* the wrath of the LORD that is poured out upon us, because our fathers have not kept the word of the LORD, to do after all that is written in this **book.**"

Don't Lose Your King James Bible

I am glad he found that book. I hope you have not lost your King James Bible. I hope it is not in some hidden place in the closet or somewhere in the basement that you cannot find it. You have to study it, read it, open it, and see. Josiah was concerned about the words of the book that was found.

- **Matthew 4:4**
  "But he answered and said, It is **written,** Man shall not live by bread alone, but by every **word** that proceedeth out of the mouth of God."

Every word is important. We have every **Word** translated accurately in our King James **Bible.** We must obey what it teaches.

- **Nehemiah 9:3**
  "And they stood up in their place, and read in the **book** of the law of the LORD their God *one* fourth part of the day; and *another* fourth part they confessed, and worshipped the LORD their God."

Nehemiah came back from captivity. He came back to Jerusalem to set up the walls. They stood up in their place when they were dedicating that wall and the temple and read in the **book** of the law of the Lord. How long did they read? A fourth part of the day. If the daylight is twelve hours, a fourth part would be three hours. For three hours they stood and read the **Words** of God. Then the other fourth part of the day they confessed. That would be three more hours. When they had heard what God demanded of them, they saw how wicked and sinful they were. That was why they were in captivity. God sent them to Babylon because of their sins. Three more hours they confessed and they worshipped the Lord.

This is a worship picture of the things of the Lord in the **book** of Nehemiah. We do not very often spend three hours reading the Scriptures and certainly not three more hours confessing and worshipping the Lord.

- **Job 19:23-25**
  "Oh that my words were now **written**! oh that they were printed in a **book**! That they were graven with an iron pen and lead in the rock for ever! For I know *that* my redeemer liveth, and *that* he shall stand at the latter *day* upon the earth:"

Job had a desire. He wanted to have his **Words written** and they are **written**. Now we have the **book** of Job. Job had the **Words** of God. God has preserved Job's words so that we can read them today.

- **Isaiah 34:16**
  "Seek ye out of the **book** of the LORD, and read: no one of these shall fail, none shall want her mate: for my mouth it hath commanded, and his spirit it hath gathered them."

Take Our Book, The Bible

As John was told by the angel, the voice which he heard from Heaven (maybe the Lord Jesus Christ Himself) said, "Go and take the little book which is open." We have to take our book, the book of Scriptures, the Bible. It is not good enough to have it. It is not good enough to know it and to let it sit. We have to read it.

You may say, "Well, I have read it once," or, "I have not read it from Genesis to Revelation, but I have read a little bit." Maybe some have said, "Well, I have read it from Genesis to Revelation, once or maybe twice or three times, but should I quit now?"

No, I say we should never quit reading, taking the **book** and reading the **Scriptures**. We are new people. Every single day, we are a different person. We have different needs, different desires, different wants. We need the grace of God and we need the **Scriptures** to tell us the way. There is no question about that. The way of the Lord must be taken, it must be used and it must be followed. So many times we will say, "I have read that before but I have never seen it just that way."

My wife and I read every day, 85 verses per day, and read that thing through. Once in a while we say, "Well, I never remembered that." I have read that thing many, many times ever since I was genuinely saved, at least once a year, if not twice or three times when I was first saved. I will say, "Well, I have never noticed that before." It behooves us to not only take the **Scriptures**, but to be faithful in our reading throughout, so that we may know the **Words** of God, know the will of God, and be willing to do the will of the living God.

Revelation 10:9

"And I went unto the angel, and said unto him, Give me the little book. And he said unto me, Take *it*, and eat it up; and it shall make thy belly bitter, but it shall be in thy mouth sweet as honey."

Here is the **eating** of a **book**. It sounds strange, but on the other hand, it says in the **Scripture** the following:

- **Jeremiah 15:16**
  "Thy **words** were found, and I did **eat** them; and thy word was unto me the joy and rejoicing of mine heart: for I am called by thy name, O LORD God of hosts."

Reading Scripture Is Like Eating

The reading of Scripture is like eating. It makes it a part of us just like food becomes a part of us. It is absorbed.

- **Psalm 19:10**
  "More to be desired *are they* than gold, yea, than much fine gold: sweeter also than honey and the honeycomb."

The **Words** of God are sweet as honey as we read it.

- **Ezekiel 2:7-10**
  "And thou shalt speak my **words** unto them, whether they will hear, or whether they will forbear: for they *are* most rebellious. But thou, son of man, hear what I say unto thee; Be not thou rebellious like that rebellious house: open thy mouth, and eat that I give thee. And when I looked, behold, an hand *was* sent unto me; and, lo, a roll of a **book** *was* therein; And he spread it before me; and it *was* written within and without: and *there was* written therein lamentations, and mourning, and woe."

Here was the case of the Lord telling Ezekiel the prophet to eat a book. A prophet is to speak God's **Words** no matter whether they will hear or not hear. Just speak them. Be faithful. Preachers and pastors should speak God's **Words** no matter whether people hear or they do not hear. Be faithful. Preach the **Word**. The prophets cannot be rebellious. It is bad enough when people are rebellious, but the preachers, pastors, and genuine Christians, should not be rebellious. How can rebels speak to rebels and expect the rebels to become unrebellious? No, the prophets, like Ezekiel, are warned by the Lord to be not rebellious.

- **John 6:53**
  "Then Jesus said unto them, Verily, verily, I say unto you, Except ye **eat** the flesh of the Son of man, and drink his blood, ye have no life in you."

Blasphemous Roman Catholic Mass

The Roman Catholics get this all wrong. They say this is the Mass. We had a lady who used to go to a local Baptist church who has turned Roman Catholic. She said to us, "The most important thing of all, is the Mass, eating Christ's flesh and drinking His blood." I said, "Ma'am, eating there and drinking there means to *appropriate* what His blood has done for you in His sacrifice on the cross. Eating His flesh means to appropriate it to yourself. That is the meaning." How could they eat the flesh of the Lord Jesus Christ when He was right there among them? They could not eat His flesh. It is a figure of speech, just like eating this book.

This was a **book** of judgment that was coming upon Israel.

- **Ezekiel 3:1-7**
  "Moreover he said unto me, Son of man, eat that thou findest; **eat** this **roll**, and go speak unto the house of Israel. So I opened my mouth, and he caused me to **eat** that **roll**. And he said unto me, Son of man, cause thy belly to **eat**, and fill thy bowels with this **roll** that I give thee. Then did I **eat** it; and it was in my mouth as honey for sweetness. And he said unto me, Son of man, go, get thee unto the house of Israel, and speak with my words unto them. For thou *art* not sent to a people of a strange speech and of an hard language, *but* to the house of Israel; Not to many people of a strange speech and of an hard language, whose words thou canst not understand. Surely, had I sent thee to them, they would have hearkened unto thee. But the house of Israel will not hearken unto thee; for they will not hearken unto me: for all the house of Israel are impudent and hardhearted."

The spiritual **eating** of a **book** is appropriating what God was telling him. The **Words** of the Lord are as honey for sweetness. As Ezekiel

ministered His **Words**, they were sweet to Ezekiel. They were not sweet
to the ones that heard them because judgment was there. Ezekiel was a
minister to his own people.

Ezekiel Was To Preach The Truth

Ezekiel was not sent to a people of a hard language.
Sometimes when you are sent to those people that are far away
with a different language and different cultures, they will
listen. But our own people, close to us, our own language
people, they do not listen. If you do not hearken to the Lord
you are not going to hearken to the Lord's prophet, as Ezekiel
was a prophet of the Lord. What a terrible testimony, or lack
of it, that Israel had. Ezekiel eating that roll was similar to this
in Revelation 10:9.

Revelation 10:10

**"And I took the little book out of the angel's hand, and
ate it up; and it was in my mouth sweet as honey: and as
soon as I had eaten it, my belly was bitter."**

Sweet Turns Bitter

Here is a picture of when sweet turns bitter. It was sweet
in his mouth, but in his stomach it turned bitter. Sin looks very
sweet, does it not? Sinners say, "Oh, what a wonderful thing.
I just do anything that I want." At the end there is bitterness.
I think this is a picture of this. It is a picture of sweetness, they
think, but it turns bitter.

- Proverbs 9:17-18
  "Stolen waters are **sweet**, and bread *eaten* in secret is pleasant.
  But he knoweth not that the dead *are* there; *and that* her guests
  are in the depths of Hell."

We are not supposed to steal anything. Stealing is **sweet** to the thief.
Drinking is **sweet** to the drunkard.

- Proverbs 23:29-30
  "Who hath woe? who hath **sorrow**? who hath contentions? who
  hath babbling? who hath wounds without cause? who hath
  redness of eyes? They that tarry long at the wine; they that go to
  seek mixed wine."

It is a picture that looks so **sweet** to the drinker. He has all kinds of
babblings and sorrow, but it looked **sweet** to him or he would not have

drunk. I remember when I was working at the University of Michigan Union Cafeteria. I was in the tray room. I would dry some trays and different things. I just had menial tasks. I was in college at that time, in the University of Michigan. We had a skinny man at one end of the trays. He would clean the trays and put them through a big cleaner and so on. He was so skinny he could hardly walk. He was haggard. They told me he was a wino. He just drank wine all day long. That was all he drank. He did not eat food, he just drank wine. He was ready to die. I am sure he died within a few years afterwards. It looked good to him, but the **sweetness** turned **bitter** at the end. Those of you who have imbibed, know full well what that means. You have seen the sweetness, and all of a sudden, the **bitterness**. Praise God, if you have been delivered from that **bitterness** and you are genuinely saved and safe.

- **Proverbs 23:31-33**
  "Look not thou upon the wine when it is red, when it giveth his colour in the cup, *when* it moveth itself aright. At the last it **biteth** like a serpent, and **stingeth** like an adder. Thine eyes shall behold strange women, and thine heart shall utter perverse things. Yea, thou shalt be as he that lieth down in the midst of the sea, or as he that lieth upon the top of a mast. They have stricken me, *shalt thou say, and* I was not sick; they have beaten me, *and* I felt *it* not: when shall I awake? I will seek it yet again."

In that drunken stupor, **pain** goes away. That is what people say when somebody is stone drunk. They say, "He feels no **pain**." This person had never learned a lesson. He thought something was **sweet** and he still thought it was **sweet**, but it is not **sweet**. It is dark. It is black. It is wicked. It turns **bitter** at the end.

- **Luke 12:16-20**
  "And he spake a parable unto them, saying, The ground of a certain rich man brought forth plentifully: And he thought within himself, saying, What shall I do, because I have no room where to bestow my fruits? And he said, This will I do: I will pull down my barns, and build greater; and there will I bestow all my fruits and my goods. And I will say to my soul, Soul, thou hast much goods laid up for many years; take thine ease, eat, drink, *and* be merry. But God said unto him, *Thou* fool, this night thy soul shall be required of thee: then whose shall those things be, which thou hast provided?"

This was a parable the Lord Jesus Christ spoke concerning the ground of a certain rich man that brought forth abundantly. Oh, what a wonderful man! He had all this ground. He was **happy**. He had all kinds of fruits and luxury. Everything was going along as the theme song of that musical *Oklahoma*, "Oh, what a beautiful morning . . . everything's going my way." This was the case. Everything was going his way. He was happy. There was great joy and **sweetness**, but all of a sudden this **sweetness** turned **bitter**.

- **Luke 12:21**
  "So *is* he that layeth up treasure for himself, and is not rich toward God."

This man had no time for God. That **sweetness** became **bitter** as his soul was required that very night.

- **Luke 15:11-19**
  "And he said, A certain man had two sons: And the younger of them said to his father, Father, give me the portion of goods that falleth to me. And he divided unto them his living. And not many days after the younger son gathered all together, and took his journey into a far country, and there wasted his substance with riotous living. And when he had spent all, there arose a mighty famine in that land; and he began to be in want. And he went and joined himself to a citizen of that country; and he sent him into his fields to feed swine. And he would fain have filled his belly with the husks that the swine did eat: and no man gave unto him. And when he came to himself, he said, How many hired servants of my father's have bread enough and to spare, and I perish with hunger! I will arise and go to my father, and will say unto him, Father, I have sinned against Heaven, and before thee, And am no more worthy to be called thy son: make me as one of thy hired servants."

I think he was a foolish father, but he was a father that said, "All right, if this young man wants half of my living, I guess it is due him." He had two sons. Half went to one and half to the other. I am sure the father thought, "I do not think it is a good idea. It is a little bit silly, but go ahead," instead of waiting for his death.

He Had Half Of His Father's Money

There was great sweetness. The youngest son had half of his father's money. Oh my, what a wonderful time he must have had! When he had spent all, there was a mighty famine in the land. The sweetness began to be bitter because he had squandered that which he should have saved. He used to have everything, all at his fingertips. Now, he was feeding swine, an unclean animal to any Jew. He would have just as soon filled his belly with the husks that the swine did eat. How bitter that sweetness had become because of his sin.

I am glad he finally realized that sweetness was back in his father's house, back in fellowship. I am glad that the son was able to change the **bitterness** into **sweetness** when he went home. The father received him, as we know. If it started with **sweet** and had gone to **bitter**, there is always **sweetness** when you go back to the Lord Jesus Christ.

Gertrude Sanborn, my mother-in-law, wrote this poem:

Bitter Waters Made Sweet

I trudged along life's barren highway;
I longed for a drink from the well;
*But the waters of Marah were **bitter**,*
*And no one a **sweetener** could tell.*

*Since then I have drunk of **sweet** waters;*
My thirst has been quenched at His well;
The Waters of Life have been flowing;
My life is a channel as well.

CODA:
Bitter** waters made **sweet
By the Cross that He bore.
***Bitter** waters made **sweet** by the Tree.*
God cast in His branch,
And I drank from the well–
It was life; it was new; It was free.

So, we who have genuinely come to the Lord Jesus Christ, are able, through His power, to make the **bitterness sweet** again.

Revelation 10:11

"And he said unto me, Thou must prophesy again before many peoples, and nations, and tongues, and kings."

Here John is a prisoner on the isle of Patmos. He must have thought, "How can this be fulfilled?" How could that come to pass? This **prophecy** from the Lord Jesus Christ, through John the apostle, in Revelation, has come before many peoples, and **nations**, and **tongues**, **and kings**.

People Read The Book Of Revelation

People of the world read the book of Revelation. They quote the book of Revelation. The four horsemen of the apocalypse–all these things, they are looking at. Many times they misinterpret it. They do not know what it means. But John, in this prophecy, has prophesied, not only in the book of Revelation, but in other books as well. God saw fit to write down God's Words through John in the Gospel of John, and his other books, 1 John, 2 John, and 3 John. The reason he was banished, was "for the Word of God and the testimony of Jesus Christ." He was a faithful apostle, a faithful preacher, and a minister of the Lord Jesus Christ.

Here are some of the verses that are going before peoples, and **nations**, and **tongues**, and **kings**, because John continues to prophesy to this very day.

- **John 1:10-13**
  "He was in the world, and the world was made by him, and the world knew him not. He came unto his own, and his own received him not. But as many as received him, to them gave he power to become the sons of God, *even* to them that believe on his name: Which were born, not of blood, nor of the will of the flesh, nor of the will of man, but of God."

These words, gospel messages, are going out to the world around us.

- **John 3:16-18**
  "For God so loved the world, that he gave his only begotten Son, that whosoever believeth in him should not perish, but have everlasting life. For God sent not his Son into the world to condemn the world; but that the world through him might be saved. He that believeth on him is not condemned: but he that believeth not is condemned already, because he hath not believed in the name of the only begotten Son of God."

This Prophecy Read Worldwide

John's words are prophesying even to this day around the world to nations, and peoples, and tongues, and kings.

- **John 3:36**
  "He that believeth on the Son hath everlasting life: and he that believeth not the Son shall not see life; but the wrath of God abideth on him."

- **John 5:24**
  "Verily, verily, I say unto you, He that heareth my word, and believeth on him that sent me, hath everlasting life, and shall not come into condemnation; but is passed from death unto life."

John's words are going out throughout the world, the gospel message.

- **John 6:47**
  "Verily, verily, I say unto you, He that believeth on me hath everlasting life."

This is the simplicity of the gospel message. John is yet prophesying before many peoples. There on the isle of Patmos, that lonely island, through his ministering, and his Words of Scripture, he is still a prophet to many.

- **John 10:27-30**
  "My sheep hear my voice, and I know them, and they follow me: And I give unto them eternal life; and they shall never perish, neither shall any *man* pluck them out of my hand. My Father, which gave *them* me, is greater than all; and no *man* is able to pluck *them* out of my Father's hand. I and *my* Father are one."

John's Words are being used to preach the gospel to many nations, tongues, kings, and people.

- **John 14:1-6**
  "Let not your heart be troubled: ye believe in God, believe also in me. In my Father's house are many mansions: if *it were* not *so*, I would have told you. I go to prepare a place for you. And if I go and prepare a place for you, I will come again, and receive you unto myself; that where I am, *there* ye may be also. And whither I go ye know, and the way ye know. Thomas saith unto him, Lord, we know not whither thou goest; and how can we know the way? Jesus saith unto him, I am the way, the truth, and the life: no man cometh unto the Father, but by me."

These are wonderful words of comfort that the Lord Jesus Christ has given John. John, I am sure, was amazed when the angel told him that he must prophesy again. John said to himself, I am sure, "How can I prophesy again? The emperor has banished me to this little island because I am a Biblical Christian, a preacher, an apostle, and I have been preaching the Lord Jesus Christ. How can I prophesy again? I do not understand. And before many peoples? There are just a few people on this island. How can that be? Many nations? All kinds of nations? There is only one **nation** on this island of Patmos. And **tongues**? Different languages? They only speak one language on this little island. And many kings? There are no **kings** here. **Kings** are all on the mainland. There are not any on the island. I have been banished for my testimony."

John had to realize, and I am sure the Lord Jesus Christ revealed, that his writing of this entire book of Revelation and all of his other books–the Gospel of John, 1 John, 2 John, and 3 John–would be preserved in a Book. Job's desire and request was, *"Oh, that my words would be put in a book"* and "I know that my redeemer liveth." Job's words were fulfilled. His words are in a Book and now John's Words are in a Book. John's Gospel probably is the most beloved Gospel of all the four.

- **John 20:30-31**
  "And many other signs truly did Jesus in the presence of his disciples, which are not written in this book: But these are written, that ye might believe that Jesus is the Christ, the Son of God; and that believing ye might have life through his name."

Bitterness Made Sweet Again

The bitterness was made sweet again. And in the imprisonment, I am sure he was happy, because the Lord Jesus Christ had promised him that he would be a prophet again. He was given another opportunity. God gives every one of us another chance, another opportunity to serve Him, if we have not served Him in the first place. It is better to serve Him in the first place, but if not, ask Him, *"Lord, give me back what I used to be and glorify Thy Name through me."*

𝕽𝖊𝖛𝖊𝖑𝖆𝖙𝖎𝖔𝖓
𝕮𝖍𝖆𝖕𝖙𝖊𝖗 𝕰𝖑𝖊𝖛𝖊𝖓

Revelation 11:1

"And there was given me a reed like unto a rod: and the angel stood, saying, Rise, and measure the temple of God, and the altar, and them that worship therein."

I want to ask the question, *"Why was our Lord crucified?"* The seven trumpet judgments are before us. The first six have sounded. The seventh will sound in the last part of this chapter. The trumpet judgments form seven of twenty-one altogether. This is still parenthetical. Chapters ten through eleven verse ten, are parenthetical in the book of Revelation.

John had this measuring **reed like a rod or a staff**. There is going to be a temple of God in the millennial reign of our Saviour, the Lord Jesus Christ. Today, the Jews are thinking about building a **temple**. There is going to be a **temple** even during the seven-year period of the tribulation. The true church, the genuine believers, will be gone. They will be out of here. No genuinely saved person will be here on earth then.

There is a measurement that has been given that is similar to when Ezekiel was told to measure the **temple**.

- **Ezekiel 40:1-3**
  "In the five and twentieth year of our captivity, in the beginning of the year, in the tenth *day* of the month, in the fourteenth year after that the city was smitten, in the selfsame day the hand of the LORD was upon me, and brought me thither. In the visions of God brought he me into the land of Israel, and set me upon a very high mountain, by which *was* as the frame of a city on the south. And he brought me thither, and, behold, *there was* a man, whose appearance *was* like the appearance of brass, with a line of flax in his hand, and a measuring **reed**; and he stood in the gate."

Ezekiel Sees The Land Of Israel

Ezekiel was brought in the visions of the Lord to the land of Israel. He was in Babylon. He was brought to Israel and set upon a very high mountain. He is speaking about the gate of the temple that is going to be built in the millennial reign of our Saviour, the Lord Jesus Christ upon this earth.

- Ezekiel 40:4-5
  "And the man said unto me, Son of man, behold with thine eyes, and hear with thine ears, and set thine heart upon all that I shall shew thee; for to the intent that I might shew *them* unto thee *art* thou brought hither: declare all that thou seest to the house of Israel. And behold a wall on the outside of the house round about, and in the man's hand a measuring reed of six cubits *long* by the cubit and an hand breadth: so he measured the breadth of the building, one **reed**; and the height, one **reed**."

That would be about nine and a half feet long. It was a big, long measuring rod. Ezekiel's **temple** is similar to what John was told to measure with a reed, as far as the millennial **temple**. It is the same **temple** of worship during the millennial reign of our Saviour.

Why A Temple In The Millennium?

Some people have said, "Why do they have a temple in the Millennium? At the temple, people had sacrifices. Do you mean there are going to be sacrifices during the millennial reign of the Lord Jesus Christ? I thought the Lord Jesus Christ's death on the cross was sufficient and that it was the last sacrifice." Well, it was the last sacrifice for sin, but there is a memorial back to that sacrifice. Just like the Old Testament sacrifices were a memorial looking forward to the sacrifice of our Lord Jesus Christ, so there will be a remembrance looking backward.

- Ezekiel 40:39
  "And in the porch of the gate *were* two tables on this side, and two tables on that side, to slay thereon the **burnt offering** and the **sin offering** and the **trespass offering**."

Reinstitution Of Blood Offerings

Yes, there will be a reinstitution of blood offerings during the millennial reign of the Lord Jesus Christ in the temple in Jerusalem. It is not as a salvation for sins, but looking back in memorial, just like we have the Lord's Supper looking back to Calvary. It is not a sacrifice like the Mass that the Roman Catholics falsely say saves. That is not the blood of the Lord Jesus Christ literally. It is not the body of the Lord Jesus Christ. It is a memorial of His death.

- Luke 22:19
  "And he took bread, and gave thanks, and brake *it*, and gave unto them, saying, This is my body which is given for you: this do in remembrance of me."

This is looking back in the millennial reign of our Saviour to Calvary and the cross of Calvary and what was done at that cross. We do not have any further sacrifices today.

- Hebrews 10:14
  "For by one offering he hath perfected for ever them that are sanctified."

The Meaning Of Worship

That word worship is an interesting word. PROSKUNEO is the word. It is a continuous worship, not just once in a while, but continually worshipping. It means *to kiss like a dog licking his master's hand.* That is what that word picture is. Among the Asians, especially the Persians, this word is *to worship and to fall down upon the knees; to touch the ground with the forehead; an expression of profound reverence.* Some Muslims do that to this day. In this verse, there is a worshipping before the Lord Jesus Christ and a continual worship in that millennial temple. The Lord Jesus Christ will reign, and the genuine believers will reign with Him, for one thousand years, as we learn in this book of Revelation.

Revelation 11:2

"But the court which is without the temple leave out, and measure it not; for it is given unto the Gentiles: and the holy city shall they tread under foot forty *and* two months."

Notice it says, *"measure it not."* There are two types of prohibitions in the Greek language. One is a present prohibition, which means to *stop an action already in progress.* The aorist prohibition means *do not even begin to do something.* This is an aorist prohibition.

Don't Measure The Court

Do not even begin to measure the court that is outside the temple. It is given to the Gentiles. Do not even bother with it. Forty and two months is 1,260 days or three and a half years. That is probably the last half of the seven-year period of Daniel's 70th week. It is Daniel's 70th week. The true church has nothing to do with this tribulation period.

- **Daniel 9:24**
  "Seventy weeks are determined upon **thy people** and upon thy holy city, to finish the transgression, and to make an end of sins, and to make reconciliation for iniquity, and to bring in everlasting righteousness, and to seal up the vision and prophecy, and to anoint the most Holy."

This is the people of **Israel**. In the times of the Gentiles in the tribulation period, the seven-year period, they are going to be ferociously against the **Jews**. The Lord Jesus Christ speaks of that.

- **Luke 21:20-22**
  "And when ye shall see **Jerusalem** compassed with armies, then know that the desolation thereof is nigh. Then let them which are in Judaea flee to the mountains; and let them which are in the midst of it depart out; and let not them that are in the countries enter thereinto. For these be the days of vengeance, that all things which are written may be fulfilled."

The Antichrist Breaks The Covenant

I believe this is the "times of the Gentiles" (Luke 21:24) which is this last half of the tribulation period. During the first half, that first three and a half years, the antichrist will bring peace. Everybody will think, "What a wonderful, peaceful man he is!" Then he will break the covenant with the Jews in the middle of that tribulation. In the last three and a half years, the antichrist, who is the Devil himself incarnate, will show his true colors.

They are not to go back to **Jerusalem** at this time.

- **Luke 21:23-24**
  "But woe unto them that are with child, and to them that give suck, in those days! for there shall be great distress in the land, and wrath upon this people. And they shall fall by the edge of the sword, and shall be led away captive into all nations: and Jerusalem shall be trodden down of the Gentiles, until the **times of the Gentiles** be fulfilled."

The Jews will be mowed down. This is prior to the battle of Armageddon. All the countries of the world will center in upon **Jerusalem**. **Jerusalem** is the center of the battle of **Armageddon**. In that particular city of **Jerusalem**, they will assemble from the east, from the north, from the west, and from the south. All of these will compass around **Jerusalem**. I believe this is the picture of Luke 21, this last half of the tribulation.

- **Luke 21:25-27**
  "And there shall be signs in the sun, and in the moon, and in the stars; and upon the earth distress of nations, with perplexity; the sea and the waves roaring; Men's hearts failing them for fear, and for looking after those things which are coming on the earth: for the powers of Heaven shall be shaken. And then shall they see the Son of man coming in a cloud with power and great glory."

This will be at the second phase of His second coming in glory. He will put down this battle of **Armageddon** and will slay thousands upon thousands that are trying to go after Jerusalem and take it.

- **Luke 21:28**
  "And when these things begin to come to pass, then look up, and lift up your heads; for your redemption draweth nigh."

Revelation 11:3

"And I will give *power* unto my two witnesses, and they shall prophesy a thousand two hundred *and* threescore days, clothed in sackcloth."

This one thousand and threescore days would be forty-two months. That will be exactly three-and-a-half years. These **two prophets** will come as witnesses unto the Lord Jesus Christ. There are some who say the witnesses are Enoch and Elijah because they never died. I believe they are Moses and Elijah because of the miracles that they perform. It seems very clear that is who they are.

Notice they are clothed in **sackcloth**. That word **sackcloth** is the Greek word SAKKOS. It is an interesting word. It just means, *a garment of the material made of a dark, coarse stuff, especially from the hair of animals, clinging to the person like a sack; worn or drawn over the tunic instead of a cloak or mantle. It is worn by mourners, penitents, suppliants, and also those who, like the Hebrew prophets, led an austere life.* These **two witnesses** will be clothed in **sackcloth**.

Revelation 11:4

"These are the two olive trees, and the two candlesticks standing before the God of the earth."

They are called **olive trees**. They are called **candlesticks**, bringing light. These are **prophets** that are prophesying three and a half years. Apparently, the first three-and-a-half years they will prophesy. Then in the middle of that week, when the antichrist will begin to kill the Jews and others that will be here, they will speak and it will be their end.

- **Zechariah 4:8-14**
  "Moreover the word of the LORD came unto me, saying, The hands of Zerubbabel have laid the foundation of this house; his hands shall also finish it; and thou shalt know that the LORD of hosts hath sent me unto you. For who hath despised the day of small things? for they shall rejoice, and shall see the plummet in the hand of Zerubbabel *with* those seven; they *are* the eyes of the LORD, which run to and fro through the whole earth. Then answered I, and said unto him, What *are* these two **olive trees** upon the right *side* of the candlestick and upon the left *side* thereof? And I answered again, and said unto him, What *be these* two **olive** branches which through the two golden pipes empty the golden *oil* out of themselves? And he answered me and said, Knowest thou not what these *be*? And I said, No, my lord. Then said he, These *are* the **two anointed ones**, that stand by the Lord of the whole earth."

Olive trees are mentioned here also. It is similar to this. <u>This is referring to the temple after the seventy years of Babylonian captivity.</u>

- **Zechariah 4:10**
  "For who hath despised the day of small things? for they shall rejoice, and shall see the plummet in the hand of Zerubbabel with those seven; they are the eyes of the LORD, which run to and fro through the whole earth."

I like verse 10 for it applies to our church. We do not despise *"small things."* If the Lord is in it, it is wonderful. I am glad that our services are going out all around the world by the Internet. This is not a *"small thing."*

In the Old Testament, the **olive trees** are there. **Olive trees** are now in the book of Revelation. Haggai, Zechariah, and Malachi were what we call post-exilic prophets. They prophesied after the exile from Babylon. They came back to Jerusalem. I believe this is a picture of these **two witnesses**. The same are called **olive trees** by the **candlestick** and they are the **anointed ones** that will stand by the Lord of the whole earth.

I looked up what **olives** are, their origin and so on. They are native to the Mediterranean region, tropical and central Asia, and various parts of Africa. They require a long, hot growing season to properly ripen the fruit. (These **witnesses**, I am sure, were ripened and ready to go.) The blossoms require a sufficient winter-chill to ensure the fruit is set. Home grown **olives** generally bring forth fruit satisfactorily in the warmer coastal valleys of California.

Virtually all U.S. commercial **olive** production is concentrated in California's central valley, with a small pocket of **olive** acreage outside Phoenix.

Olive Trees Described

The olive is an evergreen tree growing to fifty feet in height with a spread of about thirty feet. The tree can be kept to about twenty feet with regular pruning. The life expectancy of the olive tree is up to 500 or even 1,000 years. That is an old tree, is it not? (These witnesses did not last that long, as we will see in the next verse.) Commercial olive production is a multi-million dollar business in California, the Mediterranean, and in other places. These witnesses are like olive trees. They are seasoned. They are pruned. They are able to withstand things.

Revelation 11:5

"And if any man will hurt them, fire proceedeth out of their mouth, and devoureth their enemies: and if any man will hurt them, he must in this manner be killed."

The Two Witnesses' First Miracle

Here is the first miracle of these men. They will be able to proceed with fire when people try to hurt these witnesses, these men, these prophets. That is most certainly what Elijah did.

- **2 Kings 1:10**
  "And Elijah answered and said to the captain of fifty, If I *be* a man of God, then let **fire** come down from Heaven, and consume thee and thy fifty. And there came down **fire** from Heaven, and consumed him and his fifty."

He was able to bring down **fire**.

- **2 Kings 1:12**
  "And Elijah answered and said unto them, If I *be* a man of God, let **fire** come down from Heaven, and consume thee and thy fifty. And the **fire** of God came down from Heaven, and consumed him and his fifty."

The same is true. The fifty that came to take him, fire came down and consumed them.

- **Luke 9:54**
  "And when his disciples James and John saw *this*, they said, Lord, wilt thou that we command **fire** to come down from Heaven, and consume them, even as Elias did?"

The disciples, James and John, remembered Elijah's miracle.

Notice *if any man will*. That is not simply future. This is a verb that means *wills* or *desires* to hurt them. They have a fervent desire to **hurt** them.

Fire Will Devour God's Enemies

Fire will proceed and devour their enemies. If any man has a real desire to hurt these two witnesses, then that man must in this manner be killed. Fire will come out of the mouths of these witnesses, which I believe are Moses and Elijah. God does not tell us who they are, so we cannot be dogmatic. They are just two witnesses. God is going to raise up two witnesses that will prophesy against these people that are on the earth.

Revelation 11:6

"These have power to shut Heaven, that it rain not in the days of their prophecy: and have power over waters to turn them to blood, and to smite the earth with all plagues, as often as they will."

That is why many have called these men Moses and Elijah.

- **1 Kings 17:1**
  "And Elijah the Tishbite, *who was* of the inhabitants of Gilead, said unto Ahab, *As* the LORD God of Israel liveth, before whom I stand, there shall not be dew nor rain these years, but according to my word."

Elijah the prophet commanded that it would not **rain**, and it did not **rain** for three and a half years. If it is not Elijah, it is someone like Elijah that has this power to shut up the heaven that it **rain** not.

- **James 5:17**
  "Elias was a man subject to like passions as we are, and he prayed earnestly that it might not **rain**: and it **rained** not on the earth by the space of three years and six months."

Moses And Elijah's Appearances

Also, Moses and Elijah, you will remember, are the ones that appeared with the Lord Jesus Christ on the Mount of Transfiguration. The Lord Jesus Christ brought up on this mount, with him, Peter, James, and John. There appeared, on this mount, two Old Testament prophets–Moses on one hand, and Elijah on the other hand. Moses and Elijah were there on the Mount of Transfiguration. The prophetic signs are there. The miracles are there.

Then, notice, they have power over waters to turn them into blood. That was exactly what Moses was given the power to do.

- **Exodus 7:17**
  "Thus saith the LORD, In this thou shalt know that I *am* the LORD: behold, I will smite with the rod that *is* in mine hand upon the **waters** which *are* in the river, and they shall be **turned to blood.**"

Then it also says these **two witnesses** will *smite the earth with all plagues, as often as they will* to judge this earth. Of course, that is what Moses did also.

- **Exodus 9:13-14**
  "And the LORD said unto Moses, Rise up early in the morning, and stand before Pharaoh, and say unto him, Thus saith the LORD God of the Hebrews, Let my people go, that they may serve me. For I will at this time send all my **plagues** upon thine heart, and upon thy servants, and upon thy people; that thou mayest know that *there is* none like me in all the earth."

God had demanded that His people be freed to serve Him in the wilderness, and offer to Him, and to worship Him as they should. He is talking now to Pharaoh. The Lord promised to do this and He fulfilled it. The purpose of the Lord in these judgments and **plagues** in Egypt, was to turn Pharaoh's heart to the Lord. It was to deliver His people. You remember that Pharaoh said, "Let them go." The last **plague** was the death of the firstborn and the firstborn in Pharaoh's house died. Pharaoh said, "Get out of here. Flee! We do not want anything more to do with you!" The Israelites fled from Egypt and went into the wilderness, but as often is the case, Pharaoh changed his mind. He went after them with armies in order to kill and to slay them. He came to himself and said, "Who is going to build the cities? Who is going to do the work? We have lost our slaves." He went after them, but the Lord delivered the Israelites at the Red Sea. He drowned Pharaoh and his army in that sea.

Miracles During The Tribulation

Even in this time of the tribulation, the Lord Jesus Christ wants His miracle-workers—these two witnesses—to work the miracles, to have the power to turn water into blood. These are signs so that people will believe them. I am sure many people will believe them at that time when they do operate and they do show themselves. There will be no rain, the waters will be turned into blood, and there will be plagues upon the land all over the world. All over the earth there will be plagues and this will be one of them.

Revelation 11:7

"And when they shall have finished their testimony, the beast that ascendeth out of the bottomless pit shall make war against them, and shall overcome them, and kill them."

Their ministry is not like the **olive trees**, as we said, for five hundred years or more, but it was short-lived. Three and a half years is like the ministry of the Lord Jesus Christ upon the earth. It was roughly three and a half years. This is the end, at least the **beast** thinks it is. It is not the end of these two witnesses, but the **beast** will think he can get rid of them. It is just like they thought they got rid of the Lord Jesus Christ. They crucified Him, but He rose again. These prophets did also rise again.

Notice the phrase in this verse, *"And when they shall have finished their testimony."*

Do You Have A Testimony?

Do you have a testimony? That is the first question. Do I have a testimony? Are we genuinely saved? Do we know the Lord Jesus Christ as our Saviour and Redeemer? If so, we should have a testimony for the Lord Jesus Christ. We should shine as lights in the world for our Saviour.

These two had a **testimony**. They **testified** for the Saviour, I am sure, and won many to the Lord Jesus Christ. Remember, the 144,000 were there. They were soul-winners and evangelists all over the world. I believe that, as others have said, our life is here until the work that we have for the Lord Jesus Christ is finished. I believe some are cut off in the early part of their lives. Others live longer, but the ministry and the things that God has put us here to do, I believe He will keep us until our ministry and testimony has been finished.

- **Psalm 23:4**
  "Yea, though I walk through the valley of the shadow of **death**, I will fear no evil: for thou *art* with me; thy rod and thy staff they comfort me."

We must remember if we are genuinely saved (if we are born-again and have genuinely trusted the Lord Jesus Christ as Saviour, and we have accepted Him and His eternal life) God's rod and His staff comfort us even in the valley of the shadow of **death**.

- **John 4:34**
"Jesus saith unto them, My meat is to do the will of him that sent me, and to **finish** his work."

Doing The Will Of His Father

That was what He was here for, to do the will of the Father. These two witnesses finish their testimony. The Lord Jesus Christ finished His work. You may say, "How can anybody finish work in three and a half years?" That was what the Father wanted Him to do: finish His work, go to the cross of Calvary, take the sins of the world upon Himself, suffer, bleed, and die for the whole world. That was His testimony, finished. How can these men in three and a half years finish their testimony? In the same way. This is what God had for them.

- **John 19:30**
"When Jesus therefore had received the vinegar, he said, It is **finished**: and he bowed his head, and gave up the ghost."

This was at Calvary. What was **finished**? The work that the Lord Jesus Christ was given to do.

- **1 Peter 2:24**
"Who his own self bare our sins in his own body on the tree, that we, being dead to sins, should live unto righteousness: by whose stripes ye were healed."

It is **finished**. That is the **finished** work. It is not by our works that we are genuinely saved. It is not by good deeds that we are truly saved. It is not by penance, or by the Mass, or by water baptism, or by being a church member. We are saved by genuine faith in the Lord Jesus Christ. That is the work that was **finished**. He paid the price and now, as the hymn writer has said, "Jesus paid it all. All to Him I owe."

- **Acts 20:24**
"But none of these things move me, neither count I my life dear unto myself, so that I might **finish** my course with joy, and the ministry, which I have received of the Lord Jesus Christ, to testify the gospel of the grace of God."

Paul was warned, "Do not go to Jerusalem. They are going to kill you, Paul. Do not do that." What did Paul say? When he was talking about when he shall have **finished his testimony**, he said, "none of these things move me." He was not moved. He wanted to **finish** the course and that is what these two witnesses did also.

- **Colossians 4:17**
  "And say to Archippus, Take heed to the ministry which thou hast received in the Lord, that thou **fulfil** it."

Paul writes to the church at Colosse and he mentions Archippus. Maybe he was the pastor of the church, I do not know. Maybe he was an elder, or a deacon, or a leader. Every one of us, if we are genuinely saved, God has given us a ministry, a **testimony** that we should fulfill. We should not slack off and not do it. There is a ministry, whatever it might be.

- **2 Timothy 4:7**
  "I have fought a good fight, I have **finished** *my* course, I have kept the faith:"

This is Paul's last letter. This is what these two witnesses have when they have **finished their testimony**.

This **beast from the bottomless pit** is mentioned in Revelation 9:11.

- **Revelation 9:11**
  "And they had a king over them, *which is* the angel of the **bottomless pit**, whose name in the Hebrew tongue *is* Abaddon, but in the Greek tongue hath *his* name Apollyon."

These two witnesses were slain.

Revelation 11:8

"And their dead bodies *shall lie* in the street of the great city, which spiritually is called **Sodom** and Egypt, where also our Lord was crucified."

This **great city** is Jerusalem. That is where they are, right in the center.

- **Luke 17:26-30**
  "And as it was in the days of Noe, so shall it be also in the days of the Son of man. They did eat, they drank, they married wives, they were given in marriage, until the day that Noe entered into the ark, and the flood came, and destroyed them all. Likewise also as it was in the days of Lot; they did eat, they drank, they bought, they sold, they planted, they builded; But the same day that Lot went out of **Sodom** it rained fire and brimstone from Heaven, and destroyed *them* all. Even thus shall it be in the day when the Son of man is revealed."

Spiritually Sodom And Egypt

This is spiritually Sodom and Egypt. By the way, we have Sodom on our hands today in the United States of America. I ministered and preached for five years in Newton, Massachusetts as pastor of Faith Baptist Church. When that state, that used to be my state, can recognize marriages of homosexuals, sodomites, and lesbians, we are fast approaching the city of Sodom in the United States of America. That will be catching as well.

- **Hebrews 11:27**
  "By faith he forsook Egypt, not fearing the wrath of the king: for he endured, as seeing him who is invisible."

Moses forsook Egypt. The wickedness of Egypt was a terrible thing.

- **Jude 5**
  "I will therefore put you in remembrance, though ye once knew this, how that the Lord, having saved the people out of the land of Egypt, afterward destroyed them that believed not."

Egypt was a terrible cesspool. This was spiritually Egypt and **Sodom**, where **our Lord was crucified**. That is what I want to talk about a little bit. **Our Lord was crucified**.

- **Matthew 20:19**
  "And shall deliver him to the Gentiles to mock, and to scourge, and to **crucify** *him*: and the third day he shall rise again."

The Lord Jesus Christ predicted His **crucifixion**.

- **Matthew 27:31**
  "And after that they had mocked him, they took the robe off from him, and put his own raiment on him, and led him away to **crucify** *him*."

- **Mark 15:27**
  "And with him they **crucify** two thieves; the one on his right hand, and the other on his left."

They did **crucify** our Lord Jesus Christ. The question I want to ask is, "Why was He **crucified**?" We have a few verses that tell us why.

- **Romans 5:6**
  "For when we were yet without strength, in due time Christ **died** for the ungodly."

Are you ungodly? He died for the ungodly, all the ungodly of the world. I know we part company with some who teach that He only **died** for the ungodly who are the elect ungodly. No, Scriptures do not say ungodly elect, it says the ungodly, all, the whole world.

- **Romans 5:8**
  "But God commendeth his love toward us, in that, while we were yet sinners, Christ **died** for us."

Paul Writes To The Gentiles

Paul is writing to the Gentiles. He is not writing to the elect or just to the Jews or some other group. He is not writing just to the whites, or just to the blacks, just to the big, or just to the little, just to the rich, or just to the poor, just to the men or women, or just to the boys or girls. He writes to all. While all of us were yet sinners, the Lord Jesus Christ died for us, in our place, in our stead, as sinners. This is the gospel.

I am very sorry that our station that is here and all over the world has a different gospel. I am talking about WKDN, the Family Radio stations. There is a tremendous outreach and tremendous potential. They have very good music, many times excellent music, but the gospel is not there. The gospel preached by the pastors and ministers of that station, and by the false prophet Harold Camping himself, the president of that station, is that the Lord Jesus Christ only loved the elect. He did not love the sinners. Camping has a tract saying, "Does God Love You?" and sends it in various languages around the world. That tract teaches that God's love is only for the elect. No, God loves the whole world.

- **John 3:16**
  "For God so loved the world, that he gave his only begotten Son, that whosoever believeth in him should not perish, but have everlasting life."

To say, "We have a wonderful outreach at Family Radio, give to this gospel ministry," that is not the gospel. It is another gospel. The Lord Jesus Christ **died** for all of us, all sinners all over the world.

- **Romans 8:32**
  "He that spared not his own Son, but delivered him up for us all, how shall he not with him also freely give us all things?"

- **1 Corinthians 5:7**
  "Purge out therefore the old leaven, that ye may be a new lump, as ye are unleavened. For even Christ our passover is **sacrificed** for us:"

Paul speaks to the Corinthian church, which was filled with unbelief and sin. They had incest that a man should have his own father's wife and they were glorying in this. This is wickedness.

Christ Was Sacrificed For Us Sinners

The Lord Jesus Christ our passover is sacrificed for us, the genuine believers. Praise God for that. By the way, those two words *for us* are gone from the false text of Westcott and Hort. The critical text in the Greek language takes out *for us*. It is just sacrificed. They do not know who it is for. The NIV takes them out. The New American Standard takes them out. The new modern versions take away *for us*. They do not believe that He was sacrificed for anybody in particular, but it was for us, those of us who were lost.

- 1 Corinthians 15:3
    "For I delivered unto you first of all that which I also received, how that Christ **died** for our sins according to the scriptures;"

This is the gospel that he mentions. That was why the Lord Jesus Christ was **crucified**, for our sins. Because we are sinners, He had to **die** in our place. He was our substitute. Those that refuse genuinely to take Him as their substitute, will die for their own sins. They will be sent to Hell for all eternity in the lake of fire. It is a terrible thing. Why not accept and trust the Substitute for our sins?

- 2 Corinthians 5:14-15
    "For the love of Christ constraineth us; because we thus judge, that if one **died** for all, then were all dead: And *that* he **died** for all, that they which live should not henceforth live unto themselves, but unto him which died for them, and rose again."

Paul says, "the love of Christ constraineth us." It moves us along and compels us to serve. Why did He **die**? Not just to save us from Hell and give us Heaven, but that we should not any longer live to ourselves but unto Him who **died** for us and rose again. This is the motivation for living godly lives.

- 2 Corinthians 5:21
    "For he hath made him *to be* sin for us, who knew no sin; that we might be made the righteousness of God in him."

Christ Was Made Sin For All People

God the Father made God the Son to be sin for us, like a sin offering. He was sinless, otherwise He could not pay for our sins. He was sinless without any sin of His own. That is why He died, that we might be made the righteousness of God and have absolute righteousness in our standing before God.

- **Ephesians 5:2**
  "And walk in love, as Christ also hath loved us, and hath given himself for us an offering and a sacrifice to God for a sweetsmelling savour."

He has given Himself for us. That is why He **died** at Calvary.

- **1 Thessalonians 5:10**
  "Who died for us, that, whether we wake or sleep, we should live together with him."

- **Titus 2:14**
  "Who gave himself for us, that he might redeem us from all iniquity, and purify unto himself a peculiar people, zealous of good works."

This talks about the Lord Jesus Christ. There is nothing more clear. He did not just **die** to get us into Heaven, but to redeem us from sin in our lives, in our hearts, in our minds, in our words, in our actions.

If professing Christians are living for the Devil, one would wonder whether or not they are genuinely saved. God did not call anybody to salvation to live for Satan, to live for the world, to live for self, and to live for the flesh. He called us to be a peculiar people, zealous of good works.

- **1 Peter 2:21**
  "For even hereunto were ye called: because Christ also **suffered** for us, leaving us an example, that ye should follow his steps:"

The Lord Jesus Christ suffered for us, not for His own sins but for us.

- **1 Peter 4:1**
  "Forasmuch then as Christ hath **suffered** for us in the flesh, arm yourselves likewise with the same mind: for he that hath suffered in the flesh hath ceased from sin;"

- **1 John 3:16**
  "Hereby perceive we the love *of God*, because he laid down his life for us: and we ought to lay down *our* lives for the brethren."

The Lord Jesus Christ laid down His life for us. Nobody took it from Him. He laid it down as a **sacrifice**, a willing offering for sinners. The gospel songwriter has asked the question, *"Why?"* It was written by John M. Moore.

Why?

Why did they nail him to Calvary's tree;
Why, tell me why was he there?
Jesus the helper, the healer, the friend,
Why, tell me why was he there?

All my iniquities on him were laid;
He nailed them all to the tree.
Jesus, the debt of my sin fully paid,
He paid the ransom for me.

That is why our Lord Jesus Christ was **crucified**. As Revelation 11:8 says, the **dead bodies** of these two witnesses were lying in the **street of that great city**, certainly Jerusalem, which is called **spiritually Sodom and Egypt**, where also our Lord Jesus Christ was **crucified**.

John was a witness not only of the trial of our Lord Jesus Christ, but also of the crucifixion. Where were the rest of the disciples? Not a one but John was there. Peter had fled and denied Him. All the other apostles were gone. They forsook Him. John was there. The Lord Jesus Christ spoke to him at the cross and said, "Behold thy mother." Take Mary and look after her. There he was. In the midst of writing about these two witnesses being terribly killed by this antichrist, he remembers the place where our Lord Jesus Christ was **crucified**. You and I had better know why He was **crucified**. It was for our sins.

Revelation 11:9

"And they of the people and kindreds and tongues and nations shall see their dead bodies three days and an half, and shall not suffer their dead bodies to be put in graves."

All Will See The Dead Bodies

All the people all over the world shall see these two witnesses. You might say, "How can that be?" Back one hundred years ago, two hundred years ago, three hundred years ago, people might have said, "Well, we have to spiritualize this. It is impossible that the people of kindreds, and tongues, and nations shall be able to see their dead bodies all over the world." Nobody today doubts the potential of that. With our present all-purpose stations like FOX, CNN, MSNBC, CNBC, and other Internet facilities all the way around the world, we can see everything that happens. Their cameras are there and this will be the case in the future. The dead bodies will not be in graves, but they will be left out on the street for all the people of the world to see.

Revelation 11:10

"And they that dwell upon the earth shall rejoice over them, and make merry, and shall send gifts one to another; because these two prophets tormented them that dwelt on the earth."

These that are on the **earth** will be "happy as a lark," as it were. They will be happy and **rejoicing** just like they were during the calamity of Calvary.

- **Mark 15:6-14**
  "Now at *that* feast he released unto them one prisoner, whomsoever they desired. And there was *one* named Barabbas, *which lay* bound with them that had made insurrection with him, who had committed murder in the insurrection. And the multitude crying aloud began to desire *him to do* as he had ever done unto them. But Pilate answered them, saying, Will ye that I release unto you the King of the Jews? For he knew that the chief priests had delivered him for envy. But the chief priests moved the people, that he should rather release Barabbas unto them. And Pilate answered and said again unto them, What will ye then that I shall do *unto him* whom ye call the King of the Jews? And they cried out again, Crucify him. Then Pilate said unto them, Why, what evil hath he done? And they cried out the more exceedingly, Crucify him."

Pilate always released somebody at the feast of the passover. Pilate, I am sure, thought the Jews would release the Lord Jesus Christ, but the chief priests, filled with envy, moved the people that he should rather release Barabbas, this murderer. The **glee**, the **happiness**, and the **joy** you could just feel. They were absolutely out of their minds with **joy** and **gladness** to crucify the Lord of glory. The same is true here in Revelation 11:10. They will **rejoice** over these two **prophets** that are dead.

- **1 Kings 22:7**
  "And Jehoshaphat said, *Is there* not here a **prophet** of the LORD besides, that we might enquire of him? And the king of Israel said unto Jehoshaphat, *There is* yet one man, Micaiah the son of Imlah, by whom we may enquire of the LORD: but I hate him; for he doth not prophesy good concerning me, but evil. And Jehoshaphat said, Let not the king say so."

Jehoshaphat was there with Ahab. He should not have been there, but they were going to go to a battle. Ahab consulted with the **prophets** of

Baal. Jehoshaphat wanted to enquire of the Lord.

- **1 Kings 22:26-27**
  "And the king of Israel said, Take Micaiah, and carry him back unto Amon the governor of the city, and to Joash the king's son; And say, Thus saith the king, Put this *fellow* in the prison, and feed him with bread of affliction and with water of affliction, until I come in peace."

Micaiah's Good Prophecy

Micaiah gave a good prophecy. He had told the truth. These two prophets tormented them that dwell on the earth. Micaiah tormented Ahab.

- **1 Kings 22:28**
  "And Micaiah said, If thou return at all in peace, the LORD hath not spoken by me. And he said, Hearken, O people, every one of you."

- **Jeremiah 37:14-16**
  "Then said Jeremiah, *It is* false; I fall not away to the Chaldeans. But he hearkened not to him: so Irijah took Jeremiah, and brought him to the princes. Wherefore the princes were wroth with Jeremiah, and smote him, and put him in prison in the house of Jonathan the scribe: for they had made that the prison. When Jeremiah was entered into the dungeon, and into the cabins, and Jeremiah had remained there many days;"

Jeremiah Was A True Prophet

Jeremiah did not fall away to the Chaldeans. What do they do to true prophets? They put them in dungeons. They put them in prison. They stone them. They crucify them.

These were **making merry** and **giving gifts**. Some people, I guess, can **rejoice** over calamity. I do not think we should do that over any calamity, no matter what it is.

- **Proverbs 24:17**
  "**Rejoice not** when thine enemy falleth, and let not thine heart be glad when he stumbleth:"

Do not **rejoice**. These people were out of place to **rejoice** because the **two witnesses** that had **tormented** them were dead.

Tormented By Truth

What torments us? Truth torments us, I am sure. The truth about ourselves, the truth that is in the Scriptures. The truth torments unsaved people all over the world. The truth that we are lost, the truth that we are sinners, that truth that we have come short of the glory of God, that is a tormenting thing. What people want to do with that tormenting thing, if it is on the radio, is turn it off. If it is on television, turn it off. If it is in the pulpits, leave the church. There are certain things by which people are tormented–by truth and by words.

These **two prophets** had done nothing amiss any more than the Lord Jesus Christ had done anything amiss. He was perfect. He was godly. He healed the blind. He raised the dead. He fed the multitudes. He showed the way of life.

- **John 14:6**
  "Jesus saith unto him, I am the way, the truth, and the life: no man cometh unto the Father, but by me."

He had spoken good words, but He did say the things that **tormented** the Pharisees who were **hypocrites**.

- **Matthew 23:27**
  "Woe unto you, scribes and Pharisees, **hypocrites**! for ye are like unto whited sepulchres, which indeed appear beautiful outward, but are within full of dead *men's* bones, and of all uncleanness."

The Lord Jesus Christ spoke very strongly to the Pharisees.

- **John 8:44**
  "Ye are of *your* **father** the devil, and the lusts of your father ye will do. He was a murderer from the beginning, and abode not in the truth, because there is no truth in him. When he speaketh a lie, he speaketh of his own: for he is a liar, and the **father** of it."

How would you like to hear that? They were of their **father** the Devil.

There Are Two Fatherhoods

There are two fatherhoods in this world. You either have God as your Father by genuine faith in the Lord Jesus Christ, or the Devil is your father. You were born under the Devil's fatherhood and you are born-again to genuine faith in the Lord Jesus Christ and God becomes your Father.

The Pharisees despised Him from that day. They were looking for witnesses to put Him to **death**.

The Lord will raise up these **two witnesses** in the middle of the tribulation period. They will **torment** them that dwell upon the earth. It is an interesting word, the word **torment**. It is BASANIZO, which means, *to test metals by the touchstone, which is a black siliceous stone used to test the purity of gold or silver by the color of the streak produced on it by rubbing it with either metal. It means, to vex with grievous pains of body or mind; to be **harassed**; to be distressed.* Certainly, these prophets, these two witnesses, distressed and **harassed** them that dwelt on the earth, so they were **rejoicing** over their death.

As we think of these verses, and as we think of the **olive trees**, and as we think of the new **temple** that will be built in the millennial reign of the Lord Jesus Christ in Jerusalem. Let us remember, Jerusalem is the place where our Lord Jesus Christ was **crucified**. It is the very city where the **temple** will be built. It is outside that city where our Lord Jesus Christ was **crucified** on the cross of Calvary. In fact, that was near the place where Abraham offered Isaac on Mount Moriah. That is the place of ruins of the **temple** even today. It is the place where the Lord Jesus Christ was offered. It was on Mount Moriah, and Mount Zion in the city of Jerusalem.

Make Our Testimony Faithful

Remember why our Lord Jesus Christ was crucified: for you, for me, for the sins of the entire world—not just the "elect." We have to take that message to all. We have to finish our testimony.

First, we have to have a testimony and we have to be willing to finish it, come what may. No matter how many people say, "Do not tell me these things," we are to be faithful to the Lord Jesus Christ rather than to people.

Revelation 11:11

"And after three days and an half the Spirit of life from God entered into them, and they stood upon their feet; and great fear fell upon them which saw them."

The Two Witnesses Were Slain

These two witnesses that were slain by the beast, were there at Jerusalem for three and a half days. No one will bury their bodies. Here in this verse we see that, after three and a half days, the Spirit of life from God entered into them, and they stood up. Notice that great fear fell upon them which saw them. They are raised from the dead. There are others that have been revived, for instance in the Old Testament. If these two witnesses are Moses and Elijah, or Enoch and Elijah, or whoever they may be, the Bible does not tell us.

- **2 Kings 4:32-35**
  "And when Elisha was come into the house, behold, the child was dead, *and* laid upon his bed. He went in therefore, and shut the door upon them twain, and prayed unto the LORD. And he went up, and lay upon the child, and put his mouth upon his mouth, and his eyes upon his eyes, and his hands upon his hands: and he stretched himself upon the child; and the flesh of the child waxed warm. Then he returned, and walked in the house to and fro; and went up, and stretched himself upon him: and the child sneezed seven times, and the child opened his eyes."

Elisha was one who **raised** or revived someone who had died. This was a miraculous revival of life.

- **2 Kings 13:20-21**
  "And Elisha died, and they buried him. And the bands of the Moabites invaded the land at the coming in of the year. And it came to pass, as they were burying a man, that, behold, they spied a band *of men*; and they cast the man into the sepulchre of Elisha: and when the man was let down, and touched the bones of Elisha, he revived, and **stood up** on his feet."

Elisha was the one that was in charge after Elijah left. He was to be given the Spirit of God.

- **2 Kings 2:9**
"And it came to pass, when they were gone over, that Elijah said unto Elisha, Ask what I shall do for thee, before I be taken away from thee. And Elisha said, I pray thee, let a double portion of thy spirit be upon me. And he said, Thou hast asked a hard thing: *nevertheless*, if thou see me *when I am* taken from thee, it shall be so unto thee; but if not, it shall not be *so*."

Elisha saw Elijah when he went to Heaven. Elijah's miracles were seven. Elisha's miracles were fourteen, double the miracles of Elijah. This was the final miracle as someone was being buried and revived as he touched the bones of Elisha the prophet.

Christ Raised Three People

In the New Testament, the Lord Jesus Christ raised three people from the dead. Three people were raised and revived after they had died: a young girl, an older boy, and an older man.

- **Mark 5:35-42**
"While he yet spake, there came from the ruler of the synagogue's *house certain* which said, Thy daughter is dead: why troublest thou the Master any further? As soon as Jesus heard the word that was spoken, he saith unto the ruler of the synagogue, Be not afraid, only believe. And he suffered no man to follow him, save Peter, and James, and John the brother of James. And he cometh to the house of the ruler of the synagogue, and seeth the tumult, and them that wept and wailed greatly. And when he was come in, he saith unto them, Why make ye this ado, and weep? the damsel is not dead, but sleepeth. And they laughed him to scorn. But when he had put them all out, he taketh the father and the mother of the damsel, and them that were with him, and entereth in where the damsel was lying. And he took the damsel by the hand, and said unto her, Talitha cumi; which is, being interpreted, Damsel, I say unto thee, **arise**. And straightway the damsel **arose**, and walked; for she was *of the age of* twelve years. And they were astonished with a great astonishment."

This ruler was called Jairus. Jairus' daughter was dead. The ruler probably was lost. I trust that before the Lord Jesus Christ left him, he was genuinely saved. We do not know, but the Lord Jesus Christ said, "Be not afraid." He must tell us that at times of trouble, sorrow, and heartache.

Peter, James, and John were the three disciples most often mentioned together. They were with the Lord Jesus Christ on the mount of transfiguration, and they were here at this miracle of the **raising** of Jairus' daughter from the dead.

These people thought the Lord Jesus Christ was crazy or a fool of some kind. Every time somebody was **raised** from the dead, there was astonishment. There were many other emotions involved with this.

Happy The Witnesses Were Dead

When the two witnesses were dead, the people that slew them were happy. They were glad because these prophets had tormented them because of their preaching.

A second time the Lord Jesus Christ **raised up** an older boy. He was the son of the widow of Nain.

* **Luke 7:11-16**
  "And it came to pass the day after, that he went into a city called Nain; and many of his disciples went with him, and much people. Now when he came nigh to the gate of the city, behold, there was a dead man carried out, the only son of his mother, and she was a widow: and much people of the city was with her. And when the Lord saw her, he had compassion on her, and said unto her, Weep not. And he came and touched the bier: and they that bare *him* stood still. And he said, Young man, I say unto thee, **Arise**. And he that was dead sat up, and began to speak. And he delivered him to his mother. And there came a fear on all: and they glorified God, saying, That a great prophet is risen up among us; and, That God hath visited his people."

There was no father, just the mother. The Lord Jesus Christ has compassion on all those that are in affliction, those that are in difficulty, those that are sick. He is a great God of compassion, the Lord Jesus Christ. It is interesting that there is this emotion of fear. There is wonderment. There is amazement. Here there is fear; "What is this?"

There is a third man the Lord Jesus Christ **raised**. He was an older man named Lazarus.

* **John 11:14**
  "Then said Jesus unto them plainly, Lazarus is dead."
* **John 11:43-44**
  "And when he thus had spoken, he cried with a loud voice, Lazarus, come forth. And he that was dead **came forth**, bound

hand and foot with graveclothes: and his face was bound about with a napkin. Jesus saith unto them, Loose him, and let him go."

Many have said that if He had not named, *"Lazarus, come forth,"* the entire cemetery would have come forth. The power of the Lord Jesus Christ to **raise** the dead was there.

They wrapped the bodies up with graveclothes. They did not embalm them. They just laid them in the grave as soon after death as possible.

- **John 11:45**
  "Then many of the Jews which came to Mary, and had seen the things which Jesus did, believed on him."

This was the purpose of all the Lord Jesus Christ's miracles, that they would genuinely trust Him, accept the Lord Jesus Christ as Saviour and Redeemer, and realize that they should follow after Him in service.

Great Fear Fell Upon The People

In Revelation 11:11, God raised up these two witnesses after three-and-a-half days lying in the street where all could see them. By means of the television, the Internet, and everything else, this will be possible. *Great fear fell upon them which saw them.* That expression, *great fear*, is only used six times in the Scriptures.

- **Luke 8:37**
  "Then the whole multitude of the country of the Gadarenes round about besought him to depart from them; for they were taken with **great fear**: and he went up into the ship, and returned back again."

The Lord Jesus Christ had commanded the devils to go out of that man and enter into the swine. The swine with these devils in them fell headlong into the water and drowned. The people of that country were swine keepers. That was an unclean animal to the Jews. The Lord Jesus Christ had healed this poor demon-possessed man, but they did not care. "Get out of our place!" they said. God the Son is a powerful Saviour that could drive these devils out of the man into the swine.

- **Acts 5:5**
  "And Ananias hearing these words fell down, and gave up the ghost: and **great fear** came on all them that heard these things."

Ananias lied to the apostles. **Great fear** came on them all because he was slain by the Lord for lying to the Holy Spirit.

- **Acts 5:10-11**
  "Then fell she down straightway at his feet, and yielded up the ghost: and the young men came in, and found her dead, and, carrying *her* forth, buried *her* by her husband. And **great fear** came upon all the church, and upon as many as heard these things."

Ananias' wife came in and she died. **Great fear** came upon all the church because of these things.

Revelation 11:12

"And they heard a great voice from Heaven saying unto them, Come up hither. And they ascended up to Heaven in a cloud; and their enemies beheld them."

Witnesses Taken Bodily To Heaven

These two witnesses were called bodily up to Heaven. It is an interesting thing. This is approximately three and a half years in the middle of the seven-year period of the tribulation. From this *Come up hither,* some have taken this to teach a mid-tribulation rapture of the church. We take the pre-tribulation rapture of the true church in Revelation 4:1.

- **Revelation 4:1**
  "After this I looked, and, behold, a door *was* opened in Heaven: and the first **voice** which I heard *was* as it were of a trumpet talking with me; which said, Come up hither, and I will shew thee things which must be hereafter."

This verse (4:1) is the picture of when the Lord Jesus Christ will summon the true church (both living and dead in the Lord Jesus Christ) to come up to Heaven in their glorified bodies. Revelation 11:12 is in the middle of the tribulation. It is not a mid-tribulation rapture, but He did take these two witnesses up to Heaven.

This **great voice** in Revelation 11:12, I believe, is the same **voice** as in Revelation 1:10, the **voice** of the Lord Jesus Christ.

- **Revelation 1:10**
  "I was in the Spirit on the Lord's day, and heard behind me a **great voice**, as of a trumpet, Saying, I am Alpha and Omega, the first and the last: and, What thou seest, write in a book, and send *it* unto the seven churches which are in Asia; unto Ephesus, and unto Smyrna, and unto Pergamos, and unto Thyatira, and unto Sardis, and unto Philadelphia, and unto Laodicea."

That was the Lord Jesus Christ. This **voice** was none other than the Saviour.

- **1 Corinthians 15:52**
  "In a moment, in the twinkling of an eye, at the last trump: for the trumpet shall sound, and the dead shall be raised incorruptible, and we shall be changed."
- **1 Thessalonians 4:16**
  "For the Lord himself shall descend from Heaven with a **shout**, with the voice of the archangel, and with the trump of God: and the dead in Christ shall rise first:"

Taking The Saved To Heaven

That is when, I believe, He will take the genuinely saved ones up to Heaven before any part of the tribulation ever comes. There are at least five different ones that have gone to Heaven as well as these two witnesses.

- **Genesis 5:24**
  "And Enoch walked with God: and he *was* not; for God took him."
- **2 Kings 2:11**
  "And it came to pass, as they still went on, and talked, that, behold, *there appeared* a chariot of fire, and horses of fire, and parted them both asunder; and Elijah went up by a whirlwind **into Heaven**."

Enoch went up. Elijah went up. These two witnesses went up. Also I believe Paul went up **to Heaven**.

- **2 Corinthians 12:2**
  "I knew a man in Christ above fourteen years ago, (whether in the body, I cannot tell; or whether out of the body, I cannot tell: God knoweth;) such an one **caught** up to the third **Heaven**."

Here Paul talks about himself. Fourteen years ago, goes to Acts 14, when Paul was stoned at Lystra.

- **Acts 14:19-20**
  "And there came thither *certain* Jews from Antioch and Iconium, who persuaded the people, and, having stoned Paul, drew *him* out of the city, supposing he had been dead. Howbeit, as the disciples stood round about him, he rose up, and came into the city: and the next day he departed with Barnabas to Derbe."

I believe he was dead. He was **caught up to Heaven.**

The Lord Jesus Christ Himself is the fourth one that was taken up to **Heaven.**

- **Mark 16:19**
  "So then after the Lord had spoken unto them, he was received up into **Heaven**, and sat on the right hand of God."

Christ At The Right Hand Of God

This is the only gospel that has the Lord Jesus Christ sitting at the right hand of God. If you take out Mark 16:9-20, which the Westcott and Hort text takes out, the NIV removes and questions, the New American Standard Version questions, the Revised Standard Version, and the new versions, you do not have any other gospel that talks about the Lord Jesus Christ being at the right hand of God.

- **Acts 1:9**
  "And when he had spoken these things, while they beheld, he was **taken up**; and a cloud received him out of their sight."

Notice in Revelation 11:12, they ascended **up to Heaven** in a cloud.

Then there is the fifth group, the genuinely saved ones. If we are truly saved and born-again, we will be **taken up** one day.

- **1 Thessalonians 4:16-17**
  "For the Lord himself shall descend from Heaven with a **shout**, with the voice of the archangel, and with the trump of God: and the dead in Christ shall rise first: Then we which are alive *and* remain shall be caught up together with them in the clouds, to meet the Lord in the air: and so shall we ever be with the Lord."

Caught Up To Heaven

All these different ones have been caught up to Heaven, not only these two witnesses, but Enoch, Elijah, the Lord Jesus Christ, and the apostle Paul. We who are genuinely saved, one day will be caught up to Heaven as well. This is no great thing, because God is able. He who flung the stars into space, and made the world, and the universe, is able to take us to Heaven, and to transform us as He did here on earth when we were born-again.

Revelation 11:13

"And the same hour was there a great earthquake, and the tenth part of the city fell, and in the earthquake were slain of men seven thousand: and the remnant were affrighted, and gave glory to the God of Heaven."

I heard on KYW about the **earthquakes** and storms in a certain part of our country. The announcer said that it was an **earthquake** and a storm of **"Biblical proportion."** It talks about **earthquakes** in Scripture, you see. It is interesting, the reference to the Bible by a secular newscaster on KYW.

A Tenth Part Of Jerusalem

Notice a tenth part of the city, the city of Jerusalem fell. I wonder which part. Was it the part where the Jews are, or the part where the Arabs are? Absolutely all the buildings collapsed. Seven thousand were slain in that earthquake.

Notice that **the remnant were affrighted.** Remember in all these miracles people were **affrighted** with great fear and so on. Notice also what they did: <u>they gave glory to the God of Heaven.</u> That is the proper result of God's judgments–to bring glory to the God of Heaven, not to be against Him.

<u>Thirteen different times there are **earthquakes**. It is the power of God.</u>

- **Isaiah 29:6**
  "Thou shalt be visited of the LORD of hosts with thunder, and with **earthquake**, and great noise, with storm and tempest, and the flame of devouring fire."

This is talking about the **city** of David. One day this will take place. Of course, I believe it is taking place in the book of Revelation in the last days.

- **Matthew 28:2**
  "And, behold, there was a **great earthquake**: for the angel of the Lord descended from Heaven, and came and rolled back the stone from the door, and sat upon it."

Earthquake At Christ's Resurrection

This earthquake was at the resurrection of the Lord Jesus Christ our Saviour.

- **Acts 16:26**
"And suddenly there was a **great earthquake**, so that the foundations of the prison were shaken: and immediately all the doors were opened, and every one's bands were loosed."

This is when Paul and Silas were released from the prison in Philippi.

- **Revelation 6:12**
"And I beheld when he had opened the sixth seal, and, lo, there was a **great earthquake**; and the sun became black as sackcloth of hair, and the moon became as blood;"

- **Revelation 16:17-18**
"And the seventh angel poured out his vial into the air; and there came a great voice out of the temple of Heaven, from the throne, saying, It is done. And there were voices, and thunders, and lightnings; and there was a **great earthquake**, such as was not since men were upon the earth, so mighty an **earthquake**, *and* so great."

This is the seventh vial. We will see that a little bit later in Revelation 16. I do not know the seismology of it. There is a Richter Scale that goes up from zero to ten. This must have been off the scale, a **great earthquake** such as was never on earth.

Giving Glory To God In Earthquakes

Notice when the earthquake and the judgment on Jerusalem will take place, those people that were still spared (not the seven thousand that were slain) were affrighted, that is they were fearing, but gave glory to the God of Heaven. What a contrast with Revelation 9:20-21 that we talked about earlier.

- **Revelation 9:20-21**
"And the rest of the men which were not killed by these **plagues** yet repented not of the works of their hands, that they should not worship devils, and idols of gold, and silver, and brass, and stone, and of wood: which neither can see, nor hear, nor walk: Neither repented they of their murders, nor of their sorceries, nor of their fornication, nor of their thefts."

They did not repent. That was not the right way to receive God's judgment. These people in Revelation 11:13 gave glory to the God of Heaven. They did repent.

What is God's purpose in judgment?

- **2 Corinthians 7:9**
  "Now I rejoice, not that ye were made sorry, but that ye sorrowed to **repentance**: for ye were made sorry after a godly manner, that ye might receive damage by us in nothing."

God wants us to sorrow, if we are sorrowing, to **repentance**. We ought to change, if something is happening, to see what God has for us.

- **2 Peter 3:9**
  "The Lord is not slack concerning his promise, as some men count slackness; but is longsuffering to us-ward, not willing that any should perish, but that all should come to **repentance**."

That is why He judges, so that we would **repent** and have a right attitude toward God's judgment.

Revelation 11:14

"The second woe is past; *and*, behold, the third woe cometh quickly."

There are **three woes** that are mentioned in the book of Revelation. The second one is past.

- **Revelation 8:13**
  "And I beheld, and heard an angel flying through the midst of Heaven, saying with a loud voice, **Woe, woe, woe**, to the inhabiters of the earth by reason of the other voices of the trumpet of the three angels, which are yet to sound!"

- **Revelation 9:12**
  "One woe is past; *and*, behold, there come **two woes** more hereafter."

This **first woe** was the fifth trumpet judgment where people were tormented for five months. They desired to die and they could not die. They were not able to die. They were tormented for five months.

The **second woe** was the **earthquake** with **seven thousand slain. One tenth** of Jerusalem **fell** to the ground and was destroyed.

There is one more **woe** that is coming a little later in the book of Revelation. These **woes** are serious judgments upon earth during the seven-year period of tribulation when the believers, those that are genuinely saved, will have been taken to Heaven. We will not take part in any one of these **woes**.

Revelation 11:15

"And the seventh angel sounded; and there were great voices in Heaven, saying, The kingdoms of this world are become *the kingdoms* of our Lord, and of his Christ; and he shall reign for ever and ever."

All Evil Men Will Be Gone

The seventh angel is the last angel with the last trumpet to sound. The Lord Jesus Christ is going to reign. No more Bin Ladens on the face of the earth. No more Fidel Castros. No more Kruschevs, Stalins, Lenins, Mao Tse-tungs, or any Communist rulers. No terrorists, no Al Kaeda. The kingdoms of this world are going to be the kingdoms of our Saviour, the Lord Jesus Christ, and He shall reign. That is a literal reign. There is a golden rule of Bible interpretation, which says this:

"When the PLAIN SENSE of Scripture makes COMMON SENSE, SEEK NO OTHER SENSE."

This is clear sense.

- **Luke 1:33**
  "And he shall reign over the house of Jacob for ever; and of **his kingdom** there shall be no end."

This was spoken by the angel before the Lord Jesus Christ was born.

- **Romans 15:12**
  "And again, Esaias saith, There shall be a root of Jesse, and he that shall rise to **reign** over the Gentiles; in him shall the Gentiles trust."

Paul quotes Isaiah. The nations do not want the Lord Jesus Christ to **reign** over them now, but He will reign over the Gentiles, the heathen nations at the great millennial **reign** of the Lord Jesus Christ. One day they will trust in Him.

- **1 Corinthians 15:25**
  "For he must **reign**, till he hath put all enemies under his feet."

In that millennial reign of the Lord Jesus Christ, that thousand-year **reign** of our Saviour, He will have all the enemies put under His feet. Not a one of them will rise up against Him.

- **2 Timothy 2:12**
  "If we suffer, we shall also **reign** with *him*: if we deny *him*, he also will deny us:"

The apostle John talks about believers **reigning** with the Lord Jesus Christ.

- **Revelation 5:8-10**
  "And when he had taken the book, the four beasts and four *and* twenty elders fell down before the Lamb, having every one of them harps, and golden vials full of odours, which are the prayers of saints. And they sung a new song, saying, Thou art worthy to take the book, and to open the seals thereof: for thou wast slain, and hast redeemed us to God by thy blood out of every kindred, and tongue, and people, and nation; And hast made us unto our God kings and priests: and we shall **reign** on the earth."

I have said before, the four and twenty elders, I believe, are representatives of the true church, the believers, the genuinely saved ones in Glory.

When I come to Revelation 5:9, I always chide John MacArthur for his heresy on the blood of Christ. He says that blood does not mean blood; it is just a metonym (a figure of speech) for death, and that is all it is. No! Blood is blood, death is death. In this verse, both are seen. He says that the blood of Christ does not redeem, does not cleanse, and does not in any way save, but this verse in Revelation 5:9 says, *"thou wast slain."* That is His death. Then it says, *"and hast redeemed us to God by thy blood."* Redemption is by His blood. Yes, He was slain, but we are also redeemed by His blood.

Genuine believers will **reign** with the Lord Jesus Christ when He reigns.

- **Revelation 20:6**
  "Blessed and holy *is* he that hath part in the first resurrection: on such the second death hath no power, but they shall be priests of God and of Christ, and **shall reign** with him a thousand years."

The Second Death Is Hell

The second death is the death of going to Hell. The true believers who are genuinely saved and born-again, are going to be reigning with the Saviour. These are the ones who are genuinely saved and born-again in this age.

You may say, "How can I **reign**? I do not know anything about reigning." That is where we are going to have new bodies like unto His glorious body. We will be able to know how. He will tell us what to do and we will do it. We will **reign** with Him a thousand years.

- **Revelation 22:5**
  "And there shall be no night there; and they need no candle, neither light of the sun; for the Lord God giveth them light: and they shall **reign** for ever and ever."

Genuine believers will **reign** with the Lord Jesus Christ for ever and ever.

Revelation 11:16

"And the four and twenty elders, which sat before God on their seats, fell upon their faces, and worshipped God,"

The **four and twenty elders,** I believe, are representatives of the believers–the genuinely saved ones–the true church in Heaven. Notice, at this point they **fell upon their faces.** They got out of their seats and **fell on their faces and worshipped God.** In Heaven, we who are genuine believers will also **worship** the Lord God of Heaven and earth.

The Meaning Of Worship

That word for worship, as we said earlier, is PROSKUNEO. It means *like a dog licking the master's hand*; also among the Orientals, especially the Persians, it meant *to fall upon the knees and touch the ground with the forehead in expression of profound reverence.* That is what these twenty-four elders, representing the true church, the believers, the genuinely saved ones in Heaven will do at this point, and worship our God. They will have new bodies, if they represent the true church. They will be glorified bodies and they will still be worshipping the God who saved them.

Revelation 11:17

"Saying, We give thee thanks, O Lord God Almighty, which art, and wast, and art to come; because thou hast taken to thee thy great power, and hast reigned."

This is what the twenty-four elders are saying. This is what the representation of the church, the genuinely saved ones in Heaven, are saying in Glory. The first thing that comes out of their mouth is, *"We give thee thanks, O Lord God Almighty."* They were a **thankful** people. We should be a **thankful** people as well, even here on this earth, if we are genuinely saved.

- **Philippians 4:6**
  "Be careful for nothing; but in every thing by prayer and supplication with **thanksgiving** let your requests be made known unto God."

We should be **thankful**. For what have you thanked the Lord today? For what have I **thanked** the Lord today? Think about it. We should be **thankful**.

- **Colossians 2:7**
  "Rooted and built up in him, and stablished in the faith, as ye have been taught, abounding therein with **thanksgiving**."

These saints in Glory said, *"We give thee thanks."* We should give Him **thanks**.

- **Colossians 4:2**"Continue in prayer, and watch in the same with **thanksgiving**;"

There is nothing in Scripture that precludes genuine Christians from being **thankful**. No matter the circumstance, no matter whether it is difficult or easy, we are to give **thanks** unto the Lord. We are to **thank** Him in everything. Not necessarily *for* everything but *in* everything that we have, give **thanks** to the Lord.

Notice the second thing that these twenty-four elders said: *"Which art,"* That is the present. *"And wast,"* That is the past. *"And art to come;"* That is the future.

God's Eternality

Here is God's eternality, from everlasting to everlasting. This is a very important thing about God. We come, and we go, but the Lord Jesus Christ is, and was, and ever shall be. There never was a beginning of the Lord Jesus Christ and never an ending.

- **Isaiah 57:15**
  "For thus saith the high and lofty One that inhabiteth eternity, whose name *is* Holy; I dwell in the high and holy *place*, with him also *that is* of a contrite and humble spirit, to revive the spirit of the humble, and to revive the heart of the contrite ones."

God inhabits **eternity**. He has no beginning. He has no end.

- **Psalm 90:2**
  "Before the mountains were brought forth, or ever thou hadst formed the earth and the world, even **from everlasting to everlasting**, thou *art* God."

- **Psalm 93:2**
"Thy throne *is* established of old: thou *art* from everlasting."

From Everlasting To Everlasting

God is from everlasting with no beginning, not created. That is the trouble with the Jehovah's Witnesses. They believe the Lord Jesus Christ is a created being. They believe He is a creature. That is heresy. The Jehovah's Witnesses are wrong in that area and other people are wrong in that same way. The Gnostics believe the Lord Jesus Christ is a created being as well. They are wrong.

- Isaiah 40:28
"Hast thou not known? hast thou not heard, *that* the **everlasting God**, the LORD, the Creator of the ends of the earth, fainteth not, neither is weary? *there is* no searching of his understanding."
- Micah 5:2
"But thou, Bethlehem Ephratah, *though* thou be little among the thousands of Judah, *yet* out of thee shall he come forth unto me *that is* to be ruler in Israel; whose **goings forth** *have been* from of old, **from everlasting**."

This is the prophecy of the birth of the Lord Jesus Christ at His first coming. He was to be born in Bethlehem. He is the **everlasting One**, from **everlasting**, the Lord Jesus Christ.

The NIV's 1ˢᵗ Error In Micah 5:2

The New International Version (NIV) has two gross errors in this verse. The first is, instead of *"goings forth"* it says, *"whose origins."* They have the Lord Jesus Christ having an origin. He has no origin. He is from everlasting to everlasting. One of our ladies in our Bible study class, when I asked if the Lord Jesus Christ had a beginning said, "Yes." I had to straighten that out. No, He never had a beginning. As the Son of Man, born of the virgin Mary, yes. There was a beginning of His having a perfect sinless body combined with His perfect Deity, but as to His Deity, He had no beginning.

The NIV's 2ⁿᵈ Error In Micah 5:2

There is a second error in the New International Version in Micah 5:2. The King James Bible properly says, *"whose*

> *goings forth have been from of old, from everlasting."* They
> say simply, *"from ancient days."* It is more than *"ancient
> days."* It is more than just a few years back. The Lord Jesus
> Christ was <u>from everlasting.</u>

Then also the twenty-four elders say, *"because thou hast taken
to thee thy great power, and hast reigned."* God's **great power**
is mentioned.

- **2 Kings 17:36**
  "But the LORD, who brought you up out of the land of Egypt
  with **great power** and a stretched out arm, him shall ye fear,
  and him shall ye worship, and to him shall ye do sacrifice."

God has **great power**. How could anyone else but the Lord bring six or
seven million people (six hundred thousand men plus women and
children) out of Egypt? With all the Egyptian army coming after them,
it had to be God's power.

- **Nehemiah 1:10**
  "Now these *are* thy servants and thy people, whom thou hast
  redeemed by thy **great power**, and by thy strong hand."

Nehemiah was coming back from captivity. God's redemption is by His
great power.

- **Nehemiah 1:10**
  "Great *is* our Lord, and of **great power**: his understanding *is*
  infinite."

He is **great** in His **power**.

- **Psalm 147:5**
  "Great *is* our Lord, and of **great power**: his understanding *is*
  infinite."

He is **great** in His **power**.

- **Jeremiah 27:5**
  "I have made the earth, the man and the beast that *are* upon the
  ground, by my **great power** and by my outstretched arm, and
  have given it unto whom it seemed meet unto me."

We do not have evolution. We have God's creative **power, His great
power**. He created man, animals, and the entire universe.

- **Jeremiah 32:17**
  "Ah Lord GOD! behold, thou hast made the Heaven and the
  earth by thy **great power** and stretched out arm, *and* there is
  nothing too hard for thee:"

- **Genesis 1:1**
"In the beginning God created the Heaven and the earth."
How did God do this? By His **great power** and stretched out arm.
Jeremiah, looking at His **power**, and remembering His great stretched
out arm, said also, *"there is nothing too hard for thee."*

Nothing Too Hard For The Lord

**Once you remember and believe Genesis 1:1, you will
understand what Jeremiah is saying. If you once believe that
the powerful God created the Heaven and earth, you can say
with Jeremiah, *"there is nothing too hard for thee."***

There are many things that are too hard for us. There are many
difficulties and insurmountable difficulties, but there is not a single thing
that is **too hard** for the Lord, if it is His will. He created out of nothing
(*ex nihilo*) the world, man, the beasts, the trees, the shrubs, and
everything–all of these things–out of nothing. He created all the stars in
the Heavens. There is nothing **too hard** for Him, if it is His will. He
created the Lord Jesus Christ–perfect Man and perfect God–in the
womb of the virgin Mary. It was a unique miracle. Nothing is **too hard**
for Him. In all the miracles of the Lord Jesus Christ that He performed,
there was nothing **too hard** for Him.

We have to remember that we have a powerful, omnipotent God.
These twenty-four elders in Heaven, representing the true believers, the
genuinely saved ones, recognized His **great power**.

- **Mark 13:26**
"And then shall they see the Son of man coming in the clouds
with **great power** and glory."

The Battle Of Armageddon

**When the Lord Jesus Christ returns to this earth, He will
put down at the battle of Armageddon the thousands upon
thousands of armed fighters from the north, south, east, and
west. There will be multi-millions of armies when the Lord
Jesus Christ comes to put down that terrible revolt against the
city of Jerusalem. It will be with great power, might, and glory.**

Revelation 11:18

"And the nations were angry, and thy wrath is come, and the time of the dead, that they should be judged, and that thou shouldest give reward unto thy servants the prophets, and to the saints, and them that fear thy name, small and great; and shouldest destroy them which destroy the earth."

God's Many Different Judgments

Here are the nations. When they saw all of the judgments, they were angry. They were to be judged. There are many judgments in Scripture. Sin was judged at Calvary. That was a judgment of sin. As genuine believers, if we are truly saved, we should have self-judgment of our sins. There is a judgment of angels. There is a judgment of the lost at the Great White Throne judgment seat. There is a judgment of true believers at the judgment seat of the Lord Jesus Christ. There is the judgment of nations. This is spoken of here.

By the way, some have said that these **judgments** in Revelation are not individual and consecutive–seven, seven, and seven, twenty-one judgments–but are concurrent, from the beginning of the seven years until the end. For that reason, some have believed that the trumpet judgments, from the first to the seventh, span the whole seven years and that is where, at the beginning of the millennial **reign** of the Lord Jesus Christ, this is taking place. That is why they say the Lord Jesus Christ will **reign** because it was the beginning of the millennial period. Perhaps the saints that are genuinely saved during the tribulation period will be **judged** at that time as well.

- **Matthew 25:31-40**
  "When the Son of man shall come in his glory, and all the holy angels with him, then shall he sit upon the throne of his glory: And before him shall be gathered all nations: and he shall separate them one from another, as a shepherd divideth *his* sheep from the goats: And he shall set the sheep on his right hand, but the goats on the left. Then shall the King say unto them on his right hand, Come, ye blessed of my Father, inherit the kingdom prepared for you from the foundation of the world: For I was an hungred, and ye gave me meat: I was thirsty, and ye gave me drink: I was a stranger, and ye took me in: Naked,

and ye clothed me: I was sick, and ye visited me: I was in prison, and ye came unto me. Then shall the righteous answer him, saying, Lord, when saw we thee an hungred, and fed *thee*? or thirsty, and gave *thee* drink? When saw we thee a stranger, and took *thee* in? or naked, and clothed *thee*? Or when saw we thee sick, or in prison, and came unto thee? And the King shall answer and say unto them, Verily I say unto you, Inasmuch as ye have done *it* unto one of the least of these my brethren, ye have done *it* unto me."

The Judgment Of The Nations

This gives us the time of the judgment of these nations. The Jews have been safely honoured and treated well by these nations. The judgment of the nations depends on what they have done with the Lord Jesus Christ's people, His brethren.

- **Matthew 25:41-46**
  "Then shall he say also unto them on the left hand, Depart from me, ye cursed, into everlasting fire, prepared for the devil and his angels: For I was an hungred, and ye gave me no meat: I was thirsty, and ye gave me no drink: I was a stranger, and ye took me not in: naked, and ye clothed me not: sick, and in prison, and ye visited me not. Then shall they also answer him, saying, Lord, when saw we thee an hungred, or athirst, or a stranger, or naked, or sick, or in prison, and did not minister unto thee? Then shall he answer them, saying, Verily I say unto you, Inasmuch as ye did *it* not to one of the least of these, ye did *it* not to me. And these shall go away into everlasting punishment: but the righteous into life eternal."

Hell was only prepared, not for unbelievers, but for the Devil and his angels. All those who reject the Lord Jesus Christ will have to go to Hell. Apparently, the **judgment** of the nations depends upon how they treated His brethren, the Jews. Perhaps the "brethren" might also be referring to the genuinely born-again Christians. People all over the world are killing "Christians." Muslims are slaughtering "Christians" in many of the countries they control.

Revelation 11:19

"And the temple of God was opened in Heaven, and there was seen in his temple the ark of his testament: and there were lightnings, and voices, and thunderings, and an earthquake, and great hail."

All of these things are showing the glory of God in His **temple**. Many times these same loud noises and features are given.

- **Exodus 19:16**
  "And it came to pass on the third day in the morning, that there were **thunders** and lightnings, and a thick cloud upon the mount, and the **voice** of the trumpet exceeding **loud**; so that all the people that *was* in the camp trembled."

- **Exodus 20:18**
  "And all the people saw the **thunderings**, and the lightnings, and the **noise** of the trumpet, and the mountain smoking: and when the people saw *it*, they removed, and stood afar off."

This is the powerful God of the universe. There is a **temple** in Heaven. In the **temple** is the **ark** and the mercy seat. On the mercy seat, I believe, is the blood of the Lord Jesus Christ that atones for the sins of the world when sinners have genuine faith in His finished work on Calvary.

- **Revelation 4:5**
  "And out of the throne proceeded **lightnings and thunderings** and **voices**: and *there were* seven lamps of fire burning before the throne, which are the seven Spirits of God."

All this is from the **throne** of God. His **power** is manifest.

- **Revelation 8:5**
  "And the angel took the censer, and filled it with fire of the altar, and cast *it* into the earth: and there were **voices, and thunderings, and lightnings, and an earthquake.**"

- **Revelation 16:17-18**
  "And the seventh angel poured out his vial into the air; and there came a great voice out of the temple of Heaven, from the throne, saying, It is done. And there were **voices, and thunders, and lightnings; and there was a great earthquake**, such as was not since men were upon the earth, so mighty an earthquake, *and* so great."

How do you describe what the Lord is? Nobody can describe Him. All we know is, wherever the Lord is, there are **thunders, lightnings,**

earthquakes, and hail. There is power, and great things happen. There is also great **hail**.

- **Exodus 9:18**
  "Behold, to morrow about this time I will cause it to rain a very grievous **hail**, such as hath not been in Egypt since the foundation thereof even until now."
- **Revelation 16:21**
  "And there fell upon men a great **hail** out of Heaven, *every stone* about the weight of a talent: and men blasphemed God because of the plague of the **hail**; for the plague thereof was exceeding great."

This is at the seventh vial judgment, the last of the seven judgments. God will show His power by all these signs.

We praise the Lord that the **two witnesses** will be faithful. We are glad that God worked a miracle and raised them up from the dead and then said, *"Come up hither,"* just as He said in Revelation 4:1, to the genuinely born-again Christians at the rapture, *"Come up hither."* If the Lord Jesus Christ should come today, before any of the genuinely saved people die, and say, *"Come up hither,"* they will go. They will be changed. So the Lord Jesus Christ said to these two witnesses in the middle of the tribulation, *"Come up hither,"* and they went up. Their resurrection took place.

The Lord Jesus Christ's Reign

In this seventh trumpet judgment, the nations were judged and the Lord Jesus Christ will be setting up His kingdom upon this earth. The kingdoms of this world will become the kingdoms of our Lord and Saviour Jesus Christ. He will reign upon this earth literally in the millennial reign of the Lord Jesus Christ. It is not simply a spiritual reign. Many people that do not believe in the literal reign of the Lord Jesus Christ say that we are having the Millennium right now and that the Lord Jesus Christ is reigning now. He may reign spiritually now over those who are genuinely saved and a part of the kingdom God. The Lord Jesus Christ should reign over you and me if we are genuinely saved, but His physical reign over this earth, for a thousand years, will take place in the future. The Lord Jesus Christ is of great power and nothing is too hard for Him.

Revelation

Chapter Twelve

Revelation 12:1

"And there appeared a great wonder in Heaven; a woman clothed with the sun, and the moon under her feet, and upon her head a crown of twelve stars:"

The true church, the believers, the genuinely saved ones, will be in Heaven during this entire seven-year period of tribulation. This is sort of a parenthesis between the first seven judgments, and then the seven trumpet judgments, and before the vial judgments. This is a picture in Heaven.

A Picture Of Israel

This is a picture, I believe, of Israel. The Lord is not confined to time as we know it. He is from eternity past to eternity future. He is taking us back in time to the beginning of Israel. Then He is taking us to the Lord Jesus Christ's birth, His death on Calvary, and all the way through. Even though that has happened in God's timing, there is no such thing as sequence. It is all ever-present. I believe this appearing of the great wonder in Heaven is the nation of Israel.

- **Genesis 37:9**
  "And he dreamed yet another dream, and told it his brethren, and said, Behold, I have dreamed a dream more; and, behold, the **sun and the moon** and the eleven **stars** made obeisance to me."

Remember, Joseph dreamed a dream. The **sun, the moon, and the eleven stars,** are his father, his mother, and the eleven brothers. They are all part of Israel. These **twelve stars** seemingly are a picture of Israel.

The Tribulation Is For Israel

The whole seven years of the tribulation is for Israel. It has nothing to do with the true church, the genuinely born-again believers. They all will have been taken up to Heaven.

- **Jeremiah 30:7**
  "Alas! for that day *is* great, so that none *is* like it: it *is* even the **time of Jacob's trouble**; but he shall be saved out of it."

Jacob's trouble is the tribulation period for Israel to be judged. It is not going to be a pleasant thing, but he will be saved out of it.

- **Daniel 9:24**
  "Seventy weeks are determined **upon thy people** and upon **thy holy city**, to finish the transgression, and to make an end of sins, and to make reconciliation for iniquity, and to bring in everlasting righteousness, and to seal up the vision and prophecy, and to anoint the most Holy."

This is another indication that the tribulation is only **for Israel**. *"Thy people"* would be **Israel**. Seventy weeks of years, or seventy sevens, is four hundred and ninety years. Four hundred and eighty-three years already have already taken place before this tribulation period comes. This is Daniel's 70th week, the 70th week of sevens. Four hundred and eighty-three plus seven equals four hundred and ninety. There will be seventy times seven, or four hundred and ninety years in all, before this will be fulfilled literally.

"Thy holy city" is **Jerusalem**. There is no true church involved in this. I do not know how some have the true church in the midst of the tribulation and not raptured until the middle of the tribulation. I do not know where they get that. Some have the true church going all the way through the tribulation and then raptured and taken up to Heaven at the end of the seven years. There is nothing in Scripture that shows that. The entire prophetic picture is one that has to do with **Israel**, these **twelve stars**, as it were, that are upon the head of this **woman clothed with the sun**. This **woman, I believe, is the nation of Israel**.

Revelation 12:2

"And she being with child cried, travailing in birth, and pained to be delivered."

Here is **Israel, and here is Mary** from **Israel** as a **Jewish** maiden. Again, as I said, there is no time frame here. It is all eternity and it is all as if it happened today. The Lord Jesus Christ is from Israel. There is no question about the fact that He is an **Israelite**. It is part of His reign and prophecy. It has nothing to do with the true church.

- **Isaiah 7:13-14**
"And he said, Hear ye now, O house of David; *Is it* a small thing for you to weary men, but will ye weary my God also? Therefore the Lord himself shall give you a sign; Behold, a virgin shall conceive, and **bear a son**, and shall call his name Immanuel."

There are three parts of that Hebrew word for Immanuel. *Im* is "with," *anu* is "us" and *El* is "God." Immanuel means literally "*with us God*" or "*God with us.*" This is a picture of the Lord Jesus Christ Who is perfect God and perfect Man.

This woman in Revelation 12:2 is a picture of **Israel**. This is the woman from Israel, **Mary**. She was of the daughters of Israel, giving birth as a virgin, the miraculous **virgin birth** of the Lord Jesus Christ.

The liberals, modernists, and unbelievers do not believe that He was Immanuel. They do not believe that He was "God with us." That is His title and that is the prophecy that was given. It was fulfilled in the book of Matthew.

- **Micah 5:2**
"But thou, **Bethlehem** Ephratah, *though* thou be little among the thousands of Judah, *yet* out of thee shall he come forth unto me *that is* to be ruler in Israel; whose goings forth *have been* from of old, from everlasting."

This tells about where the Lord Jesus Christ was to be **born**. That is why the wise men came to **Bethlehem**.

NIV's Two Gigantic Doctrinal Errors

As I have said before about Micah 5:2, there are two gigantic doctrinal errors in the New International Version in this verse. Number one, they translate "*whose goings forth*" as "*whose origins.*" Speaking of the Lord Jesus Christ, the NIV teaches that the Lord Jesus Christ had an <u>origin</u>. The New International Version is absolutely blasphemous in Micah 5:2.

The second error in the NIV in Micah 5:2 is that they change "*from everlasting*" to "*from ancient times.*" "<u>Ancient times</u>" does not mean anywhere near the same as "<u>from everlasting</u>." "Ancient times" to us today might be in the 1800's, the 1700's, or even back to the time of the birth of the Lord Jesus Christ. This is a terrible heresy!

The Lord Jesus Christ Is A Jew

The Lord Jesus Christ is definitely from Israel. He is a Jew. Mary, travailing in birth with this child, pictures His birth.

- **Matthew 2:2**
  "Saying, Where is he that is born King of the **Jews**? for we have seen his star in the east, and are come to worship him."

This was the question of the wise men to the ruler Herod. This was the Lord Jesus Christ, connected with **Israel**. The wise men wanted to find who that King was.

- **Matthew 2:6**
  "And thou Bethlehem, *in* the land of Juda, art not the least among the princes of Juda: for out of thee shall come a Governor, that shall rule my people **Israel**."

This is referring to Micah 5:2. This man child, this Saviour, Immanuel, will be the ruler of His people **Israel**.

- **Matthew 27:11**
  "And Jesus stood before the governor: and the governor asked him, saying, Art thou the King of the **Jews**? And Jesus said unto him, Thou sayest."

In other words, yes, the Lord Jesus Christ agreed. He admitted He was the King of the **Jews**. He was a **Jewish** Saviour. He was from **Israel**.

- **Luke 1:31-33**, thou shalt **conceive** in thy womb, and **bring forth** a son, and shalt call his name JESUS. He shall be great, and shall be called the Son of the Highest: and the Lord God shall give unto him the throne of his father David: And he shall reign over the house of Jacob for ever; and of his kingdom there shall be no end."

The angel was talking to Mary. The name Jesus means "Saviour." When it says in Revelation 12:2, *"And she being with **child** cried, travailing in birth,"* it is a reference to **Israel** but it is particularly narrowing down to **Mary**, a daughter of **Israel** and speaking of the **birth** of the Lord Jesus Christ who was the One Who is to rule and to reign in Judah out of the kingdom of David forever.

Revelation 12:3

"And there appeared another wonder in Heaven; and behold a great red dragon, having seven heads and ten horns, and seven crowns upon his heads."

Here is a second **wonder**. The first **wonder** is in verse one. This is also **in Heaven**. We see that **dragon as the Devil or Satan**. He is a multi-headed beast.

- **Revelation 13:1**
  "And I stood upon the sand of the sea, and saw a **beast** rise up out of the sea, having **seven heads and ten horns**, and upon his horns ten crowns, and upon his heads the name of blasphemy."

Satan is pictured as a powerful one who has rulership. That is what heads would mean and **crowns**. He would be in charge of different kingdoms. Certainly he is the **dragon**.

- **Revelation 12:7**
  "And there was war in Heaven: Michael and his angels fought against the **dragon**; and the **dragon** fought and his angels,"

The **dragon** is **Satan**. Michael, being God's lead angel in behalf of Israel, fought against the **Devil** and his angels.

- **Revelation 12:9**
  "And the great **dragon** was cast out, that old **serpent**, called the **Devil**, and **Satan**, which deceiveth the whole world: he was cast out into the earth, and his angels were cast out with him."

The **Devil**, here, seen **in Heaven**, is cast out. He used to have access, and now he is cast out in this particular verse. He comes down to the earth. We will see that later.

- **Revelation 13:4**
  "And they worshipped the **dragon** which gave power unto the beast: and they worshipped the **beast**, saying, Who is like unto the **beast**? who is able to make war with him?"

The Political Beast

This first beast is a political beast. There are two beasts in Revelation 13. There is an entire world that worships this dragon, who is Satan. We have Satan worshippers even today. We have Satan's people and chaplains in the military. We have Satan's people getting tax-exempt status as a religion. Anton Lavey, a Satanist, (who is now dead) edited a Satanic bible.

There is worship of the Devil. It is a terrible thing to worship the Devil, is it not? When you take away the Saviour, the Lord Jesus Christ, who else is there but the power of evil and darkness, rather than the power of light?

- **Revelation 20:2**
  "And he laid hold on the **dragon**, that old **serpent**, which is the **Devil**, and **Satan**, and bound him a thousand years,"

The Devil's Fate Is Sealed

The Devil's fate is sealed. After the seven-year tribulation is finished, Satan will be bound, and he will not be loosed for the entire millennial reign of the Lord Jesus Christ. He will be gone. The people on this earth will still have the flesh and the world to tempt them, but they will not have Satanic temptation any longer. He will be bound and completely put out of commission and power over the earth.

During the tribulation, people will be worshipping Satan, just as in this age of grace, people are worshipping **Satan** himself. In fact, I think even the modernist liberals who do not accept the Deity of the Lord Jesus Christ are worshipping **Satan**. They are preaching another gospel. They are preaching a person that is not the Saviour. **Satan** has blinded their minds and their eyes.

Revelation 12:4

"And his tail drew the third part of the stars of Heaven, and did cast them to the earth: and the dragon stood before the woman which was ready to be delivered, for to devour her child as soon as it was born."

Here is the **tail** of the **dragon**. Notice what he does: *"his tail drew the third part of the stars of Heaven."* I believe the **stars** here is a picture of the angels. **Satan** was one of the angels. He was a head angel to begin with, before he sinned. In his five "**I wills**" to the Lord, finally he said, "I will be like the most high God. I will exalt my kingdom over the Lord." **Satan** drew a **third of these stars**, which I believe are the angels, to be on his side. This is a sad thing. He had that power over these angels.

Notice, it says also, *"and did cast them to the earth."* Now we have **Satan's** angels, evil spirits, on this earth working for **Satan**. **Satan** is not omnipresent, but he has the devils–other evil beings that are helping him.

A Flashback To Bethlehem

Notice, *"the dragon stood before the woman."* Again, this is not a picture of history. God has eternity and He is looking back at Bethlehem. There was Satanic opposition to the child of Mary who was from Israel. This is not in consecutive history. It is a flashback to that which took place at the birth of the Lord Jesus Christ. Satan was ready to devour the child as soon as He was born.

- Matthew 2:16
  "Then Herod, when he saw that he was mocked of the wise men, was exceeding wroth, and sent forth, and slew all the children that were in Bethlehem, and in all the coasts thereof, from two years old and under, according to the time which he had diligently enquired of the wise men."

Here we see **Satan's** plan. He used Herod. He knew that the Lord Jesus Christ would be born in **Bethlehem** because the wise men told him.

- Micah 5:2
  "But thou, **Bethlehem** Ephratah, *though* thou be little among the thousands of Judah, *yet* out of thee shall he come forth unto me *that is* to be ruler in Israel; whose goings forth *have been* from of old, from everlasting."

Herod, as wise as he was, asked the wise men, "When was He **born**? When did you see this star in the east?" They told him. He figured that it was just about two years. If he would slaughter all the children **born** from two years and under he would kill the Lord Jesus Christ. This is a picture of how **Satan, the dragon, stood before the woman ready to be delivered to devour her child as soon as it was born**. He did not succeed.

The Lord Jesus Christ escaped this devouring dragon, but the Devil had another plan. It is not mentioned in Revelation 12:4, but it is implied. He could not devour Him at His **birth** so he stirs up the evil people–the Pharisees and the publicans and the people–to let Him be crucified and kill Him. If he could not kill Him at His birth, Satan would wipe out the Lord Jesus Christ at Calvary. Satan stirred up the people. Seven days before the crucifixion the people said, "Hosanna, He that cometh in the name of the Lord." They were ready to crown Him as King. One week later, the Pharisees stirred up the people. Pilate wanted to release one of the prisoners as he always did at the Passover feast. He thought certainly they would ask for the Lord Jesus Christ to be released and not Barabbas the murderer, but the Jews were stirred up by the chief priests and the Pharisees. The people then said, "Let Jesus be crucified. Give us Barabbas!"

The Devil Thought He Won

The Devil thought he had won at Calvary. What Satan did not realize is the Lord Jesus Christ was victor over that tomb and death. Through His death He was able to atone for the sins of the entire world. That was in God's plan. Satan was fooled again. The resurrection took place.

Revelation 12:5

"And she brought forth a man child, who was to rule all nations with a rod of iron: and her child was caught up unto God, and *to* his throne."

This **man child** was destined to continue to **rule all the nations** with a rod of iron. In the despotism of men today, those that are tyrants, those that rule with authority, those that **rule** with rigor like the Communists, and the other very strong **rulers**, are men, and they are wicked and sinful. The Lord Jesus Christ is righteous and honest. When He rules with a **rod of iron,** He will be a dictator, but He will be a righteous dictator. He will tell what is right and what is wrong. He will not let evil survive. He will not let evil prevail.

A Picture Of Christ's Resurrection

Notice, *"her child was caught up unto God."* I believe this is a picture of the resurrection of the Lord Jesus Christ. The Devil tried to kill Him at His birth. He tried to kill Him at the cross. The Lord Jesus Christ is at the right hand of the throne of God even today. The resurrection, I believe, is pictured here.

- **Psalm 2:6-12**
  "Yet have I set my king upon my holy hill of Zion. I will declare the decree: the LORD hath said unto me, Thou *art* my Son; this day have I begotten thee. Ask of me, and I shall give *thee* the heathen *for* thine inheritance, and the uttermost parts of the earth *for* thy possession. Thou shalt break them with a **rod of iron**; thou shalt dash them in pieces like a potter's vessel. Be

wise now therefore, O ye kings: be instructed, ye judges of the earth. Serve the LORD with fear, and rejoice with trembling. Kiss the Son, lest he be angry, and ye perish *from* the way, when his wrath is kindled but a little. Blessed *are* all they that put their trust in him."

After The Battle Of Armageddon

This is speaking about the Lord Jesus Christ. When He comes back in His glorious return at the battle of Armageddon–when the nations are trying to slaughter and kill all the Jews gathered at Jerusalem–He will dash them like a potter's vessel. This is a picture of the Lord Jesus Christ who shall reign and rule.

- **Revelation 2:27**
  "And he shall rule them with a **rod of iron**; as the vessels of a potter shall they be broken to shivers: even as I received of my Father."

If you have a **rod** of paper, that is going to bend, but **iron** does not bend. Ruling with a **rod of iron** means a strong rule.

- **Revelation 19:15**
  "And out of his mouth goeth a sharp sword, that with it he should smite the nations: and he shall rule them with a **rod of iron**: and he treadeth the winepress of the fierceness and wrath of Almighty God."

This is when the Lord Jesus Christ comes back in His glorious return at the battle of Armageddon. He will break down all those people that are gathered from the north, south, east, and west–two hundred million and more soldiers–around Jerusalem in order to slaughter the Jews.

This is what the **man child** was to do. He was **caught up to God and His throne**. The **resurrection** and the **ascension** of the Lord Jesus Christ are given here. These are truths denied by liberals and modernists. They do not believe that He bodily rose from the grave. They do not believe that He bodily ascended into **Heaven**. They do not believe that He is going bodily to return to this earth one day, but that is what Scripture tells us.

Revelation 12:6

"And the woman fled into the wilderness, where she hath a place prepared of God, that they should feed her there a thousand two hundred *and* threescore days."

That is exactly **three and a half years**. It is **forty-two months**. I believe that the nation of Israel will be spared. There is going to be a place in the wilderness for the last half of the tribulation period. Many will be killed the first half, but God is going to **prepare a place** in the **wilderness**. Many believe that place is Petra, the rock city. Whether that is true or not, Scripture does not tell us. Many believe that is where God will feed the Israelites these three and a half years.

The Importance Of Petra

Petra was established probably about the sixth century B.C. It is called the rock city. Petra means *rock*. The crusaders constructed a fort there about the twelfth century. It was visited in the nineteenth century by the Swiss explorer Johann Ludwig Burkhardt. Petra lies about three to five hours south of Amman and about two hours north of Aqaba. Many people who visit Israel go to Petra. Brother Noah Hutchings takes people to Petra. It is a semi-arid area. There are towering hills of rust-colored sandstone. The colors range from pale yellow, to white, to rich reds. Whether that is the place or not, the rock city is where many believe God will prepare a place for Israel to flee at this time.

God **prepared a place** for His people to **flee** during the last three and a half years of the tribulation. God **prepares places** and things.

- **Exodus 23:20**
  "Behold, I send an Angel before thee, to keep thee in the way, and to bring thee into the place which I have prepared."

When Israel was in bondage in Egypt, God promised them to come into a place where He would take care of them. He would give them **food** and lodging. They did not know where it was. They had been in Egypt for over 400 years.

- **Psalm 9:7**
  "But the LORD shall endure for ever: he hath prepared his throne for judgment."

God's Prepared Judgment Throne

Another prepared thing, is His throne for judgment. People can do anything they want; it almost seems that way. They get away with murder, stealing, homosexuality, adultery, and all kinds of sin, but one day they will be held accountable. God has prepared His throne for judgment. For genuine Christian believers, it will be the judgment seat of the Lord Jesus Christ when we are taken Home to Heaven. For the unsaved, at the end of the millennial reign of the Lord Jesus Christ, it will be the great white throne judgment. Every man, woman, and child will come before the Lord Jesus Christ in one way or the other–the judgment seat of the Lord Jesus Christ, for the genuinely saved, or the great white throne for the lost. He has prepared His throne for judgment.

The Lord Jesus Christ is the Judge of all the earth and He will do right. He will never make one mistake. He will never send anyone to Hell who does not deserve it, because they have rejected the Saviour and God's Son, the Lord Jesus Christ. He will never make a mistake. Our juries and judges make constant mistakes. Not the Lord Jesus Christ. The Judge of all the earth, as Abraham said, will always do right.

- **Psalm 74:16**
  "The day *is* thine, the night also *is* thine: thou hast **prepared** the light and the sun."

That is a **prepared** thing–*the light and the sun*, a special **preparation**. He made those in the early days of Genesis, you will remember. He put the sun to rule the day and the moon to rule the night. He made the stars also. This is another thing **prepared**.

- **Proverbs 8:27**
  "When he **prepared** the Heavens, I *was* there: when he set a compass upon the face of the depth:"

God **prepared** the Heavens. The Heavens include the Heaven of Heavens. That is God's Heaven. It includes the starry Heavens, which is all the stars and planets of Heaven. It includes all the different galaxies, as we call them, with the millions and millions of stars per galaxy, and the thousands of millions of galaxies. God **prepared** the Heavens. He is a **preparing** God.

- **Jonah 1:17**
  "Now the LORD had **prepared** a great fish to swallow up Jonah. And Jonah was in the belly of the fish three days and three nights."

Jonah was wrong. Jonah fled from God. Jonah should never have fled from the Lord. He should have obeyed God. God had to punish Jonah. To do that, he prepared a special great fish to swallow up Jonah.

- **Jonah 4:6**
  "And the LORD God **prepared** a gourd, and made *it* to come up over Jonah, that it might be a shadow over his head, to deliver him from his grief. So Jonah was exceeding glad of the gourd."

This was when Jonah had been delivered from that fish's belly. I believe he died. I believe in Sheol he lifted up his eyes and prayed. It was a picture of the death, burial, and **resurrection** of the Lord Jesus Christ.

- **Matthew 12:40**
  "For as Jonas was three days and three nights in the whale's belly; so shall the Son of man be three days and three nights in the heart of the earth."

That is why I also believe that it is seventy-two hours—three days and three nights. That is why I believe that the crucifixion had to be on Wednesday, and the burial Wednesday evening (at around 6:00 p.m.) for a full three days and three nights.

After the great fish cast Jonah out on the dry land, it was hot. The sun was beating down on his head. I know what that is like having been in Okinawa as a Navy chaplain for twelve months. It was a hot sun—around 105°F or more. Jonah was complaining and the Lord took care of him. God gives us shadows in our grief. He **prepares** some things over our head.

- **Psalm 91:1**
  "He that dwelleth in the secret place of the most High shall abide under the shadow of the Almighty."

The Lord is a shelter in the time of storm—a **shelter** from the sun that beats down upon us.

- **Jonah 4:7**
  "But God prepared a worm when the morning rose the next day, and it smote the gourd that it withered."

Now there was no more shadow or **shelter**. The shade was gone. God prepared that worm. He wanted to teach Jonah a lesson.

- **Jonah 4:8**
  "And it came to pass, when the sun did arise, that God prepared a vehement east wind; and the sun beat upon the head of Jonah, that he fainted, and wished in himself to die, and said, *It is* better for me to die than to live."

Here is another **prepared** thing. God made Jonah really suffer the penalty of disobedience to the Lord. The Lord has not **prepared** a fish for you or for me when we are disobedient. He has not **prepared** a gourd, or a worm, or a vehement east wind, but the Lord has His way of judging us when we are out of His will, and when we are disobedient to what He wants us to do.

What Is Your Situation?

I do not know what your situation is. You do not know what my situation is. All I know is, God is able to get us back on the path where we should be going. When we are out of line, He knows how to put us into line. He did that to Jonah.

- **Matthew 25:41**
  "Then shall he say also unto them on the left hand, Depart from me, ye cursed, into everlasting fire, prepared for the devil and his angels:"

Here is another **prepared** thing in the judgment of the nations. Is **everlasting fire** prepared by God? Yes. Who is it **prepared** for? *For the devil and his angels.* <u>One day that is going to be the home of the Devil and all of his evil angels and everyone that has rejected the Lord Jesus Christ as Saviour and Redeemer.</u> It was not **prepared** for the sinners—the lost people—but it was **prepared** for the Devil and his angels and those that follow the Devil.

- **Luke 1:17**
  "And he shall go before him in the spirit and power of Elias, to turn the hearts of the fathers to the children, and the disobedient to the wisdom of the just; to make ready a people **prepared** for the Lord."

God Has A Prepared People

God has a prepared people. He wants us to be prepared. If we are genuinely saved, He wants us to be a prepared people for the Lord. John the Baptist was to go before and make ready a people prepared for the Lord. Are you prepared? Are you truly saved? Have you sincerely trusted the Lord Jesus Christ as your Saviour and Redeemer? Are you sure you have been truly born-again? Otherwise, you cannot be prepared for the Lord. You have to start there. After you have been genuinely saved, as you study and read the Words of God in the Scriptures and grow in grace and the knowledge of the Saviour, you can be better prepared for the Lord. He wants us prepared.

I was a Boy Scout for many years and got to be an eagle scout in rank. (Not boasting any, it was simple to do that. No problem.) The motto of the Boy Scouts is *"Be prepared."* I do not go along with the Boy Scouts of America. They are an ecumenical crowd. They are battling the homosexuals. I am glad for that. I do not know if they are going to win that battle or lose it. There are many things about them that I do not agree with, but I certainly agree with their motto.

- **John 14:2**
  "In my Father's house are many mansions: if *it were* not so, I would have told you. I go to **prepare** a place for you."

The Lord Jesus Christ is talking to His disciples. Those that love Him, those that know Him, those of us who are genuinely saved and born-again as Christians, have a place **prepared** by the Lord Jesus Christ.

- **John 14:3**
  "And if I go and **prepare** a place for you, I will come again, and receive you unto myself; that where I am, *there* ye may be also."

He has gone to **prepare** a place. He is **preparing** a place for all the genuinely saved that are truly born-again and regenerated. He is going to be in that place with us for all eternity.

- **1 Corinthians 2:9-10**
  "But as it is written, Eye hath not seen, nor ear heard, neither have entered into the heart of man, the things which God hath **prepared** for them that love him. But God hath revealed *them* unto us by his Spirit: for the Spirit searcheth all things, yea, the deep things of God."

Not the eye gate, not the ear gate, not the heart gate—it has not entered into any of those gates, the things that God has **prepared**. The Holy Spirit of God has revealed them in His Scriptures. That is speaking of Glory and Heaven.

- **Hebrews 10:5**
  "Wherefore when he cometh into the world, he saith, Sacrifice and offering thou wouldest not, but a body hast thou **prepared** me:"

This is the Lord Jesus Christ speaking to His Heavenly Father. The Lord Jesus Christ's body was specially **prepared** by God the Father. His sinews, His blood, His head, His feet, His hands—all were **prepared**. When Adam was created, he was **prepared** by God. This was a special body and it was prepared. There is not sacrifice of animals any longer, but a body—the Lamb of God that taketh away the sin of the world.

- **Hebrews 11:16**
  "But now they desire a better *country*, that is, an Heavenly: wherefore God is not ashamed to be called their God: for he hath **prepared** for them a city."

This is speaking about the pilgrims of the Old Testament–Abraham, Isaac, and Jacob. It is also speaking about the **city of Heaven**, which God has **prepared** for these faithful men of the Old Testament.

God is a **prepared** God. If you are genuinely saved, He has made provision for your salvation on the cross of Calvary.

Revelation 12:7

"And there was war in heaven: Michael and his angels fought against the dragon; and the dragon fought and his angels,"

We have **war** on earth. There has been **war** on earth for centuries–all kinds of **wars**. They are not going to be finished. There are many, many wars. Here is **war in heaven**. It is between **Michael and his angels** and the **Devil and his angels**. **Michael** is the chief prince, probably the archangel, who is supposed to be the guardian angel of the Israelites. God has **holy angels**.

- **Matthew 25:31**
  "When the Son of man shall come in his glory, and all the **holy angels** with him, then shall he sit upon the throne of his glory:"

He has **holy angels** that did not follow **Satan**.

- **Luke 9:26**
  "For whosoever shall be ashamed of me and of my words, of him shall the Son of man be ashamed, when he shall come in his own glory, and *in his* Father's, and of the **holy angels**."

- **Jude 1:9**
  "Yet **Michael** the archangel, when contending with the devil he disputed about the body of Moses, durst not bring against him a railing accusation, but said, The Lord rebuke thee."

Here are the **holy angels**, and <u>**Satan** has his **unholy angels**</u>. That is where the battle is in Heaven.

- **Psalm 78:49**
  "He cast upon them the fierceness of his anger, wrath, and indignation, and trouble, by sending **evil angels** *among them*."

- **Mark 1:39**
  "And he preached in their synagogues throughout all Galilee, and cast out **Devils**."

There are the **evil angels**–those **devils**. These are **evil beings**.

- **Luke 7:21**
  "And in that same hour he cured many of *their* infirmities and plagues, and of **evil spirits**; and unto many *that were* blind he gave sight."

These are **angels** under the control of **Satan**.

- **Luke 8:2**
  "And certain women, which had been healed of **evil spirits** and infirmities, Mary called Magdalene, out of whom went seven devils,"

Evil Angels Fight The Holy Angels

These evil angels fought with Michael and his holy angels in Heaven. The evil angels lost and Michael won. That is why Satan was cast into the earth with a third of the stars.

Revelation 12:8

"**And prevailed not; neither was their place found any more in heaven.**"

The **dragon and his angels prevailed not.** They did not win the battle. When God is the One doing the fighting, God always wins. He never is defeated–never once. It may seem like He is defeated. The Devil thought He was defeated.

Calvary Was Not A Defeat

Many people thought the Lord Jesus Christ was defeated when He was sent to Calvary, suffering, bleeding, and dying for the sins of the world, but that was not defeat. That was the very foundation of the salvation of those who genuinely trust Him. Upon His crucifixion and shed blood on the cross of Calvary, all of us who genuinely trust the Lord Jesus Christ can be redeemed.

Satan was fooled. When God is behind it, He always wins. Is God behind you? Is He behind me? Not only should He be on our side, but we should be on God's side. He is on our side if we are on His side.

- **Job 1:6-7**
  "Now there was a day when the sons of God came to present themselves before the LORD, and Satan came also among them. And the LORD said unto Satan, Whence comest thou? Then Satan answered the LORD, and said, From going to and fro in the earth, and from walking up and down in it."

- **Job 2:1-2**
  "Again there was a day when the sons of God came to present themselves before the LORD, and Satan came also among them to present himself before the LORD. And the LORD said unto Satan, From whence comest thou? And Satan answered the LORD, and said, From going to and fro in the earth, and from walking up and down in it."

Before Satan judged Job and took away all of his possessions, he was up there before the Lord. The second time, he said that he wanted to smite Job's flesh. All of his possessions were gone; now he was going to make him sick and put boils all over him, from head to toe. Satan had perfect access to Heaven at one time.

- **Luke 10:18**
  "And he said unto them, I beheld Satan as lightning fall from heaven."

Revelation 12:8 says the dragon and his angels *"prevailed not; neither was their place found any more in Heaven."* Could you be comfortable in the place called **Heaven** when Satan also is in that same place with you? I would not be comfortable. I would not be comfortable if lost people that have rejected our Saviour were in **Heaven** with us who are genuinely saved. That would be terrible discomfort. There will be no sin in **Heaven**. Angels like **Satan** will not be in Heaven, even though the heretical Gnostics taught this lie.

- **Revelation 12:10**
  "And I heard a loud voice saying in heaven, Now is come salvation, and strength, and the kingdom of our God, and the power of his Christ: for the accuser of our brethren is cast down, which accused them before our God day and night."

Satan was **cast out of Heaven** and his angels. There was **no place** for them.

Revelation 12:9

"And the great dragon was cast out, that old serpent, called the Devil, and Satan, which deceiveth the whole world: he was cast out into the earth, and his angels were cast out with him."

The Devil Has His Angels

The Devil has his angels. He is called the great dragon. Notice the titles: *the great dragon, that old serpent, the Devil, and Satan.* There are four titles right here in the same verse. Notice his occupation during the entire time when he was in Heaven and had access. His occupation is that *"which deceiveth the whole world."* <u>Deception</u>. That is continuous action present tense. He continuously deceives the whole world. He was cast out into the earth and his angels were cast out with him. He is cast from Heaven down to earth.

- **Genesis 3:1**
  "Now the **serpent** was more subtil than any beast of the field which the LORD God had made. And he said unto the woman, Yea, hath God said, Ye shall not eat of every tree of the garden?"
People have said, "Who is this **serpent**?" That **serpent** is none other than **Satan**. It is another title for him. The one that twists around. He is also a blinder of minds.

- **2 Corinthians 4:4**
  "In whom the **god of this world** hath blinded the minds of them which believe not, lest the light of the glorious gospel of Christ, who is the image of God, should shine unto them."
This is talking about deception. **Satan** has blinded the minds of those that are unbelievers. <u>That is his job—to **deceive the whole world**, and genuinely saved people as well</u>.

- **Matthew 24:11**
  "And many false prophets shall rise, and shall deceive many."
<u>The Lord Jesus Christ predicted this</u>. These are the Satanic false prophets. I maintain that every preacher and every religion that rejects the Deity of the Lord Jesus Christ, His bodily resurrection, and that He is the only Saviour of the world, is a deceiver. <u>This includes all the religions, whether Roman Catholicism or any other</u>. Those who deny that the Lord Jesus Christ is the only Saviour Who can save people from sin

by genuine faith in the Lord Jesus Christ, are **deceivers**. They are part of the Satanic one-world **deception**. <u>Satan deceives the whole world.</u>

How do you suppose the whole world is more **deceived**? It is by religious people much more than by out-and-out lost people. People are not **deceived** by the lost people who are murderers, thieves, and wicked. They know exactly that they are wicked and evil. It is like black and white. But the smooth-selling religious people that do not believe the Bible, with their smooth sweet talk, can talk people into Hell. They deny Hell. They deny Heaven, the virgin birth of the Lord Jesus Christ, and His bodily resurrection. This is Satanic religion. No matter what the guise and the pose that it comes in. There are many false prophets.

- **Revelation 20:2-3**
  "And he laid hold on the dragon, that old serpent, which is the Devil, and Satan, and bound him a thousand years, And cast him into the bottomless pit, and shut him up, and set a seal upon him, that he should deceive the nations no more, till the thousand years should be fulfilled: and after that he must be loosed a little season."

Satan Bound–Then Loosed

After that thousand-year millennial reign of Christ, Satan is going to be loosed. He is going to be able to deceive the nations. He is going to gather them together one last time to Jerusalem to overthrow the King of kings and Lord of lords. Satan will be put down again.

This **Devil**, this DIABOLOS, this **Satan** is the prince of devils, the author of evil, persecuting genuinely born-again men and women, estranging mankind from God, and enticing them to sin, afflicting them with diseases by means of devils who take possession of their bodies at his bidding. That is a terrible, frightening thing.

The **Devil** and his **angels** are going to be knocked out of Heaven, brought down to earth, subdued, and one day will be **cast** into everlasting fire prepared for the Devil and his angels. God will get the victory.

Preparing An Eternal Place For You

Of all the things that have been prepared, is the Lord Jesus Christ preparing a <u>place</u> for you? The most important preparation is that one <u>place</u>. Is He preparing a <u>place</u> for you? If you genuinely accepted Him, trusted Him, and are born-again, the Lord Jesus Christ is preparing a <u>place</u> for you. If you have rejected Him, never genuinely accepted and received Him by faith, that <u>place</u> is not for you. You will not be there. Ask yourself, "Have I genuinely trusted the Lord Jesus Christ as my Saviour? Am I sure that I have a prepared <u>place</u> that the Lord Jesus Christ is preparing for me?" If not, you need to genuinely accept Him, receive Him, and trust Him. Do it right now.

Revelation 12:10

"And I heard a loud voice saying in heaven, Now is come salvation, and strength, and the kingdom of our God, and the power of his Christ: for the accuser of our brethren is cast down, which accused them before our God day and night."

This **accuser of the brethren** is **Satan** himself. That is what he does. Those of us who are genuinely saved and born-again, **Satan** has been **accusing**, just like he did in the book of Job.

- **Job 1:6-11**
  "Now there was a day when the sons of God came to present themselves before the LORD, and Satan came also among them. And the LORD said unto Satan, Whence comest thou? Then Satan answered the LORD, and said, From going to and fro in the earth, and from walking up and down in it. And the LORD said unto Satan, Hast thou considered my servant Job, that *there is* none like him in the earth, a perfect and an upright man, one that feareth God, and escheweth evil? Then Satan answered the LORD, and said, Doth Job fear God for nought? Hast not thou made an hedge about him, and about his house, and about all that he hath on every side? thou hast blessed the work of his hands, and his substance is increased in the land. But put forth thine hand now, and touch all that he hath, and he will curse thee to thy face."

<u>Satan</u> had access to the Lord. He started **accusing** Job.

Satan–The Accuser Of The Brethren

Satan has perfect liberty to come on this earth. Satan is the accuser of the brethren. Accusations are easy. He is the main accuser. In fact, that word DIABOLOS means *accuser, one that accuses or brings a false charge.*

- **Proverbs 30:10**
  "Accuse not a servant unto his master, lest he curse thee, and thou be found guilty."
  <u>Accusations</u> are easily made.
- **Matthew 27:12**
  "And when he was **accused** of the chief priests and elders, he answered nothing."

The Lord Jesus Christ had many **accusations** brought against Him. You and I will have **accusations**. I trust that they are all false **accusations** against us because of our beliefs.

- **Mark 3:2**
  "And they watched him, whether he would heal him on the sabbath day; that they might **accuse** him."

The Pharisees watched the Lord Jesus Christ. They were just lying in wait. <u>Have you ever noticed some people just sort of lying in wait to</u> **accuse** <u>you and to</u> **accuse** <u>me</u>? They just lie in wait to see what we say, what we do, how we act.

- **Luke 3:14**
  "And the soldiers likewise demanded of him, saying, And what shall we do? And he said unto them, Do violence to no man, neither **accuse** any falsely; and be content with your wages."

John the Baptist preached a sermon to various groups. Apparently the soldiers **accused** many people falsely, put them in jail, and marked them up on charges of some kind.

- **Luke 16:1**
  "And he said also unto his disciples, There was a certain rich man, which had a steward; and the same was **accused** unto him that he had wasted his goods."

There was an **accusation** against that steward of wasting the goods. This is not what God wants us to do. **Satan is the accuser**, and in Revelation 12:10, he is cast out of Heaven. Probably that will take place in the middle of the tribulation period, three and a half years along the way.

- **Luke 23:1-2**
  "And the whole multitude of them arose, and led him unto Pilate. And they began to **accuse** him, saying, We found this *fellow* perverting the nation, and forbidding to give tribute to Caesar, saying that he himself is Christ a King."

This was at the judgment seat of the crucifixion at Calvary. That was a false **accusation**. Of what can you **accuse** the Lord Jesus Christ? What sin did He commit? He did not commit any sin. <u>He is sinless and perfect.</u>

- **Luke 20:25**
  "And he said unto them, Render therefore unto Caesar the things which be Caesar's, and unto God the things which be God's."

They had brought Him a penny. He said to go ahead and pay taxes.

- **Luke 23:14**
  "Said unto them, Ye have brought this man unto me, as one that perverteth the people: and, behold, I, having examined *him* before you, have found no fault in this man touching those things whereof ye **accuse** him:"

Pilate was willing to let Him go. Pilate did not find any fault in the Lord Jesus Christ. He is faultless. There are faults in us because we are sinners. We are genuinely saved by God's grace, but we are still sinners with the old nature. Not the Lord Jesus Christ.

- **John 8:10-11**
  "When Jesus had lifted up himself, and saw none but the woman, he said unto her, Woman, where are those thine **accusers**? hath no man condemned thee? She said, No man, Lord. And Jesus said unto her, Neither do I condemn thee: go, and sin no more."

The woman taken in adultery had **accusers** as well.

- **John 8:7**
  "So when they continued asking him, he lifted up himself, and said unto them, He that is without sin among you, let him first cast a stone at her."

In the law, it was stoning for the adulteress and the adulterer.

- **2 Timothy 3:3**
  "Without natural affection, trucebreakers, false accusers, incontinent, fierce, despisers of those that are good,"

These are signs of the last days coming upon us. <u>Killing babies certainly is not natural affection</u>. There are all kinds of breaking of promises.

- **Titus 2:3**
  "The aged women likewise, that *they be* in behaviour as becometh holiness, not false **accusers**, not given to much wine, teachers of good things;"

A Word To The Older Ladies

He has a word here to the ladies–the older women especially. One of the things that they were to be careful of, and to guard against, was to not be false accusers. Perhaps in Titus' church, and other churches, there were older-aged women who were accusing people falsely. That was to be condemned.

Revelation 12:11

"And they overcame him by the blood of the Lamb, and by the word of their testimony; and they loved not their lives unto the death."

These who were **accused** by Satan **overcame** him, that is the Devil, by the **blood of the Lamb**, and **by the word of their testimony**. **Overcoming** is conquering. They **overcame** him and conquered by the **blood of the Lamb**.

- **John 16:33**
  "These things I have spoken unto you, that in me ye might have peace. In the world ye shall have tribulation: but be of good cheer; I have **overcome** the world."

The Lord Jesus Christ has **conquered** and is victorious over the world. The world did not have anything on Him.

- **Romans 12:21**
  "Be not overcome of evil, but **overcome** evil with good."

Conquer evil with good.

- **2 Peter 2:19**
  "While they promise them liberty, they themselves are the servants of corruption: for of whom a man is **overcome**, of the same is he brought in bondage."

If something **overcomes us, we are in bondage to it.** We are not to be **overcome** of evil.

- **1 John 2:13**
  "I write unto you, fathers, because ye have known him *that is* from the beginning. I write unto you, young men, because ye have **overcome** the wicked one. I write unto you, little children, because ye have known the Father."

- **1 John 4:4**
  "Ye are of God, little children, and have **overcome** them: because greater is he that is in you, than he that is in the world."

How can we **overcome** the world and wickedness? The Holy Spirit of God is in the genuinely saved, born-again Christian. That is how we can **overcome** the world.

- **1 John 5:4-5**
  "For whatsoever is born of God **overcometh** the world: and this is the victory that **overcometh** the world, *even* our faith. Who is he that **overcometh** the world, but he that believeth that Jesus is the Son of God?"

Even by being genuinely born-again, we **overcome** the world. It is not simply a head-belief, but a heart-belief, that the Lord Jesus Christ is the Son of God.

- **Revelation 13:7**
  "And it was given unto him to make war with the saints, and to overcome them: and power was given him over all kindreds, and tongues, and nations."

This first beast is the political beast—the antichrist.

- **Revelation 17:14**
  "These shall make war with the Lamb, and the Lamb shall **overcome** them: for he is Lord of lords, and King of kings: and they that are with him *are* called, and chosen, and faithful."

The Lord Jesus Christ will **overcome** all assaults against His people, in this tribulation period, indeed.

MacArthur's Heresy On The Blood

In the book, *John MacArthur's HERESY on the Blood of the Lord Jesus*, <u>on page 8</u>, John MacArthur says, *"It was His DEATH that was EFFICACIOUS, not HIS BLOOD."* He denies the efficacy of the blood of the Lord Jesus Christ.

<u>On page 11</u>, I am quoting from Mary Baker Glover Eddy in her *SCIENCE AND HEALTH WITH KEY TO THE SCRIPTURES*. She says, *"The MATERIAL BLOOD of Jesus WAS NO MORE EFFICACIOUS TO CLEANSE FROM SIN when it was SHED UPON THE ACCURSED TREE than when flowing in his veins as he went about His Father's business."* That is the same thing MacArthur says. He says the blood of the Lord Jesus Christ was not efficacious, that is, it was not worth anything.

<u>On page 15,</u> under point F, MacArthur says, *"The SHEDDING OF BLOOD HAS NOTHING TO DO WITH BLEEDING...it simply means <u>death</u>...violent sacrificial death."* He says blood just means death and has nothing to do with bleeding.

<u>On page 17</u>, under point G, MacArthur says, *"NOTHING IN HIS [that is, CHRIST'S] HUMAN BLOOD SAVES."* This is terrible blasphemy.

<u>On page 19</u>, MacArthur says, *"JESUS WAS 100% HUMAN; HE HAD HUMAN BLOOD and He shed HUMAN BLOOD. There was nothing in the chemicals of His blood that could save.*

ATONEMENT WAS MADE THROUGH HIS DEATH. This is the historic position."

No! He was not 100% human. He is perfect Man, but also perfect God. He was not just simply a human being. MacArthur throughout denies the work of the blood of the Lord Jesus Christ.

On pages 44 through 48, I list fourteen things about the literal blood of the Lord Jesus Christ completely contrary to what John MacArthur teaches. When it says in Revelation 12:11, *"they overcame him by the blood of the Lamb,"* it does not say they overcame him by the *death* of the Lamb. There is a maxim of interpretation that we call the *Golden Rule of Bible Interpretation:* "When the plain sense of Scripture makes common sense, seek no other sense."

The first thing about the blood of the Lord Jesus Christ is that there is redemption, atonement, forgiveness, and the remission of sins. There are many verses on this point of redemption. MacArthur says it is not by the blood of the Lord Jesus Christ.

- **Acts 20:28**
  "Take heed therefore unto yourselves, and to all the flock, over the which the Holy Ghost hath made you overseers, to feed the church of God, which he hath purchased with his own **blood.**"

The words *purchase, substitution, remission,* and *salvation* all deal with the redemption through His **blood.**

The second thing through the literal **blood** of the Lord Jesus Christ is propitiation, that is, God's satisfaction.

- **Romans 3:25**
  "Whom God hath set forth *to be* a **propitiation** through faith in his blood, to declare his righteousness for the remission of sins that are past, through the forbearance of God;"

The third thing through the literal **blood** of the Lord Jesus Christ is justification.

- **Romans 5:9**
  "Much more then, being now **justified** by his **blood,** we shall be saved from wrath through him."

Through His Blood, Not His Death

When God justifies sinners, it is through His blood. It does not say, *"His death."* It is true that the Lord Jesus Christ died for our sins on the cross of Calvary and He shed His blood. The Scriptures say that the blood of the Lord Jesus Christ does fourteen things and we cannot deny it as John MacArthur does. We cannot say blood does not mean blood. When the Passover lamb was slain, the lamb died, but then the blood was taken and put in a bason and with hyssop–an ordinary weed–the blood was applied to the top and side posts of the door. When the death angel came over, they were protected by the blood of the lamb, not by the death of the lamb. All through the Old Testament, death and blood were separate entities. There was the death of the animal, and the application of the blood.

The fourth thing through the literal **blood** of the Lord Jesus Christ is fellowship.
- **Ephesians 2:13**
  "But now in Christ Jesus ye who sometimes were far off are made nigh by the blood of Christ."

The fifth thing through the literal **blood** of the Lord Jesus Christ is peace.
- **Colossians 1:20**
  "And, having made peace through the blood of his cross, by him to reconcile all things unto himself; by him, *I say*, whether *they be* things in earth, or things in `"

The sixth thing through the literal **blood** of the Lord Jesus Christ is forgiveness.
- **Ephesians 1:7**
  "In whom we have redemption through his blood, the forgiveness of sins, according to the riches of his grace;"

It does not say, *"through His death."* He did die, but the Lord Jesus Christ says it is His **blood** that is the basis of our forgiveness. He shed His **blood** for our sins.

The seventh thing through the literal **blood** of the Lord Jesus Christ is sanctification.
- **Hebrews 13:12**
  "Wherefore Jesus also, that he might sanctify the people with his own blood, suffered without the gate."

The eighth thing through the literal **blood** of the Lord Jesus Christ is reconciliation.
- **Colossians 1:20**
  "And, having made peace through the blood of his cross, by him to reconcile all things unto himself; by him, *I say*, whether *they be* things in earth, or things in heaven."

There is reconciliation with those that were opposed to Him.

The ninth thing through the literal **blood** of the Lord Jesus Christ is cleansing, purging, washing or purifying.

- **Hebrews 9:14**
  "How much more shall the blood of the Lord Jesus Christ, who through the eternal Spirit offered himself without spot to God, purge your conscience from dead works to serve the living God?"

It is the **blood** of the Lord Jesus Christ that purges and cleanses.

- **Revelation 1:5**
  "And from Jesus Christ, *who is* the faithful witness, *and* the first begotten of the dead, and the prince of the kings of the earth. Unto him that loved us, and washed us from our sins in his own blood,"

This is Scripture. We must never change it.

- **Revelation 7:14**
  "And I said unto him, Sir, thou knowest. And he said to me, These are they which came out of great tribulation, and have washed their robes, and made them white in the blood of the Lamb."

Christ's Blood Is Not Worthless!

We should not be as the modernists and the liberals who say the blood of the Lord Jesus Christ is worthless and no good. We should not say as Harry Emerson Fosdick said that Christians who worship the Scriptures in a Bible-believing way have a *"slaughterhouse religion."* In other words, he is against the blood of the Lord Jesus Christ. He does not like to speak of the blood of the Lord Jesus Christ, but the Scriptures speak of it.

The tenth thing through the literal **blood** of the Lord Jesus Christ is remembrance.

- **1 Corinthians 11:25**
  "After the same manner also *he took* the cup, when he had supped, saying, This cup is the new testament in my blood: this do ye, as oft as ye drink *it*, in **remembrance** of me."

Every time we have the Lord's Supper, it is in remembrance of His death through His **blood**.

The eleventh thing through the literal **blood** of the Lord Jesus Christ is **boldness** and access to God's throne.

- **Hebrews 10:19**
  "Having therefore, brethren, **boldness** to enter into the holiest by the blood of Jesus,"

If we are genuinely saved, we can enter into the Holy Place.

The twelfth thing through the literal **blood** of the Lord Jesus Christ is **maturity** and doing God's will.

- **Hebrews 13:20-21**
  "Now the God of peace, that brought again from the dead our Lord Jesus Christ, that great shepherd of the sheep, through the blood of the everlasting covenant, Make you **perfect** in every good work to do his will, working in you that which is wellpleasing in his sight, through Jesus Christ; to whom *be* glory for ever and ever. Amen."

Through the **blood** of the covenant, God wants us to be perfect and mature to do His will.

The thirteenth thing through the literal **blood** of the Lord Jesus Christ is **punishment, weakness, sickness, or death if we mistreat the literal blood of the Lord Jesus Christ.**

- **Hebrews 10:29**
  "Of how much sorer **punishment,** suppose ye, shall he be thought worthy, who hath trodden under foot the Son of God, and hath counted the blood of the covenant, wherewith he was sanctified, an unholy thing, and hath done despite unto the Spirit of grace?"

Christ's Blood Not "Common" Blood

A common or unholy thing is nothing but KOINOS. It is the Greek word which means, *common or ordinary.* That is exactly the sin and heresy of John MacArthur. He says that the blood of Jesus Christ is human blood, counting it an unholy thing.

- **Hebrews 10:5**
  "Wherefore when he cometh into the world, he saith, Sacrifice and offering thou wouldest not, but a body hast thou prepared me:"

The Lord Jesus Christ's body–every part of it–was prepared by the Father. It was a special body for sacrifice–His sinews, His muscles, His bones, His **blood,** His hair, His feet, His hands–all parts. He was not simply a human being like we are, with human **blood.**

- **1 Corinthians 11:27**
  "Wherefore whosoever shall eat this bread, and drink this cup of the Lord, unworthily, shall be guilty of the body and **blood** of the Lord."

Unworthiness in the Lord's Supper also partakes of judgment.

The fourteenth thing through the literal **blood** of the Lord Jesus Christ is victory over Satan.

- **Revelation 12:11**
  "And they overcame him by the **blood** of the Lamb, and by the word of their testimony; and they **loved not their lives unto the death.**"

Never Play Down Christ's Blood

The blood of the Lord Jesus Christ is a part of Scripture that we must never deprecate, deny, underplay, or discount.

Notice that this verse also says that they overcame the Devil *by the word of their testimony.* It is important that we who are genuinely saved have a good **testimony** and a good witness for our Saviour.

- **2 Timothy 1:8**
  "Be not thou therefore ashamed of the **testimony** of our Lord, nor of me his prisoner: but be thou partaker of the afflictions of the gospel according to the power of God;"

We should never be ashamed of the **testimony** and the witness of our Lord Jesus Christ. They overcame the Devil by the word of **their testimony.**

- **Hebrews 11:5**
  "By faith Enoch was translated that he should not see death; and was not found, because God had translated him: for before his translation he had this **testimony**, that he pleased God."

God had taken him from this earth to Heaven.

The Meaning Of Translation

That word *translated* is a very good word. When we talk about translation of the Bible it is the same type of word. It is from the Latin word TRANSLATUS. The first part of that is TRANS, which means *across.* LATUS is the past participle of the verb FERRO, which is *to carry.* TRANSLATUS means *to carry over or across.* In order to have a good translation, like our King James Bible, we take the Hebrew, Aramaic, and Greek words, and *carry them across* into the English.

> God took Enoch to Heaven. He took all of him. He did not leave half of him here. He did not add to him before he took him. We should not add to or subtract from the Words of God in the Hebrew, Aramaic, and Greek. The King James Bible has not done this.

Why was Enoch translated? He had a **testimony** before men that he pleased God.

- **Revelation 1:9**
  "I John, who also am your brother, and companion in tribulation, and in the kingdom and patience of Jesus Christ, was in the isle that is called Patmos, for the word of God, and for the **testimony** of Jesus Christ."

John Was A Strong Christian

John was a prisoner on this island as he wrote this book of Revelation because he stood for the Words of God. He was also standing for the testimony concerning the Lord Jesus Christ. He stood up as a true Christian. He would not back down. He was a witness. He was a strong Christian.

- **Revelation 6:9**
  "And when he had opened the fifth seal, I saw under the altar the souls of them that were slain for the word of God, and for the **testimony** which they held:"

They had a **testimony**, meaning that they were genuine Christians. In *Fox's Book of Martyrs* there are many instances of those that were slain because of their genuine faith in the Lord Jesus Christ. The early church would not reject Him or deny Him. Some did deny Him. Some did say, "I do not believe in this Lord Jesus Christ as Saviour." They were loyal to Caesar or to some other deity, but those who stood for the Lord Jesus Christ and their **testimony** for the Lord Jesus Christ, were slain. There were very difficult methods of slaying, just like the man who was slain by those murderers over there in Saudi Arabia–they severed his head. They were slain in terrible, horrific ways–tortured and slain for the **Words of God** and the **testimony** that they held.

Notice also in Revelation 12:11, *they loved not their lives unto the death.* The Lord Jesus Christ had something to say about that.

- **Matthew 10:37-39**
  "He that loveth father or mother more than me is not worthy of me: and he that loveth son or daughter more than me is not worthy of me. And he that taketh not his cross, and followeth

after me, is not worthy of me. He that findeth his life shall lose it: and he that **loseth his life** for my sake shall find it."
<u>The cross speaks of death</u>. They **loved not their lives unto the death**. In other words, they would rather be faithful to the Lord Jesus Christ than to escape **death**.

- **Acts 25:11**
  "For if I be an offender, or have committed any thing worthy of death, **I refuse not to die**: but if there be none of these things whereof these accuse me, no man may deliver me unto them. I appeal unto Caesar."

Paul had that same philosophy. He was **willing to die**.

- **Philippians 1:21**
  "For to me to live *is* Christ, and **to die *is* gain**."
- **Philippians 1:23**
  "For I am in a strait betwixt two, having a desire to depart, and **to be with Christ**; which is far better:"
- **Philippians 2:30**
  "Because for the work of Christ he was **nigh unto death**, not regarding his life, to supply your lack of service toward me."

This talks about Epaphroditus. These true Christians overcame the Devil *"by the **blood of the Lamb**, and by the **word of their testimony**; and they **loved not their lives unto the death**."*

Revelation 12:12

"Therefore rejoice, *ye* heavens, and ye that dwell in them. Woe to the inhabiters of the earth and of the sea! for the devil is come down unto you, having great wrath, because he knoweth that he hath but a short time."

When **Satan** will be **cast out** of Heaven, probably three and a half years into the tribulation, the Heavens will be glad. They do not want that rascal up there, but it says, "Woe to the inhabiters of the earth!" If you are truly born-again and the Lord Jesus Christ should return and the tribulation begins, the genuinely saved ones will be caught up, and will be in Heaven during the entire seven-year period of tribulation. To those people that are still here they will say, "Woe to those inhabiters of the earth and sea!" **Satan** needs to make up for lost time. All he will have is three and a half years. Then he is going to be bound for a thousand years during the Millennium. He is going to make up for lost time and be very, very active.

- Revelation 20:10
  "And the devil that deceived them was cast into the lake of fire and brimstone, where the beast and the false prophet *are*, and shall be tormented day and night for ever and ever."

Satan Will Meet His Doom

Satan is going to meet his doom. He is going to be bound during the millennial reign of our Saviour for a thousand years. He is going to be loosed at the end of that time to deceive the nations again.

Revelation 12:13

"And when the dragon saw that he was cast unto the earth, he persecuted the woman which brought forth the man *child*."

Here again is a picture of **persecution** of Israel, *"the woman."* Yes, it was **Mary**, but she was of the nation of **Israel**. She was of the seed of David. This is the persecution. When **Satan** comes down to the earth, he persecutes **Israel**. There will be many Jews on the earth at this time. Some will be genuinely saved through the ministry of the 144,000 evangelists.

- Matthew 10:23
  "But when they **persecute** you in this city, flee ye into another: for verily I say unto you, Ye shall not have gone over the cities of Israel, till the Son of man be come."

Antichrist Persecutes Israel

The Lord Jesus Christ pictures this in future days. The ones that persecute Israel are the antichrist's nations. There is a long, extensive picture in Matthew 24:3-21 where the Lord Jesus Christ tells Israel that Satan is going to persecute them. They will have to flee.

- Matthew 24:3
  "And as he sat upon the mount of Olives, the disciples came unto him privately, saying, Tell us, when shall these things be? and what *shall be* the sign of thy coming, and of the end of the world?
The *"sign of thy coming"* means the coming in glory. That is three and a half years after this **persecution** in this tribulation period.

- **Matthew 24:4**
  "And Jesus answered and said unto them, Take heed that no man **deceive** you.

The first thing He tells them is to not be **deceived**.

- **Matthew 24:5**
  "For many shall come in my name, saying, I am Christ; and shall **deceive** many."

The Antichrist Revealed Eventually

I believe the Lord Jesus Christ is speaking here of the antichrist who will show himself and reveal himself in three and a half years during that seven-year period of the tribulation. The antichrist will come and will say, "I am Christ!" That is the one that is going to come. He is going to pretend, imitate the Lord Jesus Christ, and act like Him, but finally he is going to turn on the Lord Jesus Christ.

- **Matthew 24:6**
  "And ye shall hear of **wars** and rumours of wars: see that ye be not troubled: for all *these things* must come to pass, but the end is not yet.

There are plenty of **wars** and rumours of **wars**.

- **Matthew 24:7**
  "For nation shall rise against nation, and kingdom against kingdom: and there shall be famines, and pestilences, and earthquakes, in divers places.

  There are plenty of nations rising against nations and kingdoms against kingdoms.

- **Matthew 24:8**
  "All these *are* the beginning of sorrows."

- **Matthew 24:9**
  "Then shall they deliver you up to be afflicted, and shall kill you: and ye shall be hated of all nations for my name's sake."

Israel Will Be Hated

During the tribulation period, Israel will be hated. The Jews are hated enough now. Just think how it will be when the antichrist is here and ruling!

- **Matthew 24:10**
  "And then shall many be offended, and shall betray one another, and shall hate one another."

Jews will betray Jews and shall hate one another.

- **Matthew 24:11-13**
  "And many false prophets shall rise, and shall **deceive** many. And because iniquity shall abound, the love of many shall wax cold. But he that shall endure unto the end, the same shall be saved."

- **Matthew 24:14**
  "And this gospel of the kingdom shall be preached in all the world for a witness unto all nations; and then shall the end come."

The *gospel of the kingdom* is the gospel that the Lord Jesus Christ is going to set up. It is a millennial kingdom. Three and a half years after this time, there will be a thousand-year reign of our Saviour.

- **Matthew 24:15**
  "When ye therefore shall see the abomination of desolation, spoken of by Daniel the prophet, stand in the holy place, (whoso readeth, let him understand:)"

The antichrist will be on the scene during the entire seven years of the tribulation. During the first three and a half years, he will be wonderful. He will be sweet. Everybody will follow him saying, "Oh, he is wonderful!"

Take the most wonderful politician you can think of—the most syrupy, the most wonderful—whether it is Ronald Reagan, George Bush, Bill Clinton, Barack Obama, or whoever—you take your pick. The one that will sell whatever you believe, is what the antichrist is going to be like.

Antichrist Will Sway The Multitudes

You pick any politician you wish. I am not going to name one, but you pick one. That is how the antichrist will be. He will sway the multitudes in this country and in the whole world. They will follow him, but he will break his covenant at three and a half years. In the middle of this seven years, he will break the covenant with Israel and with all the nations. He will reveal himself that he is really a wolf that has been in sheep's clothing. He is really a wolf.

He will offer an unclean animal in the temple at Jerusalem—perhaps a pig or some other unclean animal. That is what is spoken of by Daniel as *"the abomination of desolation."*

- **Matthew 24:16**
  "Then let them which be in Judaea flee into the mountains:"

Maybe the mountain will be Petra as we said earlier.

- **Matthew 24:17-18**
  "Let him which is on the housetop not come down to take any thing out of his house: Neither let him which is in the field return back to take his clothes."

In other words, as soon as this happens, there is going to be **persecution** against Israel.

- **Matthew 24:19-20**
  "And woe unto them that are with child, and to them that give suck in those days! But pray ye that your flight be not in the winter, neither on the sabbath day:"

- **Matthew 24:21**
  "For then shall be great tribulation, such as was not since the beginning of the world to this time, no, nor ever shall be."

This is a picture. When the **dragon** will be cast down to the earth, he **will persecute the woman, Israel**, that brought forth the man child, the Lord Jesus Christ. That **persecution will be real and genuine**. The Lord Jesus Christ predicted that in the Gospel of Matthew.

Revelation 12:14

"And to the woman were given two wings of a great eagle, that she might fly into the wilderness, into her place, where she is nourished for a time, and times, and half a time, from the face of the serpent."

The woman, or Israel, is given **two wings of a great eagle**. Many people wonder, "What are the **wings**?" These are symbols, of course, and could be airplanes. Who knows? Whatever it is, God will provide for Israel—those that are genuinely saved through the 144,000, and perhaps others as well—**to fly to the wilderness into her place**. God has provided a special **place** during the tribulation for Israel to be guarded against Satan, and against Satan's hoards and multitudes.

Israel Will Be Nourished By the Lord

Notice it says, *"where she is nourished."* That is in the present tense, continuously nourished. Everything that she needs will be taken care of—her food, her lodging (wherever it will be), her clothing—just like the Lord provided in the wilderness. For forty years, Israel was protected. They had no need of food. The manna came down. There was water from the Rock. Their clothes did not wax old. God is going to nourish

> Israel during this time. Notice also that she is nourished *"for a time, and times, and half a time."* That is three and a half years. The Lord is going to protect her.

As far as the **wings**, there are many in Scripture.

- **Exodus 19:4**
  "Ye have seen what I did unto the Egyptians, and *how* I bare you on eagles' **wings**, and brought you unto myself."

God considers His bearing them on eagles' **wings**, just like an eagle. It is a figure of speech, of course. He did not have eagles in the wilderness.

- **Deuteronomy 32:9-12**
  "For the LORD'S portion is his people; Jacob *is* the lot of his inheritance. He found him in a desert land, and in the waste howling wilderness; he led him about, he instructed him, he kept him as the apple of his eye. As an eagle stirreth up her nest, fluttereth over her young, spreadeth abroad her **wings**, taketh them, beareth them on her wings: *So* the LORD alone did lead him, and *there was* no strange god with him."

This is talking about Israel's wilderness journey. <u>The Lord's leading was like an **eagle**, scattering the foe and taking care of them.</u>

- **Deuteronomy 32:13**
  "He made him ride on the high places of the earth, that he might eat the increase of the fields; and he made him to suck honey out of the rock, and oil out of the flinty rock;"

<u>God protected Israel like an **eagle**.</u>

- **Psalm 17:8**
  "Keep me as the apple of the eye, hide me under the shadow of thy **wings**,"

- **Psalm 63:7**
  "Because thou hast been my help, therefore in the shadow of thy **wings** will I rejoice."

<u>God's shelter is like the **wings** of a bird.</u>

- **Isaiah 40:31**
  "But they that wait upon the LORD shall renew *their* strength; they shall mount up with **wings as eagles**; they shall run, and not be weary; *and they* shall walk, and not faint."

Here are **wings** as **eagles** again. Scriptures are replete with these references.

- **Malachi 4:2**
  "But unto you that fear my name shall the Sun of righteousness arise with healing in his **wings**; and ye shall go forth, and grow up as calves of the stall."

I do not know exactly how the Lord is going to do it, but I believe He is going to protect the woman, Israel–the one that brought forth the man child, the Lord Jesus Christ.

Will America Care For Israel?

The United States of America sometimes has the emblem on the dollar bills of an eagle. It is a national emblem. It could be the Americans will take care of Israel and make sure that they get over to the place of safety. Many believe that this place is Petra. It is a place of rocks. It is secure. Whatever it is, God is going to do it. Israel has a place to flee from the dragon and all the persecuting people in the last three and a half years of the tribulation period.

Revelation 12:15

"And the serpent cast out of his mouth water as a flood after the woman, that he might cause her to be carried away of the flood."

Here is water and a **flood** that comes out of the **mouth** of the **serpent**. He has power to do this.

- **Genesis 6:17**
  "And, behold, I, even I, do bring a **flood** of waters upon the earth, to destroy all flesh, wherein *is* the breath of life, from under heaven; *and* every thing that *is* in the earth shall die."

The Lord is able to bring a flood just like He brought the **flood** in Noah's time.

- **Genesis 9:11**
  "And I will establish my covenant with you; neither shall all flesh be cut off any more by the waters of a **flood**; neither shall there any more be a flood to destroy the earth."

There will be no more **floods** from the Lord. This one will be from the Serpent.

- **Isaiah 59:19**
  "So shall they fear the name of the LORD from the west, and his glory from the rising of the sun. When the enemy shall come in like a **flood**, the Spirit of the LORD shall lift up a standard against him."

Here is Satan with a **flood** of water. I do not how this is going to take place, but apparently the Lord has given him some power to have a **flood** of water chasing this woman, to drown the woman Israel, to make it so that she cannot live.

Revelation 12:16

"And the earth helped the woman, and the earth opened her mouth, and swallowed up the flood which the dragon cast out of his mouth."

The Lord made a protection again for His people Israel during this last three and a half years of tribulation. He **helped the woman**. Has the **earth opened** before? Yes.

- **Numbers 16:29-33**
  "If these men die the common death of all men, or if they be visited after the visitation of all men; *then* the LORD hath not sent me. But if the LORD make a new thing, and the **earth open** her mouth, and swallow them up, with all that *appertain* unto them, and they go down quick into the pit; then ye shall understand that these men have provoked the LORD. And it came to pass, as he had made an end of speaking all these words, that the ground clave asunder that *was* under them: And **the earth opened her mouth**, and swallowed them up, and their houses, and all the men that *appertained* unto Korah, and all *their* goods. They, and all that *appertained* to them, went down alive into the pit, and the earth closed upon them: and they perished from among the congregation."

Korah and his band wanted to be the head. They wanted to be like the priests. They wanted to be leaders like Moses and Aaron, so they rebelled. God judged Korah and his band. If you wonder why the family of Korah was also in this, it is because apparently they were a part and party to this rebellion.

God is able, as in the Old Testament, **to open up the earth**. In Revelation 12:16, He **opens up the earth** and takes care of the **flood** that Satan has tried to use to kill Israel at this time. These are miraculous things. Anything that God does is miraculous. Sometimes the thing that the Devil has been given the power to do, seems like a miracle as well. Certainly he has power, but he does not have all power.

Revelation 12:17

"And the dragon was wroth with the woman, and went to make war with the remnant of her seed, which keep the commandments of God, and have the testimony of Jesus Christ."

There is war. The **dragon is wroth with the woman, wroth** with **Israel.** She, while escaping the **flood,** and the **earth swallowing up the waters,** will make him **wroth**–absolutely, totally angry with this woman, **Israel,** and he went to **make war.**

- **Ezekiel 38:16**
  "And thou shalt come up against my people of Israel, as a cloud to cover the land; it shall be in the latter days, and I will bring thee against my land, that the heathen may know me, when I shall be sanctified in thee, O Gog, before their eyes."

War Against Israel

We see here about a war against Israel in the last time. Gog is a nation used by Satan. Satan is going to gather together all these people to come against and try to defeat Israel.

- **Revelation 16:13**
  "And I saw three unclean spirits like frogs *come* out of the mouth of the dragon, and out of the mouth of the beast, and out of the mouth of the false prophet."

The Beast Is The Political Ruler

The dragon is Satan. The beast is the political ruler, the antichrist. The false prophet is the religious leader.

- **Revelation 16:14-16**
  "For they are the spirits of devils, working miracles, *which* go forth unto the kings of the earth and of the whole world, to gather them to the battle of that great day of God Almighty. Behold, I come as a thief. Blessed *is* he that watcheth, and keepeth his garments, lest he walk naked, and they see his shame. And he gathered them together into a place called in the Hebrew tongue Armageddon."

What is their purpose? What is the mission of **Satan,** the antichrist, and the false prophet–the Satanic trinity? They are to go forth to the kings of the earth during the tribulation period to gather them together to battle.

The battle of Armageddon will be against **Israel.** All the nations from the east (China and others), the north (Gog and Magog, i.e. Russia), the west, and the south (Egypt), will be gathered against the Lord Jesus Christ's people. There will be millions of them. There are two hundred million from China alone. Who is going to win the battle? The Lord Jesus Christ Himself will win it.

- **Revelation 19:11**
  "And I saw heaven opened, and behold a white horse; and he that sat upon him *was* called Faithful and True, and in righteousness **he doth judge and make war.**"

- **Revelation 19:14**
  "And the armies *which were* in heaven followed him upon white horses, clothed in fine linen, white and clean."

Those are the genuine believers that are truly saved before the Lord Jesus Christ returns. In our new glorified bodies, we will be with the Lord Jesus Christ as He comes back, to put down this rebellion against **Israel.**

- **Revelation 19:15**
  "And out of his mouth goeth a sharp sword, that with it he should **smite the nations**: and he shall rule them with a rod of iron: and he treadeth the winepress of the fierceness and wrath of Almighty God."

- **Revelation 19:17-19**
  "And I saw an angel standing in the sun; and he cried with a loud voice, saying to all the fowls that fly in the midst of heaven, Come and gather yourselves together unto the supper of the great God; That ye may eat the flesh of kings, and the flesh of captains, and the flesh of mighty men, and the flesh of horses, and of them that sit on them, and the flesh of all *men, both* free and bond, both small and great. And I saw the beast, and the kings of the earth, and their armies, gathered together to make war against him that sat on the horse, and against his army."

Satan is gathering the multitudes of the earth against the Lord Jesus Christ, His army, and **Israel.**

- **Revelation 19:20-21**
  "And the beast was taken, and with him the false prophet that wrought miracles before him, with which he deceived them that had received the mark of the beast, and them that worshipped his image. These both were cast alive into a lake of fire burning with brimstone. And the remnant were slain with the sword of him that sat upon the horse, which proceeded out of his mouth: and all the fowls were filled with their flesh."

The Lord Jesus Christ is going to have the victory.

Notice here in Revelation 12:17, they *have the testimony of Jesus Christ*. They **keep the commandments**. These people continuously keep the Words of God. They are the ones that are victorious. These people were faithful.

- **Revelation 1:2**
  "Who bare record of the word of God, and of the **testimony** of Jesus Christ, and of all things that he saw."

- **Revelation 1:9**
  "I John, who also am your brother, and companion in tribulation, and in the kingdom and patience of Jesus Christ, was in the isle that is called Patmos, for the word of God, and for the **testimony** of Jesus Christ."

John was in the isle of Patmos, banished because of the Word of God and the **testimony** of Jesus Christ.

These things will take place. When **Satan** is cast down to the earth from Heaven, things will really begin to happen during this tribulation period. I am glad I will not be here. I am glad I will be with the Lord Jesus Christ in Heaven. If you are saved by genuine faith in the Lord Jesus Christ, genuinely born-again, and regenerated, you are not going to be on this earth. You are not going to be anywhere but with the Lord Jesus Christ in Heaven. It is a wonderful thing. We have power, just like those in the tribulation period will have power, to overcome Satan by the **blood of the Lamb**.

- **Revelation 12:11**
  "And they overcame him by the **blood of the Lamb**, and by the word of their **testimony**; and they loved not their lives unto the death."

The Power Of The Blood Of Christ

We cannot understand all the power that is in the blood of the Lord Jesus Christ, but God was in Christ reconciling the world unto Himself. It is through the blood of the Lord Jesus Christ that we can be Biblically saved, washed, and cleansed. Through that blood we can overcome the Devil and all of his angels. We ought to praise God for this victory of our Saviour. The Lord Jesus Christ is going to take care of the genuinely saved ones, even during this tribulation period on the earth.

Revelation
Chapter Thirteen

Revelation 13:1

"And I stood upon the sand of the sea, and saw a beast rise up out of the sea, having seven heads and ten horns, and upon his horns ten crowns, and upon his heads the name of blasphemy."

Beasts Out Of The Sea And Land

Chapter 13 deals with two beasts—the first beast out of the sea, and the second beast out of the land. This first beast is the political beast, the ruler that will take place in this tribulation period. The genuinely saved Christians will all be gone before any of that takes place. All the ones who are genuinely born-again will be raptured out.

This *out of the sea* means out of the **Gentiles**. I believe that this is the antichrist. This is the one that is the **political** ruler that will be revealed about the middle of the tribulation period, and take over this whole world. The **heads**, the **horns**, and the **crowns**, I think, are parallel to the book of Daniel.

- **Daniel 7:19-20**
  "Then I would know the truth of the fourth beast, which was diverse from all the others, exceeding dreadful, whose teeth *were* of iron, and his nails *of* brass; *which* devoured, brake in pieces, and stamped the residue with his feet; And of the ten **horns** that *were* in his head, and *of* the other which came up, and before whom three fell; even *of* that **horn** that had eyes, and a mouth that spake very great things, whose look *was* more stout than his fellows."

- **Daniel 7:24**
  "And the ten **horns** out of this kingdom *are* ten kings *that* shall
  arise: and another shall rise after them; and he shall be diverse
  from the first, and he shall subdue three kings."

This is apparently some ten-king kingdom, possibly the European Union,
that is going to arise.

- **Revelation 12:3**
  "And there appeared another wonder in heaven; and behold a
  great red dragon, having seven **heads** and ten **horns**, and seven
  crowns upon his heads."

Here there are lots of **horns** and **heads**. I do not pretend to know exactly
all these details, but I would assume that if the ten **horns** are ten **kings**
in Daniel 7, the ten **horns** here in Revelation 13:1 are ten **kings** also.

- **Revelation 17:3**
  "So he carried me away in the spirit into the wilderness: and I
  saw a woman sit upon a scarlet coloured beast, full of names of
  blasphemy, having seven **heads** and ten **horns**."

I would imagine the ten **horns** again are ten **kings**. I believe that the
woman is Rome, the apostate religious groups that are gathered together
with her. We will cover this when we get to Revelation 17.

- **Revelation 17:7**
  "And the angel said unto me, Wherefore didst thou marvel? I will
  tell thee the mystery of the woman, and of the beast that carrieth
  her, which hath the seven heads and ten horns."

This is a similar **beast**. At this point, the **political** ruler is going to be
underneath the religious ruler—this woman—which I believe is the
religious groups headed by Rome, apostate Protestants, and all the pagan
religions as well. I believe it will consist of all the religions of the world
including the Hindus, Muslims, Confucianists, and all the others. The ten
horns are ten kings.

- **Revelation 17:9**
  "And here *is* the mind which hath wisdom. The seven heads are
  seven mountains, on which the woman sitteth."

Many believe this is the seven hills of Rome. I agree. Not that Rome is the
only one represented by this woman, but she is the leader of the apostate
Protestants and all the other religions of the world.

The Gentile Beast Out Of The Sea

John saw this first beast rise up out of the sea. It is the sea of the Gentiles. I believe the political ruler that will come to the fore in the last half of the tribulation period—the last three and a half years—will be a Gentile out of the sea of nations. The second beast will be out of the land, which I believe will be a Jew.

You may say, "How can a man have so much **power?**" Well, how could Saddam Hussein have so much **power**—killing people, beheading people, taking off their hands, their arms, and so on? How could Castro have so much **power**? How could Adolph Hitler have the **power** that he had? How could Joseph Stalin have his **power?** Or Mao Tse-Tung in China?

Speaking of what is called "democratic" **power**, though totally different from those listed above as to the extent of his "**power**," how can Barack Hussein Obama have so much **power** in the United States of America? Rather than confining himself to the **limited powers** granted to him as president, he has repeatedly usurped **powers** never granted to him by the U. S. Constitution. He has done this despite his oath to "*preserve, protect, and defend*" that Constitution. The oath to be taken by the president on first entering office is specified in Article II, Section 1, of the Constitution is this:

> "*I do solemnly swear (or affirm) that I will faithfully execute the office of President of the United States, and will to the best of my ability, <u>preserve, protect, and defend the Constitution of the United States</u>.*"

This is what Obama promised. But he has not followed the Constitution in many of his actions. Where will Obama's **power-grab** end?

<u>This first beast here in Revelation is going to be a powerful **political beast**</u>. If the Lord Jesus Christ should come today, all these nations are right now in progress. The North Atlantic Treaty Organization (NATO) is certainly a collectivist left-wing, one-world government type of association. There is the European Union. All of those are in favor of world government. The United Nations is also for world government. There has to be a head to that world government. After the true church is gone, that head will be picked and selected. He will be the antichrist. He will be a **political** ruler. It will not be Kofi Annan. He was a cream puff compared to the antichrist. He was the head of the United Nations, but he was only a spokesman. <u>The antichrist is</u>

going to be a horrendous, powerful person. The truly born-again Christians, the genuinely saved ones, will be out of here before he ever takes over.

Revelation 13:2

"And the beast which I saw was like unto a leopard, and his feet were as *the feet* of a bear, and his mouth as the mouth of a lion: and the dragon gave him his power, and his seat, and great authority."

Three Animals In One Beast

This beast is like three different animals—a leopard, a bear, and a lion. All of them are wild animals. I would not want to meet up with any of them, would you? He is ferocious. This shows his ferocity. The power that he has is from the dragon, which we have seen before, is the Devil himself. Satan is this dragon. This antichrist—this political ruler—is empowered by Satan to do what he wants to do.

The reverse order of these animals—not **leopard, bear,** and **lion,** but **lion, bear,** and **leopard**—is found in Daniel 7. The books of Daniel and Revelation are quite similar many times. They have many similar things, indeed.

- **Daniel 7:3-7**
  "And four great **beasts** came up from the sea, diverse one from another. The first *was* like a **lion,** and had eagle's wings: I beheld till the wings thereof were plucked, and it was lifted up from the earth, and made stand upon the feet as a man, and a man's heart was given to it. And behold another **beast,** a second, like to a **bear,** and it raised up itself on one side, and *it had* three ribs in the mouth of it between the teeth of it: and they said thus unto it, Arise, devour much flesh. After this I beheld, and lo another, like a **leopard,** which had upon the back of it four wings of a fowl; the **beast** had also four heads; and dominion was given to it. After this I saw in the night visions, and behold a **fourth beast,** dreadful and terrible, and strong exceedingly; and it had great iron teeth: it devoured and brake in pieces, and stamped the residue with the feet of it: and it *was* diverse from all the **beasts** that *were* before it; and it had ten **horns.**"

Four Beasts Out Of The Sea

In Daniel, there were four great beasts that came up out of the sea. The first like a lion was Babylon. The second one like a bear was Medo-Persia. The third like a leopard was Greece. The fourth beast was Rome. These were four powerful nations.

Why does Revelation 13:2 say that all three of these are combined into one? It is because Satan has the power of all these three empires molded into one. There is the power of Babylon, the power of Medo-Persia and the power of Greece. Throw in Rome as well. All the power of these are gathered together in this one **political** ruler. He will rule the entire world.

Revelation 13:3

"And I saw one of his heads as it were wounded to death; and his deadly wound was healed: and all the world wondered after the beast."

The Lord Jesus Christ was wounded for our transgressions and bruised for our iniquities as it says in Isaiah 53.

The Deceptive Political Ruler

This is the antichrist—the political ruler—that is the mock ruler similar to the Lord Jesus Christ. He has a wound. He died, and now he comes back to life. It is an exact deception of Satan in order to try to gain this terrible miracle. Notice—*and all the world wondered after the beast.* They followed him. Later we will see that they worshipped him. They say, "Here is a resurrection. This must be God Himself!" Just like the Lord Jesus Christ, after His resurrection many went back, but some did follow Him, and some believed on Him. In fact, He appeared to more than 500 brethren at one time.

- 1 Corinthians 15:6
  "After that, he was seen of above five hundred brethren at once; of whom the greater part remain unto this present, but some are fallen asleep."

The healing of the deadly wound of the beast on one of these heads, whatever that might be, causes people to wonder and to go after this beast, and to make him like the Lord Jesus Christ in a deceitful and false fashion.

Revelation 13:4

"And they worshipped the dragon which gave power unto the beast: and they worshipped the beast, saying, Who *is* like unto the beast? who is able to make war with him?"

The Absolute Dictator

He is the absolute dictator and they worship this dragon. The dragon is Satan. That word for worship is PROSKUNEO. It means *among the Asians, especially the Persians, to fall upon the knees and touch the ground with the forehead as an expression of profound reverence.* This is the worship they gave to the dragon, that is, to the Devil.

- **Exodus 20:3**
  "Thou shalt have no other gods before me."

They are not supposed to bow down to a man, this false leader.

- **Exodus 34:14**
  "For thou shalt **worship** no other god: for the LORD, whose name *is* Jealous, *is* a jealous God:"

God is very clear on this. These people that are lost, and are on this earth after the genuinely saved people are gone into Heaven in the rapture, will **worship** this **Satan**, the **Devil**. God says, "Do not do it!"

- **Deuteronomy 30:17-18**
  "But if thine heart turn away, so that thou wilt not hear, but shalt be drawn away, and **worship** other gods, and serve them; I denounce unto you this day, that ye shall surely perish, *and that* ye shall not prolong *your* days upon the land, whither thou passest over Jordan to go to possess it."

God did not want his people, Israel, **worshipping** other gods.

- **Psalm 81:9**
  "There shall no strange god be in thee; neither shalt thou **worship** any strange god."

To **worship Satan** is a false practice. It is against the teachings of the entire Bible.

- **Isaiah 2:8**
  "Their land also is full of idols; they **worship** the work of their own hands, that which their own fingers have made:"

This antichrist is not an idol, but he is a man made into an idol. They are **worshipping** this antichrist, this **political beast**.

- **Daniel 3:18**
  "But if not, be it known unto thee, O king, that we will not serve thy gods, nor **worship** the golden image which thou hast set up."

Three Jews Did Not Worship An Idol

Shadrach, Meshach, and Abednego were told to worship an idol. They were Jews who loved the Lord God. Undoubtedly, there will be some that will not worship Satan undoubtedly, but most of the people in this tribulation period will worship this false Deity.

- **Matthew 4:9**
  "And saith unto him, All these things will I give thee, if thou wilt fall down and **worship** me."

The Lord Jesus Christ was out in the wilderness to be tempted and tested by **Satan**, the **Devil**. Satanic **worship** was right there in the New Testament, even before the antichrist comes upon the scene.

- **Matthew 4:10**
  "Then saith Jesus unto him, Get thee hence, Satan: for it is written, Thou shalt **worship** the Lord thy God, and him only shalt thou serve."

- **John 4:24**
  "God *is* a Spirit: and they that **worship** him must **worship** *him* in spirit and in truth."

This is not falling down to an idol or to a man.

- **2 Thessalonians 2:3-4**
  "Let no man deceive you by any means: for *that day shall not come*, except there come a falling away first, and that man of sin be revealed, the son of perdition; Who opposeth and exalteth himself above all that is called God, or that is **worshipped**; so that he as God sitteth in the temple of God, shewing himself that he is God."

This Man Of Sin Revealed

Here the Scriptures give us a prophecy of this man of sin—this antichrist or political ruler that will come. The *falling away* is the apostasy. This is the political ruler, the first beast out of the sea. This political beast will be worshipped just like God Himself and he says, "I am God." This is just like Hirohito in Japan. He was deity. It is just like the Roman emperor. He was god. That is why the genuine Christians failed to worship this emperor. They did not believe he was God. Many people have fallen into this error, but this antichrist will show himself that he is God and will deceive people.

- **Revelation 9:20**
  "And the rest of the men which were not killed by these plagues yet repented not of the works of their hands, that they should not **worship devils**, and idols of gold, and silver, and brass, and stone, and of wood: which neither can see, nor hear, nor walk:"

Even in the tribulation period, they are **worshipping the Devil.**

- **Revelation 13:12**
  "And he exerciseth all the power of the first beast before him, and causeth the earth and them which dwell therein to **worship** the first **beast**, whose deadly wound was healed."

There is great power to **worship this beast** and to **worship Satan**. Notice also, the **war** powers of this **political** ruler.

- **Revelation 17:14**
  "These shall make **war** with the Lamb, and the Lamb shall overcome them: for he is Lord of lords, and King of kings: and they that are with him *are* called, and chosen, and faithful."

These are ten kings that are following **Satan**. They will not get victory when the Lord Jesus Christ returns, but there is always **war**-making potential.

- **Revelation 19:11**
  "And I saw heaven opened, and behold a white horse; and he that sat upon him *was* called Faithful and True, and in righteousness he doth judge and make **war**."

The Battle of Armageddon

One day the Lord Jesus Christ is going to come back. He will make war with those armies that are gathered at Jerusalem. There will be several hundred million of them from the north, south, east, and west gathered at that great battle, the battle of Armageddon. Jerusalem is the central point. They will be after Israel's gold, and their other resources. I understand the Dead Sea has plenty of resources. They will come across from the east. The Euphrates River will be dried up and the kings of the east (China and others) will come to Jerusalem. The kings of the north will come—Moscow, Russia,

Germany, and other nations. The kings of the south will come—all of the Egyptians. They will all come for a huge, gigantic battle. They will make war with the saints and with the Lord Jesus Christ, the Saviour. The Lord Jesus Christ will return to this earth, put down that rebellion, and slay them all.

There is a whole Church of **Satan**. I found some information about that Church of **Satan** on the Internet. It began in 1966. (That is the year after we arrived here in Collingswood, New Jersey. We came here in 1965.) Anton Lavey died in 1997 and another took his place. The church of **Satan** is a real church. It is a horrible type of church. Some of the beliefs and practices may be similar to what they will practice when the antichrist is in charge. They do not worship a living deity. They do not have any god. There is a major emphasis placed on the power and authority of the individual Satanist rather than on a god or a goddess. In other words, the Satanists themselves—those that worship this false religion—will have the power and authority individualized upon themselves. Another belief they hold is that no redeemer lives.

- **Job 19:25**
  "For I know *that* my redeemer liveth, and *that* he shall stand at the latter *day* upon the earth:"

No Real Redeemer

The church of Satan does not believe in any redeemer. Each person is his or her own redeemer, fully responsible for the direction of his or her own life. That is the essence of modernism and liberalism. We have Satanism today.

- **2 Corinthians 11:13-14**
  "For such *are* false apostles, deceitful workers, transforming themselves into the apostles of Christ. And no marvel; for **Satan** himself is transformed into an angel of light."

The Church Of Satan Today

There are probably fewer than 10,000 Satanists in North America. The best-known Satanic organization is the Church of Satan. Anton Lavey wrote several books. He wrote *The Satanic Bible* in 1969. He also wrote *The Satanic Rituals* in 1972. He was the founder of the Church of Satan.

What about his **Satanic** statements? This may be the same as what the antichrist will have. Who knows?

First of all, they believe in indulgence not abstinence. They believe in vital existence—living right now. They believe in undefiled wisdom—not hypocritical self-deceit, kindness to those deserving it, vengeance—not turning the other cheek, responsibility to the responsible. They say that man is just another animal and he is the most vicious of all. These are the beliefs of the church of **Satan**. Evolutionists believe we are just animals. It is a terrible thing. They also believe in the gratification of all of one's desires. All kinds of sins are acceptable.

Some say that the **Satanic** church is the best friend the "Christian" church has ever had. Satan has kept the false churches in business for centuries. Well, that is what they say. I do not know whether these churches have kept the church of **Satan** in business, but certainly I have been speaking out against the **Devil** ever since I have been preaching. I believe that the **Devil** is revealed as a person in Scripture. He is an individual that God says is a **fallen angel**.

The Church Of Satan's Theology

What is the theology of the church of Satan? First, they say that people have created gods in many forms. Pick one that might be useful to you. Any god is all right. That is their belief. Heaven and Hell do not exist. This is a Satanic falsity about Heaven and Hell. Then they say that Satan is not a being or a living entity. He is rather a force of nature. The Bible says that he is a being. We are to beware of the Devil.

The highest of Satanic holidays is the birthday of the individual Satanist. Of lesser importance is Halloween on October 31, the Solstices on June 21 and December 21, and the Equinoxes on March 21 and September 21.

Their rituals and ceremonies have various names, including Satan, Lucifer, Belial, and Leviathan. Did you know that these are some of his names that they use? Ceremonies are pageants. They have three different types of magic rituals. There is sex magic, a healing or happiness ritual, and a destruction ritual. That destruction ritual may include: sticking pins in a doll; drawing a picture or writing a description of the victim's death; or delivering a soliloquy. A destruction ritual is best performed by a group. They get a group together and have destruction rituals to kill somebody or to wipe somebody off the face of the earth. That is what they do.

The Dress Of Male Satanists

Male Satanists usually wear full-length black robes. Young women generally wear sexually suggestive clothing. Older women wear all black. They have various traditions. They use the pentagram—the five-pointed star with one point downward and two points up. They use the goat's head and so on.

When the **Satanic** bible was written, they had a nude woman as the altar during their rituals. It was a terrible situation. They have one white candle and one black candle. For their rituals they have a bell, which is rung nine times at the beginning and end of their rituals. The **Satanic** priest rotates counterclockwise as he rings the bell. They have a chalice and other ritual tools including a gong, a sword, elixir (usually wine) and parchment.

What are some of their rules of behavior? They say that prayer is useless. I do not agree with that at all. Ritual killing of humans violates **Satanic** principles. They do not kill people, but witches do. Members enjoy indulgence instead of abstinence. If a man smites you on the cheek, smash him on the other. That is their principle. Do unto others as they do unto you, instead of as you would have them do. Engage in sexual activity freely—whether heterosexuality, homosexuality, or bisexuality—all kinds of wickedness. Membership is limited to adults of legal age.

The Satanists' Political Agenda

What is their political agenda? Termination of the myth of equality for all. Tax all the churches. Remove any religious beliefs that have been incorporated into legislation. Develop and produce artificial human companions. They are for robots and maybe also human cloning. Who knows?

Their groups are called grottos. The head man as of 2001 was Magus Peter Gilmore. He is the high priest. Blanche Barton is the high priestess. There is terrible, wicked worship of **Satan** even today. In the time of the antichrist—this political ruler—people will worship the Devil himself, the **dragon** which gave power to the **beast**.

Revelation 13:5

"And there was given unto him a mouth speaking great things and blasphemies; and power was given unto him to continue forty *and* two months."

The Power Of The Antichrist

I believe this forty two months is probably the last three and a half years of the tribulation. It will be the time when the antichrist will operate. The Lord does not want anything to do with blasphemy.

- Matthew 15:19
  "For out of the heart proceed evil thoughts, murders, adulteries, fornications, thefts, false witness, **blasphemies**:"

This wicked antichrist will have a wicked heart and he will speak **blasphemies** against God.

- Ephesians 4:29
  "Let no **corrupt** communication proceed out of your mouth, but that which is good to the use of edifying, that it may minister grace unto the hearers."

God does not want us to speak **blasphemies** like this antichrist, this political beast. We hear the **blasphemous** speech of the antichrist as we listen to various things even in our day, do we not? He will have a greater **blasphemy** than all.

Revelation 13:6

"And he opened his mouth in blasphemy against God, to blaspheme his name, and his tabernacle, and them that dwell in heaven."

This antichrist, this **political ruler**, this first **beast** opens his mouth in **blasphemy**. The Lord Jesus Christ talked about **swearing**. We are not to **swear**.

- Matthew 5:34-37
  "But I say unto you, **Swear not** at all; neither by heaven; for it is God's throne: Nor by the earth; for it is his footstool: neither by Jerusalem; for it is the city of the great King. Neither shalt thou swear by thy head, because thou canst not make one hair white or black. But let your communication be, Yea, yea; Nay, nay: for whatsoever is more than these cometh of evil."

God does not us want to speak **blasphemy** or oaths. There was an article on the Internet from the Christian Courier entitled *The Plague of Profanity*. This antichrist knows no bounds regarding **blasphemy** and **profanity**. Are you as sick of hearing it as I am (this **profanity**)? We are exposed to it at the supermarket, over the back fence, and at the ball game. It fills our novels, movies, and it is profuse on television. What is this mysterious influence? Is it **profanity**? We hear it, not just from sailors (*"to curse like a sailor"*) or from the French (*"pardon my French"*), but from all strata of society.

Filthy Speech Today

It used to be the case that a gentleman would never use profanity in the presence of a woman. Deep down he knew he shouldn't use it anywhere. Now, women can swear with the best (or the worst) of them. Small children who have not learned to discuss much of anything, yet, on an intellectual basis, they can curse profusely. Children—wicked, filthy children with their speech. It almost seems as if some of their first words are of the four-letter variety.

We had our vice president spew forth a little bit of **blasphemy** and **filthy** language as the photographers were taking pictures in the Senate. Weigh in on that if you want, but it is a horrible thing.

A recent study, by the Parents Television Council, found the use of **profanity** during the so-called "family hour" (8:00 to 9:00 p.m. Eastern time) to be up 58% from the previous two years. The nature of the language, that is **sexual explicitness**, is getting qualitatively worse. As we said before, the Words of God say we are to let no **corrupt** speech come out of our mouths. **Profanity** is all around us. This evil, first political ruler will be a **blasphemous** ruler, indeed.

Minced Oaths Dangers

There is also such a thing as "minced oaths." They arose in the time of Puritanism when they had censorship on blasphemy. They could not blaspheme so they made up these half-hearted, minced oaths:

1. *Begorra*, meaning by God;
2. *Bejabers*, meaning by Jesus;
3. *By George*, meaning by God;
4. *By golly, by gosh, by gum*—all of them mean by God. These

are minced oaths. Christians ought not to use any minced oaths either.

5. *Cripes* means Christ.

6. *Dang* means damn.

7. *Darn* is damn.

8. *Doggone* is God damn. These are things that are minced oaths.

9. *For crying out loud* means for Christ's sake.

10. *Gee means Jesus*

11. *Gee whiz refers to Jesus*

12. *Gee wilikers* refers to Jesus.

13. *Good grief* is good God. These are minced oaths used by Christians. Some of them do not know what they are saying or what they mean.

14. *Goodness gracious* means good God.

15. *Gosh* is God.

16. *Geez* means Jesus.

17. *Jiminy Cricket* means Jesus Christ.

18. *My goodness* means my God.

19. *Sam Hill* means Hell.

20. *Criminy* means Christ.

21. *Egad* means oh God.

All of these different minced oaths are around us. God does not want us as genuine believers to use these. I think of a man who is with the Lord Jesus Christ now, Bob Cook. He starts out every broadcast by saying, "How in the world are you?" He is swearing by the world. That is a minced oath. That is blasphemy.

Revelation 13:7

"**And it was given unto him to make war with the saints, and to overcome them: and power was given him over all kindreds, and tongues, and nations.**"

The Power Of The Political Beast

This political beast has great power to make war with the saints. There will be some saints that have been led to the Lord

> Jesus Christ by the 144,000 evangelists—12,000 from every one of the tribes of Israel. There will be some saints on the earth—not the born-again believers that are genuinely saved and go up in the rapture—but there are others that will be genuinely saved. This political ruler will make war with them and overcome them.

What are we to do even now as the **Devil** is attacking us?

- **James 4:7**
  "Submit yourselves therefore to God. Resist the **devil**, and he will flee from you."
- **1 Peter 5:8-9**
  "Be sober, be vigilant; because your adversary the **devil**, as a roaring lion, walketh about, seeking whom he may devour: Whom resist stedfast in the faith, knowing that the same afflictions are accomplished in your brethren that are in the world."
- **Revelation 11:7**
  "And when they shall have finished their testimony, the **beast** that ascendeth out of the bottomless pit shall make **war** against them, and shall overcome them, and kill them."

This **political** man is a **warring** man.

- **Revelation 12:17**
  "And the **dragon** was wroth with the woman, and went to make **war** with the remnant of her seed, which keep the commandments of God, and have the testimony of Jesus Christ."

Here again is the **warring beast**.

- **Revelation 17:14**
  "These shall make **war** with the Lamb, and the Lamb shall overcome them: for he is Lord of lords, and King of kings: and they that are with him *are* called, and chosen, and faithful."

Revelation 13:8

"And all that dwell upon the earth shall worship him, whose names are not written in the book of life of the Lamb slain from the foundation of the world."

All that dwell upon the earth shall **worship** the **beast**, this **political ruler**. All of them will be lining up. It almost seems like the line-up for the sale of the book of our former presidents or other famous people. Or like the books of Harry Potter. They will line up and **worship** this particular **beast**. The only ones that will **worship** him are those whose names are not written in the **book of life**. Those that are not genuinely saved will **worship** him.

- **Daniel 11:31**
  "And arms shall stand on his part, and they shall pollute the sanctuary of strength, and shall take away the daily *sacrifice*, and they shall place the abomination that maketh desolate."

There is going to be an unclean animal offered upon the altar in that rebuilt temple during the tribulation period.

- **Matthew 4:9**
  "And saith unto him, All these things will I give thee, if thou wilt fall down and **worship** me."

The man of sin is **worshipped**. Satan said, "**Worship** me" and the Lord Jesus Christ said, "Get thee hence." He would not **worship** the Devil.

- **Matthew 24:15**
  "When ye therefore shall see the abomination of desolation, spoken of by Daniel the prophet, stand in the holy place, (whoso readeth, let him understand:) "

The abomination of desolation is when he offers an unclean animal on the altar. They will **worship** him.

- **2 Thessalonians 2:3-4**
  "Let no man deceive you by any means: for *that day shall not come*, except there come a falling away first, and that man of sin be revealed, the son of perdition; Who opposeth and exalteth himself above all that is called God, or that is **worshipped**; so that he as God sitteth in the temple of God, shewing himself that he is God."

The Antichrist Will Be Worshipped

When it says, *"all that dwell upon the earth shall worship him,"* that is exactly what they will do. The antichrist—this political ruler—will sit in the temple of God. Talk about sacrilege! Talk about an abomination! People will come into that temple, not worshipping the Lord Jesus Christ, but worshipping this man, this human figure, this powerful Satanic-motivated individual.

Revelation 13:9

"If any man have an ear, let him hear."

This is a very short verse. This is repeated seven times in Revelation 2 and Revelation 3. When the Lord Jesus Christ spoke to the seven churches, He said, *"He that hath an **ear**, let him **hear** what the Spirit saith unto the churches."* He says this to the churches at Ephesus, Smyrna, Pergamos, Thyatira, Sardis, Philadelphia, and Laodicea. God wants us to **hear** what He says. Just as the believers today are to **listen** to the Scriptures, **read** the Scriptures, and know the Scriptures, so the believers in the tribulation period are to listen. They will be genuinely saved during that time as the 144,000 give the gospel and they are redeemed by genuine faith in the Lord Jesus Christ.

If any man have an **ear**, let him **hear**. Not to **hear** what **Satan** says. Not to **hear** what the man of sin, the antichrist, says, but what the Lord Jesus Christ says in His Words.

Stay With The Words Of God

As John writes this, the Lord is appealing to them to stay with the Scriptures. Stay with the Words of God. Stay with the Bible and not to go in the wrong direction—just as He said to all the churches in Asia Minor, which, by the way, is in Turkey. These very churches that used to be sound are now pagan and Muslim.

All kinds of activity is rampant there. The Lord Jesus Christ told His seven churches in that area of Turkey, *"He that hath an ear, let him **hear** what the Spirit saith unto the churches."* Because those churches did not **hear** what the Spirit of God said in the Scriptures and did not **follow** the Scriptures, they went apostate. As a result, they turned Muslim. Today, those churches are no more.

Many Churches Are Going Apostate

Sad to say, this is the fate of many churches in our land and in our world, is it not? Look at the big churches that started sound and are now apostate. How do they become that way? It is because of Satanic influence. There is Satanic influence first of all in the schools, colleges, and seminaries that train these preachers.

Take the Methodist Church. It used to be, when John and Charles Wesley were walking the earth, that the Methodist beliefs were mostly sound Scriptural beliefs. I do not agree with them on the lack of eternal security and on some other doctrines, but basically, they used to have sound Scriptural beliefs. They believed in the Deity of the Lord Jesus Christ, His bodily resurrection, and His blood atonement. But now look at the Methodist Church.

There are a few exceptions. There are a few evangelical Methodists that are still in the Methodist Church. They should come out of that United Methodist Church. It is in the World Council of Churches and the National Council of Churches. Most of the Methodist churches today are preaching modernist, liberal, apostate, and heretical doctrines. They would not be caught dead believing in the beliefs of John and Charles Wesley.

How did this come to be? It came slowly, by a process of infiltration, from the seminaries that taught atheism and unbelief in the Scriptures. They trained preachers in this heresy. This changed the whole Methodist Church structure. Now they have huge buildings, big Methodist buildings for churches that used to be fundamental. Now they are apostate.

There are Baptist buildings for churches that used to be fundamental. Now many of them are apostate. There are Lutheran buildings for churches that used to be fundamental. Now they are apostate. Let him that has an **ear**, let him **hear**. The seven churches of Asia Minor did not **hear**. Because of this, they went apostate and have disappeared. We have to **hear** lest our church and any others in our areas go apostate as well.

Revelation 13:10

"He that leadeth into captivity shall go into captivity: he that killeth with the sword must be killed with the sword. Here is the patience and the faith of the saints."

In other words, as they say, "What goes around, comes around." If you lead into **captivity**, you are going to be **captive**. If you kill with the **sword**, you must be killed with the **sword**. Evil devices have a way of returning on the heads of those that made them.

- **Esther 7:10**
  "So they hanged Haman on the gallows that he had prepared for Mordecai. Then was the king's wrath pacified."

Haman was out to kill Mordecai the Jew, and all of a sudden, he was the one that got hanged on his own gallows.

- **Psalm 9:15**
  "The heathen are sunk down in the pit *that* they made: in the net which they hid is their own foot taken."

They just get taken up in the net that they made to catch someone else.

- **Psalm 57:6**
  "They have prepared a net for my steps; my soul is bowed down: they have digged a **pit** before me, into the midst whereof they are fallen *themselves*. Selah."

Digging Pits For Enemies

Be careful. If you dig pits for your enemies, the Lord Jesus Christ may let you fall into those same pits. The ones that dug the pit for David to fall into, fell into that pit themselves.

- **Matthew 26:52**
  "Then said Jesus unto him, Put up again thy **sword** into his place: for all they that take the **sword** shall perish with the **sword**."

This was when Peter got out the **sword** to defend them there in the Garden of Gethsemane. The Lord Jesus Christ was to die. That was His mission, to take upon Himself the sins of the world. Peter did not want Him to die. He did not want the crowd to take Him, so he took out a **sword** and cut off the ear of Malchus, the high priest's servant. Here is a verse about capital punishment. They that take the **sword** and kill somebody will perish with the **sword** of capital punishment by governmental authorities.

This is God's righteousness. It will turn out all right. That is what He is saying in this case. God wants us to be **patient**. In the tribulation period, when genuine believers will be led to the Lord Jesus Christ by the 144,000 evangelist Jews, they will need **patience**. We need **patience** in the way we live today.

- **Romans 5:3**
  "And not only so, but we glory in tribulations also: knowing that tribulation worketh **patience**;"

Tribulation Worketh Patience

We do not like tribulation, but God says that tribulation worketh patience. When we see a little trouble—and we cannot get out of the trouble—after a while in the trouble, for so many minutes or hours, we get a little patience. We might say, "Well, I guess I cannot do anything. I am just going to sit down and take it easy." Tribulation works patience.

- **Romans 15:4**
  "For whatsoever things were written aforetime were written for our learning, that we through **patience** and comfort of the scriptures might have hope."

The Scriptures give us **patience**. The Scriptures teach us **patience**. We have hope because we have the **patience** and comfort of the Scriptures.

- **2 Thessalonians 1:4**
  "So that we ourselves glory in you in the churches of God for your **patience** and faith in all your persecutions and tribulations that ye endure:"

May God grant us **patience** as tribulations and troubles come upon us. God wants us to endure them, to be **patient** and to have faith in these tribulations.

- **Hebrews 10:36**
  "For ye have need of **patience**, that, after ye have done the will of God, ye might receive the promise."

God has promises when we fulfill His Word, but we have to have **patience** and wait for His promise to be fulfilled.

- **John 3:15**
  "That whosoever believeth in him should not perish, but have eternal life."

Be **patient**. You have everlasting life immediately when you are genuinely saved, but you are not going to go to Heaven until you die or are taken up in the rapture. Be **patient** for these promises. If you have done the will of God, you shall receive the promise.

- **Hebrews 12:1**
  "Wherefore seeing we also are compassed about with so great a cloud of witnesses, let us lay aside every weight, and the sin which doth so easily beset *us*, and let us run with **patience** the race that is set before us,"

The Born-Again Christian's Race

The picture is that of a great arena or race course. People are looking down from the bleachers at the runners that are running around the track. Every one of us has a different race. We must run with patience the race that is set before us. We must patiently run. You do not get to the finish line when you start. The start and the finish are not identical. There is a period of time and space that must be taken into account.

- **James 5:11**
  "Behold, we count them happy which endure. Ye have heard of the **patience** of Job, and have seen the end of the Lord; that the Lord is very pitiful, and of tender mercy."

Patience Versus Longsuffering

There are two words that are similar: patience and longsuffering. Patience means, *putting up with things.* Longsuffering means, *putting up with people.* I do not know which is harder. I think it may be harder putting up with people, although I could be wrong. Job had patience. First, his possessions went. His cattle, his animals, his servants and his children went. Finally, his own health went. He still had patience in all the things that went against him.

- **Job 13:15**
  "Though he slay me, yet will I trust in him: but I will maintain mine own ways before him."
Job's wife told him to curse God and die.
- **Job 1:21**
  "And said, Naked came I out of my mother's womb, and naked shall I return thither: the LORD gave, and the LORD hath taken away; blessed be the name of the LORD."
Job still had **patience**. I do not know whether we could have that much **patience** with all of that pain and suffering.

Through John, God is telling those who are in the tribulation period—under the czar-like oppression and sacrificial punishments of this man of sin, this antichrist, this political ruler—here is the **patience** and the faith of the saints.

Tribulation Saints And Patience

There must be patience even in the tribulation saints—those that are genuinely saved—that they may come through it successfully. God is still on the throne, even at this time of the seven-year period of tribulation, Daniel's 70th Week.

We do not want to worship the Devil in any way, shape, or form. Yet this man who will come upon the earth as the leader of many nations will clone the Lord Jesus Christ in his attributes. He will be accepted. There will be three and a half years in the beginning where he will not show his evil. In the last three and a half years he will show his power, and evil, and might, and will corrupt. People will wonder after this beast, this political ruler. The religious leader will help him to rule. Satan will be underneath all of it.

We have to realize that there is no one on this earth or in Heaven that we are to **worship** except the Lord Himself. No idols. No images. No ephods. No pictures. Just the Lord Himself, in spirit and in truth.

- **John 4:24**
  "God *is* a Spirit: and they that **worship** him must worship *him* in spirit and in truth."

We must have **patience** in all that we do, that we may glorify our Saviour, the Lord Jesus Christ.

Revelation 13:11

"And I beheld another beast coming up out of the earth; and he had two horns like a lamb, and he spake as a dragon."

The Second Beast

This is the other beast. The first beast came out of the sea whom I believe is a Gentile antichrist. This is the second beast out of the land—probably a Jew from the land of Israel, the religious leader, the false prophet. He is against Christ. He is like a lamb. He is not like the Lord Jesus Christ, but he is similar. He tries to deceive people by his looks. There are many deceptive things such as this in Scripture.

- **Genesis 27:22**
  "And Jacob went near unto Isaac his father; and he felt him, and said, The voice *is* Jacob's voice, but the hands *are* the hands of Esau."

There was a voice with different hands. Here is one who looks like a lamb, but he is really like the dragon. This false prophet **pretends** to be like the Lord Jesus Christ, but he is really of the Devil.

- **Matthew 7:15**
  "Beware of **false prophets**, which come to you in sheep's clothing, but inwardly they are ravening wolves."

Here is this **false prophet**. He looks like a lamb, but talks like the dragon.

- **Matthew 7:16**
  "Ye shall know them by their fruits. Do men gather grapes of thorns, or figs of thistles?"

- **Matthew 26:14-16**
  "Then one of the twelve, called Judas Iscariot, went unto the chief priests, And said *unto them*, What will ye give me, and I will deliver him unto you? And they covenanted with him for thirty pieces of silver. And from that time he sought opportunity to **betray** him."

Here is the colossal **deception**. Here is one that looks like an apostle, acts like an apostle chosen by the Lord Jesus Christ Himself, but he is a **false apostle**. He is an antichrist. He hates the Lord Jesus Christ.

- **Matthew 26:47**
  "And while he yet spake, lo, Judas, one of the twelve, came, and with him a great multitude with swords and staves, from the chief priests and elders of the people."

They were out there in the garden of Gethsemane to take Him. Here is one of the twelve–a **deception**. He looked like an apostle, was dressed like an apostle, but he was one of the Devil's children.

- **Mark 14:20**
  "And he answered and said unto them, It is one of the twelve, that dippeth with me in the dish."

In other words, the one that dips in that dish is the one that is going to **betray** Him. That was Judas Iscariot. He was one of the twelve.

- **Luke 22:47**
  "And while he yet spake, behold a multitude, and he that was called Judas, one of the twelve, went before them, and drew near unto Jesus to kiss him."

Satan's emissaries **seem** like they are going to worship the Lord Jesus Christ and kiss Him and adore Him. They are **fakes** and **phonies**. This is the false prophet in Revelation 13. He is a **phony**.

- **John 6:70-71**
  "Jesus answered them, Have not I chosen you twelve, and one of you is a devil? He spake of Judas Iscariot *the son* of Simon: for he it was that should **betray** him, being one of the twelve."

Why Was Judas Chosen?

The Lord Jesus Christ knew who Judas was from the start. Now you may wonder, why did the Lord Jesus Christ choose Judas? I think He chose Judas so that all of us would be on our guard—in churches, in different places, and all throughout—to guard our churches against deceivers among the members. While pretending to be genuinely saved, these deceivers are lost. The Lord Jesus Christ wanted to show us that Satan is a deceiver. Certainly among the disciples, Judas was a deceiver.

In fact, some godly men have said that, even in fundamental churches, up to 75 percent of the people are lost. Some have said, even as high as 90 or 95 percent the people are lost in fundamental churches. They make some "decision," but it is not of the heart. It is not genuine. This is a serious thing. We have this **deception** even among us. I do not know if these statistics are true, but that is what some of the older gentlemen—soldiers of the faith—have said.

Revelation 13:12

"And he exerciseth all the power of the first beast before him, and causeth the earth and them which dwell therein to worship the first beast, whose deadly wound was healed."

The Second Beast's Tasks

This second beast—this false prophet—exercises all the power of the first beast—the political ruler. This is after genuinely saved people are gone in the tribulation period. The political beast is a fake and a false Saviour. He has Satanic power. The false prophet also has great power.

- **Luke 4:6-7**
  "And the devil said unto him, All this **power** will I give thee, and the glory of them: for that is delivered unto me; and to whomsoever I will I give it. If thou therefore wilt worship me, all shall be thine."

This is when the Devil came to the Lord Jesus Christ in the wilderness to tempt Him. Satan is given some **power.** The Lord Jesus Christ did not bow down and worship him, but Satan had **power.** The **false prophet** also has **power.**

- **Luke 22:52-53**
  "Then Jesus said unto the chief priests, and captains of the temple, and the elders, which were come to him, Be ye come out, as against a thief, with swords and staves? When I was daily with you in the temple, ye stretched forth no hands against me: but this is your hour, and the **power** of darkness."

Satan has **power**—*the power of darkness.*
- **Acts 26:18**
  "To open their eyes, *and* to turn *them* from darkness to light, and *from* the **power** of Satan unto God, that they may receive forgiveness of sins, and inheritance among them which are sanctified by faith that is in me."

This was when Paul was genuinely saved and gave his testimony before Festus and Agrippa. There is **power** in Satan and in his false prophet as well.
- **Ephesians 1:21**
  "Far above all principality, and **power**, and might, and dominion, and every name that is named, not only in this world, but also in that which is to come:"

Paul talks about *all principality, and* **power**, *and might, and dominion*—speaking probably of the evil **powers**.
- **Ephesians 2:2**
  "Wherein in time past ye walked according to the course of this world, according to the prince of the **power** of the air, the spirit that now worketh in the children of disobedience:"

The *prince of the* **power** *of the air* is the Devil. He has **power**.
- **Colossians 1:13**
  "Who hath delivered us from the **power** of darkness, and hath translated us into the kingdom of his dear Son:"

Paul was talking to genuine believers in Colosse. Before we are genuinely saved, we are under the **power** of darkness.
- **2 Thessalonians 2:9**
  "*Even him,* whose coming is after the working of Satan with all **power** and signs and **lying** wonders,"

This talks about the man of sin who will one day come. He is going to have **power**.
- **Hebrews 2:14**
  "Forasmuch then as the children are partakers of flesh and blood, he also himself likewise took part of the same; that through death he might destroy him that had the **power** of death, that is, the devil;"

Satan Had The Power Of Death

The Lord Jesus Christ came unto the earth and died for our sins. Before the Lord Jesus Christ came, Satan had the power of death. There was no deliverance from death until He came. Those in the Old Testament looking forward to the cross could by faith be delivered, but Satan had them in the power and fear of death.

- **Revelation 13:2**
  "And the beast which I saw was like unto a leopard, and his feet were as *the feet* of a bear, and his mouth as the mouth of a lion: and the dragon gave him his **power**, and his seat, and great authority."

Satan has **power**. People may say, "Satan is just an image of somebody's concoction." No. He is a real person. He is a created angel that fell. He was the lead angel for a while until he said, "I will" to God.

- **Revelation 13:4**
  "And they worshipped the dragon which gave **power** unto the beast: and they worshipped the beast, saying, Who *is* like unto the beast? who is able to make war with him?"

He has **power** and the dragon gave the **power** to the beast.

- **Revelation 13:5**
  "And there was given unto him a mouth speaking great things and blasphemies; and **power** was given unto him to continue forty *and* two months."

This is three and a half years. Apparently, during the last half of the tribulation period, this beast and the false prophet will operate.

- **Revelation 13:7**
  "And it was given unto him to make war with the saints, and to overcome them: and **power** was given him over all kindreds, and tongues, and nations."

The Power Of The False Prophet

The saints—the genuinely saved Christians—will be gone, but this false prophet will have lots of power over those people that are living during the tribulation period on this earth. They will not have freedom. We talk about the freedom in the songs that we sing as *God Bless America*, and, *the land of the free and the home of the brave*. They will not have that freedom. They will be forced into worshipping this false beast. The false prophet will give power to people at that time to worship this false beast and false prophet.

Revelation 13:13

"And he doeth great wonders, so that he maketh fire come down from heaven on the earth in the sight of men,"

False Wonders Of The False Prophet

When the Lord Jesus Christ was here, He had miraculous power, as we know. He raised the dead. He gave sight to the blind. He cured lepers. He did all kinds of miracles. This false prophet—this false Christ—will also have these false wonders and miracles in order to show people that he is genuinely the Messiah. He is a false Messiah. He is a deceptive Messiah, but these are some of the things that he will be doing. The Lord Jesus Christ predicted this.

- Matthew 24:24
  "For there shall arise **false Christs**, and **false prophets**, and shall shew great **signs** and **wonders**; insomuch that, if *it were* possible, they shall deceive the very elect."

He is looking into the future. Even though He was here on earth, He is looking into the future during the tribulation period. How can a Christ be false? Well, he is a phony. He calls himself Christ. This man—the false prophet—calls himself Christ the anointed one. Remember Satan has power. (He is not all-powerful. God is all-powerful—omnipotent.)

Great Signs And Wonders

Satan is going to give to this false prophet power to show great signs, and wonders, and miracles, *insomuch that, if it were possible, they shall deceive the very elect.* If it were possible, the ones that are truly saved will be deceived by these.

I hope that the Lord will give us a spirit of discernment so that we will not ever be **deceived** by **false prophets**. We have **false prophets** today, even before the tribulation period comes. There are **false prophets** and **false teachers** all over the world and some people follow them. <u>Many of the television evangelists are **false prophets** and they are leading people astray.</u> People follow them.

- 2 Thessalonians 2:9
  "*Even him*, whose coming is after the working of Satan with all **power** and signs and **lying wonders**,"

This is a picture of the man of sin. We mentioned this earlier. Notice he is going to have great **wonders**. He makes **fire** come down from heaven. This wonder-working man is a **lying wonder**. What do we mean by **lying**? It means that it is not from the source which is God's **power**. It is Satan's **power**—lying, false wonders, and false **power**.

Faith Healers Under Satanic Powers

Some of the faith healers today, I believe, are under Satanic powers. Sometimes when people worship these false leaders they have miracles and they come away. One of the men mentioned when we were in meetings with him, that when a person is allegedly healed by one of these false healers, and then he stops believing in this Satanic man that healed him, the injury comes back. It is interesting. These are very powerful Satanic wonders even today. Many of these faith healers are frauds and people are being taken in by them. It is a sad thing, indeed.

Revelation 13:14

"**And deceiveth them that dwell on the earth by *the means of* those miracles which he had power to do in the sight of the beast; saying to them that dwell on the earth, that they should make an image to the beast, which had the wound by a sword, and did live.**"

The Deception Of The False Prophet

Here is the deception of this false prophet. This false prophet is going to do great wonders, and by the wonders, he is going to deceive. That is in the present tense. He is continually deceiving people that dwell on the earth because of these miracles that he had the power to do in the sight of this political ruler—the first beast.

He says that they should make an **image** and worship the **image**. That is what Saddam Hussein had—a big **image** of himself—and it all fell down. That was what Nebuchadnezzar had in the plain of Dura. He had a big image and said that everybody had to worship it or be killed.

- **Matthew 24:4-5**
  "And Jesus answered and said unto them, Take heed that no man deceive you. For many shall come in my name, saying, I am Christ; and shall **deceive** many."

Deception Is Terrible

Deception is terrible. We have to learn to discern and not be deceived.

Deception is not something that is far afield from a thing. It is a thing that is close. A false twenty-dollar bill is close to a regular twenty-dollar bill. Naming the name of the Lord Jesus Christ, and having **miracles**, they shall **deceive** many. This false prophet is going to be in the **deceiving** business. Many false teachers today are **deceptive** as well.

- **Matthew 27:63**
  "Saying, Sir, we remember that that **deceiver** said, while he was yet alive, After three days I will rise again."

They accused the Lord Jesus Christ of being a **deceiver**. He was a true Man. He was not a **deceiver**. Truth was and is always in His mouth.

- **Romans 16:17-18**
  "Now I beseech you, brethren, mark them which cause divisions and offences contrary to the doctrine which ye have learned; and avoid them. For they that are such serve not our Lord Jesus Christ, but their own belly; and by good words and fair speeches **deceive** the hearts of the simple."

He is talking about new evangelicals—those that are compromising the truth of Scripture. What we call "new evangelicals" are those that are not true fundamental Bible-believing Christians. They want to yoke up with the apostasy such as that which is found in the National Council of Churches and the World Council of Churches. They want to have leaders like Billy Graham, who is an example of new evangelicalism. He wants to have such apostate leaders on his radio programs, and in his evangelistic campaigns. He uses Roman Catholic priests and different Protestant apostates to lead in prayer, and then sends the converts back to these unbelieving churches. We have to be careful of **deception**.

- **Ephesians 4:14**
  "That we *henceforth* be no more children, tossed to and fro, and carried about with every wind of doctrine, by the sleight of men, *and* cunning craftiness, whereby they lie in wait to **deceive**;"

The Devil is a **deceiver**.

- **Ephesians 5:6**
"Let no man **deceive** you with vain words: for because of these things cometh the wrath of God upon the children of disobedience."
- **2 Thessalonians 2:3**
"Let no man **deceive** you by any means: for *that day shall not come*, except there come a falling away first, and that man of sin be revealed, the son of perdition;"

We Should Not Be Deceived

We should not be deceived as to when the coming of the Lord Jesus Christ should take place.

- **Titus 1:10**
"For there are many unruly and vain talkers and **deceivers**, specially they of the circumcision:"

Even in the Lord Jesus Christ's day, and in Paul's day, there were **deceivers**. There were many of them, not just one or two. We have to be careful and be on guard.

- **1 John 1:8**
"If we say that we have no sin, we **deceive** ourselves, and the truth is not in us."

Here is a **deception**.

- **2 John 7**
"For many **deceivers** are entered into the world, who confess not that Jesus Christ is come in the flesh. This is a **deceiver** and an antichrist."

The modernists do not believe that the Lord Jesus Christ, God's Son, came in the flesh. The cultists and false religions do not believe it. God says they are **deceivers** and antichrists.

- **Revelation 12:9**
"And the great dragon was cast out, that old serpent, called the Devil, and Satan, which **deceiveth** the whole world: he was cast out into the earth, and his angels were cast out with him."

Satan is the author of **deception**.

- **Revelation 20:3**
"And cast him into the bottomless pit, and shut him up, and set a seal upon him, that he should **deceive** the nations no more, till the thousand years should be fulfilled: and after that he must be loosed a little season."

During the millennial reign of the Lord Jesus Christ, Satan will be in the bottomless pit. He will not be **deceiving** anybody.

- **Revelation 20:8**
"And shall go out to **deceive** the nations which are in the four quarters of the earth, Gog and Magog, to gather them together to battle: the number of whom *is* as the sand of the sea."

This is after Satan is loosed at the end of the thousand years. Which armies are going to be gathered together? It is going to be this big united nations army. All the nations of the world gather together against the Lord Jesus Christ and against the saints at Jerusalem.

- **Matthew 24:24**
"For there shall arise false Christs, and false prophets, and shall shew great **signs** and **wonders**; insomuch that, if it were possible, they shall deceive the very elect."

The Lord Jesus Christ predicts that many people will be deceived with false prophets that will show **signs** and **wonders**.

- **2 Thessalonians 2:7-9**
"For the mystery of iniquity doth already work: only he who now letteth *will let*, until he be taken out of the way. And then shall that Wicked be revealed, whom the Lord shall consume with the spirit of his mouth, and shall destroy with the brightness of his coming: *Even him*, whose coming is after the working of Satan with all power and **signs** and **lying wonders**,"

The Holy Spirit's Hindering Of Sin

I feel that the hindering here is by the Holy Spirit of God. He will hinder sin before it erupts fully, until the rapture of the true church, and the Lord Jesus Christ takes the genuine believers Home to Glory. Then and only then shall that *Wicked* one be revealed—the antichrist. These wonders he has power to do. By these miracles he will deceive the whole world.

I hope that none of us are **deceived**. Many times people can **deceive** us. They say, "I am going to do such and such" and they do not do "such and such." They do "so and so." People **deceive** us sometimes. Ministers and preachers sometimes **deceive** the people, and then come into a church.

Removing The King James Bible

I heard that some pastor was going to come into a church that has right in its constitution, "We use and defend the King James Bible." That pastor came in there and he wants to tear

> them away from the King James Bible. That is deception. That is not proper. No man should come into that church who does not agree with the Bible they stand for. They want to deceive.

I remember when I left the Faith Baptist Church in Newton, Massachusetts. It was the second church that I took after coming out of the Navy Chaplain Corps. We had this fellow come in there. He said he believed "*this and this.*" We had it on tape recording. When I left as pastor, he did not believe "*this and this*" at all. He was a deceiver. He got into that church and almost ripped it apart.

Finally, he left and another good man came in. These are **deceivers**. People say, "Can preachers and would-be pastors deceive congregations?" You had better believe they can and they do. They fly under false colors. They come in, and then after a while, they move and change many things.

Some of the old-time churches are changed. They change their Bible versions. We know several examples of this. They had one version and all of sudden these preachers come in and they have another one. They change from the old-time hymns into the contemporary songs. They have these "worship leaders" up there with guitars and so on. This is a **deception**. When that church has been faithful, and has held sound Biblical doctrines, when they change these doctrines, this is **deception**. We must be watching for **deception**.

Revelation 13:15

"And he had power to give life unto the image of the beast, that the image of the beast should both speak, and cause that as many as would not worship the image of the beast should be killed."

Just like Shadrach, Meshach, and Abednego, they were told to worship the **image** or they would die in the fiery furnace. He is going to give life unto the **image** of the beast just like a robot. That **image** is going to talk. It is a false miracle.

- **Luke 4:6**
  "And the devil said unto him, All this **power** will I give thee, and the glory of them: for that is delivered unto me; and to whomsoever I will I give it."
- **Luke 10:19**
  "Behold, I give unto you **power** to tread on serpents and scorpions, and over all the **power** of the enemy: and nothing shall by any means hurt you."

The Lord Jesus Christ promised to give the apostles power. Satan also has **power**.

- **Luke 22:53**
  "When I was daily with you in the temple, ye stretched forth no hands against me: but this is your hour, and the **power** of darkness."

- **Acts 26:18**
  "To open their eyes, *and* to turn *them* from darkness to light, and *from* the **power of Satan** unto God, that they may receive forgiveness of sins, and inheritance among them which are sanctified by faith that is in me."

One of Paul's missions was to take people from the power of Satan.

- **Ephesians 2:2**
  "Wherein in time past ye walked according to the course of this world, according to the prince of the **power** of the air, the spirit that now worketh in the children of disobedience:"

God has delivered us from this **power** if we are genuinely saved. The antichrist will have **power**. Before the Lord Jesus Christ came, the Devil had the **power** of death. All this **power** that is given unto the Devil will be made use of by this antichrist, this **false prophet**. He will have **power** over kindreds, and tongues, and nations.

Notice also, in Revelation 13:15, that the **false prophet** gives life to the **image** of the beast that he should speak. Nobody has been able to do that as far as I know. I know there are robots and they might mumble some things. Some of them can talk and so on, but here is an inanimate object—this image—like unto the beast, the political ruler and he begins to **speak**. Notice furthermore, that as many as would not worship this **image** should be killed. They have to bow down and worship that **image** or die. There are going to be some serious questions. I would trust that those who are genuinely saved by the 144,000 evangelistic ministers in the tribulation period (not the saints that are living today—we will be out of here) will not bow down and **worship** this image of the beast. If they do not worship it, they are going to be killed. Later on, we are going to learn that if they do **worship** the beast, they are going to be in trouble with the Lord Jesus Christ. They have to decide what they are going to do.

We as a free people, on July 4, 1776, decided to be independent. Later on, we had a Constitution that gave us independence and freedom of religion, speech, and **worship**. These things will be taken away long before the tribulation period arrives, I believe.

No Religious Freedom

Certainly during this seven years, nobody is going to have religious freedom. Can you consider it to be religious freedom being forced to worship a beast and an image that talks? That is not freedom. That is slavery. Many times the first freedoms to go are the freedom of worship and the freedom of religion.

Revelation 13:16

"And he causeth all, both small and great, rich and poor, free and bond, to receive a mark in their right hand, or in their foreheads:"

Here is the **mark.** That word for mark is CHARAGMA. It is like the mark that is branded upon horses. It is something carved or sculptured. What is this **mark** of the beast? Some say it might be a microchip. There is a man by the name of Carl Sanders who is an electronics engineer. I got this from the Internet. He says that thirty-two years of his life were spent in design and engineering electronic microchips.

The Microchip For Help

In 1968, Carl Sanders was involved, by accident, in research. Somebody had a problem with a woman spy. They had this microchip that would help her. He thinks that this is the mark of the beast. The microchip is recharged by body temperature changes. Obviously, you cannot have a chip in your hand or in your forehead that has to be recharged every five minutes. This man says that over one and a half million dollars was spent on finding out that the two places in the body where the temperature changes the most rapidly are in the forehead right below the hairline (that is the primary position) and the back of the hand (that is the alternative position). That chip could survive there.

Some of the companies working on this are Motorola, General Electric, and Boston Medical Center. That is a lot of money—one and a half million dollars—they spent on this microchip. The project was almost turned into electronic acupuncture because in use of the chip you can cause behavioral modification called behavioral changes.

Microchips can also be used for migraine headaches, uppers and downers, and so on. There are 250,000 components in the microchip—250,000 components in that little tiny thing! It is no longer than a small grain of rice, they say—including a tiny lithium battery. People have been disturbed because when that lithium wears out it will do harm to the body.

Sanders says that when they developed this microchip, the identification chip became the focal point. There were several things that they wanted. They wanted a name, an image or picture of the person's face, and Social Security number with international digits on it, fingerprint identification, physical description, family history, address, occupation, income tax information, and criminal record.

Whether that is the mark of the beast, who knows? Different ones think that it is. Some think it is not. The warning is, do not let anyone for any reason inject a **chip** into your right hand or forehead. Of course, this is not the tribulation period, but even now you should not be tracked. Later on we will talk about 666, the number of the beast.

Let me just jump ahead a little bit. Here is what one of the sites said: A computer chip that is about one-quarter inch long can carry all the information of any individual. It is self-charging (as I said before, it is charged by the body's heat) and after spending one and a half million tax dollars, they found out that the best place to put the chip would be in the hand or in the forehead because of the differences in temperature. There will be eighteen digits.

You might say, "How will eighteen digits fit into 666, the number of the beast?" Here is how they figure it· The first nine are your Social Security number. The next nine is your zip code plus four. How does nine and nine have anything to do with 666? They speculate that these eighteen digits are going to be arranged, grouped by three groups of six numbers each. There are your groupings of eighteen—six, six and six. Who knows? That is what Dr. Sanders has said. This is what it might be. We can speculate, but we do not know what it is.

A Mark In The Right Hands

All we know is, they are going to have a mark in their right hands and in their foreheads. It is not going to be just the great. It is going to be the small and the great. It is going to be the rich and the poor. It is going to be the free and the bond. That would indicate to me, that in the tribulation period, there are going to be some people still in bondage.

We have slaves all over the world in Communist bondage. You might say Communism is no more. Well, is it? If Communism is no more in Russia, why did they not let the prisoners go in the Gulag? There are all kinds of prisoners still in there. They have no freedom. It is just a mirage so that they can get money from the United States.

The free and bond will receive the mark in their right hands and in their foreheads. As I said, I do not know whether it is this microchip or something else, but we do have information saying that it is possible to control people by means of a microchip.

Revelation 13:17

"And that no man might buy or sell, save he that had the mark, or the name of the beast, or the number of his name."

In the tribulation period, obviously people will want to **buy** food. They are going to have to **buy** food in order to eat and will probably want to sell some things occasionally. Nobody can do it unless they have this particular number or mark. You might say, "How will this identify people?" If you have a Social Security number, you are uniquely identified. You are already numbered. You have a zip code where you live so you are in that area. I am sure if there are duplicate Social Security numbers there are probably not duplicates in your same zip code. There is a way to do it.

Some have said that there are all kinds of determinations as far as the purpose and intent of this **chip**. It may replace, for instance, the PIN for accessing an ATM. With biometric technology, it becomes the norm, relative to accessing of accounts and services. The antichrist will most likely require the 666 prefix to access monies and services as a sign of allegiance to him. That is not freedom of worship. That is force.

Someone else on the Internet has said that with the full implementation of biometric technology, no other numbers will be required to access or distribute monies. Refusal to receive this **mark** will result in a denial of the ability to conduct even the simplest form of activity. It will render you an enemy of the state.

What The Mark Of The Beast Is

Different people have different ideas as to what this is all about and what the mark of the beast and this number will be. I will quote some of what people who have written books on Revelation have said. For instance, Dr. M. R. DeHaan said, "What this mark of the beast will be, we may not know now. Hundreds of answers have been suggested, but I do not believe that these are Scriptural. Men have tried to identify the antichrist. There have been hundreds of guesses concerning

the identity, but all of them have been wrong."
  We do not want to identify who he is going to be. He could
be living right now on this earth, that is, before the Lord Jesus
Christ comes and takes us Home. He may not be living on the
earth now.

Dr. DeHaan continues, "*It's foolish therefore to speculate
concerning his identity. The same is true with the mark of the beast.*"
Dr. DeHaan did not want to make that big statement. All we know is
there is going to be a **mark**. He thought maybe 666 would be tattooed
in the hands and in the foreheads of the followers of the **beast**.

What about Oliver B. Greene? He was another Bible commentator.
In 1963 he said, "*Yes, I believe there will be three sixes tattooed in
foreheads and right hands. Indeed, I do.*" He believed it was literal just
like John 3:16.

Dave Hunt had a statement on that in 1993. He wrote a book and
here is what he said: "*A tiny computer **chip**, painlessly and quickly
implanted just under the skin in hand or forehead will likely become the
means of fulfilling this prophecy.*" He is for the **microchip** implanted
under the skin.

Here is another one. Salem Kirban wrote a book called *Satan's
Mark Exposed* in 1978. He said:
  "*One day in the tribulation period, you'll need proper identification
  to withdraw or deposit money in your bank. The identification will
  be an invisible mark either in the back of your hand or your
  forehead.*"
He thinks it will be invisible. Some think it is invisible. Some think it is
a mark that you can see. Some think it is a microchip. Kirban continues:
  "*The Social Security number will become your identification
  number that will be prefixed by 666 and quite possibly followed by
  your own personal zip code.*"
Then there is Tim LaHaye. He and Jerry Jenkins wrote a book
called *Are We Living in the End Times?* in 1999. He quotes someone
saying, "We have settled the technology. The miniature **biochip** with the
suffix numbers embedded in it can be inserted as painlessly as a
vaccination in a matter of seconds. That's it. Just a half-inch scar is all
that will remain."

These are what some different ones have said. The point of it is,
when we are gone, there is going to be devised somewhere, somehow, in
the mind of this antichrist and the false prophet, a way to get people to
worship him, and to come to him, and to have this **mark** in order to buy
anything—food, clothing, or anything at all. This will be in the forehead

or the right hand of those that are going to worship this beast. We just do not know how. I have mentioned some of these people and their guesses. That is all it is—guess work. That is why Dr. DeHaan did not want to guess on it. <u>All we know is, in the tribulation period there is going to be forced worship of the false Christ, and forced worship of the false prophet, and the political beast</u>. People are going to have to bow down to them and worship them. If they do not, they are going to die. They are going to be killed.

The Saved Won't Enter The Tribulation

If you are genuinely saved, you will not be in the tribulation period.

Suppose a person were in the tribulation period for those seven years. Suppose that person had genuine faith in the Lord Jesus Christ, he must not bow down to any image at all. The Lord Jesus Christ is not an image. He is a Person. They who worship Him must worship Him in spirit and in truth. What if you were faced with this? There are going to be true Christians in that time. What would you do? Would you starve? Would you not take the mark? You would die. The alternative of taking the **mark of the beast** is worse than not taking it. Not taking it, you just die, and that is it. If you are genuinely saved, you go Home to be with the Lord Jesus Christ, which is far better anyway. What if you receive the mark of the beast? What does Scripture tell us if you do receive it?

Revelation 13:18

"Here is wisdom. Let him that hath understanding count the number of the beast: for it is the number of a man; and his number *is* Six hundred threescore *and* six."

What if persons decide in that tribulation period to take and receive this **number** or the name of this beast?

- **Revelation 14:9-10**
  "And the third angel followed them, saying with a loud voice, If any man worship the beast and his image, and receive *his* **mark** in his forehead, or in his hand, The same shall drink of the wine of the wrath of God, which is poured out without mixture into the cup of his indignation; and he shall be tormented with fire and brimstone in the presence of the holy angels, and in the presence of the Lamb:"

Literal Fire In Hell

I take that as literal fire. I believe there are fires of Hell
and it is literal fire. It is not just a spiritual thing. God says He
is going to deal with these who take the mark of the beast. They
will go to Hell and they will be tormented with fire and
brimstone. What other verse tells us of the fate of those that do
take the mark?

Remember, if you do not take the **mark** during the tribulation, you
are going to die. If you are genuinely saved and born-again, you will go
to Heaven. What if you do take it?

- **Revelation 14:11**
  "And the smoke of their torment ascendeth up for ever and ever:
  and they have **no rest** day nor night, who **worship** the beast
  and his image, and whosoever receiveth the **mark** of his name."

They have no rest. They are in Hell with fire and brimstone.

- **Revelation 15:1-2**
  "And I saw another sign in heaven, great and marvellous, seven
  angels having the seven last plagues; for in them is filled up the
  wrath of God. And I saw as it were a sea of glass mingled with
  fire: and them that had gotten the victory over the beast, and
  over his image, and over his mark, *and* over the number of his
  name, stand on the sea of glass, having the harps of God."

Refusing The Mark Of The Beast

These are ones in the tribulation that will be genuinely
saved and will refuse the mark of the beast. They will be killed
and will go up to Heaven. Praise the Lord for that. God has
delivered them from this beast and they should have no fear.
The beast and Satan cannot send people to Hell, but God can.
Here are the people that did not worship the beast. They are
up in Heaven.

- **Revelation 16:2**
  "And the first went, and poured out his vial upon the earth; and
  there fell a noisome and grievous sore upon the men which had
  the **mark** of the beast, and *upon* them which worshipped his
  image."

There was a grievous sore upon those who worshipped the beast and
received the **mark**. That is a serious business, indeed.

- **Revelation 19:20**
  "And the beast was taken, and with him the false prophet that wrought miracles before him, with which he deceived them that had received the **mark** of the beast, and them that worshipped his image. These both were cast alive into a lake of fire burning with brimstone."

That is the fate of those that worship the beast and have his **mark**.

- **Revelation 20:4**
  "And I saw thrones, and they sat upon them, and judgment was given unto them: and *I saw* the souls of them that were beheaded for the witness of Jesus, and for the word of God, and which had not worshipped the beast, neither his image, neither had received *his* **mark** upon their foreheads, or in their hands; and they lived and reigned with Christ a thousand years."

Result of The Mark Of The Beast

This is a picture in Heaven of those that refused the mark of the beast and were killed. Talking about beheadings, as I am preaching this sermon, every other day it seems in Iraq they are beheading. That is the way they slay people—the most bloody and most vicious way that they can. They pull their heads back and slit their throats and carve them up. Genuine Christians will be beheaded in the tribulation period. That is the way they are going to be killed, just like the Iraqi insurgents. The beheaded ones are the souls that said, "No! We are not going to take this mark. We are not going to take the mark of the beast. We are not going to have anything to do with it." Yes, they are killed, but in Glory they are in Heaven. Those that received the mark of the beast are sent to the fiery brimstone of Hell.

The first part of this chapter talks about the political ruler that will be set up during the last half of this seven-year period of tribulation—Daniel's 70th Week. He will be the political ruler that will reign over all the earth. Then they have this religious leader—the false prophet—in the last half of Revelation 13. He will cause people to worship the political leader. He will be the evangelist, as it were, for this political leader. He will force people to bow down to the image of this **beast** that lives.

I tell you, the deception that will come about is a terrible thing. You might say, "How will these people ever worship this beast? Can they not see that this is wrong?" They will be deceived. They will think this is right. They will think that this is maybe the Lord Jesus Christ Himself, and that He has come back. They will be wrong.

Guard Against Deception

May God guard us from deception of false prophets. Though they come in sheep's clothing, they are inwardly ravenous wolves. We have a lot of them now. They are not so successful unless they can be *almost* right. Just a little bit of strychnine in a glass of water will kill you. A tiny amount will kill you. We have to be careful. May the Lord give us discernment in these last days.

Revelation

Chapter Fourteen

Revelation 14:1

"And I looked, and, lo, a Lamb stood on the mount Sion, and with him an hundred forty *and* four thousand, having his Father's name written in their foreheads."

The 144,000 evangelists do not have the mark of the beast. They are ones that did not receive it. The **Father's name** is in their **foreheads**. These are genuinely born-again Jews, as we learned previously. This **Lamb** of God is mentioned throughout the Scriptures. It refers to the Lord Jesus Christ.

- **Isaiah 53:5-7**
  "But he *was* wounded for our transgressions, *he was* bruised for our iniquities: the chastisement of our peace *was* upon him; and with his stripes we are healed. All we like sheep have gone astray; we have turned every one to his own way; and the LORD hath laid on him the iniquity of us all. He was oppressed, and he was afflicted, yet he opened not his mouth: he is brought as a **lamb** to the slaughter, and as a **sheep** before her shearers is dumb, so he openeth not his mouth."

Here is the **Lamb** of God.

- **Acts 8:32**
  "The place of the scripture which he read was this, He was led as a sheep to the slaughter; and like a **lamb** dumb before his shearer, so opened he not his mouth:"

Philip was ministering in a city when the Lord called him to go into a desert place. He came to that Ethiopian eunuch who was reading in the Scripture. The place where he was reading was talking about the Lord Jesus Christ. Philip opened his mouth and preached unto him the Lord Jesus Christ.

- **John 1:29**
  "The next day John seeth Jesus coming unto him, and saith, Behold the **Lamb** of God, which taketh away the sin of the world."

John the Baptist was the forerunner of the Lord Jesus Christ. The Lord Jesus Christ is called the **Lamb** of God. He is God's sacrificial **Lamb** to die for sinners to take away the sin of the world.

- **John 1:36**
  "And looking upon Jesus as he walked, he saith, Behold the **Lamb** of God!"

John the Baptist says again the second time, "Behold the **Lamb** of God!" He wanted to repeat it. Once was not enough. He had to say it twice in Chapter One of the Gospel of John.

- **1 Peter 1:18-19**
  "Forasmuch as ye know that ye were not redeemed with corruptible things, *as* silver and gold, from your vain conversation *received* by tradition from your fathers; But with the precious blood of the Lord Jesus Christ, as of a **lamb** without blemish and without spot:"

MacArthur's Error On The Blood

Peter talks about our redemption. John MacArthur does not believe that this verse refers to the blood of the Lord Jesus Christ literally, but it does. This is His literal blood, not simply His death, but the shedding of His blood. Here is the Lamb that was slain for us. He shed His blood for us. The Lord Jesus Christ is called a Lamb.

- **Exodus 12:5**
  "Your **lamb** shall be without blemish, a male of the first year: ye shall take *it* out from the sheep, or from the goats:"

This is when the first Passover took place. The **lamb** had to be without blemish. The Lord Jesus Christ is called a *Lamb without blemish and without spot* in 1 Peter 1:19. He had to be sinless in order to take upon Himself the sins of the world.

- **Revelation 5:6**
  "And I beheld, and, lo, in the midst of the throne and of the four beasts, and in the midst of the elders, stood a **Lamb** as it had been slain, having seven horns and seven eyes, which are the seven Spirits of God sent forth into all the earth."

Again, the Lord Jesus Christ in Heaven is called a **Lamb**, the One that was slain.

- **Revelation 5:12**
  "Saying with a loud voice, **Worthy** is the **Lamb** that was slain to receive power, and riches, and wisdom, and strength, and honour, and glory, and blessing."

Worthy Is The Lamb

This is the song that was sung by those in Heaven. The Lord Jesus Christ certainly is worthy! The liberals and modernists that do not like Him say He is unworthy, but the Scriptures call Him worthy. He is worthy because He was sinless. He is worthy because He is our Saviour, the One Who died for our sins. Worthy is the Lamb.

- **Revelation 6:16**
  "And said to the mountains and rocks, Fall on us, and hide us from the face of him that sitteth on the throne, and from the wrath of the **Lamb:**"

The Lamb Is The Lord Jesus Christ

The Lord Jesus Christ came as the Lamb that took away the sin of the world the first time, but when He comes the second time at the end of the tribulation period, it is going to be for judgment. These people have rejected Him and they are calling out for the rocks to fall on them.

- **Revelation 7:9**
  "After this I beheld, and, lo, a great multitude, which no man could number, of all nations, and kindreds, and people, and tongues, stood before the throne, and before the **Lamb**, clothed with **white robes**, and palms in their hands;"

The throne is where God the Father is seated. The **Lamb** is at the Father's right hand. These clothed in **white robes** are the redeemed in Heaven.

- **Revelation 7:14**
  "And I said unto him, Sir, thou knowest. And he said to me, These are they which came out of great tribulation, and have washed their **robes**, and made them **white** in the blood of the **Lamb**."

Robes made **white** in the blood of the Lamb? That is exactly right. There are fourteen different things that the blood of the Lord Jesus

Christ does. I have mentioned these things many times from my pulpit. There are fourteen things the literal blood of the Lord Jesus Christ can do. This one here is making the people and their **robes white** through the blood of the **Lamb**. The Lord Jesus Christ's blood is said in Scripture to do many things—redeeming us, justifying us, and here, making our **robes white**.

- **Revelation 12:11**
  "And they overcame him by the **blood** of the **Lamb**, and by the word of their testimony; and they loved not their lives unto the death."

Satan Overcome By The Blood

Satan was overcome by the blood of the Lamb. If God wanted to say *the death of the Lamb*, He could have said it. Over and over, it is the *blood of the Lamb*. There is special power in the blood of the Lord Jesus Christ. Sure, He died on the cross of Calvary and shed His blood at the cross, but the blood is all throughout the Bible. Mary Baker Glover Patterson Fry Eddy, the founder of Christian Science, wrote that "*there is no more value in the blood of the Lord Jesus Christ that was shed on the cross than when it was flowing in His veins.*" That is almost the same thing that John MacArthur says. He says that the blood of the Lord Jesus Christ cannot avail—it is His death. MacArthur wrongly teaches that blood is only a metonym (figure of speech) for death. Here the blood is that which overcame Satan—*by the blood of the Lamb.*

- **Revelation 13:8**
  "And all that dwell upon the earth shall worship him, whose names are not written in the book of life of the Lamb slain from the foundation of the world."

Those whose names are not written in the book of life of the Lamb will worship the beast, this false prophet. It is the Lamb's book of life. He was *slain from the foundation of the world.* You may say, "Well, He only came and was slain at Calvary in time." No, from God's viewpoint He was slain from the foundation of the world.

- **Revelation 17:14**
  "These shall make war with the **Lamb**, and the **Lamb** shall overcome them: for he is Lord of lords, and King of kings: and they that are with him are called, and chosen, and faithful."

They are going to fight with the **Lamb**. The Lord Jesus Christ will have victory.

The **144,000** are on Mount Zion. Mount Zion is in the city of Jerusalem—the city of David.

- **Revelation 7:4**
  "And I heard the number of them which were sealed: *and there were* sealed an **hundred** *and* **forty** *and* **four thousand** of all the tribes of the children of **Israel**."

Jews Not Anglo-Saxon White Races

I believe these are literal children of Israel. They are not the Anglo-Saxons. They are not the Jehovah's Witnesses. These are Jews during the seven-year period of tribulation when the genuine believers are snatched up into Heaven. We will not be here, but the unsaved are here. There are 12,000 from every one of the tribes.

- **Revelation 7:5-8**
  "Of the tribe of Juda *were* sealed **twelve thousand**. Of the tribe of Reuben *were* sealed **twelve thousand**. Of the tribe of Gad *were* sealed **twelve thousand**. Of the tribe of Aser *were* sealed **twelve thousand**. Of the tribe of Nepthalim *were* sealed **twelve thousand**. Of the tribe of Manasses *were* sealed **twelve thousand**. Of the tribe of Simeon *were* sealed **twelve thousand**. Of the tribe of Levi *were* sealed **twelve thousand**. Of the tribe of Issachar *were* sealed **twelve thousand**. Of the tribe of Zabulon *were* sealed **twelve thousand**. Of the tribe of Joseph *were* sealed **twelve thousand**. Of the tribe of Benjamin *were* sealed **twelve thousand**."

All of these were sealed. The question is, "Do the **Jews** today know their **tribes**?" I do not know. Some do and some do not, but in the seven-year tribulation period—Daniel's 70th Week—every single **Jew** will know what **tribe** they are from. These are the ones that are sealed. God knows where they are. He will gather them together and they will be sealed. They will not have the name or the mark of the beast on them. They will be evangelists sent forth to the world that then is—a lost and dying world.

- **Revelation 7:9**
  "After this I beheld, and, lo, a great multitude, which no man could number, of all nations, and kindreds, and people, and tongues, stood before the throne, and before the **Lamb**, clothed with **white robes**, and palms in their hands;"

Evangelistic Fruits Of The 144,000

The results of their evangelism are told here. They are before the throne and before the Lamb. They are genuinely saved because of the missionary endeavors of the 144,000. I am sure they will use God's preserved written Words, the Internet, TV, radio, and all kinds of means that the Lord will give them at their disposal. People will be redeemed and will have genuinely come to the Lord Jesus Christ from all the nations of the world. These are the lost ones in that seven-year period of tribulation that perhaps had never heard of the Lord Jesus Christ. The 144,000 will be sent to China, to India, to Africa, to Russia—to all the world's kingdoms—and many will be genuinely saved.

Revelation 14:2

"And I heard a voice from heaven, as the voice of many waters, and as the voice of a great thunder: and I heard the voice of harpers harping with their harps:"

This **voice of many waters** is the Lord Jesus Christ's voice.

- **Revelation 1:15**
  "And his feet like unto fine brass, as if they burned in a furnace; and his **voice** as the **sound of many waters**."

Here is the Lord Jesus Christ speaking in Heaven. John heard it.

Then he says he sees and hears the *harpers harping*.

- **2 Samuel 6:5**
  "And David and all the house of Israel played before the LORD on all manner of *instruments made* of fir wood, even on **harps**, and on psalteries, and on timbrels, and on cornets, and on cymbals."

When the ark came into Jerusalem the **harps** were used. The **harp** is only used in the Scriptures twenty times. It is a time of joy. When the ark came into Jerusalem, the harp was played.

- **1 Chronicles 13:8**
  "And David and all Israel played before God with all *their* might, and with singing, and with **harps**, and with psalteries, and with timbrels, and with cymbals, and with trumpets."

Harps are stringed instruments. Dick Carroll, our pianist, plays on a big stringed instrument, the piano.

- **2 Chronicles 5:12**
  "Also the Levites *which were* the singers, all of them of Asaph, of Heman, of Jeduthun, with their sons and their brethren, *being* arrayed in white linen, having cymbals and psalteries and **harps**, stood at the east end of the altar, and with them an hundred and twenty priests sounding with trumpets:)"

This is when the ark was brought to the temple.

- **2 Chronicles 20:28**
  "And they came to Jerusalem with psalteries and **harps** and trumpets unto the house of the LORD."

It was a time of joy. Harping indicates joy. There is joy in Heaven, so there are harpers harping with **harps**.

- **Nehemiah 12:27**
  "And at the dedication of the wall of Jerusalem they sought the Levites out of all their places, to bring them to Jerusalem, to keep the dedication with gladness, both with thanksgivings, and with singing, with cymbals, psalteries, and with **harps**."

This is when the Jews came back from Babylonian captivity. They were seventy years in captivity before they came back to the land. They were joyful as they returned to Jerusalem, so they used **harps** on that occasion.

Revelation 14:3

"And they sung as it were a new song before the throne, and before the four beasts, and the elders: and no man could learn that song but the hundred *and* forty *and* four thousand, which were redeemed from the earth."

Here is the **song** they are **singing** in Heaven. True Christians sing here on earth. Our church people sing in our services. We have favorite hymns from those attending and from those on the Internet. In Heaven, they *sung as it were a new song*. That word *sung* is present tense continuous. There is continuous **singing** in Heaven. In the Scriptures, many times there is a **song**. The words, *new song*, are only used nine times in the Bible.

- **Psalm 33:3**
  "Sing unto him a **new song**; play skilfully with a loud noise."
- **Psalm 40:2**
  "He brought me up also out of an horrible pit, out of the miry clay, and set my feet upon a rock, *and* established my goings."

Here is David's testimony of being genuinely saved. Have you been brought up out of an horrible pit of sin? Are you genuinely saved by the redeeming grace and genuine faith in the Lord Jesus Christ?

- **Psalm 40:3**
  "And he hath put a **new song** in my mouth, *even* praise unto our God: many shall see *it*, and fear, and shall trust in the LORD."

Do you have a **new song** in your heart that the Lord has placed there and that others can see?

- **Psalm 98:1**
  "O sing unto the LORD a **new song**; for he hath done marvellous things: his right hand, and his holy arm, hath gotten him the victory."

- **Psalm 137:1-4**
  "By the rivers of Babylon, there we sat down, yea, we wept, when we remembered Zion. We hanged our **harps** upon the willows in the midst thereof. For there they that carried us away captive required of us a song; and they that wasted us *required of us* mirth, *saying*, **Sing** us *one* of the songs of Zion. How shall we sing the LORD'S **song** in a strange land?"

Judah and Benjamin were captives for seventy years in the land of Babylon. Notice, the Devil's children wanted to hear the **songs** of Zion. They want to hear them today—the good **songs**—not this junk that contemporary music puts out, but the **songs** of Zion. A strange land is the very place we need to sing the Lord's **song**. Genuine born-again Christians are living in a strange land all over the world, and we need the Lord's **song** to be **sung**, the **song** of redemption.

- **Revelation 5:9**
  "And they sung a **new song**, saying, Thou art worthy to take the book, and to open the seals thereof: for thou wast slain, and hast redeemed us to God by thy blood out of every kindred, and tongue, and people, and nation;"

Praise the Lord for this **song**.

Revelation 14:4

"These are they which were not defiled with women; for they are virgins. These are they which follow the Lamb whithersoever he goeth. These were redeemed from among men, *being* the firstfruits unto God and to the Lamb."

These **144,000** are now defined. They were **not defiled with women**—not that marriage is defiling. No, this is not speaking of that. This word for "*defile*" is MOLUNO. It means that these were not soiled by fornication or the sin of adultery. They were clean. They were "*not defiled with women*." There are **144,000**—12,000 from each of the twelve tribes.

As far as married and unmarried is concerned, Paul is very clear on this subject as to who can serve the Lord completely if that is their gift. You cannot do it if it is not your gift.

- **1 Corinthians 7:32-34**
  "But I would have you without carefulness. He that is **unmarried** careth for the things that belong to the Lord, how he may please the Lord: But he that is married careth for the things that are of the world, how he may please *his* wife. There is difference *also* between a wife and a virgin. The **unmarried** woman careth for the things of the Lord, that she may be holy both in body and in spirit: but she that is married careth for the things of the world, how she may please *her* husband."

If the gift is to be *unmarried*, an unmarried person can please the Lord in that way. I hope wives want to please their husbands. That is Scriptural. There is a distinction made—whatever the gift may be—between married or **unmarried**. These **144,000** were **unmarried**. They are **virgins**, evangelists all over the world. If they had been married, they would have had to leave their wives and families. They are evangelists serving all over the world. They can just be on their own during the seven years of tribulation. Maybe they are among the ones that were slain by the beast and the false prophet after they had fulfilled their evangelism.

Following The Lamb Continuously

Notice also, *they follow the Lamb whithersoever he goeth.* By the way, that word follow is a present tense. They are continuously following the Lamb. Are you following the Lord Jesus Christ, the Lamb, whithersoever He goeth?

- **Matthew 4:19**
  "And he saith unto them, **Follow me**, and I will make you fishers of men."
- **Matthew 8:19**
  "And a certain scribe came, and said unto him, Master, I will **follow thee** whithersoever thou goest."

That was a lie. Sometimes we lie with our mouths. Sometimes with our actions. He lied.

- **Matthew 8:20**
  "And Jesus saith unto him, The foxes have holes, and the birds of the air *have* nests; but the Son of man hath not where to lay *his* head."

I do not think that scribe **followed** Him. He had no place to go.

- **Matthew 8:21-22**
  "And another of his disciples said unto him, Lord, suffer me first to go and bury my father. But Jesus said unto him, **Follow me**; and let the dead bury their dead."

The Lord Jesus Christ is more important even than the family.

- **Matthew 8:23**
  "And when he was entered into a ship, his disciples **followed him**."

We Must Follow The Lamb

We need to follow the Lord Jesus Christ. These 144,000 men followed the Lamb whithersoever He went.

- **Matthew 9:9**
  "And as Jesus passed forth from thence, he saw a man, named Matthew, sitting at the receipt of custom: and he saith unto him, **Follow me**. And he arose, and **followed** him."

Matthew was the writer of the Gospel of Matthew. He was a tax collector. He arose and **followed the Lord Jesus Christ**, just like that.

- **Matthew 16:24**
  "Then said Jesus unto his disciples, If any *man* will come after me, let him deny himself, and take up his cross, and **follow me**."

God wants **followers** to **follow** the Lamb wherever He leads.

- **Luke 18:22**
  "Now when Jesus heard these things, he said unto him, Yet lackest thou one thing: sell all that thou hast, and distribute unto the poor, and thou shalt have treasure in heaven: and come, **follow me**."

That was a test. It is not that all of us are to make ourselves penniless, but this was a test. Would this rich man do this? He would not, so he did not **follow** the Lord Jesus Christ.

- **John 10:4**
  "And when he putteth forth his own sheep, he goeth before them, and the sheep **follow** him: for they know his voice."

If you are one of His, you **follow** Him.

- **John 10:27-28**
  "My sheep hear my voice, and I know them, and they **follow me**: And I give unto them eternal life; and they shall never perish, neither shall any *man* pluck them out of my hand."
- **John 12:26**
  "If any man serve me, let him **follow me**; and where I am, there shall also my servant be: if any man serve me, him will *my* Father honour."

We must **follow** the Lord Jesus Christ, but not like Peter. Peter **followed**, but afar off. We have to **follow** close. These **144,000 followed the Lamb** whithersoever He went.

I once put a poem in our church bulletin called *Where Shall I Work Today?* (Author unknown).

Where Shall I Work Today?

Father, where shall I work today?
And my love flowed warm and free.
Then He pointed me toward a tiny spot,
And said, "Tend that for me."

I answered quickly, "Oh, no, not that.
Why, no one would ever see,
No matter how well my work was done.
In that little place for Thee!"

And the word He spoke, it was not stern,
He answered me tenderly,
"Ah, little one, search that heart of thine;
Art thou working for them or me?

Nazareth was a little place,
And so was Galilee."

Little is much when God is in it, as the hymn writer said. We must **follow** the **Lamb** whithersoever He taketh us. We must **follow** Him. The **Lamb** has brought us to our church, to our home, and to this place. It is a little place. That is where God wants us, so here we are. We appreciate very much both those who are with us here locally, and those who are with us by the Internet.

Revelation 14:5

"And in their mouth was found no guile: for they are without fault before the throne of God."

No Guile In These Evangelists

These 144,000 had no guile. That word for guile is an interesting word. It is DOLOS. It means *to decoy*. They did not have any craft or deceit. In football, someone puts a decoy out to make a fake pass. They go out somewhere and then pass it to the other side of the line.

- **Psalm 32:2**
  "Blessed *is* the man unto whom the LORD imputeth not iniquity, and in whose spirit *there is* no **guile**."

God does not want us with **guile**. These evangelists had **no guile**.

- **John 1:47**
  "Jesus saw Nathanael coming to him, and saith of him, Behold an Israelite indeed, in whom is **no guile**!"

Nathanael Had No Guile

Nathanael had no guile, no deceit, no trickery. In other words, what you see is what you get. People sometimes do not like that. They do not want to see what they get. They want to see something that is fake and phony. If we are genuine, and our hearts are right, what we see is what we should get.

- **1 Peter 2:1-2**
  "Wherefore laying aside all malice, and all **guile**, and hypocrisies, and envies, and all evil speakings, As newborn babes, desire the sincere milk of the word, that ye may grow thereby:"

The Word of God can make us so that we have **no guile**.

- **1 Peter 2:22**
  "Who did no sin, neither was **guile** found in his mouth:"

There was no deceit at all in the Lord Jesus Christ. Also these **144,000** had **no fault**.

- **John 18:38**
  "Pilate saith unto him, What is truth? And when he had said this, he went out again unto the Jews, and saith unto them, I find in him **no fault** *at all*."

These evangelists had **no fault** and the Lord Jesus Christ had **no fault**.
- **John 19:4**
"Pilate therefore went forth again, and saith unto them, Behold, I bring him forth to you, that ye may know that I find no fault in him."
- **John 19:6**
"When the chief priests therefore and officers saw him, they cried out, saying, Crucify *him*, crucify *him*. Pilate saith unto them, Take ye him, and crucify *him*: for I find no fault in him."

Three different times Pilate found **no fault** in the Lord Jesus Christ. If you are genuinely saved, if you are born-again, if you have genuinely trusted the Lord Jesus Christ as your Saviour, God considers you to have **no fault**. Before the Lord, those who are genuinely in the Lord Jesus Christ have His righteousness. This is a tremendous thing indeed.

Revelation 14:6

"And I saw another angel fly in the midst of heaven, having the everlasting gospel to preach unto them that dwell on the earth, and to every nation, and kindred, and tongue, and people,"

The Everlasting Gospel

Here is the everlasting gospel. The millennial reign of the Lord Jesus Christ is about to be set up. This is the last part of the seven-year period of tribulation. The word gospel occurs ninety-five times. Did you know that there are nineteen different gospels? For example, there is the gospel of the kingdom. There is the everlasting gospel, which is the millennial. There is the gospel of God's grace. They are called with different names.

- **Matthew 4:23**
"And Jesus went about all Galilee, teaching in their synagogues, and preaching the **gospel of the kingdom**, and healing all manner of sickness and all manner of disease among the people."
- **Mark 1:1**
"The beginning of the **gospel of Jesus Christ**, the Son of God;"
- **Mark 16:15**
"And he said unto them, Go ye into all the world, and preach the **gospel** to every creature."

This is the **gospel** of God's grace—salvation by genuine faith in the Lord Jesus Christ

- **Acts 20:24**
  "But none of these things move me, neither count I my life dear unto myself, so that I might finish my course with joy, and the ministry, which I have received of the Lord Jesus, to testify the **gospel** of the grace of God."

This is the same **gospel** we preach today.

- **Romans 1:1**
  "Paul, a servant of Jesus Christ, called *to be* an apostle, separated unto the **gospel** of God,"
- **Romans 1:9**
  "For God is my witness, whom I serve with my spirit in the **gospel** of his Son, that without ceasing I make mention of you always in my prayers;"

This is good news about His Son, the Lord Jesus Christ.

- **Romans 1:16**
  "For I am not ashamed of the **gospel** of Christ: for it is the power of God unto salvation to every one that believeth; to the Jew first, and also to the Greek."
- **Romans 2:16**
  "In the day when God shall judge the secrets of men by Jesus Christ according to my **gospel**."
- **Romans 10:15**
  "And how shall they preach, except they be sent? as it is written, How beautiful are the feet of them that preach the **gospel** of peace, and bring glad tidings of good things!"
- **2 Corinthians 2:12**
  "Furthermore, when I came to Troas to *preach* Christ's **gospel**, and a door was opened unto me of the Lord,"
- **2 Corinthians 4:4**
  "In whom the god of this world hath blinded the minds of them which believe not, lest the light of the glorious **gospel** of Christ, who is the image of God, should shine unto them."
- **2 Corinthians 11:4**
  "For if he that cometh preacheth another Jesus, whom we have not preached, or *if* ye receive another spirit, which ye have not received, or another **gospel**, which ye have not accepted, ye might well bear with *him*."

- **Galatians 2:7**
  "But contrariwise, when they saw that the <u>gospel of the</u> <u>uncircumcision</u> was committed unto me, as *the **gospel*** <u>of the</u> <u>circumcision</u> *was* unto Peter;"

This is the Gentiles and the Jews.

- **Ephesians 1:13**
  "In whom ye also *trusted*, after that ye heard the word of truth, the **gospel** <u>of your salvation</u>: in whom also after that ye believed, ye were sealed with that holy Spirit of promise,"
- **2 Thessalonians 1:8**
  "In flaming fire taking vengeance on them that know not God, and that obey not the **gospel** <u>of our Lord Jesus Christ</u>:"
- **2 Thessalonians 2:14**
  "Whereunto he called you by <u>our **gospel**</u>, to the obtaining of the glory of our Lord Jesus Christ."
- **1 Timothy 1:11**
  "According to the <u>glorious **gospel** of the blessed God</u>, which was committed to my trust."
- **Revelation 14:6**
  "And I saw another angel fly in the midst of heaven, having the <u>everlasting **gospel**</u> to preach unto them that dwell on the earth, and to every nation, and kindred, and tongue, and people,"

John MacArthur's Twisted "Gospel"

Although there are nineteen different times, and words, and adjectives describing the gospel, it is certainly not true as John MacArthur has written in a whole book called *The Gospel According to Jesus*. He tries to make the gospel that the Lord Jesus Christ preached the same as the gospel that Paul preached. It was a different gospel.

The Lord Jesus Christ was talking about the kingdom of Heaven that He was to set up if they would receive it. Paul was talking about the good news that although the Lord Jesus Christ has not been received but rejected, He died on the cross for the sins of the world. <u>It is not just one gospel throughout. There is the gospel of the kingdom, and the everlasting gospel, speaking of the reign of our Lord Jesus Christ.</u>

Then there is another heresy that is spread abroad as far as these **gospels** are concerned. I attended Dallas Theological Seminary for five years—from 1948 through 1953. Dr. Lewis Sperry Chafer was the founder and president of that school. I was there for five years. For the first four years, Dr. Chafer was my teacher. He died in 1952, a few months after our Th.M. class had graduated. He was very clear on what the **gospel** was.

Dr. Chafer was very clear also as far as the Millennium was concerned and how the Lord Jesus Christ will one day reign during the millennial reign of the Lord Jesus Christ for a thousand years. Now they have a compromised teaching at Dallas Theological Seminary. Some teachers there have written a book that teaches that the Lord Jesus Christ is reigning now. This is a halfway **gospel** of the kingdom. It is not grace. It is almost a covenant theology that some have adopted. I hope Dallas Seminary is still dispensational, I don't know for sure since they have adopted this modified dispensationalism to some degree. Dr. Chafer would not agree with that false position, nor do I.

I am told there is another school (I do not know for sure) that has changed their theology as far as the gospel and dispensationalism are concerned. The leaders of this school say that the Lord Jesus Christ's present "reign" is not necessarily the reign of the Lord Jesus Christ for a thousand years, but they have gone into a little bit of the covenant theology.

I Preach A Different Gospel Today

There are all kinds of changes, but I know this: the gospel that I preach today, is not the same good news that the Lord Jesus Christ preached. It was good news that He had come to reign, but the Jews rejected the Messiah Who had come to reign. Having rejected the Messiah, Paul came and wrote that we have another gospel. This gospel is based upon the death of that Messiah for the sins of the world followed by His bodily resurrection.

- **1 Corinthians 15:3-4**
  "For I delivered unto you first of all that which I also received, how that Christ died for our sins according to the scriptures; And that he was buried, and that he rose again the third day according to the scriptures:"

This **gospel** of the grace of God is good news. It is sometimes accepted lightly—only in the head but not in the heart. That makes phony Christians. That makes faltering Christians. One might say, "Oh, I am a Christian. My head accepted the Lord Jesus Christ as my Saviour. My heart never did." That is a phony Christian. That is not a genuine Christian. We must have genuine faith so that the Lord Jesus Christ is our Redeemer and our Saviour. He died for our sins and we must say,

"He died for me. I have genuinely accepted and received Him. I was a sinner and I believe He died for my sins." That is the good news—the **gospel**.

Then, as soon as that faith in the Lord Jesus Christ is genuine, the Holy Spirit of God enters into the body of that Biblically saved person. The Holy Spirit of God regenerates the person. That is the good news—the **gospel** of the Lord Jesus Christ. Then God the Holy Spirit indwells us and He seals us. He glorifies the Lord Jesus Christ. That is genuine **gospel** salvation. I am afraid that there will be many, at the end of life, who will be disappointed. They thought that they were genuinely saved, but they were really lost. I hope none of you reading this are falsely thinking you are genuinely saved, but you are not sure. You must be sure and you must be genuine. You can be sure by genuinely receiving this gospel of the grace of God.

Revelation 14:7

"Saying with a loud voice, Fear God, and give glory to him; for the hour of his judgment is come: and worship him that made heaven, and earth, and the sea, and the fountains of waters."

In Heaven these that are genuinely saved and redeemed are saying, *"Fear God, and give glory to him."* We ought to be God-fearing people. That is what they are saying. The expression *fear God* is used only ten times in Scripture.

- **Genesis 42:18**
  "And Joseph said unto them the third day, This do, and live; *for* I **fear God:**"

Joseph was talking to his brothers in Egypt. Joseph **feared God.** He was in Egypt for many years, but he still feared God.

- **Exodus 18:21**
  "Moreover thou shalt provide out of all the people able men, such as **fear God,** men of truth, hating covetousness; and place *such* over them, *to be* rulers of thousands, *and* rulers of hundreds, rulers of fifties, and rulers of tens:"

This was when Moses needed helpers in the wilderness. Moses was to have men that **feared God.** The one that shakes his fist in the face of God does not **fear God.** One that rejects the Saviour does not **fear God. God-fearing** men and women are needed.

- **Job 1:9**
  "Then Satan answered the LORD, and said, Doth Job **fear God** for nought?"

Job feared God. He was **God-fearing** and he loved the Lord.

- **Psalm 66:16**
  "Come *and* hear, all ye that **fear God**, and I will declare what he hath done for my soul."

Those that **fear God**, declare, and have a testimony.

- **Ecclesiastes 8:12**
  "Though a sinner do evil an hundred times, and his *days* be prolonged, yet surely I know that it shall be well with them that **fear God**, which fear before him:"

It will be well for those that are genuinely saved—**God-fearing** people.

- **Ecclesiastes 12:13**
  "Let us hear the conclusion of the whole matter: **Fear God**, and keep his commandments: for this is the whole *duty* of man."

- **1 Peter 2:17**
  "Honour all *men*. Love the brotherhood. **Fear God**. Honour the king."

This is what we must do. God is in His Heaven and we have to realize He is a powerful God. In fact, Revelation 14:7 talks about His **creative power**.

- **Genesis 1:7**
  "And God **made** the firmament, and divided the waters which *were* under the firmament from the waters which *were* above the firmament: and it was so."

- **Genesis 1:16**
  "And God made two great lights; the greater light to rule the day, and the lesser light to rule the night: *he made* the stars also."

God's Creation–Billions Of Galaxies

Think of the creative power of Almighty God. The stars in this galaxy number in the billions. And we have billions of galaxies that are just as big. Now you just sit down and try to make one of those stars. Let me make one star. Can we do that? Absolutely not—ridiculous! God made the stars.

- **Genesis 1:25**
  "And God **made** the beast of the earth after his kind, and cattle after their kind, and every thing that creepeth upon the earth after his kind: and God saw that *it was* good."

Can we go ahead with that? Not all of them, but just one? Impossible! God did it.

- **Genesis 1:31**
  "And God saw every thing that he had **made**, and, behold, *it was* very good. And the evening and the morning were the sixth day."
- **Genesis 2:22**
  "And the rib, which the LORD God had taken from man, **made** he a woman, and brought her unto the man."

Can you make a woman? Well, yes, through natural birth, but this is God's creative hand. He made a woman and brought her unto the man. He is a powerful **Creator**.

- **Genesis 7:4**
  "For yet seven days, and I will cause it to rain upon the earth forty days and forty nights; and every living substance that I have **made** will I destroy from off the face of the earth."

This was a universal flood. All that He made was destroyed except the ones that were spared in that ark. There were two of every unclean beast and fowl—male and female—and seven pairs of the clean beasts.

- **Colossians 1:16**
  "For by him were all things **created**, that are in heaven, and that are in earth, visible and invisible, whether *they be* thrones, or dominions, or principalities, or powers: all things were **created** by him, and for him:"

Christ–Creator Of Invisible Things

This is speaking of the Lord Jesus Christ. We can see things that are visible, but we cannot see the invisible. God can. Everything that is visible is made up of invisible atoms—neutrons, protons, and electrons. When we are told to *worship him that made heaven, and earth,* that is the Lord Jesus Christ, as well as God the Father, and God the Holy Spirit. The whole Trinity was involved in the Creation.

- **Revelation 4:11**
  "Thou art worthy, O Lord, to receive glory and honour and power: for thou hast **created** all things, and for thy pleasure they are and were **created**."

That is why Colossians 1:16 says that *all things were **created** by him, and for him.* Everything that was **created** was for the Lord Jesus Christ—for His benefit. Every single thing.

- **Revelation 10:6**
  "And sware by him that liveth for ever and ever, who **created** heaven, and the things that therein are, and the earth, and the things that therein are, and the sea, and the things which are therein, that there should be time no longer:"

Worship Him that **made** all these things. This is what we should do today—to worship the Lord Himself, the **Creator** of all these things.

Revelation 14:8

"And there followed another angel, saying, Babylon is fallen, is fallen, that great city, because she made all nations drink of the wine of the wrath of her fornication."

This **Babylon** is where the two tribes of the south, Judah and Benjamin, were carried for seventy years in captivity. **Babylon** itself was a literal city, but also a figurative one. Many times Babylon refers to **Rome** and all the allegories.

Figurative Babylon Refers To Rome

Babylon was a very large famous city, the residence of the Babylonian king, situated on the banks of the Euphrates. Cyrus had formerly captured it. Darius threw down its gates and walls. Xerxes destroyed the temple of Baalis. At length, the city was reduced to almost solitude. The population had been drawn off by neighboring Seleucia, built on the Tigris. Remember, allegorically sometimes Babylon refers to Rome. Here in the seven-year period of tribulation, Babylon is fallen.

- **Isaiah 13:5-6**
  "They come from a far country, from the end of heaven, *even* the LORD, and the weapons of his indignation, to **destroy** the whole land. Howl ye; for the day of the LORD *is* at hand; it shall come as a **destruction** from the Almighty."

In the Old Testament, it is predicted that **Babylon** will **fall**.

- **Isaiah 13:19**
  "And **Babylon**, the glory of kingdoms, the beauty of the **Chaldees'** excellency, shall be as when God overthrew Sodom and Gomorrah."

God destroyed Sodom and Gomorrah and He will **destroy Babylon**. This is the prediction.

- **Isaiah 14:4-5**
"That thou shalt take up this proverb against the king of
Babylon, and say, How hath the oppressor ceased! the golden
city ceased! The LORD hath broken the staff of the wicked, and
the sceptre of the rulers."

He is going to break their staff.

- **Isaiah 14:22**
"For I will rise up **against** them, saith the LORD of hosts, and cut off
from **Babylon** the name, and remnant, and son, and nephew, saith the
LORD."

He is going to **destroy** Babylon. This is the prediction in Revelation.

- **Isaiah 21:9**
"And, behold, here cometh a chariot of men, *with* a couple of
horsemen. And he answered and said, **Babylon** is **fallen**, is
fallen; and all the graven images of her gods he hath broken
unto the ground."

The graven images of worship of **Babylon** are the reason for it being
fallen. That is why **Rome** is called the city of **Babylon**, because of its
paganism, idols, and so on.

- **Jeremiah 25:12**
"And it shall come to pass, when seventy years are
accomplished, *that* I will **punish** the king of **Babylon**, and that
nation, saith the LORD, for their iniquity, and the land of the
Chaldeans, and will make it perpetual **desolations**."

- **Jeremiah 50:2**
"Declare ye among the nations, and publish, and set up a
standard; publish, *and* conceal not: say, **Babylon** is taken, Bel
is confounded, Merodach is broken in pieces; her idols are
confounded, her images are broken in pieces."

- **Jeremiah 50:9**
"For, lo, I will raise and cause to come up against **Babylon** an
assembly of great nations from the north country: and they shall
set themselves in array against her; from thence she shall be
taken: their arrows *shall be* as of a mighty expert man; none
shall return in vain."

- **Jeremiah 51:8**
"**Babylon** is suddenly fallen and destroyed: howl for her; take
balm for her pain, if so be she may be healed."

This is all Old Testament prophecy of **Babylon** that is now mentioned
in Revelation 14.

- **1 Peter 5:13**
"The *church that is* at **Babylon**, elected together *with you*, saluteth you; and *so doth* Marcus my son."

The Judgment Of Rome

Many feel that is the church in Rome. Notice, there is judgment because they have made the *nations drink of the wine of the wrath of her fornication*. I believe there is going to be a religious Babylon. This certainly is an indication of that as well.

Revelation 14:9

"And the third angel followed them, saying with a loud voice, If any man worship the beast and his image, and receive *his* mark in his forehead, or in his hand,"

- **Revelation 13:16**
"And he causeth all, both small and great, rich and poor, free and bond, to receive a **mark** in their right hand, or in their foreheads:"

The Cost Of Developing The "Chip"

Some reports have estimated that the developers of the "chip" spent one and a half million dollars with a hundred different people confirming that the best place to put this chip is in the right hand, or in the forehead. The temperature would go back and forth causing it to charge its own batteries.

- **Revelation 15:2**
"And I saw as it were a sea of glass mingled with fire: and them that had gotten the victory over the beast, and over his image, and over his **mark**, *and* over the number of his name, stand on the sea of glass, having the harps of God."

- **Revelation 19:20**
"And the beast was taken, and with him the false prophet that wrought miracles before him, with which he deceived them that had received the **mark** of the beast, and them that worshipped his image. These both were cast alive into a lake of fire burning with brimstone."

- **Revelation 20:4**
  "And I saw thrones, and they sat upon them, and judgment was given unto them: and *I saw* the souls of them that were beheaded for the witness of Jesus, and for the word of God, and which had not worshipped the beast, neither his image, neither had received *his* **mark** upon their foreheads, or in their hands; and they lived and reigned with Christ a thousand years."

Death For Those Refusing The Mark

There are some that will not receive this mark. They will be killed by the false prophet, but they will be genuinely saved and safe.

Revelation 14:10

"The same shall drink of the wine of the wrath of God, which is poured out without mixture into the cup of his indignation; and he shall be tormented with fire and brimstone in the presence of the holy angels, and in the presence of the Lamb:"

The ones who have this **mark** will be tormented. If you have any loved ones who reject the Lord Jesus Christ as Saviour and Redeemer, and the true church has been raptured to Heaven, and they are still left here, you better tell them, "Do not receive that **mark!**" If they do receive it, they will have indignation and be **tormented**. That word for **torment** is BASANIZO. It means *applying torture; to vex with grievous pains of body and mind.* It is a terrible thing. This will be in the fire and brimstone in the presence of the holy angels. These people will be judged and sent to Hell–those who receive this **mark** of this false beast who will be raised up, will be judged by God and sent to Hell.

The Deception Of The Antichrist

The false prophet is described in the last half of Chapter 13. The false political ruler is described in the first half of Chapter 13. Both of these beasts will be against God the Father and against the Lord Jesus Christ. They will be pretending to be like the Lord Jesus Christ. That is what "anti" in the word, antichrist, means. "Anti" means not only *instead of* or *in the place of*, but also *against*. Though the antichrist will appear to be *instead of or in place of* the Lord Jesus Christ, in fact, he will be *against* Him in all of his ways. This is what they are going to do in order to confuse and deceive the people.

Praise the Lord, that these **144,000 Jews** who were called, followed the **Lamb** whithersoever He goeth. Not like Peter. Not like some of us who follow a little way, and follow afar off. Where is the Lord Jesus Christ leading you? Are you genuinely saved? Are you one of the **Lamb's** sheep? Are you one of His followers? Is He trying to lead you? Are you willing to be led by the Lord Jesus Christ? Are you willing to follow Him? I trust that will be true for every one of us who is genuinely saved and born-again.

Revelation 14:11

"And the smoke of their torment ascendeth up for ever and ever: and they have no rest day nor night, who worship the beast and his image, and whosoever receiveth the mark of his name."

Dangers Of Worshipping The Beasts

What a terrible, terrible tragedy for those during this seven-year period of tribulation. Genuine Christian believers will be raptured out. They will not be here on this earth any longer. These who are here on this earth will be worshipping these beasts—the religious beast and the political beast from Revelation 13. Because they worship these beasts, they will be cast into Hell. There is no hope for them. It is a sad thing indeed when that takes place. All those who reject the Lord Jesus Christ will end up in this fiery Hell burning with fire and brimstone. This word *smoke* in Scripture is often used for God's judgment, or else His holiness.

- **Genesis 19:28**
  "And he looked toward Sodom and Gomorrah, and toward all the land of the plain, and beheld, and, lo, <u>the **smoke**</u> of the country went up as the **smoke** of a furnace."

When God judged Sodom and Gomorrah for sodomy and all the wickedness of that day, <u>the smoke arose</u>. God judged them in fire and brimstone.

- **Exodus 19:18**
  "And mount Sinai was altogether on a **smoke**, because the LORD descended upon it in fire: and the **smoke** thereof ascended as the smoke of a furnace, and the whole mount quaked greatly."

Here is God's holiness at mount Sinai, where Moses received the ten commandments—the law. God is a fiery God. His holiness is talked about as <u>smoke of a fire</u>.

- **Isaiah 6:4**
  "And the posts of the door moved at the voice of him that cried, and the house was filled with **smoke**."

Isaiah was in the house of the Lord. The presence of God and **smoke** is part of the holiness of God.

- **Revelation 9:2**
  "And he opened the bottomless pit; and there arose a **smoke** out of the pit, as the **smoke** of a great furnace; and the sun and the air were darkened by reason of the **smoke** of the pit."

Here is the <u>smoke of judgment</u>. That **smoke** will be a terrible catastrophe indeed. This will be the **smoke** out of the pit of Hell.

- **Revelation 15:8**
  "And the temple was filled with **smoke** from the glory of God, and from his power; and no man was able to enter into the temple, till the seven plagues of the seven angels were fulfilled."

This is speaking of the Lord. This is the <u>smoke of God's presence—the smoke of His holiness</u>.

- **Revelation 18:9**
  "And the kings of the earth, who have committed fornication and lived deliciously with her, shall bewail her, and lament for her, when they shall see the **smoke** of her burning,"

This is **Babylon**—apostate religions. Here is <u>God's judgment in smoke</u>. These who **worship** the beast in Revelation 14:11 will be cast into the lake of fire. There is <u>**smoke and torment**</u>. If you think it is easy in Hell, it is not. The Scriptures depict that fire and brimstone, pain and affliction.

The Inhabitants Of Hell

All those who reject the Lord Jesus Christ, and are not genuinely saved, will be in that place. We should witness to those people. I hope nobody reading this is in that condition of having rejected the Lord Jesus Christ. They will have no rest. <u>Rest is important.</u>

- **Genesis 8:9**
  "But the dove found **no rest** for the sole of her foot, and she returned unto him into the ark, for the waters *were* on the face of the whole earth: then he put forth his hand, and took her, and pulled her in unto him into the ark."

This was when Noah sent out the dove and the raven to see whether the waters had subsided. The dove found **no rest** for the sole of her foot. <u>We need **rest**</u>.

- **Exodus 33:13-15**
  "Now therefore, I pray thee, if I have found grace in thy sight, shew me now thy way, that I may know thee, that I may find grace in thy sight: and consider that this nation is thy people. And he said, My presence shall go *with thee*, and <u>I will give thee</u> **rest**. And he said unto him, If thy presence go not *with me*, carry us not up hence."

When Moses was to lead God's people out of Egypt and into the wilderness he prayed unto the Lord. This was Moses' prayer. <u>The Lord is the only One that can give us **rest**—spiritual **rest**, resting in peace, **resting** with the Lord</u>. Moses knew that he must depend upon the Lord to get out of that terrible Egyptian bondage, and there in the wilderness journey for forty years.

- **Psalm 37:7**
  "**Rest** in the LORD, and wait patiently for him: fret not thyself because of him who prospereth in his way, because of the man who bringeth wicked devices to pass."

Just **rest**. People say, "Why worry when you can pray?" Some people have the attitude, "Why pray when you can worry?" That is just the opposite and does not make sense.

- **Isaiah 57:20**
  "But the wicked *are* like the troubled sea, when it cannot **rest**, whose waters cast up mire and dirt. *There is* no peace, saith my God, to the wicked."

Here is a picture of the wicked. <u>The sea cannot **rest**</u>. There is wave after wave after wave continuously.

<u>The Lord Jesus Christ offered **rest** to His disciples and unto you and unto me</u>.

- **Matthew 11:28-30**
  "Come unto me, all *ye* that labour and are heavy laden, and I will give you **rest**. Take my yoke upon you, and learn of me; for I am meek and lowly in heart: and ye shall find **rest** unto your souls. For my yoke *is* easy, and my burden is light."

The rest of the Lord Jesus Christ—rest from sin, rest from trouble, rest from sorrow—is there.

- **Mark 6:31**
"And he said unto them, Come ye yourselves apart into a desert place, and rest a while: for there were many coming and going, and they had no leisure so much as to eat."

We need rest for our bodies, too. Some people say, "*Come ye apart and rest, or you will come apart.*" That is certainly true. We have to have some rest.

- **Acts 2:26**
"Therefore did my heart rejoice, and my tongue was glad; moreover also my flesh shall rest in hope:"

This is David speaking about the Lord Jesus Christ's resurrection.

- **2 Thessalonians 1:7**
"And to you who are troubled rest with us, when the Lord Jesus shall be revealed from heaven with his mighty angels,"

They were going through trouble there.

- **Hebrews 4:3**
"For we which have believed do enter into rest, as he said, As I have sworn in my wrath, if they shall enter into my rest: although the works were finished from the foundation of the world."

Rest Promised To The Saved Ones

If you have genuinely trusted the Lord Jesus Christ as your Saviour—if you have been redeemed, if you have been truly born-again—you have been given His rest. No longer do you have to have turmoil and worry if you are genuinely and confidently saved—not just the head, but the heart. We can have rest. These who are in Hell have no rest day nor night. Some people are night owls and they stay up at night. They go home and they can rest. It is not so with those in Hell. There is no rest either day or night—absolutely restless. This is a terrible state. We ought to pray for our loved ones that are still lost and in need of the Lord Jesus Christ's rest.

Revelation 14:12

"Here is the patience of the saints: here *are* they that keep the commandments of God, and the faith of Jesus."

Now the scene is in Heaven, in Glory with the **saints**.

The Definition Of God's Patience

That word for patience is a very powerful word, HUPOMONE. It means, *steadfastness; endurance.* In the New Testament it means, *the characteristic of a man or woman who is not swerved from his or her deliberate purpose and loyalty to faith and piety by even the greatest trials and sufferings.* That is the definition of this word. Not swerved. We have to be firm in what we believe.

- **Hebrews 10:36**
  "For ye have need of **patience**, that, after ye have done the will of God, ye might receive the promise."
- **Hebrews 12:1**
  "Wherefore seeing we also are compassed about with so great a cloud of witnesses, let us lay aside every weight, and the sin which doth so easily beset *us*, and let us run with **patience** the race that is set before us,"

Each one of us has a separate race to run. All our races are not the same, but we must run with **patience**, being faithful to the Lord.

Keeping God's Commandments

Notice these saints also continue to *keep the commandments of God.* That is a present tense. They continue to keep His commandments and the faith of the Lord Jesus Christ. We must keep that. That word for keep, by the way, is also an interesting and important word, TEREO. It means, *to attend to carefully; taking care of something; to guard; to observe.* This is what they do continuously.

- **John 14:15**
  "If ye love me, keep my **commandments**."
That is the basis of love. That is the proof of love.
- **John 14:23**
  "Jesus answered and said unto him, If a man love me, he will keep my words: and my Father will love him, and we will come unto him, and make our abode with him."

- **John 15:10**
  "If ye **keep** my **commandments**, ye shall abide in my love; even as I have **kept** my Father's **commandments**, and abide in his love."
- **1 Timothy 6:20**
  "O Timothy, **keep** that which is committed to thy trust, avoiding profane *and* vain babblings, and oppositions of science falsely so called:"

Timothy To Keep God's Words

Timothy was a pastor at Ephesus and he was to keep the Words that were committed to his trust. That is why we must keep the Old Testament Hebrew Words that underlie our King James Bible and the New Testament Greek Words that underlie our King James Bible. We need to keep them because they are being destroyed.

- **1 John 5:3**
  "For this is the love of God, that we **keep** his **commandments**: and his **commandments** are not grievous."

We find the **commandments** in the **Words** of God, and we should **keep** them joyfully, indeed.

Revelation 14:13

"And I heard a voice from heaven saying unto me, Write, Blessed *are* the dead which die in the Lord from henceforth: Yea, saith the Spirit, that they may rest from their labours; and their works do follow them."

Saved Ones In Heaven Are Blessed

John heard a voice from Heaven. Those that die in the Lord are blessed—happy. I am not a universalist. I do not believe that everybody that dies is in the Lord Jesus Christ. I do not believe that everybody that dies is going to Heaven as some funerals seem to portray. Some pastors teach that. I do not believe that. It is only those that *die in the Lord Jesus Christ*—the happy saints.

- **Psalm 23:6**
  "Surely goodness and mercy shall follow me all the days of my life: and I will **dwell** in the **house of the LORD** for ever."

That is what is awaiting those that are genuinely saved. David was one of God's children.

- **Psalm 73:24**
  "Thou shalt guide me with thy counsel, and afterward receive me *to* Glory."

Those that **die in the Lord Jesus Christ** will go to **Glory**. There will be **Glory** by and by.

- **John 14:1-3**
  "Let not your heart be troubled: ye believe in God, believe also in me. In my **Father's house** are many mansions: if *it were* not so, I would have told you. I go to prepare a **place** for you. And if I go and prepare a **place** for you, I will come again, and receive you unto myself; that where I am, *there* **ye may be** also."

Judas was not here. He left. Only the eleven that were faithful disciples and apostles were here. That is His promise to those that **die in the Lord Jesus Christ**. It is a tremendous promise.

- **2 Corinthians 5:8**
  "We are confident, *I say,* and willing rather to be absent from the body, and to be **present with the Lord**."

No Roman Catholic Purgatory

Paul was absolutely sure that when his spirit and soul left his body—*absent from the body*—**he would be present with the Lord. There is no limbo. There is no Roman Catholic purgatory. There is no middle place. Absent from the body, immediately present with the Lord Jesus Christ. That is what happens when a genuine Christian dies in the Lord Jesus Christ. There is no separation. He or she goes directly into the presence of our Saviour.**

- **Philippians 1:23**
  "For I am in a strait betwixt two, having a desire to depart, and **to be with Christ**; which is far better:"

Paul was in a strait—a tight place—between two things. Why could Paul say that? He had been there and came back into his body again.

- **2 Corinthians 5:8**
  "We are confident, *I say,* and willing rather to be absent from the body, and to be **present with the Lord**."

Paul's Desire To Depart To Heaven

Paul was willing and would rather be absent from the body and present with the Lord. Why was he having a desire to depart? In Acts 14, when he was dragged out of the city of Lystra they thought he was dead. I think he was dead. At that point, the Lord Jesus Christ took him up to Heaven and showed him the Glory of Heaven. He came back because there was more work for him to do and he continued. Paul speaks about this in 2 Corinthians 12.

- **2 Corinthians 12:2**
  "I knew a man in Christ above fourteen years ago, (whether in the body, I cannot tell; or whether out of the body, I cannot tell: God knoweth;) such an one **caught up to the third heaven.**"

He was talking about himself. He knew what was there and he did not want anything more to do with this earth. The Lord had work for him to do, so he was willing to continue to work. He says that he was *willing rather to be absent from the body.*

- **Philippians 1:23**
  "For I am in a strait betwixt two, having a desire to depart, and **to be with Christ**; which is far better:"

Again, there is no middle ground. There is no limbo. There is no purgatory. Departing is **being with the Lord Jesus Christ** instantaneously, which is far better.

- **1 Thessalonians 4:16-18**
  "For the Lord himself shall descend from heaven with a shout, with the voice of the archangel, and with the trump of God: and the dead in Christ shall rise first: Then we which are alive *and* remain shall be **caught up together** with them in the clouds, to meet the Lord in the air: and so shall we ever be **with the Lord**. Wherefore comfort one another with these words."

What Is The Rapture Of The Church?

If the genuinely saved Christians should live until the Lord Jesus Christ's return, they will be caught up with the Lord Jesus Christ. Dying in the Lord means genuinely born-again Christians are going to be with the Lord Jesus Christ forever. These should be words of comfort. The rapture—the snatching away of the genuinely saved Christians—will come before any part of the tribulation period, the seven years that we are talking about in the book of Revelation. The redeemed ones will not be here halfway through the tribulation. They will not be here all the way through. They will be here for none of it. They will be gone.

- **Revelation 7:17**
  "For the Lamb which is in the midst of the throne shall feed them, and shall lead them unto living fountains of waters: and God shall wipe away all tears from their eyes."

What do the saints have to look forward to if they are **dying in the Lord**—saved by genuine faith in the Lord Jesus Christ? This is what awaits those who **die in the Lord** who are truly saved, born-again people, redeemed by genuine faith in the Lord Jesus Christ. The Lamb will feed them, lead them, and wipe away their tears.

- **Revelation 21:4**
  "And God shall wipe away all tears from their eyes; and there shall be no more death, neither sorrow, nor crying, neither shall there be any more pain: for the former things are passed away."

Notice what there will not be when we are with the Lord in Glory: there shall be no more death, neither sorrow, nor crying, nor any more pain. Four things will not be in Heaven for those who die in the Lord—genuinely born-again Christians.

The Saved Have Eternal Rest

Notice also in Revelation 14:13 it says, *blessed.* This means happy and rejoicing are the dead which die in the Lord, genuinely saved. There is rest, in contrast to the wicked who have no rest in Revelation 14:11. The believers who are in the Lord Jesus Christ have rest from their labours. Then it says, *their works do follow them.* The genuinely saved believers' works will be judged at the judgment seat of the Lord Jesus Christ.

- **2 Corinthians 5:10**
  "For we must all appear before the judgment seat of Christ; that every one may receive the things *done* in *his* body, according to that he hath done, whether *it be* good or bad."

Genuinely born-again believers will be judged by the Lord Jesus Christ at the judgment seat of the Lord Jesus Christ.

- **1 Corinthians 3:10-15**
  "According to the grace of God which is given unto me, as a wise masterbuilder, I have laid the foundation, and another buildeth

thereon. But let every man take heed how he buildeth thereupon. For other foundation can no man lay than that is laid, which is Jesus Christ. Now if any man build upon this foundation gold, silver, precious stones, wood, hay, stubble; <u>Every man's work shall be made manifest: for the day shall declare it, because it shall be revealed by fire; and the fire shall try every man's work of what sort it is.</u> If any man's work abide which he hath built thereupon, he shall receive a reward. If any man's work shall be burned, he shall suffer loss: but he himself shall be saved; yet so as by fire."

These verses also give a picture of that judgment. We have to be careful. <u>If you are **in the Lord**</u>—if you have been genuinely saved, redeemed, and born- again—<u>you are built on a foundation. Be careful how you build on that foundation.</u>

There are two different classes of materials. "Gold, silver, and precious stones" are small but valuable. They will abide the fire and be purified by it. "Wood, hay and stubble" are large and visible, but they will not abide the fire.

There are things that believers do that are just for people to see but are not genuine. The fire will test *every man's work of what sort it is*. <u>It is not how much it is, but what sort, what kind or what brand.</u> If all that we do after we are genuinely saved is for men, and for ourselves, and for our glory—for what people can see about it, but not for the Lord Jesus Christ—there will be no rewards.

My mother-in-law, Gertrude Sanborn, wrote a poem about her daughter's death. It talks about where Audrey is even today. She titled the poem,

Safe in Christ

Into Christ's glorious presence
Close by His pure pierced side,
Ever beholding His beauty
Our dear one has gone to abide.

Listens to songs of the angels,
Leans her dear head on His breast,
There gently we leave our beloved
Knowing how greatly she's blessed.

Tho we have grief since she's left us,
Still we have peace at the thought
That she is safe in His presence;

For her, all life's battles are fought.

That poem was about my sister-in-law, Audrey Sanborn, who *died in the Lord*, genuinely saved and safe. Her mother wrote a poem about her. In fact, we have put my mother-in-law's poems in a book of more than 400 pages. She had many poems. My wife had wanted to get them together for years. There was always one delay after another, but it has been completed. Be sure to get a copy of Gertrude Grace Sanborn's book, *With Tears in My Heart.* (It is **BFT #3196** for a gift of **$25.00 + $8.00 S&H.**)

Revelation 14:14

"And I looked, and behold a white cloud, and upon the cloud *one* **sat like unto the Son of man, having on his head a golden crown, and in his hand a sharp sickle."**

Christ With A Sharp Sickle In His Hand

Here John looks and sees one sitting on a white cloud *like unto the Son of man.* This is the Lord Jesus Christ. He has a golden crown. That means He is King of all eternity. (I trust that you and I, if we are genuinely saved, will give Him that authority and obey Him implicitly without question.) In His hand is a sharp sickle. This is a sickle of judgment. That word for sickle is DREPANON. It is *a pruning hook; a hooked vine knife such as reapers and vine dressers use to cut and reap the vines whenever they are ready.* That word sickle is only used eleven times in the Bible.

- **Joel 3:9-13**
  "Proclaim ye this among the Gentiles; Prepare war, wake up the mighty men, let all the men of war draw near; let them come up: <u>Beat your plowshares into swords, and your pruninghooks into spears</u>: let the weak say, I *am* strong. Assemble yourselves, and come, all ye heathen, and gather yourselves together round about: thither cause thy mighty ones to come down, O LORD. Let the heathen be wakened, and come up to the valley of Jehoshaphat: for there will I sit to judge all the heathen round about. Put ye in the **sickle**, for the harvest is ripe: come, get you down; for the press is full, the fats overflow; for their wickedness *is* great."

In some instances the swords are changed into plowshares when there is peace. <u>Here there is war at the battle of Armageddon when the Lord Jesus Christ comes down to judge all the nations that are gathering</u>

around Jerusalem. The valley of Jehoshaphat is the place where the battle of Armageddon will take place. Here is the **sickle** of judgment. The judgment on these nations is great because of their wickedness.

Revelation 14:15

"And another angel came out of the temple, crying with a loud voice to him that sat on the cloud, Thrust in thy sickle, and reap: for the time is come for thee to reap; for the harvest of the earth is ripe."

The Battle Of Armageddon

Here is the angel that told the Lord Jesus Christ as He was sitting on that cloud to put in the sickle. Remember, the battle of Armageddon will be taking place. Armies will come from all four points of the compass. It will take place in the area a little bit north of Jerusalem. It will be assembling all the nations from the east—over two hundred million from China alone. The Euphrates will be dried up so the kings of the east will be able to come to this great battle of Armageddon. The northern hordes from Russia and all the pagans that are up in the north will come down to that battle against the saints at Jerusalem. Egypt and Africa and all the ones from the south will come up. The westerners will also come battling the Lord Jesus Christ's people. That is when the Lord Jesus Christ comes back during the battle of Armageddon. That is when the harvest is ripe.

- Matthew 13:27-30
  "So the servants of the householder came and said unto him, Sir, didst not thou sow good seed in thy field? from whence then hath it tares? He said unto them, An enemy hath done this. The servants said unto him, Wilt thou then that we go and gather them up? But he said, Nay; lest while ye gather up the tares, ye root up also the wheat with them. Let both grow together until the **harvest**: and in the time of **harvest** I will say to the **reapers**, Gather ye together first the tares, and bind them in bundles to burn them: but gather the wheat into my barn."

Harvest Time Will Come

The Lord Jesus Christ talks about a harvest. There is going to be a harvest time. That is what the sickle signifies. It is going to be taking place at the battle of Armageddon.

Revelation 14:16

"And he that sat on the cloud thrust in his sickle on the earth; and the earth was reaped."

The Slaying Of Multitudes

The Lord Jesus Christ is the One that sat upon that cloud. The sickle was put into the earth and the battle was there. The Lord Jesus Christ does not relish a battle, slaying multitudes, but what is He going to do? Here are all these unbelievers coming in order to rase the city of Jerusalem and to take away the true believers that are there. He has nothing to do but to spare His own and judge the ones that are not His own that are trying to make war with the saints. This is a terrific battle.

Revelation 14:17

"And another angel came out of the temple which is in heaven, he also having a sharp sickle."

Here it shows that there is a <u>temple in Heaven</u>. Just as there is a tabernacle here on this earth, so there is a **temple** in **Heaven**. In fact, <u>the **temple** in **Heaven** was a pattern for the tabernacle on earth</u>. The **temple** has the holy place and the mercy seat. I believe the Lord Jesus Christ's blood is on that mercy seat. Just like the high priest had to put the blood of the goats and the lamb on the mercy seat on the day of atonement on earth, so the Lord Jesus Christ has put His blood on the mercy seat in Heaven.

The Angel Of Death

Apparently, the Lord Jesus Christ has His sharp sickle and the angel has his sharp sickle. Here is the angel of death. They are going to be joined in the reaping during this battle, which is a terrific battle. It is not a pleasant thing. It is not something to look forward to. But it is something that is very serious, indeed.

Revelation 14:18

"And another angel came out from the altar, which had power over fire; and cried with a loud cry to him that had the sharp sickle, saying, Thrust in thy sharp sickle, and gather the clusters of the vine of the earth; for her grapes are fully ripe."

Is it time to **harvest** the wicked of the earth today? Many of us feel that it is not getting any better. We have wickedness on every hand. We have the homosexuals making advances. We have the question, "Can they be married?" Some of the judges have said, "Yes" and they have married these homosexuals. They are not properly married. We have all kinds of crime, murder, and corruption. We have thievery. We have drug addiction. We have fornication and adultery. We have every kind of sin that is on the books. We have a veritable Sodom and Gomorrah as far as wickedness is concerned—in our country and all over the world. We have AIDS and HIV multiplying unto the millions in Africa. They will not have morality in order to stop AIDS. They just keep on with their filthiness, their wickedness, and their sexually transmitted diseases. You wonder, is it time to **reap**? The Lord is patient.

- **2 Peter 3:9**
  "The Lord is not slack concerning his promise, as some men count slackness; but is **longsuffering** to us-ward, not willing that any should perish, but that all should come to repentance."

We see the hand of the Lord and His grace even in Sodom and Gomorrah. Abraham pled with the Lord.

- **Genesis 18:23-32**
  "And Abraham drew near, and said, Wilt thou also destroy the righteous with the wicked? Peradventure there be fifty righteous within the city: wilt thou also destroy and not spare the place for the fifty righteous that *are* therein? That be far from thee to do after this manner, to slay the righteous with the wicked: and that the righteous should be as the wicked, that be far from thee: Shall not the Judge of all the earth do right? And the LORD said, If I find in Sodom fifty righteous within the city, then I will spare all the place for their sakes. And Abraham answered and said, Behold now, I have taken upon me to speak unto the Lord, which *am but* dust and ashes: Peradventure there shall lack five of the fifty righteous: wilt thou destroy all the city for *lack of* five? And he said, If I find there forty and five, I will not destroy *it.* And he spake unto him yet again, and said, Peradventure

there shall be forty found there. And he said, I will not do *it* for forty's sake. And he said *unto him*, Oh let not the Lord be angry, and I will speak: Peradventure there shall thirty be found there. And he said, I will not do *it*, if I find thirty there. And he said, Behold now, I have taken upon me to speak unto the Lord: Peradventure there shall be twenty found there. And he said, I will not destroy *it* for twenty's sake. And he said, Oh let not the Lord be angry, and I will speak yet but this once: Peradventure ten shall be found there. And he said, I will not destroy *it* for ten's sake."

The Lord, in His grace, said that He would spare the city for ten righteous, but He could not even find ten. Here was Lot and his wife and his two daughters. There were four people. His wife looked back and was turned into a pillar of salt. She had too many friends back in Sodom. Three people escaped. You wonder, is God ready to destroy the wicked of this earth today? He apparently sees enough righteous so that it is not time, but one day the time will come. This is not a good thing. It is a bad thing indeed.

Revelation 14:19

"And the angel thrust in his sickle into the earth, and gathered the vine of the earth, and cast *it* into the great winepress of the wrath of God."

The Winepress Of God's Wrath

Here is the great winepress of the wrath of God. That word for winepress is LENOS. It is *a tub or trough-shaped receptacle; a vat in which grapes are trodden, the lower vat dug in the ground into which the new wine flows from the press*. There is a vat on top and another in the ground where the new wine flows. That is the winepress. This word is only used fourteen times in Scripture.

- **Isaiah 63:3**
  "I have trodden the **winepress** alone; and of the people *there was* none with me: for I will tread them in mine anger, and trample them in my fury; and their blood shall be sprinkled upon my garments, and I will stain all my raiment."

- **Revelation 19:15**
  "And out of his mouth goeth a sharp sword, that with it he should smite the nations: and he shall rule them with a rod of iron: and he treadeth the **winepress** of the fierceness and **wrath** of Almighty God."

The **wrath** of God is real. The **wrath** of God is Scriptural. I do not want to have the **wrath** of God on me. I hope you do not want the **wrath** of God on you. It is real. In Scripture there are many different references to that. There is judgment because of God's **wrath** against sin.

- **Psalm 78:27-32**
  "He rained flesh also upon them as dust, and feathered fowls like as the sand of the sea: And he let *it* fall in the midst of their camp, round about their habitations. So they did eat, and were well filled: for he gave them their own desire; They were not estranged from their lust. But while their meat *was* yet in their mouths, The **wrath** of God came upon them, and slew the fattest of them, and smote down the chosen *men* of Israel. For all this they sinned still, and believed not for his wondrous works."

Here was God's provision for the Israelites in their wilderness journeys. Notice what happened. The Lord had promised to give them water and manna from Heaven for forty years wandering around in that wilderness. They had no need for food or water. Their garments did not get old. They did not have any of the diseases of Egypt. They said, "We don't like this manna. We want flesh!" They complained even though God had provided manna. The Lord made some quails to drop on the land. The Lord judged them with the wrath of God because they were gluttons. They were unthankful. I hope none of us are unthankful for the things that the Lord has provided for us. Maybe we want something better. That is what the Israelites did, and the Lord judged them for it.

- **John 3:36**
  "He that believeth on the Son hath everlasting life: and he that believeth not the Son shall not see life; but the **wrath** of God abideth on him."

God's Wrath On Your Shoulders

It is a terrible thing to have the wrath of God abiding—sitting right on the shoulders of those who reject the Lord Jesus Christ. God's wrath is real.

- **Romans 1:18**
"For the **wrath** of God is revealed from heaven against all ungodliness and unrighteousness of men, who hold the truth in unrighteousness;"

God's Wrath Revealed–Armageddon

God's wrath is revealed and God's wrath is real. At the battle of Armageddon, His wrath will be visibly seen in the judgment of all these multi-millions of people.

- **Ephesians 5:5-6**
"For this ye know, that no whoremonger, nor unclean person, nor covetous man, who is an idolater, hath any inheritance in the kingdom of the Lord Jesus Christ and of God. Let no man deceive you with vain words: for because of these things cometh the **wrath** of God upon the children of disobedience."

God has **wrath** against sin and wickedness, indeed. We wonder why He is withholding that even today. It is because of His grace and His mercy.

- **Revelation 14:9-10**
"And the third angel followed them, saying with a loud voice, If any man worship the beast and his image, and receive *his* **mark** in his forehead, or in his hand, The same shall drink of the wine of the wrath of God, which is poured out without mixture into the cup of his **indignation**; and he shall be tormented with fire and brimstone in the presence of the holy angels, and in the presence of the Lamb:"

Is this the chip that is underneath the skin of the right hand or the forehead? Possibly so. That chip can control. When Martha Stewart was to take the conviction of five months in jail, and five months at home, she would have an ankle bracelet, so they could tell just where she was. If they can do that right now with an ankle bracelet, certainly the antichrist will have the ability to monitor everything with a little chip.

They cannot buy or sell unless they have that mark of the beast, as it were. Those that do receive that mark—if they are lost people that receive the mark of the beast during this seven-year period of tribulation—they are going to go to Hell.

With Or Without The Beast's Mark

Those with the mark will be sent to Hell. Those who do not receive it, will be killed, but they will go to Heaven. Those that are genuinely saved will go to Heaven if they receive the Lord

> Jesus Christ. Those who worship the beast will *drink of the wine of the wrath of God*. The wrath of God will be poured out upon those who have the mark of the beast and worship the image of the beast.

The Lord plays for keeps. Remember the anger the Lord had when Moses came down from Mount Sinai. He had just given the Ten Commandments. As Moses came to the foot of the mountain, he heard singing. People were naked and dancing around a golden calf. Aaron was the one that had made that calf. The Lord was very **angry** with those people. He was going to smite them all. Moses asked, *"Who is on the Lord's side?"* The Levites came and slew all those who were not on the Lord's side. This included about 3,000 men. The Lord is **wrathful** against idolatry. Worshipping this beast and his image is a terrible, terrible thing indeed.

Revelation 14:20

"And the winepress was trodden without the city, and blood came out of the winepress, even unto the horse bridles, by the space of a thousand *and* six hundred furlongs."

A **furlong** is about 600 feet. That is what they estimate. Multiplying that times 1,600 equals 960,000 feet. That is about 320,000 yards. It is about 181.8 miles. This battle is going to be huge. If you can think of a battle of soldiers and the ones that were slain in various battles, whether it was the Civil War, or the Revolutionary War, or wherever it may be, the statistics are going to be tremendous. If you consider that from the east alone there will be 200 million in the Chinese contingent, how many 100 million will there be from the north? How many from the south? How many from the west?

There is going to be terrible bloodshed. The Lord Jesus Christ is going to come back at that time. It could be that they will be piled up under the compressed conditions in the valley of Jehoshaphat north of Jerusalem with all the millions there. There will be body upon body upon body with no room. The blood could be up to the horse bridles because the bodies will be piled up that way. That is one possibility that I am thinking of at least.

There are going to be 181 miles of death strewn out. How can that be? The people will not be killing these. The Lord Jesus Christ is going to be killing them. They will be killed instantaneously. There is not going to be any time gap. The **blood** will be flowing for 181 miles. How do I know that? I read it in Revelation 19:11-21. This is the second phase of the Lord Jesus Christ's return.

Two Phases Of Christ's 2ⁿᵈ Coming

The Lord Jesus Christ has one Second Coming in two phases. The first phase is the rapture where the genuine born-again Christians are caught up before the tribulation period begins. After the seven-year tribulation, the Lord Jesus Christ is going to come back in His physical presence upon the earth. That will be the second phase of His second coming. That is what is talked about in Revelation 19.

- **Revelation 19:11-16**
  "And I saw heaven opened, and behold a white horse; and he that sat upon him *was* called Faithful and True, and in righteousness he doth **judge** and **make war**. His eyes *were* as a flame of fire, and on his head *were* many crowns; and he had a name written, that no man knew, but he himself. And he *was* clothed with a vesture dipped in blood: and his name is called The Word of God. And the armies *which were* in heaven followed him upon white horses, clothed in fine linen, white and clean. And out of his mouth goeth a sharp sword, that with it he should **smite the nations**: and he shall rule them with a rod of iron: and he treadeth the **winepress** of the fierceness and **wrath** of Almighty God. And he hath on *his* vesture and on his thigh a name written, KING OF KINGS, AND LORD OF LORDS."

This is the Lord Jesus Christ Himself on that **white horse**. He would rather have people come to Him and be genuinely saved. He does not glory in killing these unbelievers. He would rather have them to be genuinely saved and born-again.

The **armies** that followed Him are the **saints, the genuine believers, the saved people with glorified bodies.** If you are genuinely saved, you will be following the Lord Jesus Christ upon a white horse. Remember the troops in Iraq are called Cavalry units—1ˢᵗ Cavalry, 2ⁿᵈ Cavalry. That means horses.

- **Revelation 19:17-21**
  "And I saw an angel standing in the sun; and he cried with a loud voice, saying to all the fowls that fly in the midst of heaven, Come and gather yourselves together unto the supper of the great God; That ye may eat the flesh of kings, and the flesh of captains, and the flesh of mighty men, and the flesh of horses,

and of them that sit on them, and the flesh of all *men, both* free and bond, both small and great. And I saw the beast, and the kings of the earth, and their armies, gathered together to make **war** against him that sat on the horse, and against his army. And the beast was taken, and with him the false prophet that wrought miracles before him, with which he deceived them that had received the mark of the beast, and them that worshipped his image. These both were cast alive into a lake of fire burning with brimstone. And the remnant were slain with the sword of him that sat upon the horse, which *sword* proceeded out of his mouth: and all the fowls were filled with their flesh."

The Flesh-Eating Fowls Will Come

The fowls will eat the flesh of these millions that are dead. This is the final judgment. This is the sickle, the reaping of the vintage of the earth, the winepress of the wrath of God upon the unbelievers that are gathered against the Lord Jesus Christ on a white horse, and against His armies that follow. It is a great battle called the battle of Armageddon. *Arm* is the Hebrew word which means, *hill.* It is the hill of Megiddo. Armageddon is two words put together. This is where the battle will take place.

Are You Genuinely Saved?

Are you genuinely saved and in the Lord Jesus Christ? It is important. If you are in the Lord Jesus Christ, you can die, and go to Heaven in peace and rest. If you are not in the Lord Jesus Christ—if you are not genuinely saved—and the Lord Jesus Christ should come in the rapture and take the truly saved ones out, you will be in this seven-year tribulation period and face terrific judgment from Almighty God. I trust that you are in the Lord Jesus Christ. It is a wonderful blessing to be in the Lord Jesus Christ and to say that departing and leaving the body is to be with the Lord Jesus Christ.

Revelation
Chapter Fifteen

Revelation 15:1

"And I saw another sign in heaven, great and marvellous, seven angels having the seven last plagues; for in them is filled up the wrath of God."

John saw another **sign**. That word for **sign** is SEMEION. It means, *transcending the common course of nature; something that is distinguished from others; remarkable events that are soon to happen.*

Seven Horrendous Last Plagues

The next events that are going to happen are the seven plagues—horrendous, terrible plagues. We have had the seven trumpets, the seven seals, and now there will be seven vials. John saw this sign in Heaven. It was a marvellous sign. We are going to see a little bit about the marvellous things of the Lord Jesus Christ, the marvellous things of God.

That word for *marvellous* is an interesting word as well: THAUMASTOS. It means, *passing human comprehension; marvellous; extraordinary; striking; surpassing.* Let us talk about some of the **marvellous** things.

- **1 Chronicles 16:12**
  "Remember his **marvellous** works that he hath done, his wonders, and the judgments of his mouth;"
These are **marvellous** things of the Lord.

- **Job 5:9**
  "Which doeth great things and unsearchable; **marvellous** things without number:"

We cannot do **marvellous** things, but the Lord Jesus Christ can—miracles and miraculous works.

- **Psalm 78:12-16**
  "**Marvellous** things did he in the sight of their fathers, in the land of Egypt, *in* the field of Zoan. He divided the sea, and caused them to pass through; and he made the waters to stand as an heap. In the daytime also he led them with a cloud, and all the night with a light of fire. He clave the rocks in the wilderness, and gave *them* drink as *out of* the great depths. He brought streams also out of the rock, and caused waters to run down like rivers."

Notice the first **marvellous** thing: **(1)** *He divided the sea.* This was the Red Sea. He just opened it right up. On either side of that sea the waters stood up. Now that is contrary to all nature. That is **marvellous**. That is unexpected. That is superhuman. Afterward, what happened? The sea came back and drowned the Egyptians.

Here is another **marvellous** thing: **(2)** *He led them with a cloud.* All the way throughout that wandering in the wilderness of Sinai for forty years, He led them with a cloud by day. That is a **marvellous** thing. Then there was the fire by night so they could find out where to go. He just kept going, by day with the cloud and with fire by night. If it moved, they followed. It was a **marvellous** thing.

Another **marvellous** thing talks about: **(3)** *He clave the rocks in the wilderness, and gave them drink.* Out of that rock that Moses spoke to and that he struck, came water. He fed them with manna and also gave them water. You might say, "How can the Lord provide water in a wilderness where there was no water?" There were six hundred thousand men that came out of Egypt plus women and children—maybe two or three million people. The Lord that made the waters, the earth, and the heavens is perfectly capable of providing water for His people and He did. It was a **marvellous** thing.

- **1 Peter 2:9**
  "But ye *are* a chosen generation, a royal priesthood, an holy nation, a peculiar people; that ye should shew forth the praises of him who hath called you out of darkness into his **marvellous** light:"

These are genuine believers. Here is the word, **marvellous**, in the New Testament. The light of the Lord Jesus Christ is indeed **marvellous**. He called us into this light. We ought not to walk in darkness.

The Seven Last Plagues Begin

This chapter is the beginning of introducing the seven last plagues. With the <u>first vial</u> plague, the angels are going to introduce in Revelation 16:2, is going to be a grievous sore on those that had the mark of the beast. (The genuine Christians are going to be caught up in the rapture. We will not be in the tribulation.) Those that receive the mark of the beast will have a grievous sore upon them.

With the <u>second vial</u> in Revelation 16:3, the sea becomes blood. Everything dies. Fish cannot live in a blood sea.

With <u>vial number three</u> in Revelation 16:4, the rivers and fountains of waters become blood. Not only do the sea creatures die, but everyone on the land. You cannot drink blood. This is a terrible **plague** and judgment.

With <u>vial number four</u> in Revelation 16:8, the sun scorches men with fire. Some people are worshippers of the sun. They go out and get sunburned and so on. This is going to be greater than ever before. God is going to change the sun in this fourth **plague**.

With <u>vial number five</u> in Revelation 16:10, there is going to be great darkness and pain with that darkness.

With <u>vial number six</u> in Revelation 16:12, the river Euphrates is going to be dried up for the kings of the east. The river Euphrates is a southern river. The Tigris is north of that. The Euphrates is going to be dried up to make way for the kings of the east to come to the great battle of Armageddon. That is China and all those of the East. It is a terrible thing.

With <u>vial number seven</u> in Revelation 16:17-18, there will be the most mighty earthquake that ever took place, much more than anything we have ever seen before.

The Wrath Of God Filled Full

The seven last plagues are going to be there. In these plagues the wrath of God will be filled to the full, and complete. That word for filled up is TELEO. It means *to perform; to execute; to complete.* It corresponds to that which has been said, a command: *to carry out the contents of a command.* God has commanded and He is going to fulfill it. The wrath of God only occurs ten times in Scripture. It is a very strong word for His anger.

- **Psalm 78:30-31**
  "They were not estranged from their lust. But while their meat *was* yet in their mouths, The **wrath of God** came upon them, and slew the fattest of them, and smote down the chosen *men* of Israel."

The Israelites were lusting after flesh. They just gorged themselves with those quail.

- **John 3:36**
  "He that believeth on the Son hath everlasting life: and he that believeth not the Son shall not see life; but the **wrath of God** abideth on him."

This wrath is God's anger on those that reject His Son. This is very important.

- **Romans 1:18**
  "For the **wrath of God** is revealed from heaven against all ungodliness and unrighteousness of men, who hold the truth in unrighteousness;"

God's wrath is against ungodliness.

- **Colossians 3:5-6**
  "Mortify therefore your members which are upon the earth; fornication, uncleanness, inordinate affection, evil concupiscence, and covetousness, which is idolatry: For which things' sake the **wrath of God** cometh on the children of disobedience:"

God pours out **wrath** on sin. Therefore genuine believers should mortify—put to death—these wickednesses and sins.

- **Revelation 14:10**
  "The same shall drink of the wine of the **wrath of God**, which is poured out without mixture into the cup of his indignation; and he shall be tormented with fire and brimstone in the presence of the holy angels, and in the presence of the Lamb:"

All those in the tribulation period that worship the beast *shall drink of the wine of the **wrath of God***. There is going to be no let up for them.

- **Revelation 14:19**
  "And the angel thrust in his sickle into the earth, and gathered the vine of the earth, and cast *it* into the great winepress of the **wrath of God**."

- **Revelation 15:7**
  "And one of the four beasts gave unto the seven angels seven golden vials full of the **wrath of God**, who liveth for ever and ever."

- **Revelation 16:1**
  "And I heard a great voice out of the temple saying to the seven angels, Go your ways, and pour out the vials of the **wrath of God** upon the earth."

A lot of the liberals and modernists say that God is not a God of **wrath**, He is not a God of anger, just a God of love. Therefore, there is no such thing as Hell. There is no such thing as the lake of fire.

The Lake Of Fire Is Real

There **is** such a thing as the lake of fire. It is prepared for the Devil and his angels. Those that reject the Lord Jesus Christ go where the Devil is. God is a God of love, yes. He also has wrath against sin. We must remember that.

Revelation 15:2

"And I saw as it were a sea of glass mingled with fire: and them that had gotten the victory over the beast, and over his image, and over his mark, *and* over the number of his name, stand on the sea of glass, having the harps of God."

Here John sees us it were a sea of glass. That is a figure of speech. It is just like glass—clear like crystal.

- **Revelation 4:1-6**
  "After this I looked, and, behold, a door *was* opened in heaven: and the first voice which I heard *was* as it were of a trumpet talking with me; which said, Come up hither, and I will shew thee things which must be hereafter. And immediately I was in the spirit: and, behold, a throne was set in heaven, and *one* sat on the throne. And he that sat was to look upon like a jasper and a sardine stone: and *there was* a rainbow round about the throne, in sight like unto an emerald. And round about the throne *were* four and twenty seats: and upon the seats I saw four and twenty elders sitting, clothed in white raiment; and they had on their heads crowns of gold. And out of the throne proceeded lightnings and thunderings and voices: and *there were* seven lamps of fire burning before the throne, which are the seven Spirits of God. And before the throne *there was* a sea of glass like unto crystal: and in the midst of the throne, and round about the throne, *were* four beasts full of eyes before and behind."

This is after the rapture when the genuine Christians are snatched up to be with the Lord Jesus Christ in Heaven. The genuine Christians are snatched away before any of this tribulation takes place. Not a single judgment will come upon those who are genuinely saved now. The four and twenty elders are representatives, I believe, of the true Church—the Christians who are genuinely saved and up in Heaven.

In Heaven, at the Father's throne, there is a **sea of glass**. It is pure. You can walk on the street of gold, but this is a **sea of glass** like unto crystal. It is beautiful, shining, and perfect. That is what it says in the Scripture and I believe it. This **sea of glass** is mingled **with fire** because judgment is here.

Who Is The Political Beast?

Notice also, he saw *them that had gotten the victory over the beast*. <u>There are two beasts in Revelation 13</u>. There is a political beast in the first half of the chapter. There is the religious beast in the last half of the chapter. The political beast is the antichrist and the religious beast is the false prophet. The false prophet will cause everybody to worship the image of this political ruler.

We do not know who it is. Is it John Kerry? Is it President Bush? Is it Obama? We do not know. Is it Putin? Nobody knows who this political ruler is, but it will be a political ruler that will be strong and popular. People will clap for him. The first three and a half years—the first half of the tribulation—they will say, "What a wonderful man!" The last half is when his colors change. The wolf is inside and the lamb outside. The wolf comes outside and they will see who he is.

Those who got the victory over the beast, over his image, over his mark, and over the number of his name (that is, 666), stand on the sea of glass. They will be in glory having victory over the beast.

- 1 Corinthians 15:57
  "But thanks *be* to God, which giveth us the **victory** through our Lord Jesus Christ."

Those that have **victory over the beast** and the **mark** are in Heaven. They did not receive the **mark** of the **beast**. Those that did receive the mark of the **beast** will perish. They will be sent to Hell and the lake of fire. The genuine believers, although the beast will kill them because they did not receive the mark of the beast, will be in **Glory**. They have **victory** over it because God takes them Home. That is real **victory**.

- **2 Samuel 23:12**
  "But he stood in the midst of the ground, and defended it, and slew the Philistines: and the LORD wrought a great **victory**."

God is a God who can give **victory**.

- **1 John 5:4**
  "For whatsoever is born of God overcometh the world: and this is the **victory** that overcometh the world, *even* our faith."

The song says, *"Faith is the victory that overcomes the world."* There is great **victory** by genuine faith in the Lord Jesus Christ. Redemption through genuine faith in Him is a great victory.

In Heaven, these saints that have been slain during the tribulation have the **harps of God**. **Harps** are used twenty different times and places in Scripture.

- **2 Chronicles 20:27-28**
  "Then they returned, every man of Judah and Jerusalem, and Jehoshaphat in the forefront of them, to go again to Jerusalem with joy; for the LORD had made them to rejoice over their enemies. And they came to Jerusalem with psalteries and **harps** and trumpets unto the house of the LORD."

The Harps Of Heaven

The harps—those stringed instruments—were instruments of joy. You may say, "Are there going to be harps in Heaven?" Well, it says that they have the harps of God. There are going to be musical instruments in Heaven. Mark Carroll plays the harp. It is an instrument of praise unto the Lord Jesus Christ that is going to be in Heaven.

Revelation 15:3

"And they sing the song of Moses the servant of God, and the song of the Lamb, saying, Great and marvellous *are* thy works, Lord God Almighty; just and true *are* thy ways, thou King of saints."

They are **singing**. That is why they have the **harps of God**. That word to **sing** is in the present tense. They continuously **sing**. People say, "Are you going to be sad in Heaven? Are you going to be happy in Heaven?" These believers who are genuinely saved by God's grace out of the tribulation—that terrible situation—are **singing**. They are **singing** continuously. We ought to **sing** in our hearts today.

- **Psalm 40:2-3**
"He brought me up also out of an horrible pit, out of the miry clay, and set my feet upon a rock, *and* established my goings. And he hath put a new **song** in my mouth, *even* praise unto our God: many shall see *it*, and fear, and shall trust in the LORD."

Songs Of Moses & Of The Lamb

Notice, they sang two types of songs. One is the song of Moses. The other is the song of the Lamb, the Lord Jesus Christ. <u>Singing is a part of Heaven.</u> That is why we love to sing in our church so much. The song of Moses is recorded in Exodus 15. You might not think of Moses as a singer. He was a great deliverer. He was a prophet. He led his people out of Israel. After the Red Sea victory—after he got victory over the Red Sea, Pharaoh and his hosts drowned, and the Israelites came through unscathed and unharmed—then Moses sang.

- **Exodus 15:1-5**
"Then **sang** Moses and the children of Israel this song unto the LORD, and spake, saying, I will **sing** unto the LORD, for he hath triumphed gloriously: the horse and his rider hath he thrown into the sea. The LORD *is* my strength and song, and he is become my salvation: he *is* my God, and I will prepare him an habitation; my father's God, and I will exalt him. The LORD *is* a man of war: the LORD *is* his name. Pharaoh's chariots and his host hath he cast into the sea: his chosen captains also are drowned in the Red sea. The depths have covered them: they sank into the bottom as a stone."

He was a **singer**. He led them in **song**. Notice, **singing** should be unto the Lord—not to men, but to the Lord. Moses knew Him to be his strength and his **song**. He had salvation because he was delivered from that terrible Red Sea instead of being slaughtered.

The LORD is a man of war when need be. In the Old Testament He certainly was. At the battle of Armageddon, He will be a man of war again.

Liberals Deny The True Red Sea

The liberals and modernists do not like the term Red Sea. They like to translate it "reed sea." They just put another "e" in there. A reed sea is six inches deep. You have one or two miracles. You take your pick. It is either the miracle that God has given in His Scripture that it is the Red Sea that is deep enough to swallow up all of Pharaoh's chariots and horses, or you take the miracle of the reed sea with six inches of water and all the horses and chariots were swallowed up in six inches of water. Either miracle you can take, but both of them are miracles. I would rather take the miracle of the Scripture.

The Lord Jesus Christ is the Lamb. He has given us great ability to sing. I know some of us cannot **sing** as well as others, but He has given us something to **sing** about.

- **Revelation 5:8**
"And when he had taken the book, the four beasts and four *and* twenty elders fell down before the **Lamb,** having every one of them **harps,** and golden vials full of odours, which are the prayers of saints."

They had **harps.** Notice what they did with those **harps.**

- **Revelation 5:9**
"And they sung a new **song,** saying, Thou art worthy to take the book, and to open the seals thereof: for thou wast slain, and hast redeemed us to God by thy **blood** out of every kindred, and tongue, and people, and nation;"

This is speaking of the Lord Jesus Christ, the only One that could open this seven-sealed book. He was the only One that was worthy. The song of the **Lamb** is redemption through the blood of the Lord Jesus Christ. John MacArthur says that blood does not mean blood, it just means death. Here you have mentioned in the same verse both the death and the blood. They are separate and distinct. Redemption is through the blood of the Lord Jesus Christ. Yes, it was while He died shedding His blood, but God specifies this redemption through His blood.

Notice also in Revelation 15:3 what song they **sang.** We have seen some marvellous works of the Lord Jesus Christ. He is called Lord God Almighty. That word for Almighty is PANTOKRATOR. PANTO is *all* and KRATOR is *strong.* It is He who holds sway over all things. He is the ruler of all, mighty God. It is a tremendous name for the Lord Jesus Christ.

God's Attributes Of "Just" & "True"

There are two attributes we want to talk about: *just* and *true*. Is He your King? Are you a Biblical saint? Have you genuinely trusted the Lord Jesus Christ? Are you redeemed? He wants to be your King and my King. That means we ought to say, "Yes, Lord," and obey Him, even while we are here.

I want you to see the attributes of God. First, God is just—absolutely righteous and just. I think the reason they sing that God is just and true, is because, in Revelation 16, He is going to pour out the wrath of God and the **wrath of the Lamb** upon the people in these seven years of the tribulation period. <u>He wants everyone to see that He is **just** in His doings.</u> There is nothing that God does that is unjust. It is well deserved.

- **Deuteronomy 32:4**
  "He is the Rock, his work *is* perfect: for all his ways *are* judgment: a God of truth and without iniquity, **just** and right *is* he."

God is **just**. He never makes a mistake. He is never unjust. All throughout Scripture He is **just**.

- **Nehemiah 9:33**
  "Howbeit <u>thou *art* **just**</u> in all that is brought upon us; for thou hast done right, but we have done wickedly:"

This was in Nehemiah's time as they came back out of the Babylonian captivity after seventy years. He came to the temple and prayed. We have to realize that we are wicked in ourselves, <u>but He is **just**</u>.

As Nehemiah prayed unto the Lord, they had just been brought out of seventy years of horrendous and very torturous captivity in Babylon. God brought them back to their land, back to Jerusalem, back to the temple, and Nehemiah prayed unto Him, "Lord, we are not going to hold you accountable."

The Lord Is Always Just

When things go bad for us many times people say, "It is the Lord's fault. Why does He do this to me? Bad things happen." Not Nehemiah. He said, "Thou art just. We have done wickedly." In other words, they got what they deserved and God is still just and righteous.

- **Isaiah 45:21**
  "Tell ye, and bring *them* near; yea, let them take counsel together: who hath declared this from ancient time? *who* hath told it from that time? *have not* I the LORD? and *there is* no God else beside me; a **just** God and a Saviour; *there is* none beside me."

God was **just**, even when He took His people Israel—the northern kingdom and the southern kingdom—into captivity. The northern kingdom went into Assyria and the southern kingdom went into Babylon. Isaiah could still say, "*Thou are a just God and a Saviour. There is none beside Thee.*"

- **Zephaniah 3:5**
  "The **just** LORD *is* in the midst thereof; he will not do iniquity: every morning doth he bring his judgment to light, he faileth not; but the unjust knoweth no shame."

He is a **just** God. You might say, "**Justice?** Do we get **justice** from men?" Sometimes we do, sometimes we do not, but we will always get **justice** from God because He is a **just** God. He will do no iniquity.

- **Zechariah 9:9**
  "Rejoice greatly, O daughter of Zion; shout, O daughter of Jerusalem: behold, thy King cometh unto thee: he *is* **just**, and having salvation; lowly, and riding upon an ass, and upon a colt the foal of an ass."

When the Lord Jesus Christ came into Jerusalem on the colt and as they spread their garments before Him, that is taken from this very verse in Zechariah 9:9. The Lord Jesus Christ was their King as He came into Jerusalem. This verse was quoted, then the next week they crucified Him.

- **Mark 11:9**
  "And they that went before, and they that followed, cried, saying, Hosanna; Blessed *is* he that cometh in the name of the Lord:"

King for a week? No! He is King forever! They just had a King for a week. We do not want a King just for a week.

- **Acts 3:14**
  "But ye denied the Holy One and the **Just**, and desired a murderer to be granted unto you;"

In Peter's sermon, he talked to those Israelites. He talked about the Lord Jesus Christ and how He came to genuinely save them. The Lord Jesus Christ is called, *the **Just***. They did not listen to the Lord Jesus Christ, but they denied Him. He is **just**. This is the very quality of the Lord Jesus Christ and God Himself—absolutely **just**.

- **Acts 7:52**
  "Which of the prophets have not your fathers persecuted? and they have slain them which shewed before of the coming of the **Just** One; of whom ye have been now the betrayers and murderers:"

Here was another sermon, this time by Stephen before he was stoned to death. The Lord Jesus Christ is called, *the Just One.* He never had any injustice. He never did anything against anybody. Why did they crucify Him? It was very strange that sinful men crucified the Man who was righteous, **just**, and sinless.

- **Acts 22:14**
  "And he said, The God of our fathers hath chosen thee, that thou shouldest know his will, and see that **Just** One, and shouldest hear the voice of his mouth."

This is part of the testimony of Paul the apostle before the court. The Lord Jesus Christ is called, *that Just One.* Paul did see the Lord Jesus Christ, the **Just** One. Remember, he was blinded by a light greater than the sun.

- **Acts 22:8**
  "And I answered, Who art thou, Lord? And he said unto me, I am Jesus of Nazareth, whom thou persecutest."

He saw the **Just** One. The Lord Jesus Christ was in Heaven. Paul was converted after the Lord Jesus Christ had gone, but now He was shown so that Paul could see that **Just** One.

- **1 Peter 3:18**
  "For Christ also hath once suffered for sins, the **just** for the unjust, that he might bring us to God, being put to death in the flesh, but quickened by the Spirit:"

The Errors Of The Mass

He suffered once—not many times like the Roman Catholic Church has mass, after mass, after mass—just once He suffered for our sins. If He were not just, He could not have suffered for us who are unjust. If He were not just, He could not have taken our sins upon His own self, die for our sins, redeem us by faith and give us everlasting life. Our God is just.

- **1 John 1:9**
  "If we confess our sins, he is faithful and just to forgive us *our* sins, and to cleanse us from all unrighteousness."

This is talking about genuine Christians, not unsaved people. They cannot get any mileage on this verse. If we are genuinely saved, redeemed, and truly born-again—if we confess our sins and agree with God that what we do, say, or think is sin—He is faithful to forgive us and He is **just** in forgiving us. He is **just** because the Lord Jesus Christ, the **Just** One, died as *the just for the unjust, that he might bring us to God.*" That is why God is **just** in forgiving us.

All Sins Forgiven To The Redeemed

Every sin that we commit in thought, word, and deed—if we are genuinely saved, if we are truly born-again, if we have been redeemed by the blood of the Lord Jesus Christ—every sin that we commit—past, present, and future—has been forgiven and cleansed. He is just in forgiving our sins if we agree.

The Greek Word For "Confess"

That word for confess is HOMOLOGEO. It comes from two Greek words. HOMO is *the same*. LOGEO is *to say*. We need to say the same thing about sin that God says and agree with God that it is sin. We need to agree with God about our thoughts of sin, our words of sin, and our actions of sin.

Notice the second of God's attributes in Revelation 15:3, just before He is going to pour out His seven last judgments. God is not only **just**, but He is also **true**. **Truth** is an attribute of God.

- **2 Samuel 7:28**
"And now, O Lord GOD, thou *art* that God, and thy words be **true**, and thou hast promised this goodness unto thy servant:" God is true. The antichrist is not **true**. The false prophet is not **true**. The political beast is not **true**. The Lord Jesus Christ, God's Words, and God Himself are all **true**—absolutely **true** with no lie and no evil of any kind.

- **Psalm 19:9**
"The fear of the LORD *is* clean, enduring for ever: the judgments of the LORD *are* **true** *and* righteous altogether."
Somebody may say, "I do not believe the Bible." Well, that is on them. The Bible is **true**. The judgments of the Lord Jesus Christ are **true**. We have to believe what God has given to us. It was not revealed by men. It was revealed by God.

God's Words Kept Intact In English

God gave us His Words by revelation—Hebrew, Aramaic, and Greek Words—and they have been translated with accurate words into our King James Bible accurately. We have Gods Words kept intact in English in our King James Bible.

- **Jeremiah 10:10**
  "But the LORD *is* the **true** God, he *is* the living God, and an everlasting king: at his **wrath** the earth shall tremble, and the nations shall not be able to abide his indignation."

Mohammad & Buddha–False Gods

The LORD is the true God—not these false prophets, but the true God. That implies there are false gods that are not true gods. Mohammad is a false god. Buddha is a false god. Shinto is a false God. In fact, let me say just very kindly: the God, that the Jews worship today, is a false god, because they do not accept the Lord Jesus Christ, the true God, the Son. They claim that they worship God, whatever that is, but the Old Testament God is the God of the New Testament as well. The Lord Jesus Christ came from the Father.

- **John 5:43**
  "I am come in my Father's name, and ye receive me not: if another shall come in his own name, him ye will receive."

They rejected the Lord Jesus. They rejected the **true** God. He is the only **true** God.

Any "god" But Our God Is False

The god of philosophy is false. The god of the Mormons is false. The god of the Jehovah's Witnesses is false. The god of Christian Science is false. The god that the Catholics worship really, in a sense, is false because they add to the God of the Scriptures such things as penance, works, the mass, Mary, the Eucharist, and all the other rituals that go with them. It is not the true God. It is God plus something. It is a change. They reject the Lord Jesus Christ's finished work. They sacrifice Him over and over again, day in and day out, mass after mass, all over the world. The Lord Jesus Christ is the true God.

- **Mark 12:14**
  "And when they were come, they say unto him, Master, we know that thou art **true**, and carest for no man: for thou regardest not the person of men, but teachest the way of God in **truth**: Is it lawful to give tribute to Caesar, or not?"

The Lord Jesus Christ is **true**. He never lied to them. He talked about His Father in Heaven. He never lied about it. When He said He would go to prepare a place for you and come again, He did not lie about that. He is going to come again. He is preparing a place for those who are genuinely saved right now. He is the **true** God. God is **true**.

- **John 3:33**
  "He that hath received his testimony hath set to his seal that God is **true**."

He is **true**, never false.

- **John 7:28**
  "Then cried Jesus in the temple as he taught, saying, Ye both know me, and ye know whence I am: and I am not come of myself, but he that sent me is **true**, whom ye know not."

He came from God the Father. These Jews did not know that **true** Father.

- **John 8:26**
  "I have many things to say and to judge of you: but he that sent me is **true**; and I speak to the world those things which I have heard of him."

The Lord Jesus Christ Never Lied

Every word that the Lord Jesus Christ spoke was from the Father and it was true. There was no lie. There was no falsehood. In order to crucify Him, they had to have lies and false witnesses with false testimonies. They had several who could not agree, so they threw them out. Finally, they got two that agreed.

- **Matthew 26:60-61**
  "But found none: yea, though many false witnesses came, yet found they none. At the last came two false witnesses, And said, This fellow said, I am able to destroy the temple of God, and to build it in three days."

He did not mean the physical temple. He meant the temple of His body.

- **John 2:19**
  "Jesus answered and said unto them, Destroy this temple, and in three days I will raise it up."

This is the bodily resurrection of our Saviour.

- **John 14:6**
  "Jesus saith unto him, I am the way, the **truth**, and the life: no man cometh unto the Father, but by me."

The Lord Jesus Christ is the **truth**, and He is the only way. You may say, "Well, does that not sound a little bit narrow-minded?" Yes, it does and yes, it is narrow-minded. <u>The Lord Jesus Christ is the only way—*the way*—not a couple of ways.</u> He is *the truth*. All the rest are false. He is *the life*. These are positive statements, dogmatic statements, and narrow-minded statements, because He *is* the only way, the only **truth**, and the only life. This is why I believe that we must give His gospel message to the whole world. He died for the sins of the world, and people need to trust and accept the Lord Jesus Christ as the way, the **truth**, and the life.

- **John 17:3**
  "And this is life eternal, that they might know thee the only **true** God, and Jesus Christ, whom thou hast sent."

The *"only **true** God"* implies that other gods are false gods—all the different idols that they worship—Baal, all the Shinto idols, and the Buddhist idols in all the temples. He is the only **true** God.

- **Romans 3:4**
  "God forbid: yea, let God be **true**, but every man a liar; as it is written, That thou mightest be justified in thy sayings, and mightest overcome when thou art judged."

Whatever men say that is contrary to God's Words, is a lie. He is **true**.

- **2 Corinthians 1:18**
  "But *as* God *is* **true**, our word toward you was not yea and nay."

God is **true**. Again, the **truth** of God is important.

- **1 Thessalonians 1:9**
  "For they themselves shew of us what manner of entering in we had unto you, and how ye turned to God from idols to serve the living and **true** God;"

These heathen people in Thessalonica turned *from idols to serve the living and **true** God*. They knew Who was **true** and who was false. They realized, when they were genuinely saved, that all these idols were false gods. They turned to the **true** God.

- **1 John 5:20**
  "And we know that the Son of God is come, and hath given us an understanding, that we may know him that is **true**, and we are in him that is **true**, *even* in his Son Jesus Christ. This is the **true** God, and eternal life."

The Lord Jesus Christ Is True God

That is a good statement for the Deity of the Lord Jesus Christ. The Son Jesus Christ *is the true God.* People say, "Well, the Scriptures never say that Jesus is God." Here is one. There are others as well. He is the true God.

- **Revelation 3:7**
  "And to the angel of the church in Philadelphia write; These things saith he that is holy, he that is **true**, he that hath the key of David, he that openeth, and no man shutteth; and shutteth, and no man openeth;"
- **Revelation 6:10**
  "And they cried with a loud voice, saying, How long, O Lord, holy and **true**, dost thou not judge and avenge our blood on them that dwell on the earth?"

Here is the **trueness** of God. He is the King of Biblical saints. These attributes of the Lord Jesus Christ will not change. They are immutable. They are changeless. They will go on forever.

Revelation 15:4

"Who shall not fear thee, O Lord, and glorify thy name? for *thou* only *art* holy: for all nations shall come and worship before thee; for thy judgments are made manifest."

We Must Glorify God's Name

After we have seen His truth and His justice, we are to glorify His name. The holiness of God leads to His judgments. Because He is holy, and because no unholiness can come into His presence, every one who is genuinely saved has to be made completely righteous.

That is only possible by what the Lord Jesus Christ has done for us. By genuinely trusting in Him, a person believes that their sins were placed upon Him, the Lord Jesus Christ, at Calvary. He is perfect Deity. Our sin was placed on Him, the sinless One, that we might be made whole and righteous. He is a righteous God.

Let us take a look at the holiness of God. It is another attribute. He is certainly **just**. He is **true**. He is also **holy**.

- **Exodus 15:11**
  "Who *is* like unto thee, O LORD, among the gods? who *is* like thee, glorious in **holiness**, fearful *in* praises, doing wonders?"

He is <u>glorious in **holiness**</u>—<u>absolutely pure</u>. You might say, "Well, can you get a spot on your clothing?" Yes, but God has no spots on Him. Can you get a spot on a rug? A spot on your car or a scratch? God is perfect. God is holy. He is absolutely perfect and glorious in **holiness**.

- **Exodus 28:36**
  "And thou shalt make a plate *of* pure gold, and grave upon it, *like* the engravings of a signet, HOLINESS TO THE LORD."

That was on Aaron's mitre, a plate of pure gold. We are not **holy** in ourselves, but God is **holy** and He makes us **holy** in the Lord Jesus Christ. He gives us His righteousness in the Lord Jesus Christ.

- **Psalm 22:3**
  "But thou *art* **holy**, *O thou* that inhabitest the praises of Israel."

- **Psalm 30:4**
  "Sing unto the LORD, O ye saints of his, and give thanks at the remembrance of his **holiness**."

The Pope Is Not "His Holiness"

I do not call the Pope, *his holiness*. I call God, His Holiness. The Pope is nothing but a sinner. If he has not genuinely trusted the Lord Jesus Christ, and Him alone, he is a lost sinner. Yet people call him, *his holiness*. He may be a nice man. I do not know him personally. I know what his church believes and teaches. I know the teachings of the church to be false and phony. I know that he believes that he cannot be saved by the Lord Jesus Christ alone, but by the mass, Mary, and other things that go along with it. I do not call him, *his holiness*. We are to give thanks to the Lord and His holiness.

- **Psalm 47:8**
  "God reigneth over the heathen: God sitteth upon the <u>throne of his **holiness**</u>."

There is <u>pure **holiness**</u> in Heaven and upon His throne.

- **Psalm 60:6**
  "God hath spoken in <u>his **holiness**</u>; I will rejoice, I will divide Shechem, and mete out the valley of Succoth."

- **Psalm 68:5**
  "A father of the fatherless, and a judge of the widows, is God in his **holy** habitation."

Is God in His **holy** habitation? Yes, He is.

- **Psalm 78:41**
  "Yea, they turned back and tempted God, and limited the **Holy** One of Israel."

God is the **Holy** One—perfectly **holy**.

- **Psalm 93:5**
  "Thy testimonies are very sure: **holiness** becometh thine house, O LORD, for ever."

God wants the true believers—the genuinely saved ones—to be **holy** as well.

- **1 Peter 1:16**
  "Because it is written, <u>Be ye **holy**; for I am **holy**</u>."

We have to be **holy**.

- **Psalm 97:12**
  "Rejoice in the LORD, ye righteous; and give thanks at the remembrance of his **holiness**."

- **Isaiah 63:15**
  "Look down from heaven, and behold from the habitation of thy **holiness** and of thy glory: where is thy zeal and thy strength, the sounding of thy bowels and of thy mercies toward me? are they restrained?"

Isaiah pleads with the Lord. Heaven is called **holy**. It is called glorious. God is there in His perfect **holiness**.

- **Psalm 145:17**
  "The LORD *is* righteous in all his ways, and **holy** in all his works."

Even in the judgment works, He is still **holy**. It is coming upon this earth as it mentions in the next chapter.

- **Isaiah 6:3**
  "And one cried unto another, and said, **Holy, holy, holy**, is the LORD of hosts: the whole earth is full of his glory."

This is the threefold **holy** God—Father, Son, and the Holy Spirit.

- **Isaiah 17:7**
  "At that day shall a man look to his Maker, and his eyes shall have respect to the **Holy** One of Israel."

Holy One, by the way, is used fifty-one times in the Bible.

- **Hebrews 12:10**
  "For they verily for a few days chastened *us* after their own pleasure; but he for *our* profit, that *we* might be partakers of his **holiness.**"

God wants genuine Christians—truly saved ones—to be partakers of His **holiness.** That is why He has given us the Scriptures. He has given us the Holy Spirit. He has given us His Words, that we might be as **holy** as He is.

Our God Is Just, True, And Holy

Here we have a God Who is just, true, and holy. In the next chapter, He is going to pour out upon this earth His seven vials of judgment. They are terrible, terrible judgments, but He is holy in doing it. There is not an unjustness about Him. He is absolutely holy in what He does. We must realize and thank Him for it. We ought to be thanking Him, if we are genuinely saved, that the just Lord Jesus Christ died for us, the unjust, that He might bring us to God. If you do not know Him as your Saviour, I hope you genuinely trust Him as your Redeemer so that you might not be lost as the world is lost.

Revelation 15:5

"And after that I looked, and, behold, the temple of the tabernacle of the testimony in heaven was opened:"

There Is A Temple In Heaven

This verse teaches very clearly, does it not, that there is a temple in Heaven. There is not only a temple on this earth. The tabernacle was a picture, and the temple was picture, but the prototype was the temple in Heaven. It is still in Heaven and as such, it has all the different articles. It has the mercy seat. I believe the blood of the Lord Jesus Christ is there on that mercy seat. It has the table of shewbread. It has the ark of the covenant.

Notice, it has *the testimony.* Here is an opening of the very presence of God. I want to take a few verses on this word *testimony. Testimony* is a reference to the Words of God, the Scriptures. There in that ark, that box up in the Holy of Holies, were the very Words of the Living God. The ten commandments were a testimony, but by extension it is all the Words of God.

- **Exodus 16:33-34**
  "And Moses said unto Aaron, Take a pot, and put an omer full of manna therein, and lay it up before the LORD, to be kept for your generations. As the LORD commanded Moses, so Aaron laid it up before the Testimony, to be kept."

This manna was the food that sustained them for forty years, all through the desert wanderings. The testimony was in the ark of the covenant. It is where the Words of God were and that is where the manna was. I believe the testimony in Heaven has the manna and some remembrances of these things that were in the earth as well.

- **Exodus 25:17-22**
  "And thou shalt make a mercy seat *of* pure gold: two cubits and a half *shall be* the length thereof, and a cubit and a half the breadth thereof. And thou shalt make two cherubims *of* gold, *of* beaten work shalt thou make them, in the two ends of the mercy seat. And make one cherub on the one end, and the other cherub on the other end: *even* of the mercy seat shall ye make the cherubims on the two ends thereof. And the cherubims shall stretch forth *their* wings on high, covering the mercy seat with their wings, and their faces *shall look* one to another; toward the mercy seat shall the faces of the cherubims be. And thou shalt put the mercy seat above upon the ark; and in the ark thou shalt put the testimony that I shall give thee. And there I will meet with thee, and I will commune with thee from above the mercy seat, from between the two cherubims which *are* upon the ark of the testimony, of all *things* which I will give thee in commandment unto the children of Israel."

The mercy seat, I believe, is in Heaven. This was a replica of it. The dimensions are given. The mercy seat is a cover on top of the ark. The ark is a box. On either end are the cherubims looking forward and down. That mercy seat is where the blood was to be applied by the high priest. I believe the Lord Jesus Christ, our Great High Priest, applied His blood there after His resurrection and ascension.

The Words Of God In Heaven

Here in Revelation 15:5, John looks and beholds *the temple of the tabernacle of the testimony in heaven.* That is the Words of God that were right there in that ark. God still can meet with us in the Scriptures, the testimony. God's communication for His earthly people was above the ark where that testimony—the Words of God—were placed. That is an important point.

- **Exodus 30:6**
  "And thou shalt put it before the vail that *is* by the ark of the testimony, before the mercy seat that *is* over the testimony, where I will meet with thee."

God is mentioning that He wants to meet with the Israelites. Does He not want to meet with us as well if we are genuinely saved in this particular age? Yes, He does. He will meet with us through the Scriptures, through the Words of God. He will meet with us through the blood of the Lord Jesus Christ if we are genuinely saved and in testimony before Him.

- **Exodus 30:36**
  "And thou shalt beat *some* of it very small, and put of it before the testimony in the **tabernacle** of the congregation, where I will meet with thee: it shall be unto you most holy."

The frankincense was to ascend up before the **tabernacle** of the testimony and before the ark of the covenant.

- **Exodus 34:29**
  "And it came to pass, when Moses came down from mount Sinai with the two tables of testimony in Moses' hand, when he came down from the mount, that Moses wist not that the skin of his face shone while he talked with him."

These were the commandments that God Himself wrote with His own finger—the Words of the ten commandments. That was the testimony specifically, but by extension all the Words of God can be considered His testimony.

Why did Moses get a shining, glistening, glorious face? Because he had been with the Lord. In our faces, our glories, our joy from the inner heart out to the facial expression should be also ours as we get into the Scriptures—the testimony, the Words of God. Moses had communed with the Lord and he came down from the mountain a different person.

As we know, later on Aaron was dancing around a calf that he had made and Moses was angry. He broke the first set of commandments, smashing them to the ground. God told him to come up and He would make another set, which He did. This was the Lord Jesus Christ and God the Father communicating with Moses.

- **Numbers 1:53**
  "But the Levites shall pitch round about the **tabernacle** of testimony, that there be no wrath upon the congregation of the children of Israel: and the Levites shall keep the charge of the tabernacle of testimony."

The Testimony–The Words Of God

Notice, it is repeatedly called *the tabernacle of testimony* because of the Words of God that are there. It is not just a shambles of tents, of curtains, of boards, and of gold and silver, which it was made of. But it is a testimony that God points out as important—the Words of the Living God. The Levites were to guard that testimony. No one was to go near that tabernacle of testimony lest they would die.

- **Numbers 17:4**
  "And thou shalt lay them up in the **tabernacle** of the congregation before the testimony, where I will meet with you."
This was the twelve rods when they were wondering who was going to be the high priest. Was it going to be Aaron or someone else? Again, it is repeated that God meets with them in that **tabernacle** of testimony.
- **2 Kings 11:12**
  "And he brought forth the king's son, and put the crown upon him, and *gave him* the testimony; and they made him king, and anointed him; and they clapped their hands, and said, God save the king."
Joash was about to be killed and Jehosheba saved him you may remember. They gave him the Words of God. <u>The king had to write out in his own hand every year the book of the law of God</u>.
- **Isaiah 8:20**
  "To the law and to the testimony: if they speak not according to this word, *it is* because *there is* no light in them."

Revelation 15:6

"And the seven angels came out of the temple, having the seven plagues, clothed in pure and white linen, and having their breasts girded with golden girdles."

The Seven Vial Judgments

Here are the angels having the seven plagues. These are called the seven vial judgments. We had the seven seals, the seven trumpet judgments, and now the seven vials. This word for plague is PLEGE. It is *a public calamity; heavy affliction.* We are going to see the first five of these terrible, terrible plagues as we go into Revelation 16.

Notice these angels were clothed in pure and white linen. There was purity of the angels. They had to be pure. Before anybody can mete out just judgment, he or she must have himself or herself pure. There must be a holiness. We cannot mete out judgment if we are unholy ourselves. We must be holy and right before the Lord.

That word for girdle is an interesting word. It is ZONE. It is *a girdle; a belt.* It serves not only to gird up the flowing garments—the men and the women both had the flowing robes and girded them up so they could run—but also, since it was hollow, to carry money. They carried money in these girdles or belts.

There are a number of **plagues** in Scripture. I would just like to allude to some of them.

- **Genesis 12:17**
  "And the LORD plagued Pharaoh and his house with great **plagues** because of Sarai Abram's wife."

Abram lied and said, "She is my sister." That was half-true, but a half-truth is a whole lie. She was a half-sister. God **plagued** Pharaoh's house until they came clean, then no more **plagues.**

- **Exodus 9:14**
  "For I will at this time send all my **plagues** upon thine heart, and upon thy servants, and upon thy people; that thou mayest know that *there is* none like me in all the earth."

He is talking to Pharaoh about the **plagues for the children of Israel** in Egypt. **Plagues** show that God's power is there.

- **Exodus 32:35**
  "And the LORD plagued the people, because they made the calf, which Aaron made."

Here is the golden calf. God plagued them because they worshipped idols.

- **Leviticus 26:21**
  "And if ye walk contrary unto me, and will not hearken unto me; I will bring seven times more plagues upon you according to your sins."

God plagues His people because of sin.

- **Numbers 11:33**
  "And while the flesh *was* yet between their teeth, ere it was chewed, the wrath of the LORD was kindled against the people, and the LORD smote the people with a very great plague."

A Plague While People Were Eating

This is an eating plague. Their eating habits were wrong. They were gluttons. They pled for meat. They did not like the manna. They did not like just water. They wanted quails. God sent them quails. You might say, "Do eating habits mean anything to God?" Well, in this case they did. How they ate, how they grabbed that food—they were not thankful. The Lord saw their hearts and their hearts were wrong on that occasion.

- **Numbers 14:37**
  "Even those men that did bring up the evil report upon the land, died by the plague before the LORD."

There were twelve spies that went out to spy out the land, to see whether or not they should go into that land. You will remember the people of Israel came out of Egypt and they were to go into the promised land. From Egypt, and across the Red Sea, they were to go right into the land of Canaan, and into Jerusalem. God told them to send in twelve spies to check out the land. Ten said, "No, we cannot do it. The giants are too strong." Two said, "Yes, we can do it." What did God do to those ten that brought back the wrong report? It says right here that they *died by the plague*—those that gave the evil report and did not say that the Lord could do it.

- **Numbers 16:35**
  "And there came out a fire from the LORD, and consumed the two hundred and fifty men that offered incense."

That was in Korah's rebellion. Korah wanted to be a priest. He wanted to be the boss. God said, "Wait a minute. I have chosen Aaron to be my priest, not you people." Two hundred and fifty of them came and offered false incense.

- **Numbers 16:41**
  "But on the morrow all the congregation of the children of Israel murmured against Moses and against Aaron, saying, Ye have killed the people of the LORD."

God slew these two hundred and fifty, so the people were angry at the Lord. "Why did you do this? You have killed the people of the Lord!"

- **Numbers 16:42**
  "And it came to pass, when the congregation was gathered against Moses and against Aaron, that they looked toward the **tabernacle** of the congregation: and, behold, the cloud covered it, and the glory of the LORD appeared."

- **Numbers 16:44-45**
  "And the LORD spake unto Moses, saying, Get you up from among this congregation, that I may consume them as in a moment. And they fell upon their faces."

All they had done was to question the judgment of God. God judged the two hundred and fifty because they were out of place.

- **Numbers 16:46**
  "And Moses said unto Aaron, Take a censer, and put fire therein from off the altar, and put on incense, and go quickly unto the congregation, and make an atonement for them: for there is wrath gone out from the LORD; the **plague** is begun."

God **plagued** them because this group wanted to be like Aaron and be priests, exalting themselves in sin.

- **Numbers 16:47-48**
  "And Aaron took as Moses commanded, and ran into the midst of the congregation; and, behold, the **plague** was begun among the people: and he put on incense, and made an atonement for the people. And he stood between the dead and the living; and the **plague** was stayed."

Aaron interceded and atonement was made between the dead and the living. God stopped the **plague**, but do you know how many people died in that **plague**—just because one man or one group wanted to be the high priests and get to be the "big cheeses," exalting themselves?

- **Numbers 16:49**
  "Now they that died in the **plague** were fourteen thousand and seven hundred, beside them that died about the matter of Korah."

- **Numbers 25:5**
  "And Moses said unto the judges of Israel, Slay ye every one his
  men that were joined unto Baalpeor."

Here is the idol Baal, the idol that said to go ahead and have immorality
and sexual relations on the part of those that were high priests. It was a
terrible, terrible religion of viciousness, falseness, and immorality.

- **Numbers 25:8-9**
  "And he went after the man of Israel into the tent, and thrust
  both of them through, the man of Israel, and the woman
  through her belly. So the **plague** was stayed from the children
  of Israel. And those that died in the **plague** were twenty and
  four thousand."

Almost 15,000 died in the plague of Korah and 24,000 died of those
worshipping Baal. God does not fool around with false worship. He did
not in the Old Testament, and He does not in the New Testament.

- **Numbers 31:16**
  "Behold, these caused the children of Israel, through the counsel
  of Balaam, to commit trespass against the LORD in the matter
  of Peor, and there was a **plague** among the congregation of the
  LORD."

- **Luke 7:21**
  "And in that same hour he cured many of *their* infirmities and
  plagues, and of evil spirits; and unto many *that were* blind he
  gave sight."

The Lord Jesus Christ was able to cure the **plagues** of those who were
there, even in His day.

- **Revelation 9:20**
  "And the rest of the men which were not killed by these **plagues**
  yet repented not of the works of their hands, that they should
  not worship devils, and idols of gold, and silver, and brass, and
  stone, and of wood: which neither can see, nor hear, nor walk:"

When People Do Not Repent

It is terrible when men and women do not repent and do
not change their minds about their sin and what they have
done that is wrong.

- **Revelation 22:18**
  "For I testify unto every man that heareth the words of the
  prophecy of this book, If any man shall add unto these things,
  God shall add unto him the **plagues** that are written in this
  book:"

There are twenty-one **plagues**: seven **plagues** of the seals; seven **plagues** of the trumpets; and seven **plagues** of the vials.

That is what they are doing with these new versions of the Bible, not only in English, but in Portuguese, Spanish, French, German, Russian and all the languages of the world. They are adding to the Words of God. This is serious. God promises that **plagues** will take place. I would not want to be in their shoes when God begins to mete that out.

- **2 Peter 3:9**
  "The Lord is not slack concerning his promise, as some men count slackness; but is longsuffering to us-ward, not willing that any should perish, but that all should come to repentance."

God Is Not On Our Timetable

God is not on our timetable. He does not necessarily plague these people in our lifetime and in their lifetimes. If they are genuinely saved, at the judgment seat of the Lord Jesus Christ they will receive their lack of reward. If they are lost, before the great white throne, God will see to it that they are punished because of their adding and subtracting of the Words of the living God. It is a terrible sin indeed.

Revelation 15:7

"**And one of the four beasts gave unto the seven angels seven golden vials full of the wrath of God, who liveth for ever and ever.**"

Remember we believe that the four beasts are representing the four leading angels. The Greek word for vial is PHIALE. It is *a broad, shallow bowl; a deep saucer*. Some of the new versions say *bowls* and so on, but to me vial is accurate.

The Vials Of The Wrath Of God

What is a vial? It is a container and that is what these are. It is all right with me—a container.

These vials are absolutely full to the brim of the wrath of God, Who liveth forever and ever. It is interesting that these last seven judgments of the twenty-one are full of the wrath of God. It is important. I talked about the wrath of God, but let us

look at some of the verses that deal with the wrath of God.
These seven vial judgments are filled with God's wrath. Is God
a God of wrath? Yes. He is a God of judgment, a God of
righteousness, and He is a God of wrath.

- **Psalm 78:30-31**
  "They were not estranged from their lust. But while their meat
  was yet in their mouths, The **wrath of God** came upon them,
  and slew the fattest of them, and smote down the chosen *men* of
  Israel."

Here again is the eating situation where they did not like the manna.
They were not satisfied with the manna for forty years. "Give us flesh to
eat!" Because their heart attitude was wrong, the **wrath of God** came
upon them.

- **John 3:36**
  "He that believeth on the Son hath everlasting life: and he that
  believeth not the Son shall not see life; but the **wrath of God**
  abideth on him."

This is a wonderful gospel verse. According to this verse, for those who
refuse to accept the Lord Jesus Christ as their Saviour, the **wrath of
God** is sitting right on them. Until they genuinely trust Him, they still
have that **wrath**. It is a terrible, terrible judgment on those that are
rejecting Him.

- **Romans 1:18**
  "For the **wrath of God** is revealed from heaven against all
  ungodliness and unrighteousness of men, who hold the truth in
  unrighteousness;"

He is **wrathful** against all ungodliness and unrighteousness of men.

- **Colossians 3:5-6**
  "Mortify therefore your members which are upon the earth;
  fornication, uncleanness, inordinate affection, evil
  concupiscence, and covetousness, which is idolatry: For which
  things' sake the **wrath of God** cometh on the children of
  disobedience:"

As genuine Christians, we are to put off all these filthy things mentioned
in this verse. **God's wrath** is heavy upon them.

- **Revelation 14:10**
  "The same shall drink of the wine of the **wrath of God**, which
  is poured out without mixture into the cup of his indignation;
  and he shall be tormented with fire and brimstone in the
  presence of the holy angels, and in the presence of the Lamb:"

Two Main Powers–God & Satan

This is those who worship the beast. There are only two powers, basically, in this earth: the power of God and the power of the Devil, or Satan. When people are worshipping Satan, God's power is there to judge them, and the wrath of God is poured out upon those that worship this religious antichrist. They will be sent to a fiery, eternal Hell.

- **Revelation 14:19**
  "And the angel thrust in his sickle into the earth, and gathered the vine of the earth, and cast *it* into the great winepress of the **wrath of God.**"

God's winepress grinds exceedingly fine.

- **Revelation 16:1**
  "And I heard a great voice out of the temple saying to the seven angels, Go your ways, and pour out the vials of the **wrath of God** upon the earth.**"

These special vials, these seven vial judgments, are the special **wrath of God** in judgment. He is angry with the wicked all day long. During that seven-year tribulation (when the Christians who are genuinely saved are caught up to be with the Lord Jesus Christ), this old world will receive judgments from God.

Notice also in Revelation 15:7, that God *liveth for ever and ever*. We have an eternal God living **for ever and ever.** Let us take a look at a few verses on God's **eternality**.

- **Exodus 15:18**
  "The LORD shall reign **for ever and ever.**"

There is no end to His reign. His reign does not cease after only four years, like that of our presidents. His reign is *"for ever and ever."*

- **Psalm 10:16**
  "The LORD *is* King **for ever and ever**: the heathen are perished out of his land.**"

- **Psalm 45:6**
  "Thy throne, O God, *is* **for ever and ever**: the sceptre of thy kingdom *is* a right sceptre.**"

- **Psalm 48:14**
  "For this God *is* our God **for ever and ever**: he will be our guide *even* unto death.**"

Is God Your "Guide Unto Death"?

Is He your guide unto death? We do not know when that will happen—not a single one of us—whatever our age is. We could meet an accident—even at a young age. Is He your guide unto death? He is forever. He was the guide of Paul who lived almost 2,000 years ago. He was the guide of John until his death, and of James, and of Peter. He can be your guide and my guide unto our deaths. He is living for ever and ever.

Are you going to change gods? God does not want us to change. There is no other god but Him. He is the only God that is true and right.

- **Psalm 90:2**
  "Before the mountains were brought forth, or ever thou hadst formed the earth and the world, even **from everlasting to everlasting**, thou *art* God."

From Everlasting To Everlasting

He was there from the beginning. He is going to be there for the ending. Nobody is going to take His place. All the idols will be smashed. All the false worship and false religions will be smashed. He alone will be King from everlasting to everlasting.

- **Psalm 93:2**
  "Thy throne *is* established of old: thou *art* **from everlasting**."
There is no beginning to the Lord. You might say, "Well, did He have a beginning? Who made Him?" Nobody made Him. He is from **everlasting**. That is hard for us to understand with our small brains, but that is what God's Words teach us. He is from **everlasting**.

- **Micah 5:2**
  "But thou, Bethlehem Ephratah, *though* thou be little among the thousands of Judah, *yet* out of thee shall he come forth unto me *that is* to be ruler in Israel; whose goings forth *have been* from of old, **from everlasting**."

The First Coming Of Christ

This is speaking of the coming of the Lord Jesus Christ at His birth. That is why the wise men came from the east. They saw His star. They knew this verse. I am especially angered at the New International Version for the translation of this verse and maybe in the Portuguese false translation, as well. The NIV makes two great serious doctrinal errors in this verse. The first one is, instead of *whose goings forth* they say, "*whose origins.*" They have the Lord Jesus Christ having an "origin" as if He was not from everlasting to everlasting. That is in the New International Version. It is terrible heresy. Then they change *from everlasting* to "from ancient times." No, my friend, it is not simply "from ancient times." It is *from everlasting.* There is a difference. It is not just a few hundred thousand years, but *from everlasting.*

I was shocked out of my boots when the NIV was read at a supposedly "fundamental" Baptist church at a Christmas pageant on one occasion. I went up to the pastor afterwards and said, "Pastor, this is horrendous! Why did you read the NIV? There are two errors in this verse for Christmas. Why wasn't the King James Bible used?" His answer was, "Well, I didn't know." I was irate because the Lord Jesus Christ does not have an origin. He is *from everlasting*, not simply from "ancient times."

- **Hebrews 1:8**
  "But unto the Son *he saith*, Thy throne, O God, *is* **for ever and ever**: a sceptre of righteousness *is* the sceptre of thy kingdom."

The Lord Jesus Christ is God **for ever and ever**, just like God the Father, and just like God the Holy Spirit.

- **Hebrews 13:8**
  "Jesus Christ the same yesterday, and to day, and **for ever**."

We Have An Unchangeable Saviour

This is a precious verse. We have an everlasting Saviour. He does not change. He does not change with the times. He does not change with the versions. He does not change with the presidents, or the governors, or the emperors. He is the same.

Some people do not like sameness. They say, "Let me go to a different restaurant or a different place. Let me get a different tie." All right, fine. We do not like sameness. We want a different car, a different color, a different rug, a different piano player. (We like the one we have!) What is wrong with the same? If the same is all right, let us keep it. The Lord Jesus is the same. Let us keep Him. He is nothing to be thrown out. These modernists trim Him, and cut Him, and change Him, and make Him just a man. They make Him not God's Son sent from Heaven and not virgin born—just a man. It is a terrible thing. He is the same. He is our God. He is our Saviour if we are genuinely trusting Him.

- **Revelation 4:9**
  "And when those beasts give glory and honour and thanks to him that sat on the throne, who liveth **for ever and ever,**"

His eternality is *for ever and ever*.

- **Revelation 4:10**
  "The four and twenty elders fall down before him that sat on the throne, and worship him that liveth **for ever and ever**, and cast their crowns before the throne, saying,"

- **Revelation 5:14**
  "And the four beasts said, Amen. And the four *and* twenty elders fell down and worshipped him that liveth **for ever and ever**."

In the book of Revelation, constantly the Lord Jesus Christ is called the One who lives **for ever and ever**. We have to get that into our heads that our Lord Jesus Christ is going to be there when our sons and daughters grow up, when our grandsons and granddaughters grow up, when our great grandsons and great granddaughters grow up and all others on down the line. He is still going to be there. He is not going to change. He was there for all the progeny in the past, from Adam right on down to the present. He is **everlasting**.

Revelation 15:8

"And the temple was filled with smoke from the glory of God, and from his power; and no man was able to enter into the temple, till the seven plagues of the seven angels were fulfilled."

That word **fulfilled** is TELEO. It means *to perform or execute or complete something, so that the thing done corresponds to what has been said.* God is going to **fulfill** these **plagues** to the letter. That is what this word **fulfilled** means: *the order or command with special reference to the subject matter; to carry out the contents of a command generally involving the notion of time performed to the last; to do just as it is commanded.* All of these things are going to be just as the Lord commanded.

I would like to speak to these two things: **the glory of God**, and the **power of God**. The whole temple was **filled** with smoke from the **glory of God** and from **His power**. Nobody could enter until these **plagues** were finished.

The *glory of God* is only used seventeen times in Scripture.

- **Psalm 19:1**
  "The heavens declare the **glory of God**; and the firmament sheweth his handywork."

The Meaning Of "Glory"

Glory means *beauty*. It means *majesty*. It means *effulgence*. It means *that which is captivating*—glorious!

- **John 11:4**
  "When Jesus heard *that*, he said, This sickness is not unto death, but for the **glory of God**, that the Son of God might be glorified thereby."

They said, "Why did you not stop it so that he would not die?" The reason was for the **glory of God**. The Lord Jesus Christ was going to raise him from the dead so as to bring **glory**. The reason was for the **glory of God**, that the Son of God may be **glorified** thereby.

- **John 17:24**
  "Father, I will that they also, whom thou hast given me, be with me where I am; that they may behold my **glory**, which thou hast given me: for thou lovedst me before the foundation of the world."

Christ's High Priestly Prayer

This is the Lord Jesus Christ's high priestly prayer. He is a glorious Saviour! We cannot behold His glory in these bodies. It would kill us. Just like Moses had to be hidden in the cleft of the rock. He could not see the complete glory of God.

There was a glimpse of the Lord Jesus Christ's **glory** on the mount of transfiguration when Peter, James, and John went up there. His garments were white as no fuller on earth could white them. Dazzling!

- **Mark 9:3**
  "And his raiment became shining, exceeding white as snow; so as no fuller on earth can white them."

- **Acts 7:55**
  "But he, being full of the Holy Ghost, looked up stedfastly into heaven, and saw the **glory of God**, and Jesus standing on the right hand of God,"

This is Stephen before he was stoned. He was about to die and he saw the **glory of God**. The Lord Jesus Christ was waiting for that martyr—the first martyr in the New Testament—to receive him unto Himself.

- **Acts 26:13**
  "At midday, O king, I saw in the way a light from heaven, above the brightness of the sun, shining round about me and them which journeyed with me."

Paul is giving his testimony. This is the third time he has given his testimony. It happened in Acts 9. He gave his testimony in Acts 22 and again in Acts 26. He is talking to King Agrippa, Bernice, and Festus. The light brighter than the sun was the **glory** of the Lord Jesus Christ. Stephen saw Him before he died. Before he was genuinely saved, Paul saw the Lord Jesus Christ and His **glory** blinded him. He was blind for three days because of the dazzling light of **the glory of God.**

- **Romans 3:23**
  "For all have sinned, and come short of the **glory of God;**"

None of us can measure up to the **glory of God,** so we need a Saviour—the Lord Jesus Christ.

- **1 Corinthians 10:31**
  "Whether therefore ye eat, or drink, or whatsoever ye do, do all to the **glory of God.**"

This is so that God's glory will be seen in all that we do, in what we say, where we go, how we talk, and how we act.

- **Revelation 21:23**
  "And the city had no need of the sun, neither of the moon, to shine in it: for the **glory of God** did lighten it, and the Lamb *is* the light thereof."

If we did not have the sun or the moon it would be dark all the time, would it not? No sunlight—nothing. In Heaven they do not need the sun or the moon. We need the **glory of God.**

Notice also, it says that *the temple was filled with smoke from the glory of God, and from his power.* God's **power** is also spoken of in Scripture. God is Omnipotent. He has no end of **power.**

- **Exodus 9:16**
  "And in very deed for this *cause* have I raised thee up, for to shew *in* thee my **power;** and that my name may be declared throughout all the earth."

The miracles and plagues of Egypt showed **God's power.**

- **Exodus 32:11**
  "And Moses besought the LORD his God, and said, LORD, why doth thy wrath wax hot against thy people, which thou hast brought forth out of the land of Egypt with great **power,** and with a mighty hand?"

He brought them out <u>with great</u> **power**. If you do not believe that is great power, just think about it. Six hundred thousand men plus women and children—two, three, or four million people—God brought out of Egypt with Pharaoh chasing them. He kept them in the wilderness for forty years. Pharaoh wanted to kill them and slaughter them. God opened up the Red Sea and made them go through on dry land, then closed the sea, and caused the soldiers with the chariots to drown. He has great power. That is the measure of His **power**.

- **1 Chronicles 29:11**
  "Thine, O LORD, *is* the greatness, and the **power**, and the glory, and the victory, and the majesty: for all *that is* in the heaven and in the earth *is thine*; thine *is* the kingdom, O LORD, and thou art exalted as head above all."

<u>God is a God of **power**</u>. He is not just a little tiny god or just a little baby that does not know how to do things. He created man—and not only man, but all the animals in the world, all the fish in the sea, all the birds of the air—and do not stop there. He also created the whole earth, all the universe. This includes the billions of stars in our galaxy and also the billions of galaxies as well. If that is not **power**, I do not know what is. For people to raise their fists against <u>the God of **power**</u> is beyond me. Instead, we should be submitting to His **power** and asking, "Lord, what wilt Thou have me to do?" That is what is necessary.

- **Psalm 66:3**
  "Say unto God, How terrible *art thou in* thy works! through the greatness of thy **power** shall thine enemies submit themselves unto thee."

- **Psalm 106:8-11**
  "Nevertheless he saved them for his name's sake, that he might make <u>his mighty **power**</u> to be known. He rebuked the Red sea also, and it was dried up: so he led them through the depths, as through the wilderness. And he saved them from the hand of him that hated *them*, and redeemed them from the hand of the enemy. And the waters covered their enemies: there was not one of them left."

This is talking about the Israelites. He saved them by <u>His **power**</u>.

- **Psalm 147:5**
  "Great *is* our Lord, and of <u>great **power**</u>: his understanding *is* infinite."

- **Matthew 22:29**
  "Jesus answered and said unto them, Ye do err, not knowing the scriptures, nor <u>the **power of God**</u>."

This speaks about the doubts of the Sadducees. They did not believe that God could raise up the dead in the Old Testament. God has great **power**.

- **Matthew 28:18**
  "And Jesus came and spake unto them, saying, All **power** is given unto me in heaven and in earth."

Christ's Bodily Resurrection

The Lord Jesus Christ, after He suffered for the sins of the world—your sins and mine, taking them on His own body—was raised bodily from the grave. This was before He ascended up bodily into Heaven to sit at the right hand of the Father. Now the Father has given to the Son the power, the authority, and the dignity in Heaven and in earth. If God the Father gave to His Son all power, all authority over Heaven and earth, who are we to not obey Him? Who are we not to say, "Aye, aye, Sir. Yes, Lord, what wilt Thou have me to do?"

- **Romans 1:20**
  "For the invisible things of him from the creation of the world are clearly seen, being understood by the things that are made, *even* his eternal **power** and Godhead; so that they are without excuse."

This talks about creation. These heathen that worship idols that they have made are going to be judged by the Lord Jesus Christ, because He made all of them. They are without excuse because His eternal **power** and His Godhead are manifest in the things that are made in creation.

- **1 Corinthians 1:18**
  "For the preaching of the cross is to them that perish foolishness; but unto us which are saved it is the **power of God**."

It is foolishness to them that perish. Who wants to preach about a dead Saviour—the preaching of the cross? The **power of God** is to redeem and to genuinely save and to switch us from going south, now north, or from east, now to go west. That is conversion. That is the **power of God**. We do not fool around with sin anymore. We do not love it. We used to love it, but if we are genuinely saved and born-again, we hate it. We despise it. We run from it. We ask God to deliver us from it—to deliver us from evil.

- **1 Corinthians 1:24**
  "But unto them which are called, both Jews and Greeks, Christ the **power of God**, and the wisdom of God."

Here he is talking about those who are genuinely saved. <u>The Lord Jesus Christ is the **power of God** and the wisdom of God</u>—not just simply foolishness, but the **power** of Almighty God.

- **2 Corinthians 4:7**
  "But we have this treasure in earthen vessels, that the excellency of <u>the **power**</u> may be of God, and not of us."

Paul looks at his body with maladies. Maybe his eyesight is gone.

- **2 Corinthians 12:7-9**
  "And lest I should be exalted above measure through the abundance of the revelations, there was given to me a thorn in the flesh, the messenger of Satan to buffet me, lest I should be exalted above measure. For this thing I besought the Lord thrice, that it might depart from me. And he said unto me, <u>My grace is sufficient for thee: for my strength is made perfect in weakness.</u> Most gladly therefore will I rather glory in my infirmities, that the **power** of Christ may rest upon me."

Vessels Of Earth

We do not know what the thorn was, so you can plug in your thorn, whatever it is—whatever malady you or I have, the *thorn* in the flesh, whatever the thing that God has given to us. He looked at his body with all this and said that we have this treasure in earthen vessels. The Lord Jesus Christ is our treasure. Earthen vessels can break. They are not pots and pans of aluminum, but *"ostraka"*–things that would smash when you drop them on the floor. We have this treasure in earthen vessels, these bodies. Why? That the excellency of the power may be of God, and not of us.

If we were dazzling, and sparkling, and great, and wonderful, and mighty, and deathless, and so on, we would have the excellency and the **glory**. God says, "No! I am just going to give you an earthly body that is built with clay, and with defects, and blemishes, because I want the **power** and the **glory** to go to Me." This treasure is in this earthen vessel. May we see, and may others see that **glory** through us and through our vessels.

- **Hebrews 1:3**
  "Who being the brightness of *his* **glory**, and the express image of his person, and upholding all things <u>by the word of his **power**</u>, when he had by himself purged our sins, sat down on the right hand of the Majesty on high;"

This talks about the Lord Jesus Christ. The Lord Jesus Christ upholds all things in the universe—the stars, the planets, the moon, the galaxies. All things are upheld by His glorious **power**.

- **1 Peter 1:5**
  "Who are <u>kept by the **power of God**</u> through faith unto salvation ready to be revealed in the last time."

This talks about those of us who are genuinely saved. We are kept by the **power of God**. There is not a one of us who is genuinely saved and born-again that is going to be lost.

Our God Of Power And Glory

God is a <u>great God of power</u>. He is a great God of glory. We ought to praise and serve Him in our years that are before us.

Revelation
Chapter Sixteen

Revelation 16:1

"And I heard a great voice out of the temple saying to the seven angels, Go your ways, and pour out the vials of the wrath of God upon the earth."

The Voice Of The Lord Jesus Christ

The voice out of Heaven is the Lord Jesus Christ's voice out of the temple. He speaks to these seven angels because there are seven vials, which are containers, or bowls, or cups. Every one of these angels has a vial or a bowl of judgment. God is angry at the sinners upon this earth that have rejected His Saviour and Son and have done vile things in every way possible and imaginable.

God is the source of the unleashing of these vials. It does not come from Satan. It does not come by accident. It does not come from men. It comes from God Himself. He is the righteous One that is going to judge this earth during the seven years of tribulation.

Revelation 16:2

"And the first went, and poured out his vial upon the earth; and there fell a noisome and grievous sore upon the men which had the mark of the beast, and upon them which worshipped his image."

Here is the first vial judgment. That word *noisome* is an interesting word. We do not use it too often. It means *injurious to health or harmful*. Sometimes it means *having a bad odor; foul-smelling*. It is a terrible, terrible judgment. As you know, sometimes **sores** are very, very bad smelling. Putrefaction takes place. It is almost like the smell of death. This is going to be put upon the men and the women that are here on this earth.

Notice the ones that are going to have this **sore** are those that had the **mark of the beast**—those that took this **mark** of 666, whatever it is, on their foreheads and their right hands.

Constant Worship Of The Beast

That word worship, by the way, is in the present tense, continuous action. They are continuously worshipping this beast. This beast is the false prophet. He is the one who is from Satan. He is the wrong one to worship. We are supposed to worship the Lord. They worship this beast so this is poured out upon them.

Certainly Job had many **sores**, from the top of his head down to his feet. They were terrible **sores**. He had to scrape his flesh because of the sores and boils.

- **Job 5:18**
  "For he maketh **sore**, and bindeth up: he woundeth, and his hands make whole."

We May Get Sores From God

We may have sores that God brings to us. He is also the One that binds them up and helps us to get back into shape and back into health.

- **Psalm 38:11**
  "My lovers and my friends stand aloof from my **sore**; and my kinsmen stand afar off."

Apparently, David had some sort of **sore**. It was a terrible grievous **sore**, so the people just stayed away. You do not like to see **sores**, do you? We went to the hospital to visit someone. He had his leg all open. It was a terrible thing. He had to have an amputation of a small toe.

- **Psalm 77:2**
  "In the day of my trouble I sought the Lord: my **sore** ran in the night, and ceased not: my soul refused to be comforted."

Sometimes our **sores** and our pains run and they do not cease.

- **Isaiah 1:6**
  "From the sole of the foot even unto the head *there is* no soundness in it; *but* wounds, and bruises, and putrifying **sores**: they have not been closed, neither bound up, neither mollified with ointment."

Putrifying **sores** are **sores** that smell, that are dead. That is the condition of every man, woman, and child on this earth—just like putrefying sores and bruises. God looked at Israel in that same way.

- **Luke 16:20-21**
  "And there was a certain beggar named Lazarus, which was laid at his gate, full of **sores**, And desiring to be fed with the crumbs which fell from the rich man's table: moreover the dogs came and licked his **sores**."

This is the man that God took to Heaven because he had genuinely trusted Him. You know, dogs can lick and clean things up. They licked Lazarus' **sores**. They clean up their puppies. Cats clean their kittens and make them clean.

A Noisome And Grievous Sore

This terrible first vial was a noisome and grievous sore upon the men which had taken the mark of the beast and worshipped his image. It is a terrible thing to be pagan in their worship.

Revelation 16:3

"And the second angel poured out his vial upon the sea; and it became as the blood of a dead *man*: and every living soul died in the sea."

Every living soul in the sea died—a terrible catastrophe. I looked up on the Internet and found that there are at least 2,000 creatures under the **sea**. We do not name all of them, but there are many animals in the sea. There is coral and coral reefs. Coral is a live sort of an animal even though it is a hard substance. There are some dangerous sea animals such as sharks. There are crabs, echinoderms, fishes of all kinds, whales, jellyfish, lobsters, mollusks, octopus, sea anemones, sea lions, walrus, sea turtles, sponges, manatee, penguins, seahorses. Every one of these creatures dies because the **sea** is turned into **blood**. When the water turns to **blood** the creation cannot function. I am not a knowledgeable person on fish. We do not have an aquarium in our house, but I suppose if you put pure **blood** in the **fish** tank every one of them would die. **Fish** have to have oxygen and conditions that are balanced.

God's Judgment On The Fish

God poured out His judgment upon the fish of the sea and the waters turned into blood. That is literal blood. It is not simply death. You will remember John MacArthur says that blood in the Bible does not mean blood. He says that it is just a figure of speech or a metonym for death. This is blood. It is real blood.

- **Exodus 4:9**
  "And it shall come to pass, if they will not believe also these two signs, neither hearken unto thy voice, that thou shalt take of the water of the river, and pour *it* upon the dry *land*: and the water which thou takest out of the river shall become **blood** upon the dry *land*."

God used this before when Moses was there. There were ten plagues in Egypt and one of them was the waters turned into **blood**.

- **Exodus 7:17**
  "Thus saith the LORD, In this thou shalt know that I *am* the LORD: behold, I will smite with the rod that *is* in mine hand upon the waters which *are* in the river, and they shall be turned to **blood**."

That was the promise and God did this.

- **Exodus 7:19**
  "And the LORD spake unto Moses, Say unto Aaron, Take thy rod, and stretch out thine hand upon the waters of Egypt, upon their streams, upon their rivers, and upon their ponds, and upon all their pools of water, that they may become **blood**; and *that* there may be **blood** throughout all the land of Egypt, both in *vessels* of wood, and in *vessels* of stone."

No matter where the vessels were, they would become as **blood**.

- **Exodus 7:21**
  "And the fish that *was* in the river died; and the river stank, and the Egyptians could not drink of the water of the river; and there was **blood** throughout all the land of Egypt."

Blood is a terrible-smelling substance, as we know. This is the judgment that God pours out during the seven-year period of tribulation upon this earth where all the waters and fountains of water become **blood**.

Revelation 16:4

"And the third angel poured out his vial upon the rivers and fountains of waters; and they became blood."

Here is the third vial. The second vial was poured out by the second angel and the sea became blood.

All Water Becomes Blood

Now, God goes into the inlets and into the land where the rivers and the fountains of water are. They became blood also. It continues—the blood in all waters—just like in the days of Moses in the land of Egypt. There was no drinking water. You can imagine what happens. If they do not drink any water they are going to die. This is a terrible plague upon all the waters during the seven years of tribulation upon this earth. It is a judgment from the Lord Jesus Christ.

You may say, "Is that fair? Is God doing what is right and righteous to put all these things upon men and women during these seven years of tribulation, after the genuine believers (or saints) are gone into Heaven?"

Revelation 16:5

"And I heard the angel of the waters say, Thou art righteous, O Lord, which art, and wast, and shalt be, because thou hast judged thus."

Here is the **angel of the waters** that became **blood**. He says of the Lord, *"Thou art righteous."* The Lord Jesus Christ is present, past, and future. We talked about the eternality of the Godhead. He is forever.

Righteousness Defined

That word righteous, DIKAIOS, is used of the Lord Jesus Christ. It is used of people that are righteous. It is used of the one whose thinking, and feeling, and acting is wholly conformed to the will of God who therefore needs no rectification or straightening out of the heart or life. The Lord Jesus Christ is absolutely fair and righteous.

- **Psalm 7:9**
  "Oh let the wickedness of the wicked come to an end; but establish the just: for the **righteous** God trieth the hearts and reins."

The **righteous** God tries or tests out our reins—our inside heart.

- **Psalm 11:7**
  "For the **righteous** LORD loveth righteousness; his countenance doth behold the upright."

His whole nature is **righteous**. He wants us to be **righteous** if we are genuinely saved by grace through real faith in the Lord Jesus Christ, and we have been truly born-again. We have that old nature that is wicked, but we have a new nature that is **righteous**. Genuine Christians ought to walk by the new nature and by the power of the Holy Spirit.

- **John 17:25**
  "O **righteous** Father, the world hath not known thee: but I have known thee, and these have known that thou hast sent me."

This was the high priestly prayer of the Lord Jesus Christ. God the Father is a **righteous** Father. Notice, the **righteous** Father sent His Son, the Lord Jesus Christ, to the cross of Calvary because the Father knew the penalty had to be paid for the sins of the world. Therefore, the **righteous** Father caused His Son to pay that penalty in His death on Calvary.

- **Romans 2:5**
  "But after thy hardness and impenitent heart treasurest up unto thyself wrath against the day of wrath and revelation of the **righteous** judgment of God;"

God's Judgments Are Righteous

When God judges and puts His wrath upon this whole world, it will be a righteous judgment. There is no question about it. The people that are being judged will not think it is righteous any more than our children when they have done something amiss and we discipline them. They do not think that is righteous either. A lot of them just whine and carry on and cry, but if they need it, they need it. God is a righteous God with righteous judgment.

- **2 Thessalonians 1:5**
  "*Which is* a manifest token of the **righteous** judgment of God, that ye may be counted worthy of the kingdom of God, for which ye also suffer:"

<u>Nothing that God does is unrighteous.</u> In fact, God told Abraham what he was going to do before the judgment of Sodom and Gomorrah.

- **Genesis 18:25**
  "That be far from thee to do after this manner, to slay the **righteous** with the wicked: and that the **righteous** should be as the wicked, that be far from thee: Shall not the Judge of all the earth do right?"

He is **right** and He is **righteous** in His judgment.

- **1 John 1:9**
  "If we confess our sins, he is faithful and just to forgive us *our* sins, and to cleanse us from all unrighteousness."

Our sins were put upon the Lord Jesus Christ and He is the One that paid the penalty, so He is just in forgiving our sins.

- **1 John 2:1**
  "My little children, these things write I unto you, that ye sin not. And if any man sin, we have an advocate with the Father, Jesus Christ the **righteous:**"

Our Advocate is a Lawyer. He is the One Who intercedes for us. His title is Jesus Christ the **righteous**. He is **righteous** in all that He is and all that He does.

- **1 John 2:29**
  "If ye know that he is **righteous**, ye know that every one that doeth **righteousness** is born of him."

God Pours Out Righteous Judgments

Our God who is pouring out these righteous judgments upon the earth is righteous in everything that He does and every judgment that He makes. He is righteous in these seven vials of judgment, and in the seven seals, and in the seven trumpet judgments on this earth in the book of Revelation.

Revelation 16:6

"For they have shed the blood of saints and prophets, and thou hast given them blood to drink; for they are worthy."

The Lord is **righteous** in judging the earth and making them drink that blood. The, water being blood, they would have to drink it. He made them to **drink** the **blood**. These mentioned in this verse had shed the **blood** of martyrs. The antichrist will kill off many thousands, and probably millions of genuine Christian believers in that seven-year period of tribulation. God judges them and makes them **drink** of that **blood**.

There is a war with the **saints** and the **prophets**.

- **Revelation 13:7**
  "And it was given unto him to make war with the **saints**, and to overcome them: and power was given him over all kindreds, and tongues, and nations."

The battle of the antichrist was against the **saints**, the genuine believers, those that are truly saved upon this earth.

Many Saved During The Tribulation

Remember there are 144,000 Jewish evangelists that will preach the gospel and many will be genuinely saved during that seven-year period of tribulation. As soon as they are genuinely saved, the antichrist will kill them. They will be given a choice: the mark of the beast, or else be slaughtered. The genuine Christians will say, "I am not going to have the mark." They will be killed and go to Heaven. There will be a terrible, terrible judgment.

- **Revelation 17:6**
  "And I saw the woman drunken with the blood of the **saints**, and with the blood of the martyrs of Jesus: and when I saw her, I wondered with great admiration."

This woman is Babylon the great, which I believe is Rome, Roman Catholicism, and Protestantism that is combined with them in the end-time religious apostasy of all the world religions. There is going to be a persecution by the false religions against everyone that is genuinely saved during this period of tribulation.

- **Revelation 18:24**
  "And in her was found the blood of **prophets**, and of **saints**, and of all that were slain upon the earth."

Babylon The Great's Final Apostasy

This again is Babylon the great, which is the final apostasy of religion. There will be terrible persecution by the so-called religions. Just because they are religious, does that mean they do not persecute and slay? If you do not believe it, just look at the countries now where the Muslims have been slaying the "Christians."

We had an e-mail from Iraq where our friend, Dr. DiVietro, went to set up a church there. He said everything was fine. They put the cross up. Then they got a message: "Take that cross down!" Now they are persecuted because the Muslims in Iraq are killing and destroying "Christian" churches. There is great persecution by this false Muslim religion. They hate the Jews. They hate the "Christians." This is the fundamental teaching of Mohammad.

Revelation 16:7

"And I heard another out of the altar say, Even so, Lord God Almighty, true and righteous *are* thy judgments."

Here again there is a confirmation of the <u>righteousness</u> of these judgments.

- **Psalm 19:9**
  "The fear of the LORD *is* clean, enduring for ever: the **judgments** of the LORD *are* true *and* **righteous** altogether."

God's **judgments** are **righteous**. They are **true**.

- **Revelation 19:2**
  "For **true** and **righteous** *are* his **judgments**: for he hath judged the great whore, which did corrupt the earth with her fornication, and hath avenged the blood of his servants at her hand."

The great whore is the religious system. There is no unrighteousness with the Lord Jesus Christ in any way at all in His **judgments**. There is **truth** that is involved.

Revelation 16:8

"And the fourth angel poured out his vial upon the sun; and power was given unto him to scorch men with fire."

Here is the fourth **vial** judgment on the **sun**.

Facts About Our Sun

I want to take a little bit of time on the sun. You might say, "Well, how can the sun scorch men and burn them with fire?" It is horrendous. According to Internet information, the sun is a normal main sequence G2 star. (Some of this is true and some of it may not be true because these are not genuine Christians that write these things. Most of it, I suppose, is all right.) It is one of more than 100 billion stars just in our galaxy. There are billions of galaxies. On the surface, the temperature of the sun is 5800 K. In the center it is 15.5

> million K. The sun is by far the largest object in our solar system. It contains more than 98.8% of the total mass of our solar system. Jupiter contains the rest of most of it. Just think, 98% is the sun. We have other things in this solar system, but the sun is huge.

The sun is personified in many mythologies. The Greeks called the sun Helios. The Romans called it Sol. They have all kinds of stories about it.

At present, the **sun** is about 70% hydrogen and 28% helium. Everything else is metals, less than 2%. There is a differential rotation. The center of the **sun** rotates so many days and the outside rotates differently. It is hard for us to understand that. The surface rotates every 25 days and the core takes 36 days to get around altogether.

The **sun** is not a solid body like the earth. (I did not know that.) It is filled with gas. <u>The earth is solid, but not the sun</u>. It is a gas like the gas planets. The core of the **sun** rotates as a solid body, but it is not a solid body. It is interesting. The condition on about 25% of the radius of the **sun's** core is extreme temperatures. It is 15.6 million Kelvin degrees with the pressure of 250 billion atmospheres.

The **sun's** energy output is tremendous. <u>This **sun** is the thing that is going to scorch the people on this earth during the seven-year period of tribulation</u>. In fact, solar energy is so great that it produces nuclear fusion reaction in the **sun**. We talk about nuclear fusion and fission of atomic bombs. Each second, about 700 million tons of hydrogen are converted to about 695 million tons of helium and over five million tons of energy.

More About The Sun's Structure

The surface of the sun is called the photosphere and that is 5800 K. The small region on top of that is the chromosphere. Then there is the corona above the chromosphere. That is about one million K, as far as the heat is concerned. The sun's magnetic field is very strong by terrestrial standards. There is also what is known as solar wind that blows on the sun. That makes interferences and causes the Aurora Borealis, the Northern Lights as we call them, because of this wind. A spacecraft went up to measure that wind. Solar wind has effects on the tails of comets. It blows them around.

What is the **sun's** output? It is constant. It has the same amount of heat always. It was the same in the 17th century as today. They say that the sun is 4.5 billion years old. I disagree with this point about the sun. I do not believe a word of it. The creation of the world is about 4,000 B.C. It is at the most 6,000 or so years old. Of course, they do not believe in creation and they think the sun is 4.5 billion years old.

Scientists Deny Bible Truth

No, during the very first part of the Lord's creation there was the sun. One particular person also says that half the hydrogen at the sun's core has been used up. The sun he says, will "radiate peacefully" for another 5 billion years. They do not know anything about the Bible. They do not know anything about the judgment of God. One day, whenever the true Church, the real believers, the genuinely saved people are raptured and taken Home to Heaven, seven years of tribulation will come. Then, when this fourth vial plague or judgment comes along, that sun is no longer peaceful. That sun is going to scorch men and women and boys and girls on this earth. It will be a terrible calamity and judgment. It is not going to "radiate peacefully" for another 5 billion years. I would like to see what they say about that.

The Sun And Other Planets

Then of course, we have the sun's satellites or the ones that rotate around it, the planets, and so on. The smaller ones are not called planets so there is a big discussion about how many planets there are. One person believes there are nine planets rotating around the sun. When this sun scorches people, I do not know what is going to happen to these planets. Whether they will change rotation or whatever, I do not get into that. There is Mercury, Venus, the Earth, Mars, Jupiter, Saturn, Uranus, Neptune, and Pluto. Those are the different planets that revolve around the sun.

Geocentricity Vs. Heliocentricity

Of course, some people do not believe the planets revolve around the sun. They believe the earth is the center of the universe. That is called geocentricity versus heliocentricity. I believe there is something to be said about that particular view. These people work on another basis and from another frame of reference. It is my opinion that the Bible argues for geocentricity in all of its references that bear on this theme. I side with the Bible on this.

There was a second article on the **sun** I found on the Internet. It tells about the same story but with a little bit added here and there. This one says that the **sun** is the most prominent feature in our solar system. Can you imagine what would happen if there was no **sun** of any kind?

The Sun–The Largest Heavenly Body

It is bad enough when the poles have so little light from the sun that there are long, long nights. We have a sun that comes up and goes down on a regular basis. We are glad for that. The sun is the most prominent feature in our solar system. As the largest object, it contains approximately 98% of the total solar system mass. As we said before, it is not solid as the earth is but it is filled with gas.

The Exact Size Of The Sun

How big is the sun? You take 109 earths and they would fit across the sun's surface. What about if you stuffed the earths into the core of the sun? Do you know how many earths it would take to get into that sun? Imagine how big the sun is—1.3 million earths! The sun's outer visible layer, the photosphere, is about 6,000 centigrade or 11,000 degrees Fahrenheit. That is the normal as we know it today.

11,000 Degrees Fahrenheit

You know and I know that we cannot touch anything even boiling, which is 212 degrees Fahrenheit. The sun is not 212 degrees, it is 11,000 degrees Fahrenheit. This is tremendous. I do not know what it is going to be heated up to, but we know that it is going to scorch the people on this earth. The sun will be hotter than ever. The temperature of solar energy created deep within the sun is 15 million degrees centigrade and 27 million degrees Fahrenheit. Nuclear reactions take place because it is so hot in that center core.

Sun Not A Million Years Old!

Here is another lie: The energy generated in the sun's core takes a million years to reach its surface. The sun has not been around a million years, so that is all a fable. This is what some scientists believe. Imagine that. Here you have the energy down in the core of the sun taking a million years to reach the surface. They just figure millions and billions of years. They throw those figures around like they are peanuts or something like that.

The energy generated in the **sun's** core is that every second, 700 million tons of hydrogen are converted to helium. That is a tremendous production of helium. In the process, five million tons of pure energy are released. Therefore, as time goes on they say the sun is becoming lighter. Well, that is all right. Let it be light. Nothing is going to happen to it.

This second article agreed with the first one that the **sun** appears to have been active for 4.6 billion years. At least they say, *appears*. They are not sure. It is just guesswork. They also say the sun has enough fuel to go on for another five billion years or so. Well, it is not going to last that long.

- **Matthew 24:35**
  "Heaven and earth shall pass away, but my words shall not pass away."
- **Mark 13:31**
  "Heaven and earth shall pass away: but my words shall not pass away."
- **Luke 21:33**
  "Heaven and earth shall pass away: but my words shall not pass away."

One day Heaven and earth will pass away. That means the **sun**, the solar system, and all the stars of heaven one day will pass away.

These scientists who really do not even know when the **sun** was created, and do not believe that God created it, have a prediction of what is going to happen at the end of the **sun's** life. They say that at the end of its life, the **sun** will start to fuse helium into heavier elements and begin to swell up. It is going to swell up just like a balloon apparently, according to them. They say it will ultimately grow so large that it will swallow up the earth. (We are going to be long gone and the earth is going to be gone.) Then they say that after a billion years, as a red giant, the sun will suddenly collapse into a white dwarf. They have some fanciful ideas about the **sun**. They say that the final end product of a star like ours may take a trillion years to cool off completely. It is just fanciful trillions, billions, and millions. We know that God created the universe in about 4000 B.C. if we take the Scriptural chronology as accurate.

What are some of the Scriptures that have to do with the **sun**? We are told here, in Revelation 16, that the fourth angel poured out his **vial** upon the **sun,** and power was given to him (the angel) to **scorch men with fire.** The **sun** is a **fire.** Imagine, 11,000 degrees Fahrenheit on the outside and millions of degrees Fahrenheit at the core. How is that going to happen?

- **Psalm 121:6**
"The **sun** shall not smite thee by day, nor the moon by night."
Here is a guarantee. Because God wrote this into the Psalms, apparently the **sun** is able to smite. In other words, it could really hurt. We know that we can get sunburn.

- **Isaiah 30:25-26**
"And there shall be upon every high mountain, and upon every high hill, rivers *and* streams of waters in the day of the great slaughter, when the towers fall. Moreover the light of the moon shall be as the light of the **sun**, and the light of the **sun** shall be sevenfold, as the light of seven days, in the day that the LORD bindeth up the breach of his people, and healeth the stroke of their wound."

The Sun Seven Times Hotter

This is in the judgment of this earth. There is going to be a time, probably during this tribulation period, when the light of the moon will be like the light of the sun. In other words, at night it will be so hot it will be like the sun was out. Can you imagine the sun being seven times hotter? It reminds me of the furnace that Shadrach, Meshech, and Abednego were cast into by Nebuchadnezzar because they would not worship the image. They heated up that fire seven times hotter. That is what is going to happen to the sun. This, I believe, explains why they are going to be scorched with heat. The sun will be seven times hotter than it ever has been.

- **Isaiah 49:10**
"They shall not hunger nor thirst; neither shall the heat nor **sun** smite them: for he that hath mercy on them shall lead them, even by the springs of water shall he guide them."
There is protection. It means that the **sun** is able to smite them and the heat is able to hurt. That will take place in this fourth **vial judgment.**

Revelation 16:9

"And men were scorched with great heat, and blasphemed the name of God, which hath power over these plagues: and they repented not to give him glory."

The result of the **sun** smiting the earth is that men were **scorched**. You and I know that if we are **scorched** we are not going to live. My wife mentioned about a poor pastor's family in New York near Johnstown and how the **fire** and smoke came and they were killed by inhalation of smoke and fumes. Our son David had 31% of his body burned. He had a Christmas tree and some man who was a horrible bum, as far as I am concerned, was playing around putting his cigarette lighter near the tree and then withdrawing it. Pretty soon that thing got so near the tree it went up in flames. David was not burned, but he was **scorched**—not by fire but by the heat. Finally, he got out the window and he was spared, but 31% of his body was burned. When heat is there, you do not even have to have the fire on you. It will burn you just like in an oven. There is heat in there.

Blaspheming The Name Of God

This verse says that in the tribulation period they *were scorched with great heat.* What was their reaction? I would not have this reaction, but they *blasphemed the name of God.* They cursed Him and swore against Him instead of turning to Him and saying, "What must I do to be saved?" They blasphemed His name. He could have stopped it.

When Moses was here on earth and the plagues were there to kill all the different Israelites (24,000 and 31,000), he prayed unto the Lord to stop the plague. He turned to the Lord and the Lord stopped the plague.

Notice also in this verse that *they* **repented not to give him glory.** This is a statement in the aorist tense. That means they did not even begin to **repent**. That is what God wants us to do, to give repentance and to change our minds if we are sinners, to come unto Him and be genuinely saved.

As far as **blasphemy** is concerned, the Lord Jesus Christ tells where this all comes from.

- **Mark 7:20-23**
  "And he said, That which cometh out of the man, that defileth the man. For from within, out of the heart of men, proceed evil thoughts, adulteries, fornications, murders, Thefts,

covetousness, wickedness, deceit, lasciviousness, an evil eye, **blasphemy**, pride, foolishness: All these evil things come from within, and defile the man."

These people, with their **blasphemy** against the Lord, were **burning up**. With their last breath they **cursed** and **swore** against the Lord Jesus Christ and against God the Father instead of asking Him to save them and deliver them from death. That is what Hell is going to be. It is going to be a tremendously **scorching**, burning, fiery Hell, burning with **fire** and brimstone.

- **Colossians 3:8**
  "But now ye also put off all these; anger, wrath, malice, **blasphemy**, filthy communication out of your mouth."

Blasphemy Should Be Gone

<u>God wants our mouths clean and our blasphemy gone once we are genuinely saved and born-again.</u> We may have sworn a blue streak before we were genuinely saved and that was the way that people always around us had done, but once we are genuinely saved and redeemed, God wants to get a hold of our mouths, and our tongues, and clean us up.

- **Revelation 13:1**
  "And I stood upon the sand of the sea, and saw a beast rise up out of the sea, having seven heads and ten horns, and upon his horns ten crowns, and upon his heads the name of **blasphemy**."

<u>This beast out of the sea is a political beast.</u> The antichrist is going to be **blasphemous** against God the Father and against the Lord Jesus Christ.

- **Revelation 13:5-6**
  "And there was given unto him a mouth speaking great things and **blasphemies**; and power was given unto him to continue forty *and* two months. And he opened his mouth in **blasphemy** against God, to **blaspheme** his name, and his tabernacle, and them that dwell in heaven."

<u>This antichrist is going to **swear** and **blaspheme** God, Heaven, and all the Biblical saints that are in Heaven.</u> He is going to speak up and **blaspheme** and speak evil of the things of the Lord Jesus Christ instead of **worshipping** Him. <u>I do not know where these people that **blaspheme** the Lord Jesus Christ get all their hatred for Him, but they certainly have a lot on television and radio.</u> Their speech is no longer censored. They can **blaspheme** and use God's name. It is terrible.

You would think, after the Lord Jesus Christ showed them Who was boss, they would have **repented**. They should have said, "Uncle," as it were. You know when you are wrestling around, and you are ready to press somebody to the mat, you say, "Say Uncle," that is, "Give up!" They did not do it. They **repented not**. Strange.

- **Luke 5:32**
  "I came not to call the righteous, but sinners to **repentance**."

That is why the Lord Jesus Christ came. He wants us to **repent** of sin and come to Him. Once we are genuinely saved, we should still change our minds regarding sin. We should hate sin. Love the Lord Jesus Christ and hate sin.

- **Luke 15:7**
  "I say unto you, that likewise joy shall be in heaven over one sinner that **repenteth**, more than over ninety and nine just persons, which need no **repentance**."

He talked about the man that had 100 sheep and one went astray. They need **repentance**, but they do not think they do. Every one of us needs **repentance**. That word for **repentance** is METANOIA. It means *a change of mind*—a change of mind regarding our sin, to hate it instead of loving it.

- **Luke 24:47**
  "And that **repentance** and remission of sins should be preached in his name among all nations, beginning at Jerusalem."

That is what God wants us to do—to preach **repentance** and remission of sins.

- **Acts 20:21**
  "Testifying both to the Jews, and also to the Greeks, **repentance** toward God, and faith toward our Lord Jesus Christ."

Definition Of Repentance

Many times, people do not want to say anything about repentance, but repentance is a change of mind concerning sin. That means we used to love it, now we should hate it. Then we turn in genuine faith unto the Lord Jesus Christ.

- **Acts 26:20**
  "But shewed first unto them of Damascus, and at Jerusalem, and throughout all the coasts of Judaea, and *then* to the Gentiles, that they should **repent** and turn to God, and do works meet for **repentance**."

When Paul was genuinely saved, the Lord Jesus Christ said He would send him to the Gentiles. <u>After we repent, we ought to do works that follow.</u>

- **2 Peter 3:9**
  "The Lord is not slack concerning his promise, as some men count slackness; but is longsuffering to us-ward, not willing that any should perish, but that all should come to **repentance**."

These people in the tribulation period that have been **scorched** by the heat and are ready to die, should come to **repentance** and genuinely trust the Lord Jesus Christ as Saviour and Redeemer.

- **Revelation 9:20**
  "And the rest of the men which were not killed by these plagues yet **repented not** of the works of their hands, that they should not worship devils, and idols of gold, and silver, and brass, and stone, and of wood: which neither can see, nor hear, nor walk:"

Repentance Needed After Judgment

Way back, even in Revelation 9, they did not repent. You would think after the Lord Jesus Christ got a hold of them, and got their attention, they would say, "Wait a minute. Who gave these judgments? Lord, did You give these judgments? Did You pour this upon me? I had better turn to Thee and repent of my sins. I am going to turn to the Lord Jesus Christ and be genuinely saved."

Revelation 16:10

"And the fifth angel poured out his vial upon the seat of the beast; and his kingdom was full of darkness; and they gnawed their tongues for pain,"

The Fifth Vial Judgment

<u>Here is the fifth vial judgment.</u> This angel poured out his vial on the seat, or throne, where the beast was. That will probably be in Jerusalem in the temple where he is usurping the authority of God. This is a switch. The fourth vial judgment had to do with the sun scorching men with the heat and light. Now there is no light, but just pitch darkness.

Notice what they did. *They gnawed their tongues for pain.* I do not know how that would ease the **pain** if you chew your tongue or

gnawed on your **tongue.** They continuously **gnawed.** There was such pain I guess they wanted to feel the **pain** of the **tongue** rather than the other **pain** they were experiencing. God brings **pain** many times and judges. This is what is going to happen in that fifth **vial** judgment, a judgment of **pain.**

Revelation 16:11

"And blasphemed the God of heaven because of their pains and their sores, and repented not of their deeds."

Can you imagine that? **Darkness, pain, gnawing** their **tongues,** and still not using their **tongues** to say, "Lord, deliver me. I believe in the Lord Jesus Christ as my Saviour. I want to be genuinely saved and I want to come to Thee." Instead of that, they **blasphemed** God. Because of their pains, they were blaming it on Him instead of themselves for their sin. They did not **repent** of their deeds.

- **Jeremiah 30:23**
  "Behold, the whirlwind of the LORD goeth forth with fury, a continuing whirlwind: it shall fall with **pain** upon the head of the wicked."

That is exactly what happened here during this tribulation—**pain** upon the head of the wicked ones that **worshipped** the **beast,** the false prophet, and had the mark of the **beast.**

- **Ezekiel 30:4**
  "And the sword shall come upon Egypt, and great **pain** shall be in Ethiopia, when the slain shall fall in Egypt, and they shall take away her multitude, and her foundations shall be broken down."

God has a way of ministering **pain** unto those who reject Him, those who refuse Him, and those who do not love Him.

Revelation 16:12

"And the sixth angel poured out his vial upon the great river Euphrates; and the water thereof was dried up, that the way of the kings of the east might be prepared."

This is the sixth **vial** judgment. The **Euphrates River** is a long river. The word **Euphrates** occurs only 21 times in the entire Bible. It runs from Assyria and Syria all the way down to Babylon. It is a long river. The Tigris is above it.

Euphrates River Dried Up

God says that the Euphrates River is going to be dried up. The whole river will be dried up. The purpose in the end-time is *that the way of the kings of the east might be prepared*. The kings of the east (that would be east of Jerusalem) would take in Babylon, Assyria, and especially China. They are noted to be the kings of the eastern part of the world. They will be prepared to come in for battle against Jerusalem, at the Battle of Armageddon. That is the purpose of this. The word Euphrates is first found in Genesis 2:14.

- **Genesis 2:14**
  "And the name of the third river *is* Hiddekel: that *is* it which goeth toward the east of Assyria. And the fourth river *is* **Euphrates**."

These are the rivers out of the garden of Eden.

- **Genesis 15:18**
  "In the same day the LORD made a covenant with Abram, saying, Unto thy seed have I given this land, from the river of Egypt unto the great river, the river **Euphrates**:"

This talks about the possessions that Abraham was given by the Lord. Israel has never possessed their promised land completely. The river of Egypt is probably the Nile River. That is all to be his possession all the way up to that great river **Euphrates**. They have never had all of this land, but they will one day in the millennial reign of our Saviour the Lord Jesus Christ. This was promised to Abraham.

The Influence Of China

I looked up a few things from the Internet about China. I believe they are the distinguishing feature of the kings of the east. It says, later in the book of Revelation, there will be 200 million people in that battle of Armageddon. That may be just from the eastern area of China itself. It will be a tremendous battle. We have never had 200 million in one place coming down to Jerusalem in that one spot on the earth's surface.

In **China**, they have a very temperate climate. They have a huge population. The date of establishment of the People's Republic of China was October 1, 1949. That is when they revolted and that is when the Communist **China** split from the free Chinese. That is when Taiwan left and went to the Taiwanese Formosa. There was a terrific revolution and battle, as we know. At that time there were 542 million in **China**. Today there are 1.2 billion. The population has mushroomed. It is a tremendous group of people. They are still under Communist rule.

In 1970, their birth rate was 33 per thousand. Now, because they are penalizing births and saying you cannot have more than one child, they were down to 15 per thousand in 1999. They have cut the birth rate by their laws. I do not know what they do with the babies. Maybe they kill them. I am not sure what they do. They limit them so that the birth rate is down, but they still have 1.2 billion people.

The Euphrates River Dried Up

There are plenty of people to come into this battle with the kings of the east. That whole body of water will be dried up, just as the Red Sea was dried up for the Israelites as they fled from Egypt. God permitted them to walk across it. They could not have done it otherwise.

The national flag of **China** is a Communist flag. Their economic growth in 1995 was ten percent. In 2000 it was down to eight percent. There is a lot of Chinese history for thousands of years. They had the Great Wall of China and various other architectural wonders of that land. The state organs are the National People's Congress and the Supreme People's Court. Of course, it is all the Communist regime. They have a Constitution. They have a Liberation People's Army, the ruling army of the Communist Party of China. The current president's name is Hu Jintao. I do not know whether he is going to be president when the battle of Armageddon takes place. Whoever it is, will bring his armies across the Euphrates River and into the land of Palestine for judgment. God is going to judge them at that time.

Their working days are the same as ours, Monday to Friday. Most people do not work on the weekends in **China**. They have different family names.

The Many Religions In China

There are many religions in China. The big three are Buddhism, Taoism, and Islam. They have some Catholicism and some Protestantism. Communism does not really allow them to practice religion generally. In fact, there have been some persecutions of "Christians" in China. We have read about these in David Cloud's *Friday News Notes*. They have a television system. It is run by the government. The Internet also is run by the government.

God's Omnipotence Proven

The Euphrates River goes from the mountains of Armenia, flows through Assyria and Syria, Mesopotamia and the city of Babylon, and empties into the Gulf of Persia. That is a huge, huge river. How is God going to dry it up? He can do that because of His omnipotence. He has no problem drying up rivers. He had no problem creating rivers, or creating all the universes, all the galaxies, all the stars, and all the planets. He has no problem with that. That is going to take place in the future to prepare for this battle.

Revelation 16:13

"And I saw three unclean spirits like frogs *come* out of the mouth of the dragon, and out of the mouth of the beast, and out of the mouth of the false prophet."

Here is the **Satanic trinity**. The **dragon** is the Devil, the **beast** is the political ruler of Revelation 13 and there is the **false prophet**. This is a threefold **trinity**. We have the Trinity of the Godhead—God the Father, God the Son, and the God Holy Spirit. **Satan has his trinity.**

Unclean Spirits Like Frogs

Notice, out of the mouths of these three triumvirates of evil (the dragon, the beast, and the false prophet) came *unclean spirits like frogs*. Unclean spirits are very serious. They are like frogs. I am going to take you on a frog expedition in just a minute, because the Bible says they are *like frogs*. I do not know much about frogs, so I looked it up. These are unclean spirits that are similar to frogs.

- Matthew 10:1
  "And when he had called unto *him* his twelve disciples, he gave them power *against* **unclean spirits**, to cast them out, and to heal all manner of sickness and all manner of disease."

Apostolic Power Over Devils

When the disciples were sent out and commissioned, the Lord Jesus Christ gave them power over *unclean spirits, to cast them out.* God's power is great over these unclean spirits, and He does not deal with them nicely. He casts them out.

- **Mark 1:27**
"And they were all amazed, insomuch that they questioned among themselves, saying, What thing is this? what new doctrine *is* this? for with authority commandeth he even the **unclean spirits**, and they do obey him."

The people were amazed when the Lord Jesus Christ cast them out. These **unclean spirits** in the end time, will be sent out by the **Satanic trinity**, and be doomed by the Lord Jesus Christ, just like during His earthly ministry.

- **Mark 5:13**
"And forthwith Jesus gave them leave. And the **unclean spirits** went out, and entered into the swine: and the herd ran violently down a steep place into the sea, (they were about two thousand;) and were choked in the sea."

Unclean spirits had entered into a man. The Lord Jesus Christ got them out of the man and the **unclean spirits** said, "Where shall we go?" Here were some swine (pigs) feeding—unclean animals. The **unclean spirits** did go out and enter into the swine. About 2,000 were choked in the sea. That gives you an idea of the Lord's power over the devils and these evil spirits, but also the power of the number in one man—2,000 evil, devilish, **unclean spirits**.

- **Luke 6:18**
"And they that were vexed with **unclean spirits**: and they were healed."

People who had **unclean spirits** were healed by the Lord Jesus Christ.

Frogs are only used 14 times in Scripture. This is part of God's plague system—**frogs**. Why He picks that, I do not know.

- **Exodus 8:2**
"And if thou refuse to let *them* go, behold, I will smite all thy borders with **frogs**:"

He is talking to Pharaoh about the people of Israel. Frogs were a judgment of the Lord. He is going to be doing this in the tribulation time. The true believers or genuinely saved ones will be gone, raptured out of this place before any part of this seven-year period of Daniel's 70th Week.

- **Daniel 9:24**
"Seventy weeks are determined upon thy people and upon thy holy city, to finish the transgression, and to make an end of sins, and to make reconciliation for iniquity, and to bring in everlasting righteousness, and to seal up the vision and prophecy, and to anoint the most Holy."

This is 70 weeks of years—70 times seven or 490 years. It has nothing to do with the true Church, nothing to do with the genuine believers of this age. They will be gone.

- **Exodus 8:5**
  "And the LORD spake unto Moses, Say unto Aaron, Stretch forth thine hand with thy rod over the streams, over the rivers, and over the ponds, and cause **frogs** to come up upon the land of Egypt."

They were **frogs** that were living in ponds, and streams, and water.

- **Psalm 78:45**
  "He sent divers sorts of flies among them, which devoured them; and **frogs**, which destroyed them."

You might say, "Frogs? What can they do?" If you have enough of them, you will be in serious trouble. You cannot walk. You cannot eat. You cannot sleep. They are all over the place.

- **Psalm 105:30**
  "Their land brought forth **frogs** in abundance, in the chambers of their kings."

The Lord speaks of what God did to the **frogs** in Exodus. We had some animals crawling up in our chimney. There were squirrels and raccoons. Now they are gone. We finally put a lid on top. I would be uncomfortable with animals. They have their own houses, so let them go. With the **frogs**, it is the same way.

Information About Frogs

What about frogs? What are they? They are vertebrates and amphibians. They go on both land and sea like the Marines. They are land and sea. They are amphibians. A frog's body temperature is the same as the surrounding temperature. They are cold-blooded animals so as the temperature is, their body goes to the same temperature. They have lungs. They do not have to drink water because their bodies absorb water. They can still survive. They have strong hind legs to leap over things and great distances. Their front legs are short and they prop up the frog when it jumps.

How big is the biggest **frog**? (I am sure that is of great interest to all of us.) There is a Goliath **frog**. Would you believe it is one foot long? I did not know that. Then there is a very small **frog** of one and a half inches. There are different kinds of **frogs**. I do not know what kind of spiritual **frogs** are coming out of the mouths of this evil trinity, but they are going to be *like frogs*.

Frogs can breathe because they have lungs, but they also can breathe through their skin because of their hearts. They only have three heart compartments instead of four.

Where do frogs live? Practically everywhere except Antarctica. They do not do well there. They freeze. They are mostly in tropical places. I think if the Lord Jesus Christ is going to send spiritual **frogs** He will hit the Antarcticans, too. He will make not make an exception. I am sure the evil spirits, like **frogs**, go everywhere.

Some **frogs** never even go into the water except for mating purposes. Some live in trees. They have different kinds of feet. Some have webbed feet for swimming. Some have suction cups so they can climb. These would be the tree **frogs**. Some dig or burrow in the ground. Some can fly or glide.

How does a **frog** catch an insect? They have a tongue that is sharp and sticky to grab insects. My wife and I always used to say that when the modernistic preachers would preach, they would talk about different things that did not have anything to do with the Bible. I feel like I am doing the same thing here, but God talks about **frogs** so I go into the **frog** aspect.

How does a **frog** protect itself from enemies? They do have enemies. Bats like them. Heron, fish, raccoons, turtles, snakes, and some human beings eat **frogs**. It is not on my menu, generally. By way of protection, some of them have poison glands. People die when they eat them. In fact, some of the Indians use the poison to put on their arrows. Sometimes the frogs change colors so that they frighten off predators. Some have camouflage and different things. There are all kinds of different **frogs**. Singing **frogs** have a good voice, I guess. Their life cycle does not last too long. They go from a tadpole up to a frog. Sometimes it takes months, sometimes a few weeks. They do get rid of pests and they eat insects, so they are all right.

Frogs From All Three Creatures

Getting back to the Scripture in Revelation 16:13, these unclean or evil spirits come out of the mouths of all three of these creatures—the dragon, the beast, and the false prophet. They are evil, unclean spirits *like* frogs. We do not know what kind they are, but they are coming out and doing evil to the people of this land.

Revelation 16:14

"For they are the spirits of devils, working miracles, *which* **go forth unto the kings of the earth and of the whole world, to gather them to the battle of that great day of God Almighty."**

The Devil's Working Miracles

Notice these evil "spirits of devils." They work miracles. You might say, "How can the Devil work miracles?" He can work some. You will remember in Egypt when Moses had the plague miracles, with the first two plague miracles the Satanic evil magicians also worked the same miracles. They had a limit. They could not go beyond that. You might say, "What about all these miracle workers today? Are they God's miracle workers?" I do not believe that they are. I believe that they are Satan's and they have the power of Satan.

In fact, Brother Joseph Chambers gave a message on some of these faith healers and charismatics. He said that some people were healed. It seemed like a Satanic healing, because whenever they found out that this man was of the Devil, and they forsook that particular speaker, and served the Lord Jesus Christ, their illness came back. Dr. Chambers believes this is one of the proofs to show that as long as they are worshipping the Devil, they are free of the illness.

Evil Miracles From Evil Spirits

There are evil miracles and these evil spirits working miracles go forth unto the kings of the earth and the whole world. The purpose of these spirits is to gather them to the battle of that great day, the Battle of Armageddon. Before we get to the battle, let us take a look at some of these devils.

- **Leviticus 17:7**
  "And they shall no more offer their sacrifices unto **devils**, after whom they have gone a whoring. This shall be a statute for ever unto them throughout their generations."

The sacrifices that Israel had made were unto the **devils**. The sacrifices of people that worship idols today we believe are under **devils'** domination. Whether it is in China, or Russia, or Africa, or wherever it may be, it is **Devil** worship.

- **Deuteronomy 32:17**
  "They sacrificed unto **devils**, not to God; to gods whom they knew not, to new *gods that* came newly up, whom your fathers feared not."

Now some people say, "Why is this **devils**? There is only one **Devil**." Well, you have the **Devil's** helpers. Many say, "It should be demons." No, it is **devils**. Demons are the gods that the people following Greek mythology and present day New Age people worship. Anyway, I am all right with it being *devils*. There is no problem with that. They are little **devils**. We have the big **Devil**, the main **Devil**, and the little ones. There is no problem as far as I am concerned.

- **2 Chronicles 11:15**
  "And he ordained him priests for the high places, and for the **devils**, and for the calves which he had made."

This is talking about Jeroboam, the one that split the kingdom of Israel. He worshipped **devils**.

- **Psalm 106:37**
  "Yea, they sacrificed their sons and their daughters unto **devils**,"

All of the human sacrifices in the Old Testament were unto **devils**. The **devils** wanted them to kill their children. I suppose we could say that the **devils** want them to kill their children today with all these abortions. There are about 1.5 million abortions per year in this country alone. They were sacrificing unto **devils** in the Old Testament. Why not today? **Devils** are high, wide, and handsome. Many of these people are having even late-term abortions. Even President Clinton would not sign off on that. Perhaps the current president will. These are terrible things— sacrificing unto **devils**—killing them.

- **Luke 8:27**
  "And when he went forth to land, there met him out of the city a certain man, which had **devils** long time, and ware no clothes, neither abode in *any* house, but in the tombs."

This man was possessed with **devils**.

- **James 2:19**
  "Thou believest that there is one God; thou doest well: the **devils** also believe, and tremble."

God warns us about believing only as the **devils** and not really being genuine. It has to be a heart belief in the Lord Jesus Christ, God's Son.

- **2 Thessalonians 2:6-10**
  "And now ye know what withholdeth that he might be revealed in his time. For the mystery of iniquity doth already work: only he who now letteth *will let,* until he be taken out of the way. And

then shall that Wicked be revealed, whom the Lord shall consume with the spirit of his mouth, and shall destroy with the brightness of his coming: *Even him,* whose coming is after the working of **Satan** with all power and signs and **lying wonders,** And with all deceivableness of unrighteousness in them that perish; because they received not the love of the truth, that they might be saved."

This talks about the end time when the man of sin will be revealed, the wicked one. **Satan** will have **lying wonders.**

- **Revelation 19:20**
  "And the **beast** was taken, and with him the **false prophet** that wrought **miracles** before him, with which he deceived them that had received the mark of the **beast,** and them that worshipped his image. These both were cast alive into a lake of fire burning with brimstone."

The **false prophet** will be a miracle-working prophet in the time of the tribulation period.

What about the **battle of Armageddon?** There are five passages that deal with that. I will just go through them very briefly.

- **Ezekiel 38:14-16**
  "Therefore, son of man, prophesy and say unto Gog, Thus saith the Lord GOD; In that day when my people of Israel dwelleth safely, shalt thou not know *it?* And thou shalt come from thy place out of the north parts, thou, and many people with thee, all of them riding upon horses, a **great company,** and a mighty army: And thou shalt come up against my people of Israel, as a cloud to cover the land; it shall be in the latter days, and I will bring thee against my land, that the heathen may know me, when I shall be sanctified in thee, O Gog, before their eyes."

Gog, The Probable Russian Capital

God addresses Gog, which is the northern capital, probably Russia and that area. This is the picture of the great Battle of Armageddon. Coming from the north country will be Russia, Gog, Magog and all of Germany. From the east, there will be the kings of the east, centering in upon Jerusalem.

- **Ezekiel 39:1-4**
  "Therefore, thou son of man, prophesy against Gog, and say, Thus saith the Lord GOD; Behold, I *am* against thee, O Gog, the chief prince of Meshech and Tubal: And I will turn thee back,

and leave but the sixth part of thee, and will cause thee to come up from the north parts, and will bring thee upon the mountains of Israel: And I will smite thy bow out of thy left hand, and will cause thine arrows to fall out of thy right hand. Thou shalt fall upon the mountains of Israel, thou, and all thy bands, and the people that is with thee: I will give thee unto the ravenous birds of every sort, and *to* the beasts of the field to be devoured."

Eating The Flesh Of The Dead

After the Battle of Armageddon, the birds and the ravenous beasts will eat the flesh of those that are killed in that battle.

- **Ezekiel 39:11-20**
"And it shall come to pass in that day, *that* I will give unto Gog a place there of graves in Israel, the valley of the passengers on the east of the sea: and it shall stop the *noses* of the passengers: and there shall they **bury Gog** and all his multitude: and they shall call *it* The valley of Hamongog. And seven months shall the house of Israel be burying of them, that they may cleanse the land. Yea, all the people of the land shall bury *them*; and it shall be to them a renown the day that I shall be glorified, saith the Lord GOD."

"And they shall sever out men of continual employment, passing through the land to **bury** with the passengers those that remain upon the face of the earth, to cleanse it: after the end of seven months shall they search. And the passengers *that* pass through the land, when *any* seeth a man's bone, then shall he set up a sign by it, till the **buriers** have **buried** it in the valley of Hamongog."

"And also the name of the city *shall be* Hamonah. Thus shall they cleanse the land. And, thou son of man, thus saith the Lord GOD; Speak unto every feathered fowl, and to every beast of the field, Assemble yourselves, and come; gather yourselves on every side to my sacrifice that I do sacrifice for you, *even* a great sacrifice upon the mountains of Israel, that ye may eat flesh, and drink blood."

"Ye shall eat the flesh of the mighty, and drink the blood of the princes of the earth, of rams, of lambs, and of goats, of bullocks, all of them fatlings of Bashan. And ye shall eat fat till ye be full, and drink blood till ye be drunken, of my sacrifice which I have sacrificed for you. Thus ye shall be filled at my table with horses and chariots, with mighty men, and with all men of war, saith the Lord GOD."

The Decaying Flesh Is Putrid

In other words, the smell of the decaying flesh will be so great it will stop their noses. It will take seven months to bury them. How great this will be! God calls it His sacrifice. God is judging these people and the birds and ravenous beasts are going to be eating their flesh. Just like whenever an animal is killed—we call it "road kill"—whether it is a deer or whatever it is, those vultures and different animals come and eat it. They clean up things. They are the cleaning establishment. We do not have to pay to clean it. They take care of it. This is the same way here.

- **Zechariah 14:1-4**
  "Behold, the day of the LORD cometh, and thy spoil shall be divided in the midst of thee. For **I will gather all nations** against Jerusalem to battle; and the city shall be taken, and the houses rifled, and the women ravished; and half of the city shall go forth into captivity, and the residue of the people shall not be cut off from the city. Then shall the LORD go forth, and fight against those nations, as when he fought in the day of battle. And his feet shall stand in that day upon the mount of Olives, which is before Jerusalem on the east, and the mount of Olives shall cleave in the midst thereof toward the east and toward the west, *and there shall be* a very great valley; and half of the mountain shall remove toward the north, and half of it toward the south."

The Day Of The Lord Battle

This Battle of Armageddon is called *the day of the LORD.* It is another title for it. This is going to be a terrible battle for Israel. The Lord Jesus Christ will come back in the second phase of His second coming. On the eastern side of Jerusalem is the mount of Olives. My wife and I stayed there when Mom and Dad sent us over there in the 1980's. That mount will be moved north and south so that the east and west will open up and the fresh water will take care of it. The Lord Jesus Christ is going to come back and He is going to fight against those nations.

- **Revelation 19:11-12**
"And I saw heaven opened, and behold a white horse; and he that sat upon him *was* called Faithful and True, and in righteousness he doth judge and **make war**. His eyes *were* as a flame of fire, and on his head *were* many crowns; and he had a name written, that no man knew, but he himself."

This is the Lord Jesus Christ Himself.

- **Revelation 19:13-14**
"And he *was* clothed with a vesture dipped in **blood**: and his name is called The Word of God. And the **armies** *which were* in heaven followed him upon white horses, clothed in fine linen, white and clean."

Those are the true saints, the genuine believers, following the Lord Jesus Christ at this **battle**.

- **Revelation 19:15-16**
"And out of his mouth goeth a sharp sword, that with it he should smite the nations: and he shall rule them with a rod of iron: and he treadeth the winepress of the fierceness and wrath of Almighty God. And he hath on *his* vesture and on his thigh a name written, KING OF KINGS, AND LORD OF LORDS."

- **Revelation 19:17-18**
"And I saw an angel standing in the sun; and he cried with a loud voice, saying to all the fowls that fly in the midst of heaven, Come and **gather yourselves together** unto the **supper** of the great God; That ye may eat the flesh of kings, and the flesh of captains, and the flesh of mighty men, and the flesh of horses, and of them that sit on them, and the flesh of all *men, both* free and bond, both small and great."

It is called the *supper of the great God*. This is the same thing that Ezekiel was saying.

- **Revelation 19:19-21**
"And I saw the beast, and the kings of the earth, and their armies, gathered together **to make war** against him that sat on the horse, and against his army. And the **beast** was taken, and with him the **false prophet** that wrought miracles before him, with which he deceived them that had received the **mark** of the beast, and them that worshipped his image. These both were cast alive into a lake of fire burning with brimstone. And the remnant were slain with the sword of him that sat upon the horse, which *sword* proceeded out of his mouth: and all the fowls were filled with their flesh."

God Wins The Armageddon Battle

God is going to finish the Battle of Armageddon. It will be favorable to Him. I might say that the Lord Jesus Christ never enters a battle that He does not win. There is never a battle that the Lord Jesus Christ is engaged in that He does not win. He never has a "no win" policy like some people you know. We do not believe that. He is a victorious Lord and He will win the Battle of Armageddon.

Revelation 16:15

"Behold, I come as a thief. Blessed *is* he that watcheth, and keepeth his garments, lest he walk naked, and they see his shame."

<u>He comes as a thief</u>. We do not know when it is going to be. These people living in the tribulation period do not know that there are seven years only. They do not know He is going to come back at a certain time. <u>He is going to come as a **thief**</u>.

- **2 Peter 3:10**
  "But the day of the Lord will come as a **thief** in the night; in the which the heavens shall pass away with a great noise, and the elements shall melt with fervent heat, the earth also and the works that are therein shall be burned up."

- **Revelation 3:3**
  "Remember therefore how thou hast received and heard, and hold fast, and repent. If therefore thou shalt not watch, I will come on thee as a **thief**, and thou shalt not know what hour I will come upon thee."

The false teacher, Harold Camping, on Family Radio, said that the Lord Jesus Christ came already. It is the same old false prophecy. No, He is coming as a thief. No one knows the hour. We must be watching. Even today we can apply this. Even though this is for the tribulation saints, we must be **watching**. We must continue to keep our garments clean.

- **Matthew 24:42**
  "**Watch** therefore: for ye know not what hour your Lord doth come."

- **Matthew 26:41**
  "**Watch** and pray, that ye enter not into temptation: the spirit indeed *is* willing, but the flesh *is* weak."

- **Acts 20:31**
  "Therefore **watch**, and remember, that by the space of three years I ceased not to warn every one night and day with tears."
Paul is speaking to the church at Ephesus. We have to be watchful.
  - **1 Corinthians 16:13**
  "Watch ye, stand fast in the faith, quit you like men, be strong."
  - **Colossians 4:2**
  "Continue in prayer, and **watch** in the same with thanksgiving;"
Why does God want us to **watch**? Because evil is all around us! It reminds me of the joke that people said about former President Reagan. Many times, as he spoke, he looked down. They asked him, "Why do you look down?" He said, "You'd look down too if you lived on a ranch."

We're Surrounded By Evil

We have to be careful. Evil people are all around us. No matter where we are, we must be watchful. Watch. Do not sleep. Endure all things. Endure afflictions. The end is near.

- **1 Peter 4:7**
  "But the end of all things is at hand: be ye therefore sober, and **watch** unto prayer."
God wants us to be careful and to **watch** at all times. These people in the tribulation period also should be watching.

Revelation 16:16

"And he gathered them together into a place called in the Hebrew tongue Armageddon."

The Hill Of Megiddo–Armageddon

Armageddon is the Hebrew word for the hill of Megiddo. HAR is the word for *hill* and with MEGIDDO it is the hill of Megiddo. The valley of Esdraelon is a little bit north of Jerusalem and that is where the battle is going to take place.

He **gathered them together**. I believe this is the Lord Jesus Christ. The Lord says in Ezekiel that He is going to **gather** these nations. They will have their own ideas about why they are coming there. They are after the wealth of Jerusalem. There are millions and billions of dollars of wealth they say in the Dead Sea. There are all kinds of wealth there. It is the center of wealth. As far as God is concerned, He is going to gather all these nations together to judge them because of their rejection of His Son, the Lord Jesus Christ.

There are a lot of books and movies made on Armageddon. Many of them are fanciful. They do not know what is going to happen. We looked at least five passages that I believe talk Scripturally about what is going to happen at **Armageddon**.

Revelation 16:17

"And the seventh angel poured out his vial into the air; and there came a great voice out of the temple of heaven, from the throne, saying, It is done."

This is the **seventh angel** and the seventh **vial** judgment. In that judgment, there are many things happening. The angel said, *"It is done."* It is poured out. It is finished. It is done.

Revelation 16:18

"And there were voices, and thunders, and lightnings; and there was a great earthquake, such as was not since men were upon the earth, so mighty an earthquake, *and* so great."

Here is God's judgment of **earthquakes**. This is the greatest of all. Sometimes God does use **earthquakes** to wake us up and shake us up. Certainly, it literally does shake us up and rumble us.

- **Matthew 27:54**
  "Now when the centurion, and they that were with him, watching Jesus, saw the **earthquake**, and those things that were done, they feared greatly, saying, Truly this was the Son of God."

This was at the Lord Jesus Christ's crucifixion. God quaked the earth at the crucifixion.

- **Matthew 28:2**
  "And, behold, there was a great **earthquake**: for the angel of the Lord descended from heaven, and came and rolled back the stone from the door, and sat upon it."

There was also an **earthquake** at the Lord Jesus Christ's resurrection.

- **Acts 16:26**
  "And suddenly there was a great **earthquake**, so that the foundations of the prison were shaken: and immediately all the doors were opened, and every one's bands were loosed."

Paul was in prison. God released Paul with an **earthquake**.

- **Revelation 6:12**
  "And I beheld when he had opened the sixth seal, and, lo, there was a great **earthquake**; and the sun became black as sackcloth of hair, and the moon became as blood;"
- **Revelation 8:5**
  "And the angel took the censer, and filled it with fire of the altar, and cast *it* into the earth: and there were voices, and thunderings, and lightnings, and an **earthquake**."
- **Revelation 11:13**
  "And the same hour was there a great **earthquake**, and the tenth part of the city fell, and in the **earthquake** were slain of men seven thousand: and the remnant were affrighted, and gave glory to the God of heaven."

There was a great **earthquake** after the two witnesses were raised from the dead.

- **Revelation 11:19**
  "And the temple of God was opened in heaven, and there was seen in his temple the ark of his testament: and there were lightnings, and voices, and **thunderings**, and an **earthquake**, and great hail."

Earthquakes only occur 13 times in Scripture, but God has a way of getting our attention. You know that an **earthquake** gets attention just like rain, storms, and floods get our attention. That is what God has done.

Let me just depart and say a little bit about **earthquakes**. We do not know what kind of **earthquake** it is going to be, but it is going to be a great one—greater than any before.

Earthquakes Described

What is an earthquake? Well, I am not an earthquake specialist, but it has to do with a violent changing of earth faults. A fault is a gap in the earth and it either goes up, or down, or it splits. There are all kinds of earthquakes based upon these faults. There are three main groups. There is a normal fault, which is pulling or tension. Then there is a thrust or reverse fault, a squeezing. Then there is a third one, a strike-slip lateral fault.

Then they talk about the "focal depth." How deep is an **earthquake**? Where does the **earthquake** come from? I do not know about this great **earthquake**. This is going to be greater than anything since man was created on earth. Do not believe the scientists who say man is billions and billions of years old. That is absolutely false. You take the Bible's chronology and go back about 6,000 years and that is it. The creation of man and the universe was about 4,000 B.C. or so.

There is a small **earthquake** called a shallow **earthquake** that goes down 43 miles under the earth. In other words, that is where the earthquake starts. Then there is a normal **earthquake**—more or less a middle-of-the-ground **earthquake**—and that goes down 186 miles. Then there is a tremendous **earthquake**—the deep **earthquake** that goes down 435 miles.

How Deep Will This Earthquake Go?

How many miles down do we have in the earth to the center? There are 3,000 miles before you get to the center of the earth. There will be a great earthquake, greater than ever since man was created on the earth 6,000 years ago. It will be greater than all. I do not know how deep the Lord Jesus Christ is going to go down for that. I am sure it will be deep. It will go down to the center and just explode the whole thing. It is going to be a tremendous thing.

They talk about the epicenter, which is exactly where the focus is. They talk about some of the **earthquakes** on the ocean floor. There are huge waves of the tsunamis that Japan dreads, some forty-nine feet tall and that reach the velocity of 597 miles an hour. Can you imagine what that does?

Maybe this **earthquake** is going to be in the ocean's floor, which would be even greater destruction perhaps than the other. Forty-nine feet high—can you imagine that? Our house is probably about forty-nine feet high. That is a huge wave. It engulfs all coastal areas and sometimes causes liquefaction. God is going to do this as part of the seventh and final vial judgment of the Lord Jesus Christ during this tribulation period.

Revelation 16:19

"And the great city was divided into three parts, and the cities of the nations fell: and great Babylon came in remembrance before God, to give unto her the cup of the wine of the fierceness of his wrath."

Here is the **great city**. It is probably Jerusalem. It does not say. This earthquake divided Jerusalem, and the cities of the nations fell. All the different nations—eastern Europe probably, western Europe, the

United States, all the nations that are on this earth—fell because of this great **earthquake.**

Earthquakes In Many Places At Once

Normally, earthquakes as we know, are centered in one place. The Lord Jesus Christ said in the prophetic picture in the book of Matthew in the end-time that there will be earthquakes in *divers places* or different places at the same time. That is what it means. If this is the result of the seventh vial judgment when earthquakes on this earth will be in different places, that is why it says in Revelation 16:19 *the cities of the nations fell.* Can you imagine cities just collapsing? We saw the Twin Towers fall because of the explosion from beneath and planes from above, but just think, city after city just falling down.

Babylon is a city in Iraq. There is also an allegorical picture of **Babylon.** We will take that up in Revelation 17. That is religious **Babylon,** allegorically speaking of **Rome** as the most corrupt seat of idolatry and the enemy of Biblical Christianity. If this is literal **Babylon,** it is the area where Nebuchadnezzar ruled, and Ur of the Chaldees where Abraham came from. That is where the present conflict is.

- **Revelation 14:8**
  "And there followed another angel, saying, **Babylon** is fallen, is fallen, that great city, because she made all nations drink of the wine of the wrath of her fornication."

Religious **Babylon** is filled with idolatry, evil, and worship of devils.

- **Revelation 18:2**
  "And he cried mightily with a strong voice, saying, **Babylon** the great is fallen, is fallen, and is become the habitation of devils, and the hold of every foul spirit, and a cage of every unclean and hateful bird."

If this is religious **Babylon,** if this is religious **Rome,** it does not say what that *great whore* is in Revelation 17. There are the seven hills of Rome and so on.

Rome And All Religious Systems

In my judgment, I believe that Rome is the core of this terrible wicked idolatry. Then from Rome, and from the Pope, and from that system, is drawn in together the religious systems of apostate Protestantism, apostate Judaism, and all

the world religions—Hinduism, Buddhism, Taoism, New Age,
and all the others. They will be caught into this. It is a terrible,
disgraceful thing.

- **Revelation 18:10**
  "Standing afar off for the fear of her torment, saying, Alas, alas,
  that great city **Babylon**, that mighty city! for in one hour is thy
  judgment come."

Revelation 16:20

**"And every island fled away, and the mountains were
not found."**

What else happens at this seventh **vial** judgment? To have an island
flee away means that it disappears, it seems like to me. Maybe that is
why this **earthquake** is going to be from the ocean. That certainly
would cause **islands** to wash away and disappear, would it not?

- **Isaiah 40:4**
  "Every **valley** shall be exalted, and every **mountain** and hill
  shall be made low: and the crooked shall be made straight, and
  the rough places plain:"

Maybe this is the time.

- **Revelation 6:14**
  "And the heaven departed as a scroll when it is rolled together;
  and every **mountain** and **island** were moved out of their
  places."

Rearranging Of This Earth

God is going to do some rearranging of this earth. I do not
understand the details of it, but in this case, God says that
every island fled away. That includes, I suppose, here in New
Jersey. We have some islands out here off the coast. That
means the islands in San Francisco and in the area of
California. There are all kinds of islands. That means the
Philippines and all the islands all over the world.

Why are islands there? I think the flood is the reason for that. The
flood brought water upon the earth. When the water rises up, there is
just a little bit of the top of the **mountains** left. In fact, they say if you
go down in the depth of the ocean you go down deeper than mountains
are high. This shows that God rearranges the whole earth and the seas
as well.

Revelation 16:21

"And there fell upon men a great hail out of heaven, *every stone* **about the weight of a talent: and men blasphemed God because of the plague of the hail; for the plague thereof was exceeding great."**

Here is another part of this last vial judgment—*great hail out of heaven.* A talent of silver is 100 pounds. A **talent** of gold is 200 pounds. Can you imagine being hit by 100 or even 50 pounds? It is going to be terrific **hail.** Instead of saying, "Lord, what must I do to be saved?" they blasphemed God. They hated Him because of the plague of the **hail.** Hail is only used 34 times in Scripture.

- **Exodus 9:18**
  "Behold, to morrow about this time I will cause it to rain a very grievous **hail,** such as hath not been in Egypt since the foundation thereof even until now."

- **Exodus 9:25**
  "And the **hail** smote throughout all the land of Egypt all that was in the field, both man and beast; and the **hail** smote every herb of the field, and brake every tree of the field."

That was a little hail. This one here is a huge **hail.** Just think what that will do.

- **Psalm 78:47**
  "He destroyed their vines with **hail,** and their sycomore trees with frost."

- **Revelation 8:7**
  "The first angel sounded, and there followed **hail** and fire mingled with blood, and they were cast upon the earth: and the third part of trees was burnt up, and all green grass was burnt up."

- **Revelation 11:19**
  "And the temple of God was opened in heaven, and there was seen in his temple the ark of his testament: and there were lightnings, and voices, and thunderings, and an earthquake, and great **hail.**"

The blasphemy instead of prayer unto the Lord to deliver them from the hail is strange.

- **Revelation 16:9**
  "And men were scorched with great heat, and **blasphemed** the name of God, which hath power over these plagues: and they repented not to give him glory."

After the people were scorched with great heat in the fourth vial judgment, they **blasphemed** the name of God again. They **blasphemed** Him and cursed Him just like they do on television, radio, in the newspapers, and on the streets today. It is a sad thing.

- **Revelation 16:11**
  "And **blasphemed** the God of heaven because of their pains and their sores, and repented not of their deeds."

Looking into **hail** again, Texas does things big around there. In Texas, there was a storm with **hail** that was three to four and a half inches in diameter. That is the size of a baseball. Some are five inches in diameter. The damage that they do includes breaking of windows. God is going to do some damage. People get shot by bullets. People kill people by coming up behind them and choking them to death, but from Heaven itself—hail?

We have had little hail storms. You know those little tiny things. You hear them on your car and on your windows. These will be hailstones that will be able to kill people. They will be the size of a **talent**. There will be destruction and damage to buildings.

Blasphemy Instead Of Praise

God is going to judge. Instead of praising the Lord and praying to Him, "Lord, deliver me from this," they blaspheme Him. To me, that is illogical. That is unreasonable. The God who made the hail, could He not protect the people from that hail judgment if they would turn to Him? He is able. Nothing is impossible with the Lord Jesus Christ. Instead, they blaspheme His name.

We have our work cut out for us, do we not? Before this terrible judgment, I am glad that those of us who are genuinely saved and born-again will not be here during this Battle of Armageddon. It is going to be a terrific battle. The Scriptures speak of it as so great, and so awful, that not only will it take seven months to bury the dead, but it will take all the fowls of heaven and the beasts of the earth to eat up the flesh that is decaying. It is a terrific battle.

Some People Deny This Possibility

Some people say, "I do not believe this. This must be figurative." Well, the fowls of the air are not figurative. Eating flesh and blood is not figurative. The Lord Jesus Christ's return and touching the mount of Olives and having it split, fighting against them and putting down this battle is not figurative. He will destroy them with the brightness of His coming.

- 2 Thessalonians 2:8
  "And then shall that Wicked be revealed, whom the Lord shall consume with the spirit of his mouth, and shall destroy with the brightness of his coming:"

The Lord Jesus Christ is going to put down that final battle, the **Battle of Armageddon**, against His people and against Jerusalem at that time. He will not put up with it.

- Psalm 2:1
  "Why do the heathen rage, and the people imagine a vain thing?"

Win People To Christ Now!

The Lord Jesus Christ is going to put down this rebellion against Him. Our job is cut out for us, to lead people to the Lord Jesus Christ before this tribulation ever takes place that they may come to Him and know Him as their Saviour and Redeemer.

Revelation
Chapter Seventeen

Revelation 17:1

"And there came one of the seven angels which had the seven vials, and talked with me, saying unto me, Come hither; I will shew unto thee the judgment of the great whore that sitteth upon many waters:"

- **Revelation 17:9**
  "And here *is* the mind which hath wisdom. The seven heads are seven mountains, on which the woman sitteth."

Why do I say this is **Rome** and the martyrs' blood? This **great whore** that is spiritually prostituting the various religions of the world is sitting on seven hills. John was on the isle of Patmos. He was a prisoner because **Rome** put him out there to banish him. He knew the **Roman** government. He did not want to name who it was. It does not say who it was, but I am of the opinion that the **Roman** Catholic system is what we are talking about in Revelation 17. The **seven hills** are the **seven hills** of **Rome**. I do not think it is only **Rome**, but I think **Rome** is the head. I think **Rome** includes the Protestant apostates, the Jewish religion, the Hindus, the Muslims, and all the religions of the world. **Rome** is going to collect them all together. That is the **great whore** that is spoken of here.

The **whore**, the prostitute, could be spiritual or physical prostitution—sex for money. In Scripture, at least eighteen times, the word **whore** is used in a spiritual sense of false religions.

- **Exodus 34:15**
  "Lest thou make a covenant with the inhabitants of the land, and they go a **whoring** after their gods, and do sacrifice unto their gods, and *one* call thee, and thou eat of his sacrifice;"

In other words, **whoring** is taking another god instead of the true God and making a false god out of it.

- **Leviticus 17:7**
  "And they shall no more offer their sacrifices unto devils, after whom they have gone a **whoring**. This shall be a statute for ever unto them throughout their generations."

This is spiritual adultery and **whoredom** and prostitution.

- **Leviticus 20:5**
  "Then I will set my face against that man, and against his family, and will cut him off, and all that go a **whoring** after him, to commit **whoredom** with Molech, from among their people."

This is false religion and **Rome** has a false religion. They are, in that sense, going after false gods.

- **Judges 8:33**
  "And it came to pass, as soon as Gideon was dead, that the children of Israel turned again, and went a **whoring** after Baalim, and made Baalberith their god."

Again, spiritual **whoredom** is mentioned.

- **Ezekiel 6:9**
  "And they that escape of you shall remember me among the nations whither they shall be carried captives, because I am broken with their **whorish** heart, which hath departed from me, and with their eyes, which go a whoring after their idols: and they shall lothe themselves for the evils which they have committed in all their abominations."

The **prostitution** of religion against the Lord is called spiritual **whoredom**. There was an article on the Internet about the plain truth about the **Roman** Catholic Church. Let me give a background.

- **Matthew 16:18**
  "And I say also unto thee, That thou art Peter, and upon this rock I will build my church; and the gates of Hell shall not prevail against it."

The **Roman** Catholic Church claims it was started in Matthew 16. That is false. **Rome** is none other than the pagan mystery religion of ancient Babylon.

After the persecutions of the **Roman** government in 65-300 A.D. most of the professing Christians went through a gradual departure from New Testament doctrine. That was where the local churches ceased to be autonomous and began to be ruled over by hierarchies like **Rome**. The ministers became priests. Pagans became "Christians" by simply being sprinkled with water. This tolerance of *"unregenerate membership"* only made things worse. Sprinkled paganism is about the best definition of

Roman Catholicism. That is what Constantine the Great did when he brought in "Christianity" as a religion into the **Roman** Empire.

Satan Ruled Europe

Through popes, bishops, and priests, Satan ruled Europe. Biblical Christianity became illegal. This is the way it was in Rome. True Christians, such as the Waldensians and Anabaptists, would not conform to the Roman system. Many of them paid for it by being killed by Rome.

No Popes In The New Testament

In the New Testament, there is no mention of the Roman Catholic system of popes and priests. It destroys the true dispensational approach. It inserts the Old Testament priests into the New Testament. It mixes Israel and the Church. It is also forbidden in the New Testament to call any man *Father.*

- **Matthew 23:9**
  "And call no *man* your father upon the earth: for one is your **Father**, which is in heaven."

The **worship of Mary** is another pagan **prostitution** of religion. The Roman Catholic Church teaches that Mary, the mother of Jesus, remained a virgin after the birth of Jesus, and was sinless all of her life. She is worshipped by the Catholic Church as the "mother of God." In fact, the Church says that she was immaculately conceived, and that she was conceived with no sin at all. No, she was a sinner that needed to be truly saved by God's grace through genuine faith.

The Heresy Of Purgatory

The Roman Catholic Church has the false doctrine of purgatory. The Catholic Church teaches that "Christian" souls must burn in purgatory after death until all their sins have been purged. To speed up the purging process, money may be paid to a priest so he can pray and have special masses for an earlier release from purgatory. That is absolutely unbiblical and unscriptural.

The Catholic Church has created the **mass**, which they believe to be a continual sacrifice of the Lord Jesus Christ. This is spiritual **whoredom** and spiritual **apostasy** indeed. The Catholic Church teaches that the "holy mass" is the literal eating and drinking of the literal flesh and blood of the Lord Jesus Christ. That is absolutely pagan.

The Images And Relics Of Rome

The Catholic religion is filled with all sorts of symbols, images, and relics. The catechism of the Council of Trent states this: *"It is lawful to have images in the church and to give honor and worship unto them."* This is from their own religious system. They say, "Oh, we do not worship them." The Council of Trent says that it is all right to worship the images.

Salvation by works is another false teaching of Rome through infant baptism, keeping sacraments, church attendance, going to mass, praying to Mary, and confession, just to mention a few. The Catholic Church has developed a system of salvation through works.

The Scripture says that the Lord Jesus Christ paid it all.

* Ephesians 2:8-9

  "For by grace are ye saved through faith; and that not of yourselves: *it is* the gift of God: Not of works, lest any man should boast."

Revelation 17:1 talks about the judgment of the **great whore**. It is a woman that sitteth upon many waters. Many waters, we believe, are all the different nations of the world.

Revelation 17:2

"With whom the kings of the earth have committed fornication, and the inhabitants of the earth have been made drunk with the wine of her fornication."

The Roman Church Is Worldwide

This is worldwide. Some of the Baptist churches are not worldwide. Some of the Presbyterian churches are not worldwide. The Lutheran church is not worldwide. The Episcopal church is not worldwide. The Roman Catholic Church is all over the world, in all kinds of places–even in Communist countries and various other places.

- **Isaiah 23:17**
  "And it shall come to pass after the end of seventy years, that the LORD will visit Tyre, and she shall turn to her hire, and shall commit **fornication** with all the kingdoms of the world upon the face of the earth."

Here is spiritual **fornication**.

- **Revelation 2:20**
  "Notwithstanding I have a few things against thee, because thou sufferest that woman Jezebel, which calleth herself a prophetess, to teach and to seduce my servants to commit **fornication**, and to eat things sacrificed unto idols."

There is both spiritual **fornication** and physical **fornication**. It can be both, but probably spiritual in this case.

- **Revelation 14:8**
  "And there followed another angel, saying, Babylon is fallen, is fallen, that great city, because she made all nations drink of the wine of the wrath of her fornication."

Jesuits Are All Over The World

Is Rome worldwide? The order of Jesuits, called the Society of Jesus, was founded by Ignatius Loyola in 1534. It was recognized and empowered by Pope Paul III in 1540. The Jesuits are all over the world. They are loyal to the Pope. They hate the Protestants. They hate anything that is not Catholic and they are out to maintain Rome at all costs. They are all over the world.

There is some literal **fornication** in the church of Rome, as well. An article on the Internet talked about the Roman Catholic Church's sex abuse scandal. In the late twentieth century, and especially at the turn of the twenty-first century, the Catholic Church was hit by a series of allegations concerning sexual abuse of children under the legal age of consent by Catholic clergy, the overwhelming majority of whom are priests.

Three Charges Against Rome

1. Sexual abuse by religious and secular clergy of children with whom they had contact in the community.

2. Sexual abuse of children in religion-run houses (orphanages and schools) by both clergy and laity.

3. The policy of Catholic clergy in dealing with the abuse,

namely a failure to report what were criminal acts to the local police and efforts to pressure the victims, their families, and independent witnesses into not reporting the incidents to civil authorities. Internal church law is often given priority over the secular criminal law, an action which led some Catholic Church leaders to be accused of perverting the course of justice, which is itself a criminal act.

The **fornication** in **Rome** is not only spiritual because of their false doctrine, but it is also physical and literal. There have been multitudes of stories. In fact, at least one **Roman** Catholic seminary is for homosexual priests to come and be trained. There are sexual relations with priests and nuns, priests with priests, and nuns with nuns. It is a terrible, terrible thing. There is spiritual fornication. There is also physical degradation.

There was another article on the Internet called *The Roman Catholic Church and Homosexuality 2002 to Now*. In 2002 and 2003 there was the sexual child abuse scandal. Donald Cousins was the author of this report. He reported that by the end of the mid-1990s it was estimated that some 600 priests had been named in abuse cases and more than half a billion dollars had been paid in jury award settlements with legal fees—half a billion dollars in order to quiet things down!

John sees a woman and the nations drunk with the wine of her fornication. Again, is Rome worldwide?

Compromising With Rome

There was an article by David Cloud called *United Bible Societies and Rome*. It stated the United Bible Societies was an international body formed in 1946 composed of 142 national Bible societies. We have an American Bible Society here. There is a German one, an Italian one, and the British & Foreign Bible Society. The United Bible Societies have worked with the Roman Catholic Church in various ways from the beginning. These joint endeavors have become commonplace today. It should be noted that the growth of this partnership between Bible Societies and the Catholic Church has coincided closely with the proliferation of new texts and versions of Scripture. The corruption of the Bible is a product of apostasy.

In the 1960s, there was the work of joint Bible translation and distribution between Protestants and Catholics. It was encouraged. They wanted a common-language Bible that Protestants and Catholics could both use. In 1965, the Second Vatican Council approved this form of cooperation. In 1966, the *Today's English Version of the New Testament* was made by Rome. The best-selling Bible translation in history has been cleared for use by Catholics as well as Protestants. In 1970, it was a big year for the distribution by the Vatican of the different versions of Scripture.

Infiltration Of Bible Societies

In fact, Bishop Abodini said that two Catholic priests were working for the Italian Bible Society. What does this mean? That means the 142 Bible Societies all over the world have been infiltrated strongly with Roman Catholic presence and they are over all. This is true of what is mentioned here in Revelation 17:2, *the inhabitants of the earth have been made drunk with the wine of her fornication.*

As far as the **Roman** Catholics in position of leadership in the United Bible Societies, in the 1970s, a Catholic woman named Maria Porcile Santiso was employed in the ecumenical cause in Mexico.

Rome's Approved Greek Text

In 1967, Roman Catholic Carlo Martini, a cardinal of the Roman Catholic Church, was named one of the editors of the United Bible Societies' Greek New Testament. That and the Nestle-Aland Greek New Testament are used at Bob Jones University, Detroit Baptist Seminary, Central Baptist Seminary, and Calvary Baptist Seminary—fundamentalist schools—in addition to the new evangelical schools like Dallas Seminary and others.

Here you have four Protestant heretics on the committee to tell the churches and the students at these seminaries what Bible version to use and what the Greek text is—four Protestant apostates and one Roman Catholic cardinal. Rome has infiltrated. They push it on our fundamentalist brethren.

Fundamentalism Infiltrated Also

It is not simply the Roman Catholics and the Protestant apostates and the new evangelicals like at Wheaton College that use this version, but also some fundamentalist schools use this. Rome has certainly infiltrated and inserted itself all over the world. It is true that they have not only committed fornication, but *the inhabitants of the earth have been made drunk with the wine of her fornication.*

There is not a country in the world that has not been influenced by Rome. We do not believe it is proper and doctrinally sound to have done so. That is why we send missionaries to the various mission fields of the world, in order to make the gospel clear and plain, and not a perversion of Rome.

Revelation 17:3

"So he carried me away in the spirit into the wilderness: and I saw a woman sit upon a scarlet coloured beast, full of names of blasphemy, having seven heads and ten horns."

A Woman Out Of Place

Here John is taken to the wilderness and again sees a woman. The false religion is named as a woman. A woman is out of place in leadership in religion. She has no place to be a pastor and no place to have anything to do with spiritually ministering the Words of God to congregations. Yet, throughout the Protestant world, they have women preachers. This is a woman out of place. It is Jezebelism.

The Woman Riding The Beast

There are two beasts in Revelation 13. There is the political beast and the religious beast, the false prophet. This woman was sitting upon him. In other words, here is Rome in control of the political system. Later on in Revelation, the beast gets a little tired of being dictated to by a false religious system. He throws that woman off and kills her and turns against this false religion. For a time, the political rulers will make common cause with the religious apostate rulers of Rome and all the other nations gathered together in this tribulation period when the believers will be gone up to Heaven.

The **seven heads** and **ten horns** are repeated in Revelation 17:7 and 17:9. The **woman is riding the beast**. Someone who is riding something, if he is any kind of a horse person, is in control of that animal. Some riders do not know how to control their horses, but <u>this woman sitting and riding is in control</u>. There are other places in Scripture that have the **seven heads** and **ten horns**.

- **Daniel 7:24**
  "And the **ten horns** out of this kingdom *are* **ten kings** *that* shall arise: and another shall rise after them; and he shall be diverse from the first, and he shall subdue three kings."

Horns in Daniel are kings. Apparently, <u>the **horns** here in Revelation 17 are **kings**. There are going to be ten kings that are ruled over by this woman</u>.

- **Revelation 12:3**
  "And there appeared another wonder in heaven; and behold a great red dragon, having **seven heads** and **ten horns**, and seven crowns upon his heads."

<u>The great red dragon is the Devil.</u>

- **Revelation 13:1**
  "And I stood upon the sand of the sea, and saw a **beast** rise up out of the sea, having **seven heads** and **ten horns**, and upon his horns **ten crowns**, and upon his heads the name of **blasphemy**."

<u>This is a terrible **blasphemous** situation of this beast.</u> Some people have said the **ten horns** or ten powers may be the European Union. Well, it may be the European Union, but the problem is they do not have ten. Maybe they will finally have ten, but according to an article on the Internet, they had member states of fifteen and then ten more came in, so there are 25 of them: Austria, Belgium, Denmark, Finland, France, Germany, Greece, Ireland, Italy, Luxembourg, Netherlands, Portugal, Spain, Sweden, United Kingdom, and the ones that were added.

There is a European Commission Service, European Science Foundation, European Central Bank, European Patent Office, and Virtual Tourism in Europe. They have a number of others.

We're In The Age Of Grace

We are not in the tribulation period at this point. We are still in the age of grace and the genuine believers will be raptured and taken out—those that are truly saved—before this seven years of tribulation ever comes. When that comes, there will be ten, apparently, and not 25. There will be a union of these ten powers and these ten kings.

Revelation 17:4

"And the woman was arrayed in purple and scarlet colour, and decked with gold and precious stones and pearls, having a golden cup in her hand full of abominations and filthiness of her fornication:"

To me, this pictures **Rome** very clearly. There is an array of **colors** in the **vestments** of **Rome**, **colors** of pageantry, all different **colors** in their garments. There are a total of 21 **vestments** for the Roman Catholic priests, bishops, and cardinals. There are fourteen regular ones and then seven additional ones.

1. The **amice** is a helm to protect against Satan's assaults. These priests need to do more than to just wear an **amice** to protect. They have been assaulted and they assault others—the young people as we have seen in some instances.

2. The **alb** is white. It signifies the purity of body and soul for which he prays. They ought to get more **albs**, I guess, because there is a lot of impurity in the Roman Catholic priesthood—not all, but certainly many, and they are covering it up.

3. The **cincture** symbolizes purity in thoughts and actions. It binds the **alb** and spiritually binds the concupiscence of the priest. They need a lot of **cinctures** as far as I am concerned. I am speaking only of some. I am not speaking of all the priests. I am sure there are some that try to be godly, holy, and right—even though they are spiritually wrong and doctrinally wrong—but as far as being moral, they are not going after young boys, or nuns, or anyone else. I am speaking of those that are morally wrong. The immoral priests need to have their concupiscence bound indeed.

4. The **maniple** is worn on the left arm and is symbolic of good works.

5. The **miretta** is worn as the priest goes up and down the altar.

6. The **papal tiara** has three crowns with certain meanings.

7. The **mitre** has two points, speaking of the Old and New Testaments.

8. The **crozier** is the Latin cross.

9. The **humeral veil** is worn by the priests.

10. The **stole** is also worn by the priests.

11. The **chasuble** is the proper liturgical color.

12. The **surplice** is ordinarily a white garment.

13. **The cassock** is usually black and symbolizes death. The priest is supposed to be dead to the world, and dead to sin. The pope's **cassock** is white, the bishop's is violet and the cardinal's is red. Here is the purple and scarlet mentioned in Revelation 17:4.
14. **The cape** is worn by the priest.
15. **The archbishop's pallium** is made of white wool.
16. **The bishop's glove** is silk.
17. **The bishop's pallium** is made of white wool.
18. **The bishop's gremiale** is a small cloth with golden lace. Here is the gold on the vestments of a bishop.
19. **The bishop's ring**
20. **The cardinal's hat** is scarlet in color.
21. **The pectoral cross** is usually made of precious metal. Here are the precious stones.

Rome Will Be In Full Blossom

I do not know whether it is the priests' garments that are mentioned in Revelation 17:4. All I know is, this woman who is an apostate woman—whom I believe is Rome and all of her minions—is in full blossom during the tribulation period after the true church is gone. She is arrayed with all these different colors, purple and scarlet, gold and precious stones and pearls, having a golden cup full of abominations and filthiness. I do not know the exact worth of the church of Rome, but I am told its wealth is into the millions and billions of dollars. Where did she get that wealth? Well, people give her wealth. When you have somebody trying to get out of purgatory, for example, you have to pay money to get your loved one out of purgatory. Many millions of dollars are paid into the church of Rome.

Revelation 17:5

"And upon her forehead *was* a name written, MYSTERY, BABYLON THE GREAT, THE MOTHER OF HARLOTS AND ABOMINATIONS OF THE EARTH."

Here again it is a **woman, the religious system**. She is not alone. That is why I say I believe that this final woman will be the church of **Rome** with all the other minions together with her. The Protestant apostates will join them. The Jews will join them. The false religions of Hindus, Muslims, and Taoists will join **Rome**. I think she is the mother of harlots. She is the one that organizes. She is the one that has the money. She is the one that has the organization worldwide.

Background Of Babylon

Babylon literally is a place or territory. That was where Abraham came from, Ur of the Chaldees. That is where God took the southern two tribes of Israel into captivity for 70 years. Babylon can be literal Babylon, but also allegorical Babylon. Rome is the most corrupt seat of idolatry, the enemy of true Christianity. That is what is in our reference books as to symbolism and allegory. Rome is called here, *the mother of harlots and abominations of the earth.* Will she gain ground after the rapture of the true believers, the genuinely saved ones? I believe she will. Will she gain money? I believe she will. Will she gain power? I believe she will.

The fact of the matter is, **Rome** has welcomed Protestant denominations within her grasp. "Come and join us!" This is ecumenical—a one worldwide outfit. Some denominations are entering. They are coming into the tentacles of **Rome**. What if some are even Bible believing? **Rome** does not care. "Come in anyway. It will be all right. Everything is fine." Come on in, the water is fine! One big one-world religion!

Revelation 17:6

"And I saw the woman drunken with the blood of the saints, and with the blood of the martyrs of Jesus: and when I saw her, I wondered with great admiration."

Here again is the woman. I believe it is the **Roman** Catholic system. Brother David Cloud has written an excellent article on the Catholic commission and how they perverted the **martyr** statistics. If this woman is **Rome** and her minions, they will be active, especially in the seven-year tribulation, after the genuine believers are gone. She has **killed** saints—not **Roman** Catholic saints, but genuine believers, truly saved people. There is a commission of new martyrs of the Vatican Jubilee. They came out in May 2000 with some statistics. Brother Cloud feels from his analysis, and other documents, that these lists are inaccurate.

Rome Killed Over 50,000,000

For example, it has been estimated by careful and reputed historians about the Catholic Inquisition that more than 50 million people were slaughtered for the crime of "heresy." The Catholic Inquisition was against non-Catholic genuine believers. If we talk about the blood of the martyrs of the Lord Jesus Christ, that is a lot of people. That was the Roman Catholic Inquisition. What was their crime? They did not believe in Rome. They believed in the Lord Jesus Christ as the only way to God the Father in Heaven. We do not need Mary. We do not need the saints. We do not need extreme unction. We do not need any of the Catholic system. We do not need the Mass.

For that crime of "heresy," 50 million met with **death** by **Roman** persecutors between 606 and 1850 A.D. In 1,200 years, 50 million people died in the Catholic Inquisition. This is the number cited by John Dowling in *The History of Romanism*. It is a large volume. In Clarke's Martyrology (that is a big word that means, *the study of martyrs*), he counts the number of Waldensian martyrs.

The Fate Of The Waldensians

The Waldensians were Bible-believing Christians that loved the Lord Jesus Christ and served Him faithfully down through their history. During the first half of the thirteenth century (that would be from 1200 to 1250 A.D.), in France alone, two million Waldensians were visited and were killed. From 1160 to 1560 A.D., the Waldensians that dwelled in the Italian Alps were visited with 36 different fierce persecutions that spared neither sex nor age. This comes from Thomas Armitage in *The History of the Baptists*.

Rome Killed Millions More

The blood of the martyrs is on Rome's hands. National authentic testimony from 1540 to 1570 A.D. proves that nearly one million Protestants were publicly put to death in various European countries. This is in addition to all those who were privately destroyed, of whom no human record exists. The Catholic historian, Vergerius, admits gleefully that during the pontification of Pope Paul IV (1555-1559 A.D.), the Inquisition alone—by tortures, starvation, or the fire—murdered more than 150,000 Protestants.

Did Rome kill those that disagreed? Yes, they did. Did they kill just a few? No, they did not. They **killed** many. They killed **multiplied millions** throughout their history. Is Revelation 17:6 a picture possibly of the **Roman** Catholic system, where John says, *"I saw the woman drunken with the blood of the saints, and with the blood of the martyrs of Jesus?"* I believe it is. I believe it pictures the **Roman** Catholic system. They have **blood** on their hands.

Calvin Also Killed People

If there are Protestants that kill people, I am against that, too. If it is Calvin in Geneva that killed Servetus and nailed him to the stake because he did not turn to be a Calvinist, that is wrong. There were at least a few instances in Geneva, not millions like in Rome. We have a serious situation, a serious problem.

Is it possible to be **killed** in foreign countries such as Argentina and other places where you do not knuckle under to the **Roman** Catholics? Yes, we still have reports of that in foreign countries, in Latin America, where Protestants are being slaughtered. They are being **killed**. There is not religious liberty and freedom as we have in our country here.

Revelation 17:7

"And the angel said unto me, Wherefore didst thou marvel? I will tell thee the mystery of the woman, and of the beast that carrieth her, which hath the seven heads and ten horns."

Here is the **woman** again. We believe it is **Rome** and her minions, the mother of harlots. The **beast** that carries her is the political system. The **woman** is riding that **beast**. We will see in Revelation 17:9 that the **seven heads** are seven mountains.

- **Daniel 7:24**
  "And the **ten horns** out of this kingdom *are* **ten kings** *that* shall arise: and another shall rise after them; and he shall be diverse from the first, and he shall subdue three kings."

The **horns** are **kings.** That is why it is said that, in the last days in the tribulation time, there will be a ten-nation united kingdom.

- **Revelation 12:3**
  "And there appeared another wonder in heaven; and behold a great red dragon, having **seven heads** and **ten horns**, and seven crowns upon his heads."

Again, there are **seven heads** and **ten horns**, heads being kingdoms and kings.

- **Revelation 13:1**
  "And I stood upon the sand of the sea, and saw a **beast** rise up out of the sea, having **seven heads** and **ten horns**, and upon his horns **ten crowns**, and upon his heads the name of blasphemy."

Rome Riding The Beast

He marvelled because of the beast that carried her. David Hunt has written a book called *A Woman Rides the Beast*. This is the picture of Rome riding the beast, which is the political power. Is it true that the Vatican of Rome has sway over political powers? Yes, it is true. They can push. They say this, they can say that. They can take away their blessing of political powers all over the world. It is going to get increasingly worse during the seven-year period of tribulation. They will control and they will be in charge. They will ride until the beast gets tired of it, as we will see later in the book of Revelation, and throws that woman off and kills her and her children.

Revelation 17:8

"The beast that thou sawest was, and is not; and shall ascend out of the bottomless pit, and go into perdition: and they that dwell on the earth shall wonder, whose names were not written in the book of life from the foundation of the world, when they behold the beast that was, and is not, and yet is."

The Beast's Fake Resurrection

Here John is told that the beast was and is not. Here is a beast that lives. He was, is not, and now he is. The devilish powers of the evil spiritual trinity (Satan, the false prophet,

> and the antichrist) will cause a resurrection similar to the Lord Jesus Christ—a miracle they will work in this time. That is what this verse is talking about.

Revelation 13:3
"And I saw one of his heads as it were **wounded to death**; and his deadly wound was healed: and all the world wondered after the beast."

Something *wounded to death* means it dies. Here is healing by the false miracle of **resurrection** of a Satanic person, bringing him back to life.

- ### Revelation 13:15
  "And he had power to give life unto the image of the **beast**, that the image of the **beast** should both speak, and cause that as many as would not worship the image of the **beast** should be killed."

Satan will bring life to the image and his head being wounded will become alive again. He is **resurrected** and this is a false miracle. Just as the Lord Jesus Christ's miracle of rising bodily from the grave was to prove that He was Deity, this is the false proof and a false miracle.

Is your name in the **book of life**? I trust that it is, if you have genuinely trusted the Lord Jesus Christ as your Saviour.

- ### Philippians 4:3
  "And I intreat thee also, true yokefellow, help those women which laboured with me in the gospel, with Clement also, and *with* other my fellowlabourers, whose names *are* in the **book of life**."

When we genuinely trust the Lord Jesus Christ as Saviour, our names are written in the **book of life**.

- ### Revelation 3:5
  "He that overcometh, the same shall be clothed in white raiment; and I will not blot out his name out of the **book of life**, but I will confess his name before my Father, and before his angels."

Those that are genuinely trusting the Lord Jesus Christ as Saviour and Redeemer will not be blotted out. They are in the **book of life**.

- ### Revelation 13:8
  "And all that dwell upon the earth shall worship him, whose names are not written in the **book of life** of the Lamb slain from the foundation of the world."

As far as God is concerned, the Lamb is *slain from the foundation of the world.* He came into the world. Thirty-three years after the Lord Jesus

Christ's miraculous virgin birth, He was slain. Those that are not genuinely saved, that are not true Christians, will worship the beast.

- **Revelation 20:12**
  "And I saw the dead, small and great, stand before God; and the books were opened: and another book was opened, which is *the book* of life: and the dead were judged out of those things which were written in the books, according to their works."

This is the Great White Throne Judgment.

- **Revelation 20:15**
  "And whosoever was not found written in the **book of life** was cast into the lake of fire."

Again I ask, is your name in the **book of life**? It can be by true faith in the Lord Jesus Christ, genuinely trusting in Him as Redeemer. Realizing that you are a lost sinner, and understanding that you are to hate that sin, and genuinely coming to Him, your name can be written there.

- **Revelation 21:27**
  "And there shall in no wise enter into it any thing that defileth, neither *whatsoever* worketh abomination, or *maketh* a lie: but they which are written in the Lamb's **book of life**."

Nobody can enter Heaven but only those who are written in the Lamb's book of life who are genuinely saved.

- **Revelation 22:19**
  "And if any man shall take away from the words of the book of this prophecy, God shall take away his part out of the **book of life**, and out of the holy city, and *from* the things which are written in this book."

Warning To Bible Perverters

Here is a verse for Bible and translation perverters. In these new versions, they are adding, subtracting, and changing the Hebrew, Aramaic, and Greek Words. If that is the case, *God shall take away his part out of the book of life.*" We believe the *part*—not his name—is the reward. There is no longer a reward. If these are genuine believers that are making these bad versions, taking away the words out of the book of prophecy of Revelation or any part of the Scriptures, I believe their reward will be gone. There are some genuine believers who are doing this. Shame on them! This is a serious thing, indeed.

Revelation 17:9

"And here *is* the mind which hath wisdom. The seven heads are seven mountains, on which the woman sitteth."

The Seven Mountains Of Rome

Again, here are the seven mountains of Rome. That is a fact of history. Does Philadelphia have seven mountains? No. Does Collingswood have seven mountains? Name all the different places of the world. I am not a geographer and I am not acquainted with all the different places. I have never been to all the places of the world. I would venture to say that there is no other place but Rome that has seven hills, or seven mountains altogether—not three, or four, or six, but seven.

There is a fanciful tale about how those **seven mountains** got there. It is not true, but tradition says that **Rome** was founded in 753 B.C. by Romulus and Remus. The hills looking over the Tiber River are the seven hills. Then they say the **seven hills** mean they worship seven planets, maybe one from each of the **hills**. They worship the sun, the moon, Mercury, Venus, Mars, Jupiter, and Saturn. They named the hills Palatine, Aventine, Capitoline, Quirinal, Viminal, Esquiline and Caelian. Between these **hills** were marshy valleys.

There is an article on the Internet on the seven hills of **Rome**. You can see what they are. I saw a story of Romulus and Remus. You do not have to believe that. That is a fanciful thing. They list what Palantine hill is, a four-sided plateau, and what is on there. They even have a picture of **Rome** and the seven hills in the article and exactly where the seven hills are. It talks about how high one hill is over another. It talks about the details.

The Capitoline hill is of **Roman** authority—*caput mundi*, the head of the world. This system is going to be the head of the world, the world ruler of the religious sphere. All these different hills are mentioned.

I believe that is why most of the major Bible expositors have made the church of **Rome** as the one who is this **woman** in this many-colored attire. This **woman** that is called the **great whore** and the **mother of harlots** and is filled with the **abominations** of the world around her, is because of these **seven hills** of Rome.

The Battle On Our Hands

We have a battle on our hands. As a church, or as Christian people who love the Lord Jesus Christ and follow His Words, we not only have the battle with liberals, modernists, unbelievers, homosexuals, and various others trying to dictate our course of action and life, but we also have a battle with the church of Rome. The church of Rome influences governments. It says where churches can be built. Secular buildings require building permits. This is true of churches as well. Many times a permit is denied. You do not know why it is denied. Nobody says, "I am a Roman Catholic" on the commission, but many times there is an influence. They do not want Bible-believing fundamental churches.

Our pastors who have tried to start churches in certain localities have been affected adversely by the church of **Rome**. It is a powerful church. We have a Roman Catholic church right down the street.

Rome Stronger After The Rapture

After the rapture of the true church, Rome will be stronger than ever before, and millions will probably be hurt. When she rides that beast, the political beast, she will be in charge. She can say to that political beast and ruler, "Get this one. Kill that one. Take away these true believers. Wipe it out. Burn this one down." She will be all powerful. This is going to be a serious situation. I am glad I will be out of here. I will be in Heaven with the Lord Jesus Christ before any part of this terrible seven-year period of tribulation begins.

Revelation 17:10

"And there are seven kings: five are fallen, and one is, *and* the other is not yet come; and when he cometh, he must continue a short space."

I do not know who the **seven kings** are. I talked about **ten kings** in the earlier verses of Revelation 17. I believe that the seven hills that the **woman**—the **whore** or religious **prostitute**—sits on, are the **seven hills** of **Rome**. It is a mystery in this end-time during the tribulation period. This is all talking about when the genuine believers, the saved ones, are caught up to be with the Lord Jesus Christ, which is far better. We will not be on this earth during the seven-year period of tribulation,

Daniel's 70th week. Those nations that will be here during the tribulation will know who the seven kings are and who the antichrist is.

John, A Prisoner Of Rome

The apostle John, you will remember, was a prisoner of Rome. He was out on the isle of Patmos. To have John write about Rome and to mention that this was Rome, might have caused him to be killed. For this reason, he writes in figures and different symbols. We will not know about this for sure until the time comes.

Revelation 17:11

"And the beast that was, and is not, even he is the eighth, and is of the seven, and goeth into perdition."

Two Beasts In Revelation

This is a ruler. Remember there were two beasts in Revelation 13. There is the beast out of the sea that is the political beast. The beast out of the earth is the religious beast, the false prophet. Whoever these seven kings are, and wherever they are, this eighth one—the antichrist—will come from that source.

- Revelation 13:12
  "And he exerciseth all the power of the first **beast** before him, and causeth the earth and them which dwell therein to worship the first **beast**, whose deadly wound was healed."

The beast was resurrected. It is a picture like the Lord Jesus Christ was resurrected from the dead. This is a phony, fake antichrist with the miracle of resurrection so that people would believe on him and accept him.

- Revelation 13:15
  "And he had power to give life unto the image of the **beast**, that the image of the **beast** should both speak, and cause that as many as would not worship the image of the **beast** should be killed."

Here is the image of the **beast**.

- Revelation 17:8

"The **beast** that thou sawest was, and is not; and shall ascend out of the bottomless pit, and go into perdition: and they that dwell on the earth shall wonder, whose names were not written in the **book of life** from the foundation of the world, when they behold the **beast** that was, and is not, and yet is."

The Political Beast's Judgment

This is speaking of the resurrection of this political beast of power. Notice, it says he goes *into perdition*. That is a statement as to where this political ruler is headed. He is antichrist. He is against the Lord Jesus Christ. "Anti" means *against,* but it also means, *in place of* or *instead of.* Antichrist is in place of Christ and he goes into perdition. That is the status of where he is going to be headed. That word perdition is APOLEIA. It has many different meanings. One of them is, *the destruction which consists of eternal misery and Hell.* This is where this beast is headed—for Hell.

- John 17:12

"While I was with them in the world, I kept them in thy name: those that thou gavest me I have kept, and none of them is lost, but **the son of perdition;** that the scripture might be fulfilled."

This is the High Priestly prayer of the Son to the Father. The *son of perdition* is Judas Iscariot. Judas was bound for **Hell.** Why did the Lord Jesus Christ pick him? In order to keep us, I believe, on our toes that people that seem like they are saved and seem like they are Christians are not necessarily genuine Christians.

- Matthew 7:22-23

"Many will say to me in that day, Lord, Lord, have we not prophesied in thy name? and in thy name have cast out devils? and in thy name done many wonderful works? And then will I profess unto them, I never knew you: depart from me, ye that work iniquity."

Why Was Judas Picked?

We have to be careful. I think the Lord picked Judas, *the son of perdition,* so that we would be on our toes and not claim that everybody that looks like a Christian is a genuine Christian. As I have said many times before, just because you are in the garage does not make you a car. Am I right? Just because you are in church does not make you a genuine Christian either.

- **2 Thessalonians 2:3**
  "Let no man deceive you by any means: for *that day shall not come*, except there come a falling away first, and that man of sin be revealed, the **son of perdition;**"

This *man of sin* is called *the son of perdition*. He is on his way to **Hell**, this antichrist.

- **1 Timothy 6:9**
  "But they that will be rich fall into temptation and a snare, and *into* many foolish and hurtful lusts, which drown men in destruction and **perdition.**"

All they care about is riches. It does not mean that all rich men are going to **Hell**, but those that *will be rich*—that is all that they want. They have no time for God, just for making wealth. Many times they are drowned in **perdition.**

- **Hebrews 10:39**
  "But we are not of them who draw back unto **perdition**; but of them that believe to the saving of the soul."

We ought to flee **Hell**. We should not want anything to do with it.

- **2 Peter 3:7**
  "But the heavens and the earth, which are now, by the same word are kept in store, reserved unto fire against the day of judgment and **perdition** of ungodly men."

The World Is Headed For Hell

The whole earth is headed for perdition—not for a flood any more, like in Noah's day—but by fire. Those that are lost will go into perdition. God is preparing a place in Hell for two kinds of people: the Devil and his angels. There is a third kind of a person that will go there—those that reject the Lord Jesus Christ's way out of Hell. It is not prepared for them, but they will go to Hell if they do not genuinely trust in Him.

- **Revelation 17:8**
  "The beast that thou sawest was, and is not; and shall ascend out of the bottomless pit, and go into **perdition**: and they that dwell on the earth shall wonder, whose names were not written in the book of life from the foundation of the world, when they behold the beast that was, and is not, and yet is."

There are verses that talk about **Hell**. That is where this **beast** is going to be. <u>Hell is a real place.</u> This **beast** will not escape the **perdition**.

- **Matthew 23:33**
  "*Ye* serpents, *ye* generation of vipers, how can ye escape the damnation of **Hell**?"

<u>The Lord Jesus Christ speaks of **Hell**.</u> Many people think, "Well, He is a loving Saviour. He would not talk about **Hell**." Would He not? He is the One Who spoke about **Hell** more than any other Person in the Scriptures. Here He is talking about the Pharisees. The Lord Jesus Christ really calls them names. How would you like to be called a viper or a serpent? These hypocrites, these Pharisees, were not genuine.

- **2 Peter 2:4**
  "For if God spared not the angels that sinned, but cast *them* down to **Hell**, and delivered *them* into chains of darkness, to be reserved unto judgment;"

<u>There were many angels that fell.</u> <u>Satan was one of them.</u> He was the leader, Lucifer, that fell. If God cast these angels down to **Hell**, how shall those escape who are rejecting the Lord Jesus Christ today? That is the issue of 2 Peter 2:4.

- **Revelation 1:18**
  "*I am* he that liveth, and was dead; and, behold, I am alive for evermore, Amen; and have the keys of **Hell** and of death."

<u>Who has the keys of Hell and death?</u> Who sends them to **Hell** or keeps them out of **Hell**? The Lord Jesus Christ is the One with the keys. This also speaks of the bodily resurrection of our Saviour. He is the only One that can send somebody to **Hell**.

- **John 14:6**
  "Jesus saith unto him, I am the way, the truth, and the life: no man cometh unto the Father, but by me."

The Lord Jesus Christ has the keys of **Hell** and death.

- **Revelation 20:13-14**
  "And the sea gave up the dead which were in it; and death and Hell delivered up the dead which were in them: and they were judged every man according to their works. And death and **Hell** were cast into the lake of fire. This is the second death."

<u>This is at the Great White Throne judgment.</u> This is a serious business. The political beast goes into **Hell**, into **perdition**.

Revelation 17:12

**"And the ten horns which thou sawest are ten kings,
which have received no kingdom as yet; but receive power
as kings one hour with the beast."**

Who Are The Ten Kings?

We talked about the ten kings when Pastor Kevin Kline
was at our church. When we chatted back and forth he said,
"You know, there are some that believe that these are regions
of the world, not necessarily the ten European nations." I
looked it up some more. Yes, there are some who believe that
it is the regionalization of the world. These ten kings at the
tribulation time are going to be regionalized. They are the ten
horns, these ten leaders. It is part of the United Nations, the
Beast System. <u>That is what one article on the Internet talks
about—the Beast System.</u>

As for the United Nations, they are antichrist. You can not have
prayer at any of the doings of the United Nations. There are all kinds of
Communist nations that are in there. They have no regard for the Lord
Jesus Christ in any way. This article says that the United Nations will
divide the world into ten regions. The man that wrote the article believes
that the ten regions are the ten kings during the time of the tribulation.
There is a map of the ten horns drawn up to see what it is going be in the
end-time and who is going to rule over what part of the world. This is all
planned.

These fellows have done this and it could be these are the ten horns.
**Though these regions on the map are not completely clear, it
seems like these are the following regions listed on this map:**
Region #1–the United States, Canada and Mexico.
Region #2–Europe.
Region #3–Japan
Region #4–South Africa
Region #5–Russia
Region #6–South America
Region #7–Northern Africa
Region #8–Central Africa
Region #9–India
Region #10–China
There are the ten horns. They have it all ready and divided up.

The Ten Kings Take Power

During the tribulation (it has not come yet—the seven years have not begun), when the true Church is raptured and taken up to Heaven, that is when it begins. Only then will these ten kings take the power, but you see they have this thing already set up. According to the article, right or wrong, let me just give you, at least from one man's point of view, what is going to happen and who got this thing up. The article maintains it is the New World Order that has concocted these ten divisions. That is a phrase that presidents have used. The former presidents used it. All over the world it has been used.

The Communist leaders have used it. They are trying to get away from any independence and merge us into one world. The Bilderbergers, for instance, are part of that organization, as well as the Council on Foreign Relations, the Trilateralists, and all these money-making people. The New World Order is basically made up of the Rothschild banking and political system. These are powerful financial people that are leading this thing.

The Communist control of Russia was set up by these money-makers. The control of the Nazis in Germany was all set up by these same people. Henry Ford and other financiers all over the world supported this. The Nazi movement and the Communist movement were founded by the Rothschilds' wealth.

These are some things that are strange to our ears, but these are facts that some have shown to be true. The great financial powers in Europe, the empires of the Rothschilds and the Rockefellers are competitors for this. The Rockefellers include the Council on Foreign Relations (which, by the way, most presidents have been affiliated with for many years in our country), the Trilateral Commission, and Zionism. These are under this overall umbrella.

The Bilderbergers, and, in fact, the Mafia, are a part of the financial world. Can you imagine the crooks that are all a part of this heavy financial institutional set-up that wants control? The European community wants large conglomerates of nations and to break down independence so that boundaries are diminished.

The United Nations Will Rule

The United Nations is for the rule of the whole world. They want to break down the individual nations that are under them. They do not want the United States to be under our Constitution. They do not want us to have freedom and power that we have always had. They want to break us down so we have to say, "Yes" to the big ruler, the United Nations, that is running things.

Russians and eastern Europe are part of this, encompassing all of Asia, to establish these **ten regions.** The United States is certainly a part of it. Instead of having 50 states in the United States, it would be like having **ten regions,** so the individual states would not have any more power. We are the United States of America and we should have states' power, but this is what they would like to take us to.

Funding The United Nations

Who funds and gives the money to this world organization, the New World Order? The troops will be supplied from other countries. According to this article, the funding will come from the United States. We have the billions and billions. We can do anything with it, so that is where the money will come from, according to this article. It means the United States will fund the United Nations in its various global projects of trying to bring resistant nations under the control of the U.N.

There are some nations that will resist this. They will say, "Wait a minute! We are our own people. We elect our own rulers. We are not going to be brought under domination." This is where they have to fund the power to do this. Europe itself will be organized slowly and gradually under Rothschild organizations and various leaders of countries that are working with the Rothschilds energy. Many of the countries of Europe right now are strengthening the United Nations, which is a central world-governing body. That is what they are trying to do now.

This article mentions there are thirteen families—a group of super-wealthy individuals and groups—involved in this world conquest. Rothschilds are the most notable. The European Union is mentioned. Originally, Washington, D.C. was not a part of the United States. It was a separate ten square miles. Now it almost rules the whole country.

Skull And Bones Society

In 1933, Adolph Hitler spoke of the New World Order. Did you know that? It is not just our present people, but Adolph Hitler. He tried to do it by power, force, and by killing and slaughter, instead of gradualism. He tried his best. By the way, the Skull and Bones Society, which George Bush and John Kerry are a part of, was an offshoot of the Skull and Bones Society in Nazi Germany. Did you know that? They are all connected. It is interesting.

The New World Order will be worse than Hitler. What could be worse than Hitler? This is all part of the **ten nation** confederation that will be set up after the genuine believers are raptured to Heaven. How could it be worse? Hitler's effort to promote the world order by force, invading country after country and killing the people, will be much worse when the tribulation will take place because they have much more deadly weapons. They have all kinds of things that they can use. With tanks, guns, planes, smart bombs, and everything else, it will be much, much worse. The mass control of mass murder will be much worse than Hitler's time and that was bad enough.

It is quite likely that these political controls will begin to become imprisonment controls. We talked about our Attorney General making room for prisons for those that are of some type of beliefs. Imprisonment controls will be keeping entities under greater and greater **control** for the purpose of certain individuals.

The Rothschilds' estate is in England, but they have an independent colony. They are a sovereign territory. The Rothschilds have millions and billions—multi-billionaires—and they have a sovereign territory in Great Britain. They are not a part of the Great Britain laws. The English have no control over them, just as Washington, D.C. was originally supposed to be separate and independent. It is a foreign land right in England without any control from England at all. This particular article believes that the Rothschild millions and billions will be the head or the horn of this beast that will rule—the antichrist. Well, it could be or it could not be, but the Rothschild purpose, is control, first with them and twelve other super-wealthy families associated and riding the coattails of the Rothschilds. There are thirteen major families. There are approximately 300 families that are powerful families ruling the world, but thirteen are major families made up of the international **banking** community.

- 1 Timothy 6:10
  "For the **love of money** is the root of all evil: which while some coveted after, they have erred from the faith, and pierced themselves through with many sorrows."

Not **money,** but *the love of money* is the root of all evil. These super-wealthy, I mean multi-billionaires, are all over the world—three hundred families and thirteen families are the largest of those.

Here are some of the organizations that they control:

1. **International Banking Community** (You wonder why your rates go up or down?)
2. **The Bilderbergers**
3. **The Council on Foreign Relations**
4. **Secret cults**
5. **Masonry**
6. **The Tong Organization** (I do not know what that is.)
7. **The Mafia**

All of these are suborders of the International Banking Community and these families. I do not know whether this is true or false. I just simply give it to you as somebody's idea as to what the **ten regions** are. I know this, they have divided the whole world into **ten sections.** I have seen that in other sources. Why ten? Revelation 17:12 talks about the **ten horns, which are ten kings.** It seems to me it is possible that this would be a fulfillment at the end-time when this will take place. They do not have the power yet, but that is what they are aiming for. That is their goal.

Revelation 17:13

"These have one mind, and shall give their power and strength unto the beast."

Satan Will Give Nations One Mind

All of these ten rulers or kings will be united. You know and I know that nations are not united today. There are all kinds of divisions. They fight. They war. They carry on. They debate. When the antichrist rules, when this power of Satan is upon this earth—after the true Church is gone, and the tribulation period takes place—they will have one mind. The antichrist will just transform the ten kings into one mind. I do not understand it, but they will have one mind. Then they will give their power and strength unto the beast. The ten nations have one mind, then they turn that one mind over to one ruler. There is the antichrist, the political ruler that one day will rule this whole world after the true Church is gone.

Is the **power** to Satan, or is the **power** to the Lord Jesus Christ? That is the battle. They have one mind and give the **power** to the Satanic beast. We should have one mind for the Lord Jesus Christ our Saviour.

- **Romans 15:6**
  "That ye may with **one mind** *and* one mouth glorify God, even the Father of our Lord Jesus Christ."

Our Church Should Be Of One Mind

That is what we should be in our church and our outreach, our missions—one mind. We should be single-minded to glorify the Lord Jesus Christ, not one mind to give our strength to the beast and the Devil.

- **2 Corinthians 13:11**
  "Finally, brethren, farewell. Be perfect, be of good comfort, be of **one mind**, live in peace; and the God of love and peace shall be with you."

That does not mean all of us agree on every detail of our lives. You may have a red carpet, I may have a blue carpet. You may have a Volkswagen, I may have a Buick or a Ford. Our doctrinal mentality should be unity. The belief in the Bible as God's Words and our doctrines of the faith should be of **one mind**. The Corinthian church was divided all kinds of ways.

- **1 Corinthians 1:12**
  "Now this I say, that every one of you saith, I am of Paul; and I of Apollos; and I of Cephas; and I of Christ."

There were all different divisions. They were to be of **one mind**.

- **Philippians 1:27**
  "Only let your conversation be as it becometh the gospel of Christ: that whether I come and see you, or else be absent, I may hear of your affairs, that ye stand fast in **one spirit**, with **one mind** striving together for the faith of the gospel;"

We should not be striving against each other and battling, as many churches do, but striving together with **one mind** in the Lord Jesus Christ *for the faith of the gospel.* That is the thing that should unify every Bible-believing church—the faith of the gospel, **one mind**.

- **Philippians 2:2**
  "Fulfil ye my joy, that ye be likeminded, having the same love, *being* of one accord, of **one mind**."

These nations give their **one mind** to the Devil's beast, the antichrist. God wants us to give our minds to the Lord Jesus Christ. <u>This is important for churches, instead of fighting, carrying on, splitting, going away in a huff, and moving around all over the place.</u>

- **1 Peter 3:8**
  "Finally, *be ye* all of **one mind**, having compassion one of another, love as brethren, *be* pitiful, *be* courteous:"

<u>If we have **one mind**, we are going to love each other as brethren</u>—those that love the Lord Jesus Christ. Do not be brazen and ugly. This is **one mind** for genuine believers.

Satan has some **power**, as it says in Revelation 17:13. <u>I believe these kings will be under Satan's **power**.</u> They will not be genuinely saved rulers. They will be unsaved, I believe. Let us look at Satan's **power**, similar to this verse.

- **Luke 22:53**
  "When I was daily with you in the temple, ye stretched forth no hands against me: but this is your hour, and the **power** of darkness."

The Lord Jesus Christ was in the Garden of Gethsemane and all these people were coming out with staves to take Him and crucify Him. Judas, you will remember, came up to Him and kissed Him.

- **Luke 22:48**
  "But Jesus said unto him, Judas, betrayest thou the Son of man with a kiss?"

The Power Of Present Darkness

Darkness has power in this world and the power of darkness is what led the Lord Jesus Christ to be crucified. Satan's power was there with these people.

- **Acts 26:18**
  "To open their eyes, *and* to turn *them* from darkness to light, and *from* the **power** of Satan unto God, that they may receive forgiveness of sins, and inheritance among them which are sanctified by faith that is in me."

When Paul was genuinely saved, he gave his testimony. That was Paul's mission when he was genuinely saved by the Lord Jesus Christ. He was turned around on the road to Damascus. <u>The Lord Jesus Christ can deliver us from the **power** of Satan.</u>

- **Ephesians 2:2**
  "Wherein in time past ye walked according to the course of this world, according to the prince of the **power** of the air, the spirit that now worketh in the children of disobedience:"

Now, if you are genuinely saved, you are no longer under that **power**. Satan has **power**. These kings surrendered their **power** to the beast, the antichrist.

- **2 Thessalonians 2:9**
  "*Even him*, whose coming is after the working of Satan with all **power** and signs and lying wonders,"

During this tribulation period, the antichrist and the false prophet will have lying wonders—miracles that are not true miracles, but they will be lying wonders. They will look like miracles. They will actually seem like miracles, but they will be lying. Satan has **power**.

Tribulation Christians–What To Do?

What should genuine believers do? These Satanically-motivated kings—these ten kings with one mind—give their power and strength to the beast, the antichrist in the tribulation period. What should be our desire if we are genuinely saved and born-again Christians? Who should we give our power to and where is the source of our power? It is in the Lord Jesus Christ.

- **Matthew 6:13**
  "And lead us not into temptation, but deliver us from evil: For thine is the kingdom, and the **power**, and the glory, for ever. Amen."

This is called the Lord's Prayer. I call it the Disciples' Prayer. The **power** is God's **power**, not ours.

- **Matthew 9:6**
  "But that ye may know that the Son of man hath **power** on earth to forgive sins, (then saith he to the sick of the palsy,) Arise, take up thy bed, and go unto thine house."

The Lord Jesus Christ has the **power** to forgive sins.

- **Matthew 28:18**
  "And Jesus came and spake unto them, saying, All **power** is given unto me in heaven and in earth."

He has the **power, not Satan.**

- **Acts 1:8**
  "But ye shall receive **power**, after that the Holy Ghost is come upon you: and ye shall be witnesses unto me both in Jerusalem, and in all Judaea, and in Samaria, and unto the uttermost part of the earth."

God promised that genuine believers would receive **power**. The **power** of God would help the genuine believers to witness.

- **Romans 1:16**
  "For I am not ashamed of the gospel of Christ: for it is the **power** of God unto salvation to every one that believeth; to the Jew first, and also to the Greek."

God's **power** is what we should be strong in.

- **1 Corinthians 1:18**
  "For the preaching of the cross is to them that perish foolishness; but unto us which are saved it is the **power** of God."

They do not want anything to do with it.

- **1 Corinthians 1:24**
  "But unto them which are called, both Jews and Greeks, Christ the **power** of God, and the wisdom of God."

The Lord Jesus Christ is the **power** of God. He is the One Who can give us **power**.

- **2 Corinthians 12:9**
  "And he said unto me, My grace is sufficient for thee: for my strength is made perfect in weakness. Most gladly therefore will I rather glory in my infirmities, that the **power** of Christ may rest upon me."

When Paul had a thorn in the flesh, he asked the Lord to take it away three times and three times the Lord said, "No." The **power** of Christ is the source of **power**—not in Satan's **power**—the **power** of the Lord Jesus Christ.

- **Ephesians 3:20**
  "Now unto him that is able to do exceeding abundantly above all that we ask or think, according to the **power** that worketh in us,"

If we are genuinely saved, the Holy Spirit of God indwells us. We have His **power**. Since we have His **power**, we can use that **power** and not rely upon our sinful flesh.

- **Ephesians 6:10**
  "Finally, my brethren, be strong in the Lord, and in the **power** of his might."

Spiritual power is the **power** of His might.

- **Colossians 1:11**
  "Strengthened with all might, according to his glorious **power**, unto all patience and longsuffering with joyfulness;"

It is God's **power** that strengthens us.

- **Revelation 4:11**
  "Thou art worthy, O Lord, to receive glory and honour and **power**: for thou hast created all things, and for thy pleasure they are and were created."

The Lord Jesus Christ is worthy to receive **power.** He is the One Who has the **power** for us who need it. The Lord Jesus Christ is also our strength.

- **Mark 12:30**
  "And thou shalt love the Lord thy God with all thy heart, and with all thy soul, and with all thy mind, and with all thy **strength**: this *is* the first commandment."

Our **strength** should be to love the Lord, not to join in battle with the Devil and be wrong and evil.

- **Romans 5:6**
  "For when we were yet without **strength**, in due time Christ died for the ungodly."

We do not have **strength** of our own to win the battles. God's grace and His **strength** is made perfect in weakness.

- **Philippians 4:13**
  "I can do all things through Christ which **strengtheneth** me."

Christ The Christian's Strength

Our strength and power must come from the Lord Jesus Christ. The false Greek text does not have *Christ* in this verse. That is why the New International Version takes it out. It takes Christ right out of that verse. The New American Standard, the Revised Standard, and all the new versions have the wrong Greek text. They say, "I can do all things through Him who strengthens me." They do not know Who it is. It could be the "Force." God's power should be uppermost and we should rely upon His power.

As it says in the song, *It Took a Miracle,* my Father is Omnipotent. He has all power. That you can not deny. He is a God of might and miracles. It is written in the sky. The greatest **power** of all is to genuinely save a soul and to trust the Lord Jesus Christ. That salvation and **power** can be yours when you genuinely trust the Lord Jesus Christ as your Saviour.

Revelation 17:14

"These shall make war with the Lamb, and the Lamb shall overcome them: for he is Lord of lords, and King of kings: and they that are with him *are* called, and chosen, and faithful."

These, that is these **ten kings** during the seven-year period of tribulation, probably at the **Battle** of Armageddon, will **make war with the Lamb**. The Lamb is the Lord Jesus Christ.

- **John 1:29**
  "The next day John seeth Jesus coming unto him, and saith, Behold the **Lamb** of God, which taketh away the sin of the world."

Christ Is The Lamb Of God

He is the Lamb. Why do they make war with Him? Why did the Pharisees make war with Him? Why did they crucify Him? Because they hated Him. They will hate the righteousness of the Lamb. They will make war with the Lamb. What will be the result of it? The Lamb shall overcome them because He is Lord of all lords. All these ten kings giving their power and might to the antichrist—the Lord Jesus Christ is Lord of Lords and He is King of kings. This is the victory of the Lamb of God.

- **1 Corinthians 15:57**
  "But thanks *be* to God, which giveth us the **victory** through our Lord Jesus Christ."

Through our Lord Jesus Christ, we have **victory** over sin, death, and Hell.

- **2 Thessalonians 2:8**
  "And then shall that Wicked be revealed, whom the Lord shall consume with the spirit of his mouth, and shall **destroy** with the brightness of his coming:"

The Lord Jesus Christ is going to **destroy** Satan and be the **Victor**.

- **Revelation 15:2**
"And I saw as it were a sea of glass mingled with fire: and them that had gotten the **victory over the beast,** and over his image, and over his mark, *and* over the number of his name, stand on the sea of glass, having the harps of God."

Victory Is In The Lord Jesus Christ

There is victory in the Lord Jesus Christ and the Lamb will prevail. Notice also, in Revelation 17:14, we who are genuinely saved with new bodies will be with the Lamb when He overcomes these ten kings on this earth. Genuinely saved people will be with Him. Notice, we are *called, and chosen, and faithful.* I would like to look at some people who were faithful followers of the Lamb.

- **Matthew 25:21**
"His lord said unto him, Well done, *thou* good and **faithful** servant: thou hast been **faithful** over a few things, I will make thee ruler over many things: enter thou into the joy of thy lord."
May we be **faithful** in our service.
- **Luke 16:10**
"He that is **faithful** in that which is least is **faithful** also in much: and he that is unjust in the least is unjust also in much."
God wants us **faithful.**
- **1 Corinthians 4:2**
"Moreover it is required in stewards, that a man be found **faithful.**"

The Duty Of A Steward

A steward is one who has charge of his master's goods. We were told recently that one of our churches in our area has called a pastor who was unfaithful in money. He stole money from a former church. He did not go to jail because Mom and Dad bailed him out, but now they have called him as their pastor. I asked someone who was very much in the know in that particular local church, "How is that situation coming?" They said, "Oh, everything is all right. He told the church about it and they don't care." Well, I care. You do not put a fox in charge of the chickens unless you are stupid. Right? You do not put a thief in charge of money. God wants us faithful. It is required in stewards. We must be faithful. We pay all our bills by checks and give an accounting of all the funds that come into our local church. Faithfulness is required in stewards, not unfaithfulness.

Here are eight men listed specifically as being **faithful**.

- **1 Corinthians 4:17**
  "For this cause have I sent unto you Timotheus, who is my beloved son, and **faithful** in the Lord, who shall bring you into remembrance of my ways which be in Christ, as I teach every where in every church."

Timothy was **faithful**.

- **Galatians 3:9**
  "So then they which be of faith are blessed with **faithful** Abraham."

God calls Abraham faithful.

- **Ephesians 6:21**
  "But that ye also may know my affairs, *and* how I do, Tychicus, a beloved brother and **faithful** minister in the Lord, shall make known to you all things:"

Tychicus was a **faithful** minister in the Lord.

- **Colossians 1:7**
  "As ye also learned of Epaphras our dear fellowservant, who is for you a **faithful** minister of Christ;"

Epaphras was a **faithful** minister of Christ.

- **Colossians 4:9**
  "With Onesimus, a **faithful** and beloved brother, who is *one* of you. They shall make known unto you all things which *are done* here."

Onesimus was a **faithful** and beloved brother.

- **1 Timothy 1:12**
  "And I thank Christ Jesus our Lord, who hath enabled me, for that he counted me **faithful**, putting me into the ministry;"

Paul was **faithful**.

- **2 Timothy 2:2**
  "And the things that thou hast heard of me among many witnesses, the same commit thou to **faithful** men, who shall be able to teach others also."

This is one of Dan's favorites in his young people's meetings. That is what we seek to do here in our Bible for Today Baptist Church–to commit these things to **faithful** people that they will teach others also.

- **1 Peter 5:12**
"By Silvanus, a **faithful** brother unto you, as I suppose, I have written briefly, exhorting, and testifying that this is the true grace of God wherein ye stand."
Silvanus refers to Silas. He was a **faithful** brother.

- **Revelation 2:13**
"I know thy works, and where thou dwellest, *even* where Satan's seat is: and thou holdest fast my name, and hast not denied my faith, even in those days wherein Antipas *was* my **faithful** martyr, who was slain among you, where Satan dwelleth."
Antipas was the Lord Jesus Christ's **faithful** martyr. Sometimes, **faithfulness** leads us to death. In the case of Antipas, he was **faithful**.

- **Revelation 2:10**
"Fear none of those things which thou shalt suffer: behold, the devil shall cast *some* of you into prison, that ye may be tried; and ye shall have tribulation ten days: be thou **faithful** unto death, and I will give thee a crown of life."
Those that follow the Lamb overcome. Those that are following Him are **faithful,** and chosen, and called.

Revelation 17:15

"And he saith unto me, The waters which thou sawest, where the whore sitteth, are peoples, and multitudes, and nations, and tongues."

The waters in Scripture is apparently a figure of speech, as it mentions here. Remember in Revelation 17:9 we talked about who this **whore** was. We talked about the seven hills. She sits on seven hills. One of the only places that I know anything about where there are seven hills in one town is the **seven hills** of **Rome**. This is not **Roman** Catholicism alone, as we said before. It is not **Rome** alone, but **Rome** and all of her children.

Rome Wants All To Join Her

The Roman Catholic Church wants all people to come in under her wings—all the Protestant unbelievers and anybody who would want to join—the compromisers. She wants the Jews to come in and to worship. She wants the Hindus, the Muslims, and all the world religions. I believe that will be the whore, the religious prostitute. There is great influence in Roman Catholicism all over the world. Kings are crowned because Rome wants the king to be crowned. Rulers are put down because Rome does not want the ruler. There are all kinds of power and billions upon billions of dollars in Rome.

Revelation 17:16

"And the ten horns which thou sawest upon the beast, these shall hate the whore, and shall make her desolate and naked, and shall eat her flesh, and burn her with fire."

Here are these **ten horns** introduced, which are called **ten kings** in Revelation 17:12. They are the ones that gave their power with one mind to this **beast**, this political ruler. They are going to **hate** this religious system. They say, "Long enough that you have been in charge of us! We are not going to be any more under your yoke."

- **Revelation 17:7**
  "And the angel said unto me, Wherefore didst thou marvel? I will tell thee the mystery of the **woman**, and of the beast that carrieth her, which hath the **seven heads** and **ten horns**."

You know and I know that no beast is going to carry you that does not want to carry you. You try to get onto a horse that has never been broken—never had a saddle, never had a rider—you will be off in a matter of seconds, regardless.

This prostitute type of a religious evil person, is riding the beast. She is on top of that beast, in control. The antichrist will throw away all the powers of this Roman Catholic system and all the unbelievers in the religious systems of the world.

After The Church Is Raptured

You will remember when this happens the true Church—the genuine believers, the truly saved ones—will be raptured. They will be in Heaven with the Lord Jesus Christ. We will all be gone. All that is left will be the unsaved, godless people—unsaved Romanists, unsaved Protestants, unsaved Jews, unsaved Hindus, Muslims, and the whole crop. They are the ones that will finally say, "I have had enough!" The rulers—these ten kings in the ten different regions of the world—will say, "Off with her head! Kill her! String her up!" They will burn down all of her churches, as it were.

Revelation 17:17

"For God hath put in their hearts to fulfil his will, and to agree, and give their kingdom unto the beast, until the words of God shall be fulfilled."

The Ten Coming Kings

Here is God putting in the hearts of these ten kings to fulfill His will. Apparently, the Lord Jesus Christ does not go with this religious system that is false. He does not go along with the Roman Catholic hierarchy and all the religions of the world—this whore, as it mentions—that are wrong and evil. His will is to put the religious system, which is pagan, to death.

You may remember the story about when the emperor Constantine allegedly saw a cross in the sky which said something like: "*By this cross you will conquer.*" Constantine misinterpreted this cloud. Some people today might see a sign that reads "*P.C.*" and they might interpret it, "*Preach Christ,*" when it might really mean, "*Plow Corn.*" Constantine interpreted this sign to mean that he was now the new leader of the religious system of that day. **Rome** combined true faith with apostasy and paganism. That is the **Roman** Catholic system to this day.

God always **fulfills His Words**.

- **Isaiah 46:11**
  "Calling a ravenous bird from the east, the man that executeth my counsel from a far country: yea, **I have spoken** *it*, I will also **bring it to pass; I have purposed** *it*, I will also do it."

- **Jeremiah 4:28**
  "For this shall the earth mourn, and the heavens above be black: because **I have spoken** *it*, I have **purposed** *it*, and will not repent, neither will I turn back from it."

What God says, He will fulfill. Reading through the book of Ezekiel, many times God speaks of **fulfilling His Words**.

- **Ezekiel 22:14**
  "Can thine heart endure, or can thine hands be strong, in the days that I shall deal with thee? **I the LORD have spoken** *it*, and **will do** *it*."

- **Ezekiel 24:14**
"I the LORD have spoken *it*: it shall come to pass, and I will do *it*; I will not go back, neither will I spare, neither will I repent; according to thy ways, and according to thy doings, shall they judge thee, saith the Lord GOD."
- **Ezekiel 36:36**
"Then the heathen that are left round about you shall know that I the LORD build the ruined *places, and* plant that that was desolate: **I the LORD have spoken** *it*, and **I will do** *it*."
- **Ezekiel 37:14**
"And shall put my spirit in you, and ye shall live, and I shall place you in your own land: then shall ye know that **I the LORD have spoken** *it*, and **performed** *it*, saith the LORD."

God keeps His Words. We can bank upon it—take it to the bank, as they say. When God's Words are promised, He **will fulfill** that which He has spoken.

Revelation 17:18

"And the woman which thou sawest is that great city, which reigneth over the kings of the earth."

Babylon The Great

That great city, also called Babylon the great and mystery Babylon, is this religious set-up. She was reigning over these ten kings as well until the ten kings said, "I've had enough!" and threw her off and burned her up and ate her flesh and dismantled all that she stood for.

The power that these evil kings had was of one mind—ten kings giving their power and strength to the antichrist, this beast. God wants us, if we are genuinely saved, to get the power from the Lord Jesus Christ.

- **Matthew 28:18-20**
"And Jesus came and spake unto them, saying, All **power** is given unto me in heaven and in earth. Go ye therefore, and teach all nations, baptizing them in the name of the Father, and of the Son, and of the Holy Ghost: Teaching them to observe all things whatsoever I have commanded you: and, lo, I am with you alway, *even* unto the end of the world. Amen."

- **Acts 1:8**
  "But ye shall receive **power**, after that the Holy Ghost is come upon you: and ye shall be witnesses unto me both in Jerusalem, and in all Judaea, and in Samaria, and unto the uttermost part of the earth."

We Must Keep Being Faithful

That should be our goal. May God give us that power as our church sends forth missionary agencies and the missionaries that God has given to us. As we faithfully proclaim His Words through radio, Internet, the printed page, and in other places, may the Lord continue to bless and use us as a church.

Revelation

Chapter Eighteen

Revelation 18:1

"And after these things I saw another angel come down from heaven, having great power; and the earth was lightened with his glory."

The believers will be gone. <u>This is the tribulation period. The true saints, the ones that are born-again, will be out of this world.</u> We will not be here in this tribulation period. This *angel came down from heaven, having **great power***. Notice, *the earth was lightened with his **glory***. He had the **glory** from the Lord Jesus Christ Himself and the **light** from the **glory** of God was there. There is a lot of Scripture about **light** and **glory**.

- **Genesis 1:16**
  "And God made two great **lights**; the greater **light** to rule the day, and the lesser light to rule the night: *he made* the stars also."

These **lights** that are created by God are **lights** of **glory**. That is where this angel got the **light**.

- **Exodus 13:21**
  "And the LORD went before them by day in a pillar of a cloud, to lead them the way; and by night in a pillar of fire, to give them **light**; to go by day and night:"

- **Isaiah 60:19**
  "The sun shall be no more thy **light** by day; neither for brightness shall the moon give **light** unto thee: but the LORD shall be unto thee an everlasting **light**, and thy God thy **glory**."

Here is **light** and **glory**. Here the angel coming from Heaven mixes **light** and **glory**.

- **Luke 2:9**
  "And, lo, the angel of the Lord came upon them, and the **glory** of the Lord shone round about them: and they were sore afraid."

Angels have glory. This angel had **glory**.

- **Revelation 22:5**
  "And there shall be no night there; and they need no candle, neither **light** of the sun; for the Lord God giveth them **light**: and they shall reign for ever and ever."

The Lord God is **light**. The Lord is **power**. The Lord is great **glory** as well, and He will take care of this world. This angel came down with that.

Revelation 18:2

"And he cried mightily with a strong voice, saying, Babylon the great is fallen, is fallen, and is become the habitation of devils, and the hold of every foul spirit, and a cage of every unclean and hateful bird."

Babylon Here Speaks Of Rome

Babylon is a city, but there is also an application allegorically. One writer has said that it speaks allegorically of Rome as the most corrupt seat of idolatry and the enemy of true Christianity. I believe this is what the Lord Jesus Christ is speaking of in this entire chapter 18 of the book of Revelation. It is not only Rome itself, but the whole World Council of Churches—Rome, all the apostate Protestants, Jews, and all the world religions gathered together.

Babylon is fallen. One day it is going to be **fallen**. Notice what has happened to this terrible religious system of **Rome**, all the non-Roman religious apostasy, and all the apostasy in all the world religions. It is a **habitation of devils**. This speaks of false doctrine everywhere it is mentioned.

- **Deuteronomy 32:17**
  "They sacrificed unto **devils**, not to God; to gods whom they knew not, to new *gods that* came newly up, whom your fathers feared not."

Devils and gods are together. This is false religion and false worship.

- **Psalm 106:37-38**
  "Yea, they sacrificed their sons and their daughters unto **devils**, And shed innocent blood, *even* the blood of their sons and of their daughters, whom they sacrificed unto the idols of Canaan: and the land was polluted with blood."

Behind every idol is the **Devil**. This is talked about in this verse as well.

- **1 Corinthians 10:20-21**
  "But *I say,* that the things which the Gentiles sacrifice, they sacrifice to **devils,** and not to God: and I would not that ye should have fellowship with **devils.** Ye cannot drink the cup of the Lord, and the cup of **devils:** ye cannot be partakers of the Lord's table, and of the table of **devils.**"

Again, the sacrifice to **devils** is worshipping false gods. That is **Rome.** It certainly is.

- **1 Timothy 4:1**
  "Now the Spirit speaketh expressly, that in the latter times some shall depart from the faith, giving heed to seducing spirits, and doctrines of **devils;**"

Certainly, **Rome** is filled with such doctrines.

- **James 2:19**
  "Thou believest that there is one God; thou doest well: the **devils** also believe, and tremble."

Oh, they are religious **devils.** They do not have a heart belief, but only a head belief. They know there is a God. Religious worship is false.

- **Revelation 9:20**
  "And the rest of the men which were not killed by these plagues yet repented not of the works of their hands, that they should not worship **devils,** and **idols** of gold, and silver, and brass, and stone, and of wood: which neither can see, nor hear, nor walk:"

The **devils** and the **idols** go together. Not only is it *the habitation of devils,* but the *hold of every foul spirit.*

- **Leviticus 19:31**
  "Regard not them that have **familiar spirits,** neither seek after wizards, to be defiled by them: I *am* the LORD your God."

Again, this is false religious worship.

- **2 Kings 23:24**
  "Moreover the *workers with* **familiar spirits,** and the wizards, and the images, and the **idols,** and all the abominations that were spied in the land of Judah and in Jerusalem, did Josiah put away, that he might perform the words of the law which were written in the book that Hilkiah the priest found in the house of the LORD."

He put away these wicked things.

- **1 Timothy 4:1**
  "Now the Spirit speaketh expressly, that in the latter times some shall depart from the faith, giving heed to **seducing spirits,** and doctrines of **devils;**"

This is what is talked about, *every foul spirit.*

- **1 John 4:1**
  "Beloved, believe not every spirit, but try the spirits whether they are of God: because many false prophets are gone out into the world."

There are many **false spirits.** This **foul spirit of Rome** and false teaching are there.

- **Revelation 16:13**
  "And I saw three **unclean spirits** like frogs *come* out of the mouth of the dragon, and out of the mouth of the beast, and out of the mouth of the false prophet."

Remember we talked about this in Revelation 16. Religious worship is **devils** and **foul spirits** working together. This system of **Rome**—this **Babylonian** religious system of **Rome** and all of her children—are **foul spirits.** Not only that, but *a cage of every unclean and hateful bird.* **Birds** are spoken of as evil wherever they are in Scripture.

- **Leviticus 11:13-19**
  "And these *are they which* ye shall have in **abomination** among the **fowls;** they shall not be eaten, they *are* an abomination: the eagle, and the ossifrage, and the ospray, And the vulture, and the kite after his kind; Every raven after his kind; And the owl, and the night hawk, and the cuckow, and the hawk after his kind, And the little owl, and the cormorant, and the great owl, And the swan, and the pelican, and the gier eagle, And the stork, the heron after her kind, and the lapwing, and the bat."

- **Jeremiah 5:27**
  "As a cage is full of **birds,** so *are* their houses full of deceit: therefore they are become great, and waxen rich."

Here is a picture of **birds** and deceit—bad, bad things indeed.

- **Romans 1:23**
  "And changed the glory of the uncorruptible God into an image made like to corruptible man, and to birds, and fourfooted beasts, and creeping things."

They even made **birds** into **idols.** This is a **bird idol** in the saying that it has become a cage of every hateful and **unclean bird.**

Revelation 18:3

"For all nations have drunk of the wine of the wrath of her fornication, and the kings of the earth have committed fornication with her, and the merchants of the earth are waxed rich through the abundance of her delicacies."

Here are these nations that have gone unto **Rome** and unto this religious system. Remember, if **Rome** is bad now with all of her **pedophiles** and **homosexual priests** and various other problems today, with all her idolatry, just think what it is going to be after the true believers—the saints, the born-again ones—are raptured and taken up to Heaven. She will be very seriously more evil than ever. This is, of course, the situation with the nations that have trafficked with Rome and made deals with Rome and traded with **Rome**—the kings of the earth—the wrath of her **fornication**.

Idolatry Is Spiritual Fornication

Spiritual fornication is idolatry. Certainly, the idols are there. The kings of the earth have committed fornication with her, and the merchants of the earth are waxed rich. Rome can grant special privilege and this is where the nations that have the "smile of Rome" have gained riches, because they are powerful. The Vatican is a special kingdom. In fact, it has been a new thing recently that we sent an ambassador to the Vatican. Years ago, we never had any ambassador to the Vatican. We had nothing to do with Rome. Now, all of a sudden we are cozying up to this system and the political nation of Rome.

Revelation 18:4

"And I heard another voice from heaven, saying, Come out of her, my people, that ye be not partakers of her sins, and that ye receive not of her plagues."

I believe that even as bad as it is today, when **Rome** is riding high in the tribulation period, when the genuine believers are gone, there will be some that will be truly saved. Remember in the earlier chapters of Revelation, God sanctified 12,000 from each of the twelve tribes—144,000 evangelists all over the world—and some will be genuinely saved. Yes, the Antichrist will kill some, but God still has some of His people during this seven years of tribulation. That is what this verse speaks to. This is not an earthly voice. This is a Heavenly voice.

I heard a testimony of sorts on WTMR. Every once in a while our son, Dan, takes the car and he likes to hear the news on WTMR, so it was there, and this man was a Roman Catholic. He said he was saved. At first he thought he would leave the Catholic church, but now he is just staying right in among them. He is wrong–dead wrong. Stay in Rome? We have some folks in our church today who are former Roman Catholics. They have **come out.**

Come Out Of Apostasy!

This is the cry even in the tribulation period in this verse—*Come out of her, my people.* Why? *That ye be not partakers of her sins, and that ye receive not of her plagues.* It is a bad place to be in that terrible apostasy—whether it is Rome or Protestant apostasy or whatever it is.

I want to talk a little bit about Bible separation from sin and separation from false doctrine.

- **Genesis 15:14**
  "And also that nation, whom they shall serve, will I judge: and afterward shall they **come out** with great substance."

God's people **came out** of Egypt. God wanted them to **come out** of Egypt. There is a "**come out**" of wickedness.

- **Numbers 1:1**
  "And the LORD spake unto Moses in the wilderness of Sinai, in the tabernacle of the congregation, on the first *day* of the second month, in the second year after they were **come out** of the land of Egypt, saying,"

God's people **came out** of Egypt, out of that evil place. No question about it.

- **Numbers 22:5**
  "He sent messengers therefore unto Balaam the son of Beor to Pethor, which *is* by the river of the land of the children of his people, to call him, saying, Behold, there is a people **come out** from Egypt: behold, they cover the face of the earth, and they abide over against me:"

We should **come out** from Egypt, the genuine believers of this age, not only in the tribulation age. All of us should **come out** from wickedness.

- **Ezra 8:35**
  "Also the children of those that had been carried away, which were **come out** of the captivity, offered burnt offerings unto the God of Israel, twelve bullocks for all Israel, ninety and six rams, seventy and seven lambs, twelve he goats *for* a sin offering: all *this was* a burnt offering unto the LORD."

Here in Ezra's time it speaks about those that **came out** of the captivity of Babylon and Assyria. They came back to Jerusalem. They **came out** of that captivity. We should not have anything to do with captivity, and wickedness, and evil of any kind, whether religious or immorality or whatever.

- **Isaiah 52:11**
  "Depart ye, depart ye, go ye out from thence, touch no unclean *thing*; **go ye out** of the midst of her; be ye clean, that bear the vessels of the LORD."

We Must Separate From Sin

This is speaking of an apostate condition. Those of us who are genuinely saved today, in this dispensation, bear the vessels of the Lord. <u>Our bodies are the temples of the Holy Spirit and we ought to be clean.</u> That is what it says here. If we are dirty, if we are mixed with the world, the flesh, the devil, and the unsaved, we can not be clean and we can not fittingly bear the vessels of our Lord Jesus Christ. He wants us to do that.

- **2 Corinthians 6:17**
  "Wherefore **come out from among** them, and **be ye separate**, saith the Lord, and touch not the unclean thing; and I will receive you,"

Paul is quoting from Isaiah. God says He will receive us.

What about **separation** from unbelievers? It is clear in Scripture that we should have no close affiliation with unbelievers.

- **2 Corinthians 6:14-18**
  "Be ye not unequally yoked together with unbelievers: for what fellowship hath righteousness with unrighteousness? and what communion hath light with darkness? And what concord hath Christ with Belial? or what part hath he that believeth with an infidel? And what agreement hath the temple of God with idols? for ye are the temple of the living God; as God hath said, I will dwell in them, and walk in *them*; and I will be their God, and they shall be my people. Wherefore **come out from**

among them, and **be ye separate**, saith the Lord, and touch not the unclean *thing*; and I will receive you, And will be a Father unto you, and ye shall be my sons and daughters, saith the Lord Almighty."

What Bible Separation Means Today

This is what we call the norm of Bible separation. There is nothing in common with them. We must separate from them. That applies to the National Council of Churches. That applies to the World Council of Churches. That applies to Islam. That applies to false religions. That applies to all these things that are evil. That applies to all kinds of wicked associations. That applies to the cults. That applies, I believe, to the Masons and to these who are false religious systems—these oath-bound secret societies. There is nothing in common. Somebody asked the question, "What's wrong with the Masons? It seems like a religious organization." I said, "There is plenty wrong with them." We have a number of materials on that. God will be a Father if we obey Him and come out from apostasy.

- **Romans 16:17**
  "Now I beseech you, brethren, mark them which cause divisions and offences contrary to the doctrine which ye have learned; and **avoid** them."

We Must Avoid False Doctrines

God says we are to avoid those that have false doctrines—those that deny the Deity of the Lord Jesus Christ, deny His virgin birth, deny His bodily resurrection, deny His miracles, deny salvation by grace through faith, deny the cleansing of the blood of the Lord Jesus Christ. Have nothing to do with them. Avoid them.

- **Ephesians 5:11**
  "And have **no fellowship** with the unfruitful works of darkness, but rather reprove *them*."

What are we to do with these works of darkness? Reprove is ELEGCHO, *bring them to light*. We are to throw the light upon them and expose them because of what they are—evil.

- **2 Timothy 3:1-5**
  "This know also, that in the last days perilous times shall come. For men shall be lovers of their own selves, covetous, boasters, proud, blasphemers, disobedient to parents, unthankful, unholy, Without natural affection, trucebreakers, false accusers, incontinent, fierce, despisers of those that are good, Traitors, heady, highminded, lovers of pleasures more than lovers of God; Having a form of godliness, but denying the power thereof: from such **turn away.**"

We Are In Perilous Times Today

We are certainly in those perilous times today. We see the *forms*. We see religious churches all over. We have three on our street. They have big buildings. They have a *form of godliness*. Some have more power than others. What does God say to do with those *having a form of godliness, but denying the power thereof*? We are to just separate from them and have no fellowship in a close way. We cannot go out of the world. There are going to be people that are lost that we do business with, but a close fellowship? Stay away from close ties with those that are lost and unbelieving.

- **2 John 9-11**
  "Whosoever transgresseth, and abideth not in the doctrine of Christ, hath not God. He that abideth in the doctrine of Christ, he hath both the Father and the Son. If there come any unto you, and bring not this doctrine, **receive him not** into *your* house, neither bid him God speed: For he that biddeth him God speed is partaker of his evil deeds."

The Teachings About Christ

The doctrine of the Lord Jesus Christ is His Deity, His bodily resurrection, the blood atonement—all the doctrines the Bible tells us about our Saviour.

Do not let the Jehovah's Witnesses come into your house. Do not let the Seventh Day Adventists come into your house. Do not let any false religious system come into your house. **Do not receive them.** They do not have the doctrine of the Lord Jesus Christ as we do.

Separation From The Disorderly

There is another aspect of Biblical separation, that is separation from disorderly believers. A lot of people say we should separate from the unsaved but not from true Christians that are disorderly.

- **Matthew 18:15-17**
  "Moreover if thy brother shall trespass against thee, go and tell him his fault between thee and him alone: if he shall hear thee, thou hast gained thy brother. But if he will not hear *thee, then* take with thee one or two more, that in the mouth of two or three witnesses every word may be established. And if he shall neglect to hear them, tell it unto the church: but if he neglect to hear the church, let him be unto thee **as an heathen man** and a publican."

In other words, **separate** from that brother or sister that thumbs his or her nose at the Lord's people and at the true Church.

- **Romans 16:17**
  "Now I beseech you, brethren, mark them which cause divisions and offences contrary to the doctrine which ye have learned; and **avoid them.**"

We use this for unbelievers, but we can use it also for genuine believers.

- **2 Corinthians 6:14-18**
  "**Be ye not unequally yoked together** with unbelievers: for what fellowship hath righteousness with unrighteousness? and what communion hath light with darkness? And what concord hath Christ with Belial? or what part hath he that believeth with an infidel? And what agreement hath the temple of God with idols? for ye are the temple of the living God; as God hath said, I will dwell in them, and walk in *them*; and I will be their God, and they shall be my people. Wherefore **come out from among them**, and **be ye separate**, saith the Lord, and **touch not** the unclean *thing*; and I will receive you, And will be a Father unto you, and ye shall be my sons and daughters, saith the Lord Almighty."

Obey Biblical Separation Teachings

One of the doctrines that we have learned and that Paul has taught us clearly is the doctrine of Biblical separation from apostasy. If they are not following that doctrine, we are to not have anything to do with them. We are to obey this rule to avoid them. For instance, there is the apostasy of Rome and the apostasy of the National Council of Churches in disbelief. There is Dr. Billy Graham. Much of what he says is Biblical, but he invites Roman Catholic priests to the platform. He invites apostate Protestants to the platform. Then in the inquiry room, he sends these who are presumably converted (I hope they are) back to the apostate Roman Catholic church, or back to the Jewish temples and synagogues, and back to the Protestant apostate churches. No, if it is contrary to the doctrine you have learned, avoid them!

- **1 Corinthians 5:9-11**
  "I wrote unto you in an epistle **not to company** with fornicators: Yet not altogether with the fornicators of this world, or with the covetous, or extortioners, or with idolaters; for then must ye needs go out of the world. But now I have written unto you **not to keep company**, if any man that is called a brother be a fornicator, or covetous, or an idolater, or a railer, or a drunkard, or an extortioner; with such an one no not to eat."

This was about the incestuous man—a genuine believer. They were to put him out of their assembly, this true Christian that was walking disorderly. Do not even eat with him. We should **not have fellowship** with genuine believers that are disorderly until they repent—and they should repent.

- **2 Thessalonians 3:6-7**
  "Now we command you, brethren, in the name of our Lord Jesus Christ, that ye **withdraw yourselves** from every brother that walketh disorderly, and not after the tradition which he received of us. For yourselves know how ye ought to follow us: for we behaved not ourselves disorderly among you;"

This is another very important verse about **separation** from disorderly believers. This is not just a suggestion. What about the brethren? Should they be restored? Yes, brothers should be restored. After they are restored, we can have fellowship with them.

- **Galatians 6:1**
  "Brethren, if a man be overtaken in a fault, ye which are spiritual, restore such an one in the spirit of meekness; considering thyself, lest thou also be tempted."

<u>We are to restore our brethren and then have fellowship after that.</u>

- **Numbers 31:7**
  "And they warred against the Midianites, as the LORD commanded Moses; and they slew all the males."

You may remember Balaam was that hireling prophet that wanted to curse Israel. **He never separated** from the Midianites. There he was with them and not with Israel.

- **Numbers 31:8**
  "And they slew the kings of Midian, beside the rest of them that were slain; *namely,* Evi, and Rekem, and Zur, and Hur, and Reba, five kings of Midian: Balaam also the son of Beor they slew with the sword."

He was in the wrong place at the wrong time. Because **he was not separated** from that godless crowd, he fell.

Separate From Rome!

The plain truth about the Roman Catholic church, about the papacy and priesthood, is *Come out of her, my people.* There is no papacy or priesthood in Scripture or the worship of Mary. There is no such thing as purgatory. We either go straight to Heaven or straight to Hell. The mass is not the sacrifice of the Lord Jesus Christ—it is paganism. Image worship—*Come out of her, my people.* There is no such thing as worshipping images. God says, "Do not do it!" Salvation by works—one work or another—is paganism. God very clearly says, *"Come out of her, my people, that ye be not partakers of her sins."* Rome is certainly one that we should come out of—and all paganism and unbelief—completely.

Revelation 18:5

"For her sins have reached unto heaven, and God hath remembered her iniquities."

Sin reaches to Heaven. There is no way we can keep them, whether we are genuinely saved or lost. Sin will be remembered before Heaven. Here are the sins of this apostate group, which I believe is headed up by Rome. As we read in earlier chapters, this is the one that is on seven hills—the seven hills of Rome. There is no other big place in the world that I know anything about (maybe you can find one) that has seven hills. There is the city—the seven hills of Rome.

John Was Condemned By Rome

The apostle John, writing from Patmos, was condemned by Rome. He was condemned because he was a true Christian and because he was an apostle. He was on the small island of Patmos. He did not dare spell out in writing about the Roman religious system. They would have killed him for sure, but he did write these things talking about seven hills. I believe that these are the sins of Rome as the leader.

As we said before, she is not alone. Rome wants to take into her arms every apostate Protestant, Jew, and false religion. During the tribulation period when the true believers are gone, this will be accomplished. Her **sins have reached unto Heaven**. What about the sins that have been **covered** by the Lord Jesus Christ?

- **Psalm 32:1-2**
  "*A Psalm* of David, Maschil. Blessed *is he whose* transgression *is* **forgiven**, *whose* sin *is* covered. Blessed *is* the man unto whom the LORD imputeth not iniquity, and in whose spirit *there is* no guile."

Our sins, if we are in the Lord Jesus Christ, are **covered** and **forgiven**. That is a wonderful blessedness, and wonderful happiness, is it not? We have not the iniquity and the sin that the Lord Jesus Christ took upon Himself. It does not mean that genuine believers are sinlessly perfect. It means that He has **forgiven** us all sins past, present, and future. As to the fellowship with the Lord, that depends on 1 John 1:9.

- **1 John 1:9**
  "If we confess our sins, he is faithful and just to **forgive** us our sins, and to cleanse us from all unrighteousness."

Instant Cleansing For Fellowship

That has to do with fellowship. He can cleanse from sins for fellowship. When we sin, we should keep short close accounts with the Lord and confess the sins. He will restore us. He is faithful to forgive us and bring us back to fellowship. He is righteous to forgive us, because the Lord Jesus Christ paid the price for all sins past, present, and future.

- **Colossians 2:13**
  "And you, being dead in your sins and the uncircumcision of your flesh, hath he quickened together with him, having **forgiven** you all trespasses;"

It is an interesting thing. <u>The sins of Rome and all that religious system have reached unto Heaven. God hath remembered her iniquities. The Lord is omniscient. He can remember.</u>

- **Hebrews 10:17**
  "And their sins and iniquities will I **remember no more.**"

He is able to remember but He says, "I am not going to do it." Our sins are paid for by our Saviour the Lord Jesus Christ. We have a choice. <u>We either pay for our own sins and go to Hell for eternity, or let the Lord Jesus Christ pay for our sins and trust and accept Him.</u>

Revelation 18:6

"Reward her even as she rewarded you, and double unto her double according to her works: in the cup which she hath filled fill to her double."

Here are some **doublings**. We talk about **double** indemnity and **double** this and **double** that. The Scriptures talk about paying **double**. Did you know that? This is certainly true of this terrible apostate religious system.

- **Exodus 22:4**
  "If the theft be certainly found in his hand alive, whether it be ox, or ass, or sheep; he shall restore **double.**"

Here is the **doubling** up of restoration for a thief. This **doubling** up of sin as payment for sin is not just simply in the New Testament, but it is in the Old Testament as well.

- **Exodus 22:7**
  "If a man shall deliver unto his neighbour money or stuff to keep, and it be stolen out of the man's house; if the thief be found, let him pay **double.**"

<u>Is God righteous to pay</u> **double**? <u>Yes.</u> What is the effect of paying **double**? It would seem to me, if I were to have to pay **double**, I would think twice about repeating that offense. Wouldn't you?

- **Isaiah 40:2**
  "Speak ye comfortably to Jerusalem, and cry unto her, that her warfare is accomplished, that her iniquity is pardoned: for she hath received of the LORD'S hand **double** for all her sins."

<u>God chastened His people Israel</u> **double** <u>for her sins, but He has also pardoned her iniquity.</u>

- **Jeremiah 16:18**
  "And first I will recompense their iniquity and their sin **double**; because they have defiled my land, they have filled mine inheritance with the carcases of their detestable and abominable things."

God is righteous in causing them to pay **double** when there is great and grievous iniquity and sin. This is the case in Jeremiah.

- **Zechariah 9:12**
  "Turn you to the strong hold, ye prisoners of hope: even to day do I declare *that* I will render **double** unto thee;"

Doubling Payment Not New

This doubling of rendering pay and judgment is not new. It is in the Old Testament as well as the New Testament. If God, the righteous Judge, sees fit to double the payment of sin and double the judgment, He is fair in doing so. God will do that to this terrible religious apostate system.

Revelation 18:7

"How much she hath glorified herself, and lived deliciously, so much torment and sorrow give her: for she saith in her heart, I sit a queen, and am no widow, and shall see no sorrow."

She is **glorifying** herself. This religious system **glorified herself**. You know and I know that is not the thing that we are to do today. <u>We are not to **glorify** ourselves, we are to **glorify** the Lord</u>.

- **Psalm 86:12**
  "I will praise thee, O Lord my God, with all my heart: and I will **glorify** thy name for evermore."

She **glorified herself**. We do not **glorify ourselves**. We should never glorify ourselves.

- **Matthew 5:16**
  "Let your light so shine before men, that they may see your good works, and **glorify** your Father which is in heaven."

He is the One to be **glorified**, not us.

- **John 17:1**
  "These words spake Jesus, and lifted up his eyes to heaven, and said, Father, the hour is come; **glorify** thy Son, that thy Son also may **glorify** thee:"

This is the High Priestly prayer of the Lord Jesus Christ. <u>The **glory** that is due to the Lord Jesus Christ should be given to Him, not to ourselves.</u>

- **Romans 15:6**
  "That ye may with one mind *and* one mouth **glorify** God, even the Father of our Lord Jesus Christ."

Give **glory** to Him. Praise His name and thank Him for all that He is.

- **1 Corinthians 6:20**
  "For ye are bought with a price: therefore **glorify** God in your body, and in your spirit, which are God's."

Why We Should Glorify Our Lord

This gives us a reason why we are to glorify our Lord and not ourselves. If you are genuinely saved, you do not own your body. You do not own your lips. You do not own your ears. You do not own your hands, your feet, your heart, or any part of you. God owns you, and therefore you are to glorify God in your spirit, your soul, and your body.

- **1 Peter 2:12**
  "Having your conversation honest among the Gentiles: that, whereas they speak against you as evildoers, they may by *your* good works, which they shall behold, **glorify** God in the day of visitation."

<u>Many people do speak of us as evildoers.</u> We should give God the **glory**.

Notice, it says in Revelation 18:7 that she lives deliciously, she has **glorified herself**. Give her torment and give her sorrow. The Lord Jesus Christ is going to judge her. She is going to be a widow. **Sitting as a queen** is again a picture of Rome. It is in the Old Testament.

- **Jeremiah 7:18**
  "The children gather wood, and the fathers kindle the fire, and the women knead *their* dough, to make cakes to the **queen of heaven**, and to pour out drink offerings unto other gods, that they may provoke me to anger."

Mary–The Queen Of Heaven

I am going to identify this with Rome because that is what they call Mary—*"the queen of heaven."* It is right there in Scripture.

- **Jeremiah 44:17**
  "But we will certainly do whatsoever thing goeth forth out of our own mouth, to burn incense unto the **queen of heaven**, and to pour out drink offerings unto her, as we have done, we, and our fathers, our kings, and our princes, in the cities of Judah, and in the streets of Jerusalem: for *then* had we plenty of victuals, and were well, and saw no evil."

The false **queen of heaven** was worshipped. That is Tamuz or some other false deity.

- **Jeremiah 44:18**
  "But since we left off to burn incense to the **queen of heaven**, and to pour out drink offerings unto her, we have wanted all *things*, and have been consumed by the sword and by the famine."

They had it wonderfully when they were worshipping this false idol, the **queen of heaven**.

- **Jeremiah 44:19**
  "And when we burned incense to the **queen of heaven**, and poured out drink offerings unto her, did we make her cakes to worship her, and pour out drink offerings unto her, without our men?"

- **Jeremiah 44:25**
  "Thus saith the LORD of hosts, the God of Israel, saying; Ye and your wives have both spoken with your mouths, and fulfilled with your hand, saying, We will surely perform our vows that we have vowed, to burn incense to the **queen of heaven**, and to pour out drink offerings unto her: ye will surely accomplish your vows, and surely perform your vows."

Well, what do you know! On a website there is a picture of Mary as the **Queen of Heaven**. It says, "Welcome to the website of the Blessed Virgin Mary, **Queen of Heaven**." Then another page says, "Holy Queen, we ask for mercy. Thank you for visiting the **Queen of Heaven** site." Then there is another site on the Internet on pagan sun worship and Catholicism, the sunburst image and Baal. In that, there is the coronation of the Virgin. There is a picture of the Virgin Mary being crowned. She is crowned the **Queen of Heaven**. Rome crowns her. In fact, in 1954, Pope Pius XII officially declared Mary the **Queen of Heaven**. She is officially the **Queen**. There has been a complete substitution of Mary for the Lord Jesus Christ in the work of salvation.

On November 21, 1964, one of the constitutions of the church said, "Finally the Immaculate Virgin...is exalted by the Lord as Queen of the Universe." Then there is even a rite in the Catholic church that involves crowning statues or idols of Mary as the **Queen of Heaven**. This is one of their rituals—crowning her as **Queen of Heaven**. Once placed on the statue, the crown remains permanently. The title, *"queen of heaven"* can be found in Scripture, but not in reference to Mary.

Popes Bow To Mary

We saw Pope John Paul II bowing down and paying homage to a crowned statue of Mary, the Queen of Heaven, in direct violation of the commandment of God. Paganism!

Rome admits that she sits as queen. She is on the seven hills. It is a strange thing. She does not know and recognize that she is a widow. She has sorrow and she shall see torment, indeed.

Revelation 18:8

"Therefore shall her plagues come in one day, death, and mourning, and famine; and she shall be utterly burned with fire: for strong *is* the Lord God who judgeth her."

The woman is going to be **burned**. You remember in Revelation, first the woman was riding the beast in charge.

- **Revelation 17:16**
  "And the ten horns which thou sawest upon the beast, these shall hate the whore, and shall make her desolate and naked, and shall eat her flesh, and **burn her with fire**."

The political rulers will rebel against the religious system.

- **Daniel 2:40-42**
  "And the fourth kingdom shall be **strong** as iron: forasmuch as iron breaketh in pieces and subdueth all *things*: and as iron that breaketh all these, shall it break in pieces and bruise. And whereas thou sawest the feet and toes, part of potters' clay, and part of iron, the kingdom shall be divided; but there shall be in it of the strength of the iron, forasmuch as thou sawest the iron mixed with miry clay. And *as* the toes of the feet *were* part of iron, and part of clay, *so* the kingdom shall be partly **strong**, and partly broken."

The ten horns of these kings are like the ten toes of Daniel. Remember, the fourth kingdom with the ten toes is the kingdom of Rome. There was Babylon, Medo-Persia, Greece, and then Rome.

I am glad our Lord Jesus Christ is **strong**.

- **Psalm 24:8**
  "Who *is* this King of glory? The LORD **strong** and mighty, the LORD mighty in battle."
- **Psalm 71:7**
  "I am as a wonder unto many; but thou *art* my **strong** refuge."

The Lord Jesus Christ is our **strong** refuge. Are we weak today? He is **strength.**

- **Psalm 89:8**
  "O LORD God of hosts, who *is* a **strong** LORD like unto thee? or to thy faithfulness round about thee?"
- **Psalm 89:13**
  "Thou hast a mighty arm: **strong** is thy hand, *and* high is thy right hand."
- **Proverbs 18:10**
  "The name of the LORD *is* a **strong** tower: the righteous runneth into it, and is safe."

We can be safe in our Lord Jesus Christ. Safe in the hurricanes. I think of all those people in a recent hurricane who thought they could make it on their own. They stayed in their homes and did not evacuate. Bodies were found. They had dogs sniffing around. It was terrible. They did not have a **strong** tower. In our God and our Saviour we do have a **strong** tower, our Saviour the Lord Jesus Christ.

- **Isaiah 40:26**
  "Lift up your eyes on high, and behold who hath created these *things*, that bringeth out their host by number: he calleth them all by names by the greatness of his might, for that *he is* **strong** in power; not one faileth."

God is not only **strong, but He is a good Judge**.

- **Genesis 18:25**
  "That be far from thee to do after this manner, to slay the righteous with the wicked: and that the righteous should be as the wicked, that be far from thee: Shall not the **Judge** of all the earth do right?"

Yes, He will do right.

- **Psalm 9:8**
  "And he shall **judge** the world in righteousness, he shall minister **judgment** to the people in uprightness."

When He **judges** this prostitute whore—this religious system of Rome and all the other apostate religions—He will do it in righteousness.

- **Psalm 67:4**
"O let the nations be glad and sing for joy: for thou shalt **judge** the people righteously, and govern the nations upon earth. Selah."
- **Psalm 75:2**
"When I shall receive the congregation I will **judge** uprightly."
- **Psalm 75:7**
"But God *is* the **judge**: he putteth down one, and setteth up another."
- **Psalm 96:10**
"Say among the heathen *that* the LORD reigneth: the world also shall be established that it shall not be moved: he shall **judge** the people righteously."
- **Psalm 98:9**
"Before the LORD; for he cometh to **judge** the earth: with righteousness shall he **judge** the world, and the people with equity."

Our God will never do anything in a wrong or unrighteous way. He will **judge** this woman righteously also.

Revelation 18:9

"And the kings of the earth, who have committed fornication and lived deliciously with her, shall bewail her, and lament for her, when they shall see the smoke of her burning,"

There are going to be **kings** in this tribulation period attached, assigned, and close by this religious system. When they see her **burning, they see all of their profits up in smoke.** Just as in 9/11 when we saw the towers **burning**, it took several days before our economic structure could get back into high gear. When they see her **burning up, they will lament for her. It is a combination of religious systems with political systems in connection with them.**

Revelation 18:10

"Standing afar off for the fear of her torment, saying, Alas, alas, that great city Babylon, that mighty city! for in one hour is thy judgment come."

These political leaders will stand afar off as they see this religious system go down. It will go down because the system is wrong and because the Lord Jesus Christ is **judging** that system. He is a strong

Lord that **judges** her. They will say, "**Alas**, woe unto me!" They are going to be crying for **fear** of the **torment**, but they are mainly going to be crying because of the possessions they have lost and the trade-in potential. They are going to count goods more than anything else in the world. If we can come through a battle and still be living, though we have lost all, we are still living. We can come through a terrible hurricane, as many of our people have done. They are alive, with a little water and a little food. Mrs. Wallnofer said that Josh was up there in Alabama. He did not have much food. He had a little water and he was eating Pop Tarts. That is what she said he was eating. I tell you, at least he was spared. Those that have been **spared** should be thankful. Martin Luther's hymn said:

> *Let goods and kindreds go,*
> *This mortal life also—*
> *The body they may kill;*
> *God's truth abideth still:*
> *His kingdom is forever.*

All Job's Riches Left

That was the idea that Job had. Look at his riches! Look at his wealth! Look at his possessions! Look at his servants! Look at his children! They all went. His wife was not happy with him.

- **Job 13:15**
  "Though he slay me, yet will I **trust** in him: but I will maintain mine own ways before him."

God spared his life. If things ruin our houses and our lives, yes, it hurts us, but if God **spares** us, we should put more value on life than on what we have.

Revelation 18:11

"And the merchants of the earth shall weep and mourn over her; for no man buyeth their merchandise any more:"

Again it is a question of **financial loss**. **Financial loss** is before her and she can not stand that.

Revelation 18:12

"The merchandise of gold, and silver, and precious stones, and of pearls, and fine linen, and purple, and silk, and scarlet, and all thyine wood, and all manner vessels of ivory, and all manner vessels of most precious wood, and of brass, and iron, and marble,"

These were **luxurious things** that she was trading. Yet, it was gone. It reminds me of the church in Laodicea.

- **Revelation 3:16-18**
  "So then because thou art lukewarm, and neither cold nor hot, I will spue thee out of my mouth. Because thou sayest, I am rich, and **increased with goods**, and have need of nothing; and knowest not that thou art wretched, and miserable, and poor, and blind, and naked: I counsel thee to buy of me gold tried in the fire, that thou mayest be rich; and white raiment, that thou mayest be clothed, and *that* the shame of thy nakedness do not appear; and anoint thine eyes with eyesalve, that thou mayest see."

The Laodicean Church Picture

<u>This is when God pronounced the judgments on the seven churches. We believe Laodicea is the church of the end-time.</u> Here is the apostasy of Rome, the apostasy of this Laodicean church, and the apostasy of Protestantism today. This religious system of Rome and apostasy is rich, but in the tribulation period when Rome falls, all the riches will go along with her. I hope that all of us will remember, especially in this context, that the place of the genuine believers in the tribulation period is, *Come out of her, my people.* The place of God's people in this dispensation, before the tribulation ever comes is, *Come out of her, my people,* and be not partakers of her plagues. This is what we need to do. Separation is in two

phases: first, it is unto God and then from sin. That is what the Thessalonians did.

- **1 Thessalonians 1:9**
  "For they themselves shew of us what manner of entering in we had unto you, and how ye **turned to God** from idols to serve the living and true God;"

If you do not **separate** yourself to the Lord Jesus Christ first, all the **separation** from sin will not do you a bit of good. The people with grass shirts—monks in monasteries—with little food, are in favor of separation from evil but not unto the Lord Jesus Christ. If they are not genuinely saved, that will not do them a bit of good. May God help us to be separate that we may be "*clean, that bear the vessels of the Lord*" (Isaiah 52:11).

Revelation 17 seems to be referring to apostate religious Babylon and Revelation 18 refers to the political arm of Babylon. There are some similarities and there are also some differences. They are both called, *Babylon the Great*. They both have committed **spiritual fornication** with the kings of the earth. They both have a full cup. They both are burned with fire. Both are destroyed because of the judgment of God. Both are called, *that great city*. Both are responsible for the blood of the Biblical saints. These are the things that are similar.

Then there is the contrast. Their destructions are announced by two different angels. The revelation of the second angel is given at a later time than the first angel. The first Babylon is a religious center. The second Babylon is an economic power. The first Babylon is destroyed by the ten kings and they follow the beast, while the second Babylon seemed to be destroyed by God Himself. The ten kings destroy the first Babylon, but the kings of the earth lament the destruction of the second Babylon.

Babylon The Great Contrasts

There are contrasts, but they are one picture of Babylon the great. There is the religious element and a political and economic element as well. The first Babylon points to Rome. The second Babylon is probably located on the historic site of Babylon, which is in Iraq. Probably political Babylon will rebuild Babylon, as far as that is concerned. These are some of the similarities and the contrasts. Also, religious Babylon is *mystery* and the political Babylon is *the great*. There are different contrasts and symbols that are used for these two different Babylons. There are two different time periods. Babylon began in the garden of Eden with the rivers Tigris and

Euphrates. It especially began with Nimrod after the flood and the building of the big tower in Babel. Babylon began there. There is the Babylon of the Old Testament. Then there will be a restored Babylon in the future.

Revelation 18:13

"And cinnamon, and odours, and ointments, and frankincense, and wine, and oil, and fine flour, and wheat, and beasts, and sheep, and horses, and chariots, and slaves, and souls of men."

Categories Of Babylon's Wealth

These are the goods of this economic Babylon—wealthy indeed. In fact, there are twenty-eight different items of desirable merchandise. They could be divided up into categories.

1. Money—the gold, silver, and precious stones.
2. Clothing—this Babylon is rich in fine linen, purple, silk, and scarlet.
3. Furniture—thyine wood and ivory to make furniture.
4. Building materials—wood, bronze, iron, and marble.
5. Fragrances—cinnamon, incense, fragrant oil, and frankincense.
6. Staples—oil, wine, fine flour, and wheat.
7. Livestock—cattle and sheep.
8. Weapons and transport—chariots and horses.
9. Men—bodies and souls of men.

Wealth was there. The **souls** of men have been commented on by different ones at different times. John sees this commodity as slavery. It was a common thing in Rome to have **slaves.** The Jews in the Old Testament had slaves. Traffic in the dead and living was a viable enterprise.

Cloning Of Humans And Animals

One commentary mentions the harvesting of fetal material and future cloning of humans and animals. It is possible.

There may be trafficking in the souls of men and the body parts of executed "Christians," for instance. With lack of food because of the different judgments, possibly cannibalism might not be far off. There will be human slavery during this time.

Human Slavery

Another commentary on the bodies and souls of men mentioned that the application was first, undoubtedly, the practice of slavery, which will not be abolished until the millennial reign of our Saviour. The slaves were bartered in human lives and vessels of bronze for merchandise. Such traffic could be related to prostitution where men and women barter their bodies and souls for some trifle, something that at best could afford but a monetary satisfaction. When we talk about the souls of men, this terrible religious and political system has bartered in these areas, which is something that is wrong and against the will of God and the Words of God. All these things mentioned in Revelation 18:12-13 show that this Babylon the great was rich. Babylon is located in the country of Iraq today. It is going to be destroyed.

Revelation 18:14

"And the fruits that thy soul lusted after are departed from thee, and all things which were dainty and goodly are departed from thee, and thou shalt find them no more at all."

All that they loved—all these **material blessings** and benefits to them, these twenty-eight different things that they had—are all **gone**. This idea of **lust** after **material goods** is something that I want to talk about because this is important. <u>In Scripture, we find a number of those who **lusted** after **material things**</u>.

- **Numbers 11:4**
  "And the mixt multitude that *was* among them fell a **lusting**: and the children of Israel also wept again, and said, Who shall give us flesh to eat?"

Meat Versus God's Manna

The children of Israel wanted food that was animal food. God had provided the manna for them. Manna was perfectly capable of handling all of their needs—all of the vitamins, all the minerals—but they wanted something more than what God provided. If that is what we lust after—something more than what God has provided—we have to watch ourselves. They were wrong in that lusting after food.

- **Numbers 11:31-32**
  "And there went forth a wind from the LORD, and brought quails from the sea, and let *them* fall by the camp, as it were a day's journey on this side, and as it were a day's journey on the other side, round about the camp, and as it were two cubits *high* upon the face of the earth. And the people stood up all that day, and all *that* night, and all the next day, and they gathered the quails: he that gathered least gathered ten homers: and they spread *them* all abroad for themselves round about the camp."

God answered their **lust**.

- **Numbers 11:33-34**
  "And while the flesh *was* yet between their teeth, ere it was chewed, the wrath of the LORD was kindled against the people, and the LORD smote the people with a very great plague. And he called the name of that place Kibrothhattaavah: because there they buried the people that **lusted**."

Should we **lust** after evil things? No, we should not. We should not **lust** after anything that is wrong for us. These people did that. This particular incident is mentioned in other places.

- **Psalm 78:17-19**
  "And they sinned yet more against him by provoking the most High in the wilderness. And they tempted God in their heart by asking meat for their **lust**. Yea, they spake against God; they said, Can God furnish a table in the wilderness?"

Certainly, God can furnish a table anywhere. For forty years in that wilderness, He provided manna—angels' food, very good things—but they wanted more. They **lusted** after flesh.

- **Psalm 78:25-32**
  "Man did eat angels' food: he sent them meat to the full. He caused an east wind to blow in the heaven: and by his power he brought in the south wind. He rained flesh also upon them as dust, and feathered fowls like as the sand of the sea: And he let

it fall in the midst of their camp, round about their habitations. So they did eat, and were well filled: for he gave them their own desire; They were not estranged from their **lust**. But while their meat *was* yet in their mouths, The wrath of God came upon them, and slew the fattest of them, and smote down the chosen *men* of Israel. For all this they sinned still, and believed not for his wondrous works."

I guess the *"fat"* ones did not need to have any more meat. They had more, I guess, than the slim ones. Regardless of God smiting them, they still did not get the point.

We Should Heed God's Judgment

When you and I sin, I trust that when the Lord Jesus Christ condemns and judges us, I hope we will get whatever it is that He is trying to say to us and will profit by it. The Israelites did not do that. They did not profit. They still continued to sin.

- **Psalm 106:13-14**
  "They soon forgat his works; they waited not for his counsel: But **lusted** exceedingly in the wilderness, and tempted God in the desert."

This incident is mentioned again. We have to wait for God's counsel found in His Words.

- **Psalm 106:15**
  "And he gave them their request; but sent leanness into their soul."

This is a pathetic verse. Which is more important, strong healthy souls or strong healthy bodies? God wants the soul and He wants us to be strong. Sometimes God does answer poor requests, wrong requests, and sinful requests like those of the Israelites.

- **Mark 4:18-19**
  "And these are they which are sown among thorns; such as hear the word, And the cares of this world, and the deceitfulness of riches, and the **lusts** of other things entering in, choke the word, and it becometh unfruitful."

The four different soils were the wayside, the thorns, the hard stony ground, and the good soil. This was the thorny soil. As soon as that seed got into the soil, all of a sudden, the lusts of other things sidetracked the Words of God and the people did not grow and did not produce. It was unfruitful.

- **John 8:44**
"Ye are of *your* father the devil, and the **lusts** of your father ye will do. He was a murderer from the beginning, and abode not in the truth, because there is no truth in him. When he speaketh a lie, he speaketh of his own: for he is a liar, and the father of it."

Children Of Satan

Every unsaved person is a child of this Satan, this Devil. Every unsaved person is awash in sin. The Lord Jesus Christ was bold enough to tell those Pharisees that the lusts of their father they would do.

- **Romans 6:12**
"Let not sin therefore reign in your mortal body, that ye should obey it in the **lusts** thereof."

Stop The Sin Nature Reign

The sin nature should not reign. We should not give in to the lusts of the flesh. Stop letting sin reign. God does not want sin.

A lady called me who listened to our shortwave broadcast in the middle of the night. She was afraid. She claimed to be "saved," but she wondered if Satan was trying to influence her life. We talked about the **lusts** of the flesh. I said that every one of us who is genuinely saved still has this flesh. We are still capable of producing the works of the flesh manifested in Galatians.

- **Galatians 5:19-21**
"Now the works of the flesh are manifest, which are *these*; Adultery, fornication, uncleanness, lasciviousness, Idolatry, witchcraft, hatred, variance, emulations, wrath, strife, seditions, heresies, Envyings, murders, drunkenness, revellings, and such like: of the which I tell you before, as I have also told *you* in time past, that they which do such things shall not inherit the kingdom of God."

God wants us to walk after the Holy Spirit of God who indwells the genuinely saved ones, that we not fulfill the **lusts** of the flesh.

- **Romans 13:14**
"But put ye on the Lord Jesus Christ, and make not provision for the flesh, to *fulfil* the **lusts** *thereof.*"

You have heard about the drunks that want to stop drinking. For a day or two, they stop and lay aside the bottle, but they have hidden one in the back closet just in case. <u>If we make provision for the flesh, chances are</u> <u>we are going to take it up whenever we are weak</u>. Do not even make provision.

- **1 Corinthians 10:5-6**
  "But with many of them God was not well pleased: for they were overthrown in the wilderness. Now these things were our examples, to the intent we should not lust after evil things, as they also **lusted**."

You may wonder, "<u>Why do we have the Old Testament?</u>" It is in order to make examples for us. God gives us examples. You can have an example that is a good example. You can profit by it and walk therein. You can also have an example that is a bad example and be far from it. It will teach you to avoid those bad examples as well.

- **Galatians 5:16:17**
  "*This* I say then, Walk in the Spirit, and ye shall not fulfil the lust of the flesh. For the flesh **lusteth** against the Spirit, and the Spirit against the flesh: and these are contrary the one to the other: so that ye cannot do the things that ye would."

This is true. Every genuine believer has the Holy Spirit of God inside of them. The flesh is also here with the old nature. <u>Do not listen to the</u> <u>sinless perfectionist people that say they can all of a sudden reach a point</u> <u>in their life that they are totally sanctified and totally apart from any evil</u>. Ask their spouse, their child, their relatives, or their neighbors, and see if it pans out. No. We have the flesh, but God says we are to walk in the Spirit.

- **Titus 2:12-13**
  "Teaching us that, denying ungodliness and worldly **lusts**, we should live soberly, righteously, and godly, in this present world; Looking for that blessed hope, and the glorious appearing of the great God and our Saviour Jesus Christ;"

- **1 Peter 2:11**
  "Dearly beloved, I beseech *you* as strangers and pilgrims, abstain from fleshly **lusts**, which war against the soul;"

The fleshly **lusts** war against the soul. God wants our souls strong and in love with Him and walking with Him.

- **1 John 2:15-17**
  "Love not the world, neither the things *that are* in the world. If any man love the world, the love of the Father is not in him. For all that *is* in the world, the **lust** of the flesh, and the lust of the eyes, and the pride of life, is not of the Father, but is of the world. And the world passeth away, and the **lust** thereof: but he that doeth the will of God abideth for ever."

Stop Loving The World

<u>Stop loving the world</u>. God so loved the world, but this means the world of sin, wickedness, and corruption. Here is the lust again that God speaks of in Revelation 18:14, *the fruits that thy soul lusted after are departed from thee*—the lust of the flesh. The lust of the eyes may be television, Internet, magazines, books, or whatever it might be. The pride of life—many are proud. They may say, "I've escaped the lust of the eyes. I've escaped the lust of the flesh. I'm pretty good." They still have the pride of life. Every lust that you can have or think of is going to pass away. We must do the will of God.

Revelation 18:15

"The merchants of these things, which were made rich by her, shall stand afar off for the fear of her torment, weeping and wailing,"

The Torment Of The City

Here are the merchants that are standing afar off for fear of the torment of this city, <u>Babylon the great, probably rebuilt in the area of Iraq</u>. Notice, they were made rich by her. There are a number of Bible verses on riches. We have to be careful how we use them.

- **Psalm 37:16**
  "A little that a righteous man hath *is* better than the **riches** of many wicked."

This is a good verse.

- **Psalm 49:6-7**
  "They that trust in their wealth, and boast themselves in the multitude of their **riches**; None *of them* can by any means redeem his brother, nor give to God a ransom for him:"

<u>Riches</u> will not redeem, but the Lord Jesus Christ can.

- **Psalm 52:7**
  "Lo, *this is* the man *that* made **riches** not God his strength; but trusted in the abundance of his, *and* strengthened himself in his wickedness."

<u>Riches</u> can bring wickedness, not necessarily always, but we have to not trust in them.

- **Psalm 62:10**
  "Trust not in oppression, and become not vain in robbery: if **riches** increase, set not your heart *upon them*."

Just keep on in a steady way.

- **Proverbs 13:7**
  "There is that maketh himself **rich**, yet *hath* nothing: *there is* that maketh himself poor, yet *hath* great **riches**."

We have **riches** of eternal things—**riches** of glory.

- **Matthew 13:22**
  "He also that received seed among the thorns is he that heareth the word; and the care of this world, and the deceitfulness of **riches**, choke the word, and he becometh unfruitful."

Riches are deceitful. People often think, "Oh, what a wonderful thing if we only had these **riches**!" They are deceitful.

- **Ephesians 3:8**
  "Unto me, who am less than the least of all saints, is this grace given, that I should preach among the Gentiles the unsearchable **riches** of Christ;"

There are spiritual **riches** far more important than any **riches** we may have. We must have some **riches** in order to live.

- **2 Corinthians 8:9**
  "For ye know the grace of our Lord Jesus Christ, that, though he was **rich**, yet for your sakes he became poor, that ye through his poverty might be **rich**."

We do not believe in the **riches** gospel, but **rich** in spiritual things. God wants us all to be **rich** in them.

Revelation 18:16

"And saying, Alas, alas, that great city, that was clothed in fine linen, and purple, and scarlet, and decked with gold, and precious stones, and pearls!"

Here are the merchants. **Clothing is important to God, but how are we clothed?**

- **Psalm 45:13**
  "The king's daughter is all glorious within: her **clothing** is of wrought gold."

This is a verse my mother-in-law always used to tell my wife and her two sisters.

- **Proverbs 31:25**
  "Strength and honour *are* her **clothing**; and she shall rejoice in time to come."

- **1 Timothy 6:6-8**

  "But godliness with contentment is great gain. For we brought nothing into *this* world, *and it is* certain we can carry nothing out. And having food and **raiment** let us be therewith content."

Raiment is something to wear.

I heard on the news that one of the billionaires died at age 76 or so. He was a billionaire, but where are those **riches** now? Did he take them? You cannot take them, that is, the coin of this world. He died and he left his riches behind. I do not know whether he was genuinely saved or lost. He was not content with **raiment**. He wanted many other things.

I noticed also on the news that there are more billionaires now in our country than ever before—a recent count shows that there are more than 300 billionaires. The man who is still the highest is Bill Gates of Microsoft.

- **1 Peter 3:1-6**

  "Likewise, ye wives, *be* in subjection to your own husbands; that, if any obey not the word, they also may without the word be won by the conversation of the wives; While they behold your chaste conversation *coupled* with fear. Whose **adorning** let it not be that outward *adorning* of plaiting the hair, and of wearing of gold, or of putting on of apparel; But *let it be* the hidden man of the heart, in that which is not corruptible, *even the ornament* of a meek and quiet spirit, which is in the sight of God of great price. For after this manner in the old time the holy women also, who trusted in God, **adorned** themselves, being in subjection unto their own husbands: Even as Sara obeyed Abraham, calling him lord: whose daughters ye are, as long as ye do well, and are not afraid with any amazement."

Inner And Outer Adorning

The adorning means what the lady wears. This is a different kind of clothing completely. We have to be careful of the different types of decking with gold and ornaments. The inner adorning is more important than the outer adorning. That goes for men as well as women.

Revelation 18:17

"For in one hour so great riches is come to nought. And every shipmaster, and all the company in ships, and sailors, and as many as trade by sea, stood afar off,"

<u>Riches fly away</u>. You may remember that parable of Luke 12.

- **Luke 12:15-21**
  "And he said unto them, Take heed, and beware of covetousness: for a man's life consisteth not in the abundance of the **things** which he possesseth. And he spake a parable unto them, saying, The ground of a certain **rich** man brought forth plentifully: And he thought within himself, saying, What shall I do, because I have no room where to bestow my fruits? And he said, This will I do: I will pull down my barns, and build greater; and there will I bestow all my fruits and my **goods**. And I will say to my soul, Soul, thou hast much **goods** laid up for many years; take thine ease, eat, drink, *and* be merry. But God said unto him, *Thou fool*, this night thy soul shall be required of thee: then whose shall those **things** be, which thou hast provided? So *is* he that layeth up **treasure** for himself, and is not **rich** toward God."

<u>We have to be **rich** toward God</u>.

- **Luke 12:22-24**
  "And he said unto his disciples, Therefore I say unto you, Take no thought for your life, what ye shall **eat**; neither for the body, what ye shall **put on**. The life is more than meat, and the body *is more* than **raiment**. Consider the ravens: for they neither sow nor reap; which neither have storehouse nor barn; and God **feedeth** them: how much more are ye better than the fowls?"

- **Luke 12:27-31**
  "Consider the lilies how they grow: they toil not, they spin not; and yet I say unto you, that Solomon in all his glory was not **arrayed** like one of these. If then God so **clothe** the grass, which is to day in the field, and to morrow is cast into the oven; how much more *will he clothe you*, O ye of little faith? And seek not ye what ye shall **eat**, or what ye shall **drink**, neither be ye of doubtful mind. For all these things do the nations of the world seek after: and your Father knoweth that ye have need of these things. But rather seek ye the kingdom of God; and all these things shall be added unto you."

<u>God knows we have need of **food, drink, and clothing**</u>.

- **Psalm 62:10**
  "Trust not in oppression, and become not vain in robbery: if **riches** increase, set not your heart *upon them.*"
- **Proverbs 23:5**
  "Wilt thou set thine eyes upon that which is not? for *riches* certainly make themselves wings; they fly away as an eagle toward heaven."

If you do not believe that, just think back to the **stock market** crash of 1929. I was two years old when the crash came. There may be other crashes. There was a lot of downsizing in stocks recently. In fact, cut not quite in half, but almost. <u>Riches fly away as eagles toward Heaven.</u>

- **1 Timothy 6:17**
  "Charge them that are **rich** in this world, that they be not highminded, nor trust in uncertain **riches**, but in the living God, who giveth us **richly** all things to enjoy;"

We have to trust in God.

This Does Not Refer To Rome

<u>I do not believe that Revelation 18:16 refers to Rome.</u> It is the political area of the original Babylon, which is right on the Euphrates River. It is not in the Persian Gulf. The Euphrates River is navigable for some 500 miles. It is not a seaport, but it is accessible. It is 370 miles up river to Babylon. You can shuttle from the Gulf by smaller barges or you can go over land. There is great trading and all these people, the shipmasters, are crying after Babylon because their money is gone. Their trade is gone. That is why they are angry.

Revelation 18:18

"And cried when they saw the smoke of her burning, saying, What *city is* **like unto this great city!"**

It was a great city, but the city is no more. It is gone. It is **burned** up. The Lord Jesus Christ has judged this great political city in the tribulation period. The true Church—the genuine believers—will be gone.

Revelation 18:19

"And they cast dust on their heads, and cried, weeping and wailing, saying, Alas, alas, that great city, wherein were made rich all that had ships in the sea by reason of her costliness! for in one hour is she made desolate."

Immediate Destruction

This happened immediately, almost like 9/11 when everything was gone in the Twin Towers. Everything was gone in part of the Pentagon. These were terrible things that happened immediately.

There is great trading in this end-time political Babylon. We have to be careful that we do not trust in uncertain riches, but in the living God.

Revelation 18:20

"Rejoice over her, *thou* heaven, and *ye* holy apostles and prophets; for God hath avenged you on her."

Here is **rejoicing** because of God's **avenging**. Though God does not want us to take **vengeance**, He is a God Who does take **vengeance** on those who are unbelievers. We have to realize that.

- **Deuteronomy 32:43**
  "Rejoice, O ye nations, *with* his people: for he will avenge the blood of his servants, and will render **vengeance** to his adversaries, and will be merciful unto his land, *and* to his people."

God will **judge** those who are unbelievers.

- **Psalm 58:10**
  "The righteous shall rejoice when he seeth the **vengeance**: he shall wash his feet in the blood of the wicked."

The Vengeance Of God

Does that mean He is always avenging? No, He is a God of righteousness and love, but He is also a God of justice. He will avenge, but we are not to take vengeance on others.

- **Proverbs 24:17**
"**Rejoice not** when thine enemy falleth, and let not thine heart be glad when he stumbleth:"
We are not supposed to rejoice because, who knows? We are going to trip up ourselves and stumble. God does not want us to do that. The Lord Jesus Christ does **avenge**.

  - **Deuteronomy 32:43**
"Rejoice, O ye nations, *with* his people: for he will **avenge** the blood of his servants, and will render **vengeance** to his adversaries, and will be merciful unto his land, *and* to his people."

  - **2 Kings 9:7**
"And thou shalt smite the house of Ahab thy master, that I may **avenge** the blood of my servants the prophets, and the blood of all the servants of the LORD, at the hand of Jezebel."

God is **avenging** His servants the prophets and those who speak for Him.

  - **Jeremiah 46:10**
"For this *is* the day of the Lord GOD of hosts, a day of **vengeance**, that he may **avenge** him of his adversaries: and the sword shall devour, and it shall be satiate and made drunk with their blood: for the Lord GOD of hosts hath a sacrifice in the north country by the river Euphrates."

Vengeance is part of the character of our God.

  - **Luke 18:7-8**
"And shall not God **avenge** his own elect, which cry day and night unto him, though he bear long with them? I tell you that he will **avenge** them speedily. Nevertheless when the Son of man cometh, shall he find faith on the earth?"

He will **avenge** his elect, the genuine believers, one day. It may not be in this life.

  - **Romans 12:19**
"Dearly beloved, **avenge** not yourselves, but *rather* give place unto wrath: for it is written, **Vengeance** is mine; I will repay, saith the Lord."

That is the character of God—to repay. The modernists and liberals do not think that is part of God's character. They say, "He is just a God of love and that is all He does. Everything is all right." No, He is also a God of justice and of **vengeance**.

Revelation 18:21

"And a mighty angel took up a stone like a great millstone, and cast *it* into the sea, saying, Thus with violence shall that great city Babylon be thrown down, and shall be found no more at all."

The analogy or picture is like a big **millstone**. I understand there is a lower **millstone** and an upper one to grind the corn. This is like someone just throwing that **millstone** into the sea with a big splash. That is exactly how Iraq, or rebuilt Babylon, will be.

What is going to happen to that city Babylon? That is what a friend of ours, Dr. Kirk DiVietro, and several pastors, were trying to find. They were trying to go on that road to go to Babylon. One was killed. The terrorists opened fire. Dr. DiVietro was injured, but it was an unnecessary trip. He admits that. It was not a spiritual mission. They just wanted to go sightseeing to see the old Babylon and he almost got killed. The Lord spared his life. We are glad for that, but one pastor—a godly man—was slain.

The Destruction Of Babylon

Babylon will be destroyed. How? Will it be the atomic bomb? Will it be something like that? God knows about that. He is able to destroy what He says is going to be destroyed *with violence*. That city that is wicked and against the Lord Jesus Christ and is rebuilt with all of its wealth, glory, pomp, and power, God is going to knock down and knock apart.

Revelation 18:22

"And the voice of harpers, and musicians, and of pipers, and trumpeters, shall be heard no more at all in thee; and no craftsman, of whatsoever craft *he be*, shall be found any more in thee; and the sound of a millstone shall be heard no more at all in thee;"

There Are Many Sounds

Here are the different voices and sounds. With nobody there to play, it is almost like when hurricanes come. The streets are empty. Nobody is there. We see pictures on television of every one of the hurricanes. Here is a deserted street that used to be filled with cars. So in this case, when God destroys this political Babylon that hates Him and despises His Son the Lord Jesus Christ.

There will be **no harpers**. Our pianist will not be there. He is genuinely saved and is going to be out of there. They will not hear the lost **harpers** and **musicians** anymore. The lost **pipers** and **trumpeters** will be heard no more at all. There will be no **craftsmen**. They will not even be working at their jobs. Nothing will be done. Not a single craft will be anymore in Babylon. Grinding and preparing food will be gone. It will be a puff of smoke–wiped out completely.

Revelation 18:23

"And the light of a candle shall shine no more at all in thee; and the voice of the bridegroom and of the bride shall be heard no more at all in thee: for thy merchants were the great men of the earth; for by thy sorceries were all nations deceived."

No More Light

There will be no candle and no light. The bride and bridegroom—happiness—they are gone. Everything is gone in this judgment of God on this terrible city of restored Babylon. The *merchants were the great men of the earth.* Now look at them. They have nothing. They are penniless. In the 1929 stock market crash, those that used to have money, had no money. Many of them jumped from high buildings to their death. Why? Because their whole life was built upon their possessions. Their whole life was built upon, "What do I have? What do I own?" They had nothing more, so what is life? End it all.

Notice also, *by thy sorceries were all nations* **deceived.** PHARMAKEIA is the Greek word. It means, *sorceries, drugs.* The nations were **deceived** by drugs.

- **Isaiah 47:1-13**
  "Come down, and sit in the dust, O virgin daughter of Babylon, sit on the ground: *there is* no throne, O daughter of the Chaldeans: for thou shalt no more be called tender and delicate. Take the millstones, and grind meal: uncover thy locks, make

bare the leg, uncover the thigh, pass over the rivers. Thy nakedness shall be uncovered, yea, thy shame shall be seen: I will take vengeance, and I will not meet *thee as* a man. *As for* our redeemer, the LORD of hosts *is* his name, the Holy One of Israel. Sit thou silent, and get thee into darkness, O daughter of the Chaldeans: for thou shalt no more be called, The lady of kingdoms. I was wroth with my people, I have polluted mine inheritance, and given them into thine hand: thou didst shew them no mercy; upon the ancient hast thou very heavily laid thy yoke. And thou saidst, I shall be a lady for ever: *so* that thou didst not lay these *things* to thy heart, neither didst remember the latter end of it. Therefore hear now this, *thou that art* given to pleasures, that dwellest carelessly, that sayest in thine heart, I *am,* and none else beside me; I shall not sit *as* a widow, neither shall I know the loss of children: But these two *things* shall come to thee in a moment in one day, the loss of children, and widowhood: they shall come upon thee in their perfection for the multitude of thy sorceries, *and* for the great abundance of thine enchantments. For thou hast trusted in thy wickedness: thou hast said, None seeth me. Thy wisdom and thy knowledge, it hath perverted thee; and thou hast said in thine heart, I *am,* and none else beside me. Therefore shall evil come upon thee; thou shalt not know from whence it riseth: and mischief shall fall upon thee; thou shalt not be able to put it off: and desolation shall come upon thee suddenly, *which* thou shalt not know. Stand now with thine enchantments, and with the multitude of thy sorceries, wherein thou hast laboured from thy youth; if so be thou shalt be able to profit, if so be thou mayest prevail. Thou art wearied in the multitude of thy counsels. Let now the astrologers, the stargazers, the monthly prognosticators, stand up, and save thee from *these things* that shall come upon thee." This is a prophetic picture, perhaps, of this last time. This is Isaiah looking forward to this end-time of the rebuilt Babylon. Do you think that Satan is riding high, wide, and handsome today? Just think of what it will be in the tribulation period, during those seven years when the genuine believers will be gone. There will be **sorceries**, enchantments, Ouija boards, Satanic rituals, and so on.

God sees all of us everywhere we go, night or day. That is the trouble today. Knowledge perverts. You may say, "Well, how can knowledge pervert?" Right here in the Philadelphia area we had a man raping some girls in the dormitories. In a college?

Knowledge Often Perverts

Is knowledge the answer to all life? No, it perverts. Not all knowledge perverts, but it is not the final answer. It has to be the heart as well as knowledge.

The attitude of a lot of people is, "I am." They have rejected the Lord Jesus Christ. Let the Ouija boards and their **sorceries** and all these Satanic things save and deliver them from problems. Notice, it says that the **sorceries** have **deceived**.

- **Jeremiah 37:7-9**
  "Thus saith the LORD, the God of Israel; Thus shall ye say to the king of Judah, that sent you unto me to enquire of me; Behold, Pharaoh's army, which is come forth to help you, shall return to Egypt into their own land. And the Chaldeans shall come again, and fight against this city, and take it, and burn it with fire. Thus saith the LORD; **Deceive** not yourselves, saying, The Chaldeans shall surely depart from us: for they shall not depart."

Deception Goes With Drugs

Deception comes with drugs. There was a drunken man arrested just this past week for killing two people. He worked at night. He came off work and went to the saloon and took a lot of whiskey, or whatever it was, and drove and ran off the street and killed two people. Sorcery or drugs of any kind, whether alcohol or whatever it may be, deceives us and we cannot function.

- **Matthew 24:4-5**
  "And Jesus answered and said unto them, Take heed that no man **deceive** you. For many shall come in my name, saying, I am Christ; and shall **deceive** many."
- **Romans 16:18**
  "For they that are such serve not our Lord Jesus Christ, but their own belly; and by good words and fair speeches **deceive** the hearts of the simple."

In the last days there is **deception**. We have all kinds of preachers **deceiving** people. They say they believe this, and then they do that. They say they want to do this, but they do something else. This is **deception** of *the hearts of the simple.*

- **Ephesians 4:14**
  "That we *henceforth* be no more children, tossed to and fro, and carried about with every wind of doctrine, by the sleight of men, *and* cunning craftiness, whereby they lie in wait to **deceive;**"

Deception is a terrible thing.

- **2 Timothy 3:13**
  "But evil men and seducers shall wax worse and worse, **deceiving,** and **being deceived.**"

Who is the cause of this? Who is the source?

- **Revelation 12:9**
  "And the great dragon was cast out, that old serpent, called the Devil, and Satan, which **deceiveth** the whole world: he was cast out into the earth, and his angels were cast out with him."

Use Of Drugs Is Rampant

Sorcery—drugs—is rampant. What about drugs in Iraq? There was an article on the Internet recently talking about that. Cocaine smuggling from Iran to Iraq was spiraling. Iraqi police forces were apparently unable to stop it. They especially had some called "box sniff." They sniffed it up into their nostrils. It was terrible. Narcotics were being sold with newspapers at traffic lights by Iraqi children in Baghdad. People in the past were afraid even to tell a joke about drugs in public. Now you can see the children at traffic lights coming to you and asking if you need a newspaper or some capsules. If that was true today in Iraq, what about after the true Church is gone in the tribulation? This is a two-way street. The sorcery is a devilish type of thing, but it also means PHARMAKEIA, like the pharmacy. It is the same word. It means, *drugs.*

Revelation 18:24

"And in her was found the blood of prophets, and of saints, and of all that were slain upon the earth."

We have told before about the Roman Catholic **slaughter** of genuine Christians down through the centuries. Brother David Cloud has an article, *Catholic Commission Perverts Martyr Statistics.* He says, for example, that it has been estimated by careful and reputed historians of the Catholic inquisition that 50 million people were **slaughtered** for the crime of heresy. That was from 606 to 1850 A.D. This is Rome. In the 1900's there was another study that says that 27 million died at the hands of the Communists, the Nazis, the Islamic regimes and so on.

Nazis are reported to have **slaughtered** six million (maybe more or less), not only the Jews but also others. One reference says that Communism **killed** over one hundred million people in the last century.

John, who wrote the book of Revelation, was banished to the isle of Patmos. He was not martyred or killed, but he was put out of commission. Many of the apostles and holy men of God in the early New Testament were not that privileged. *Fox's Book of Martyrs* relates the terrible **martyrdom** of genuine Christians down through the centuries. They were eaten by beasts and animals, put into lions' dens, and tortured. Paul was not so fortunate either.

- **2 Timothy 4:6**
  "For I am now ready to be **offered**, and the time of my departure is at hand. I have fought a good fight, I have finished *my* course, I have kept the faith: Henceforth there is laid up for me a crown of righteousness, which the Lord, the righteous judge, shall give me at that day: and not to me only, but unto all them also that love his appearing."

This was his second Roman imprisonment. He had been in prison one time and God delivered him from the first Roman imprisonment. Then they put him back again. You would think that if Paul were smart (in the world's smartness), he would have quit preaching the Lord Jesus Christ. He would not have been put into prison again, but Paul was not *"smart"* in this world's *smartness*. He was honoring the Lord Jesus Christ. He kept preaching the Scriptures. He kept preaching the Lord Jesus Christ and was put right back into prison again. In the second Roman imprisonment, spoken of in 2 Timothy 4, he died.

The Blood Of The Martyrs

The blood of the martyrs is said to be the seed of the true Church. The more Rome slaughtered, the more Christians believed. It almost reminds me of the ones that were gathered around trying to be volunteers in Iraq for police officers. A car pulled up and machine-gunned them and with a hand grenade slaughtered them all. One of the newscasters said that when that happened, a hundred more stood up and volunteered to take the place of the ones that were slaughtered.

May God give us wisdom to go forth with the Lord Jesus Christ our Saviour. If blood comes upon us, so be it. We must be faithful.

Revelation Chapter Nineteen

Revelation 19:1

"And after these things I heard a great voice of much people in heaven, saying, Alleluia; Salvation, and glory, and honour, and power, unto the Lord our God:"

The Heavenly Alleluia To The Lord

Here is a great multitude in Heaven—true saints, genuinely saved, born-again, regenerated—up there with new bodies and saying, *Alleluia*. It is from two Hebrew words: HALAL is *praise ye* and YAHH (for JEHOVAH) is *the Lord*. Praise ye the Lord! Notice these four other things they say to the Lord God of Heaven and earth. The four words are salvation, glory, honour, and power. Let us look at a few verses that remind us of God as salvation.

- **Acts 4:12**
  "Neither is there **salvation** in any other: for there is none other name under heaven given among men, whereby we must be saved."
- **Acts 13:47**
  "For so hath the Lord commanded us, *saying*, I have set thee to be a light of the Gentiles, that thou shouldest be for **salvation** unto the ends of the earth."

That was where Paul was commissioned by the Lord Jesus Christ.

- **Romans 1:16**
  "For I am not ashamed of the gospel of Christ: for it is the power of God unto **salvation** to every one that believeth; to the Jew first, and also to the Greek."
- **2 Corinthians 6:2**
  "(For he saith, I have heard thee in a time accepted, and in the day of **salvation** have I succoured thee: behold, now is the accepted time; behold, now is the day of **salvation**.)"

We should not put it off. Today, if we are not Biblically **saved**, we have to trust Him and be genuinely **saved**.

- **Titus 2:11**
  "For the grace of God that bringeth **salvation** hath appeared to all men,"

God's Grace To All People

It is God's grace that brings salvation, and it has appeared to all men. All men can genuinely trust the Lord Jesus Christ if they would. It is not just to the elect, not just to a certain group, but salvation has appeared to all and they can trust the Lord Jesus Christ as Saviour and Redeemer as they hear the gospel, repent of sin, and genuinely trust Him.

- **Hebrews 2:3**
  "How shall we escape, if we neglect so great **salvation**; which at the first began to be spoken by the Lord, and was confirmed unto us by them that heard *him;*"

We cannot neglect **salvation**.

- **Hebrews 5:9**
  "And being made perfect, he became the author of eternal **salvation** unto all them that obey him;"

This is speaking of the Lord Jesus Christ. Eternal **salvation** does not stop. It does not end. We do not get genuinely **saved** today and lost tomorrow. No matter what, it is eternal.

- **Revelation 7:10**
  "And cried with a loud **voice**, saying, **Salvation** to our God which sitteth upon the throne, and unto the Lamb."

This second word the multitude is saying to our God is **salvation**. Notice the next word, *glory*.

- **Luke 9:32**
  "But Peter and they that were with him were heavy with sleep: and when they were awake, they saw his **glory**, and the two men that stood with him."

Peter, James, and John went up with the Lord Jesus Christ to the mount of Transfiguration. They were heavy with sleep. They fell asleep, but they saw His **glory**, the **glory** of the Lord Jesus Christ.

- **Luke 21:27**
  "And then shall they see the Son of man coming in a cloud with power and great **glory**."

His second coming will be a **glorious** coming.

- **John 1:14**
  "And the Word was made flesh, and dwelt among us, (and we beheld his **glory**, the **glory** as of the only begotten of the Father,) full of grace and truth."

The **glory** was veiled in His perfect human body, but still there was **glory** there. John says, "We saw his **glory**."

- **1 Corinthians 2:8**
  "Which none of the princes of this world knew: for had they known it, they would not have crucified the Lord of **glory**."

They did not think He had any **glory**. They did not think He was the Lord of **glory**. They thought He was just a human, just a man.

- **Hebrews 1:3**
  "Who being the brightness of *his* **glory**, and the express image of his person, and upholding all things by the word of his power, when he had by himself purged our sins, sat down on the right hand of the Majesty on high;"

This is speaking of the Lord Jesus Christ again. The brightness of God's **glory** was the Lord Jesus Christ, His Son. He was veiled in His perfect human body, but He was the brightness of His **glory**.

- **Hebrews 2:9**
  "But we see Jesus, who was made a little lower than the angels for the suffering of death, crowned with **glory** and honour; that he by the grace of God should taste death for every man."

That is eternal **salvation** to every man, woman, and child that genuinely trusts Him. That, to me, shows that it is for every man that will sincerely believe, not just a limited number.

- **Jude 1:24**
  "Now unto him that is able to keep you from falling, and to present *you* faultless before the presence of his **glory** with exceeding joy,"

The **glory** in Heaven, when we see it, will be <u>effulgent glory</u>, bright **glory** with exceeding joy. That is the second word after ***Alleluia***.

Notice there is also ***honour*** unto the Lord. We should give **honor** to Him. The Heavenly host does. Why shouldn't we?

- **John 5:23**
  "That all *men* should **honour** the Son, even as they **honour** the Father. He that **honoureth** not the Son honoureth not the Father which hath sent him."

It is not enough to **honor** the Father. You cannot get to Heaven by only **honoring** the Father. As the Jews say, "Let us go worship God." It cannot be Allah or anyone else. We have to come to the Son.

- **Hebrews 2:9**
  "But we see Jesus, who was made a little lower than the angels for the suffering of death, crowned with **glory** and **honour**; that he by the grace of God should taste death for every man."

He is an **honorable** Saviour and we must **honor** Him.

- **Revelation 4:11**
  "Thou art worthy, O Lord, to receive **glory** and **honour** and power: for thou hast created all things, and for thy pleasure they are and were created."

The last word is *power*. All the hosts of Heaven say, *"power, unto the Lord."*

- **Matthew 28:18**
  "And Jesus came and spake unto them, saying, All **power** is given unto me in heaven and in earth."

He is a **powerful** Saviour.

- **Romans 1:16**
  "For I am not ashamed of the gospel of Christ: for it is the **power** of God unto **salvation** to every one that believeth; to the Jew first, and also to the Greek."

- **1 Corinthians 1:18**
  "For the preaching of the cross is to them that perish foolishness; but unto us which are saved it is the **power** of God."

If you do not believe it, just try to give the gospel to one of the lost people that will not accept it. It is foolishness to them. Do you mean you can be saved by genuinely trusting the Lord Jesus Christ who died on a cross? Yes. The cross preaches the **power** of God.

- **1 Corinthians 1:24**
  "But unto them which are called, both Jews and Greeks, Christ the power of God, and the wisdom of God."

That is His title: *the power of God.*

- **1 Corinthians 2:5**
  "That your faith should not stand in the wisdom of men, but in the **power** of God."

It is God's **power** that our faith should stand in, not in some man's wisdom.

- **2 Corinthians 12:9**
  "And he said unto me, My grace is sufficient for thee: for my strength is made perfect in weakness. Most gladly therefore will I rather glory in my infirmities, that the **power** of Christ may rest upon me."

After Paul asked the Lord three times to remove the thorn in the flesh, the Lord said, "No," three times. Paul wanted God's **power** and the Lord Jesus Christ's **power**.

- **1 Peter 1:5**
  "Who are kept by the **power** of God through faith unto **salvation** ready to be revealed in the last time."

Kept By The Power Of God

Peter says that we are kept by the power of God. Those who are truly saved, those that are born again, those that have been redeemed through genuine faith in the Lord Jesus Christ, are kept. They are secured by the power of God. It is through faith, but it is the power of God that keeps us. We do not get lost every time we sin. We may get out of fellowship with the Lord, but we are not lost.

- **Revelation 4:11**
  "Thou art worthy, O Lord, to receive **glory** and **honour** and **power**: for thou hast created all things, and for thy pleasure they are and were created."

No wonder the hosts of Heaven could sing, "Praise ye the Lord—**Alleluia!**" and then, "**Salvation** unto Thee, **glory** unto Thee, **honour** unto Thee, and **power** unto Thee." He is a great Lord and a great God, indeed. The reason for their singing all these different things unto Him is found in Revelation 19:2.

Revelation 19:2

"For true and righteous *are* his judgments: for he hath judged the great whore, which did corrupt the earth with her fornication, and hath avenged the blood of his servants at her hand."

The Four Alleluias Here

There are four *Alleluias* in the first part of this chapter: in Revelation 19:1, 19:3, 19:4, and 19:6. This *Alleluia* is because He has *judged the great whore*, this Babylonian system and this Roman Catholic system, the Roman Catholic one-world

> church gathering up all the different religions of the world.
> Political Babylon is judged as well, which did continue to
> *corrupt the earth with her fornication*—idolatry (physical or
> spiritual), all kinds of fornication.

Then notice, He has *avenged the blood of his servants.* We see
God's **righteous judgments** in Scripture.

- **Psalm 19:9**
  "The fear of the LORD *is* clean, enduring for ever: the
  judgments of the LORD *are* true *and* **righteous** altogether."

There is not a single lie in the Words of God. That is why we use our King
James Bible, because it is accurately translated from the proper Hebrew,
Aramaic, and Greek Words into English.

- **Psalm 119:7**
  "I will praise thee with uprightness of heart, when I shall have
  learned thy **righteous judgments**."

Righteous judgments have nothing sinful about them.

- **Psalm 119:62**
  "At midnight I will rise to give thanks unto thee because of thy
  righteous judgments."

If we do not know God's Words, we are not going to know they are
righteous. We want to know them and we should know them.

- **Psalm 119:106**
  "I have sworn, and I will perform *it*, that I will keep thy
  righteous judgments."

David cannot keep God's **righteous judgments**, and you and I cannot
keep God's **righteous judgments** unless we consider these three
things:

1. We must know what God's judgments are.
2. We must be willing to keep God's judgments.
3. We must ask God's power to help us keep God's judgments.

In our own strength, we cannot keep anything. Then we may be able
to keep with David *thy righteous judgments.*

- **Psalm 119:160**
  "Thy word is true *from* the beginning: and every one of **thy
  righteous judgments** <u>*endureth* for ever</u>."

God's **judgments** endure for ever. That is why we believe in **Bible
preservation.** That is one of the battles in our fundamentalist world
today. Two big books have been written that I have answered on the
radio. The sequel to *From the Mind of God to the Mind of Man,* which
is a Bob Jones University production (graduates and teachers and so on),

is *God's Word in Our Hands, the Bible Preserved For Us.* They have the wrong idea of **preservation.**

A second book was written by the head of the language department of Bob Jones University, Dr. Samuel Schnaiter and another man by the name of Ron Tagliapietra. They also talk about Bible **preservation,** but they are incorrect on it.

These fundamentalists do not believe what the Bible is. The only Bible they have preserved is the thoughts of the Bible, the messages of the Bible, the Word not the Words, the ideas of the Bible, the truth of the Bible, not the Words. That is not the Bible. God gave us a Bible and He spoke Hebrew, a little Aramaic, and Greek. If you talk about Bible preservation, you have to believe in the Words of the Hebrew, Aramaic, and Greek being preserved to this day. They do not do that. They say there are errors and all kinds of mistakes. David said, *"Every one of thy righteous judgments endureth for ever."*

Proper Bible Preservation

I believe in Bible preservation. Because we have the preserved Hebrew, Aramaic, and Greek Words, and our King James translators used those preserved Words, we have God's preserved Words in the English language in the King James Bible—preserved and translated for us accurately. Pardon that soapbox, but I thought I would get that in. It *endureth for ever.*

- **Psalm 119:164**
  "Seven times a day do I praise thee because of **thy righteous judgments.**"

God's **judgments** are **righteous.**

Notice also, in Revelation 19:2, they are thankful to the Lord Jesus Christ because He has **avenged his saints.** God does **avenge.**

- **Deuteronomy 32:43**
  "Rejoice, O ye nations, *with* his people: for he will **avenge the blood of his servants,** and will render **vengeance** to his adversaries, and will be merciful unto his land, *and* to his people."

The Lord Jesus Christ is the One that will **avenge.** That is part of His attributes.

- **2 Kings 9:7**
  "And thou shalt smite the house of Ahab thy master, that I may **avenge** the blood of my servants the prophets, and the blood of all the servants of the LORD, at the hand of Jezebel."

Jezebel slaughtered God's servants, many of them, and God is **avenging** their blood righteously.

- **Jeremiah 46:10**
  "For this is the day of the Lord GOD of hosts, a day of **vengeance**, that he may avenge him of his adversaries: and the sword shall devour, and it shall be satiate and made drunk with their blood: for the Lord GOD of hosts hath a sacrifice in the north country by the river Euphrates."

Is God a **vengeful** God? He is a God of love, but He also has righteous judgment against His adversaries that are against Him.

- **Luke 18:7-8**
  "And shall not God **avenge** his own elect, which cry day and night unto him, though he bear long with them? I tell you that he will **avenge** them speedily. Nevertheless when the Son of man cometh, shall he find faith on the earth?"

He will **avenge** those of us who cry unto Him.

- **Romans 12:19**
  "Dearly beloved, **avenge** not yourselves, but *rather* give place unto wrath: for it is written, **Vengeance** is mine; I will repay, saith the Lord."

Vengeance Belongs To The Lord

God does not want us to do it ourselves. Just stay away from wrath. When the Lord Jesus Christ repays, He will do it righteously. He will not make any mistakes. He will not do it in anger. He will do it properly. Everything will be right when He has vengeance in these judgments.

Revelation 19:3

"And again they said, Alleluia. And her smoke rose up for ever and ever."

Again, here is the multitude, as it says in Revelation 19:1. There is a great **voice** of much people in Heaven. Here is the **smoke** of the judgment of political Babylon and religious Babylon. So they said again, **"Praise the Lord!"**

When Our Enemies Fall

God tells us we should not rejoice when our enemy falls into a pit. We should not rejoice when he stumbles, but here are the saints in Heaven saying, "Praise the Lord!" I guess we can praise the Lord Jesus Christ when this terrible religious and political system that has rejected the Lord Jesus Christ is burned up and smoke is rising. They are praising the Lord Jesus Christ for it. We can at least do that. If the Heavenly hosts can, I guess we can. We have to be careful about being too clever and too happy when our enemies fall into trouble. The Lord Jesus Christ said, *"Love your enemies."*

- Matthew 5:44
  "But I say unto you, Love your enemies, bless them that curse you, do good to them that hate you, and pray for them which despitefully use you, and persecute you;"

The true saints in Heaven are saying to the Lord Jesus Christ, "Alleluia."

Revelation 19:4

"And the four and twenty elders and the four beasts fell down and worshipped God that sat on the throne, saying, Amen; Alleluia."

Here is another *Alleluia*, the third one. These **four and twenty elders**, you remember, I say are a picture probably of the true Church in Heaven. The **four beasts**, I believe, are representatives of the leading angels. Both the representatives of the true Church and the angelic beings **fell down and worshipped God**. That is Who we should **worship**. We should **worship** none other than God. In fact, later on in the chapter, we will see in Revelation 19:10 that John was going to **worship** an angel. He said, "Get up." We do not **worship** a man. We have to be careful of that.

- Psalm 29:2
  "Give unto the LORD the glory due unto his name; **worship** the LORD in the beauty of holiness."

Holiness means to say, "No," to sin. Our **worship** should come out of pure, cleansed hearts, confessing known sins unto the Lord.

- **Matthew 4:10**
  "Then saith Jesus unto him, Get thee hence, Satan: for it is written, Thou shalt **worship** the Lord thy God, and him only shalt thou serve."

The Lord Jesus Christ always quoted the Scripture in the three temptations of Satan in the wilderness.

GEGRAPTAI Is In The Perfect Tense

That word for *it is written* is GEGRAPTAI. That is the perfect tense of GRAPHO. GRAPHO is the word, *to write*, like graphite pencils, graphic arts, and so on. GEGRAPTAI, the perfect tense, means *that which has been written in the past,* when Moses wrote it, *and that which continues to the present and on into the future.* That is Bible preservation again. The Lord uses this some fifteen or twenty times in the New Testament.

The object of our **worship** is not men, not movie stars, not football, basketball, or hockey players, but the Lord Himself—not preachers, not people, but the Lord.

- **John 4:24**
  "God *is* a Spirit: and they that **worship** him must **worship** *him* in spirit and in truth."

That is Who He is. We must **worship** Him in spirit with the proper attitude, and in truth with the Scriptures before us, truly presented.

- **Philippians 3:3**
  "For we are the circumcision, which **worship** God in the spirit, and rejoice in Christ Jesus, and have no confidence in the flesh."

Our **worship** of the Lord should be in the spirit and having no confidence in the flesh.

- **Revelation 4:10**
  "The four and twenty elders fall down before him that sat on the throne, and **worship** him that liveth for ever and ever, and cast their crowns before the throne, saying,"

We have all these churches in these modern days with contemporary services. Some have contemporary services for one hour and then worship service the next hour. They have all these **worship** leaders. They go up there with their instruments or whatever they have. That is not what the Lord means by **worship**. This is, I think, a pollution of the real meaning of **worshipping** the Lord in the beauty of holiness.

Revelation 19:5

"And a voice came out of the throne, saying, Praise our God, all ye his servants, and ye that fear him, both small and great."

Praise defined used to be *to set a price upon.* Appraisal of your house—what is your price? That is the old meaning literally. Now it means to *commend the worth of something, to express approval, the admiration of, to laud, to glorify, to extol.* When we **praise** the Lord, we express approval.

- **Psalm 7:17**
  "I will **praise** the LORD according to his righteousness: and will sing **praise** to the name of the LORD most high."

That word, by the way, is in the present tense. It is a continuous action, continually **praising** the Lord.

- **Hebrews 13:15**
  "By him therefore let us offer the sacrifice of **praise** to God continually, that is, the fruit of our lips giving thanks to his name."

Praise God Continuously

This is for us. Praise to God continuously—how is that done? Giving thanks to His name. That is God's praise and that is what every one of us who names the Name of the Lord Jesus Christ should do continually.

- **1 Peter 4:11**
  "If any man speak, *let him speak* as the oracles of God; if any man minister, *let him do it* as of the ability which God giveth: that God in all things may be glorified through Jesus Christ, to whom be **praise** and dominion for ever and ever. Amen."

Praise By Giving Thanks

We must extol and honor and praise our Saviour, the Lord Jesus Christ, in everything that we do with the fruit of our lips, giving thanks to His Name.

Revelation 19:6

"And I heard as it were the voice of a great multitude, and as the voice of many waters, and as the voice of mighty thunderings, saying, Alleluia: for the Lord God omnipotent reigneth."

Here again are the **voices** in Heaven, a **great multitude**, strong, loud, again saying, "**Alleluia**," the fourth **Alleluia. Praise ye the Lord!** Notice, the reason they are **praising** the Lord, *for* (in the sense of because) *the Lord God omnipotent reigneth*. This is the only time in the Bible the word *omnipotent* is used. It means *all powerful*. It is one of God's attributes.

This is near the end of the tribulation period. Genuine believers will be in Heaven. All of us who are genuinely saved will be gone from the earth. We will be raptured up with the Lord Jesus Christ. Those that are lost will be on this earth. Up in Heaven, the multitude will say, *"the Lord God omnipotent reigneth."* It would be good if the Lord would reign over every one of our hearts and lives. It would be good, if even down here, He would reign and rule. Lord means, *master*. Lord means, *someone to whom we yield allegiance*. It means, *someone to whom we say, "Not my will, but thine be done."* One thing is certain—when we are in glory, He will reign and we will be glad of it. We will reign with Him. Soon, at the end of this tribulation period, there will be the marriage supper of the Lamb and the millennial reign of our Saviour. He will reign with an **omnipotent** and righteous reign.

A Republic, Not A Democracy

You may ask, "Is it going to be a democracy?" No. Democracy is probably the weakest of all governments. A republic is what we have in the United States of America. I do not care how they talk about democracy, democracy, the people rule. No, it is a democracy as far as we have a democratic republic, but it is a republic of states.

When the Lord Jesus Christ reigns, it will be a **beneficent dictatorship**. Usually, that has a bad connotation. If you want to use another word, it will be a **monarchy**. One man rules.

Christ's Righteous Monarchy

The Lord Jesus Christ will be the King of kings and Lord of lords. It will not be, "What do I think about it? What does somebody else think about it? We will take a vote on it." No. He is going to be righteous. Every dictator or monarch that ever lived on this earth, could not be completely righteous, because they are sinners. Our Saviour is righteous. He will rule with a rod of iron. It will be a monarchy. He will reign omnipotent.

Revelation 19:7

"Let us be glad and rejoice, and give honour to him: for the marriage of the Lamb is come, and his wife hath made herself ready."

The **marriage of the Lamb** is come. We are going to be reading something about the **marriage** supper, what it means in historical fashion. Before we do that, let me just notice, the Lord says, *"Let us be glad and rejoice, and give honour to him."* That to *be glad* is a present continuous action. Let us continue to **be glad**. So is *rejoice* a present continuous action. Let us continue to **rejoice**. Let us not let up in our **gladness** and **joy**.

- **Psalm 9:2**
  "I will be **glad** and **rejoice** in thee: I will sing praise to thy name, O thou most High."

- **Psalm 32:11**
  "Be **glad** in the LORD, and **rejoice**, ye righteous: and shout for **joy**, all *ye that are* upright in heart."

- **Psalm 40:16**
  "Let all those that seek thee **rejoice** and be **glad** in thee: let such as love thy salvation say continually, The LORD be magnified."

Glad is a good word—continuously.

- **Psalm 64:10**
  "The righteous shall be **glad** in the LORD, and shall trust in him; and all the upright in heart shall glory."

- **Psalm 68:3**
  "But let the righteous be **glad**; let them **rejoice** before God: yea, let them exceedingly **rejoice**."

- **Psalm 104:34**
  "My meditation of him shall be sweet: I will be **glad** in the LORD."

Why should we be so gloomy and so downcast? We should be **glad** in the Lord.

- **1 Peter 4:13**
  "But **rejoice**, inasmuch as ye are partakers of Christ's sufferings; that, when his glory shall be revealed, ye may **be glad** also with exceeding **joy**."

There is **gladness** in serving the Lord. We can serve the Lord in **gladness**, not in sadness, but in **gladness**.

Revelation 19:7 says not only to be continuously **glad**, but also to continuously **rejoice**. Keep on **rejoicing**.

- **Matthew 5:11-12**
  "Blessed are ye, when *men* shall revile you, and persecute *you*, and shall say all manner of evil against you falsely, for my sake. **Rejoice**, and be exceeding **glad**: for great *is* your reward in heaven: for so persecuted they the prophets which were before you."

Blessings Even When Reviled

How is it a blessing when men revile you? God says that it is a blessing. Since when is persecution a blessing? The Lord Jesus Christ says that it is, and it is. What He says, He means. Blessing? Yes. The Lord Jesus Christ prepares us for persecution.

- **Romans 5:2**
  "By whom also we have access by faith into this grace wherein we stand, and **rejoice** in hope of the glory of God."

Rejoice! We have a hope. The world does not have any hope.

- **Philippians 2:16**
  "Holding forth the word of life; that I may **rejoice** in the day of Christ, that I have not run in vain, neither laboured in vain."

When Paul preached to them he said, "I want to **rejoice** because you true Christians at Philippi are genuinely saved."

- **Philippians 4:4**
  "**Rejoice** in the Lord alway: *and* again I say, **Rejoice**."

How could Paul, a prisoner in the jail at Philippi and in Rome, **rejoice**? Does he have something that you do not have? No, he had the Holy Spirit of God, same as you and I have, if you are genuinely saved and born-again. We are obligated to **rejoice** in any circumstance, whatever it may be.

- **1 Thessalonians 5:16**
  "**Rejoice** evermore."

Rejoice always. Never stop.

- **1 Peter 1:8**
  "Whom having not seen, ye love; in whom, though now ye see *him* not, yet believing, ye **rejoice** with **joy** unspeakable and full of glory:"

This is speaking of the Lord Jesus Christ.

- **1 Peter 4:13**
  "But **rejoice**, inasmuch as ye are partakers of Christ's sufferings; that, when his glory shall be revealed, ye may **be glad** also with exceeding **joy**."

Notice also in Revelation 19:7, that it says, *"give honour to him: for the marriage of the Lamb is come, and his wife hath made herself ready."* His *wife* means, all *those who are born-again and genuinely saved.* Are you **ready**? There are many verses that tell us we have to be **ready** for many things.

- **Matthew 24:44**
  "Therefore be ye also **ready**: for in such an hour as ye think not the Son of man cometh."

We do not know when the rapture of the true Church will be, taking us Home.

- **Acts 21:13**
  "Then Paul answered, What mean ye to weep and to break mine heart? for I am **ready** not to be bound only, but also to die at Jerusalem for the name of the Lord Jesus."

Paul Was Ready To Die

People said to Paul, "Do not go to Jerusalem. They are going to bind you. They are going to kill you. They are going to take you to be slaughtered in Rome." This was Paul's answer. He was ready to die.

- **Romans 1:15**
  "So, as much as in me is, I am **ready** to preach the gospel to you that are at Rome also."

- **1 Timothy 6:18**
  "That they do good, that they be rich in good works, **ready** to distribute, willing to communicate;"

They were to be **ready** to distribute, **ready** to give, **ready** to communicate the funds to the Lord's work.

- **2 Timothy 4:6-7**
  "For I am now **ready** to be offered, and the time of my departure is at hand. I have fought a good fight, I have finished *my* course, I have kept the faith:"

This was Paul's last **readiness**. It was his second Roman imprisonment. Paul was **ready**. We have to be **ready**.

- **1 Peter 3:15**
  "But sanctify the Lord God in your hearts: and *be* **ready** always to *give* an answer to every man that asketh you a reason of the hope that is in you with meekness and fear:"

We need to be **ready** to give an answer. "Why do you believe like this?" Know the Scriptures. Give an answer.

- **1 Peter 5:2**
  "Feed the flock of God which is among you, taking the oversight *thereof*, not by constraint, but willingly; not for filthy lucre, but of a **ready** mind;"

He talks about the **ready** mind of preachers here.

Now there is **readiness** for the marriage.

- **2 Corinthians 11:2**
  "For I am jealous over you with godly jealousy: for I have espoused you to one husband, that I may present *you* as a chaste virgin to Christ."

There should be **readiness** for the marriage.

- **John 14:6**
  "Jesus saith unto him, I am the way, the truth, and the life: no man cometh unto the Father, but by me."

That is the only way we can be **ready** to meet the Lord Jesus Christ in the air. As far as the **marriage supper of the Lamb**, let us just go through briefly some of the things that are there.

Seven Pictures Of The True Church

The word *bride* is one of the seven pictures of the true Church–those who are genuinely saved. There are seven pictures.

1. Sheep–the Lord Jesus Christ is the Shepherd and we are the sheep.
2. Branches–He is the Vine and we are the branches.
3. Lively Stones–He is the cornerstone. We are the lively, or living stones.
4. Pearl–He is the One that searches for us and we are the pearl of great price.
5. Servants and Priests–He is our Master. We are servants and priests of God.
6. Body–We are the Body of Christ.
7. Bride–We are the Bride of Christ.

There are three parts of the **marriage** ceremony of Israel in Jewish history.

1. The first part is the legal **marriage,** often arranged by the parents of the bride and bridegroom, in which the dowry is paid. The young people are formally married in a legal sense. They have not yet come together. The dowry for us who are His bride was paid by the shedding of the blood of the Lord Jesus Christ in His death at the cross of Calvary. That is the dowry. That is the price–the Lord Jesus Christ's death on the cross, shedding His blood for our sins.
2. The second part of the **marriage, subsequent to the legal marriage, is when the bridegroom, according to the custom, would go with his companions to the house of the bride to claim his bride for himself and take her back to his own home.** The Lord Jesus Christ, in the rapture, will take His bride one day Home to Heaven, to His Father's house. It may be today. So shall we ever be with the Lord.
3. The third part of the **marriage supper** is the bridal procession, followed by the **marriage feast,** which often lasts for many days. That is the Oriental **marriage.** That is basically the **marriage supper** of the Lamb–three parts: the legal **marriage,** which is a dowry; secondly, the groom taking the

bride to his house, claiming her for his own; and then the **marriage supper** is the third thing following that. Rejoice! The **marriage of the Lamb** is come.

Revelation 19:8

"And to her was granted that she should be arrayed in fine linen, clean and white: for the fine linen is the righteousness of saints."

The bride should have **clean fine linen.** That is why those of us who are genuinely saved and are part of the **bride** of the Lord Jesus Christ should have **clean** lives—clean *fine linen.* **Brides** wear **white** generally. What does it speak of? It speaks of **purity.**

Brides In White Should Be Clean

I am going to step on some people's toes, I guess, but in my judgment as a pastor, white should indicate purity of the bride. If it is not a pure situation, it should not be white. That is just my opinion. What does a symbol mean? I realize white can be a million things, but if it means, as it means here, the Lord Jesus Christ's bride, the ones that are genuinely saved and clean with new bodies, we will have fine linen, clean and white.

- **Genesis 41:41-42**
  "And Pharaoh said unto Joseph, See, I have set thee over all the land of Egypt. And Pharaoh took off his ring from his hand, and put it upon Joseph's hand, and arrayed him in vestures of **fine linen,** and put a gold chain about his neck;"

Joseph was in prison. He was in Pharaoh's dungeon. He was given wonderful clothing after coming out of prison.

- **Esther 8:15**
  "And Mordecai went out from the presence of the king in royal apparel of blue and **white,** and with a great crown of gold, and with a garment of **fine linen** and purple: and the city of Shushan rejoiced and was glad."

Mordecai was elevated and he had **fine linen.**

Notice also, *the fine linen is the righteousness of saints.* It just so happens that is in the plural. It could be just as well *righteousnesses* or *righteous* deeds.

- **Genesis 15:6**
  "And he believed in the LORD; and he counted it to him for **righteousness.**"

This is talking about Abraham. Faith equals **righteousness** in the Words of God.

- **Romans 3:21-22**
  "But now the **righteousness** of God without the law is manifested, being witnessed by the law and the prophets; Even the **righteousness** of God *which is* by faith of Jesus Christ unto all and upon all them that believe: for there is no difference:"

Faith is unto all, but *upon **all them that believe.*** Those that genuinely trust in the Lord Jesus Christ have the **righteousness** of God.

- **Romans 4:5**
  "But to him that worketh not, but believeth on him that justifieth the ungodly, his faith is counted for **righteousness.**"

How do we get this **righteousness** of the saints? We get God's righteousness by genuine faith in the Lord Jesus Christ. That is a transaction. That is an imputation. That is giving of something we do not deserve if we are trusting Him as Saviour and Redeemer.

- **Romans 10:10**
  "For with the heart man believeth unto **righteousness**; and with the mouth confession is made unto salvation."

Genuine faith in the Lord Jesus Christ equals **righteousness** in God's sense. The Lord Jesus Christ gives us **righteousness**.

- **2 Corinthians 5:21**
  "For he hath made him *to be* sin for us, who knew no sin; that we might be made the **righteousness** of God in him."

Righteous Standing Before God

This is a beautiful picture of God's method of bestowing His righteousness upon us. God the Father made God the Son to be sin for us. He knew no sin—not any sin at all. This is the only way we have a righteous standing before God. That is our standing. Our state is what we are right here. I hope it is not unrighteous. We ought to aim for the righteousness we have, as far as our standing is concerned. As we have said many times, "If you aim at nothing, you will hit it every time." Aim for the standing so our state will be righteous. As it says, *"Be ye holy for I am holy."*

Notice the fruits of **righteousness**. There are some verses that tell us that if we have a **righteous** standing before God, our lives should also be **righteous**.

- **Ephesians 2:8-10**
  "For by grace are ye saved through faith; and that not of yourselves: *it is* the gift of God: Not of **works**, lest any man should boast. For we are his workmanship, created in Christ Jesus unto **good works**, which God hath before ordained that we should walk in them."

Saved Unto Good Works

We are not saved by good works, but *unto good works.* God wants every believer that is genuinely saved and justified to righteously walk in the good works that He has laid out before us in His Words.

- **Philippians 1:11**
  "Being filled with the fruits of **righteousness**, which are by Jesus Christ, unto the glory and praise of God."

Roots And Fruits

Fruits are derived from roots. The root is our righteous standing before God—salvation. We should have fruits, which are by the Lord Jesus Christ to the glory and praise of God—*filled with the fruits.*

- **2 Timothy 2:22**
  "Flee also youthful lusts: but follow **righteousness**, faith, charity, peace, with them that call on the Lord out of a pure heart."

You may be declared **righteous** by God. That is your standing, but let your state follow after it.

- **2 Timothy 3:16-17**
  "All scripture *is* given by inspiration of God, and *is* profitable for doctrine, for reproof, for correction, for instruction in **righteousness**: That the man of God may be perfect, throughly furnished unto all good works."

Instruction in **righteousness**—that is the Words of God. That is why it is given. That is the purpose of it. We say that every Lord's Day in our church, because I believe that is the purpose—the *instruction in* **righteousness**. There are fruits of **righteousness**. We must not only be **righteous**, but we must follow after **righteousness**.

- **Titus 2:11-13**
  "For the grace of God that bringeth salvation hath appeared to all men, Teaching us that, denying ungodliness and worldly lusts, we should live soberly, **righteously**, and godly, in this present world; Looking for that blessed hope, and the glorious appearing of the great God and our Saviour Jesus Christ;"

Denying Ungodliness and Lusts

Using a negative command, Pastor Titus was to be teaching us who are genuinely saved that we are to be *denying ungodliness and worldly lusts*. We are to absolutely deny them. We should live soberly, righteously, and godly. Where? In Heaven? No, in this present world, looking unto the Lord Jesus Christ, the *blessed hope*. That is what we are to do—follow after righteousness.

- **Titus 3:5**
  "Not by works of **righteousness** which we have done, but according to his mercy he saved us, by the washing of regeneration, and renewing of the Holy Ghost;"

Our works do not save, but after we are genuinely saved, God wants us to **work**.

- **Philippians 2:12**
  "Wherefore, my beloved, as ye have always obeyed, not as in my presence only, but now much more in my absence, **work out** your own salvation with fear and trembling."

Harvest Salvation's Fruits

It is not that you work for salvation, but you work it out. God has worked it in, the true Christian should work it out. Harvest it. Just like you plant seeds (and I am not a planter of seeds, by the way). I understand if you plant seeds and take care of them, they will bloom. God wants us to have the fruits of righteousness. What is in us should come out.

- **1 Peter 2:24**
  "Who his own self bare our sins in his own body on the tree, that we, being dead to sins, should live unto **righteousness**: by whose stripes ye were healed."

We Should Live Righteously

Live unto righteousness. Live righteously. That is the way that God wants us to do. The bride is to do that. She hath made herself ready—ready because the Lord Jesus Christ has made us ready.

The **righteousness** of the saints is the fine linen, clean and white. You may remember, the judgment seat of the Lord Jesus Christ is what determines what we bring in to this marriage supper of the Lamb.

Two Kinds Of Building Materials

There are two different types of materials: the things that will stand the fire; and the things that will burn up in the fire.

Talking about the fire, one of the news commentators mentioned about the Mount Saint Helens eruption in 1980, how immediately (instantaneously) it erupted and shot out rocks and lava and heat at the speed of sound (761 miles per hour). That heat wave reached fifteen miles away from Mount Saint Helens and burned everything in its wake to a crisp and to ash. Trees four feet in diameter were burned to ashes. People in their homes were burned—fifty-seven dead.

The Judgment Seat Of Christ

The judgment seat of the Lord Jesus Christ will reckon two types of materials. One is combustible, the other is not. We build on the foundation of the Lord Jesus Christ. Is it gold, silver, and precious stones? Or is it hay, wood, and stubble? The fire shall try every man's work of what sort it is—not how much it is—but what sort it is. The Lord Jesus Christ died for us that we should live unto righteousness.

Revelation 19:9

"And he saith unto me, Write, Blessed *are* they which are called unto the marriage supper of the Lamb. And he saith unto me, These are the true sayings of God."

We ought to be thankful, if we are genuinely saved, to be **called to the marriage supper** of the Lamb. Mrs. Waite sings a song called *Come and Dine*. That third stanza is very appropriate:

> Soon the Lamb will take His bride
> To be ever at His side,

All the host of Heaven will assembled be;
O 'twill be a glorious sight,
All the saints in spotless white;
And with Jesus they will feast eternally.

That is the **marriage of the Lamb,** feasting with the Lord Jesus Christ eternally. Are you ready? Are you one of His? Will you be there? I hope you will.

Revelation 19:10

"And I fell at his feet to worship him. And he said unto me, See *thou do it* not: I am thy fellowservant, and of thy brethren that have the testimony of Jesus: worship God: for the testimony of Jesus is the spirit of prophecy."

We are not to **worship** any man, anyone, whoever it may be. This is taught very clearly. I trust that we may have the **testimony of the Lord Jesus Christ**. We should not drag His name in the dirt in any way. That is why some genuine Christians do not want to be known as "Christians" in any sense of the word, because their lives do not measure up. If people knew they were genuine Christians and they live the way they live, the world would point to them and say, "Oh, what a horrible situation that is!" May our **testimony** be clean and right before the Lord. Notice, it says, *I am thy fellowservant.* We need **fellowservants.** One man cannot do it all.

- **Colossians 1:7**
  "As ye also learned of Epaphras our dear **fellowservant,** who is for you a faithful minister of Christ;"

We need **fellowservants,** fellow slaves of the Lord Jesus Christ, fellow people that will do His will.

- **Colossians 4:7**
  "All my state shall Tychicus declare unto you, *who is* a beloved brother, and a faithful minister and **fellowservant** in the Lord:"

We need **fellowservants.** I pray that everyone in our church will help us as a group to serve the Lord Jesus Christ. We do not worship each other. We are to worship the Lord Jesus Christ, but we need **fellowservants** to help us in the tremendous battle that is before us. We may be few in number in our church, but we have a big God and a big Saviour, a big Master. He will help us.

The Marriage Supper Of The Lamb

We have talked about the marriage supper of the Lamb. The Lord Jesus Christ has paid for us, the bride, with the dowry of His shed blood on the cross of Calvary. One day, He will call us and take us Home to His Father's house in the rapture. Then there will be the marriage supper of the Lamb for those of us who will be there.

I trust that you and I may be living for Him who died for us. We should not wait until we get to Heaven to be arrayed in fine linen, white and clean, but may our garments be white and clean down here as well.

Revelation 19:11

"And I saw heaven opened, and behold a white horse; and he that sat upon him was called Faithful and True, and in righteousness he doth judge and make war."

Two Phases Of Christ's Coming

The Lord Jesus Christ's second coming is in glory. There are two phases of His second coming, as we know. There is the rapture that comes before the tribulation, the seven-year period that we have been reading about in this book of Revelation. That is pre-tribulation. He takes us into the air. He will snatch away genuine believers, the born-again ones. The second phase of the coming is post-tribulation, after the tribulation is over, after the seven years are completed. Then it will not be in the air, but to the ground, His feet touching on the Mount of Olives, and then setting up His millennial kingdom to reign.

- **Matthew 24:27**
  "For as the lightning cometh out of the east, and shineth even unto the west; so shall also the **coming** of the Son of man be."
That is exactly the second phase of His **coming**.
- **Matthew 24:29-30**
  "Immediately after the tribulation of those days shall the sun be darkened, and the moon shall not give her light, and the stars shall fall from heaven, and the powers of the heavens shall be shaken: And then shall appear the sign of the Son of man in

heaven: and then shall all the tribes of the earth mourn, and
they shall see the Son of man **coming** in the clouds of heaven
with power and great glory."

The World Will See Christ

The world will see Him. At the rapture, before the
tribulation, caught up together, the genuine believers will see
and meet Him—not the unsaved. They will not know what
happened to us. Here, in the second phase of His second
coming, after the tribulation, they will *see the Son of Man*
coming in the clouds of heaven with power and great glory.
It will be a glorious coming.

- **1 Thessalonians 3:13**
  "To the end he may stablish your hearts unblameable in holiness
  before God, even our Father, at the **coming** of our Lord Jesus
  Christ with all his saints."

Paul wrote to the true Christians at Thessalonica. There is a **coming** of
the Lord Jesus Christ *for* His saints. There is a **coming** *with* His saints,
after the Biblical saints have been taken out before the tribulation, and
we will come back with Him. Revelation 19:11 includes the genuinely
saved, the born-again ones, redeemed with new bodies **coming** back
with the Lord Jesus Christ. He is **coming** with His saints.

- **2 Thessalonians 2:8**
  "And then shall that Wicked be revealed, whom the Lord shall
  consume with the spirit of his mouth, and shall destroy with the
  brightness of his **coming:**"

That Wicked one, that man of sin, that antichrist during this tribulation
period, this political ruler will be put down at the **coming** of the Lord
Jesus Christ. Revelation 19:11 tells about what will happen and on
through this chapter.

Notice, the Lord Jesus Christ said Heaven was opened, and the Lord
Jesus Christ is in Heaven. He went Home to Heaven with His Father.
This is the true Saviour, the true Christ. In Revelation 6:2, there is the
antichrist. He also had a white horse.

- **Revelation 6:2**
  "And I saw, and behold a white horse: and he that sat on him
  had a bow; and a crown was given unto him: and he went forth
  conquering, and to conquer."

There is a fake horse that is white, and a true horse that is white. The
Lord Jesus Christ is on this true white horse. Notice the attributes of the
Saviour as He comes to judge and to make war. Notice first, He is called

the *Faithful* One. That means, *someone you can depend upon.* If somebody says that he is going to do something, he does it. That is **faithful**.

- **Hebrews 2:17**
  "Wherefore in all things it behoved him to be made like unto *his* brethren, that he might be a merciful and **faithful** high priest in things *pertaining* to God, to make reconciliation for the sins of the people."

The Lord Jesus Christ is our High Priest. We do not believe in priests on earth, other than that all genuine believers are believer-priests. We are all believer-priests if we are genuinely saved. We do not have some priest we go to for confession that can forgive our sins, but we do have a great High Priest, who has passed into the heavens, even the Lord Jesus Christ. He is merciful, but He is also **faithful**. He deals with us in **faithfulness**.

- **Hebrews 3:1-2**
  "Wherefore, holy brethren, partakers of the heavenly calling, consider the Apostle and High Priest of our profession, Christ Jesus; Who was **faithful** to him that appointed him, as also Moses *was faithful* in all his house."

God the Father appointed the Lord Jesus Christ to do what He should have done: come to the cross of Calvary, be a **faithful** witness and testimony, and then go to that cross. The Lord Jesus Christ was **faithful** to Him that appointed Him. Then, when God the Father raised Him from the dead, the Lord Jesus Christ is a **faithful** High Priest. He is **faithful** to Him that appointed Him.

- **Revelation 3:14**
  "And unto the angel of the church of the Laodiceans write; These things saith the Amen, the **faithful and true** witness, the beginning of the creation of God;"

Christ Our Faithful High Priest

This is speaking of the Lord Jesus Christ. You know, if we do not have a faithful Saviour, then we are in trouble. If you are not saved, you do not have a faithful Saviour, a faithful Redeemer and a faithful High Priest. He is faithful to those who have genuinely believed and trusted in Him. If you are not saved, He is faithful to forgive your sins and to take you to Heaven and give you eternal life if you will but trust and genuinely receive Him, repent of your sins, and have a different attitude toward sin. Say, "I do not want that sin anymore," and trust in the Lord Jesus Christ. He will save you. He is faithful in to keeping His Words. That is why I believe John 3:16 is something we must believe by genuine faith.

- **John 3:16**
  "For God so loved the world, that he gave his only begotten Son, that whosoever believeth in him should not perish, but have everlasting life."

That is eternal security. God so loved the world—not just the world of the elect—but all the world, everybody in it. He died for the sins of the world. He is **faithful** to keep His promise of everlasting life.

Our Saviour Is Also True

Notice the second attribute of our Saviour. He is not only faithful, He is true. This man on a white horse, our Saviour, is faithful and true.

- **Matthew 22:16**
  "And they sent out unto him their disciples with the Herodians, saying, Master, we know that thou art **true**, and teachest the way of God in **truth**, neither carest thou for any *man*: for thou regardest not the person of men."

Even the Herodians, who despised the Lord Jesus Christ, saw that He spoke the **truth**.

- **John 1:9**
  "*That* was the **true** Light, which lighteth every man that cometh into the world."

This was spoken of the Lord Jesus Christ. He is the **true** Light, not a false light, but the **true** Light.

- **John 1:14**
  "And the Word was made flesh, and dwelt among us, (and we beheld his glory, the glory as of the only begotten of the Father,) full of grace and **truth**."

He is **faithful** and He is **true**. He does not have any lies about Him.

- **John 8:44**
  "Ye are of *your* father the devil, and the lusts of your father ye will do. He was a murderer from the beginning, and abode not in the **truth**, because there is no **truth** in him. When he speaketh a lie, he speaketh of his own: for he is a liar, and the father of it."

The Devil is the father of liars, but the Lord Jesus Christ is the **Truth**.

- **John 1:17**
"For the law was given by Moses, *but* grace and **truth** came by Jesus Christ."

<u>The Lord Jesus Christ is the One that brought His **truth** to us upon His incarnation.</u>

- **John 6:32-33**
"Then Jesus said unto them, Verily, verily, I say unto you, Moses gave you not that bread from heaven; but my Father giveth you the **true** bread from heaven. For the bread of God is he which cometh down from heaven, and giveth life unto the world."

He is speaking of when He multiplied the loaves for 5,000 men plus women and children. There must have been more than 10,000 that were eating.

- **Matthew 14:21**
"And they that had eaten were about five thousand men, beside women and children."

- **Matthew 15:38**
"And they that did eat were four thousand men, beside women and children."

At that occasion, the Lord Jesus Christ remarked about the manna from Heaven and how Moses was given that manna for forty years for the children of Israel. The Father gave the bread then. The Lord Jesus Christ is the **true** Bread. If a man partake of that Bread, he will have life eternal. <u>He was and is the **true** Bread that giveth life unto the world.</u>

- **John 4:13-14**
"Jesus answered and said unto her, Whosoever drinketh of this water shall thirst again: But whosoever drinketh of the water that I shall give him shall never thirst; but the water that I shall give him shall be in him a well of water springing up into everlasting life."

The woman at the well found everlasting life when she came to that well and He gave her living water.

- **John 7:18**
"He that speaketh of himself seeketh his own glory: but he that seeketh his glory that sent him, the same is **true**, and no unrighteousness is in him."

Christ Sought God's Glory

<u>The Lord Jesus Christ is **true**.</u> He sought the glory of His Father. He never tried to push Himself. He never tried to maintain Himself as an ego-maniac. We have many ego-

maniacs in the world, I am afraid. They push themselves ("I, I, I"), but the Lord Jesus Christ pointed to the Father and that was His purpose. The *same is true.*

- John 14:6
  "Jesus saith unto him, I am the way, the **truth**, and the life: no man cometh unto the Father, but by me."

The Saviour is **Truth. Faithful** and **true** is the Son of God on that white horse.

- John 15:1
  "I am the **true** vine, and my Father is the husbandman."

Christ The Only True Vine

There are many other vines, but they are not true. There are many other branches, many other religions, but not true. The Lord Jesus Christ is the *true vine* and if we are genuinely saved, we are branches of that vine. God wants us to bring forth fruit.

- John 15:5
  "I am the vine, ye *are* the branches: He that abideth in me, and I in him, the same bringeth forth much fruit: for without me ye can do nothing."

Christ The Righteous Judge

Notice also, an attribute of the Lord Jesus Christ as He judges: He is righteous. He is true, faithful, and in righteousness He judges and makes war. To have a judgment, to have a war that is unrighteous is wrong. A lot of people say, "Are we for defending our country?" Yes, in righteous wars. Who defines what righteous war is and what it is not? We maintain that the war of independence, for example, in 1776, was a righteous war. Different people have different ideas on it. I believe it was a righteous war. The Lord Jesus Christ makes war in absolute righteousness. There is no question about it. We may question the righteousness of some of our wars. Is it Korea? Is it Viet Nam? Is it Iraq? There are all kinds of questions. I am not going to come down on one side or the other. We may question and people may question, but when the Lord Jesus Christ makes war, no one can question the righteousness of this war. He is absolutely, totally righteous.

- **John 5:30**
  "I can of mine own self do nothing: as I hear, I **judge**: and my judgment is **just**; because I seek not mine own will, but the will of the Father which hath sent me."
- **John 8:16**
  "And yet if I **judge**, my **judgment** is **true**: for I am not alone, but I and the Father that sent me."
- **John 12:47**
  "And if any man hear my words, and believe not, I judge him not: for I came not to **judge** the world, but to save the world."

To Save First, Then To Judge

When the Lord Jesus Christ came the first time, it was not to judge. His mission, the first time He came, was to save the world, but the second phase of His second coming is to judge the world.

- **Acts 17:31**
  "Because he hath appointed a day, in the which he will **judge** the world in righteousness by *that* man whom he hath ordained; *whereof* he hath given assurance unto all *men*, in that he hath raised him from the dead."

God the Father will **judge** the world *by that man whom he hath ordained*—the Lord Jesus Christ. In righteousness will the **judgment** take place.

It says that He will **judge** and make war. People say, "Well, my, does the Lord Jesus Christ have anything to do with **war**?"

- **Exodus 15:3**
  "The LORD *is* a man of **war**: the LORD *is* his name."

God Wars Against Satan

This is in the song of Moses. God is warring against Satan. He is warring against evil of all kinds. He is a warring God of righteousness. In righteousness He makes war and we will see that as we move along in this chapter and the verses that follow. He is a man of war and He judges. The Lord Jesus Christ is the Judge of all the earth. He will judge the angels. We will be with Him in that judgment. He will judge the genuine believers at the judgment seat of the Lord Jesus Christ. He will judge the unsaved at the great white throne judgment. He will judge the nations. He will judge Israel. The Lord Jesus Christ is the Judge.

Revelation 19:12

"His eyes _were_ as a flame of fire, and on his head _were_ many crowns; and he had a name written, that no man knew, but he himself."

Here are the Lord Jesus Christ's **eyes** again. I remember our friend, Pastor Bob Rogers, in Ohio. He had a family of three sisters and two brothers, I believe. He would always tell the story about whenever he and his brothers and sisters were out of line, his father would give them the **eye** and bring them into line with his **eye**. Pastor Rogers would say, "_Don't eye me, Daddy!_" Bob was a good friend and a faithful servant of the Lord Jesus Christ. He is with the Lord now.

Christ's Piercing Eyes

The Lord Jesus Christ's eyes _were as a flame of fire_. I believe the flame of fire indicates that they were piercing eyes. I believe they were penetrating eyes. There is no shield. When you have an x-ray, the x-ray attendant goes behind a shield so that he or she does not get any of the x-rays, but there is no shield from the eyes of the Saviour. He penetrates into the very recesses of our souls. If there is anything that He does not like in that soul of ours, He sees it. He despises it. He says in His Words that we should get rid of it. Those are His penetrating eyes, a flame of fire.

- **Revelation 1:14**
  "His head and _his_ hairs _were_ white like wool, as white as snow; and his **eyes** _were_ as a **flame of fire;**"
- **Revelation 2:18**
  "And unto the angel of the church in Thyatira write; These things saith the Son of God, who hath his **eyes** like unto a **flame of fire**, and his feet _are_ like fine brass;"

This is a figure of speech, the **flaming eyes** of the Lord Jesus Christ.

He had **many crowns** on His **head**. He had **many crowns** because He is more worthy than any king, president, or emperor in all the world. Everyone who thinks he is in power has, as it were, a **crown** to signify his power. The Lord Jesus Christ has **on His head _many_** _**crowns**_ to take care of Russia, the United States, China, and all other countries. He is in charge of all the **crowns** of the world.

Then He has _**a name written, that no man knew, but he himself.**_ Later on, He says what that name is, as we will see.

Revelation 19:13

"And he _**was**_ **clothed with a vesture dipped in blood: and his name is called The Word of God."**

Why was His **vesture dipped in blood?**

- **Revelation 14:19-20**
  "And the angel thrust in his sickle into the earth, and gathered the vine of the earth, and cast _it_ into the great winepress of the wrath of God. And the winepress was trodden without the city, and **blood** came out of the winepress, even unto the horse bridles, by the space of a thousand _and_ six hundred furlongs."

Vesture Dipped In Blood

That is why His vesture was dipped in blood, because this is the battle of Armageddon spoken of here. This is the battle where many will perish—the unsaved, the godless, the beast, the political ruler, all the kings, and the millions that are gathered together to Jerusalem on that day of battle. His vesture was dipped in blood. By the way, I know some are not Baptists, but that word _dipped_ is a good word—BAPTO. It means, _to immerse._

Notice, His name is called **The Word of God.**

A furlong is approximately 582 feet. There are 5,280 feet in a mile and 1,600 furlongs times 582 feet divided by 5,280. I did not do the math. I will leave that up to you, but that is a huge, tremendous distance where **blood** will flow.

When armies assemble, even from China alone, the kings of the east, there will be 200 million of them in that time. That is just one nation, China, that has millions of people. Two hundred million will be there from China, the kings of the east. What about the north, the kings of the north, Gog and Magog—Russia and all the huge number of population they have there? They will be lined up. You know and I know whenever you have a crowd, for whatever occasion, in Washington, D.C. or anywhere else, you do not gather in one corner. You spread out. These people that are against the Lord Jesus Christ and His people and Jerusalem to take over, are spread out—1,600 furlongs, 200 million.

How much space does it take to fit in 200 million from China, 200 million from Russia, 200 million, maybe from the United States? I do not know, but that is a lot of blood. **His vesture was dipped**—*immersed*—**in blood.**

Revelation 19:14

"And the armies *which were* in heaven followed him upon white horses, clothed in fine linen, white and clean."

Christ's Armies Are Believers

The armies which followed Him are the genuine believers, the saved ones with resurrected bodies. The true Christians will be with Him at this judgment at the battle of Armageddon. They are the armies who follow Him. The genuinely saved ones will follow Him there, but oh, that we would follow Him here as well as there! We will be on white horses, clothed in fine linen, white and clean. We will have gone through the judgment seat of the Lord Jesus Christ. The genuinely saved ones will have their fine linen, white and clean.

You may remember, when the disciples were called by the Lord Jesus Christ, He said, "**Follow** me." They were fishing.

- **Matthew 4:19**
  "And he saith unto them, **Follow** me, and I will make you fishers of men."

You may also remember in the last chapter of the gospel of John, the Lord Jesus Christ said about the apostle John that he would do this, this, and this.

- **John 21:21**
  "Peter seeing him saith to Jesus, Lord, and what *shall* this man do? Jesus saith unto him, If I will that he tarry till I come, what *is that* to thee? **follow** thou me."

Do not worry about the other fellow. That is our problem. We worry about the other fellow. The Lord Jesus Christ speaks to us, "*Follow thou me.*"

They **follow** Him on **white horses.** We will have a part of this judgment at the battle of Armageddon with the Lord Jesus Christ. We are on the Lord's side, by the way. We are not on the Devil's side. We will have **clean** and **white linen** and redeemed bodies up in glory. We will **follow** Him.

Revelation 19:15

"And out of his mouth goeth a sharp sword, that with it he should smite the nations: and he shall rule them with a rod of iron: and he treadeth the winepress of the fierceness and wrath of Almighty God."

Smiting Like A Sharp Sword

Out of the mouth of the Lord Jesus Christ—we do not know the nature of what that is, but we know the results. He will smite the nations. Out of His mouth—our powerful Creator God—the Lord Jesus Christ will smite. That which goeth out of His mouth is like a sharp sword. He will smite the nations. Then it says that *He shall rule them with a rod of iron.*

The **rod of iron** is mentioned in many places in Scripture.

- **Psalm 2:9**
  "Thou shalt break them with a **rod of iron**; thou shalt dash them in pieces like a potter's vessel."

Prophetically, this speaks of the Lord Jesus Christ.

- **Revelation 2:27**
  "And he shall **rule them with a rod of iron**; as the vessels of a potter shall they be broken to shivers: even as I received of my Father."

That is what is going to happen in the millennial reign of the Lord Jesus Christ. He will be ruling *with a rod of iron.* Every disobedience will be judged immediately by our Saviour.

- **Revelation 12:5**
  "And she brought forth a man child, who was to rule all nations with a **rod of iron**: and her child was caught up unto God, and *to* his throne."

This is the Lord Jesus Christ.

- **Deuteronomy 13:17**
  "And there shall cleave nought of the cursed thing to thine hand: that the LORD may turn from the **fierceness of his anger**, and shew thee mercy, and have compassion upon thee, and multiply thee, as he hath sworn unto thy fathers;"

- **Joshua 7:26**
"And they raised over him a great heap of stones unto this day. So the LORD turned from the **fierceness of his anger.** Wherefore the name of that place was called, The valley of Achor, unto this day."

This was because of Achan and his sin. The Lord Jesus Christ has **fierceness of anger** and He turns from it if the conditions are right.

- **2 Kings 23:26**
"Notwithstanding the LORD turned not from the **fierceness of his great wrath,** wherewith his anger was kindled against Judah, because of all the provocations that Manasseh had provoked him withal."

God has **fierceness of anger.**

- **2 Chronicles 30:8**
"Now be ye not stiffnecked, as your fathers *were, but* yield yourselves unto the LORD, and enter into his sanctuary, which he hath sanctified for ever: and serve the LORD your God, that the **fierceness of his wrath** may turn away from you."

This was during Hezekiah's reign. Serve Him so that **wrath** will not come upon you.

- **Revelation 16:19**
"And the great city was divided into three parts, and the cities of the nations fell: and great Babylon came in remembrance before God, to give unto her the cup of the wine of the **fierceness of his wrath.**"

Fierceness Against Sin

The Lord Jesus Christ has fierceness. When we are in the Lord Jesus Christ, we are shielded. We have a Refuge that we have fled to, and a Fortress in our Saviour.

Revelation 19:16

"And he hath on *his* vesture and on his thigh a name written, KING OF KINGS, AND LORD OF LORDS."

King Of Kings, Lord Of Lords

Here is the Name of the Lord Jesus Christ. He is the King of all the other kings. There is no other king that is over Him. He is over every one of them. He is the Lord of all the lords.

> There is no lord that is above Him. This will be the case in the
> millennial reign of the Lord Jesus Christ. He will be King of all
> and Lord of all.

- 1 Timothy 6:15
  "Which in his times he shall shew, *who is* the blessed and only
  Potentate, the **King of kings, and Lord of lords;**"
- Revelation 17:14
  "These shall make war with the Lamb, and the Lamb shall
  overcome them: for he is **Lord of lords, and King of kings:**
  and they that are with him *are* called, and chosen, and faithful."

Here the titles are inverted. Either way, He is the **Lord of all the lords**
and **King of all the kings.**

Revelation 19:17-18

**"And I saw an angel standing in the sun; and he cried
with a loud voice, saying to all the fowls that fly in the
midst of heaven, Come and gather yourselves together
unto the supper of the great God; That ye may eat the
flesh of kings, and the flesh of captains, and the flesh of
mighty men, and the flesh of horses, and of them that sit
on them, and the flesh of all *men, both* free and bond, both
small and great."**

This is the **supper** of the **fowls**, the birds, that will take place at the
battle of Armageddon.

- Jeremiah 7:32-33
  "Therefore, behold, the days come, saith the LORD, that it shall
  no more be called Tophet, nor the valley of the son of Hinnom,
  but the valley of slaughter: for they shall bury in Tophet, till
  there be no place. <u>And the carcases of this people shall be meat
  for the **fowls** of the heaven,</u> and for the beasts of the earth; and
  none shall fray *them* away."

<u>This **battle of Armageddon** has been predicted where the **fowls** of the
air will eat the **flesh** and feed on the dead that are there.</u>

- Revelation 16:16
  "And he gathered them together into a place called in the
  Hebrew tongue **Armageddon.**"

The Hill Of Megiddo

HAR means *hill.* Armageddon is the *hill of MEGIDDO.* The plain of Esdraelon is a little bit south of the sea of Galilee. That is where this will take place. That is probably where the 1,600 furlongs are that stretch from Jerusalem all the way up there.

The **battle of Armageddon** is also spoken of prophetically in the book of Ezekiel.

- **Ezekiel 39:1-4**

  "Therefore, thou son of man, prophesy against Gog, and say, Thus saith the Lord GOD; Behold, I *am* against thee, O Gog, the chief prince of Meshech and Tubal: And I will turn thee back, and leave but the sixth part of thee, and will cause thee to come up from the north parts, and will bring thee upon the mountains of Israel: And I will smite thy bow out of thy left hand, and will cause thine arrows to fall out of thy right hand. Thou shalt fall upon the mountains of Israel, thou, and all thy bands, and the people that *is* with thee: I will give thee unto the ravenous **birds** of every sort, and *to* the beasts of the field to be devoured."

Russia, Moscow, And Tobolsk

I believe Gog is Russia. Many believe Meshech is Moscow and Tubal is Tobolsk. He is saying that Gog and Magog are coming down the mountains of Israel at this battle of Armageddon that we are speaking of. Here again, the birds are eating the flesh of those that are dead.

- **Ezekiel 39:11-20**

  "And it shall come to pass in that day, *that* I will give unto Gog a place there of graves in Israel, the valley of the passengers on the east of the sea: and it shall stop the *noses* of the passengers: and there shall they bury Gog and all his multitude: and they shall call *it* The valley of Hamongog. And seven months shall the house of Israel be burying of them, that they may cleanse the land. Yea, all the people of the land shall bury *them*; and it shall be to them a renown the day that I shall be glorified, saith the Lord GOD. And they shall sever out men of continual employment, passing through the land to bury with the passengers those that remain upon the face of the earth, to cleanse it: after the end of seven months shall they search. And the passengers *that* pass through the land, when *any* seeth a man's bone, then shall he set up a sign by it, till the buriers have buried it in the valley of Hamongog. And also the name of the city *shall* be Hamonah. Thus shall they cleanse the land. And, thou son of man, thus saith the Lord GOD; Speak unto every feathered **fowl**, and to every beast of the field, Assemble yourselves, and come; gather yourselves on every side to my sacrifice that I do sacrifice for you, *even* a great sacrifice upon the mountains of Israel, that ye may **eat flesh**, and drink **blood**. Ye shall eat the **flesh** of the mighty, and drink the **blood** of the princes of the earth, of rams, of lambs, and of goats, of bullocks, all of them fatlings of Bashan. And ye shall eat fat till ye be full, and drink blood till ye be drunken, of my sacrifice which I have sacrificed for you. Thus ye shall be filled at my table with horses and chariots, with mighty men, and with all men of war, saith the Lord GOD."

The Great Slaughter

Here are the birds again, even in the prophecy of the Old Testament. That is a gruesome description. Let us face it, that is a horrendous description. Nobody likes to tell it like it is, but many times, battles are just exactly that. You cannot but hear about the news of people that blow themselves up, car bombs that burst and slaughter people—body parts all over, and blood all over.

It is a different picture. This is a picture of the Lord Jesus Christ Himself putting down atheistic, godless, Christ-hating nations that are at war against the Saviour and against His people. This is a different thing. The Lord Jesus Christ is faithful in this judgment. He is righteous in judgment and He is true, but this is a terrible, terrible picture.

You may say, "Can this really take place?" With the Lord Jesus Christ, all things are able to take place. He could bring the quails when the Israelites demanded **flesh to eat** from all parts of the earth and give them meat. (The quails did not last long because they were lusting with their sinful flesh. He got so fed up with the ones that just stuffed and stuffed themselves that He slew many of them and the quails left.) If He can bring the quails, He can bring the **birds**. If He can say to the animals, two of every beast of the animals that were living in Noah's day,

"Come into the ark," and they could come, our God is able to call animals to Himself for His purposes.

I do not have any question in my mind that when this takes place, there will be animals enough that **eat flesh**. You know and I know that when we see some of the nature films, for example, the lions pounce upon deer, and wildebeasts, and various other things and slaughter them and **eat** them. It is a gruesome scene. God is able to draw them to this feast, this **supper**. It is not the **marriage supper of the Lamb**, but the **supper of Almighty God**. In judgment, it will take place and we must realize that.

No Favorites In This Battle

The Lord Jesus Christ is not going to have any favorites in this battle and this judgment. There are going to be kings—the leaders. There are going to be captains. That word is CHILIARCHOS, *rulers of a thousand*. That is the word for *captains* here. There will be mighty men, horses and them that sit on them—all men, whether they are free or bond. There will be slavery here at the Lord Jesus Christ's return, of one kind or another. Whether they are free or bond, there is no difference.

Can a **bondperson** trust the Lord Jesus Christ and be genuinely saved? Yes, he can trust the Lord Jesus Christ and be truly saved. Paul was a prisoner in Rome. In the first Roman imprisonment, he wrote four godly, wonderful, blessed books. While he was a prisoner in the second Roman imprisonment, he wrote at least one book, 2 Timothy, if not 1 Timothy and Titus. He led many to the Lord Jesus Christ who were also prisoners. The **bound** can come to the Lord Jesus Christ.

There is no excuse. "Oh, I am in prison. I cannot do anything!" Listen, we have prisoners writing to us every single week asking us for Bibles, gospel tracts, and so on. We do the best we can, when possible, to send them what we can. Prisoners, bond or free, can genuinely trust the Lord Jesus Christ. If they are opposed to the Lord Jesus Christ, they will suffer alike. There is both **small and great**, the little and the big. He is going to have justice, faithfulness, and judgment in righteousness on the small as well as the great.

As I said, this is not a pleasant sight, but the Lord Jesus Christ has given it to us in His Words. He has predicted it and I believe it will come to pass. How else can the Lord Jesus Christ initiate a proper millennial reign? Ask yourself that.

1. Here are the seven years of tribulation.
2. Here is the first beast, the political beast, in Revelation 13.
3. Here is the second beast, the religious beast, also in Revelation 13.
4. Here are the multiplied millions and billions of people at that tribulation time.

The judgments have not destroyed all of them. They are still there and coming against the Lord Jesus Christ. He has to wipe them out before the millennial reign of the Lord Jesus Christ, the new heavens and the new earth. That is what will happen.

God Is Just In His Punishments

If that seems to you to be unjust, think of the fires of Hell. That is what is lying in wait for these people. God is not unjust. He never has been and never will be. He must punish those that are out to kill His Son, His Son's people, and genuine believers.

Revelation 19:19

"And I saw the beast, and the kings of the earth, and their armies, gathered together to make war against him that sat on the horse, and against his army."

This is the political **beast** of Revelation 13 and the **kings of the earth**. They followed this **beast** in the tribulation time. He will be the ruler or the dictator—the antichrist—over all the kings of the earth. They will do whatever he says. I do not know whether that will be the revised and revived United Nations or what it is going to be, but the antichrist is going to be in charge of it. I do not know who it is going to be, but somebody is going to have enough power that when he speaks, they will follow.

We have had 138,000 of our men in Iraq. Russia has had multiplied thousands and tens of thousands in their armies. China has multiplied millions in their armies. Russia and China and all the others are going to follow the beast.

The Nations Gather Against Christ

Notice what these nations are going to do. They are going to gather together to make war against the One that sat on the white horse—the Lord Jesus Christ. He is the target. He is the object of their hatred and their war. These nations are also against the Lord Jesus Christ's army and all the true saints who are following Him. They are against the One on the white horse and those that followed Him, the genuine believers, the redeemed who are also there. They are going to be against His army as well. They are fighting.

What about war against the Lord Jesus Christ?

- **Ezekiel 38:14-16**

  "Therefore, son of man, prophesy and say unto Gog, Thus saith the Lord GOD; In that day when my people of Israel dwelleth safely, shalt thou not know *it*? And thou shalt come from thy place out of the north parts, thou, and many people with thee, all of them riding upon horses, a great company, and a mighty army: And thou shalt come up against my people of Israel, as a cloud to cover the land; it shall be in the latter days, and I will bring thee against my land, that the heathen may know me, when I shall be sanctified in thee, O Gog, before their eyes."

Horses Or Tanks?

Here again, I believe Gog is Russia. You might say, "Why is it horses? Maybe it will be tanks." Well, number one, it could be with an oil shortage, they may revert to horses. Number two, this could be the method of warfare in the Day of the Lord here, in John's day. It could be other methods and powers, but for my part, it is horses.

- **Zechariah 14:1-2**

  "Behold, the day of the LORD cometh, and thy spoil shall be divided in the midst of thee. For I will gather all nations against Jerusalem to battle; and the city shall be taken, and the houses rifled, and the women ravished; and half of the city shall go forth into captivity, and the residue of the people shall not be cut off from the city."

That is why the Lord Jesus Christ is coming, faithful and true, **to judge and make war,** because He is attacked first. This is self defense. We have always taken the position in battle, or in protection of our homes, our children, our families, and our loved ones, that self defense is always right–defending yourself, not too much, but self defense.

- **Zechariah 14:3**
  "Then shall the LORD go forth, and **fight against those nations,** as when he fought in the day of battle."

The word that begins this verse is, *Then.* After all this takes place, *then*–what then? Who is this LORD that is going to **fight against those nations?**

- **Zechariah 14:4**
  "And his feet shall stand in that day upon the mount of Olives, which *is* before Jerusalem on the east, and the mount of Olives shall cleave in the midst thereof toward the east and toward the west, *and there shall be* a very great valley; and half of the mountain shall remove toward the north, and half of it toward the south."

The Mount Of Olives Will Split

The Lord Jesus Christ is the LORD. The mountain goes north and south, and the valley east and west. We know what is going to happen. The Lord Jesus Christ will come forth and will put down all the forces of the enemies that are going against Israel, against the Lord Jesus Christ, and against His armies.

Revelation 19:20

"And the beast was taken, and with him the false prophet that wrought miracles before him, with which he deceived them that had received the mark of the beast, and them that worshipped his image. These both were cast alive into a lake of fire burning with brimstone."

The Literal Fires Of Hell

The *beast that was taken* is the political ruler, the first beast of Revelation 13. The *false prophet* is the second beast of Revelation 13, the religious beast. Their purpose is deception. Notice what happened: *These both were cast alive into a lake of fire burning with brimstone.* There is a literal fire in Hell. Billy Graham in the 1950s denied it. He has denied it all through his ministry. Others have denied it. New Evangelicals have denied it. Modernists have always denied it. Even some fundamentalists, I am afraid, are denying it, but the Lord Jesus Christ does not deny it. I will go with the Lord Jesus Christ any day, as far as His description of Hell.

- **Matthew 3:12**

  "Whose fan *is* in his hand, and he will throughly purge his floor, and gather his wheat into the garner; but he will **burn up** the chaff with unquenchable **fire.**"

That sounds like **fire** to me.

- **Matthew 13:40-42**

  "As therefore the tares are gathered and **burned** in the **fire**; so shall it be in the end of this world. The Son of man shall send forth his angels, and they shall gather out of his kingdom all things that offend, and them which do iniquity; And shall cast them into a furnace of **fire**: there shall be wailing and gnashing of teeth."

That sounds like **fire** to me also.

- **Matthew 25:41**

  "Then shall he say also unto them on the left hand, Depart from me, ye cursed, into **everlasting fire**, prepared for the devil and his angels:"

Hell Prepared For Satan

The fires of Hell were not prepared for people. They were *prepared for the devil and his angels*, but those that reject our Saviour go there.

- **2 Thessalonians 1:7-9**

  "And to you who are troubled rest with us, when the Lord Jesus shall be revealed from heaven with his mighty angels, In **flaming fire** taking vengeance on them that know not God, and that obey not the gospel of our Lord Jesus Christ: Who shall be punished with everlasting destruction from the presence of the Lord, and from the glory of his power;"

The second phase of His second coming will be with *flaming fire*.

- Revelation 20:10

  "And the devil that deceived them was cast into the **lake of fire and brimstone,** where the beast and the false prophet *are,* and shall be tormented day and night for ever and ever."

That sounds like fire to me. The beast and the false prophet were cast into the **lake of fire,** this **fire** burning with **brimstone,** 1,000 years before the Devil is cast into that same lake, but it still says where the beast and the false prophet *are*—present tense. They do not get **burned** up. They suffer the pains of Hell and **fire** for eternity. It is a very important point.

- Revelation 20:14-15

  "And death and Hell were cast into the **lake of fire.** This is the second death. And whosoever was not found written in the book of life was cast into the **lake of fire.**"

Fire Is Not Just A Figure Of Speech

That sounds like fire to me. Again, the fire is real. The Lord Jesus Christ did not say that it is *like* fire. He did not say that it is a figure of speech that sort of resembles fire. He talked about fire that burns. He talked about fire that lasts. Some of the New Evangelicals have the idea that after a little bit of time in Hell, they are going to get out, that there is going to be an escape, so they say that it is a limited Hell. No, it is everlasting. It is just as everlasting as everlasting life. Are you going to break out of Heaven, those of you who are genuinely saved and going to Heaven? Will you just go back to earth or back to Hell one day? No, you cannot break out of Heaven. It is everlasting life. There is everlasting death and everlasting punishment as well.

Revelation 19:21

"And the remnant were slain with the sword of him that sat upon the horse, which *sword* proceeded out of his mouth: and all the fowls were filled with their flesh."

Here is the **great supper of God.** It handles the first and second beasts, the false prophet, and the political beast, but then the *remnant*—those that were remaining, those that followed the false leaders—were also *slain with the sword of him that sat upon the horse,* the Lord Jesus Christ. As I said, we do not know the nature of that **sword** that comes **out of His mouth,** but we know the results—death. I do not want to be on the receiving end of that **sword.** The Word of God is like a **sword,** but this **sword** is a **sword** of death.

- **Hebrews 4:12**

  "For the word of God is quick, and powerful, and sharper than any twoedged **sword,** piercing even to the dividing asunder of soul and spirit, and of the joints and marrow, and *is* a discerner of the thoughts and intents of the heart."

Again, the fowls—the birds—will be at this **great supper of God.** This is a terrible calamity, but it is the second phase of the second coming of the Lord Jesus Christ, portrayed right here before our very eyes. He is coming in the first phase to take those that are truly born-again and genuinely saved to Himself and out of this world. He will snatch us away. He will not come to this earth. It has nothing to do with this earth, but **in the air.**

- **1 Thessalonians 4:16-17**

  "For the Lord himself shall descend from heaven with a shout, with the voice of the archangel, and with the trump of God: and the dead in Christ shall rise first: Then we which are alive *and* remain shall be caught up together with them in the clouds, to meet the Lord **in the air**: and so shall we ever be with the Lord."

The Pre-Tribulation Rapture

The Lord Jesus Christ shall come and snatch us away *in the air.* The genuinely saved ones will be taken up to be with Him and *so shall we ever be with the Lord*—forever. After that seven-year period of tribulation, the genuinely saved will not be here in any part of it, He will come back in the second phase of His second coming to judge.

Are you ready? Am I ready? I trust that is the case in every one of our hearts—ready for His coming to take us unto Himself, if we are genuinely saved. If you are not genuinely saved, you can be. The Lord Jesus Christ is a great God. Remember, He is called faithful and true and righteous. He is going to judge and He is going to make war with the enemy forces.

- **Romans 12:19**
"Dearly beloved, avenge not yourselves, but *rather* give place unto wrath: for it is written, **Vengeance** *is* mine; I will repay, saith the Lord."

Revelation

Chapter Twenty

Revelation 20:1

"And I saw an angel come down from heaven, having the key of the bottomless pit and a great chain in his hand."

Here John is seeing the **angel** who is going to come with a **key**. The **key** and the **chain** are for Satan. They are for the **bottomless pit**, the **abyss**, which is mentioned seven times in Scripture.

- **Revelation 9:1**

    "And the fifth angel sounded, and I saw a star fall from heaven unto the earth: and to him was given the **key** of the **bottomless pit**."

A **key** is that which opens and that which shuts—that which locks.

- **Revelation 9:2**

    "And he opened the **bottomless pit**; and there arose a smoke out of the pit, as the smoke of a great furnace; and the sun and the air were darkened by reason of the smoke of the pit."

Where there is smoke there is fire. This **abyss**, this **bottomless pit**, is a smoking fiery **pit**.

- **Revelation 9:11**

    "And they had a king over them, *which is* the angel of the **bottomless pit**, whose name in the Hebrew tongue *is* Abaddon, but in the Greek tongue hath *his* name Apollyon."

There is an angel of this **bottomless pit** whose name is Abaddon or Apollyon.

- **Revelation 11:7**

    "And when they shall have finished their testimony, the beast that ascendeth out of the **bottomless pit** shall make war against them, and shall overcome them, and kill them."

You may remember there are two witnesses that speak and preach. Whether they are Moses and Elijah or whoever (I think that they are Moses and Elijah), the devils—this evil angelic power—slay them.

- **Revelation 17:8**

  "The beast that thou sawest was, and is not; and shall ascend out of the **bottomless pit**, and go into perdition: and they that dwell on the earth shall wonder, whose names were not written in the book of life from the foundation of the world, when they behold the beast that was, and is not, and yet is."

The beast has access to the **bottomless pit**. Now this angel comes with a key and will bind him in this **bottomless pit**. He was free, apparently, to come and go.

- **Revelation 20:3**

  "And cast him into the **bottomless pit**, and shut him up, and set a seal upon him, that he should deceive the nations no more, till the thousand years should be fulfilled: and after that he must be loosed a little season."

This is the **bottomless pit** where Satan is going to be cast. This angel is the angel that has the **key** and a great **chain**. A **chain** is to bind people, either hands or feet or whatever. It is to bind them so that they cannot move.

- **Acts 28:20**

  "For this cause therefore have I called for you, to see *you*, and to speak with *you*: because that for the hope of Israel I am bound with this **chain**."

Paul was in **chains**. He was in prison. He was in **chains** and he could not move. He was in prison, just before he went to Rome, in Caesarea.

- **2 Timothy 1:16**

  "The Lord give mercy unto the house of Onesiphorus; for he oft refreshed me, and was not ashamed of my **chain**:"

Different Kinds Of Chains

There are all kinds of chains to bind things. That word for chain is HALUSIS. It means, *a chain bound to the body; a bond by which the body or any part of it, hands or feet, is bound.* That is the chain and that is what this angel had—a chain to take care of the old Devil during this millennial reign of the Lord Jesus Christ. The true church is gone during this tribulation period for the whole seven years.

When we read Revelation 20:2 and following, I want you to notice we talk about the *thousand years*. Before we read the verse, let us remember that there are a number of **thousand years** references here. There are, in fact, six of them: in verses two, three, four, five, six, and seven. There are six different references to a **thousand years**.

Years ago, when Mr. Camping of Family Radio was on the air with his call-in program, I called up. It was probably 25 years ago. (How many years ago, who knows? Thirty years, maybe. I have been here a long time.)

I said, "Now, Mr. Camping, this is very clear. There are a **thousand years** in the Millennium." He said that it does not mean a **thousand years**, that it is just a general idea. We argued back and forth. I never called him again. That was the end of it. He cannot understand the plain sense of Scripture and see that it is a **thousand years**. He does not believe in the Millennium. He does not believe there is any such thing as that. He has all kinds of other crazy notions. He says that we are right now in the tribulation.

My wife and I were coming back from visiting our son, David, in Glassboro, NJ. We visited him every month, and took him out to eat. I asked my wife if we should tune in and listen to Mr. Camping. She said that we might as well listen to what he had to say. We heard him say that the Lord Jesus Christ has already come as a Judge, but nobody saw Him. He said that He was going to come in real life in 2011. Where he got that is beyond me. At that time, he declared that right now we are in the tribulation and that the church was gone. He said that we should come out of the churches because there is no such thing as the church.

I want us to see that this **thousand years** is clear. Here is the "Golden Rule of Bible Interpretation" that is in our *Defined King James Bible*. This is the thing that anchors down hermeneutics or interpretation of Scripture.

"When the PLAIN SENSE of Scripture makes COMMON SENSE, SEEK NO OTHER SENSE. Therefore, take EVERY WORD at its primary, ordinary, usual, literal meaning, UNLESS the facts of the immediate context, studied in the light of related passages, and axiomatic and fundamental truths, indicate CLEARLY otherwise. God, in revealing His Word, neither intends nor permits the reader to be confused. He wants His children to understand."

1,000 Years Means 1,000 Years

So pardon me if I just take this at its usual, common, ordinary meaning. A thousand years means a thousand years. Every time in Scripture, when it talks about Adam lived so many years, and the kings so many years, that is it. Here, a thousand years is a thousand years.

Revelation 20:2

"And he laid hold on the dragon, that old serpent, which is the Devil, and Satan, and bound him a thousand years,"

Here is the first mention of a **thousand years**. Here are four different names for the **Devil**.

- **Revelation 12:3**

  "And there appeared another wonder in heaven; and behold a great red **dragon**, having seven heads and ten horns, and seven crowns upon his heads."

That was **Satan**.

- **Revelation 12:4**

  "And his tail drew the third part of the stars of heaven, and did cast them to the earth: and the **dragon** stood before the woman which was ready to be delivered, for to devour her child as soon as it was born."

This is speaking of devouring the child—the Lord Jesus Christ. The woman, of course, is Mary, the mother, in picture form.

- **Revelation 12:7**

  "And there was war in heaven: Michael and his angels fought against the **dragon**; and the **dragon** fought and his angels,"

The dragon is another name for **Satan**.

- **Revelation 12:9**

  "And the great **dragon** was cast out, that old **serpent**, called the **Devil**, and **Satan**, which deceiveth the whole world: he was cast out into the earth, and his angels were cast out with him."

- **Revelation 13:4**
  "And they worshipped the dragon which gave power unto the beast: and they worshipped the beast, saying, Who is like unto the beast? who is able to make war with him? "

The Satanic Trinity

There is a Satanic trinity. There is the dragon, the first beast, and the second beast. The dragon is Satan. The first beast is the political ruler. The second beast is the religious ruler, the false prophet.

- **Revelation 16:13**
  "And I saw three unclean spirits like frogs come out of the mouth of the **dragon**, and out of the mouth of the beast, and out of the mouth of the false prophet."

These are the pictures of the **dragon**.

The Meaning Of "Dragon"

What does that word dragon mean? It is a great serpent. It is a name for Satan. DRAKON is almost the same as dragon in the Greek language.

Let us take a look at the second name. It says that the **dragon** is *that old serpent*.

- **Genesis 3:1**
  "Now the **serpent** was more subtil than any beast of the field which the LORD God had made. And he said unto the woman, Yea, hath God said, Ye shall not eat of every tree of the garden?"

Here we meet the **serpent**. This is the **serpent** in the garden of Eden, which questioned God's Words. Yes, God did say that exactly. The **serpent** quoted it, but he did not quote the next verse.

- **Genesis 2:17**
  "But of the tree of the knowledge of good and evil, thou shalt not eat of it: for in the day that thou eatest thereof thou shalt surely die."

The **serpent** quoted just one verse accurately, but he did not quote the context.

- **2 Corinthians 11:3**

  "But I fear, lest by any means, as the **serpent** beguiled Eve through his subtilty, so your minds should be corrupted from the simplicity that is in Christ."

Satan Corrupts Minds

We have to see this Devil and his deceptive devices. The mind can be corrupted by Satan and his hordes. We have to be careful and guard our minds. That is one of his strategies. Paul was concerned about those Corinthian Christians, that their minds would not be corrupted.

- **Revelation 12:9**

  "And the great dragon was cast out, that old **serpent**, called the **Devil**, and **Satan**, which deceiveth the whole world: he was cast out into the earth, and his angels were cast out with him."

- **Revelation 12:14-15**

  "And to the woman were given two wings of a great eagle, that she might fly into the wilderness, into her place, where she is nourished for a time, and times, and half a time, from the face of the **serpent**. And the serpent cast out of his mouth water as a flood after the woman, that he might cause her to be carried away of the flood."

This is the **Devil** working in the tribulation period. True born-again Christians are going to be gone—those that are genuinely saved will be out of this world. The old **Devil**, the serpent, is the one that is going to attack the people of the Lord Jesus Christ in that tribulation time.

What Does "Satan" Mean?

Notice, the serpent's name is also *Satan*. The word *Devil* is used 57 times in the New Testament. That word is an interesting term. It has several different meanings. DIABOLOS is a Greek word. It means, *prone to slander; accusing falsely; a metaphor applied to a man who by opposing the cause of God may be said to act the part of the Devil or to side with him; Satan, the prince of the devils, the author of evil, persecuting good, estranging mankind from God, enticing them to sin.* This is all part of what the Devil does. He is a usurper, a slanderer, and a false accuser.

- **Matthew 4:1**
  "Then was Jesus led up of the Spirit into the wilderness to be tempted of the **devil**."

The **Devil** was a tempter or a tester of the Lord Jesus Christ.

- **Matthew 13:39**
  "The enemy that sowed them is the **devil**; the harvest is the end of the world; and the reapers are the angels."

The Wheat And The Tares

Do you remember the wheat and the tares? The Lord Jesus Christ sows the wheat, but it says here very clearly that the enemy that sowed the tares is the Devil. We have the Devil working even today, sowing his falsities in among the wheat. That is where the modernists, the false prophets, the cults, the "isms," the false Protestants, and the Roman Catholic type of churches are sowing tares—falsities among the wheat. The Devil is the one that is behind the false tares.

- **Matthew 25:41**
  "Then shall he say also unto them on the left hand, Depart from me, ye cursed, into everlasting fire, prepared for the devil and his angels:"

This is the judgment of the nations. Hell was prepared for the **Devil** and his angels, not for the unbelievers. The unsaved people go there because they are following the **Devil**.

- **John 6:70**
  "Jesus answered them, Have not I chosen you twelve, and one of you is a **devil**?"

The Lord Jesus Christ spoke of His disciples. The Lord Jesus Christ knew when He chose Judas that he was a **devil**. The Lord Jesus Christ chose him so those in true Christian churches should not be surprised to find some of the people that attend—and some even that are members in fundamental churches—to be **devils**, that is, unsaved people. Oh, they talk the good talk. Listen, Judas talked the talk. Maybe he walked the walk too, but he was devilish and he was not of God. These are the **Devil's** deceitful things and devices.

- **John 8:44**

    "Ye are of *your* father the **devil**, and the lusts of your father ye will do. He was a murderer from the beginning, and abode not in the truth, because there is no truth in him. When he speaketh a lie, he speaketh of his own: for he is a liar, and the father of it."

This is the subtilty. The lusts of their father—the lying—that is **devilish**. We have to be careful of his devices of lies.

- **John 13:2**

    "And supper being ended, the **devil** having now put into the heart of Judas Iscariot, Simon's *son*, to betray him;"

The **Devil** is the one that put into Judas' heart to betray the Lord Jesus Christ. That betraying is important, indeed. It is not a good thing. It shows the **Devil's** power to corrupt.

- **Acts 13:10**

    "And said, O full of all subtilty and all mischief, *thou* child of the **devil**, *thou* enemy of all righteousness, wilt thou not cease to pervert the right ways of the Lord?"

There Are Two Fatherhoods

Paul addresses one who was the Devil's child. Here was a false prophet and Paul just comes right out and says he was a child of the Devil.

We only have two fatherhoods—either the Devil, or God the Father. When every one of us is born, we have the Devil as our father. We are born into his family. When we are genuinely born-again, we are born into God's family. That is the different fatherhood. The universal fatherhood of God that the modernists spew forth from their churches is absolutely false. There is not a universal fatherhood. If there is a universal fatherhood, I would rather say it was the fatherhood mostly of the Devil. That is the most universal—the Devil's children. Very few are in the fatherhood of God. There is no universal fatherhood. That is false. There are two fatherhoods.

- **Ephesians 4:27**

    "Neither give place to the **devil**."

Do not give him any room. If you do, he will take it. Do not give him any place. Just say, "I am going to stand right here."

- **Ephesians 6:11**
  "Put on the whole armour of God, that ye may be able to stand against the wiles of the **devil**."

"Wiles" are *strategies, cleverness*. Oh, he will come as an angel of light. He will come in many ways. He is wily.

- **1 Timothy 3:6-7**
  "Not a novice, lest being lifted up with pride he fall into the condemnation of the **devil**. Moreover he must have a good report of them which are without; lest he fall into reproach and the snare of the **devil**."

We are not to ordain a man to the gospel ministry to be a pastor-bishop-elder who is a novice. The **Devil** has snares. The **Devil** is pushing for pride. We have to be very careful of the **Devil** and his strategies.

- **2 Timothy 2:26**
  "And *that* they may recover themselves out of the snare of the **devil**, who are taken captive by him at his will."

The Devil's Snares And Traps

The Devil has snares and traps. <u>A trap will never work if you see it coming</u>. It is always hidden. <u>As soon as you walk into it, it is too late</u>. We have to walk in a circumspect way. CIRCUM is, *around* (360 degrees). SPECTOS is, *to look—Looking around 360 degrees*.

- **Ephesians 5:15**
  "See then that ye walk circumspectly, not as fools, but as wise,"

- **Hebrews 2:14**
  "Forasmuch then as the children are partakers of flesh and blood, he also himself likewise took part of the same; that through death he might destroy him that had the power of death, that is, the **devil**;"

The Lord Jesus Christ came to this earth. He was a partaker of flesh, a perfect human body. Before He came, the **Devil** had the power of death. Nobody could snap those fetters. The Lord Jesus Christ came to break that power.

- **James 4:7**
  "Submit yourselves therefore to God. Resist the **devil**, and he will flee from you."

Just resist him and he will flee. Do not move. He is the one to move. It is his move.

- **1 Peter 5:8-9**

  "Be sober, be vigilant; because your adversary the **devil**, as a roaring lion, walketh about, seeking whom he may devour: Whom resist stedfast in the faith, knowing that the same afflictions are accomplished in your brethren that are in the world."

- **1 John 3:8**

  "He that committeth sin is of the **devil**; for the **devil** sinneth from the beginning. For this purpose the Son of God was manifested, that he might destroy the works of the **devil**."

Continuous Sinners

That is in the present tense—*continues* in sin. People that are constant sinners are of the Devil. They are the Devil's children. You cannot get away from that. It does not mean that true Christians do not fall into sin occasionally, but this is committing sin continuously. They are of the Devil. God does not want us to continue in sin.

- **Revelation 12:9**

  "And the great **dragon** was cast out, that old **serpent**, called the **Devil**, and **Satan**, which deceiveth the whole world: he was cast out into the earth, and his angels were cast out with him."

Here is another name. We have the *dragon,* the *serpent* and the *Devil.* Now we have the word, *Satan,* which is used 49 times in the Bible.

- **Job 1:6**

  "Now there was a day when the sons of God came to present themselves before the LORD, and **Satan** came also among them."

- **Job 2:7**

  "So went **Satan** forth from the presence of the LORD, and smote Job with sore boils from the sole of his foot unto his crown."

Satan has power to smite with disease as he did with Job.

- **Matthew 4:10**
  "Then saith Jesus unto him, Get thee hence, **Satan**: for it is written, Thou shalt worship the Lord thy God, and him only shalt thou serve."

- **Matthew 16:21-23**
  "From that time forth began Jesus to shew unto his disciples, how that he must go unto Jerusalem, and suffer many things of the elders and chief priests and scribes, and be killed, and be raised again the third day. Then Peter took him, and began to rebuke him, saying, Be it far from thee, Lord: this shall not be unto thee. But he turned, and said unto Peter, Get thee behind me, **Satan**: thou art an offence unto me: for thou savourest not the things that be of God, but those that be of men."

Satan Did Not Indwell Peter

This does not mean that Satan indwelled Peter, but he used Peter. Can a true Christian be possessed of the Devil? No, I do not believe he can, but he can be wrongly influenced by the Devil. We better watch out if we rebuke the Lord Jesus Christ. No man should rebuke our Saviour. <u>Is Peter the first pope</u>? <u>No</u>! When we are used of the Devil—influenced by the Devil—the Lord Jesus Christ will say the same to us. I hope that does not happen. Give no place for the Devil.

- **Mark 4:15**
  "And these are they by the way side, where the word is sown; but when they have heard, **Satan** cometh immediately, and taketh away the word that was sown in their hearts."

You may remember the four soils: the way side soil, the stony soil, the thorny soil and the good soil. Here the Word is sown. It is a good Word, but bad soil. This is **Satan,** taking away of the Word of God that is in their hearts.

- **Luke 22:3**
  "Then entered **Satan** into Judas surnamed Iscariot, being of the number of the twelve."

When **Satan** entered Judas, he became a **devilish** person. He was a betrayer of the Lord Jesus Christ.

- **Luke 22:31-32**
  "And the Lord said, Simon, Simon, behold, **Satan** hath desired *to have* you, that he may sift *you* as wheat: But I have prayed for

thee, that thy faith fail not: and when thou art converted, strengthen thy brethren."

Satan wanted to use Peter, and the Lord Jesus Christ prayed for him.

- **John 13:25-27**

  "He then lying on Jesus' breast saith unto him, Lord, who is it? Jesus answered, He it is, to whom I shall give a sop, when I have dipped *it*. And when he had dipped the sop, he gave *it* to Judas Iscariot, *the son* of Simon. And after the sop **Satan** entered into him. Then said Jesus unto him, That thou doest, do quickly."

- **Acts 26:18**

  "To open their eyes, *and* to turn *them* from darkness to light, and *from* the power of **Satan** unto God, that they may receive forgiveness of sins, and inheritance among them which are sanctified by faith that is in me."

These were some of Paul's commissioning Words from the Lord Jesus Christ. He mentioned them when he was talking to King Agrippa. **Satan** has power over people that are lost.

- **Romans 16:20**

  "And the God of peace shall bruise **Satan** under your feet shortly. The grace of our Lord Jesus Christ *be* with you. Amen."

I am glad that **Satan** can be bruised, that he can be hurt and harmed.

- **1 Corinthians 7:5**

  "Defraud ye not one the other, except *it be* with consent for a time, that ye may give yourselves to fasting and prayer; and come together again, that **Satan** tempt you not for your incontinency."

In marriage, we have to be careful. **Satanic** powers are in the bedrooms of husbands and wives.

- **2 Corinthians 2:10-11**

  "To whom ye forgive any thing, I *forgive* also: for if I forgave any thing, to whom I forgave *it*, for your sakes *forgave I it* in the person of Christ; Lest **Satan** should get an advantage of us: for we are not ignorant of his devices."

Forgiveness Is Important

Forgiveness is important. Lack of forgiveness is Satan's advantage. If we keep ourselves apart and there is no reconciliation or forgiveness, Satan is going to get the better

of us, whether it is a family, a church, or whatever it may be.
Be very careful of that.

- **2 Corinthians 11:13-15**
  "For such *are* false apostles, deceitful workers, transforming
  themselves into the apostles of Christ. And no marvel; for **Satan**
  himself is transformed into an angel of light. Therefore *it is* no
  great thing if his ministers also be transformed as the ministers
  of righteousness; whose end shall be according to their works."

We are talking now about modernistic preachers, Roman Catholic
priests—those that are unsaved that are in the pulpits.

Satan–A Phony Angel Of Light

Satan is transformed into an angel of light. He is not one,
but he is transformed into one. He is made into one. He has
ministers, people that sound like they are in the light, but they
are in the darkness. It is a sad situation. Satan is most effective
when he comes as an angel of light. We do not understand who
he is. He looks like one of us, if we are genuinely saved. He
looks like those who are in the light. He comes and sometimes
he may use genuine Christians who are in the light to get us
off base and off the track. Be careful of that. Satan appears as
an angel of light.

- **1 Thessalonians 2:18**
  "Wherefore we would have come unto you, even I Paul, once and
  again; but **Satan** hindered us."

Sometimes **Satan** hinders us from doing what God wants us to do.

- **2 Thessalonians 2:8-9**
  "And then shall that Wicked be revealed, whom the Lord shall
  consume with the spirit of his mouth, and shall destroy with the
  brightness of his coming: *Even him*, whose coming is after the
  working of **Satan** with all power and signs and lying wonders,"

This is speaking of the second phase of the second coming of the Lord
Jesus Christ. This antichrist will be smitten by the Lord Jesus Christ in
the second phase of His coming. The antichrist has a terrible record of
lying wonders.

- **1 Timothy 5:14-15**

  "I will therefore that the younger women marry, bear children, guide the house, give none occasion to the adversary to speak reproachfully. For some are already turned aside after **Satan**."

Some of the young widows were not living Scripturally and were turned aside after **Satan**.

- **Revelation 12:9**

  "And the great **dragon** was cast out, that old **serpent**, called the **Devil**, and **Satan**, which deceiveth the whole world: he was cast out into the earth, and his angels were cast out with him."

What does this *serpent* mean? To the ancients, the **serpent** was an emblem of cunning and wisdom. The **serpent** who deceived Eve was regarded by the Jews as the **Devil**. I believe he was the **Devil**. He is DIABOLOS. He is a slanderer.

Satan Is An Adversary

What about Satan? That word is SATANAS. It means, *an adversary; one who opposes another in purpose or act; the prince of the evil spirits; inveterate adversary of God and Christ.* He incites apostasy from God, circumventing men by his wiles. The worshippers of idols are said to be under his control. By his devils, he is able to take possession of men and inflict them with diseases. By God's assistance, he is overcome. When the Lord Jesus Christ returns from Heaven to rule and reign on the earth, Satan will be bound with chains.

Revelation 20:3

"And cast him into the bottomless pit, and shut him up, and set a seal upon him, that he should deceive the nations no more, till the thousand years should be fulfilled: and after that he must be loosed a little season."

The Devil Is A Deceiver

The Devil's object is deception. When it says, *"that he should deceive the nations no more,"* that means he is doing it right now. He is deceiving the nations. That is his method of operation, that is his *modus operandi*, as they say, his "MO."

- **Jeremiah 17:9**
  "The heart *is* **deceitful** above all *things*, and desperately wicked: who can know it?"

Satan is a **deceiver** and our hearts are deceptive.

- **Matthew 24:4-5**
  "And Jesus answered and said unto them, Take heed that no man **deceive** you. For many shall come in my name, saying, I am Christ; and shall **deceive** many."

We should not be **deceived** for any reason. There are people even on the earth today saying, "I am Christ. I am the Messiah." Do not believe them. The Lord Jesus Christ said that they are **deceivers**.

- **1 Corinthians 15:33**
  "Be not **deceived**: evil communications corrupt good manners."

Associations Can Corrupt Us

Evil communications are evil associations. Stay away from the Devil's crowd in a close-knit sense. Do not fellowship with that crowd. If you do, your manners will be corrupt. Do not be deceived.

- **Galatians 6:7**
  "Be not **deceived**; God is not mocked: for whatsoever a man soweth, that shall he also reap."

Stop being **deceived**. You may say, "Well, I am going to sow evil and I am going to get good." No. You sow evil, you get evil. You sow good, you get good. You sow beans, you get beans. You do not get apples. What you sow, you reap. Do not be **deceived**. People feel that they can do anything. They are going to reap the whirlwind one of these days if they sow to the flesh, and not to the Holy Spirit of God.

- **2 Thessalonians 2:9-10**
  "*Even him*, whose coming is after the working of Satan with all power and signs and lying wonders, And with all **deceivableness** of unrighteousness in them that perish; because they received not the love of the truth, that they might be saved."

The Antichrist Will Be Slick

<u>This is the man of sin, this antichrist.</u> Why do people accept the antichrist? It is because of his deception. He is slick. You may have heard the expression, *"Slick Willy."* People who are slick put things over very easily on people because they are suave. Maybe they are handsome or beautiful, whatever it may be. They can corrupt by being deceptive, looking one way and being another.

- 2 Timothy 3:13
  "But evil men and seducers shall wax worse and worse, **deceiving**, and **being deceived**."

<u>Deception is the work of the Devil.</u>

- James 1:22
  "But be ye doers of the word, and not hearers only, **deceiving** your own selves."

To be hearing without doing, that is **deception**. We can **deceive** ourselves.

- 1 John 1:8
  "If we say that we have no sin, we **deceive** ourselves, and the truth is not in us."

No One Is Sinless But Christ

No man, woman, or child can ever say, "We have no sin." We have the sin nature within us. It will never be gone until we have our new bodies. If some of these people in Christian churches say they are sinlessly perfect, they deceive themselves. The truth is not in them.

- 2 John 1:7
  "For many **deceivers** are entered into the world, who confess not that Jesus Christ is come in the flesh. This is a **deceiver** and an antichrist."

Deceivers Deny The Incarnation

If someone says that the Lord Jesus Christ has not come in the flesh, as perfect God and perfect Man, he is a deceiver. Not only that, but he is an antichrist. This is every modernist

and liberal that denies the incarnation, that God became flesh and dwelled among us.

- **1 Timothy 3:16**

  "And without controversy great is the mystery of godliness: **God was manifest in the flesh**, justified in the Spirit, seen of angels, preached unto the Gentiles, believed on in the world, received up into glory."

Every modernist and liberal that denies His **incarnation**, perfect God and perfect Man, is not only a **deceiver**, he is an **antichrist**. We have antichrists in pulpits all over the world. It is a sad thing. Whether it is the Jews—they deny that the Lord Jesus Christ has come in the flesh—they are **antichrist**. Whether it is the Muslims—they deny that the Lord Jesus Christ is come in the flesh—they are **antichrist**. Whether it is the Christian Scientists or any cult that you can name—**antichrist**. This is Scripture. It is not my idea. This is God's idea. You may say, "Is that not harsh on some of these other religions?" The Bible is harsh against other religions.

- **John 14:6**

  "Jesus saith unto him, I am the way, the truth, and the life: no man cometh unto the Father, but by me."

- **Revelation 12:9**

  "And the great **dragon** was cast out, that old **serpent**, called the **Devil**, and **Satan**, which **deceiveth** the whole world: he was cast out into the earth, and his angels were cast out with him."

I am glad that the **Devil** is going to be bound for the **thousand years** because during that **thousand years**, if we are genuinely saved and born-again, we are going to be with new bodies ruling and reigning with the Lord Jesus Christ. We will not have the **Devil** to put up with. I am very happy about that.

Revelation 20:4

"And I saw thrones, and they sat upon them, and judgment was given unto them: and *I saw* the souls of them that were beheaded for the witness of Jesus, and for the word of God, and which had not worshipped the beast, neither his image, neither had received *his* mark upon their foreheads, or in their hands; and they lived and reigned with Christ a thousand years."

Those Who Are Beheaded

Those who were witnesses of the Lord Jesus Christ were beheaded during the tribulation period. These saints, I think, will be standing along with those that are genuine believers who are in Heaven before the tribulation. Those of us who are genuinely saved who are here today, will be with them. This beheading is a terrible thing.

Matthew 14:10

"And he sent, and **beheaded** John in the prison."

We have **beheadings** in Iraq. The beheadings of Rome was their method of capital punishment. It was **decapitation**. The executioners had a short sword about 18 inches long, a cubit long. They would use one fell swoop. That is not the way they do it over there in Iraq. They want to hurt and to harm. They pull the head back and then, with a knife, just hack at the neck. That is not what they did here.

I am against **beheading**, do not get me wrong, but if that is the method of execution—like the guillotine—it was a merciful way. Even though you think it is a horrible thing to cut off somebody's head, at least that knife came down and the prisoners were out of their misery. It was not a question of suffering. I am sure that the antichrist who **beheads** the Christians during the tribulation period is not merciful. They are probably just like the Iraqis. The most suffering they could possibly inflict is given.

The Saints Will Be Judges

Revelation 20:4 speaks of the thrones. The saints (genuinely saved people) are on those thrones, the ones that are going to reign and rule with the Lord Jesus Christ a thousand years. It says in Scripture that the Biblical saints shall judge the world. These saints shall judge angels. These are the ones on those thrones. Judgment was given unto them. They had not received the mark of the beast in this tribulation period. These are the tribulation saints. The saints lived and reigned with the Lord Jesus Christ a thousand years. This is the Millennium—one thousand years.

Revelation 20:5

"But the rest of the dead lived not again until the thousand years were finished. This _is_ the first resurrection."

There is a **first resurrection** and there is a second resurrection. These Biblical saints that were raised here were part of the **first resurrection**, but the ones who were not in this, are with the rest of the dead. They did not live until the **thousand years were finished**.

- **John 5:29**
  "And shall come forth; they that have done good, unto the **resurrection** of life; and they that have done evil, unto the resurrection of damnation."

The Lord Jesus Christ speaks of **resurrections**. I understand, _they that have done good,_ to mean those who have genuinely trusted the Lord Jesus Christ as Saviour. That is the only good you and I can do. I would understand, _they that have done evil,_ to mean those that have rejected the Saviour. In between these two **resurrections**—life and damnation—there is a **thousand years**. That is the distinction.

- **John 11:25-26**
  "Jesus said unto her, I am the **resurrection**, and the life: he that believeth in me, though he were dead, yet shall he live: And whosoever liveth and believeth in me shall never die. Believest thou this?"

Christians Never Die Spiritually

If we believe in Him, we will never die, because we have eternal life. We may die physically, but not spiritually—not in eternity. We have eternal life.

- **1 Corinthians 15:23-24**

  "But every man in his own order: Christ the firstfruits; afterward they that are Christ's at his coming. Then *cometh* the end, when he shall have delivered up the kingdom to God, even the Father; when he shall have put down all rule and all authority and power."

We see there is a special order. The Lord Jesus Christ is the One that was raised bodily from the dead after three days. *They that are Christ's at his coming* are the ones that are raptured. <u>There are three phases of the resurrection.</u>

- **1 Peter 1:3**

  "Blessed *be* the God and Father of our Lord Jesus Christ, which according to his abundant mercy hath begotten us again unto a lively hope by the **resurrection** of Jesus Christ from the dead,"

<u>What is awaiting for those of us who are saved?</u>

- **1 Peter 1:4**

  "To an inheritance incorruptible, and undefiled, and that fadeth not away, reserved in heaven for you,"

<u>That is a "*reservation*" that those of us who are truly saved have received by genuine faith in the Lord Jesus Christ.</u>

Revelation 20:6

"**Blessed and holy *is* he that hath part in the first resurrection: on such the second death hath no power, but they shall be priests of God and of Christ, and shall reign with him a thousand years.**"

No Second Death For The Saved

There is no second death to those who are in the first resurrection—those who are truly born-again, those that are genuinely saved, that is, those who have sincerely come to the Lord Jesus Christ. There is the first death that every one of us will experience unless the Lord Jesus Christ should return in the rapture and take us Home and transform our bodies, the mortal becoming immortal. If that does not come in our lifetime, every one of us will pass through the first death. If we are genuinely saved and born-again, there will be no second death. If we are not genuinely saved, there is going to be a second death and that is Hell itself. It is terrible.

- **Revelation 2:11**

  "He that hath an ear, let him hear what the Spirit saith unto the churches; He that overcometh shall not be hurt of the **second death**."

- **Revelation 20:14**

  "And death and Hell were cast into the lake of fire. This is the **second death**."

This is a horrible thing. Many people are afraid to die the first death. Wait until they get to the **second death** if they are lost—a horrible, horrible situation.

- **Revelation 21:8**

  "But the fearful, and unbelieving, and the abominable, and murderers, and whoremongers, and sorcerers, and idolaters, and all liars, shall have their part in the lake which burneth with fire and brimstone: which is the **second death**."

The Second Death Explained

This second death is not going to be a picnic. It is not going to last just for five seconds, as a sudden heart attack that takes us in our first death. It is not going to last a week or two weeks, as a lingering illness. It is not going to last three weeks or four weeks, whatever that first death may bring to us. This will be for eternity. There is no end to it.

Some of the new evangelicals and others are saying, "We do not believe in everlasting Hell any longer. It is just a portion or a partial thing. Pretty soon we will be released from it." They say that it is not eternal. No, it is eternal. The Lord Jesus Christ said so. I believe Him. I do not know where some of these theologians get some of these ideas, but they get them and they are wrong ideas.

Literal Burning Fire

The second death is a place that burns with fire and brimstone and it is literal fire.

As we have said before, way back in the 1950s I wrote a doctoral dissertation on Billy Graham in the first ten years and his effect as a speaker in Purdue University. I heard his speeches in the 1950's and I heard him say very clearly that there is no fire in Hell. That was well over 50 years ago. Others have followed in his train, saying that no fire is there. There is going to be judgment and it is going to be serious, this **second death.**

Revelation 20:7

"And when the thousand years are expired, Satan shall be loosed out of his prison,"

Satan is going to be **loosed.** During the millennial reign of the Lord Jesus Christ, He will rule people with a rod of iron. People will be obedient, but many of them will not be converted. Some will be converted. Some will be genuinely saved during the thousand years, there is no question about that, but not all will be saved. Not all will be converted. They will be Satan's children, obeying externally the wishes of the Lord Jesus Christ because He will rule over them with a rod of iron. Any infraction will mean swift justice. It will not be like our courts today—slow and sometimes with injustice. It will be swift and it will be just. Satan will be bound. The thing about it is, afterwards, people will see who these people really are. They will be revealed.

Longevity Will Be Restored

Longevity, you may remember, will be extended. Many feel that the days will be as the days of a tree, like a big Sequoia tree—a thousand years. Various things in the book of Isaiah have told us the length of the days will be extended. It will be just like in the time before Noah, where Methuselah lived 969 years, almost a thousand years, because there will be climatic changes. In the millennial reign of the Lord Jesus Christ, the climate will be changed. It will probably be as it was in pre-flood times, for all we know.

Revelation 20:8

"And shall go out to deceive the nations which are in the four quarters of the earth, Gog and Magog, to gather them together to battle: the number of whom *is* as the sand of the sea."

Satan Will Gather The Nations

This Gog and Magog are people from the north, maybe in Russia or wherever up in the north part of the world—in that direction. The Devil was a deceiver before he went into the prison a thousand years earlier. Now, after he comes out of the prison, he is still a deceiver. His number one item is deception, deception, deception! These were unconverted nations. They were ruled by the Lord Jesus Christ and they were obedient to Him, but they were Satan's children. As soon as Satan is released from his prison, he will gather the nations together to battle in the Jerusalem area.

- Zechariah 14:1-4

  "Behold, the day of the LORD cometh, and thy spoil shall be divided in the midst of thee. For I will **gather all nations** against Jerusalem **to battle**; and the city shall be taken, and the houses rifled, and the women ravished; and half of the city shall go forth into captivity, and the residue of the people shall not be cut off from the city. Then shall the LORD go forth, and fight against those nations, as when he fought in the day of battle. And his feet shall stand in that day upon the mount of Olives, which is before Jerusalem on the east, and the mount of Olives shall cleave in the midst thereof toward the east and toward the west, *and there shall be* a very great valley; and half of the mountain shall remove toward the north, and half of it toward the south."

It is with God's permissive power that Satan will **gather all nations** against Jerusalem. The mount will split north and south so that east and west the wonderful river from the temple will come through.

- Revelation 16:16

  "And he **gathered them together** into a place called in the Hebrew tongue Armageddon."

The Battle of Armageddon

Here is the battle of Armageddon. Satan is the instigator of it to gather all the nations—Russia, China, Africa, the United States, Europe, Australia, all the Muslim nations, and all the others. All of them are gathered from the four corners of the earth to battle against the Lord Jesus Christ.

Satan is a master **deceiver**. I hope that when you and I, if we are genuinely saved and born-again, will never ever be duped by him and his deceptive tactics. There are many things Satan wants to do. We must continue to resist him, steadfast in the faith. That is why we have to know the Scriptures—know the Words of God. Be like the Lord Jesus Christ was. Three times, when He was tempted and tested of the Devil, He quoted Scripture, *It is written, it is written, it is written.* We must do the same to defeat the one who is against our souls, against our God, and against our Saviour, the Lord Jesus Christ.

Revelation 20:9

"And they went up on the breadth of the earth, and compassed the camp of the saints about, and the beloved city: and fire came down from God out of heaven, and devoured them."

This is referring to Gog, Magog, and the other nations **compassing** the great **city**, Jerusalem. This is after the Devil has been released. He was bound for a thousand years and now he is released. He **gathers all these nations together.**

God wants to judge these nations and He will. Who is this LORD? It is the Lord Jesus Christ in His second coming in glory.

- **Revelation 16:16**

  "And he **gathered them together** into a place called in the Hebrew tongue Armageddon."

Armageddon is *the hill of Megiddo.* It is to the north of Jerusalem.

When this takes place, just think of **all the nations**—two hundred million strong, the kings of the east—**gathered** against Jerusalem. That will be from the northern areas of Russia and all the east, which will be China, and the south, which will be Egypt, and of course, the west, the whole western European countries and probably the United States at that time. They will **compass** the city about, a huge two hundred million contingent from the east alone. This **fire will devour them**.

- **2 Thessalonians 1:7-10**

  "And to you who are troubled rest with us, when the Lord Jesus shall be revealed from heaven with his mighty angels, In flaming **fire** taking vengeance on them that know not God, and that obey not the gospel of our Lord Jesus Christ: Who shall be punished with everlasting destruction from the presence of the Lord, and from the glory of his power; When he shall come to be glorified in his saints, and to be admired in all them that believe (because our testimony among you was believed) in that day."

That judgment, that devouring by **fire**, will take place in these nations.

- **2 Thessalonians 2:8**

  "And then shall that Wicked be revealed, whom the Lord shall consume with the spirit of his mouth, and shall destroy with the brightness of his coming:"

This is another reference to this very thing. That *brightness*, in this case, will be a **fire** that will judge.

Revelation 20:10

"And the devil that deceived them was cast into the lake of fire and brimstone, where the beast and the false prophet *are*, and shall be tormented day and night for ever and ever."

The End Of The Millennium

Here is the end of the Millennium. The Lord Jesus Christ will destroy the Devil. He will have destroyed the nations that had come. The Devil will be cast into the lake of fire. You will remember that before, he was cast into the abyss, the bottomless pit. He will be in chains for a thousand years during that millennial reign of the Lord Jesus Christ.

By the way, I mentioned Mr. Camping and that he did not believe in the Millennium. At the time, I was down in the basement. Family Radio was on as I was getting something. Lo and behold, a question was asked about the Millennium and the dispensations. He said that the dispensationalists were all wrong because they believe there will be a literal Millennium. He is off on that. There is going to be a Millennium and at the end of that time, **Satan will be cast into the lake of fire.**

Notice, it says, *"where the beast and the false prophet are."* They are still there. They have not been destroyed and shall be tormented day and night forever.

- **Revelation 19:20**

  "And the **beast** was taken, and with him the **false prophet** that wrought miracles before him, with which he deceived them that had received the mark of the beast, and them that worshipped his image. These both were cast alive into a **lake of fire** burning with brimstone."

This talks about the religious beast and the political beast. The judgment of **fire** is in Scripture in many places.

- **Matthew 13:39-42**

  "The enemy that sowed them is the devil; the harvest is the end of the world; and the reapers are the angels. As therefore the tares are gathered and burned in the **fire**; so shall it be in the end of this world. The Son of man shall send forth his angels, and they shall gather out of his kingdom all things that offend, and them which do iniquity; And shall cast them into a furnace of **fire**: there shall be wailing and gnashing of teeth."

This is speaking of the judgment at the great white throne of those that are lost—burned in the **fire**. That is a literal **fire**.

- **Matthew 25:41**

  "Then shall he say also unto them on the left hand, Depart from me, ye cursed, into everlasting **fire**, prepared for the devil and his angels:"

The Judgment Of The Nations

This is the judgment of the nations—the sheep on the right and the goats on the left. As we have said many times, the Devil and his angels had this judgment of fire, not people, but if they follow the Devil, they will go where the Devil goes.

- **Mark 9:45**

  "And if thy foot offend thee, cut it off: it is better for thee to enter halt into life, than having two feet to be cast into Hell, into the **fire** that never shall be quenched:"

This is a very serious place. It is not a pleasant place by any means. It is a place of literal **fire**.

- **2 Thessalonians 1:7-9**

  "And to you who are troubled rest with us, when the Lord Jesus shall be revealed from heaven with his mighty angels, In flaming **fire** taking vengeance on them that know not God, and that obey not the gospel of our Lord Jesus Christ: Who shall be punished with everlasting destruction from the presence of the Lord, and from the glory of his power;"

The Uses Of Fire In The Bible

Fire is in Scripture in judgment in many places. When the beast and the false prophet were cast into the lake of fire, it says in Revelation 20:10, *"where the beast and the false prophet are."* They are still there. When you cast a piece of paper into a burning fiery furnace, the paper burns up and you have ashes. Here, you have people with some sort of bodies that will not be burned up. They are not glorified bodies, but they will be some kind of bodies that will not be burned up. They will be in pain. They will be tormented for ever and ever. They will feel the pain of the fire, but they are still there after a thousand years. This is something to remember. They do not escape.

That word for **torment** is BASANIZO. It is a very strong word. It means, *to torture; to vex with grievous pains of body or mind; to torment.* It is a very serious thing.

The **Devil that deceived them** is mentioned here in Revelation 20:10. That word for **deception** is PLANAO. We get the word *planet* from that. A planet wanders all over. This word PLANAO means, *to lead away from the truth; to lead into error; to deceive; to go astray; to wander; to roam about; taken away.* That is what the Devil has done. He has **deceived** the people. He **deceives** people now in the age of grace. He will not be there during the Millennium to **deceive**, but as soon as he gets out, there will be **deception** again. It is like the thing that we used to get at the fair—cotton candy. You think it is big. It is huge, but when you bite into it, it is not there. It just disappears. The Devil is a **deceptive** being.

Torment is in Scripture in many places.

- **Luke 16:28**

  "For I have five brethren; that he may testify unto them, lest they also come into this place of **torment**."

This is the rich man and Lazarus. The rich man was an evil man. He rejected the Lord, apparently, and he was in HADES or Hell in **torment**. HADES, we believe, is an intermediate state of the spirits and souls of those that die. It is not the **lake of fire** yet, but HADES is the place where the spirits and souls of those that are lost go as soon as they die. The Old Testament word for that is SHEOL. There used to be two divisions. There was a blessed section and a section for the damned or the unsaved. I think that is talked about in the account of the rich man and Lazarus in Luke 16. Before Christ's resurrection, Abraham's bosom was in the paradise section of HADES. That is where Abraham was and that is where the poor man, Lazarus, was. The rich man was in HADES or Hell in the section of the damned people—those that are judged and unsaved. That is where the **torment** will be. Later on, we are going to talk about HADES.

Translating HADES As Hell

The King James Bible translates HADES. It does not transliterate HADES. It translates it as Hell, which is true. There is a little Hell and a big Hell—Hell "A" and Hell "B." Hell "A" is HADES, which is the damned, tormented section of every soul and spirit that dies before they are cast eventually into Hell "B" which is the lake of fire. This is their final destination. Both places are Hell. Both involve torment. One place is for the spirits and souls. The other place is for the spirits, souls, and bodies. We will see more of this a little bit later in this chapter.

- **Luke 16:24**

  "And he cried and said, Father Abraham, have mercy on me, and send Lazarus, that he may dip the tip of his finger in water, and cool my tongue; for I am **tormented** in this flame."

One of the preachers in one of our churches locally, their assistant pastor, said that all this picture of the rich man and Lazarus was just a parable. No, I believe it is a true story. It is not a parable. It is a true story that the Lord Jesus Christ told. This **torment** in the flame is a literal flame. It is painful and that is what He is talking about here.

- **Revelation 14:10**

  "The same shall drink of the wine of the wrath of God, which is poured out without mixture into the cup of his indignation; and he shall be **tormented** with fire and brimstone in the presence of the holy angels, and in the presence of the Lamb:"

This is those that receive the mark of the beast. There is a **torment** for those that receive the mark of the beast during this seven-year period of tribulation. The true believers, the genuinely saved ones, will be gone. We will be raptured out. For those that are still here, that is their fate. That is a serious situation.

- **Revelation 14:11**

  "And the smoke of their **torment** ascendeth up for ever and ever: and they have no rest day nor night, who worship the beast and his image, and whosoever receiveth the mark of his name."

Those that have received the mark of the beast say, "I want money. I want food. I am going to worship this false prophet. I am going to worship this false political ruler, the beast. I am going to bow down and I am going to get his mark in my right hand and in my forehead. Therefore, I can buy, I can sell, and I am going to do wonderful things."

The Mark Of The Beast

Well, the fate of every one of those during the seven-year period of tribulation that receives the mark of the beast in his right hand and his forehead will be torment and suffering in fire and brimstone forever. It is true that when the antichrist tells the true believers of that time—the genuinely saved ones that are in tribulation and are really born-again at that time, and in that seven-year period—the antichrist will say, "Do this or die!" Many of the Biblical Christians at that time will die. They will suffer. They will go to Heaven. Far better to die in the body, and the spirit and soul go immediately to Heaven than, to receive the mark of the beast and go to the lake of fire. That is the choice that they have.

This everlasting **torment** is forever.

- **Matthew 18:8-9**

  "Wherefore if thy hand or thy foot offend thee, cut them off, and cast *them* from thee: it is better for thee to enter into life halt or maimed, rather than having two hands or two feet to be cast into **everlasting fire**. And if thine eye offend thee, pluck it out, and cast *it* from thee: it is better for thee to enter into life with one eye, rather than having two eyes to be cast into Hell fire."

When President John F. Kennedy died, they had at his grave site in Massachusetts what they call an eternal flame. It is always burning. You may have seen it on television. They keep it lighted. This Hell, this lake of fire, is an eternal flame of fire as well. God is the One that is making it eternal. It is not man that puts gas into it or whatever makes it burn.

- **Matthew 25:41**
"Then shall he say also unto them on the left hand, Depart from me, ye cursed, into **everlasting fire**, prepared for the devil and his angels:"

These are the ones in the goat nations—the ones that have not genuinely trusted the Lord Jesus Christ and have not been kind to Israel His people.

- **Matthew 25:46**
"And these shall go away into everlasting **punishment**: but the righteous into life eternal."

There Is No Purgatory

The punishment is not just for a day or for an hour. I do not know how or where the Roman Catholic church gets the idea of a purgatory and that you can pray your way out of this intermediate place of torment. There is no way out.

I remember on one of the talk programs what one man said to the woman who was leading the discussion. He said, "Yes, my grandmother died the other day and I lit a candle for her." I thought to myself, "What on earth is that candle going to do?" That lady was either genuinely saved or lost. It was a candle to get her out of purgatory. Of course, when people buy the candles, the church gets the money.

I wonder what the pope is going to do when he dies. Is he going to go to purgatory, too, or is he going straight to Heaven? If he is genuinely saved, he will go straight to Heaven. If he is lost, he will go straight to Hell. This is a serious thing. It is an everlasting state that cannot be modified. It is too late once you die. You may have no time for faith, no time for the Lord Jesus Christ, no time for anything, but you will have time to die.

Revelation 20:11

"And I saw a great white throne, and him that sat on it, from whose face the earth and the heaven fled away; and there was found no place for them."

Here is the **white throne** of judgment. Notice it says, *"and him that sat on it."* Who was it that sat on that throne? I want to show you it is the Lord Jesus Christ. He is the One that is going to do all the

judging, not the Father, not the Holy Spirit.

- **John 5:22**
  "For the Father **judgeth** no man, but hath committed all **judgment unto the Son:**"

He is the One and He is on that **throne** and powerful.

- **John 5:27**
  "And hath given him authority to execute **judgment** also, because he is the Son of man."

All **judgment** is by the Lord Jesus Christ. He is the One on that **throne**.

- **Jude 14-15**
  "And Enoch also, the seventh from Adam, prophesied of these, saying, Behold, the Lord cometh with ten thousands of his saints, To execute **judgment** upon all, and to convince all that are ungodly among them of all their ungodly deeds which they have ungodly committed, and of all their hard *speeches* which ungodly sinners have spoken against him."

This is the Lord Jesus Christ's return. When He comes, He will be the One on that **throne**. He is going to execute the **judgment**.

- **Acts 17:31**
  "Because he hath appointed a day, in the which he will **judge** the world in righteousness by *that* man whom he hath ordained; *whereof* he hath given assurance unto all *men*, in that he hath raised him from the dead."

The Saviour Will Be The Judge

It is the Saviour that is going to be the Judge. He came the first time to save men, women, boys, and girls by His death on the cross, that they would genuinely trust Him and be truly saved, but He is one day going to come as their Judge.

- **Romans 2:16**
  "In the day when God shall **judge** the secrets of men by Jesus Christ according to my gospel."

Christ On The Great White Throne

The Lord Jesus Christ is the Judge. He is the One on that white throne.

- 1 Corinthians 4:5
  "Therefore **judge** nothing before the time, until the Lord come, who both will bring to light the hidden things of darkness, and will make manifest the counsels of the hearts: and then shall every man have praise of God."

The Lord Jesus Christ's Coming

Here is the coming of the Lord Jesus Christ. He will make all things open and above-board. Hidden things of darkness will come out. I am sure those that are at that great white throne judgment, those that are lost, will not want some of the things to come out. It will be very embarrassing, but He will bring them out.

- Revelation 16:20
  "And **every island fled away,** and the mountains were not found."

This was at the fall of Babylon. The power of God causes no place to be found for them as the Lord Jesus Christ is there. The chorus of a song my wife sings says,

> *And O, what a weeping and wailing,*
> *As the lost were told of their fate;*
> *They cried for the rocks and the mountains,*
> *They prayed, but their prayer was too late.*

It was too late, and it is too late at that time.

Revelation 20:12

"And I saw the dead, small and great, stand before God; and the books were opened: and another book was opened, which is *the book* of life: and the dead were judged out of those things which were written in the books, according to their works."

The Great White Throne Judgment

Here are the dead, small and great, standing before God. Here is the judgment of the Lord Jesus Christ. They are standing before God the Son and they are going to be judged.

These are all lost people. They are not genuinely saved people. Saved people have already been judged at the judgment seat of the Lord Jesus Christ.

The Lord Jesus Christ never does anything that is untoward or that is half-hearted or that is in any way unjust. He opens up the **books** and He shows in the books all the deeds and all the lives of every one of these that are standing before Him. Did they genuinely trust the Lord Jesus Christ when the gospel was preached or did they reject Him? They did not receive Him. Here is another occasion. You heard the gospel message on the radio, television–or whatever–and you rejected it. All the **books are open.** That is what it says in the book of Romans. They will be **without excuse**–without any excuse whatever.

- **Romans 1:20**
  "For the invisible things of him from the creation of the world are clearly seen, being understood by the things that are made, *even* his eternal power and Godhead; so that they are **without excuse:**"

They will not be in this **book of life.**

- **Philippians 4:3**
  "And I intreat thee also, true yokefellow, help those women which laboured with me in the gospel, with Clement also, and *with* other my fellowlabourers, whose names *are* in the **book of life."**

Is Your Name In The Book Of Life?

I hope your name is in the book of life. If you are genuinely trusting in the Lord Jesus Christ, I know your name is in the book of life. That is a very important book. It was open in addition to the book of judgment.

- **Revelation 3:5**
  "He that overcometh, the same shall be clothed in white raiment; and I will not blot out his name out of the **book of life**, but I will confess his name before my Father, and before his angels."
- **Revelation 13:8**
  "And all that dwell upon the earth shall worship him, whose names are not written in the **book of life** of the Lamb slain from the foundation of the world."

Those Not In The Book Of Life

These that are following the antichrist—the false Christ—their names are not written in that book.

- **Revelation 17:8**

  "The beast that thou sawest was, and is not; and shall ascend out of the bottomless pit, and go into perdition: and they that dwell on the earth shall wonder, whose names were not written in the **book of life** from the foundation of the world, when they behold the beast that was, and is not, and yet is."

They will wonder about this beast. They will be confused. They will say, "Look at that powerful man!" Those whose names are written in the **book of life** will know who he is, but those that will not genuinely trust the Lord Jesus Christ will wonder after that beast.

- **Revelation 21:27**

  "And there shall in no wise enter into it any thing that defileth, neither *whatsoever* worketh abomination, or *maketh* a lie: but they which are written in the Lamb's **book of life**."

The Book Of Life Continues

The word *is* in Revelation 20:12, "*which is the book of life,*" is a present tense <u>continuous action</u>. It is never going to change. It continues to be. God is not going to wipe it out. The Devil cannot steal it. It is there and it is there for all to behold—the book of life.

- **Revelation 22:19**

  "And if any man shall take away from the words of the book of this prophecy, God shall take away his part out of the **book of life,** and out of the holy city, and *from* the things which are written in this book."

<u>I believe his name will not be removed, but his *part.* I have always believed that the part is the rewards. That Christian whose name is there, if he takes away from the Words of the book of Revelation</u>—the Words of God—his part or rewards of the **book of life** will be taken away.

These books of judgment are mentioned. There are lots of works that are mentioned. They will be judged about those things that are **written** in the books. By the way, that word *written,* GEGRAPTAI, is in the perfect tense. That is an action in the Greek language which was in the past. They were **written** down and they are still **written** down today. In the future they will still be written down. Nobody is going to erase that either. These are indelible actions and **works** of these people that are up before the Judge of all the earth, the Lord Jesus Christ. They will be judged by their **works**. There are a lot of names and places where **works** are mentioned—some good, some bad.

- **Matthew 5:16**
  "Let your light so shine before men, that they may see your good **works**, and glorify your Father which is in heaven."

Christians Should Shine As Lights

The Lord Jesus Christ tells this to His disciples, and to all of us. Those are good works. Those are not the bad works that are going to be in this last judgment. God wants us to shine. He wants us to be lights in the world to shine that they may behold our good works and not glorify us. Not that they would say, "What a wonderful man, woman, boy, or girl this is," but to glorify the Father which is in Heaven.

- **Matthew 7:21-23**
  "Not every one that saith unto me, Lord, Lord, shall enter into the kingdom of heaven; but he that doeth the will of my Father which is in heaven. Many will say to me in that day, Lord, Lord, have we not prophesied in thy name? and in thy name have cast out devils? and in thy name done many wonderful **works**? And then will I profess unto them, I never knew you: depart from me, ye that **work** iniquity."

The Lord Jesus Christ warns of wrong **works**. Is there superficial salvation? Sometimes there is. Is there just head knowledge of the Lord Jesus Christ? Yes, many times there is. If it is not all the way down to the heart and genuine, people are lost. No matter how much they profess with their mouth and their lips, "I am saved, I did this or I did that, I prayed a little prayer," if it is not genuine, they are lost.

Some Prayers Not Genuine

I believe there are some people in this world (I hope not those who are reading this) that believe they are genuinely saved. They had a little prayer. They said some light little thing and they are lost. They are not saved. They are not genuine. Why do I say that? Because of what the Lord Jesus Christ says

> in Matthew 7:21-23. They did wonderful things in His name, they prophesied and did many wonderful works. The Lord Jesus Christ said, "I looked at your heart and I never knew you." He is going to say that to Judas Iscariot and others, professing but not possessing.

- **Matthew 16:27**

    "For the Son of man shall come in the glory of his Father with his angels; and then he shall reward every man according to his **works**."

This is the second phase of His second coming.

- **Matthew 23:3**

    "All therefore whatsoever they bid you observe, *that* observe and do; but do not ye after their **works**: for they say, and do not."

The Lord Jesus Christ talks about the Pharisees to His disciples. We know some people like that, do we not? They say and they do not. What they say sometimes is all right, but it is a sham. The Pharisees were fakes.

- **Matthew 23:5**

    "But all their **works** they do for to be seen of men: they make broad their phylacteries, and enlarge the borders of their garments,"

That is a bad motive. If unsaved people do works to be seen of men, it is not going to count for eternity. All these **works** will be brought up at that great white throne judgment for unbelievers.

- **John 6:28-29**

    "Then said they unto him, What shall we do, that we might **work** the **works** of God? Jesus answered and said unto them, This is the **work** of God, that ye believe on him whom he hath sent."

They wanted to really **work the works** of God—do a good deed. Faith in the Lord Jesus Christ is the only **work** that anybody can do—and that is not a **work** as we usually think of a "**work**." Do not worry about what you do. First, genuinely trust in the Lord Jesus Christ as Saviour.

- **John 7:7**

    "The world cannot hate you; but me it hateth, because I testify of it, that the **works** thereof are evil."

He testifies of evil **works**. These are some of the **works** that will be brought up at the white throne judgment.

- **Acts 7:41**

  "And they made a calf in those days, and offered sacrifice unto the idol, and rejoiced in the **works** of their own hands."

According to their **works** they will be judged. The **works** of their own hands—this calf—all the idolatry in all the world is a **work** of their hands. That will not be good enough.

- **Acts 9:36**

  "Now there was at Joppa a certain disciple named Tabitha, which by interpretation is called Dorcas: this woman was full of good **works** and almsdeeds which she did."

Here is a good type of **works**. Many churches have a Dorcas room, a Dorcas club, or a Dorcas kind of group. These are good **works**. I believe she was genuinely saved. This is different from the works on the part of those that are lost.

- **Romans 4:2**

  "For if Abraham were justified by **works**, he hath *whereof* to glory; but not before God."

These men, women, boys, and girls that are standing before God and the Lord Jesus Christ at the great white throne judgment, think that they can be saved by what they do. This is not going to glorify God and will not be suitable to the Lord Jesus Christ. That is what this verse teaches.

- **2 Corinthians 11:15**

  "Therefore *it is* no great thing if his ministers also be transformed as the ministers of righteousness; whose end shall be according to their **works**."

Satan has ministers. Whether it is a Lutheran minister, or Baptist minister, or Roman Catholic priest, or whoever it is, Satan has his ministers. You and I had better know. You and I had better stay clear of Satan's ministers. They appear righteous, but they are the Devil's people. Some of them are very clever as they preach. Others are not so clever. It is very obvious to tell the difference, but he has ministers. Every one of Satan's ministers will stand before the Lord Jesus Christ at the **great white throne** judgment and their **works** will be judged. The Lord Jesus Christ will open up the **books**. He will say, "Oh, you were a minister. You preached this and you believed this. You denied this and you did not believe this. You did not accept My Son." It is part of the **works** of these ministers, which are Satan's ministers.

- **Ephesians 2:9-10**
"Not of works, lest any man should boast. For we are his workmanship, created in Christ Jesus unto good **works**, which God hath before ordained that we should walk in them."

No One Saved By Works

People are not genuinely saved by works at all. We are to walk in good works. That is important for us. Saved people are not going to be in the white throne judgment, but God wants them to have good works.

- **2 Timothy 1:9**
"Who hath saved us, and called *us* with an holy calling, not according to our **works**, but according to his own purpose and grace, which was given us in Christ Jesus before the world began,"

We are not genuinely saved by **works**. We are truly saved by His Grace, but God wants us to do good **works**.

- **2 Timothy 4:14**
"Alexander the coppersmith did me much evil: the Lord reward him according to his **works**:"

Here is a situation where works are going to go before the **great white throne** judgment. This is Paul's last letter. He was ready to be offered and the time of his departure was at hand. He names the name of this Alexander the coppersmith. He will be receiving what his works were. He is going to be rewarded according to his **works.**

God looks at **works**, good or bad, for reward. Do I believe that there are going to be differences of severity of punishment in Hell? Yes, I believe so. The Lord Jesus Christ said that those that disbelieved His miracles in this day and age are going to be in Hell, but their punishment is going to be far worse than in the Old Testament. In other words, there seems to be a gradation. They are all in Hell. They are all suffering very seriously, but there will be gradations. That is why I believe it says they will be judged according to their **works.**

- **Matthew 11:21-24**
"Woe unto thee, Chorazin! woe unto thee, Bethsaida! for if the mighty works, which were done in you, had been done in Tyre and Sidon, they would have repented long ago in sackcloth and ashes. But I say unto you, It shall be more tolerable for Tyre and Sidon at the day of judgment, than for you. And thou,

Capernaum, which art exalted unto heaven, shalt be brought
down to Hell: for if the mighty **works**, which have been done in
thee, had been done in Sodom, it would have remained until this
day. But I say unto you, That it shall be more tolerable for the
land of Sodom in the day of judgment, than for thee."

They will all be there. They will all be lost. There seems to be in Scripture
some differences in punishment, but they will all be punished in Hell in
eternal fire.

- **Titus 1:16**

    "They profess that they know God; but in **works** they deny *him*,
    being abominable, and disobedient, and unto every good **work**
    reprobate."

This is an indication of some of the people that will be there at the **great
white throne**. There are some that profess to know God.

We had a letter from a lady who is a relative of my wife. She has a
big cross on her stationery and talks about God. We do not believe she
knows the Lord and Saviour in any way, shape, or form—relative or no
relative—but she has a lot of religious talk.

- **Revelation 2:23**

    "And I will kill her children with death; and all the churches
    shall know that I am he which searcheth the reins and hearts:
    and I will give unto every one of you according to your **works**."

Differences Of Rewards

This is the church at Thyatira. I believe that even at the
judgment seat of the Lord Jesus Christ there will be
differences of rewards in Heaven. Everyone who is genuinely
saved and born-again will go to Heaven, but they will not all
receive the rewards of Heaven, the crowns of Heaven. That is
what the judgment seat of the Lord Jesus Christ is all about.

- **1 Corinthians 3:12-15**

    "Now if any man build upon this foundation gold, silver,
    precious stones, wood, hay, stubble; Every man's **work** shall be
    made manifest: for the day shall declare it, because it shall be
    revealed by fire; and the fire shall try every man's **work** of what
    sort it is. If any man's work abide which he hath built thereupon,
    he shall receive a reward. If any man's work shall be burned, he
    shall suffer loss: but he himself shall be saved; yet so as by fire."

- **2 Corinthians 5:10**

"For we must all appear before the judgment seat of Christ; that every one may receive the things *done* in *his* body, according to that he hath done, whether *it be* good or bad."

Differences Of Judgment Results

All will be there, but there will be differences in the results of the believers' judgments. They will be saved, yet so as by fire. The fire shall judge the works that they built upon the foundation of the Lord Jesus Christ.

If true Christians build on the Lord Jesus Christ as the Foundation, hay, wood, and stubble, it will be burned up. They will be saved, but just barely. If they build on Him gold, silver, and precious stones, that will be purified by the fire of judgment. They will be rewarded throughout all eternity. Gradations in Heaven? Yes—rewarded or not rewarded, crowns or no crowns. Gradations in Hell? They will all be there, but there seem to be some gradations found in Scripture.

- **Revelation 18:6**

  "Reward her even as she rewarded you, and double unto her double according to her **works**: in the cup which she hath filled fill to her double."

This is Babylon. God has **books**. People will say that some group has two sets of books. In an organization right close by to us here, a man who was the bookkeeper told me many times, "His organization has two sets of **books**." He knew because he was the bookkeeper. They had another set. One is one way and the other is another way. This is illegal. He said he was going to show me and give me the **books** before he died, to prove that this was the situation. Then he got cold feet. Now he is dead.

God's Books Are Well Kept

God's books never perish. God's books never have two sets, just one—the truth, always the truth. It is the truth that will either make us free or, in this case of the great white throne judgment, it will condemn these to eternal Hell. They will be without excuse. Every mouth shall be shut and the whole world guilty.

---

* **Romans 3:19**
  "Now we know that what things soever the law saith, it saith to them who are under the law: that every mouth may be stopped, and all the world may become guilty before God."

Revelation 20:13

"And the sea gave up the dead which were in it; and death and Hell delivered up the dead which were in them: and they were judged every man according to their works."

Here is the final analysis of what happens. Here is what they do. The bodies that have gone into the **sea** and have decayed, the fish have eaten them up. These are unsaved dead. They will be delivered up.

Reunion Of Bodies, Spirits, & Souls

Then notice, *death and Hell.* Death is THANATOS, *the grave.* The bodies of those that have died and are unsaved will be delivered up. Hell is the translation of HADES. It is the spirits and souls of those that have died before this time in torment. They will be resurrected and reunited with their bodies.

"Death" refers to their bodies. "Hell" refers to their spirits and souls. There the bodies of those in the sea, and the bodies of those in the graves, are reunited with their spirits and souls and **delivered up**. Here spirit, soul, and body will be reunited at that time of that judgment. It is important that we see this. Nobody can escape the judgment just because they are in the sea. The Lord Jesus Christ is going to take care of those that are in the sea.

John Kennedy, Jr. ("John John," as we used to call him) was the little boy at his father's funeral, who stood there and saluted. He died in a plane crash. His plane crashed into the **sea**. They found the body. They picked it up. They had a funeral service of some kind. They cremated his body to ashes and then threw him back into the sea.

I do not know if his family thought that was going to prevent the judgment. If he was genuinely saved, that is one thing, but if he was unsaved, the sea will give up the dead which were in it. **Death and Hell** will give up the **dead** which were in them and they will be **judged**.

Revelation 20:14

"And death and Hell were cast into the lake of fire. This is the second death."

That is the second phase judgment for the unsaved. The first phase was when their spirits and souls were cast into the punishments of Hell (HADES) immediately after their physical **death**. Finally, at this point, as this first declares, the spirits and souls of the unsaved will be united with their resurrected bodies and will be cast into the **lake of fire**. The **lake of fire** is only found four times in our Bible.

- **Revelation 19:20**

  "And the beast was taken, and with him the false prophet that wrought miracles before him, with which he deceived them that had received the mark of the beast, and them that worshipped his image. These both were cast alive into a **lake of fire** burning with brimstone."

- **Revelation 20:10**

  "And the devil that deceived them was cast into the **lake of fire** and brimstone, where the beast and the false prophet *are*, and shall be tormented day and night for ever and ever."

- **Revelation 20:14**

  "And death and **Hell** were cast into the **lake of fire**. This is the second death."

- **Revelation 20:15**

  "And whosoever was not found written in the book of life was cast into the **lake of fire**."

Hell Fire Is Real Eternal Fire

Do not listen to those pastors, preachers, and evangelists that say the lake of fire is not real fire. If there is anything that is clear in Scripture, it is that it is fire. It is burning. There is smoke. Remember the old saying, "Where there is smoke, there is fire." This is true. It is a real eternal fire.

Then it talks about this final casting into the **lake of fire**. It is called *the second death.*

- **Hebrews 9:27**

  "And as it is appointed unto men once to die, but after this the judgment:"

That is the **second death** if you are lost. The **second death** also is only found four times in Scripture.

- **Revelation 2:11**
  "He that hath an ear, let him hear what the Spirit saith unto the churches; He that overcometh shall not be hurt of the **second death.**"

- **Revelation 20:6**
  "Blessed and holy *is* he that hath part in the first resurrection: on such the **second death** hath no power, but they shall be priests of God and of Christ, and shall reign with him a thousand years."

- **Revelation 21:8**
  "But the fearful, and unbelieving, and the abominable, and murderers, and whoremongers, and sorcerers, and idolaters, and all liars, shall have their part in the lake which burneth with fire and brimstone: which is the **second death.**"

You know, it is one thing if you go through the first death. If we are genuinely trusting the Lord Jesus Christ and are redeemed, saved, and know it—genuinely saved—may the Lord Jesus Christ give us victory as we pass from this life into Heaven above in the first death. If the Lord Jesus Christ returns in the rapture, the genuinely saved Christians will not have to undergo physical death. Woe unto any human being that has to go through the **second death**. People that are lost do not realize that there is a **second death**. Many of them say, "Well, I'll just die and I don't care."

Some people have Dr. Kevorkian or someone like him to come and to kill them. They are in pain and so forth. Let the Lord Jesus Christ take the dying in their own time. Many people do not believe there is anything to fear. They have these "near death" experiences. They come back and say, "Oh, there were wonderful lights," and other visions. It is false. It is the Devil's mirage. The **second death** is serious indeed. People do not understand it.

Revelation 20:15

"And whosoever was not found written in the book of life was cast into the lake of fire."

Getting Into The Book Of Life

How do we get into the book of life? I want to give some Scriptures. The first thing I think that a person has to do is to admit that he is a sinner. If nobody admits that he or she is a sinner, why would they need a Saviour? If a drowning man or woman does not admit they are drowning, who needs the lifeguard? They just do not call. They just go under the water and die.

- Romans 3:23
  "For all have **sinned**, and come short of the glory of God;"

A Change Of Mind Is Needed

The second thing is, there needs to be repentance concerning sin—*a change of mind* concerning sin. If people do not think they are sinners, if they do not think they need to change their minds about their sin, that it is wrong, they will not look for a Saviour.

- Acts 3:19
  "**Repent** ye therefore, and be converted, that your sins may be blotted out, when the times of refreshing shall come from the presence of the Lord;"

Trust In The Lord Jesus Christ

Thirdly, there must be a genuine trust and reception of the Lord Jesus Christ as your Saviour and Substitute.

- John 1:11-12
  "He came unto his own, and his own received him not. But as many as **received him**, to them gave he power to become the sons of God, *even* to them that **believe** on his name:"

- **John 3:16**

  "For God so loved the world, that he gave his only begotten Son, that whosoever **believeth** in him should not perish, but have everlasting life."

  That is how we get into the **book of life**.

- **John 3:18**

  "He that **believeth** on him is not condemned: but he that believeth not is condemned already, because he hath not believed in the name of the only begotten Son of God."

- **John 3:36**

  "He that **believeth** on the Son hath everlasting life: and he that believeth not the Son shall not see life; but the wrath of God abideth on him."

- **John 5:24**

  "Verily, verily, I say unto you, He that heareth my word, and **believeth** on him that sent me, hath everlasting life, and shall not come into condemnation; but is passed from death unto life."

Getting Into The Book Of Life

That is how to get into the book of life—to trust the Saviour that came to seek and to save that which was lost. Wonderful, wonderful good news we have to share with other people, lest they come to the great white throne judgment. I do not want any friend of mine, any enemy of mine, or anybody to have to come to the great white throne judgment. Far better that they be written in the book of life by faith in the Lord Jesus Christ—genuine faith—and be truly saved. Let us pray that we may be used of the Lord to bring others to Him.

Revelation
Chapter Twenty-One

Revelation 21:1

"And I saw a new heaven and a new earth: for the first heaven and the first earth were passed away; and there was no more sea."

The **new heaven** and the **new earth** are mentioned in Scripture in other places.

- **Isaiah 65:17**

  "For, behold, I create **new heavens** and a **new earth**: and the former shall not be remembered, nor come into mind."

- **Isaiah 66:22**

  "For as the **new heavens** and the **new earth**, which I will make, shall remain before me, saith the LORD, so shall your seed and your name remain. "

The Jews will maintain themselves as a nation.

- **2 Peter 3:10-13**

  "But the day of the Lord will come as a thief in the night; in the which the heavens shall pass away with a great noise, and the elements shall melt with fervent heat, the earth also and the works that are therein shall be burned up. *Seeing* then *that* all these things shall be dissolved, what manner *of persons* ought ye to be in *all* holy conversation and godliness, Looking for and hasting unto the coming of the day of God, wherein the heavens being on fire shall be dissolved, and the elements shall melt with fervent heat? Nevertheless we, according to his promise, look for **new heavens** and a **new earth**, wherein dwelleth righteousness."

Cleansing Comes After Judgment

Right after the great white throne judgment comes this cleansing. There is the fire. There is the new Heaven and the new earth. Then comes eternity. After the Millennium is finished, there is this cleansing.

Revelation 21:2

"And I John saw the holy city, new Jerusalem, coming down from God out of heaven, prepared as a bride adorned for her husband."

The New Jerusalem From Heaven

Here John sees in the Spirit this holy city, the new Jerusalem. We believe that Jerusalem is going to be coming down from Heaven. It will be in Heaven. We will see later on that it will have four dimensions. Some have thought it is a pyramid. No, it is a cube. It is just as high, and broad, and wide from end to end. It will hover over the renovated earth, the new heaven and the new earth, *coming down from God out of heaven, prepared as a bride adorned for her husband.*

That word, *prepared,* is used many places in Scripture. It is in the perfect tense. It was **prepared** in the past, it is continuing to be prepared and prepared into the future. It will still remain prepared **as a bride.**

Brides should be prepared. This **Heavenly city** is *prepared as a bride adorned for her husband.*

- **Revelation 3:12**

  "Him that overcometh will I make a pillar in the temple of my God, and he shall go no more out: and I will write upon him the name of my God, and the name of the city of my God, *which is* **new Jerusalem,** which **cometh down out of heaven** from my God: and *I will write upon him* my new name."

The Church At Philadelphia

The church at Philadelphia is told about this new Jerusalem. This is a Heavenly city. During the millennial reign of the Lord Jesus Christ, many feel that the city will come down from Heaven also. Who knows whether it is at the end of the Millennium or during the Millennium?

If it be the case, the genuine believers, the saints, will be in that new holy **city** during the time that they will be working on this earth during the Millennium. People will be unsaved. We will be governing at that time, helping the Lord Jesus Christ. Some will take five cities, some ten cities, and so on. We will be used during the day on the new earth, but we will go back at night to that holy **city** up in Heaven. Some believe that is the case during the millennial reign as well as the **city** that will be eternal and a **city** which is **Heavenly**. Both of these may be true.

The Heavenly City

In the eternal city, many believe that the Biblical saints of this age or dispensation—the true church saints, the believers that are genuinely saved—will be in that new Jerusalem, the Heavenly city, hovering over the earthly Jerusalem. The genuinely saved Israelites during eternity will be in the earthly Jerusalem, not in the Heavenly. I will take that up a little bit later, but this is what many believe.

Revelation 21:3

"**And I heard a great voice out of heaven saying, Behold, the tabernacle of God *is* with men, and he will dwell with them, and they shall be his people, and God himself shall be with them, *and be* their God.**"

Here God Himself is going to be **dwelling** with the genuinely saved people. There is a foreshadowing in 2 Corinthians 6.

- **2 Corinthians 6:14-18**

  "Be ye not unequally yoked together with unbelievers: for what fellowship hath righteousness with unrighteousness? and what communion hath light with darkness? And what concord hath Christ with Belial? or what part hath he that believeth with an infidel? And what agreement hath the temple of God with idols?

for ye are the temple of the living God; as God hath said, I will dwell in them, and walk in *them*; and I will be their God, and they shall be my people. Wherefore come out from among them, and be ye separate, saith the Lord, and touch not the unclean *thing*; and I will receive you, And will be a Father unto you, and ye shall be my sons and daughters, saith the Lord Almighty."

<u>God wants us separated from the world, the flesh, and the Devil.</u> Right here on this earth, **He will dwell with us.** We have the Spirit of God within our bodies if we are genuinely saved and truly born-again. *Wherefore come out from among them*—these apostates, these unbelievers.

Separated Christians

All Biblical Christians have God as their Father, but separated Christians, according to this verse, have God as a real, close fellowshipping Father. The worldly Christians have God as their Father, but not in this sense. One day, God will dwell completely with us in that glorious time.

Revelation 21:4

"And God shall wipe away all tears from their eyes; and there shall be no more death, neither sorrow, nor crying, neither shall there be any more pain: for the former things are passed away."

A Picture of Heaven

Here is a picture of Heaven. Here is the picture of the saints, those that are genuinely saved, those that are truly born-again. That is our Heavenly city. These are some of the things that will not be there in that city. There are many references of tears in the Bible in different places.

- **Job 16:20**

  "My friends scorn me: *but* mine eye poureth out *tears* unto God."

- **Psalm 6:6**

  "I am weary with my groaning; all the night make I my bed to swim; I water my couch with my **tears**."

In Heaven, there will be no more **tears**.

- **Psalm 116:8**

  "For thou hast delivered my soul from death, mine eyes from **tears**, *and* my feet from falling."

This is a beautiful verse of God's perfect plan for the genuine believers that are walking with Him.

- **Isaiah 25:8**

  "He will swallow up death in victory; and the Lord GOD will wipe away **tears** from off all faces; and the rebuke of his people shall he take away from off all the earth: for the LORD hath spoken *it*."

- **Isaiah 38:5**

  "Go, and say to Hezekiah, Thus saith the LORD, the God of David thy father, I have heard thy prayer, I have seen thy **tears**: behold, I will add unto thy days fifteen years."

Hezekiah was sick unto death. God said, "Make preparation. You are going to die, Hezekiah." God saw Hezekiah's **tears**. The Lord then changed His mind and added fifteen years.

- **Jeremiah 13:17**

  "But if ye will not hear it, my soul shall weep in secret places for *your* pride; and mine eye shall weep sore, and run down with **tears**, because the LORD'S flock is carried away captive."

Jeremiah's Message Spurned

Jeremiah the preacher said, "Turn from your sins or you are going into captivity in Babylon." They did not turn, but he was a weeping prophet.

- **Acts 20:19**

  "Serving the Lord with all humility of mind, and with many **tears**, and temptations, which befell me by the lying in wait of the Jews:"

There was weeping in the apostle Paul's ministry. He was talking to the elders at Ephesus. Why do you suppose Paul had **tears**? He served the Lord, but there were **tears**. It was because he was dealing with people. Sometimes, yea many times, people bring us **tears**. The people brought Paul **tears**—many **tears**.

- **Acts 20:31**

  "Therefore watch, and remember, that by the space of three years I ceased not to warn every one night and day with **tears**."

He continues to talk to the elders at Ephesus here. Paul was a warning preacher. We have to be *warning preachers, and teachers,* and Biblical Christians as well—warning people of the compromises of our day. Notice, Paul says that he warned *every one night and day with **tears**.* He warned them with **tears**.

- **Acts 20:29-30**

  "For I know this, that after my departing shall grievous wolves enter in among you, not sparing the flock. Also of your own selves shall men arise, speaking perverse things, to draw away disciples after them."

Paul had **tears** because he knew what would happen to that local church in Ephesus. That is true with many churches. A pastor friend and I talked about different churches as we ate lunch and supper together. We discussed how these churches had gone astray. These churches were Scripturally founded, and then they were gone. What has happened to them? They went back into modernism. He believes, and I believe, that a church is just one pastor away from modernism or apostasy—just one pastor, that is all. There is no guarantee that any church will maintain its position of Bible belief (*Thus saith the Lord*) and separation, and lack compromise after that one pastor is gone. There is no guarantee.

- **2 Corinthians 2:4**

  "For out of much affliction and anguish of heart I wrote unto you with many **tears**; not that ye should be grieved, but that ye might know the love which I have more abundantly unto you."

The Sin Of Incest Covered-Up

Paul had scolded the Corinthians because they wickedly kept an incestuous man right in the church instead of disciplining him out. Many of them said, "Oh, it's all right. Let's have this sinner in our church." Paul said, "Get that man out!" No leaven must be there. We are a new lump. We are to purge out the old leaven. They were upset. Paul was a man with tears.

- **Hebrews 5:7**
  "Who in the days of his flesh, when he had offered up prayers and supplications with strong crying and **tears** unto him that was able to save him from death, and was heard in that he feared;"

This speaks of the Lord Jesus Christ, probably in the garden of Gethsemane.

- **Matthew 26:39**
  "And he went a little further, and fell on his face, and prayed, saying, O my Father, if it be possible, let this cup pass from me: nevertheless not as I will, but as thou *wilt.*"

Heaven Is For All The Saved

Heaven is for every genuinely born-again one. It is for every one who has genuinely received the Lord Jesus Christ as their Saviour. Look at the conditions in Heaven in Revelation 21:4. Tears are gone. Death is gone, because genuine believers will have new bodies—undying bodies, incorruptible and immortal bodies—not subject to death. There will be no sorrow, because there will be no sin in Heaven. There will be no crying nor weeping, because tears are gone. There is nothing to weep over. It will be perfect, not like our situations here on this earth. Neither will there be any more pain. Those of you who have pain, whatever it may be, that is gone. No more pain.

What about this "*place*"? As we said before, the **new Jerusalem** was coming down out of Heaven **as a bride prepared for her husband.** I wish more **brides** would be **prepared** for their husbands as they ought to be **prepared.**

- **John 14:1-6**
  "Let not your heart be troubled: ye believe in God, believe also in me. In my Father's house are many **mansions:** if *it were* not *so,* I would have told you. I go to prepare a **place** for you. And if I go and **prepare a place** for you, I will come again, and receive you unto myself; that where I am, *there* ye may be also. And whither I go ye know, and the way ye know. Thomas saith unto him, Lord, we know not whither thou goest; and how can we know the way? Jesus saith unto him, I am the way, the truth, and the life: no man cometh unto the Father, but by me."

This is a **prepared place**. The Lord Jesus Christ told His disciples, His believers, that He was going to **prepare a place**. That is the Biblical saints' Heavenly Home, this **place** in Heaven with the Lord Jesus Christ. It is a **prepared place** for a **prepared** people.

Thomas did not know what He was talking about. The only ones that will be in Heaven will be the saints—not the Roman Catholic saints, but the genuine believers that are truly born-again. Those are the saints— the ones who are in the Lord Jesus Christ. They will be there because they have come to the Father through His Son.

- **1 Corinthians 2:9**

   "But as it is written, Eye hath not seen, nor ear heard, neither have entered into the heart of man, the things which God hath **prepared** for them that love him."

Paul tries to give a picture of Heaven. Again, it is a **prepared place** for **prepared** people.

- **2 Corinthians 5:6**

   "Therefore *we are* always confident, knowing that, whilst we are at home in the body, we are absent from the Lord: (For we walk by faith, not by sight:) We are confident, *I say*, and <u>willing rather to be absent from the body, and to be present with the Lord</u>."

Paul Willing To Go To Heaven

Why was Paul willing? I believe he had been to Heaven. <u>I believe he died in Acts 14</u>. They dragged him out of the city at Lystra after he had been stoned, supposing he was dead. I believe he was dead. <u>He talks about it in 2 Corinthians 12</u>.

- **2 Corinthians 12:2-5**

   "I knew a man in Christ above fourteen years ago, (whether in the body, I cannot tell; or whether out of the body, I cannot tell: God knoweth;) such an one caught up to the third heaven. And I knew such a man, (whether in the body, or out of the body, I cannot tell: God knoweth;) How that he was caught up into paradise, and heard unspeakable words, which it is not lawful for a man to utter. Of such an one will I glory: yet of myself I will not glory, but in mine infirmities."

Paul Had More Work To Do

I think Paul had been there and God sent him back to this earth because there was more work for him to do. <u>Acts 14 was not the end of the Acts.</u> He had not completed his writing of the books of Scripture. He had many more things to do, but that is how he knew that it is better to be with the Lord. <u>He was willing to be absent from the body.</u>

Most of us, perhaps, are not willing to be **absent** from the body. Think of yourself. Ask yourself the question. I do not care what your age is. You could be younger or older, but are we willing? <u>What if it is God's will to take us? Are we willing?</u> Paul knew what was on the other side of life. He knew it was Heaven. He knew it was glorious. He knew it was in Heaven that a Home had been prepared. That is why he was willing. People say, "Well, I know when I get older I will die. If I am genuinely saved, I know I will go to Heaven, but I'm not willing to go now." <u>If the Lord should call you, are you willing?</u> It is very important that every one of us ask that question.

- **2 Corinthians 5:9**

  "Wherefore we labour, that, whether present or **absent**, we may be accepted of him. For we must all appear before the judgment seat of Christ; that every one may receive the things done in *his* body, according to that he hath done, whether *it be* good or bad."

He was not "pie in the sky, by and by." The judgment seat of the Lord Jesus Christ is when He will judge those who are genuinely saved. Paul says we are to be accepted of Him and living for Him, not wasting our lives in any way.

- **Philippians 1:20**

  "According to my earnest expectation and *my* hope, that in nothing I shall be ashamed, but *that* with all boldness, as always, so now also Christ shall be magnified in my body, whether *it be* by life, or by **death**."

Paul's First Roman Imprisonment

Paul again knew whereof he spoke. He was writing from prison, the first Roman imprisonment. He wrote four books from prison: Ephesians, Philippians, Colossians, and Philemon. He knew that death might come to him there in prison. He wanted the Lord Jesus Christ to be glorified.

- Philippians 1:21
  "For to me to live *is* Christ, and to die *is* gain."

Paul Had Been To Heaven

How did he know? I believe he went to Heaven. He saw Heaven and God brought him back. Because of this, he knew that to die was "*gain*."

- Philippians 1:22-23
  "But if I live in the flesh, this *is* the fruit of my labour: yet what I shall choose I wot not. For I am in a strait betwixt two, having a desire to **depart**, and to be with Christ; which is far better:"

Paul Desired To Depart To Heaven

Here again, he was not only willing to depart, but he had a desire to depart. If you were as Paul with no home, with no food (except what the Lord provided), with no friends to speak of in many cities where you preached, you would be ready to go Home, too. He knew what Home was. It is far better. If the unbelievers are right and there is no Heaven, as Paul said, we are of all men most miserable.

- 1 Corinthians 15:19
  "If in this life only we have hope in Christ, we are of all men most miserable."

We genuine believers try to live for the Lord Jesus Christ. We are not out drinking, eating, and making merry with the world. If there is no resurrection, "*we are of all men most miserable.*" The Lord Jesus Christ is risen from the dead.

- 1 Corinthians 15:20
  "But now is Christ risen from the dead, *and* become the firstfruits of them that slept."

We must try to live for the Lord Jesus Christ here on earth.

- **Philippians 1:24-25**
  "Nevertheless to abide in the flesh *is* more needful for you. And having this confidence, I know that I shall abide and continue with you all for your furtherance and joy of faith;"

When I was one year of age, my grandmother, Mae Andrews Peirce, wrote a poem about Heaven. She probably prayed for me, that I would be genuinely saved. It is called, *Just Home.*

Just Home

In childhood's days, my thoughts of Heaven
Are pearly gates and streets of gold;
In the gathering of the years,
When time within its fading leaf,
With eyes perchance bedimmed with tears,
And hearts oft overwhelmed with grief,
We look beyond the pearly gates,
Beyond the clouds of sin's dark night,
And see a place where loved ones wait,
A place all beautiful and bright;
And over all, we'll see the face
Of Him who will bring us to our Home,
Not to some far-off, distant place;
For Heaven is, after all, just Home.

Grandma Peirce was a genuinely saved grandmother. She was a Methodist when the Methodist church was sound. She brought my Mom up in the Methodist church and my Mom was a genuinely saved woman. I just wish that Mom would have left the Methodist church when it turned modernist. She did not, but her son did leave that apostate church. Praise God for Grandma Peirce. I remember her very well.

Revelation 21:5

"And he that sat upon the throne said, Behold, I make all things new. And he said unto me, Write: for these words are true and faithful."

The One that is sitting on the throne is the Lord Jesus Christ Himself. In Scripture there are many **new** things.

- **2 Corinthians 5:17**

    "Therefore if any man *be* in Christ, *he is* a **new** creature: old things are passed away; behold, all things are become new."

There is a **new** relationship, a **new** Heavenly Father, a **new** brotherhood, a **new** Saviour that is our elder Brother, **new** believers.

- **Galatians 6:15**

    "For in Christ Jesus neither circumcision availeth any thing, nor uncircumcision, but a **new** creature."

We are a **new** creature, when we are genuinely saved. We are neither Jew nor Gentile, but a **new** creature.

- **Ephesians 4:24**

    "And that ye put on the **new** man, which after God is created in righteousness and true holiness."

We are a brand **new** man once we are genuinely saved.

- **Hebrews 10:20**

    "By a **new** and living way, which he hath consecrated for us, through the veil, that is to say, his flesh;"

There will be a **new** Heaven. These words are **true and faithful**. They never change.

Revelation 21:6

"And he said unto me, It is done. I am Alpha and Omega, the beginning and the end. I will give unto him that is athirst of the fountain of the water of life freely."

I believe that this is a picture of Heaven. It is spoken by the Lord Jesus Christ. He is the **Alpha**. He is the **Beginning**. He is the **End**. He is the very **beginning**, eternal past, and eternal future. Right in this age in which we live, the **water** of life is available by faith in the Lord Jesus Christ. Everyone can come unto Him and be genuinely saved.

- **Revelation 1:8**

    "I am **Alpha and Omega**, the **beginning and the ending**, saith the Lord, which is, and which was, and which is to come, the Almighty."

- **Revelation 1:11**
  "Saying, I am **Alpha and Omega**, the **first and the last**: and, What thou seest, write in a book, and send *it* unto the seven churches which are in Asia; unto Ephesus, and unto Smyrna, and unto Pergamos, and unto Thyatira, and unto Sardis, and unto Philadelphia, and unto Laodicea."
- **Revelation 22:13**
  "I am **Alpha and Omega**, the **beginning and the end**, the **first and the last**."
- **Revelation 22:17**
  "And the Spirit and the bride say, Come. And let him that heareth say, Come. And let him that is **athirst** come. And whosoever will, let him take the **water of life freely**."

No Hyper-Calvinist Approach

We believe that is Scriptural—not a hyper-Calvinist approach where only the elect can come. *Whosoever* means, *whosoever will*. Let him come and take the water of life freely. That is the Lord Jesus Christ in this dispensation. Before Heaven comes, this is available to *whosoever will*.

Revelation 21:7

"He that overcometh shall inherit all things; and I will be his God, and he shall be my son."

There are many verses on **overcoming**. These are referring to the genuinely saved ones.

- **1 John 5:4-5**
  "For whatsoever is born of God **overcometh** the world: and this is the victory that **overcometh** the world, *even* our faith. Who is he that **overcometh** the world, but he that believeth that Jesus is the Son of God?"

That is the **overcoming** faith.

- **Revelation 2:7**
  "He that hath an ear, let him hear what the Spirit saith unto the churches; To him that **overcometh** will I give to eat of the tree of life, which is in the midst of the paradise of God."

- **Revelation 2:11**

  "He that hath an ear, let him hear what the Spirit saith unto the churches; He that **overcometh** shall not be hurt of the second death."

- **Revelation 2:17**

  "He that hath an ear, let him hear what the Spirit saith unto the churches; To him that **overcometh** will I give to eat of the hidden manna, and will give him a white stone, and in the stone a new name written, which no man knoweth saving he that receiveth *it*."

These are all things that are predicated of true believers, genuinely saved ones in Heaven.

- **Revelation 3:5**

  "He that **overcometh**, the same shall be clothed in white raiment; and I will not blot out his name out of the book of life, but I will confess his name before my Father, and before his angels."

- **Revelation 3:21**

  "To him that **overcometh** will I grant to sit with me in my throne, even as I also **overcame**, and am set down with my Father in his throne."

All these **overcomers** will be in Heaven with rich rewards. By contrast, let us read Revelation 21:8.

Revelation 21:8

"But the fearful, and unbelieving, and the abominable, and murderers, and whoremongers, and sorcerers, and idolaters, and all liars, shall have their part in the lake which burneth with fire and brimstone: which is the second death."

All these people that have these terrible attributes are unsaved people, unbelieving. They cannot enter the city of Heaven.

Three Attributes Of The Unsaved

Abominable means, *to render foul; to abhor; to turn one's self away on account of the stench.* In the Old Testament, homosexuality was called an abomination.

> **Whoremongers** is in the masculine. It is PORNOS. It means, *a male prostitute; one who prostitutes his body to another's lust for hire.* It could be again, a homosexual situation.
>
> **Sorcerers** are *those who prepare magical remedies.* That word is PHARMAKEUS. Satan is the father of lies.
>
> That word **burneth** with fire is *continuous action*—continuously **burning**. Hell is real. These who have rejected the Saviour will not be in Heaven above. They will not be in the Heavenly city with the saints.

Revelation 21:9

"And there came unto me one of the seven angels which had the seven vials full of the seven last plagues, and talked with me, saying, Come hither, I will shew thee the bride, the Lamb's wife."

We see that the angel that had one of the **seven vials**, one of the plagues, was the one that came and showed John the **Lamb's wife**, the **bride**. There is a connection between the Lord Jesus Christ and His bride.

- **John 3:29**
  "He that hath the **bride** is the **bridegroom**: but the friend of the **bridegroom**, which standeth and heareth him, rejoiceth greatly because of the **bridegroom's** voice: this my joy therefore is fulfilled."

- **Revelation 22:17**
  "And the Spirit and the **bride** say, Come. And let him that heareth say, Come. And let him that is athirst come. And whosoever will, let him take the **water of life** freely."

Once the **bride** is married, the **bride** becomes His **wife**. The **bride** is the **Lamb's wife** after the marriage supper of the Lamb. The **water of life** is a free gift of God, not by works of righteousness.

- **Ephesians 5:22-25**
  "**Wives**, submit yourselves unto your own husbands, as unto the Lord. For the husband is the head of the wife, even as Christ is the head of the church: and he is the saviour of the body. Therefore as the church is subject unto Christ, so *let* the wives *be* to their own husbands in every thing. Husbands, love your **wives**, even as Christ also loved the church, and gave himself for it;"

Genuinely saved people are the **bride** of the Lord Jesus Christ. For the husbands, it is a more difficult task than for the wives. The **wives** do not believe it, but it is more difficult. *Husbands, love your wives,* it does not stop there, *even as Christ also loved the church, and gave himself for it.* That is the toughest part. We are to love our **wives** no matter what they are, what they say, what they do. We are to love them as the Lord Jesus Christ loved the church and gave Himself for it. That is a tough, hard, difficult task, but that is the picture.

- **Ephesians 5:32**
  "This is a great mystery: but I speak concerning Christ and the church."

Notice, the Heavenly city came down. The angel was going to show John the **bride**, the **Lamb's wife.** It is, no doubt, a reference to the inhabitants of that city, those that live in the city.

There is an article on the Internet called, *Dispensationalism in Transition.* I am a dispensationalist. Our church is a dispensational church. We believe in the dispensations. We believe that the innocence in the garden of Eden is different from conscience. It is different from human government. It is different from promise. It is different from the law. It is different from grace. When the kingdom comes, that will be a different dispensation as well. We believe there is a difference between Israel, God's earthly people, and the church, the genuine believers of this age.

There is a whole school of the dispensationalists that are in transition and are obliterating the distinctions between Israel and the church. This particular article is leaving the old-time dispensationalism and is in transition. The fellow that wrote the article is a transitional man, but he quotes Dr. Don Campbell who I went to school with in Dallas Theological Seminary. He was the president of the school for several years. He says, "Some dispensationalists make a sharp distinction between Israel as God's earthly people and the church as God's Heavenly people, both continuing throughout eternity. Others favor a blurring of such distinctions in eternity." He quotes Dr. Charles Ryrie, who is also a dispensationalist of the old school. He believes that distinction will be maintained throughout eternity.

I Was Taught By Dr. Lewis S. Chafer

I was taught by Dr. Lewis Sperry Chafer in Dallas. He was the founder and our teacher for four years of our class from 1948 to 1952. He died and went Home to be with the Lord in the summer of 1952. He was a Presbyterian and I am a Baptist, but he was a dispensationalist—a godly man, a spiritual man. We were taught that there was a distinction. I am an old dispensationalist, not one of these new kind that are switching and turning and drifting like some politicians do.

Israel And The Church Are Separate

We were taught that Israel was Israel and will remain so throughout eternity. The church is the genuine believers and that will maintain throughout eternity. As a result, the old-time dispensationalists (and I am one of the old-timers) believe that in eternity, there will be the Heavenly Jerusalem suspended above the earth where the true church, the body of the Lord Jesus Christ, will dwell for eternity. The redeemed, genuinely saved Israel will dwell on the new earth. There will be new heavens for the Biblical Christian believers and the new earth for the Jews that are genuinely saved and born-again. Israel will be *"born at once"* (Isaiah 66:8) These are some of the things that the bride, the Lamb's wife, is a picture of coming down from Heaven. Probably, the inhabitants are referred to in that particular time and picture.

Revelation 21:10

"And he carried me away in the spirit to a great and high mountain, and shewed me that great city, the holy Jerusalem, descending out of heaven from God,"

Heaven Is God's Design & Purpose

There is nothing that man can do to go to Heaven. The city comes from God. Heaven is God's design, God's purpose. God made this very earth where we are. He put the animals here. He made the heavens. He made the planets. He made the stars. He made the sun. He created man in His own image. Adam named the animals that were there. God said that it was not good for man to be alone, so He created woman out of Adam's rib. He made a woman on this earth. This earth was a creation of God, but it was not a perfect place because He created man and woman with a will that was capable of choosing not only for the Lord, but against the Lord. It was not a perfect place because it had imperfect people.

Why did not God make Adam and Eve automatons? He made them with free will because He wanted the free-willed people to worship Him willingly—and so today. Nobody, if you are genuinely saved, was ever hit over the head with a two-by-four and made to trust in the Lord Jesus Christ as Saviour. God led you. God drew you through the Scripture and His Words, but you were willing to come unto Him and be genuinely saved. That is God's way. What we have here is a group of willing people, if we are genuinely saved and born-again, serving Him willingly. We are not pushed and forced. We are willingly serving. The Lord is pleased with willing serving.

God will make this **Heaven**, the **new Heaven** and the **new earth**, in a different fashion. No longer will He populate the **new Heaven** and the **new earth** with human beings like Adam and Eve with free will. The Biblical Christians will have new bodies just like the Lord Jesus Christ's body. We will be sinless. We will have no tears. We will have no death. We will have no sorrow. We will have no pain.

All the former things will be passed away. There, in the **new Heaven** and the **new earth,** is a Heavenly place come down from Heaven that God made. He not only made Heaven itself, the **new Heaven** and the **new earth,** but He made the people dwelling in that Heaven. All the sinners and the lost people will not be there. They will be somewhere else. The **city descending** out of Heaven from God is a Heavenly creation.

What about those that do not believe that God can create the **new Heaven?** Well, that is too bad. They will not be there. If they do not believe in a God that is able to create a **new Heaven** and a **new earth,** they will be lost. They do not even believe in the Lord Jesus Christ as their Saviour and Redeemer. They will not be able to enter. A **new Heaven** and a **new earth** will come down from God out of Heaven.

Revelation 21:11

"Having the glory of God: and her light *was* like unto a stone most precious, even like a jasper stone, clear as crystal;"

The Holy Jerusalem

This light that John saw coming down was the holy Jerusalem, a great city, a huge city. You can imagine 1,200 cubits high, 1,200 cubits wide, 1,200 cubits deep—a huge city. I figured 1,200 cubits is about 1,400 miles—north, south, east, and west. It is a huge city, a large city. Notice, it has the glory of God, the city's light. It will not need the sun. We will see that in the next part of the chapter. There is no light there. There is no need of light. The Lamb is the light thereof.

- John 8:12
  "Then spake Jesus again unto them, saying, I am the **light** of the world: he that followeth me shall not walk in darkness, but shall have the **light** of life."

The Jasper Stone

It is a wonderful thing. A jasper stone is a precious stone of various colors. Some jaspers are purple. Some jaspers are blue. Some are green. Others are the color of brass. This is a beautiful, wonderful stone, *clear as crystal*, but it is light. It is light like a stone that is just glistening. There will be no sin there. There will be no death there. It is a beautiful city, come down from God out of Heaven.

Revelation 21:12

"And had a wall great and high, *and* had twelve gates, and at the gates twelve angels, and names written thereon, which are *the names* of the twelve tribes of the children of Israel:"

The Wall Of The City

Here is a great wall, high so that nobody can get in there. We will see a little later on just how high that wall is—a tremendous wall, high and great with twelve gates. Notice, God leaves nothing to chance. At the gates, there are twelve angels guarding those gates. Nobody is going to get in there that does not belong. Do you remember in Genesis 3:24 when God threw the people out of the garden of Eden?

- **Genesis 3:24**

  "So he drove out the man; and he placed at the east of the garden of Eden **Cherubims**, and a flaming sword which turned every way, to keep the way of the tree of life."

Cherubims are **angelic beings**. They were to keep, that is to guard, the way of the tree of life.

God is not through with the **twelve tribes** of Israel. They are His eternal earthly people.

- **Exodus 24:4**

  "And Moses wrote all the words of the LORD, and rose up early in the morning, and builded an altar under the hill, and twelve pillars, according to the twelve tribes of Israel."

Israel is in the Old Testament.

- **Exodus 28:21**

  "And the stones shall be with the names of the children of Israel, twelve, according to their names, *like* the engravings of a signet; every one with his name shall they be according to the **twelve tribes**."

The high priest had the names of the **twelve tribes** of the children of Israel on his breastplate. God is not through with the children of Israel.

- **Ezekiel 47:13**
  "Thus saith the Lord GOD; This *shall be* the border, whereby ye shall inherit the land according to the **twelve tribes** of Israel: Joseph *shall have two* portions."

There will be a new millennial temple. The **tribes** of Israel will have a say as to the land.

- **Matthew 19:28**
  "And Jesus said unto them, Verily I say unto you, That ye which have followed me, in the regeneration when the Son of man shall sit in the throne of his glory, ye also shall sit upon twelve thrones, judging the **twelve tribes** of Israel."

The Lord Jesus Christ was talking to His apostles. There is going to be a judgment of Israel. The apostles will have a hand in it. The genuine believers will have a hand in it. The Lord Jesus Christ will judge the **twelve tribes** of Israel. The genuinely saved Jews will be in that Heavenly city as far as the gates thereof—the names of the tribes. They are in remembrance of this and they will be guarded by these **twelve angels**, each of the **angels** at each gate.

Revelation 21:13

"On the east three gates; on the north three gates; on the south three gates; and on the west three gates."

These are the **gates** of the city, the **new Jerusalem** as it were coming down from God out of Heaven. These **gates** will be guarded by the angels—and guarded very carefully so that nobody can come in.

- **Revelation 21:8**
  "But the fearful, and unbelieving, and the abominable, and murderers, and whoremongers, and sorcerers, and idolaters, and all liars, shall have their part in the lake which burneth with fire and brimstone: which is the second death."

These will not enter—nothing that defiles. There will be **gates** that we can go in and out. I believe that, if indeed it is true that the Heavenly Jerusalem, the **holy Jerusalem** coming down from God out of Heaven, is also a part of the millennial reign of the Lord Jesus Christ, the true believers that are genuinely saved during that millennial reign will reign with the Lord Jesus Christ for a thousand years. If the genuinely saved are inhabiting that new Jerusalem, they will go back there, as I have said, after work on earth is done in that particular day. If that be the case, then we will be there and the apostles will, at least, have their names on the foundations.

Revelation 21:14

"And the wall of the city had twelve foundations, and in them the names of the twelve apostles of the Lamb."

There were **twelve tribes** of Israel. That is the Old Testament, God's holy people, the Israel of the Old Testament, the earthly people. Now, here in the New Testament, are the **apostles of the Lamb**, that is, the Heavenly people, the genuine believers, the true church of the Lord Jesus Christ and the wall with **twelve foundations**. Later on, we will see there are different precious stones in each one of these **twelve foundations**. I think it is like when you build a bridge. You have a big foundation of cement and so on. Cement is something that holds that thing up. Each of those foundational places will have precious stones.

- **Matthew 10:2-4**
  "Now the names of the **twelve apostles** are these; The first, Simon, who is called Peter, and Andrew his brother; James *the son* of Zebedee, and John his brother; Philip, and Bartholomew; Thomas, and Matthew the publican; James *the son* of Alphaeus, and Lebbaeus, whose surname was Thaddaeus; Simon the Canaanite, and Judas Iscariot, who also betrayed him."

- **Matthew 19:28**
  "And Jesus said unto them, Verily I say unto you, That ye which have followed me, in the regeneration when the Son of man shall sit in the throne of his glory, ye also shall sit upon twelve thrones, judging the **twelve tribes** of Israel."

There is a future for the **twelve apostles** and a future for the **twelve tribes**.

- **Luke 22:14**
  "And when the hour was come, he sat down, and the **twelve apostles** with him."

You remember what happened to Judas. He committed suicide. The apostles had an election in the first chapter of the book of Acts and Matthias was selected. I do not think Matthias is the one. I believe it was Paul. Why do I say that?

- **1 Corinthians 4:9**
  "For I think that God hath set forth us the apostles last, as it were appointed to death: for we are made a spectacle unto the world, and to angels, and to men."

Paul wrote to the Corinthians, "*us.*"

- **1 Corinthians 9:5**
  "Have we not power to lead about a sister, a wife, as well <u>as other</u> **apostles**, and *as* the brethren of the Lord, and Cephas?"

<u>Paul is one of the</u> **apostles**.

- **1 Corinthians 15:9**
  "For I am the least of the **apostles**, that am not meet to be called an apostle, because I persecuted the church of God."

- **Galatians 1:17**
  "Neither went I up to Jerusalem <u>to them which were</u> **apostles** <u>before me</u>; but I went into Arabia, and returned again unto Damascus."

The City–A Picture Of Heaven

The Heavenly city is a picture of Heaven where the Biblical saints will dwell for eternity. Are you a saint? Not a Roman Catholic canonized saint, but are you truly born-again by genuine faith in the Lord Jesus Christ? If you are, you will dwell in the city. If not, your place will be in the fires of Hell. Heaven is a wonderful place and it is, after all, as my Grandma Peirce said, "*Just Home.*" Paul was willing to go Home and he was desirous and eager to go Home. May you and I—not that we do not want to work down here—but may we be willing at any time the Lord Jesus Christ should call us Home.

Revelation 21:15

"**And he that talked with me had a golden reed to measure the city, and the gates thereof, and the wall thereof.**"

This is a measuring rod and the angel measures the city. I believe the city is the city that came down from Heaven from the Lord. I mentioned that in the first part of the chapter. This will be the Home of the genuine believers throughout the entire millennial reign of the Lord Jesus Christ, I believe, and possibly even the Heavenly Home. I am not certain of that, but it seems like it is the Heavenly Home as well as that home for a thousand years when the Lord Jesus Christ reigns.

The Measurements Of The City

The measurements are of the city itself, the gates thereof, and the wall. Those are the three areas that the angel measured. There is plenty of room for all to dwell. I believe that this city will come down from God out of Heaven and will be suspended over the earth during that thousand years. The earthly new Jerusalem will be for those that are living in this world, those people that enter into the Millennium. Many of them will be genuinely saved. There will be many people born during that thousand years that are lost and they will not be saved.

This Heavenly Jerusalem will be suspended over the earthly Jerusalem. You may ask, "How can the Lord do that?" Let me ask you this—how can man go to the moon? How can man have space stations? How can man do all these things he does? The Lord who created the heavens, the earth, the planets, the stars, the sky, the sun, and the moon, He is able to do that. I believe that is the way it seems to fall in place as we see the Scriptures.

Revelation 21:16

"And the city lieth foursquare, and the length is as large as the breadth: and he measured the city with the reed, twelve thousand furlongs. The length and the breadth and the height of it are equal."

This right here is the **measurement** of the city. That is what the angel is told to do. It seems to me it is a cube. There are some Bible scholars, for some reason or another (I do not understand it), that have said this is a *pyramid*. It seems to be to be foursquare right and left, breadth and height. It should go straight up, so it is a *cube* as far as I am concerned.

The Size Of The Foursquare Cube

It is more easy to understand. It is foursquare. Mathematically, a furlong is about 600 feet. If you multiply 12,000 by 600 feet you get 7.2 million feet. Divide that by 5,280 miles it gets about 1,363 miles—almost 1,400 miles wide, 1,400 miles long, and 1,400 miles high. There is plenty of room for all the genuinely saved and redeemed of all times. It is about 3,000 miles from one coast of the United States to the other. Half of that would be halfway across the United States of America wide, and then deep and of course all the way up high. These are the dimensions of this city that came down.

As I said before, it came down from God. It was constructed of God and we will see some of the construction. It is beautiful, like unto no other city that has ever been built or ever even dreamed to be built as we will see. As I said, it is definitely the time of the millennial reign.

- Luke 19:17-19

  "And he said unto him, Well, thou good servant: because thou hast been faithful in a very little, have thou authority over ten **cities**. And the second came, saying, Lord, thy pound hath gained five pounds. And he said likewise to him, Be thou also over five **cities**."

Millennial Duties Of The Saved

I believe the genuine believers in renovated, resurrected bodies will have day jobs reigning over the cities. The Lord Jesus Christ will reign for a thousand years and we will reign with Him, those of us who are genuinely born-again, for a thousand years. I believe we will leave that Heavenly place, that city, and go down and do whatever we have to do to help Him to reign over this wicked world. Of course, He will rule with a rod of iron. There will be plenty of unsaved people, but they will obey. If not, He will see to it just like that. We are going to go back in the evening time to our city. That is the way it seems to work—at least to me.

Revelation 21:17

"And he measured the wall thereof, an hundred *and* forty *and* four cubits, *according to* the measure of a man, that is, of the angel."

The Large Wall

The wall was measured. The city was 1,400 miles wide, 1,400 miles long and 1,400 miles high—a cube. The wall is a tremendous size. A cubit is about 18 inches. One hundred and forty and four times 18 inches equals 2,592 inches. Divided by 12, it is 216 feet tall. That is a big wall. If the room we are in is ten and a half feet high, it would equal 20 of these rooms, right straight up.

People have been known to break out of different prisons. They scale the wall somehow and they come down. I heard on the news that one man scaled the wall. It was the second time he broke out in one week. The first time, his wife forged a letter from an attorney or sheriff or some other official. A sergeant in the police department, said, "He is free to go," so they let him out. That was false, so they brought him back. Then he jumped from the second-story window and broke his legs as he attempted to get out again.

Listen, I would not think anyone would jump from this **wall 216 feet high**. It is a **wall** of protection. It is a **wall** of blessing. That is a big **wall**, a tall **wall**, and I do not think any of our **walls** of any buildings that we know about are that tall. This is the wall that is an hundred and forty and four cubits—**over 200 feet** high—so that we will be safe in there and nobody will come in who is not supposed to come in through those **gates**.

Revelation 21:18

"And the building of the wall of it was *of* jasper: and the city *was* pure gold, like unto clear glass."

What a beautiful and expensive city this is! The **building** was of **jasper**. According to references, jasper is a precious stone of various colors. I do not know which color is which, because they say that some are purple, others are blue, others are green, and others are the color of brass. I do not know which color this is, but it is a **jasper**. That is the wall—the **jasper wall**.

Then the city itself is **pure gold**. We know that **gold** is expensive. One of our presidents took us off the **gold** standard. Then one of our other presidents came along and took us off the silver standard. Now we have no standard, just paper money. We are in seriously sad shape because of it. It says, in the Constitution of the United States, that Congress will have power to *coin* money. You cannot coin paper. It has to be **gold** or silver. That is what our forefathers wanted us to have.

An Expensive City

Anyway, it is an expensive city—pure gold. You may ask, "How can the Lord get that much gold?" Do not worry about it. If He can take care of this universe, take care of the earth, and take care of building people—making Adam and Eve, you and me, and all the animals—He will not have any problem finding enough gold to make that city. It is of pure gold and like unto clear glass. It is not only gold, but *pure* gold like glass. The city is an expensive, beautiful city because the Lord made it. We who are genuinely saved will dwell in it.

Revelation 21:19

"And the foundations of the wall of the city *were* garnished with all manner of precious stones. The first foundation *was* jasper; the second, sapphire; the third, a chalcedony; the fourth, an emerald;"

God does not do things in a slipshod manner. Years ago, in one of the presidential debates, one of the candidates said the Iraq war was done *"on the cheap."* I had never heard that expression in my life. I guess that means they did not want to spend a lot of money on it. The Lord is not doing anything *on the cheap*. When He wanted to redeem us, He redeemed us with the precious blood of the Lord Jesus Christ. It is not cheap. When He is building a city, He is building for beauty with wonderful and expensive materials.

I take it that the wall had **foundations** just like a bridge. You go down deep and there is a **foundation** that goes into the earth and then you put a pillar on it. The quotations of the meanings of these stones is from the *Oxford English Dictionary Unabridged*.

The first **foundation** is **jasper**. That is "the name among the ancients for any bright-coloured chalcedony except carnelian, the most esteemed being of a green colour."

The second **foundation** is **sapphire**. That is a precious stone. I asked my wife, "Honey, what is a **sapphire**?" She said, "That is blue." She knows her colors. In fact, she said that is the stone of the forty-fifth anniversary. We made that and I guess I never gave her a **sapphire** because I do not know the color. She says it is blue. Some say, "It is a precious stone of a beautiful transparent blue. It is a variety of native alumina akin to the ruby."

The third **foundation** is **chalcedony**. The reference says that is a precious stone of misty grey color, clouded with blue, yellow, or purple. All these are misty colors.

The fourth **foundation** is an **emerald**. This is "a precious stone of bright green colour; in modern use exclusively applied to a variety of the Beryl species." These **walls** had **foundations** that were of **precious stones**—valuable stones.

Revelation 21:20

"The fifth, sardonyx; the sixth, sardius; the seventh, chrysolite; the eighth, beryl; the ninth, a topaz, a chrysoprasus; the eleventh, a jacinth; the twelfth, an amethyst."

You wonder, why does the Lord name all these stones? Why does He have these **foundations garnished**? The word **garnished** means, *beautifying*. The Lord enjoys beauty. Remember the garments of the high priest—they were for beauty as well as practicality. The Lord wants us to have beautiful things. He made these foundations beautiful.

The fifth **foundation** is a **sardonyx**, which is "a variety of onyx or stratified chalcedony having white layers alternating with one or more strata of sard."

The sixth **foundation** is a **sardius**, which is "a precious stone mentioned by ancient writers."

The seventh **foundation**, is a **chrysolite**, which is "a name formerly given to several different gems of a green colour, such as zircon, tourmaline, topaz, and apatite. . . . Its colour varies from pale yellowish green (the precious stone) to dark bottle-green." There appears to be some gold in it.

The eighth **foundation** is a **beryl**, "a transparent precious stone of a pale-green colour passing into light-blue, yellow, and white; distinguished only by colour from the more precious emerald."

The ninth **foundation** is a **topaz**, which is "the name given (with or without distinguishing adjunct) to several highly valued precious stones." Some say it is a yellowish precious stone.

The tenth **foundation** is a **chrysoprasus** which is "the ancient name of a golden-green precious stone, now generally believed to have been a variety of the beryl, or to have included that among other stones of similar appearance. It was one of the stones to which in the Middle Ages was attributed the faculty of shining in the dark. It is hard to pronounce. That is a stone of green color. It is inclined to that of gold, so it is green but it is toward the gold type of a green."

The eleventh **foundation** is a **jacinth**. It is "among the ancients, a gem of a blue colour, probably sapphire."

Finally, the twelfth **foundation** is an **amethyst**. It is "a precious stone of a clear purple or bluish violet colour, of different degrees of intensity, consisting of quartz or rock-crystal coloured by manganese, or, according to Heintz, by a compound of iron and soda."

These are the beautiful colors of the foundations of this new city that God is bringing down from Heaven, His creation. He knows no expense. No expense is too great for the city that is pure gold with the jasper walls and all these **foundations** of precious stones.

If we were to make a city and we were to make **walls**, we would make them out of brick and mortar, maybe steel, but the Lord has precious stones. You may ask, "How can He make **precious stones** strong enough to withstand the pressures of that **wall**?" He has no bounds as far as making things strong enough to withstand any pressures of any weight that is coming down upon those. It is no problem with the Lord.

Revelation 21:21

"And the twelve gates *were* twelve pearls; every several gate was of one pearl: and the street of the city *was* pure gold, as it were transparent glass."

The Gates Are Always Open

Here are the twelve gates of the city with a tall wall. We will see later that the gates are never closed. Every one of the

> twelve gates is a pearl. You can have fake pearls that are cheap, but genuine pearls are expensive. I cannot tell the difference and probably most people cannot, but a jeweler can.

I remember one time my wife bought a **pearl** necklace for someone (I do not remember who). I do not know whether that someone who got the **pearl** necklace knew if it was real or fake, but it was a genuine **pearl** necklace. Every one of these gates was of one pearl. You may ask, "How can you get a gate of a **pearl**?" Well, that is up to the Lord again, but apparently, a gate will go back and forth and turn and open, or perhaps it is a gate that comes up and down. We are not sure which kind of gates they would be, but every one of those gates is a solid pearl. A solid pearl is expensive and the Lord has it. It is beautiful. It is garnished and it is arranged so that it will be functional, I am sure. This is the street of the city—pure gold. The city is **pure gold** and the street. The genuinely saved will walk on the street of **gold**.

I remember one of the schools that was formerly approved by the General Association of Regular Baptist Churches used to be called the Grand Rapids Baptist Bible College. Then they took Baptist out and became Grand Rapids Bible College. Then they took Bible off. Then it became Cornerstone College and Cornerstone University. They have changed their name a few times.

One of their professors said there was no such thing as a street of **gold**, that it was fake. He was one of the teachers there. Some of the pastors came down from the northern part of Michigan when they put this teacher on the "hot seat." They had a lot of talk back and forth with this man. Finally, the guy left the school, but that school has been going soft for many years.

When Plain Sense Makes Good Sense

If the Bible says the city is pure gold, it is pure gold. There is no question. It is the old, *When the plain sense of Scripture makes good sense, seek no other sense.* That is the golden rule of Bible interpretation. I have no problem with the Lord doing whatever He wants. He is sovereign. He is great. He is omnipotent. He can do it.

Revelation 21:22

"And I saw no temple therein: for the Lord God Almighty and the Lamb are the temple of it."

Just think, no **temple**. A **temple** is for two things in the Old Testament. One was for sacrifice—where they brought the lambs and the goats and the bullocks for sacrifice. The second is for fellowship. God was there in that **temple**. He dwelled over the mercyseat. His presence was there. The shekinah glory was there.

Why do you need a **temple** for sacrifice? There is no sacrifice. It has been finished. There was one sacrifice for all the sins of the world, so there is no need for a **temple** for that purpose. Then for fellowship, the Lamb is there. God the Father is there. The fellowship is there. We do not need a **temple** for that. We have the real thing. God Himself will be there.

Let us look at a few things about the **temple** in the Scripture.

- **Isaiah 6:1**

  "In the year that king Uzziah died I saw also the Lord sitting upon a throne, high and lifted up, and his train filled the **temple**."

God's presence was filling the **temple** of Isaiah's day.

- **Ezekiel 8:16**

  "And he brought me into the inner court of the LORD'S house, and, behold, at the door of the **temple** of the LORD, between the porch and the altar, *were* about five and twenty men, with their backs toward the **temple** of the LORD, and their faces toward the east; and they worshipped the sun toward the east."

Here were idolaters worshipping idols in the **temple** of the LORD. There will be a temple like the one in Ezekiel's day. People say, "Will there be the law of Moses again?" We do not know whether it is the law, but there will be a **temple**. There will be sacrifices again. You may ask, "Why do they have sacrifices of animals—blood offerings?" It is looking back, just like the high priest before the cross looked forward. Our Lord's Supper is a memory of the death of the Lord Jesus Christ until He comes. There is no sacrifice, but Ezekiel's **temple** speaks about sacrifices, blood offerings looking back. Here, the **temple** of the LORD's house was filled with sun worshippers.

- **Habakkuk 2:20**
  "But the LORD is in his holy **temple**: let all the earth keep silence before him.""

That is sometimes quoted in churches that are noisy. Some quote this verse to make people to keep quiet in church. The LORD is in His **temple**, meaning that is where He dwells. That is the presence of the LORD for fellowship.

- **Haggai 2:18**
  "Consider now from this day and upward, from the four and twentieth day of the ninth *month, even* from the day that the foundation of the LORD'S **temple** was laid, consider *it*."

Haggai, Zechariah, and Malachi were post-exilic prophets. After the exile, after Babylon, they came back to re-build the wall and the **temple**. They laid the foundation of the temple as soon as they came back out of captivity. That **temple** was erased. It was broken down. It was ruined and they laid those foundations.

- **Zechariah 6:12**
  "And speak unto him, saying, Thus speaketh the LORD of hosts, saying, Behold the man whose name is The BRANCH; and he shall grow up out of his place, and he shall build the **temple** of the LORD:"

That BRANCH is the Lord Jesus Christ Himself. The Lord Himself shall build the **temple**.

- **Zechariah 6:15**
  "And they *that are* far off shall come and build in the **temple** of the LORD, and ye shall know that the LORD of hosts hath sent me unto you. And *this* shall come to pass, if ye will diligently obey the voice of the LORD your God."

You will remember that the king gave permission for the Jews to leave. Ezra and Nehemiah were given permission to leave Babylon to go to Jerusalem and to build the **temple**. Nehemiah laid the foundation, and Ezra began to re-build the walls and build the **temple** again, so that Israelites could have sacrifices that the Lord had told them to do and also fellowship with the Lord in His temple.

God's Presence In The Tabernacle

Remember even in the tabernacle, the very presence of God was over the mercy seat and over the ark of the covenant. That was where the cloud abode. That is how they could tell when the Lord wanted them to move somewhere. The cloud moved. Whenever it was, by day or by night, when that cloud moved from off that tabernacle, the Levites and the priests had to break all that tabernacle down and fold it up.

The Merarites had four wagons. The Gershonites had two wagons. The Kohathites had no wagons—they put the vessels on their shoulders with staves, because they were the implements of the tabernacle itself. They had to move every time that cloud moved. The Israelites moved 43 times, if my count is correct, in the 40 years—an average of once a year. Sometimes it was just a day, sometimes a week, sometimes a month, sometimes a year. In the book of Numbers it tells all the places where they moved.

The Lord's **presence** was there in the tabernacle. They wanted to have the Lord back again.

- **Malachi 3:1**

    "Behold, I will send my messenger, and he shall prepare the way before me: and the Lord, whom ye seek, shall suddenly come to his **temple**, even the messenger of the covenant, whom ye delight in: behold, he shall come, saith the LORD of hosts."

This is a prediction of the Lord Jesus Christ Himself that He would one day come, and He did come to the **temple** in His first coming.

- **Matthew 24:1-2**

    "And Jesus went out, and departed from the **temple**: and his disciples came to *him* for to shew him the buildings of the **temple**. And Jesus said unto them, See ye not all these things? verily I say unto you, There shall not be left here one stone upon another, that shall not be thrown down."

The **temple** that Herod built was thrown down in 70 A.D. This was a terrible situation. They had no **temple** after that time. The Lord Jesus Christ predicted it.

- **Matthew 27:51**

    "And, behold, the veil of the **temple** was rent in twain from the top to the bottom; and the earth did quake, and the rocks rent;"

The Veil Of The Temple

At the crucifixion, the temple again comes into play. It was not man that did it. It was a very heavy veil, indeed. The NIV does not ever use the word *veil*, just a *curtain*, so veil is gone. Nobody knows what the veil is if they have a New International Version. That veil was rent by the Lord. That signified that the very way into Heaven itself was available because the Lord Jesus Christ had died. His flesh was the veil, as it says in the book of Hebrews.

- **Hebrews 10:20**

  "By a new and living way, which he hath consecrated for us, through the **veil**, that is to say, his flesh;"

- **1 Corinthians 3:16**

  "Know ye not that ye are the **temple** of God, and *that* the Spirit of God dwelleth in you?"

Paul teaches us a little bit more about the **temple**. He is speaking of the genuine believers, the born-again ones. It is not a **temple** of rock and stone, but the believers. If you are genuinely saved, if you are born-again, your body is the **temple** of God. That is what he said to these Christians at Corinth.

- **1 Corinthians 3:17**

  "If any man defile the **temple** of God, him shall God destroy; for the temple of God is holy, which *temple* ye are."

That is why we should not have defilement in our bodies—whatever defiles—whether it is nicotine, or whatever. Some people are defiled by caffeine. (I am going to get off that subject very quickly.) I tell you, it is all kinds of drugs and all kinds of narcotics—anything that defiles the body. Lack of sleep defiles the body. Overeating defiles the body. God says, "Ye are holy." We should not defile the **temple** of God.

- **1 Corinthians 6:19-20**

  "What? know ye not that your body is the **temple** of the Holy Ghost *which is* in you, which ye have of God, and ye are not your own? For ye are bought with a price: therefore glorify God in your body, and in your spirit, which are God's."

We are bought with a price and our bodies are His dwelling place.

- **2 Corinthians 6:16**

   "And what agreement hath the **temple** of God with idols? for ye are the temple of the living God; as God hath said, I will dwell in them, and walk in *them*; and I will be their God, and they shall be my people."

God dwells in us. We are the **temple** of Almighty God.

Revelation 21:23

"And the city had no need of the sun, neither of the moon, to shine in it: for the glory of God did lighten it, and the Lamb *is* the light thereof."

The Lamb Is The Light Here

The city has no need for light. There is no night there. The Lamb is the light. There is no need of the sun or the moon because the glory of God lightens it. God's SHEKINAH glory–bright glory–lightens that city. Throughout eternity, throughout the Millennium, we will need no light bulbs or anything at all. It will be light everywhere we go. There is no night there, either in the millennial reign of the Lord Jesus Christ when we are up there in the suspended city of God, or in all eternity. If that is the same city for eternity, which many feel that it is, there will be no lights needed.

I wrote two emails to Dr. Jung, because my wife asked me a question. He called and I asked him, "What kind of power do you have over in Korea? Is it 110 or 220?" He said, "Oh, I have 220." Of course, all of our implements are 110, but he said, "That's all right. We have an adapter. Plug it in. It's all right. No problem." I said, "All right. That is fine." I did not want to blow out my notebook computer. I did not want to blow out my tape recorder. I did not want to blow out anything. We will not have to worry about that in the **Heavenly city**. There will be **no night** there, no power, no need for **lights**, no need for anything. The **Lamb is the light** thereof.

- **Genesis 1:3**

   "And God said, Let there be **light**: and there was **light**."

God needed and wanted light in this world.

- **Genesis 1:16**
  "And God made two great **lights**; the greater **light** to rule the day, and the lesser **light** to rule the night: *he made* the stars also."

The sun and the moon were created by the Lord. He made **lights** in this world and we need the **lights** as long as we are living here.

- **Matthew 4:16**
  "The people which sat in darkness saw great **light**; and to them which sat in the region and shadow of death **light** is sprung up."

Christ Is The Light Of The World

This is a spiritual light that is caused. This is the coming of the Lord Jesus Christ Himself. He is the Light of the world. The heathen people and the Jewish people that were in darkness saw that Light. This is a prediction of the Lord Jesus Christ.

- **Luke 2:29-32**
  "Lord, now lettest thou thy servant depart in peace, according to thy word: For mine eyes have seen thy salvation, Which thou hast prepared before the face of all people; A **light** to lighten the Gentiles, and the glory of thy people Israel."

Simeon talked about the Lord Jesus Christ, the **Light** of the world. We call it the *nunc dimittis*, the old Latin phrase, *now lettest thy servant depart in peace*. He saw the Lord Jesus Christ. He was an old man ready to die. The Lord said, "You will not die until you see the Saviour, the Messiah, the Christ." He is the **Light** for us who are Gentile people. The Lord Jesus Christ came to give us **light** and salvation.

- **John 1:4-5**
  "In him was life; and the life was the **light** of men. And the **light** shineth in darkness; and the darkness comprehended it not."

Christ's Light Still Shines

This is speaking of the Lord Jesus Christ. He is still shining in darkness in this world today. The darkness did not understand it, did not hold it down, but the Light is still shining. People are still rejecting the Light of the world, which is the Lord Jesus Christ.

- **John 8:12**

  "Then spake Jesus again unto them, saying, I am the **light** of the world: he that followeth me shall not walk in darkness, but shall have the **light** of life."

God does not want those that have the **Light** of the world to walk in darkness. Is that sinless perfection? No, but it certainly is an idea and a goal for every one of us if we are genuinely saved and truly born-again. We should not walk in the darkness of our former life, but walk in His light.

- **John 9:5**

  "As long as I am in the world, I am the **light** of the world."

As long as He is there, He is the **Light**. Later on He says, "Ye are the **light** of the world," but as long as He is there, He is the **Light**. He told His disciples, "Ye are the **light**." We have to shine.

- **John 12:46**

  "I am come a **light** into the world, that whosoever believeth on me should not abide in darkness."

Saved Not To Abide In Darkness

He does not want us who are genuinely saved and truly born-again to abide in the darkness of sin and wickedness, worldliness, or satanic worship of any kind.

- **Acts 9:3**

  "And as he journeyed, he came near Damascus: and suddenly there shined round about him a **light** from heaven:"

Three times, Paul talks about this. First, is when it happened in Acts 9. Next, is his testimony in Acts 22. Third, is another testimony in Acts 26 before King Agrippa. The *light from heaven* is the Lord Jesus Christ.

- **Acts 9:8**

  "And Saul arose from the earth; and when his eyes were opened, he saw no man: but they led him by the hand, and brought *him* into Damascus."

The Light blinded him. You may ask, "Did the Lord Jesus Christ reveal His glory on this earth?" No. All of us would have been blinded if we were there. He did not. With new bodies we will be able to see the **Light** of the world.

- **Acts 22:6**

   "And it came to pass, that, as I made my journey, and was come nigh unto Damascus about noon, suddenly there shone from heaven a great **light** round about me."

The time was noon. That is when the sun is the highest. The *great light* is the Lord Jesus Christ from Heaven. <u>He is the **Light** of the world.</u>

- **Acts 22:11**

   "And when I could not see for the glory of that **light**, being led by the hand of them that were with me, I came into Damascus."

Because of the *glory of that light*, he could not even see. He was blinded for several days. I think the Lord Jesus Christ wanted Paul to realize that he was not "somebody." He wanted to take him down a few notches. Paul fell to the earth. The Lord Jesus Christ blinded Paul to let him see he must trust in the One who had blinded him. You and I must do the same thing. We must trust the Lord Jesus Christ and Him alone.

- **Acts 26:13**

   "At midday, O king, I saw in the way a **light** from heaven, above the brightness of the sun, shining round about me and them which journeyed with me."

Again, he was speaking of the noon hour when the sun was the brightest it could be. The Lord Jesus Christ shines brighter. <u>The Lord Jesus Christ shines fairer than any **light** that could be on this earth.</u>

- **Acts 26:18**

   "To open their eyes, *and* to turn *them* from darkness to **light**, and *from* the power of Satan unto God, that they may receive forgiveness of sins, and inheritance among them which are sanctified by faith that is in me."

Paul Received A Great Commission

   After Paul saw the Light of the world and after he was blinded, the Lord Jesus Christ gave him a commission to open their eyes and to turn people who are sinners from darkness to light. That was Paul's commission. He saw the Light, the Lord Jesus Christ. He was blinded by the Light. He was told to turn people from darkness to His light.

- **2 Corinthians 4:3-4**

  "But if our gospel be hid, it is hid to them that are lost: In whom the god of this world hath blinded the minds of them which believe not, lest the **light** of the glorious gospel of Christ, who is the image of God, should shine unto them."

The reason for people not coming to the **Light** is made very clear. <u>The god of this world</u> is Satan. The lost ones are blinded by Satan. Therefore, he wants to keep them blinded so they cannot understand the **Light**. We have to preach the gospel anyway and let the gospel shine forth.

- **2 Corinthians 11:14**

  "And no marvel; for Satan himself is transformed into an angel of **light**."

Satan As An Angel Of Light

Satan knows the power of light. He knows that in order to be acceptable, he must be almost like the Lord Jesus Christ, the Light of the world, so he is transforming himself into an angel of light. How many angels of light have you seen this past week? Think of it. Maybe they were on television. Maybe they were out walking around in your shopping centers. Maybe they were in churches. Satan transforms himself into an angel of light in order to confiscate and darken people's hearts and blind them further.

- **Ephesians 5:8**

  "For ye were sometimes darkness, but now *are ye* light in the Lord: walk as children of light:"

<u>We are not to walk in the darkness any more. If we have the **Light** of the world in us, we are to walk as children of **light**</u>.

- **1 Thessalonians 5:5**

  "Ye are all the children of **light**, and the children of the day: we are not of the night, nor of darkness."

<u>Those that are genuinely saved are children of **light**</u>.

- **1 Peter 2:9**

  "But ye *are* a chosen generation, a royal priesthood, an holy nation, a peculiar people; that ye should shew forth the praises of him who hath called you out of darkness into his marvellous **light**:"

<u>That is our mission—as genuine believers and saved people—to show forth His marvellous **light**</u>.

- **1 John 1:5**
  "This then is the message which we have heard of him, and declare unto you, that God is **light**, and in him is no darkness at all."

This talks about the character of the Lord. There is not a single particle of darkness. That is why God cannot have sinners in Heaven. He is all **light** and no darkness.

- **1 John 1:7**
  "But if we walk in the **light**, as he is in the **light**, we have fellowship one with another, and the blood of Jesus Christ his Son cleanseth us from all sin."

A hymn writer has put it in verse form:

The Light of the World is Jesus.

The whole world was lost
In the darkness of sin,
*The **Light** of the world is Jesus!*
Like sunshine at noonday,
His glory shone in.
*The **Light** of the world is Jesus!*

Then it talks about Heaven in verse four of that hymn.

No need of the sunlight
In Heaven we're told;
*The **Light** of the world is Jesus!*
The Lamb is the Light
In the city of gold,
*The **Light** of the world is Jesus!*

Then the hymn writer says:

*Come to the **light**, 'tis shining for thee;*
*Sweetly the **light** has dawned upon me.*
Once I was blind, but now I can see:
*The **Light** of the world is Jesus!*

The **Lamb is the Light** thereof. There is **no night** there and no need of any light, because the **Lamb is the Light**, the Lord Jesus Christ Himself. The glory of God did lighten it.

Revelation 21:24

"**And the nations of them which are saved shall walk in the light of it: and the kings of the earth do bring their glory and honour into it.**"

Apparently, this is during the Millennium. We who are genuinely saved will be there. The kings who are genuinely saved will bring their honour into it.

"Them Which Are Saved" Is Gone

I want all genuine Christians to know that the phrase, *them which are saved*, is omitted in the Westcott and Hort false Greek texts. It does not say that at all. It does not say that in the versions that are based upon this false text. The New International Version does not have *them which are saved*. Neither do the NASB, the Revised Standard, the New Revised and so on. They have, *the nations shall walk in the light of it*. It is only the nations *which are saved* that shall walk in the light of it. That is a false Greek text and a false reason. They will bring their glory and honour into this city through those gates. Those gates will be guarded, as we said, by the angels. They will bring in those that are proper, those that are right.

Revelation 21:25

"And the gates of it shall not be shut at all by day: for there shall be no night there."

If it is not **shut** by day, you imply that it will be **shut** at night. That is what we normally say, but He reminds us there is **no night** there. The gates will be open all the time. **Gates** do two things: they keep out marauders; they keep in the people that are in that particular city.

The gate of salvation is open for the sinners today. There are no closed **gates**. The Lord Jesus Christ says that He is the Way, the Truth, and the Life. He is the Door.

- **John 10:9**
  "I am the door: by me if any man enter in, he shall be saved, and shall go in and out, and find pasture."

Just as there are no **gates** that will be closed there, there is no **gate** for salvation that is closed to anybody in this world.

- **2 Corinthians 6:2**
  "(For he saith, I have heard thee in a time accepted, and in the day of salvation have I succoured thee: behold, now *is* the accepted time; behold, now *is* the day of salvation.)"

Today is the day of salvation. We can genuinely trust in the Lord Jesus Christ by faith, immediately, any time.

No gates will be **shut**. All twelve of them will be **open**. The genuine believers will have access to the city foursquare.

Revelation 21:26

"And they shall bring the glory and honour of the nations into it."

These are the **nations** that will be genuinely saved. They are the **nations** that will be truly born-again, the genuine believers that are there. <u>Glory and honour shall be brought into this city through the **gates** that will not be shut.</u>

The Glory In The Millennium

You may ask, "What glory is there in the nations? What honour is there?" It is whatever they have done for the Lord. As the little phrase says, *one life, t'will soon be past, only what's done for Christ will last.* These nations that have honoured the Lord Jesus Christ in this time of the Millennium will bring their honour and their glory into that. That will be a great thing to have and to see. What the glory and honour is, we are not told. Whether it is gold, or actions, or deeds—whatever it may be—whatever is glorious, will be brought into the city.

There is a very bad cult that is called the cultural mandate heresy. They contrast the missionary mandate (Go ye into all the world and preach the gospel to every creature) with the cultural mandate, which they say is to culturalize the world. Bring "Christianity" to the world. Make it "Christian." "Christianize" it.

There was a teacher who taught with me at Shelton College in Cape May, New Jersey, where I was professor of Greek and Speech. I was there for about three years (1965–1968). Dr. Nigel Lee from South Africa was a hyper-Calvinist. He also believed in the cultural mandate. He said that as far as he was concerned, all the good things of this world are going to be in Heaven, all the cultural things—good music, good painting. I never could accept that. I do not accept that. That is what he believed. That is what they call the cultural mandate. We have people that believe in that. In fact, I have heard that preached recently. The man who was the head of Coral Ridge Ministries, Dr. Kennedy, preached the cultural mandate. I heard him with my own ears saying something about the cultural mandate. This, of course, comes from Genesis.

The Lord does not subdue the whole world, but what glory and honour that will be brought into the city, I am sure, will not be the old things that we have done on this earth. They will be burned up and all the works thereof, as far as that is concerned. The things that we think are so high and mighty, whether it is music, or paintings, or whatever it is, the Lord Jesus Christ does not look at those things that we look at. In fact, you see some of these new paintings—modern art—I do not even think most human beings would think much of them. They are just sticks, and lines, and squiggles, but they get prizes at exhibits. That is the thing I do not understand. There will be **glory and honour** and kings will bring it in.

Revelation 21:27

"And there shall in no wise enter into it any thing that defileth, neither *whatsoever* worketh abomination, or *maketh* a lie: but they which are written in the Lamb's book of life."

God is going to guard those **twelve gates** so that nothing of defiling, or abomination, or lying will **enter** into that city—just those who are in the **Lamb's book of life**. My question to you is, "Are you in the **Lamb's book of life?** Are you sure you are genuinely saved?" I talked to a gentleman and asked him, "Are you saved? Are you going to Heaven?" We talked earlier about our Heavenly Home. He said, "I hope so." I said, "You have to do more than hope so." I trust that his name will be in that **book of life.**

- **Philippians 4:3**
  "And I intreat thee also, true yokefellow, help those women which laboured with me in the gospel, with Clement also, and *with* other my fellowlabourers, whose names *are* in the **book of life.**"

The Book Of Life

The book of life is a book of names of people who are born-again and genuinely saved. Only those who are genuinely saved are in that book and only those that are in the Lamb's book of life are going to be entering that city. There is no access to others.

- **Revelation 20:12**
  "And I saw the dead, small and great, stand before God; and the books were opened: and another book was opened, which is *the* **book of life**: and the dead were judged out of those things which were written in the books, according to their works."

- **Revelation 20:15**
  "And whosoever was not found written in the **book of life** was cast into the lake of fire."

You are either in the **book** or you are out of the **book**. There is no halfway. There is no middle ground. There is no purgatory. There is no middle place. You are either in or you are out. The Lord is so clear. This is the city that will be pure. Since the Lamb is there (sinless, spotless, perfect), since God the Father is there, and since God the Holy Spirit is there, absolutely righteous.

You can rest assured nothing of impurity will enter that city. That is why you and I, if we are genuinely saved, if we are truly born-again, must have new, glorified bodies when this life is over in order to enter that city.

The genuine Christian's new bodies will be sinless. We will no longer have the old sinful nature and the new nature combined, fighting, flesh versus spirit, warring. We will have new bodies as the Lord Jesus Christ's body.

No Night In The Heavenly City

The Lamb will be the light of that city. There will be no night, only light. Are you going to be there? Ask yourself that question. The next question is, "Are you positive?" It is important.

𝕽𝖊𝖛𝖊𝖑𝖆𝖙𝖎𝖔𝖓
𝕮𝖍𝖆𝖕𝖙𝖊𝖗 𝕿𝖜𝖊𝖓𝖙𝖞-𝕿𝖜𝖔

Revelation 22:1

"And he shewed me a pure river of water of life, clear as crystal, proceeding out of the throne of God and of the Lamb."

The Pure Water Of Life

Here John is taking a look at the throne of God in Heaven. God's *water of life* is *pure*. It is salvation that is full and free. That *water of life* is what makes us genuinely saved, the *water of life*, spiritually speaking.

- **John 4:10**
  "Jesus answered and said unto her, If thou knewest the gift of God, and who it is that saith to thee, Give me to drink; thou wouldest have asked of him, and he would have given thee **living water**."

Here was a woman with five husbands and the one she was living with was not her husband. The Lord Jesus Christ said, "If you drink of this **water**, you are going to thirst again. I will give thee **living water**." That is a very important thing. That is eternal life. Salvation is **living water**.

When we are thirsty and parched, what we need is **water** for our bodies. We can live without food for a long time, but without **water**, not as long.

- **John 4:11**
  "The woman saith unto him, Sir, thou hast nothing to draw with, and the well is deep: from whence then hast thou that **living water**?"

She wondered, "Where could He get it?" It was a big, deep well, 90 feet deep. Mrs. Waite and I were visiting the place where they think this well was. The guide said they had a well they thought was Jacob's well when we were there in the holy land. I think there was 70 feet of air in that well and 20 feet of **water** in those 90 feet, if I remember correctly. They dropped a pebble or a rock down and waited until it hit the **water** to hear the splash. The Lord Jesus Christ was not speaking of physical **water**, He was speaking of **living water**, spiritual **water**, eternal life.

- **John 4:13-14**
  "Jesus answered and said unto her, Whosoever drinketh of this **water** shall thirst again: But whosoever drinketh of the **water** that I shall give him shall never thirst; but the **water** that I shall give him shall be in him a well of **water** springing up into everlasting life."

Every one of us have gotten thirsty for physical **water**. We will thirst again. **Water** is good for us. We should drink **water**, but the Lord Jesus Christ said to the woman, "whosoever drinketh of the **water** that I shall give him shall never thirst." The person who drinks of the water the Lord Jesus Christ gives him will never spiritually thirst again. Everlasting life by genuine faith in the Lord Jesus Christ is a well of **water** springing up in the Biblical Christian to everlasting life. That is the **living water** in Revelation 22:1. This **living water** is a pure river, not polluted. We have streams all over our country that are polluted streams. This is a pure river, clear as crystal.

- **John 7:37**
  "In the last day, that great *day* of the feast, Jesus stood and cried, saying, If any man thirst, let him come unto me, and **drink.**"

Drinking Living Spiritual Water

Obviously, you cannot drink of a person, but spiritually, you can drink of what He offers. He has offered forgiveness of sins and eternal life. That is like water, refreshing water. Come unto me if you are thirsty and drink.

- **John 7:38**
  "He that believeth on me, as the scripture hath said, out of his belly shall flow rivers of **living water**."

This is speaking of the Holy Spirit of God Who indwells those of us who are genuinely saved that are true believers. These rivers of **living water** are available to every genuinely saved person.

- **Revelation 21:6**
  "And he said unto me, It is done. I am Alpha and Omega, the beginning and the end. I will give unto him that is athirst of the fountain of the **water of life** freely."

That is the promise of the Lord Jesus Christ.

- **Revelation 22:17**
  "And the Spirit and the bride say, Come. And let him that heareth say, Come. And let him that is athirst come. And whosoever will, let him take the **water of life** freely."

Salvation For "Whosoever Will"

There are some who think that only a certain group of people can be genuinely saved. They claim that the ones who are not part of the "elect" cannot be truly saved. You can preach the gospel until you are blue in the face, but unless the people are part of the "elect," they cannot come to the Lord Jesus Christ and be genuinely saved. They are lost and they will go to Hell. No, the Lord Jesus Christ said, "*Whosoever will.*" It has to be our will. *Whosoever will,* let him take the water of life freely. Those that do not wish to take the water of life, (the Lord Jesus Christ), will go to Hell.

- **John 3:36**
  "He that **believeth** on the Son hath everlasting life: and he that **believeth** not the Son shall not see life; but the wrath of God abideth on him."

If God is the only One that can choose and the person cannot accept the Lord Jesus Christ no matter how much he might want to, how can God send a person to Hell who has not had the ability to genuinely **trust** the Lord Jesus Christ?

Our Ability Of Credence

Every one of us, as Pastor Carl Drexler used to say, has the ability of credence or belief, so that whosoever will may come. Not everyone wants to come. Not all the people in the world want to come to the Lord Jesus Christ, but the ones that do come can have everlasting life. Whosoever will, let him take the water of life freely.

Revelation 22:2

"In the midst of the street of it, and on either side of the river, *was there* the tree of life, which bare twelve *manner* of fruits, *and* yielded her fruit every month: and the leaves of the tree *were* for the healing of the nations."

Here is the **tree of life** on **either side of the river.** Either it was a big **tree,** or they had some on the one side of the river, one side or the other side, but this **tree of life** is mentioned only ten times in Scripture.

- **Genesis 2:9**
  "And out of the ground made the LORD God to grow every **tree** that is pleasant to the sight, and good for food; the **tree of life** also in the midst of the garden, and the tree of knowledge of good and evil."

Here is the **tree of life** and the tree of the knowledge of good and evil right in the garden of Eden.

- **Genesis 3:22**
  "And the LORD God said, Behold, the man is become as one of us, to know good and evil: and now, lest he put forth his hand, and take also of the **tree of life**, and eat, and live for ever:"

They were banished from the garden.

- **Genesis 3:24**
  "So he drove out the man; and he placed at the east of the garden of Eden Cherubims, and a flaming sword which turned every way, to keep the way of the **tree of life.**"

Here in Heaven, there is a **tree of life.** If they had eaten of the **tree of life** and had lived forever in a fallen state, their bodies would be decaying. In the garden of Eden, the tree of life was forbidden. It would not be proper. It would be a horrible thing. The Lord did not want this. He wants resurrected bodies of those of us who are genuinely saved and not ones that would be dilapidated and so on, so He did not let Adam and Eve take of that **tree of life.** That may be one of the reasons they were put out of the garden of Eden.

- **Revelation 2:7**
  "He that hath an ear, let him hear what the Spirit saith unto the churches; To him that overcometh will I give to eat of the **tree of life**, which is in the midst of the paradise of God."

This is the New Testament. In Heaven, we have the **tree of life.** We can eat of the **tree of life.** There is no problem.

- **Revelation 22:14**
"Blessed *are* they that do his commandments, that they may have right to the **tree of life**, and may enter in through the gates into the city."

The **tree of life** is there in Heaven. Notice in Revelation 22:2, it also says that the tree will *bear twelve manner of fruits, and yielded her fruit every month: and the leaves of the tree were for the healing of the nations.*

If that is going to be in Heaven, you may ask, "How can **leaves heal** anybody?" Well, if you look it up on the Internet, you will see some of the **leaves** that are used for herbal medicines even today. The Indians in the desert lands used seven basic plants and they had **healing** of the different diseases. I looked this up and here is a summary of medicinal uses of desert plants—**leaves** for the **healing of the nations.**

Desert Plants As Medicines

1. **Mesquite.** A tea made from the bark is used to treat bladder infections. Black gum known to the mesquite is used for chapped lips, rashes, and sunburn. Sometimes it is used as a laxative. Dried mesquite leaves, ground to powder, can be used for pink eye. These are treatments that the Indian tribes used. The inner yellow sap wood induces vomiting if that is needed.

2. **Prickly Pear.** A pad of this pear is broken off and passed over an open fire to burn off the spines. Then it is split in half and warmed for 20 seconds in a microwave oven, for instance. It is then bound to the chest with a cloth for rheumatic and asthmatic symptoms. Similarly, earaches are treated by cleaning one of these prickly pear pads, cutting it in half and placing it over the ear. It is a very effective remedy for an earache. Likewise, hemorrhoids are relieved with a pad of the prickly pear. The gooey juice of the pear is used for sunburn and minor rashes. These are some of the different healing things that are mentioned. It is also used for snake bites, insect bites, burns, rashes and minor abrasions. This is the prickly pear cactus used by the Indians.

3. **Agave.** It is used as a compress for local infections and fresh wounds to heal them. Similarly, a compress is used for relieving chest congestion. Raw agave leaves induce vomiting if that is needed. The pulp is used to treat chapped lips, rashes,

sunburn and snow blindness. All kinds of things can be treated with the agave.

4.   Yucca. The black ashes of burnt yucca are made into paste and used to break a fever. Yucca is also used as a diuretic or an emetic. It is also used to treat dandruff and associated hair and scalp problems, making a shampoo of the root of the yucca. The young shoots of the yucca serve as a pain reliever when mashed and boiled. It will also induce vomiting if needed.

5.   Cholla. The Hopi Indians chew on the roots of the cholla to treat diarrhea. The Navajos commonly used poultices made of the cholla. They are split and used to relieve the pain of arthritis. I do not know whether arthritis was something that they had a lot of, but they used the cholla for that.

6.   Ocotillo. This was used by the Apache Indians. Fatigue was effectively relieved by bathing in water with crushed roots and flowers of the ocotillo. Many Indian tribes report that the flowers and roots were used to stem bleeding.

7.   Creosote Bush. The Apache Indians used this as a cure for diarrhea. A strong tea made of dried creosote bush leaves was commonly used to treat the common cold. The resinous leaf nodes soothe bruises and wounds. A tea from the leaves can relieve kidney pain. Generally speaking, even small doses of this plant are sufficient.

God says that the **tree of life** in Revelation 22:2, with **twelve manner of fruits,** yielded the **fruit every month** and the **leaves were for the healing of the nations.** This may be during the millennial reign of the Lord Jesus Christ. Sometimes the chapters are mixed between the thousand-year reign of the Lord Jesus Christ (the Millennium) and the eternal state. Certainly, during the Millennium, there will be sickness. There will be unsaved people. There will be people that are living on this earth. The saints, the genuine believers, the truly saved ones will be, I believe, in the Heavenly Jerusalem that comes down, which is like a cube. We who are truly saved will be there with new resurrected bodies. Those who are on earth will have just regular earthly bodies and they will have sicknesses. The **leaves** of this special **tree** will be for the **healing of the nations.** God is able to do it. God who made the bodies is able to heal the bodies by the special **leaves** of this **tree of life.**

Revelation 22:3

"And there shall be no more curse: but the throne of God and of the Lamb shall be in it; and his servants shall serve him:"

The Curse Will Be Removed

Think of the curse that God pronounced upon this world because of sin. There will be no more curse. Think of the curse of the animals. In the millennial reign of the Lord Jesus Christ, they will be no longer under bondage, but they will be free. They will not be wild any more. They will be tame. That is part of the curse. The animals in the millennial reign of the Lord Jesus Christ will not be eating one another. They will not be eating us. They will not be attacking us. The curse will be removed.

- Romans 8:19-21
  "For the earnest expectation of the creature waiteth for the manifestation of the sons of God. For the creature was made subject to vanity, not willingly, but by reason of him who hath subjected *the same* in hope, Because the creature itself also shall be delivered from the bondage of corruption into the glorious liberty of the children of God."

No Curse On Ground Or Man

There will be no more curse on the ground or on man. One of the curses, you will remember, was the nettles and the thorns and the thistles that were growing up in the land so that Adam would have difficulty getting his food. The curse was upon the land. The curse was upon the man. The curse was upon the woman. They had a fallen nature from this curse. They had a nature that would be sinful and sin-laden. That was a part of the curse.

In Heaven, there will be no more **curse**. The **throne of God and of the Lamb shall be in it.**

- **Genesis 8:21**
  "And the LORD smelled a sweet savour; and the LORD said in his heart, I will not again **curse** the ground any more for man's sake; for the imagination of man's heart *is* evil from his youth; neither will I again smite any more every thing living, as I have done."

No More Curse Of A Flood

This is after Noah and his ark rested on Mount Ararat. The Lord is never going to put a curse of the flood upon this earth. He will judge by fire at the end of the time, but not any more with the water on this earth.

- **Galatians 3:10**
  "For as many as are of the works of the law are under the curse: for it is written, **Cursed** *is* every one that continueth not in all things which are written in the book of the law to do them."

There is another **curse** and that is the **curse** of sin. Those who try to keep the law of Moses are under the **curse** because you cannot keep it. You cannot be genuinely saved by keeping the law of Moses or any other law of works. If you do everything except one point of the law, whether it is the thousands of different laws the Jews have made or whether it is the law of Moses, if you just fail at one place, you are **cursed** of all. There are many different laws. There is no way that anybody can keep all of the law.

- **Galatians 3:13**
  "Christ hath redeemed us from the **curse** of the law, being made a curse for us: for it is written, **Cursed** *is* every one that hangeth on a tree:"

The Curse Of The Cross

The curse of sin was placed upon the Lord Jesus Christ on the cross. He was hanging on a tree between Heaven and earth. The Old Testament says if you hang suspended like that, as Absalom was, that was a curse, a cursed thing. You remember, his head got caught in the tree and he was suspended and cursed. All those on the cross were under the curse. The Lord Jesus Christ was taken down before the weekly Sabbath or the holy day. The thieves were taken down because it was a curse. The Lord Jesus Christ has redeemed us from this curse of the law. He took our sin that we might have His eternal life. That is a very important part of Scripture. Why would Almighty God the Father make His Son become a curse? In order that we would not have to be cursed, that is why. Certainly, the Lord Jesus Christ is our substitute for sin. The Lord Jesus Christ was made a curse for us.

Notice also in Revelation 22:3 it says, *"and his servants shall serve him."* You may ask, "In Heaven, will we have nothing to do?" If we are His servants, we are going to be **serving Him**. We are going to be **working for Him**. If this is the millennial reign of our Saviour, we are going to be **working for Him** and **serving Him** and we will reign with Him a thousand years. We will be over different cities and different nations and different states. We are going to be serving Him. We should **serve Him** now, even before we get to Heaven.

A servant is supposed to **serve**. If he is not **serving**, then something is wrong with the servant. That is what we are supposed to do. There were many times people did not like slavery because that was too much of a harsh situation of service. Those that were enslaved said, "We are not going to do that any more." All of a sudden, many of them are still serving. All of us should **serve**, regardless of whether we are slaves or not slaves. We are to **serve** the Lord Jesus Christ if we are servants of His. In Heaven, we will have plenty to do in order to **serve** our Saviour.

Revelation 22:4

"And they shall see his face; and his name *shall be* in their foreheads."

The servants, those that are genuinely saved, **shall see God's face** in the face of the Lord Jesus Christ. That was not true in the Old Testament. That was not true ever in Scripture. It was not possible.

- **Exodus 33:18-20**
  "And he said, I beseech thee, shew me thy glory. And he said, I will make all my goodness pass before thee, and I will proclaim the name of the LORD before thee; and will be gracious to whom I will be gracious, and will shew mercy on whom I will shew mercy. And he said, Thou canst not see my **face**: for there shall no man see me, and live."

Moses was talking to the Lord Himself. He wanted to see the glory of the Lord. If you see the **face** of the Lord, you will die. The holiness of God, the glory of God, would cause us to die.

- Exodus 33:21-23
  "And the LORD said, Behold, there is a place by me, and thou shalt stand upon a rock: And it shall come to pass, while my glory passeth by, that I will put thee in a clift of the rock, and will cover thee with my hand while I pass by: And I will take away mine hand, and thou shalt see my back parts: but my **face** shall not be seen."

Seeing The Face Of God

There was no way that the face of God could be seen in the Old Testament. Here in Revelation 22:4 it says, *"they shall see his face."*

- John 1:18
  "No man hath seen God at any time; the only begotten Son, which is in the bosom of the Father, he hath declared *him*."

Christ's Perfect Sinless Humanity

The Lord Jesus Christ had to be clothed with a perfect human body. If He manifested His perfect Deity, nobody could even look upon Him. Just like when Moses went with the Lord, even though He was in the clift of the rock and seeing the back parts of the Lord, his face shone. He had to put a veil over his face. If the people who were living in the time of Lord Jesus Christ would have seen His full glory, they would have died. Therefore, He was clothed with humanity. He was clothed with a body—perfect humanity. He has declared the Father. No man hath seen God at any time. The closest that they came was on the mount of Transfiguration when Peter, James, and John went up and He was transfigured before them. His garments were white—whiter than any fuller could whiten them. They saw and they beheld on that occasion, but they still did not see God as such.

- 1 Timothy 6:16
  "Who only hath immortality, dwelling in the light which no man can approach unto; whom no man hath seen, nor can see: to whom *be* honour and power everlasting. Amen."

They Shall See His Face

This is speaking of God the Father and the Lord Jesus Christ, God the Son. As long as we are in these bodies, no man can see, no man can even approach unto the Lord. He is glorious and we are not glorious. We are sinful and therefore we cannot be in His presence and see Him. Yet in Heaven, *they shall see his face*, it says.

- 1 John 3:2
  "Beloved, now are we the sons of God, and it doth not yet appear what we shall be: but we know that, when he shall appear, we shall be like him; for we shall see him as he is."

This is another verse on the seeing of the Lord Jesus Christ. There are two promises in this verse. <u>First of all, *we shall be like him*</u>. The resurrected bodies of the Lord Jesus Christ's genuinely saved ones will be like unto His glorious body. We will be like Him. <u>Secondly, *we shall see him as he is*</u>. We shall see Him **face to face** in Glory.

- 1 John 4:12
  "No man hath **seen** God at any time. If we love one another, God dwelleth in us, and his love is perfected in us."

We cannot see God. Yet in glorified bodies, *they shall see his face*.

Notice also in Revelation 22:4 it says, *"his name shall be in their foreheads."* <u>The Lord's name is different from the **mark** of the beast</u>.

- **Revelation 13:16**
  "And he causeth all, both small and great, rich and poor, free and bond, to receive a **mark** in their right hand, or in their foreheads:"

The genuine believers will reject that. They will say, "No, we do not want that **mark**." <u>In Glory, God's name shall be in their foreheads—the name of glory, the name of beauty—and not the name of the antichrist</u>.

Revelation 22:5

"And there shall be no night there; and they need no candle, neither light of the sun; for the Lord God giveth them light: and they shall reign for ever and ever."

<u>There shall be **no night** there</u>.

- **Revelation 21:25**
  "And the gates of it shall not be shut at all by day: for there shall be **no night** there."

No Night There

It will be daytime all the time. It reminds Mrs. Waite and me of when we flew from here to South Korea. We flew in a westerly direction and it took fourteen and a half hours because we had headwinds. Coming back, it took twelve and a half hours because we had tailwinds. As we flew from JFK in New York City toward the west, there was no night there. Everything was day. We left in the morning hours. We arrived in different hours and it was still daylight. We could not figure it out. We saw the sun rise and we saw the sun was still there. It was amazing. We passed the International Date Line. We lost a day. It was a day later. It was the next day.

In this case of the Lord Jesus Christ in Heaven itself, there will be **no night,** only day. Because of that, we will have **no need of candles.** **Candles** are used (not just the Roman Catholic candles to get somebody out of purgatory, which certainly is not going to help any), but **candles** are for light. In those days, we will not need a **candle,** *neither the light of the sun; for the Lord God giveth them light.* The Lamb is the **light.**

- **Revelation 21:23**
  "And the city had **no need of the sun,** neither of the moon, to shine in it: for the glory of God did lighten it, and the Lamb *is* the light thereof."

The **Lamb is the light** of the world.

Then it says, *"they shall **reign** for ever and ever."*

- **2 Timothy 2:12**
  "If we suffer, we shall also **reign** with *him:* if we deny *him,* he also will deny us:"

We are going to be **reigning** forever.

- **Revelation 5:10**
  "And hast made us unto our God kings and priests: and we shall **reign** on the earth."

- **Revelation 20:6**
  "Blessed and holy *is* he that hath part in the first resurrection: on such the second death hath no power, but they shall be priests of God and of Christ, and **shall reign** with him a thousand years."

You may say, "I do not know anything about **reigning.**" The Lord Jesus Christ will help you. We will have new bodies. We will have new minds. We will be like unto the Lord Jesus Christ. The millennial **reign** of the

Lord Jesus Christ—a 1,000-year **reign** upon this earth—will need some helpers. The Lord Jesus Christ is omnipresent, that is true, but in His resurrected body, He is in one place at a time. He has genuine believers, truly saved people, thousands and millions of those who are redeemed. They will have new bodies.

- **Luke 19:17**
  "And he said unto him, Well, thou good servant: because thou hast been faithful in a very little, have thou authority over ten cities."

Reigning In New Bodies

What does that mean? That means the resurrected believers in their new bodies will reign and rule with Him. It says so in Scripture over and over again. We must take it and accept it literally as it will be. If you do not know how to reign, the Lord Jesus Christ will give you that wisdom. We will have new bodies. We will have new understanding. He will take care of the reigning for a thousand years.

I wanted to look up the **sun** again. We looked at it before. You remember earlier in the book of Revelation, the **sun** will be so hot it will scorch men and kill them. What about the **sun**? That is one of the **lights** that God made. The **sun** was to rule the day and the moon to rule the night—two great lights, a great light and a lesser light. Now, it says there will be no sun. We will not need it any more. Men have worshipped the **sun** for years—Indians and others. There were **sun** worshippers in the book of Ezekiel—even in the temple they had **sun** worshippers it says.

The Size Of The Sun

The sun is the more prominent feature in our solar system. It is the largest object and contains approximately 98% of the local solar system mass—98% of our solar system is the sun. Think of how big that is. It means that it is 98% of all the stars and planets in our galaxy. <u>Do you know how many earths it would take to fit across the front of the sun? It would take 109 earths just to fit across.</u> Do you know how many earths it would take to fit into the interior of the sun—to actually take up the whole interior? It would take a total of 1.3 million earths. Yet God says here that there will be no need of the sun any more. It will be gone.

How hot is it? On the surface, it is 11,000 degrees Fahrenheit. In the inner core, it is 27 million degrees Fahrenheit. That is why in the book of Revelation, where men will be scorched by the heat of the sun, God will somehow turn some of this heat right on this earth to scorch the people.

I do not believe some of this nonsense where they say energy generated in the **sun's** core takes a million years to reach the surface. We have not had the **sun** a million years. I believe the Creation took place about 6,000 years ago, so this is a nonsensical theory.

Every second, 700 million tons of hydrogen are converted into helium. In the process, five million tons of pure energy are released. Therefore, as time goes on, the **sun** is becoming lighter. In other words, it is not as heavy as it used to be.

Lies About The Earth's Age

Another lie says that the sun has been active for 4.6 billion years. We do not believe that at all. It has been 6,000 years. The Lord made the sun. Human beings with evolutionary theories of how things were made say, "It has to be so many billions of years old." No. They say the sun has enough fuel to go on for another five billion years. It may have that much fuel, but it certainly is not that old, because, in the beginning God created the heaven and the earth.

Whether these theories are true or false, I do not know, but some say that at the end of the **sun's** life, it will start to fuse helium into heavier elements, begin to swell up, and ultimately grow so large that it will swallow the earth. After a billion years as a red giant, it will then suddenly collapse into a white dwarf. The final end-product will take a trillion years to cool off. All that stuff is not going to take place. All I know is there will be no need of the sun. It is not going to be swelling up and so on. The Lord is going to take care of it.

New Heaven And New Earth

We will have a new heaven and a new earth and we will not need the sun, the stars, the light of the moon, or anything of the kind.

In the chemistry of the **sun**, 92% is hydrogen. There is a **little** helium, oxygen, carbon, nitrogen, neon, iron, silicon, magnesium, sulfur, and other elements. I do not know how scientists get the percentages. I do not know how they figure it, but they have this all figured out. Talking about the rotation of the **sun**, it takes 25 to 36 days at the poles.

The Lord Knows About The Sun

The Lord knows all about the sun. He made it and when He has no more need of the light of the sun, He will cause the light of the sun to stop. It will not take a million years. Whenever God wants to do it, He will do it. We will not need the sun any more. The sun is used for the earth and the earth's light, but in Heaven we will have the Son of God as the Light of the world. We will not need any earthly sun to lighten up things. There will be no night there, so we will not need any sun to lighten up anything.

Revelation 22:6

"And he said unto me, These sayings *are* faithful and true: and the Lord God of the holy prophets sent his angel to shew unto his servants the things which must shortly be done."

Here the angel said to John that the *sayings are faithful and true*. That means all the sayings of this book of Revelation are **faithful sayings**. They will come to pass. They are true sayings, whether it is the twenty-one judgments that God has pronounced upon this earth, or all the different things about the sun and the various other things. All the things in Revelation are **faithful things**. They are true things. The Lord Jesus Christ sent His angel to show this to John. John was told to write these things.

- **Revelation 1:3**
  "Blessed *is* he that readeth, and they that hear the words of this prophecy, and keep those things which are written therein: for the time *is* at hand."

God's "Shortly" Not Ours

These things have not come to pass. John has been dead many hundreds of years and yet it says, *"the things which must shortly be done."* God's *shortly* is different from our shortly. To us, shortly must be done in a few minutes. God is an eternal Being. He has no beginning and no time. Shortly, to Him, could be a thousand years, or it could be whatever. It has been almost 2,000 years now since this was written and still the things are not completed. One day, they will be completed. The things that are being said here are faithful. They are true. God wants us to know them and understand them.

Revelation 22:7

"Behold, I come quickly: blessed *is* he that keepeth the sayings of the prophecy of this book."

Here is the Lord Jesus Christ telling John, *"I come quickly."* Again, He has not come yet. It has been 2,000 years and He still has not returned to this earth. It says, *"I come quickly."* That means, *at any moment.* I believe in the imminent return of the Lord Jesus Christ.

Then He says, *"Blessed* (or happy) *is he that keepeth the sayings of the prophecy of this book."* There are a number of verses in regard to **keeping** the Words of God, not only the sayings of this book, but keeping the Words of God in general. It is very important that we keep them.

- **John 14:21**
  "He that hath my commandments, and **keepeth** them, he it is that loveth me: and he that loveth me shall be loved of my Father, and I will love him, and will manifest myself to him."

God wants us to **keep the sayings** of the **prophecy of this book** and the **sayings** of His Words generally. It is not enough to know the Words of God. We must **keep** them. We must follow them.

- **John 14:24**
  "He that loveth me not **keepeth** not my sayings: and the word which ye hear is not mine, but the Father's which sent me."

Keeping God's Words

That is a measure of our love. People say, "Oh, I love the Lord." Do they keep His Words? Do they read His Words and know His Words? No? Then how can they love Him?

The first thing about **keeping** the Words of God and the commands of God is to know the commands of God. We must know the Scriptures from Genesis to Revelation. We must read and study God's Words.

Once we know what it is, the second thing is to **keep** what we know. That is a more difficult process than simply reading and studying—**keeping** and following.

- **1 John 2:4**
  "He that saith, I know him, and **keepeth** not his commandments, is a liar, and the truth is not in him."

There is a term to be used for those that say they know the Lord and do not **keep** His commandments. He is a liar, and the truth is not in him.

- **1 John 2:5**
  "But whoso **keepeth** his word, in him verily is the love of God perfected: hereby know we that we are in him."

We may not be perfectly capable of **keeping** all that God wants us to keep, but we should have a desire to want to keep His Words and know His Words so that we can **keep** them.

Our Mission In South Korea

That was the purpose of our mission in South Korea. It was a Bible conference and it was centered around the King James Bible. There is a Korean Bible faithful to the King James Bible, the Textus Receptus, and the Hebrew and Aramaic Words. Dr. Jung has produced that Bible. It is accurate and has all the verses that it ought to have. This is part of the Korean life, to keep God's Words. They have them. Now may they keep them. As we have His Words in our King James Bible, we also should keep them.

- **1 John 3:24**
  "And he that **keepeth** his commandments dwelleth in him, and he in him. And hereby we know that he abideth in us, by the Spirit which he hath given us."

What does this word, *keep,* mean? It is the word *TEREO*. It is a *continuous present tense*—he that continues to **keep**. What does it mean? The first meaning is, *to attend to carefully; be attentive to what God has said; to take care of.* Another meaning of TEREO is, *to guard.* Guard the very Words of God—observe and **guard**.

Guarding God's Words Needed

Guarding and keeping the sayings of God—that is one of the battles we have, as I said, over in Korea. We have it in this country. We have it in all the nations of the world, to keep the Words of God. We believe the Scriptures are clear that God gave us His Hebrew, a little Aramaic in the Old Testament, and the New Testament Greek Words. He has promised to keep those Words. He has promised to guard those Words for us, so

> we have them even to this day. We believe He has preserved and protected them. We have to guard those Words and then translate those Words into other languages.

During the course of the recent conference in South Korea, Pastor Jung, who was, at that time, the associate pastor of our host Church in Seoul, and I compared different verses that were wrong in the false Greek text of Westcott and Hort. They are wrong in the versions in our country—wrong in the New International Version, wrong in the New American Standard, and so on.

One of the men brought up to him the Regular Standard Korean Bible, which is produced by the United Bible Society.

The Korean Bible Analyzed

As we compared the verses of Dr. Jung's Bible, which were accurate, as in our King James Bible, he read the verses in the Korean Bible that is used generally in that country. In every place where error was, error was in the Korean Bible. There are 356 doctrinal passages altogether that are wrong because of the wrong Greek text. I put 158 of those in *Defending the King James Bible* in chapter five. We went over about twenty-five of those and compared them with the Korean Bible. Twenty-four out of the twenty-five were the exact same errors they had in their Korean Bible. That is why Dr. Jung, one of our missionaries, has worked on and has produced a Korean Bible, which is accurate. It has all these verses and all the Words properly translated. God wants us to keep His Words and guard them.

Revelation 22:8

"And I John saw these things, and heard *them*. And when I had heard and seen, I fell down to worship before the feet of the angel which shewed me these things."

The word for **angel** is *AGGELOS*. It means *a messenger*. Apparently he was one of the servants of the Lord Jesus Christ. It was a Heavenly angel that John fell down to worship. He was glad to see this angel.

Revelation 22:9

"Then saith he unto me, See *thou do it* not: for I am thy fellowservant, and of thy brethren the prophets, and of them which keep the sayings of this book: worship God."

Here again, the **angel** tells John to *keep the sayings*—continue to **keep the sayings.** God does not want us to **worship** men or anything else.

- **1 John 5:21**
  "Little children, keep yourselves from **idols.** Amen."

We have many **idol worshippers.** Many people worship Billy Graham. They believe what Billy Graham says must be true. We should not **worship** any man. In the past, some have **worshipped** Jack Hyles, who was from Indiana. We should not worship him. Some **worship** even David Cloud. David Cloud has written a lot of good things, but we cannot put him up on a pedestal to worship him. Some **worship** the pope. Some **worship** Bill Gothard. They will say, "What does Bill say about it?" Well, what does the Bible say? Some **worship** the GARBC, the Regular Baptist Fellowship, or the Independent Baptist Fellowship, or something else. Some **worship** schools like Bob Jones University, or Dallas Theological Seminary, or something else.

Worship The Lord, Not Men

We have to worship the Lord Jesus Christ. You cannot worship any preacher. Do not worship me or anyone else. We must follow the things of the Lord Jesus Christ. The apostle John was rebuked by this servant of the Lord Jesus Christ. We are not to worship any one individual. We are to worship God. The Lord Jesus Christ is God the Son. We are to worship Him and God the Father in spirit and in truth. It is very important that we do this.

Revelation 22:10

"And he saith unto me, Seal not the sayings of the prophecy of this book: for the time is at hand."

Two Types Of Prohibitions

As we have said many times before, this is a prohibition. There are two types of prohibition in the Greek language. One is an aorist prohibition, which says, "Do not even begin to do something." The other is the present prohibition, which means, "Stop an action already in the process of doing." Which one is this? This is the aorist. Do not even begin to seal up the sayings of the prophecy of this book. The time is at hand. That *at hand* is already 2,000 years. If it was *at hand* in John's day, it is much more *at hand* even today.

What does it mean to **seal**? Since these things are **sealed** up, they are concealed as the contents of a letter. It means, *to hide; to keep in silence; to keep secret.* God wants His Book, His Words, His Scripture, His Revelation—all the Words of Scripture—not to be **sealed**, not to be hidden, not to be secret or kept in silence. Do not even begin to **seal** the *sayings of the prophecy of this book: for the time is at hand.* What **time**? It is the **time** for this to be fulfilled.

The Time For Many Things

Again, if it was time in John's day, it is much more time today in our day—the time of the tribulation. It will be the time when the antichrist shall reign; the time of seven years of terrible chaos on this earth; and the time of the rapture—the taking up of genuine believers out of this earth before the tribulation. Then, after the seven years, it will be the time of the millennial reign of the Lord Jesus Christ. After that thousand years, time shall be no more. The time is at hand. Do not even begin to seal up the sayings of the Book.

The popes for years have tried to **seal** up the Bible. The popes for years said, "Don't you lay people ever touch and open the Bible! The clergy will tell you what the Bible says. We will tell you how to interpret it." Now, I guess they are able to read the Bible, but the interpretation is left up to the priests and different leaders in the church. God says, "**Do not even begin to seal up the sayings.**" We want to let the Bible loose. <u>We want every genuine Christian, and every truly born-again believer to read the Bible himself or herself, to know what God's Words say. That is why we have the battle for the right Bible, our King James Bible.</u>

Bible Preservation Is Important

Now we have to battle some of the fundamentalist schools and universities that do not even believe that God promised to preserve His Hebrew, Aramaic, and Greek Words. I am talking about the big four schools. I have said it many times. Bob Jones University is the leader, along with Detroit Baptist Seminary, Central Seminary, and Calvary Seminary. They do not believe God preserved His Words or that He even promised to, so we have errors in the Hebrew and errors in the Greek. They go ahead with their New American Standard Version and the New International Version and those are sealing up the Words of God.

- **Amos 8:11**
"Behold, the days come, saith the Lord GOD, that I will send a famine in the land, not a famine of bread, nor a thirst for water, but of hearing the words of the LORD:"

Do not even begin to seal up the sayings. Let them have free course—all of the Words of God.

Revelation 22:11

"He that is unjust, let him be unjust still: and he which is filthy, let him be filthy still: and he that is righteous, let him be righteous still: and he that is holy, let him be holy still."

You may wonder, "Why is this verse here?" The situation is that the Lord Jesus Christ may come at any time. There is no time to make any changes. He is going to come back. Whether this is at the rapture or at the millennial reign of the Lord Jesus Christ, there is no time for change. Just stay right where you are. It is not that God justifies being unjust or **filthy**. He does not. He wants people to be **righteous** and holy. This is just as before the flood.

- **Matthew 24:37-39**
"But as the days of Noe *were*, so shall also the coming of the Son of man be. For as in the days that were before the flood they were eating and drinking, marrying and giving in marriage, until the day that Noe entered into the ark, And knew not until the flood came, and took them all away; so shall also the coming of the Son of man be."

They will not know what hit them. That is why I think this verse is in there. The **unjust** keep going. The **unholy** keep going. The **filthy**, the **righteous**, the just—there is no time to change. Of course, that is true of anybody that is about to die. There is no time to change in that venue either unless you genuinely trust the Lord Jesus Christ at the very end of the line. Sometimes the medications that doctors use and give to the patients to relieve the pain mean there is no thinking ability left. If you try to lead that person to the Lord Jesus Christ at his death bed, he cannot understand what you are saying. I have seen this as I have ministered to different ones that are in hospitals. We have to be ready because the Lord Jesus Christ may come at any time.

Revelation 22:12

"And, behold, I come quickly; and my reward *is* with me, to give every man according as his work shall be."

The Lord Jesus Christ is speaking here. He is going to be **coming**. He is going to come in the rapture. Notice, it says that his **reward** is with Him. That word reward is MISTHOS. It means, *dues paid for work.* It can be, *reward,* but it is also, *punishments.* MISTHOS is *wages* and in both senses—**rewards** and punishments. Both the genuine believer and the unbeliever are going to be **rewarded** or judged *according as his work shall be.* God judges by what our works are after we come to the Lord Jesus Christ as genuine believers.

- **1 Corinthians 3:9-11**
  "For we are labourers together with God: ye are God's husbandry, ye are God's building. According to the grace of God which is given unto me, as a wise masterbuilder, I have laid the foundation, and another buildeth thereon. But let every man take heed how he buildeth thereupon. For other foundation can no man lay than that is laid, which is Jesus Christ."

He is our foundation.

- **1 Corinthians 3:12-15**
  "Now if any man build upon this foundation gold, silver, precious stones, wood, hay, stubble; Every man's work shall be made manifest: for the day shall declare it, because it shall be revealed by fire; and the fire shall try every man's work of what sort it is. If any man's work abide which he hath built thereupon, he shall receive a reward. If any man's work shall be burned, he shall suffer loss: but he himself shall be saved; yet so as by fire."

These are genuinely believing people. This is the judgment seat of the Lord Jesus Christ. This is for genuine Christians. It is the judgment of the works that have been done after they have genuinely come to the Lord Jesus Christ. The works of true believers will be tested. The genuine believers that have built nothing on the Lord Jesus Christ except *"wood, hay, and stubble"*—things of this life, things that are big, but not genuine—will be burned up with the fire. The genuine believers will be safe, but all of their works will be burned up. They will have no **rewards**.

The Five Crowns Of Scripture

There are five crowns of rewards for true believers. We have mentioned this many times before. I always use the memory hint "R GIRL." Those are the five crowns.

R is the crown of righteousness.

G is the crown of glory.

I is the incorruptible crown.

R is the crown of rejoicing.

L is the crown of life.

- **1 Thessalonians 2:19**
  "For what *is* our hope, or joy, or **crown** of rejoicing? *Are* not even ye in the presence of our Lord Jesus Christ at his coming?"

That is a soulwinner's **crown, apparently.**

- **1 Peter 5:4**
  "And when the chief Shepherd shall appear, ye shall receive a **crown** of glory that fadeth not away."

That is the Shepherd's **crown** for people who are serving the Lord Jesus Christ as pastors, ministers, missionaries, and maybe moms and dads who are serving—those who are faithful.

- **1 Corinthians 9:25**
  "And every man that striveth for the mastery is temperate in all things. Now they *do it* to obtain a corruptible **crown**; but we an incorruptible."

That is the incorruptible **crown** for being faithful in the race.

- **2 Timothy 4:8**
  "Henceforth there is laid up for me a **crown** of righteousness, which the Lord, the righteous judge, shall give me at that day: and not to me only, but unto all them also that love his appearing."

Those that love His appearing will get a **crown** of righteousness.

- **James 1:12**
"Blessed *is* the man that endureth temptation: for when he is tried, he shall receive the **crown** of life, which the Lord hath promised to them that love him."

- **Revelation 2:10**
"Fear none of those things which thou shalt suffer: behold, the devil shall cast *some* of you into prison, that ye may be tried; and ye shall have tribulation ten days: be thou faithful unto death, and I will give thee a **crown** of life."

The Judgment Seat Of Christ

The Lord Jesus Christ says, "*I am coming quickly.*" We do not know when. All who are genuinely saved and truly born-again are going to be in Heaven for all eternity. Some will have rewards and some will not have rewards. Some of the works will be burned up. Some works will be preserved and maintained. Fire takes away the impurities of gold, silver, and precious stones, but fire burns up wood, hay, and stubble.

What about the unbelievers? The Lord Jesus Christ is going to judge them according to their works also. I believe there will be gradations in Hell, as well. They are going to be judged according to their works. They all are going to be in Hell suffering, just as all the genuine Christians are going to be in Heaven rejoicing. Some unbelievers will have more severe judgments than others.

- **Revelation 20:11-12**
"And I saw a great white throne, and him that sat on it, from whose face the earth and the heaven fled away; and there was found no place for them. And I saw the dead, small and great, stand before God; and the books were opened: and another book was opened, *which is* the book of life: and the dead were judged out of those things which were written in the books, according to their works."

The big and the little, the rich and the poor, and the handsome and the ugly, will stand before the Lord Jesus Christ and will be judged by Him. These are lost people.

- **Matthew 11:21-24**
"Woe unto thee, Chorazin! woe unto thee, Bethsaida! for if the mighty works, which were done in you, had been done in Tyre and Sidon, they would have repented long ago in sackcloth and ashes. But I say unto you, It shall be more tolerable for Tyre and Sidon at the day of judgment, than for you. And thou,

Capernaum, which art exalted unto heaven, shalt be brought down to Hell: for if the mighty works, which have been done in thee, had been done in Sodom, it would have remained until this day. But I say unto you, That it shall be **more tolerable** for the land of Sodom in the day of judgment, than for thee."
I believe there is going to be a gradation in Hell. All the lost are going to be suffering in Hell, but they are going to be judged according to their works, even though they are lost. What have they done? What type of works do they have? They will be lost. They have not received the Lord Jesus Christ. According to the above verse, it will be *"more tolerable"* for some than for others in Hell.

The Lord Jesus Christ says, *"I come quickly; and my reward is with me."* That word for reward is MISTHOS.

- **Romans 6:23**
  "For the wages of sin *is* death; but the gift of God *is* eternal life through Jesus Christ our Lord."

That word MISTHOS is **reward**, but it also means His punishments will be coming, as well as the reward. The **reward** will be for the true believers that are genuinely saved, and punishment will be for those that are unbelievers.

Revelation 22:13

"I am Alpha and Umega, the beginning and the end, the first and the last."

Christ Is The Alpha And Omega

Here is a title of the Lord Jesus Christ. Alpha and Omega are the first and last letters of the Greek alphabet. There is nothing that was before the Lord Jesus Christ. He was eternally the Son of God and God the Son. He will be in eternity to come with no ending. Everything is first with Him and everything is last as well.

- **Revelation 1:8**
  "I am **Alpha and Omega**, the **beginning and the ending**, saith the Lord, which is, and which was, and which is to come, the Almighty."

- **Revelation 1:11**
  "Saying, I am **Alpha and Omega**, the **first and the last**: and, What thou seest, write in a book, and send *it* unto the seven churches which are in Asia; unto Ephesus, and unto Smyrna, and unto Pergamos, and unto Thyatira, and unto Sardis, and unto Philadelphia, and unto Laodicea."
- **Revelation 21:6**
  "And he said unto me, It is done. I am **Alpha and Omega**, the **beginning and the end**. I will give unto him that is athirst of the fountain of the water of life freely."

Christ Is Complete For The Saved

Four times, the Lord Jesus Christ is called the Alpha and Omega. There is nothing that is more important than accepting the Lord Jesus Christ. He is the very beginning and the very ending. Our life is full if we have the Lord Jesus Christ. Without Him, it is empty. <u>Without Him, there is no eternal life</u>. There is no peace. There is no joy. <u>There are not all the different gifts of the Spirit of God</u>. With Him, we can have the beginning and the ending, the Alpha and Omega, everything we need. There is a gospel song that says, *Christ is all I need*. Certainly, if He is Alpha and Omega, the beginning and the end, the first and last, you cannot name a need that He cannot meet as the omnipotent Saviour. If you are genuinely saved and have trusted in Him and are truly born-again, He will supply.

- **Philippians 4:19**
  "But my God shall supply all your need according to his riches in glory by Christ Jesus."

Paul wrote this when the Philippian Christians gave him an offering for his ministry. They gave of their necessity and poverty to Paul. Paul said, "God is going to supply your need as well," and He will.

Revelation 22:14

"Blessed *are* they that do his commandments, that they may have right to the tree of life, and may enter in through the gates into the city."

This is apparently the millennial city, that city which is hovering above the earth, a city foursquare. What about these **commandments**? Are we genuinely saved by doing **commandments** and works? No. The only **commandments** that we must do in order to be genuinely saved and have the right to the tree of life are the **commandments** such as:

- **Matthew 11:28**
  "**Come unto me**, all *ye* that labour and are heavy laden, and I will give you rest."

That is an order. The Lord Jesus Christ invites those who are lost to **come** unto Him.

- **Acts 16:28-31**
  "But Paul cried with a loud voice, saying, Do thyself no harm: for we are all here. Then he called for a light, and sprang in, and came trembling, and fell down before Paul and Silas, And brought them out, and said, Sirs, what must I **do** to be saved? And they said, **Believe** on the Lord Jesus Christ, and thou shalt be saved, and thy house."

The Philippian jailer was about to kill himself. He thought people had escaped out of his prison in Philippi. He asked what he had to "*do*" to be saved. The answer was to "*believe on the Lord Jesus Christ.*" That is the answer. That is **doing** what He **commands** us to do.

- **John 6:28-29**
  "Then said they unto him, What shall we **do**, that we might **work** the works of God? Jesus answered and said unto them, This is the <u>**work**</u> of God, that ye **believe** on him whom he hath sent."

That is the <u>**work**</u> of God. Those that do His commandments—in other words, genuinely <u>**trusting Him**</u> as Saviour and Redeemer—have the **right to the tree of life**. That is the **tree** from which Adam and Eve were banished in the garden of Eden after they ate of the **tree** of the knowledge of good and evil. They were sinners. They were lost and God closed down that **tree of life**. In the millennial reign of the Lord Jesus Christ, and certainly in eternity, those who are genuinely saved will have the "*right to the tree of life.*"

Revelation 22:15

"**For without** *are* **dogs, and sorcerers, and whoremongers, and murderers, and idolaters, and whosoever loveth and maketh a lie.**"

That *without* is **without** the city, the holy Jerusalem. They are not going to have entrance into this gate of the city. They are lost people.

- **Philippians 3:2**
  "Beware of **dogs**, beware of evil workers, beware of the concision."

The Bible's Use Of "Dogs"

That term, *dogs*, is a term that is used many times in Scripture to refer by metaphor to a man of impure mind, an impudent man. Sometimes it refers to the homosexuals in the Old Testament. Dogs—those that are unbelievers, impure—are going to be outside the city.

The second ones outside are the *sorcerers*. <u>Sorcerers are people that have to do with magical arts.</u> They are not going to be in the city. They are lost people.

- **Exodus 7:11**
  "Then Pharaoh also called the wise men and the **sorcerers**: now the magicians of Egypt, they also did in like manner with their enchantments."

- **Daniel 2:2**
  "Then the king commanded to call the magicians, and the astrologers, and the **sorcerers**, and the Chaldeans, for to shew the king his dreams. So they came and stood before the king."

The king was going to kill all of them unless they showed the dream. What was the dream? Not simply the interpretation—he did not even remember his dream.

- **Malachi 3:5**
  "And I will come near to you to judgment; and I will be a swift witness against the **sorcerers**, and against the adulterers, and against false swearers, and against those that oppress the hireling in *his* wages, the widow, and the fatherless, and that turn aside the stranger *from his right*, and fear not me, saith the LORD of hosts."

<u>God does not want **sorcerers**, those that use magical arts.</u>

- **Revelation 21:8**
  "But the fearful, and unbelieving, and the abominable, and murderers, and **whoremongers, and sorcerers, and idolaters, and all liars**, shall have their part in the lake which burneth with fire and brimstone: which is the second death."

We have Satanic people all around us in this country and in other countries as well. Satanism with Satanic powers and all the evil spirits will be outside the city in the millennial reign of the Lord Jesus Christ

.

The Homosexual Males

Another group of people outside the city is the *whoremongers*. This word PORNOS is in the masculine. It is *a man who prostitutes his body to another's lust for hire; a male prostitute*. It could be a homosexual male.

- **1 Timothy 1:9-10**
  "Knowing this, that the law is not made for a righteous man, but for the lawless and disobedient, for the ungodly and for sinners, for unholy and profane, for murderers of fathers and murderers of mothers, for manslayers, For **whoremongers**, for them that defile themselves with mankind, for menstealers, for liars, for perjured persons, and if there be any other thing that is contrary to sound doctrine;"

- **Hebrews 13:4**
  "Marriage *is* honourable in all, and the bed undefiled: but **whoremongers** and adulterers God will judge."

There is a judgment of the **whoremongers**.

- **Revelation 21:8**
  "But the fearful, and unbelieving, and the abominable, and murderers, and **whoremongers, and sorcerers, and idolaters, and all liars**, shall have their part in the lake which burneth with fire and brimstone: which is the second death."

These are things that are outside the city. There is another group, *murderers*. This is only used nine times in Scripture—those that kill people.

We have **murderers** all the time. We had a man in Philadelphia who gave himself up. His lawyer came in with no fight, no struggle. He shot one of the students in one of the fifth district middle schools for $50 that he owed him. He shot him dead, killed him. He is a **murderer**. I taught in that fifth district of Philadelphia years ago—for 18 years, in fact. **Murderers** are all around us.

- **Acts 7:52**
  "Which of the prophets have not your fathers persecuted? and they have slain them which shewed before of the coming of the Just One; of whom ye have been now the betrayers and **murderers**:"

The death of the Lord Jesus Christ was **murder**.

- **1 Timothy 1:9**
  "Knowing this, that the law is not made for a righteous man, but for the lawless and disobedient, for the ungodly and for sinners, for unholy and profane, for **murderers** of fathers and **murderers** of mothers, for manslayers,"

The Purpose Of Laws

Again, what is the law made for? It is not for the righteous or godly man, but for the ungodly. One of those things the law is made for is murderers. People say, "Why do you have a law against murder?" That is one of the reasons in the New Testament for laws against these things.

- **Revelation 21:8**
  "But the fearful, and unbelieving, and the abominable, and **murderers**, and **whoremongers**, and **sorcerers**, and **idolaters**, and all liars, shall have their part in the lake which burneth with fire and brimstone: which is the second death."

There is another group of people who are going to be outside the holy city, the *idolaters*—those that worship images. An idol is something that can be seen. EIDOS is from the Greek word, *to see*. LATREUO means, *to worship; to bow down*.

- **1 Corinthians 5:11**
  "But now I have written unto you not to keep company, if any man that is called a brother be a fornicator, or covetous, or an **idolater**, or a railer, or a drunkard, or an extortioner; with such an one no not to eat."

Genuine believers are not to fellowship with those who practice these evil things.

- **1 Corinthians 6:9-10**
  "Know ye not that the unrighteous shall not inherit the kingdom of God? Be not deceived: neither fornicators, nor **idolaters**, nor adulterers, nor effeminate, nor abusers of themselves with mankind, Nor thieves, nor covetous, nor drunkards, nor revilers, nor extortioners, shall inherit the kingdom of God."

Those that are redeemed are going to Heaven, but the **idolaters** are on the outside of the holy city.

- **1 Corinthians 10:7**
  "Neither be ye **idolaters**, as *were* some of them; as it is written, The people sat down to eat and drink, and rose up to play."

Paul warns them, speaking of Israel, against worshipping of images and idols. All over the world, they have **idolatry**.

- **1 John 5:21**
  "Little children, keep yourselves from **idols**. Amen."

Those might refer to **idols** of stone, wood, gold, or silver. <u>They might be human idols.</u> We should not worship people either.

Another classification of those who will have their part in the lake of fire and brimstone are *those that loveth and maketh a lie*—constant liars. The Devil is the source of **liars**. The word, **liars**, is used eight times in Scripture.

- **Jeremiah 50:36**
  "A sword *is* upon the **liars**; and they shall dote: a sword *is* upon her mighty men; and they shall be dismayed."

- **1 Timothy 1:9**
  "Knowing this, that the law is not made for a righteous man, but for the lawless and disobedient, for the ungodly and for sinners, for unholy and profane, for **murderers** of fathers and **murderers** of mothers, for manslayers,"

The law, again, was made for various unrighteous people—not for righteous people. <u>One of the things the law was made for was **liars**.</u> That is why we must have the truth in advertising. People are not to lie about what they put in food. People are not to lie when they testify in court. They raise their hands and affirm they will tell the truth, the whole truth, and nothing but the truth. Liars are part of Satan's kingdom and they will be outside that holy city. The Devil is the father of lies.

- **John 8:44**
  "Ye are of *your* father the devil, and the lusts of your father ye will do. He was a murderer from the beginning, and abode not in the truth, because there is no truth in him. When he speaketh a **lie**, he speaketh of his own: for he is a **liar**, and the father of it."

Revelation 22:16

"I Jesus have sent mine angel to testify unto you these things in the churches. I am the root and the offspring of David, and the bright and morning star."

The Root And Offspring Of David

The Lord Jesus Christ affiliates and associates Himself with *the root and the offspring of David*. He is the Son of David. He is of the Davidic line. He is of royalty and He will sit on the throne of His father David in the millennial reign of the

Lord Jesus Christ in Palestine and Jerusalem. He also says
that He is *the bright and morning star*. That is a title for the
Lord Jesus Christ, the *morning star*.

That is one of the things we have against the New International
Version because of its rendering in Isaiah 14:12 of *morning star*, which
is a title for the Lord Jesus Christ.

- **Isaiah 14:12**
  "How art thou fallen from heaven, O Lucifer, son of the
  morning! *how* art thou cut down to the ground, which didst
  weaken the nations!"

This is a picture of Satan. The NIV, reads, *"How you have fallen from
heaven, morning star, son of the dawn!"* Our King James Bible rightly
renders it, *"How art thou fallen from heaven, O Lucifer, son of the
morning!"* There is no *morning star* there. Morning is *BOQER* and
star is *KOKAB*. Neither one is there, but it is *Lucifer*. That word in
Hebrew is *HEYLEL*. It means, *the bright one; the shining one*. Lucifer
is a good Latin term. *LUX* is *light*. *FEROS* is *to carry*. It is a bearer of
light, a light bearer. The NIV has the morning star for Satan! That is one
of the things that is very, very wrong in the New International Version.
That is why people are worshipping Lucifer.

People Worship Satan Today

There are Luciferian cults and they are worshipping
Lucifer. The NIV plays into this, it seems. In this section of
Isaiah, which is depicting Satan, the NIV translators are
calling him the morning star just as the Lord Jesus Christ is
called here in Revelation 22:16.

Revelation 22:17

**"And the Spirit and the bride say, Come. And let him
that heareth say, Come. And let him that is athirst come.
And whosoever will, let him take the water of life freely."**

All of this invitation is to *whosoever will*. As we have said many
times before, there is a whole family of theologians in the world called
hyper-Calvinists that do not believe that **whosoever will**. They say that
salvation is not for **whosoever will**, but it is only for the elect, a certain
group of people. If you are not one of that group, there is nothing that
you can do to trust the Lord Jesus Christ. That is contrary to this verse.

13 Verses On "Whosoever Will"

I would like to look at 13 verses that say that the Lord's salvation is for whosoever will, in addition to this one here.

- **Isaiah 53:6**
  "All we like sheep have gone astray; we have turned every one to his own way; and the LORD hath laid on him the iniquity of us <u>all</u>."

This is not just simply the elect, not just simply Jews, but **all** people.

- **Matthew 11:28**
  "**Come unto me, <u>all</u>** ye that labour and are heavy laden, and I will give you rest."

He does not say, "just the elect" or "just the Jews," but **all**.

- **John 1:29**
  "The next day John seeth Jesus coming unto him, and saith, Behold the Lamb of God, which taketh away the **sin of the world**."

He removed the punishment of sin for the **whole world** if they will genuinely trust Him. He made provision for them, but they must genuinely trust Him.

- **John 3:14-15**
  "And as Moses lifted up the serpent in the wilderness, even so must the Son of man be lifted up: That **whosoever believeth** in him should not perish, but have eternal life."

He did not lift up the serpent for a certain elect group of the Israelites. **Anyone** could look at that serpent on the pole and be delivered and saved physically from poison and death. So at Calvary, it is that same way.

- **John 3:18**
  "**He that believeth** on him is not condemned: but he that believeth not is condemned already, because he hath not believed in the name of the only begotten Son of God."

Notice the reason **he that believeth** not is condemned already. He is condemned already, but not because he is not one of the elect. Everyone who rejects the Lord Jesus Christ is condemned because he believeth not on the only begotten Son of God. God condemns them because they do not believe. If they cannot believe, how can God condemn somebody who has no possibility of believing? Everyone has the ability of credence, as Pastor Carl Drexler used to tell us in the little white church.

- **Romans 5:6**
  "For when we were yet without strength, in due time **Christ died for the ungodly**."

That is not simply the **ungodly** who are the elect. It is all the **ungodly** of the world—all the Jews, the Gentiles, everyone. He died in the place of the **ungodly**.

- **2 Corinthians 5:19**
  "To wit, that God was in Christ, **reconciling the world** unto himself, not imputing their trespasses unto them; and hath committed unto us the word of reconciliation."

He has **reconciled the world**, not simply the world of the elect, but all the truly saved people are **reconciled**. They are all made able to be genuinely saved because the Lord Jesus Christ died for their sins—all of them, not simply a portion of them.

- **1 Timothy 2:5-6**
  "For *there is* one God, and one mediator between God and men, the man Christ Jesus; Who gave himself a **ransom for all**, to be testified in due time."

These verses refute limited atonement. It does not say, "all the elect only." It does not say, "all the Jews only," or "all the Catholics only," but for the big and the little, the men and the women—**for all**.

- **Hebrews 2:9**
  "But we see Jesus, who was made a little lower than the angels for the suffering of death, crowned with glory and honour; that he by the grace of God should taste **death for every man**."

This is another verse that refutes limited atonement. Every man is every person, everyone of mankind—not just the elect. The Lord Jesus Christ died for the sins of the whole world.

- **2 Peter 2:1**
  "But there were false prophets also among the people, even as there shall be false teachers among you, who privily shall bring in damnable heresies, even denying the Lord that **bought them**, and bring upon themselves swift destruction."

Here is another refutation of limited atonement. Here were some false prophets and false teachers. Notice what it says about them: *"even denying the Lord that bought them."* He died for the sins even of the unbelievers, these false prophets. Not that they are genuinely saved. They are not coming to Him and truly trusting Him, but they have been bought and their sins have been paid for if they will really accept the One that **bore their sins**.

- **1 John 4:14**
  "And we have seen and do testify that the Father sent the Son *to be* the **Saviour of the world**."

Here is another verse against limited atonement. <u>He is the **Saviour of the world**, not simply the world of the elect</u>. His salvation is offered to the **world**. Those that are genuinely trusting the Lord Jesus Christ are truly saved by Him, but also, the invitation is extended to the **world**.

- **1 John 2:2**
  "And he is the propitiation for our sins: and not for ours only, but also for *the sins of* the **whole world**."

This is not just the world of the elect. I believe that this limited atonement, hyper-Calvinist belief, is a heretical belief. Mr. Harold Camping of Family Radio preached it every single day of the year on his program. He taught that if you are one of the elect, then you can be genuinely saved. If you are not, you cannot be genuinely saved. It is apostasy and it is heretical.

Hyper-Calvinism Breaks Friendships

I got into trouble with some of my Presbyterian friends overseas because I wrote very clearly on this subject in *The Bible for Today Newsreport* years ago. They broke fellowship with me ("We don't want anything to do with you!") because I said, "The Lord Jesus Christ died for the sins of the world." He died for the sins of whosoever will. Let him come and take the water of life freely. That is Bible. All these verses—14 of them, and there are others—are very clear.

Revelation 22:18-19

"For I testify unto every man that heareth the words of the prophecy of this book, If any man shall add unto these things, God shall add unto him the plagues that are written in this book: And if any man shall take away from the words of the book of this prophecy, God shall take away his part out of the book of life, and out of the holy city, and *from* the things which are written in this book."

These two verses are together. I preached a message on this called, *The Peril of Bible Perverters*. God pronounces a curse on those that *add* or those that *take away from the words of the prophecy of this*

book. There are 15 verses that show God is against those that take away His Words. He wants all of His Words there.

Words Added, Subtracted & Changed

Yet, in the <u>New King James Version</u>, I found over 2,000 examples of either adding to the Hebrew, Aramaic, and Greek Words, subtracting, or changing them. In the <u>New American Standard Version</u>, I found over 4,000 examples of dynamic equivalency—adding, subtracting, or changing God's Words. In the <u>New International Version</u>, I found 6,653 examples (and I stopped counting) of adding, subtracting, and changing. I maintain that these who translate, pervert, or paraphrase these versions are Bible perverters. They are under the judgment of Revelation 22:18-19. Is God against this? Yes, He is.

- **Deuteronomy 4:2**
  Ye shall not **add** unto the word which I command you, neither shall ye **diminish** *ought* from it, that ye may keep the commandments of the LORD your God which I command you."

<u>God does not want us to **add**. He does not want us to **subtract**.</u>

- **Deuteronomy 8:3**
  "And he humbled thee, and suffered thee to hunger, and fed thee with manna, which thou knewest not, neither did thy fathers know; that he might make thee know that man doth not live by bread only, but by **every** *word* that proceedeth out of the mouth of the LORD doth man live."

<u>How can he live by **every word** if he does not have **every word** in the translation?</u>

- **Deuteronomy 12:32**
  "What thing soever I command you, observe to do it: thou shalt **not add** thereto, **nor diminish** from it."

This is as clear as crystal. <u>Do **not add**. Do **not subtract**.</u>

- **Deuteronomy 29:29**
  "The secret *things belong* unto the LORD our God: but those *things which are* revealed *belong* unto us and to our children for ever, that *we* may do **all the words** of this law."

<u>How can you "do all the **words**" if you do not have **all the words** translated in the language like we have in our King James Bible?</u>

- **Job 23:12**
  "Neither have I gone back from the commandment of his lips; I have esteemed the **words of his mouth** more than my necessary *food.*"

If you do not have the **words—all of them—**how can you esteem them more than your necessary food? Do not miss the meal!

- **Proverbs 30:6**
  "**Add thou not** unto his words, lest he reprove thee, and thou be found a liar."

Why do these translators **add**?

- **Isaiah 55:11**
  "So shall **my word** be that goeth forth out of my mouth: it shall not return unto me void, but it shall accomplish that which I please, and it shall prosper *in the thing* whereto I sent it."

The **word** that goes out of God's mouth will be blessed, not the words that men have **added** or **subtracted**.

- **Jeremiah 15:16**
  "**Thy words** were found, and I did eat them; and thy word was unto me the joy and rejoicing of mine heart: for I am called by thy name, O LORD God of hosts."

The **words** were found, but if you cannot find **all the words** because of the false translations with the false Hebrew, Aramaic, and Greek Words, we are in serious trouble.

- **Jeremiah 23:30**
  "Therefore, behold, I *am* against the prophets, saith the LORD, that **steal my words** every one from his neighbour."

Steal His Words? If you take out a Hebrew word, you are **stealing God's Words**. If you take out a Greek word, you are **stealing God's Words**. God says, "I am against the prophets."

- **Jeremiah 23:36**
  "And the burden of the LORD shall ye mention no more: for every man's word shall be his burden; for ye have **perverted the words** of the living God, of the LORD of hosts our God."

That is why I called this message, *The Peril of Bible Perverters.* Translators who give wrong translations are *perverters* of the **Words of God.**

- **Jeremiah 26:2**
  "Thus saith the LORD; Stand in the court of the LORD'S house, and speak unto all the cities of Judah, which come to worship in the LORD'S house, **all the words** that I command thee to speak unto them; **diminish not a word:**"

Jeremiah could not take a single **word** back. If he did not have **all the words,** how could he preach in the Lord's house?

- **Jeremiah 29:23**
  "Because they have committed villany in Israel, and have committed adultery with their neighbours' wives, and have spoken **lying words** in my name, which I have not commanded them; even I know, and *am* a witness, saith the LORD."

In these versions that are **adding to the Words of God,** God did not command these words. Yet they **add and add, or subtract and subtract.**

- **Amos 8:11**
  "Behold, the days come, saith the Lord GOD, that I will send a famine in the land, not a famine of bread, nor a thirst for water, but of **hearing the words of the LORD:**"

I think we are in this position of famine right now. If we do not have **all the Words, we are not going to hear all the Words.** Our King James Bible accurately translates into the English language **all the** original Hebrew, Aramaic, and Greek **Words** that God has preserved. In the other English versions, you do not have them all properly translated.

- **Matthew 4:4**
  "But he answered and said, It is written, Man shall not live by bread alone, but by **every word** that proceedeth out of the mouth of God."

How can you live by **every word,** if you do not have them? God is against this destruction of His **Words.**

- **Luke 9:26**
  "For whosoever shall be ashamed of me and of **my words,** of him shall the Son of man be ashamed, when he shall come in his own glory, and in his Father's, and of the holy angels."

- **Luke 21:33**
  "Heaven and earth shall pass away: but **my words** shall not pass away."

The Lord Jesus Christ's Hebrew and Aramaic Old Testament **Words** shall not pass away. His Greek **Words** shall not pass away. I believe He has preserved those **Words** down to the present. Why then do the fundamentalist schools' leaders say, "God never even promised to preserve His **Words?**" Yet, He says right here, *"my Words shall not pass away."*

Bob Jones University teaches that He never promised to preserve His **Words,** therefore He has not. Detroit Baptist Seminary teaches that He never promised to preserve His **Words,** therefore He has not.

Calvary Baptist Seminary in Lansdale, Pennsylvania teaches that He has not promised to preserve His **Words,** therefore He has not. Central Baptist Seminary in the Minneapolis area teaches that He has not even promised to preserve His **Words,** therefore He has not.

Unbelief In God's Preservation Promise

They say, "There are mistakes in the Hebrew and mistakes in the Greek, therefore why are we fighting about Bible versions?" They do not even believe that God has promised to preserve His Words. They say, "Oh, He has promised to preserve His *Word,* but not His *Words.*" You might say, "Wait a minute! I thought Word and Words were the same." They are the same in the Bible, but these schools have a new definition for the Word. They say, "He preserved His *Word,* but not His *Words*—not His Hebrew, Aramaic, and Greek Words—just His *Word.*" They mean only His message, His thoughts, His ideas, His concepts, His truths, but not His *Words.* Any old words you want to put in there are all right, just so the general message is there. This is a terrible heresy among our fundamentalist Bible-believing colleges, seminaries, and universities. They are fundamental in other areas, but apostate in this doctrine of the Bible. It is sad to say.

I would not want to be in their shoes, if they are genuinely saved, at the judgment seat of the Lord Jesus Christ—adding and subtracting from His **Words.** Plagues are promised by the Lord Jesus Christ—not necessarily in this life.

Then it says in Revelation 22:19, plagues are promised by the Lord *if any man shall take away from the words of the book of this prophecy, God shall take away his part out of the book of life.* What does that mean? Does it mean they are going to be losing salvation? No, I believe the word *part* means, *his rewards.* He will be in the book of life, but his *part* or rewards will be removed. His rewards will be gone, because he has added to or subtracted from the **Words** of God.

ABWE'S Bengali Perversion

The Association of Baptist World Evangelists (ABWE) used to be near us in Cherry Hill. They had a translation team on the Bengali language in Bangladesh. The lady from ABWE who wrote a little tract on that said, "The nationals were upset when we were taking so many liberties with the Bengali language in the Bengali Bible." They looked at this verse, *if any man shall take away from the words of the book of this prophecy, God shall take away his part out of the book of life,* and said, "We cannot do this!" She said they should take it to the field council, so they made some exceptions and changed it. The nationals understood clear, plain language. They knew

this woman was taking liberties with their Bible, because they knew that they were adding words that were not in the Bible. It is as clear as anything. I do not understand how these men and women can add, subtract, and change. God says, "Do not do it!"

Revelation 22:20

"He which testifieth these things saith, Surely I come quickly. Amen. Even so, come, Lord Jesus."

This is the **coming of the Lord Jesus** for His own. He is coming. Are you ready?

- **1 Corinthians 1:7**
  "So that ye come behind in no gift; waiting for the **coming of our Lord Jesus Christ:**"

Are you waiting for Him? The **rapture** will take place one of these days to snatch out the genuine believers.

- **1 Thessalonians 2:19**
  "For what *is* our hope, or joy, or crown of rejoicing? *Are* not even ye in the presence of our Lord Jesus Christ at his **coming?**"

Paul was looking for the **coming** of the Lord Jesus Christ.

- **1 Thessalonians 4:15-18**
  "For this we say unto you by the word of the Lord, that we which are alive *and* remain unto the **coming** of the Lord shall not prevent them which are asleep. For the Lord himself shall descend from heaven with a shout, with the voice of the archangel, and with the trump of God: and the dead in Christ shall rise first: Then we which are alive *and* remain shall be caught up together with them in the clouds, to meet the Lord in the air: and so shall we ever be with the Lord. Wherefore comfort one another with these words."

Here is when and how the **rapture** will take place. Paul was looking for the **coming** of the Lord Jesus Christ even in his day. Those who have died who are genuinely saved, are going to rise first when that **rapture** takes place. If we still are living when the **rapture** takes place, we will be caught up together with them. The first phase of His **coming** is going to be in the air, not to earth. Paul was looking for His **coming**.

The Lord Jesus Christ says, *"I come quickly."* Quickly has been over 2,000 years. We are still waiting.

- **1 Thessalonians 5:23**
"And the very God of peace sanctify you wholly; and *I pray God* your whole spirit and soul and body be preserved blameless unto the **coming** of our Lord Jesus Christ."

We have to be preserved in our spirits, souls, and bodies—blameless.

- **2 Thessalonians 2:1**
"Now we beseech you, brethren, by the **coming** of our Lord Jesus Christ, and *by* our gathering together unto him,"

That is the **rapture**—*gathering together unto Him.*

- **James 5:7**
"Be patient therefore, brethren, unto the **coming** of the Lord. Behold, the husbandman waiteth for the precious fruit of the earth, and hath long patience for it, until he receive the early and latter rain."

Be patient. We do not know when it is going to be.

- **James 5:8**
"Be ye also patient; stablish your hearts: for the **coming** of the Lord draweth nigh."

It was nigh even in James' day. How much more nigh and near is it today?

- **1 John 2:28**
"And now, little children, abide in him; that, when he shall appear, we may have confidence, and not be ashamed before him at his **coming**."

Will you be ashamed before Him at His **coming**? We should not be ashamed before Him. We should live for Him. We should live to please Him. On His foundation, we should be building gold, silver, and precious stones—things that cannot be seen, but are valuable for the Lord Jesus Christ.

Only one life, 'twill soon be past.
Only what's done for Christ will last.

If it is wood, hay, and stubble we are building on the foundation, it will be burned up. We will be ashamed before Him at His **coming**. The judgment seat of the Lord Jesus Christ will be at His **coming** and if we are not living for Him, we will be ashamed before Him.

- **Titus 2:11-13**
  "For the grace of God that bringeth salvation hath appeared to all men, Teaching us that, denying ungodliness and worldly lusts, we should live soberly, righteously, and godly, in this present world; Looking for that blessed hope, and the glorious **appearing** of the great God and our Saviour Jesus Christ; "

It May Be Today

By Gertrude Grace Sanborn

One day, and it may be today,
We shall hear His great commanding shout,
And while we are busy at our tasks,
He will come to take us out.

"Come up, come up hither!"
And, in a moment—"a twinkling"—it will be.
We shall be with Him
Whom we so long have yearned to see.

With wondrous joy, we shall hear His voice
Which bids the dead to rise and leave earth's shroud.
Our dear, dear dead that we have missed so long
They rise in beauty to meet us in the cloud.

Fulfilled His promise, we'll rise
And leave behind earth's tears and fears—
The things we could not understand or comprehend
To be together with Him, eternal years.

To be with Him, whatever that may be,
Our glorious Lord, in His blest company.
So let us wait and sing hope's sweetest song:
One day! Hold fast! It won't be long.

Revelation 22:21

"The grace of our Lord Jesus Christ be with you all. Amen."

God's Grace Is To All People

The grace of God has appeared to all men, not just to the elect. That *blessed hope* is the coming of the Lord Jesus Christ in the rapture, being caught up in the air to be with the Lord Jesus Christ forever. The *glorious appearing* is His second coming to earth. He will appear in glory and His feet will touch the Mount of Olives and it will be split. He will come and reign in the millennial reign of the Lord Jesus Christ for 1,000 years, but the *blessed hope* is seven years before that *glorious appearing*. The rapture will take us Home to be with the Lord Jesus Christ, which is far better.

That word *grace* is *CHARIS*. It means, *that which affords joy and pleasure; delight; sweetness; charm; loveliness; grace of speech; good will; lovingkindness; favor*. All of these are words for that word CHARIS or **grace**. God wants us to be gracious. He wants us to be filled with His grace. God wants the **grace** of our Saviour to be with every true believer who is genuinely saved. This is how John ends this letter.

"Amen"–The Universal Word

Then he says this word, "Amen." It is an interesting word. It is a most remarkable word. It was transliterated, not translated, letter-for-letter, from the Hebrew into the Greek of the New Testament and then into Latin and into English and into many other languages. It is practically a universal word. It has been called the best-known word in human speech. The word is directly related—in fact, almost identical—to the Hebrew word for believe. The word for believe is AMAN. That is the Hebrew word for, *I believe* or *faithful*. Thus, it came to mean, *sure* or *truly; an expression of absolute trust and confidence*. The apostle John was absolutely confident that the Lord Jesus Christ is coming. He was confident in Revelation 22:20. "I believe it," says John. He is confident in Revelation 22:21. So be it.

We have to have a gracious spirit if we are genuinely saved and born-again. We must remember that in this last chapter of Revelation, especially in verses 18 and 19, <u>there is a terrible peril to those who are</u> <u>Bible-perverters, who **change, add, or subtract** from God's Words.</u> God has pronounced a judgment on them. I have not pronounced that judgment. This is in the Book. You may ask, "Is this only for the people who add to the book of Revelation?" Revelation is the last book of the Bible. If anyone presumes to have God's revelation and **adds** to any of the books of the Bible, they are under the **curse**.

The Book of Mormon is an addition. That is under this **curse**. Mary Baker Glover Patterson Fry Eddy's *Science and Health, With Key to the Scriptures* is under the **curse**. There are all kinds of wrongful additions. The charismatic movement adds words to the Bible. They claim to get special gifts of prophecy from the Lord and say, "This is what the Lord told me." That is under the **curse**.

I believe that those who say that the King James Bible is a **"revelation** from God" rather than a **"translation"** of the Words of God are also under God's **curse**. That is the position of Peter Ruckman, Gail Riplinger, and all of their dupes and followers. They repudiate the Hebrew, Aramaic, and Greek Words that God has revealed to us and substitute for those Words man's translation of those Words as given in the King James Bible. They wrongly claim that the King James Bible was a *new* God-breathed *and God-inspired* revelation in 1611. They teach that there is no more need for God's Words that He has preserved in Hebrew, Aramaic, and Greek. Therefore, no one should ever look up any of these Words in any lexicon or dictionary since they are no longer needed or even relevant. This is one of the most serious errors of Ruckmanism, Riplingerism, and their blind and unscriptural followers. The King James Bible is not a new revelation. It is the only accurate, true, and reliable English translation of God's preserved Hebrew, Aramaic, and Greek Words that underlie it. I believe that in the King James Bible, because of its excellent translation of the preserved underlying Hebrew, Aramaic, and Greek Words, we have God's Words kept intact in English.

INDEX OF WORDS AND PHRASES

.

About the Author

The author of this book, Dr. D. A. Waite, received a B.A. (Bachelor of Arts) in classical Greek and Latin from the University of Michigan in 1948, a Th.M. (Master of Theology), with high honors, in New Testament Greek Literature and Exegesis from Dallas Theological Seminary in 1952, an M.A. (Master of Arts) in Speech from Southern Methodist University in 1953, a Th.D. (Doctor of Theology), with honors, in Bible Exposition from Dallas Theological Seminary in 1955, and a Ph.D. in Speech from Purdue University in 1961. He holds both New Jersey and Pennsylvania teacher certificates in Greek and Language Arts.

He has been a teacher in the areas of Greek, Hebrew, Bible, Speech, and English for over thirty-five years in ten schools, including one junior high, one senior high, four Bible institutes, two colleges, two universities, and one seminary. He served his country as a Navy Chaplain for five years on active duty; pastored three churches; was Chairman and Director of the Radio and Audio-Film Commission of the American Council of Christian Churches; since 1969, has been Founder, President, and Director of THE BIBLE FOR TODAY; since 1978, has been President of the DEAN BURGON SOCIETY; has produced over 700 other studies, books, cassettes, VHS's, CD's, or VCR's on various topics; and is heard on a thirty-minute weekly radio program IN DEFENSE OF TRADITIONAL BIBLE TEXTS, on radio, shortwave, and streaming on the Internet at BibleForToday.org, 24/7/365.

Dr. and Mrs. Waite have been married since 1948; they have four sons, one daughter, and, at present, eight grandchildren, and twelve great-grandchildren. Since October 4, 1998, he has been the Pastor of the Bible For Today Baptist Church in Collingswood, New Jersey.

Order Blank (p. 1)

Name:_____

Address:_____

City & State:_____Zip:_____

Credit Card #:_____Expires:_____

Latest Books

[ ] Send Revelation–Preaching Verse by Verse, by Pastor D. A.
Waite, 1032 pages, perfect bound ($50+$10 S&H)

[ ] Send 2 Timothy–Preaching Verse by Verse, by Pastor D. A.
Waite, 248 pages, perfect bound ($11+$5 S&H) fully indexed.

[ ] Send *A Critical Answer to God's Word Preserved* by Pastor D.
A. Waite, 192 pp. perfect bound ($11.00+$4.00 S&H)

The Most Recently Published Books

[ ] Send *8,000 Differences Between Textus Receptus & Critical Text*
by Dr. J. A. Moorman, 544 pp., hd. back ($20+$5+ S&H)

[ ] *Early Manuscripts, Church Fathers, & the Authorized
Version* by Dr. Jack Moorman, $18+$5 S&H. Hardback

[ ] Send *The LIE That Changed the Modern World* by Dr.
H. D. Williams ($16+$5 S&H) Hardback book

[ ] Send *With Tears in My Heart* by Gertrude G. Sanborn.
Hardback 414 pp. ($25+$5 S&H) 400 Christian Poems

Preaching Verse by Verse Books

[ ] Send 1 Timothy–Preaching Verse by Verse, by Pastor D. A.
Waite, 288 pages, hardback ($11+$5 S&H) fully indexed.

[ ] Send *Romans–Preaching Verse by Verse* by Pastor D. A.
Waite 736 pp. Hardback ($25+$5 S&H) fully indexed

[ ] Send *Colossians & Philemon–Preaching Verse by Verse* by
Pastor D. A. Waite ($12+$5 S&H) hardback, 240 pages.

[ ] Send *Philippians–Preaching Verse by Verse* by Pastor D.
A. Waite ($10+$5 S&H) hardback, 176 pages.

[ ] Send *Ephesians–Preaching Verse by Verse* by Pastor D. A.
Waite ($12+$5 S&H) hardback, 224 pages.

[ ] Send *Galatians–Preaching Verse By Verse* by Pastor D. A.
Waite ($12+$5 S&H) hardback, 216 pages.

Send or Call Orders to:
THE BIBLE FOR TODAY
900 Park Ave., Collingswood, NJ 08108
Phone: 856-854-4452; FAX:–2464; Orders: 1-800 JOHN 10:9

Order Blank (p. 2)

Name:_____

Address:_____

City & State:_____Zip:_____

Credit Card #:_____Expires:_____

More Preaching Verse by Verse Books

[ ] Send *First Peter–Preaching Verse By Verse* by Pastor D. A. Waite ($10+$5 S&H) hardback, 176 pages.

Books on Bible Texts & Translations

[ ] Send *Defending the King James Bible* by DAW ($12+$5 S&H) A hardback book, indexed with study questions.

[ ] Send *BJU's Errors on Bible Preservation* by Dr. D. A. Waite, 110 pages, paperback ($8+$4 S&H) fully indexed

[ ] Send *Fundamentalist Deception on Bible Preservation* by Dr. Waite, ($8+$4 S&H), paperback, fully indexed

[ ] Send *Fundamentalist MIS-INFORMATION on Bible Versions* by Dr. Waite ($7+$4 S&H) perfect bound, 136 pages

[ ] Send *Fundamentalist Distortions on Bible Versions* by Dr. Waite ($6+$3 S&H) A perfect bound book, 80 pages

[ ] Send *Fuzzy Facts From Fundamentalists* by Dr. D. A. Waite ($8.00 + $4.00) printed booklet

[ ] Send *Foes of the King James Bible Refuted* by DAW ($10 +$4 S&H) A perfect bound book, 164 pages in length.

[ ] Send *Central Seminary Refuted on Bible Versions* by Dr. Waite ($10+$4 S&H) A perfect bound book, 184 pages

[ ] Send *The Case for the King James Bible* by DAW ($7 +$3 S&H) A perfect bound book, 112 pages in length.

[ ] Send *Theological Heresies of Westcott and Hort* by Dr. D. A. Waite, ($7+$3 S&H) A printed booklet.

[ ] Send *Westcott's Denial of Resurrection*, Dr. Waite ($4+$3)

[ ] Send *Four Reasons for Defending KJB* by DAW ($3+$3)

Send or Call Orders to:
THE BIBLE FOR TODAY
900 Park Ave., Collingswood, NJ 08108
Phone: 856-854-4452; FAX:–2464; Orders: 1-800 JOHN 10:9
E-Mail Orders: BFT@BibleForToday.org; Credit Cards OK

Order Blank (p. 3)

Name:_____

Address:_____

City & State:_____Zip:_____

Credit Card #:_____Expires:_____

More Books on Texts & Translations

[ ] Send *Holes in the Holman Christian Standard Bible* by Dr. Waite ($3+$2 S&H) A printed booklet, 40 pages

[ ] Send *Contemporary Eng. Version Exposed*, DAW ($3+$2)

[ ] Send *NIV Inclusive Language Exposed* by DAW ($5+$3)

[ ] Send *26 Hours of KJB Seminar* (4 videos) by DAW($50.00)

Books By Dr. Jack Moorman

[ ] Send Manuscript Digest of the N.T. (721 pp.) By Dr. Jack Moorman, copy-machine bound ($50+$7 S&H)

[ ] *Early Manuscripts, Church Fathers, & the Authorized Version* by Dr. Jack Moorman, $18+$5 S&H. Hardback

[ ] Send *Forever Settled–Bible Documents & History Survey* by Dr. Jack Moorman, $20+$5 S&H. Hardback book.

[ ] Send *When the KJB Departs from the So-Called "Majority Text"* by Dr. Jack Moorman, $16+$5 S&H

[ ] Send *Missing in Modern Bibles–Nestle-Aland/NIV Errors* by Dr. Jack Moorman, $8+$4 S&H

[ ] Send *The Doctrinal Heart of the Bible–Removed from Modern Versions* by Dr. Jack Moorman, VCR, $15 +$4 S&H

[ ] Send *Modern Bibles–The Dark Secret* by Dr. Jack Moorman, $5+$3 S&H

[ ] Send *Samuel P. Tregelles–The Man Who Made the Critical Text Acceptable to Bible Believers* by Dr. Moorman ($2+$1)

[ ] Send *8,000 Differences Between TR & CT* by Dr. Jack Moorman [$65 + $7.50 S&H] Over 500-large-pages of data

[ ] Send *356 Doctrinal Errors in the NIV & Other Modern Versions*, 100-large-pages, $10.00+$6 S&H.

Send or Call Orders to:
THE BIBLE FOR TODAY
900 Park Ave., Collingswood, NJ 08108
Phone: 856-854-4452; FAX:–2464; Orders: 1-800 JOHN 10:9
E-Mail Orders: BFT@BibleForToday.org; Credit Cards OK

Order Blank (p. 4)

Name:_____

Address:_____

City & State:_____Zip:_____

Credit Card #:_____Expires:_____

Books By or About Dean Burgon

[ ] Send *The Revision Revised* by Dean Burgon ($25 + $5
S&H) A hardback book, 640 pages in length.

[ ] Send *The Last 12 verses of Mark* by Dean Burgon ($15+$5
S&H) A hardback book 400 pages.

[ ] Send *The Traditional Text* hardback by Burgon ($16+$5
S&H) A hardback book, 384 pages in length.

[ ] Send *Causes of Corruption* by Burgon ($15+$5 S&H)
A hardback book, 360 pages in length.

[ ] Send *Inspiration and Interpretation*, Dean Burgon ($25+$5
S&H) A hardback book, 610 pages in length.

[ ] Send *Burgon's Warnings on Revision* by DAW ($7+$4
S&H) A perfect bound book, 120 pages in length.

] Send *Westcott & Hort's Greek Text & Theory Refuted by
Burgon's Revision Revised–Summarized* by Dr. D. A.
Waite ($7.00+$4 S&H), 120 pages, perfect bound.

[ ] Send *Dean Burgon's Confidence in KJB* by DAW ($3+$3)

[ ] Send *Vindicating Mark 16:9-20* by Dr. Waite ($3+$3S&H)

[ ] Send *Summary of Traditional Text* by Dr. Waite ($3 +$3)

[ ] Send *Summary of Causes of Corruption*, DAW ($3+$3)

[ ] Send *Summary of Inspiration* by Dr. Waite ($3+$3 S&H)

More Books by Dr. D. A. Waite

[ ] Send *Making Marriage Melodious* by Pastor D. A. Waite
($7+$4 S&H), perfect bound, 112 pages.

Send or Call Orders to:
THE BIBLE FOR TODAY
900 Park Ave., Collingswood, NJ 08108
Phone: 856-854-4452; FAX:–2464; Orders: 1-800 JOHN 10:9
E-Mail Orders: BFT@BibleForToday.org; Credit Cards OK

Order Blank (p. 5)

Name:_____

Address:_____

City & State:_____Zip:_____

Credit Card #:_____Expires:_____

Books by D. A. Waite, Jr.

[ ] Send *Readability of A.V. (KJB)* by D. A. Waite, Jr. ($6+$3)

[ ] Send *4,114 Definitions from the Defined King James Bible* by D. A. Waite, Jr. ($7.00+$4.00 S&H)

[ ] Send *The Doctored New Testament* by D. A. Waite, Jr. ($25+$5 S&H) Greek MSS differences shown, hardback

[ ] Send *Defined King James Bible* lg. prt. leather ($40+$7.50)

[ ] Send *Defined King James Bible* med. prt. leather ($35+$6)

Miscellaneous Authors

[ ] Send *The Pure Words of God* by Dr. H. D. Williams, perfect bound ($15.00 + $5 S&H)

[ ] Send *Hearing the Voice of God* by Dr. H. D. William, perfect bound ($18.00 + $5.00 S&H)

[ ] Send *The Attack on the Bible's Canon* by Dr. H. D. Williams, perfect bound ($15.00 + S&H)

[ ] Send *Word-For-Word Translating of The Received Texts* by Dr. H. D. Williams, 288 pages, paperback ($10+$5 S&H).

[ ] Send *Guide to Textual Criticism* by Edward Miller ($7+$4) Hardback book

[ ] Send *Scrivener's Greek New Testament Underlying the King James Bible*, hardback, ($14+$5 S&H)

[ ] Send *Scrivener's Annotated Greek New Testament*, by Dr. Frederick Scrivener: Hardback–($35+$5 S&H); Genuine Leather–($45+$5 S&H)

[ ] Send *Why Not the King James Bible?–An Answer to James White's KJVO Book* by Dr. K. D. DiVietro, $10+$5 S&H

[ ] Send Brochure #1: *"1000 Titles Defending the KJB/TR"* No Charge

Send or Call Orders to:
THE BIBLE FOR TODAY
900 Park Ave., Collingswood, NJ 08108
Phone: 856-854-4452; FAX:–2464; Orders: 1-800 JOHN 10:9
E-Mail Orders: BFT@BibleForToday.org; Credit Cards OK

The Defined

𝕶𝖎𝖓𝖌 𝕵𝖆𝖒𝖊𝖘 𝕭𝖎𝖇𝖑𝖊

Uncommon Words Defined Accurately

I. Deluxe Genuine Leather

✦Large 𝖕𝖗𝖎𝖓𝖙–𝕭lack or 𝕭urgundy✦

1 for $40.00+$7.50 S&H

✦Case of 12 for✦

$30.00 each+$30 S&H

✦𝕸edium 𝖕𝖗𝖎𝖓𝖙–𝕭lack or 𝕭urgundy ✦

1 for $35.00+$6 S&H

✦Case of 12 for✦

$25.00 each+$24 S&H

II. Deluxe Hardback Editions

1 for $20.00+$7.50 S&H (Large Print)

✦Case of 12 for✦

$15.00 each+$30 S&H (Large Print)

1 for $15.00+$6 S&H (Medium Print)

✦Case of 12 for✦

$10.00 each+$24 S&H (Medium Print)

Order Phone: 1-800-JOHN 10:9

Pastor D. A. Waite, Th.D., Ph.D.

Banished For The Words Of God

The Main Character. Though there are many other characters mentioned throughout this book of Revelation, the Lord Jesus Christ is the main character. He is seen in every one of the twenty-two chapters. He is the "Lamb" who shed His blood for the forgiveness of sins. He is the One Who is *"worthy"* to open the seals of the book of the earth's *redemption*. He is the mighty One Who will be the Victor at the Armageddon battle. He is seen in many other ways.

The Human Writer. The Lord chose the Apostle John to write this book. He is the apostle whom Jesus loved. He was the only one of the twelve who followed the Lord Jesus Christ all the way to the cross of Calvary. He not only wrote this book of Revelation, but also the Gospel of John, 1 John, 2 John, and 3 John. He was one of apostles, along with Peter and James who shared a very close fellowship with our Saviour.

The Location Of The Writing. The book was written while the Apostle John was on the Isle of Patmos. Though the other apostles met very painful deaths at the hands of their non-Christian enemies, John was banished to the Isle of Patmos to live out his life. This banishment was *"for the Word of God, and for the testimony of Jesus Christ."* He refused to deny the Words of God, or renounce his testimony.

www.BibleForToday.org

BFT 3495 BK   **ISBN #978-1-56848-080-6**

CPSIA information can be obtained at www.ICGtesting.com
Printed in the USA
BVOW02s1631140115

382593BV00011B/39/P